The Economics of Choice, Change and Organization

The Economics of Choice, Change and Organization

Essays in Memory of Richard M. Cyert

Edited by

Mie Augier
Post-doctoral Fellow, Stanford University, USA

and

James G. March
Professor Emeritus, Stanford University, USA

Edward Elgar
Cheltenham, UK • Northampton, MA, USA

Published by
Edward Elgar Publishing Limited
Glensanda House
Montpellier Parade
Cheltenham
Glos GL50 1UA
UK

Edward Elgar Publishing, Inc.
136 West Street
Suite 202
Northampton
Massachusetts 01060
USA

A catalogue record for this book is available from the British Library

Library of Congress Cataloging-in-Publication Data
The economics of choice, change, and organization : essays in memory of Richard M. Cyert / [edited by] Mie Augier and James G. March.
p. ; cm.
Includes bibliographical references and index.
1. Organizational behavior. 2. Organizational learning. I. Augier, Mie, 1972– II. March, James G. III. Cyert, Richard Michael, 1921–

HD58.7 . E285 2002
338.5–dc21

2002018834

ISBN 1 84064 321 8
Printed and bound in Great Britain by MPG Books Ltd, Bodmin, Cornwall

Contents

Figures

Tables

Contributors

Mie Augier Post-doctoral Fellow, Stanford University, CA, USA.

Joel A.C. Baum Canadian National Chair in Strategic Management, Rotman School of Management, University of Toronto, Canada.

Christopher S. Boerner Doctoral candidate in Business and Public Policy, Haas School of Business, University of California, Berkeley, CA, USA.

Philip Bromiley Curtlis L. Carlson Chair in Strategic Management, University of Minnesota, Minneapolis, MN, USA.

William W. Cooper Foster Parker Professor of Finance and Management (Emeritus), Graduate School of Business at the University of Texas at Austin, TX, USA.

Rickard Danell Research Assistant, INFORSK research group, Umeå University, Sweden.

Richard H. Day Professor of Economics, University of Southern California, Los Angeles, CA, USA.

Giovanni Dosi Professor of Economics, Sant'Anna School of Advanced Studies, Pisa, Italy.

Massimo Egidi Professor of Economics and co-director, with Axel Leijonhufvud, Computable and Experimental Economics Laboratory, University of Trento, Italy.

Lars Engwall Professor of Management, Department of Business Studies, Uppsala University, Sweden.

Lee Fleming Assistant Professor in Technology and Operations Management, Harvard Business School, Boston, MA, USA.

Paul Ingram David W. Zalaznick Associate Professor of Business, Columbia Business School, New York, USA.

Sok-Hyon Kang Associate Professor of Business Administration, George Washington University, Washington, DC.

Alfred Kieser Chaired Professor of Business Administration and Organizational Behavior, Business School, University of Mannheim, Germany.

Ulrich Koch Research Assistant at the Sonderforschungsbereich (Research Program) 'Rationality, Decision Making and Economic Modeling' and at the Department of Business Administration and Organizational Behavior, Business School, University of Mannheim, Germany.

Praveen Kumar Professor of Finance, Bauer College of Business, University of Houston, TX, USA.

Daniel A. Levinthal Julian Aresty Professor of Management and Economics, Wharton School, University of Pennsylvania, Philadelphia, PA, USA.

Brian J. Loasby Honorary and Emeritus Professor of Economics, University of Stirling, Scotland.

Franco Malerba Professor of Industrial Economics and Director of CESPRI (Research Center on Innovation and Internationalization Processes) at Bocconi University, Milan, Italy and editor of *Industrial and Corporate Change*.

James G. March Professor Emeritus, Stanford University, CA, USA.

John M. Mezias Assistant Professor of Business, University of Miami, FL, USA.

Anne S. Miner Henry Ford Motor Company Distinguished Professor of Management and Human Resources, School of Business, University of Wisconsin-Madison, Madison, WI, USA.

Richard Nelson George Blumenthal Professor of International and Public Affairs, Columbia University, New York, USA.

Luigi Orsenigo Professor of Economics and Industrial Organization and Deputy Director of CESPRI (Research Center on Innovation and Internationalization Processes), Bocconi University, Milan, Italy.

J. Lamar Pierce Doctoral student in Business and Public Policy, Haas School of Business, University of California, Berkeley, CA, USA.

Thekla Rura-Polley Senior Lecturer in Management, University of Technology, Sydney, Australia.

Susan R. Salgado Doctoral student, Stern School of Management, New York University, NY, USA.

Sridhar Seshadri Associate Professor of Operations Management, Stern School of Business, New York University, NY, USA.

Zur Shapira Research Professor of Management, Stern School of Business, New York University, NY, USA.

Herbert A. Simon (1916–2001) Was Richard K. Mellon University Professor of Computer Science and Psychology, Carnegie-Mellon University, Pittsburgh, PA, USA.

William H. Starbuck ITT Professor of Creative Management, Stern School of Business, New York University, NY, USA.

David J. Teece Mitsubishi Bank Professor and Director of the Institute of Management, Innovation and Organization, Haas School of Business, University of California, Berkeley, CA, USA.

Oliver E. Williamson Edgar Kaiser Professor of Business, Professor of Economics, and Professor of Law, University of California, Berkeley, CA, USA.

Sidney G. Winter Deloitte and Touche Professor of Management, Wharton School, University of Pennsylvania, Philadelphia, PA, USA.

Preface

This book is a story, a prolegomenon, a memorial and a testament. It is a story of a set of ideas in economics, statistics, and organization studies. It is a prolegomenon to contemporary work elaborating those ideas. It is a memorial to a leading architect of the ideas – Richard M. Cyert. And it is a testament to the affection with which Dick Cyert is remembered by his colleagues.

The ideas illuminate some of the central issues of modem economics – issues of choice, particularly choices made by and in business firms; issues of information and judgment; issues of organizational change through learning and evolution; and issues of organizational structure. Topics include behavioral theories of the firm, cognitive factors in organization and economic action, the place of rules in organizations, learning from experience and from the knowledge of others, selection in economic change, the impact of information technology, and the evolution of organizational forms.

Our success in securing the contributions of such a distinguished group of scholars suggests something of the respect that Dick Cyert earned from his associates. He probably would have rejected the notion of a personal intellectual memorial; he consistently eschewed the glorification of self, preferring always to stimulate discussions of scholarly ideas rather than individual scholars. We have tried to honor that sentiment by asking each author to focus on the ways in which Cyert's ideas have been elaborated and extended, rather than explicating their original presentation or enumerating the many personal linkages with him that they recall. Our strictures have not always been followed rigorously, but in general (after a few introductory comments in the first chapter) the emphasis in the book is not on Cyert the man but on the ideas with which he was associated and their current place in economic thought.

After an introduction that tries to review the Cyert legacy briefly, the book is organized into four parts, each highlighting a major area of his work. Part I looks at the economics of choice, and considers the theory of the firm. Part II deals with information and the cognitive basis of action, in particular with behavioral considerations in assessing the role of information in the making of choice. Part III considers the economics of change with special attention to ideas about learning in organizations (Section A) and the evolution of populations of organizations (Section B). Part IV examines the economics of organization, exploring some ideas about the organizational structure of firms.

We are grateful to the authors for their contributions and for their willingness to forgo royalties from sales of the book. At the suggestion of Margaret Cyert, all authors' and editors' royalties will be contributed to the Carnegie-Mellon University Library.

Mie Augier
James G. March
Stanford, California, USA
September, 2000

1. Introduction Richard M. Cyert: the work and the legacy*

Mie Augier and James G. March

This volume is dedicated to the memory of Richard M. Cyert. It reflects the respect and love that he engendered among his colleagues, students, and friends; but most of all, it reflects the ways in which his ideas are manifested in contemporary thinking about economic choice and change. Cyert worked extensively within the fields of behavioral economics, microeconomics, statistics, decision theory, and management (Day and Sunder, 1996). Some of his more important contributions included *A Behavioral Theory of the Firm* written with James G. March (Cyert and March, 1963), *Bayesian Analysis and Uncertainty in Economic Theory* written with Morris DeGroot (Cyert and DeGroot, 1987), and *The Management of Nonprofit Organizations* (Cyert, 1990a). Although they contain other themes, each of these books – as the remainder of his work – can be seen as reflecting a behavioral vision for economics. Indeed, Cyert was one of the fathers of this tradition (Earl, 1988; 1995), and the Carnegie Institute of Technology Graduate School of Administration, within which he worked during the early years of his career is now recognized as having had at that time an unusual cluster of significant social scientists on its faculty.

1 THE MAN AND THE INSTITUTION

Richard M. Cyert was born on July 22, 1921, and died on October 7, 1998. He was a remarkable person, a distinguished scholar, and a profoundly effective academic administrator. He came to the Carnegie Institute of Technology (the predecessor of Carnegie-Mellon University) in 1948 as an instructor of economics and spent his entire professional career there. From 1962 to 1972 he was dean of the Graduate School of Administration (GSIA), and from 1972 to 1990 he was president of the university. Over the course of fifty years, he was a major contributor to the university and to the field of economics.

Cyert before Carnegie

Richard Cyert was unpretentious, helpful, and a believer in hard work. He was born into a working class family in Minnesota, and he never forgot the lessons of the deep economic depression of the 1930s. He frequently recalled the economic disaster of the depression, which hit his family hard and which shaped his own sense of himself. As Margaret Cyert observed, '[H]e was a poor boy. He learned to make it on his own' (in Cyert, 1990b, p. 22), and 'Dick and I believe it is easy to go up but hard to come down. So we've always lived simple, been frugal and very careful with money'.[1] Cyert himself recalled, 'I was the first person in my family going to college, and my notion was to somehow get yourself prepared so that you could get a better job, so you weren't always worrying about unemployment and so on' (ibid.). He remembered delivering papers as a young child to help make ends meet and sleeping on the floor so his two young sisters could sleep on the cots.[2] The attitudes and values of the depression years in Minnesota and concerns about the effects of business cycles on ordinary people framed both his interest in economics and his approach to his experiences throughout his life.[3]

As a young man, Cyert was an energetic and enthusiastic student with an interest in mathematics. He enrolled at the University of Minnesota in 1939, working in the library to pay his tuition. At the university, he considered the fields of statistics and applied mathematics but settled on economics. He graduated with an economics degree in 1943. After serving as officer in the US Navy for three years during the Second World War and marrying Margaret Shadick in 1946, he entered the doctoral program in economics at Columbia University in New York City. Cyert studied economics and statistics under Abraham Wald, Arthur Burns and George Stigler, one of his professors from Minnesota who had taken a position at Columbia and became Cyert's principal advisor. Stigler and Cyert remained friends and respected each other throughout their lives, but Cyert drifted a good deal from a Stiglerian perspective on economic rationality. In an interview late in his life, Cyert recalled: 'When I was studying with Stigler I thought that anybody who assumed that entrepreneurs did not maximize profits was stupid. I surely changed my view on this but I am sure Stigler never did'.[4] The drift began early. In his thesis, he looked for confirmation of economic theories of price setting in oligopolistic markets. He could find rather little support for the theories, and though he never lost confidence in economic theory as a *prescription* for managerial behavior, he came to recognize severe behavioral limits in it as a *description*.

Carnegie before Cyert

When Cyert came to Carnegie, the school had little tradition in economics.[5] The Carnegie Institute of Technology had been founded in 1912 by Andrew Carnegie and had established itself as one of the better engineering schools in the country (on the early years of Carnegie, see Schaefer, 1992). In 1948, the school was under the leadership of a dynamic president, Robert Doherty, who had come from Yale in 1936 and an equally dynamic provost, Elliott Dunlap Smith, whom Doherty recruited from Yale in 1946. Doherty wanted Carnegie Tech to be a leader in research and hence, to 'place less emphasis upon routine know-how and miscellaneous technical information, and much more upon [the] intellectual skills [and] fundamental knowledge ... essential to coping with practical situations'.[6]

In Doherty's view, the education of engineers involved exposure not only to the technical aspects of engineering subjects but also to the fundamental science underlying them and to broader aspects of society. A key element in this vision of engineering education was instruction in the interdisciplinary, particularly social, aspects of engineering. In 1940, in keeping with this perspective, Doherty put forward a set of guidelines that became known as the 'Carnegie Plan' for engineering education (Schaefer, 1992; Fenton, 2000). The essence of the plan was the idea that Carnegie Tech would strive to cultivate: '(1) the ability to think independently ... (2) the ability to ... deal with the whole problem or situation and not only part of it ... (3) the ability to learn from each new experience ... [and] (4) competence and interest in dealing with the responsibilities of citizenship'.[7]

After the war, Doherty and Smith decided that the time was right for developing distinct programs in economics and management as part of the Carnegie Plan (Gleeson and Schossman, 1996; Fenton, 2000). Early in 1946 they hired an economist, George Leland Bach and charged him with vitalizing economics at Carnegie. Bach was a banker's son from Iowa who had received his PhD in economics from the University of Chicago. He had absorbed the (at that time) characteristic Chicago creed that interdisciplinary thinking was vital to innovation, that social science should be linked to public service, and that social science must be theoretically sophisticated to be useful as a guide to practical action. The intellectual tools were courses in measurement, logic, statistics, and so on.

Bach wanted to staff his department with economists who combined intellectual skills and experience in applying theory to real-world situations.[8] He also wanted to establish economics at Carnegie as a major player among American university departments of economics. The vision was ambitious. As Bach later recalled:

> I was young, smart, and brash. I was going to build the best economics department in the country from scratch. When I arrived at Carnegie, there was nothing going on at all outside of science and engineering ... The economics faculty began publishing a lot. We worked long hours and (sometimes) neglected our families. It was a hardball place. (Quoted from Gleeson and Schlossman, 1996, p. 13)

Carnegie Tech's economics department could offer its faculty neither prestige nor salary equivalent to that provided by more highly rated departments, but Bach saw an opportunity to attract outstanding young economists by providing a creative intellectual environment, free from the skeptical oversights of older, more traditional colleagues who were wary of theory and quantification. The first faculty member he hired was William W. Cooper whom he had known during Cooper's days as chair of an interagency task force on the government's wartime problems of statistical analysis. A short time later, he hired Cyert. When Bach visited Columbia in search of faculty, his friend, George Stigler suggested Cyert. On the basis of Stigler's recommendation, Bach offered Cyert a job at Carnegie Tech, initially to work with Cooper on a course on quantitative controls in business.

Cyert and Carnegie

The experience of the depression, his service in the navy, and his doctoral training at Columbia all shaped Cyert's approach to economics and higher education and laid the foundation for his long association with the Carnegie Institute of Technology and Carnegie-Mellon University. When he came to Pittsburgh to join the Carnegie Tech economics faculty in 1948, Cyert had not yet finished his thesis. As was common at the time, he took the job at Carnegie and finished the thesis there. He expected to stay at Carnegie only a few years while writing his dissertation, and then to move to a major research university. As things turned out, however, he stayed nearly 50 years and became one of the principal architects of making the institution into a major research university.

Soon after Cyert arrived, the playing field became broader than academic economics. While Bach was assembling his economics department he had found himself drawn toward the broader field of management education by Doherty and by outside sources, in particular the Ford Foundation (Gleeson and Slossenman, 1996, p. 13) which had hired H. Rowan Gaither from the RAND Corporation. Gaither had been helping RAND president Collbohm with its reorganization in 1948 and had been 'discovered' by Henry Ford when he wanted someone to do a study of the objectives of the foundation. Experienced in working with both scientists and funding institutions, and eager to find ways to strengthen the US economy in the post-Second World War period, Gaither was a strong advocate for better management in the US:

> If we are to achieve a better realization of democratic goals within the United States and for the peoples of the world, our domestic economy must stand as an example before the world as a strong and growing economy characterized by high output, the highest possible level of constructive employment and a minimum of destructive instability. (Kaplan, 1983, p. 61; see also pp. 127–9)

Bach resonated both with Gaither's vision and with Doherty's interest in broad social science and the idea of linking business practice to fundamental research. Bach recalled,

> We were social scientists who had discovered, in one way or another, that organizational and business environments provided a fertile source of basic research ideas and who therefore did not regard 'basic' and 'applied' as antithetical terms. Accurately or not, we perceived business education as a wasteland of vocationalism that needed to be transformed into science-based professionalism, as medicine and engineering had been transformed a generation or two earlier.[9]

When a gift from William Larimer Mellon provided an endowment that allowed Carnegie to establish a new Graduate School of Industrial Administration, Bach became the first dean of the school. Cyert was then an assistant professor. In a remarkably short time, GSIA became the home of an exceptional collection of scholars bound together by an unabashed commitment to transforming economics, organization studies, and management education. During the next few years, Bach hired (among others) Harold Guetzkow, Charles Holt, Harold Leavitt, James G. March, Alan Meltzer, Merton Miller, Franco Modigliani, Herbert A. Simon, Victor Vroom, and Harrison White. They recruited a group of doctoral students that included (among others) Albert Ando, Dwight Crane, William Dill, Edward Feigenbaum, Julian Feldman, Dale Mortensen, John Muth, Allan Newell, Edward Prescott, William Pounds, William Starbuck, and Oliver Williamson, and a group of new faculty and extended visitors that included (among others) Robert Lucas, Jacob Marschak, Richard Nelson, and Thomas Sargent.

During the 1950s, Cyert and his colleagues at GSIA built a new model for US business schools[10] and laid the research foundations for a series of contributions to organizational and behavioral economics. It was a period of ferment and experimentation, and Cyert was a key innovator. For example, he was among the first to see the potential for using computers in research and teaching. Along with others at Carnegie Tech, he argued for the use of computer simulation in simulating economic and organizational processes and for the use of gaming as an instructional tool. In 1959, Cyert and others at GSIA began developing the Carnegie Tech Management Game; a device both for using computers to simulate management problems and for encouraging students to use computers in solving problems.

In 1960, Cyert was named full professor and in 1962, he was persuaded to take over the deanship of GSIA. The persuasion was not difficult. In the late 1950s, studies of business education had criticized US business school education (Schaefer, 1992). The GSIA vision of a more scholarly and more research-oriented business school became the model, and Cyert moved to consolidate the gains initiated by G.L. Bach. The deanship suited Cyert well. 'I've always liked to run things', he said, 'and coming from my background, I saw a deanship as a promotion not as a step down out of scholarship'.[11]

Ten years later, in 1972, he became president of the university. Carnegie Tech had become Carnegie-Mellon University in 1967, and when H. Guyford Stever left the presidency to become director of the National Science Foundation, Cyert was chosen to succeed him. Allen Meltzer, a member of the search committee and a colleague at GSIA, explained what attracted the committee and the board to Cyert:

> He was a good scholar and had a great analytical mind. He listened well. He liked to run things and had great enthusiasm. He was curious and innovative. He really believed this place could be great. But two things were probably decisive. One was that Dick was thoroughly knowledgeable about Carnegie Mellon, and we were in a crisis and didn't have a year or two to break in an outsider. Also, Dick was tough and not afraid to make hard decisions. We needed some quick hard choices.[12]

Although he might not have said so, Cyert had a similar conception of himself. He saw himself as someone who solved problems and made choices: 'My deepest belief is in the need for people to deal with problems, both personal and societal. ... I value intellectual activity very highly because it is our best weapon to deal with problems. Disciplined thought is critical'.[13] He was a problem solver, and he had a sense of mission. He thought of higher education and Carnegie-Mellon as making society better. In his 1973 presidential inaugural speech, he said:

> [O]ur opportunity to contribute to the development of outstanding young men and women and to contribute to the solution of the problems of society is great. Our only enemy is discouragement and loss of commitment. If we maintain our dedication to our goals, our courage to innovate, and our energy to work, we will, we must accomplish our goals. The future greatness of our society depends in the end on institutions like this one. Our goal is greatness for us and for our society. Through success we can help lead the way to a better world for everyone.[14]

It was a romantic hope, as befitted a romantic man. Cyert was a romantic, but he was not just a romantic. He combined an unbounded capacity for optimism (nurtured perhaps by having been a Pittsburgh Pirate baseball fan during the 1950s when the Pirates were habitual losers) with a strong administrative talent. One year after he became president, a projected $1.4 million deficit became a $150,000 surplus. In the ensuing years he presided over a change of the university's image from that of a good engineering school, to an internationally recognized research university. Carnegie-Mellon became a prime example of a university that used strong leadership to make itself both more distinguished and more solvent (Schaefer, 1992).

Cyert threw considerable energy into his administrative efforts as dean of GSIA and as president of the university. Nevertheless, he continued to publish scholarly articles and books throughout his administrative years and afterwards. Indeed, much of his work with Morris DeGroot was carried out during the time of his service as president. At that time, Allen Meltzer commented that Cyert 'may be the only American university president who continues to do serious research'.[15]

2 THE WORK

Richard M. Cyert was a student of the firm, a statistician, and an academic leader; and each of his three main clusters of contributions was attached to one of those roles. In each case, he was deeply an economist. He worked within the general frame of economic theories of rational choice, using those theories when they seemed to make sense, suggesting modifications when they did not.

The Behavioral Theory of the Firm

The mantra of Cyert's contributions to behavioral and organizational economics was his insistence that economic theories be as realistic as possible in their assumptions. He argued that the characterization of economic actors in the theory of the firm should be consistent with what is known about the way individuals in firms actually behave, and that arguments to the contrary were both specious and pernicious (see, for example, Cyert, 1970; 1973).[16] The focus on real behavior and real decision practices led, in turn, to a commitment to make economics more attentive to other social and behavioral sciences.

> If you are doing behavioral economics you have to think about actual behavior and you also have to have the ability to move to the field of organization theory, and to borrow ideas from other fields too, such as psychology. ... On the theoretical level it is important ... to learn to deal with bounded rationality and uncertainty. You have to deal with the real world – and the real world is messy and people make a lot of mistakes.[17]

Cyert's emphasis on interdisciplinary openness and empirical realism was reflected especially in his collaboration with Herbert A. Simon and James G. March in trying to understand the internal decision-making processes of business firms. Simon, who had a doctorate from the University of Chicago and had been on the faculty at the University of California, Berkeley, and Illinois Institute of Technology, came to Carnegie Tech in 1949 with an already established reputation as a leading student of organizations and administration. In 1953 Simon invited March, who had just received his PhD from Yale University, to join the GSIA faculty.

In 1955 Simon published two papers, one in a major economics journal and the other in a major psychology journal (Simon, 195 5, 1956), which sketched some key elements of a theory of bounded rationality. Over the ensuing ten years, Cyert, Simon, and March published two books and numerous articles that elaborated a vision of a revised theory of the firm (for example, March and Simon, 1958; Cyert and March, 1955, 1956, 1963; Cyert et al., 1958). That period at GSIA was, Cyert recalled, 'the most exciting environment in which I have ever lived'.[18] When asked to choose which period of his productive life was most important to him, Richard Cyert replied:

> Of course, I think of the period when Jim [March] and Herb [Simon] and I were developing behavioral economics. I am sure as one reads the history of economic thought from a different perspective, he could pick a different period, but I would pick the later 50s and early 60s.[19]

Cyert's association with March grew out of one of the intense professional relationships that were frequent at GSIA in the 1950s. As Cyert described it:

> I came to Carnegie in 1948 and Jim came in 1953, and we really hit it off. I had been doing quite a bit of reading and had come to the conclusion that we weren't ever going to get a theory of how oligopoly priced without going inside the firm. And I talked to Jim about it and thought that we might be able to do something with organization theory and oligopoly theory. Fortunately, Jim was very interested and we started having our lunches together. ... [I]t was really an exciting time, because we would talk, get ideas, write something down and eventually we would produce a paper. ... [I]t was

> a big thrill for us and the school of course was pleased as well. So we continued working together. ... I was (and I still am) very pleased with our work. ... That became the basis of deciding to do a book together. We had I think 8–10 papers that were different and were all beginning to focus on the same thing called behavioral economics. We worked together even though I became the dean of the school in 1962 and it was a really exciting time. By that time we had finished the book and it was published in 1963. ... That is really how the *Behavioral Theory of the Firm* got started. (Interview with Richard Cyert, p. 8)

It was to be a friendship that lasted until Cyert's death (March, 1998). Their first co-authored paper, 'Organizational structure and pricing behavior in an oligopolistic market' was published in the *American Economic Review* in 1955, and about seven years later they completed *A Behavioral Theory of the Firm*. Their last collaborative work was the 'Epilogue' to the second edition of that work, published in 1992.

A Behavioral Theory of the Firm outlined a theory that was built around a political conception of organizational goals, a bounded rationality conception of expectations, an adaptive conception of rules and aspirations, and a set of ideas about how the interactions among these factors affect decisions in a firm. The *goals* of a firm were pictured as reflecting the demands of a political coalition, changing as the composition of that coalition changes. Thus, the theory treated the demands of shareholders, managers, workers, customers, suppliers, and creditors as components of the operational goals of a firm. At the same time, not all goals are salient at all times. Rather, specific goals are evoked by the presence of coalition members in the decision neighborhood, by the divisional organization of the firm, and by the recognition of particular problems. Aspirations with respect to each dimension of the goals were pictured as changing in response to the experience of the organization and its components as well as the experience of others to whom they compare themselves.

Expectations were portrayed as the result of making inferences from available information. This led to attention both to the processes by which information is made available and to the processes of drawing inferences. Within the boundedly rational assumptions of the theory, information is not automatically and costlessly available. Rather, information is generated by search activity. The intensity of search depends on the performance of the organization relative to aspirations and the amount of organizational slack. The direction of search is affected by the location (in the organization) of search activity and the definition of the problem stimulating the activity.

Choice was assumed to take place in response to a problem, to use standard operating procedures and other routines, and to involve finding an alternative that is acceptable from the point of view of current aspiration levels for evoked goals. Choice is affected, therefore, by the definition of a problem, by existing rules (which reflect past learning by the organization), by the order in which alternatives are considered (which reflects the location of decision making in the organization and past experience), and by anything that affects aspirations and attention.

The theory was described in the *Behavioral Theory of the Firm* as depending on four central concepts. The first was the *quasi-resolution of conflict*, the idea that firms function with considerable latent conflict of interests but do not necessarily resolve that conflict explicitly. Overt conflict is avoided, first, by treating goals as independent constraints, thus as not requiring determination of explicit trade-offs. Conflict is avoided, second, by local rationality, through delegation and specialization that results in evoking only a subset of the goals at any particular decision point. Conflict is avoided, third, by using acceptable-level, satisficing decision rules.

And conflict is avoided, fourth, by sequential attention to goals. The resulting time buffers among goals reduce the likelihood of confronting inconsistent demands at any particular time.

The second concept was *uncertainty avoidance*. Although firms try to anticipate an unpredictable future insofar as they can, they also try to restructure their worlds in order to minimize their dependence on anticipation of the highly uncertain future. They do this, in part, by making extensive use of feedback-react decision procedures in which they monitor changes in their environments and develop capabilities for responding quickly to them when they are detected, rather than trying to forecast them. And they do it, in part, by negotiating their environments, rather than simply reacting to an exogenous environment. Jointly with their competitors, they establish rules for good practice that reduce uncertainty in competition. Within the firm, they establish budgets and rules that reduce internal uncertainty.

The third concept was *problemistic search*, the idea that search within a firm is stimulated primarily by problems and directed to solving those problems. It is depressed by the absence of problems. Moreover, search is local in two senses. First, search occurs initially in the neighborhood of a problem symptom, particularly the organizational neighborhood. Second, search occurs initially in the neighborhood of existing policy. Finally, search is biased by the special competencies or experiences of the searching units, by the interaction of hopes and expectations, and by deliberate falsifications attributable to unresolved conflict.

The fourth concept was *organizational learning*. The theory assumes that firms learn from their own experiences and the experiences of others. That learning affects three critical aspects of decision making in firms. First, aspirations adapt, tracking experience. Second, attention rules adapt. Experience teaches which criteria and which parts of the environment deserve attention. Third, search rules adapt, increasing the use of rules associated with success and decreasing the use of rules associated with failure.

Sequential Choice and Bayesian Updating

Cyert also collaborated at Carnegie with Robert Trueblood and Morris DeGroot. With Trueblood he worked on statistical sampling in accounting, work that was influential in introducing modem sampling methods and statistical decision theory to accounting practice (Trueblood and Cyert, 1957). More well known among academic students of economics, however, is his collaboration with Morris DeGroot. DeGroot was trained in Bayesian statistics (see, for example, Cyert and DeGroot, 1970, 1975, 1984, 1986, 1987) and came to Carnegie to help develop the field of statistical decision theory at GSIA. In the late 1960s Cyert and DeGroot started working together. They published their first paper in 1970, and their book, *Bayesian Analysis and Uncertainty in Economic Theory*, was published in 1987.

Although the structure and intent of 'Bayesian' updating seem on the surface to be rather distant from 'behavioral' economics, Cyert saw his Bayesian work as having been initiated by and feeding upon his work on the behavioral theory of the firm (see Day and Sunder, 1996):

> [T]he stuff with DeGroot ... is definitely in the same direction as the behavioral theory of the firm. It is trying to study decision making under uncertainty ... and to do it in a way that relates back to the behavioral theory of the firm. So that book and the research Jim and I did really started this.[20]

The emphasis on uncertainty was a natural one, since it fit into modern thinking about choice both in statistical decision theory and in behavioral economics (see Earl, 1988). The attraction is made explicit in his 1987 book with DeGroot.

> We were attracted to the Bayesian approach because it seemed the best analytical framework available for dealing with decision making under uncertainty, and the research presented in this book has only served to strengthen our belief in the appropriateness and usefulness of this methodology. (Cyert and DeGroot, 1987, p. ix)

In doing this work, Cyert was less interested in contributing to statistical theory than in building a theory of real economic behavior under uncertainty. In some ways, he returned to his thoughts from his thesis on oligopoly theory. Traditional theory not only lacked any specification of the decision process, it was also bereft of any learning on the part of the firm or its decision makers. Models like the 'kinked demand curve', he felt, could not be sustained under learning (see in particular Cyert and DeGroot, 1971). Cyert and DeGroot argued that 'the concept of organizational learning is fundamental to decision making under uncertainty in economics and the Bayesian framework is the most appropriate for developing that concept' (Cyert and DeGroot, 1987, p. x). Thus, sequential sampling and Bayesian updating became a framework for exploring learning by economic actors (see, especially Cyert and DeGroot, 1975, and 1987, Chapters 6 and 7).

Cyert combined his early training in sequential sampling with Bayesian ideas to provide a framework for understanding how economic actors cope with uncertainty by updating their beliefs on the basis of observations. The essential notion was that actors learn from their actions, modifying their expectations and the expected utilities of their alternatives as a consequence of their experiences. The central idea is illustrated in the work on adaptive utility. The point of departure was the difficulty of fitting standard economic ideas about decision making to choice under uncertainty, particularly the Allais paradox (Cyert and DeGroot, 1975). Observed choices of decision makers appear to be inconsistent with a theory that assumes a fixed utility for alternatives (Allais, 1953; Cyert and DeGroot, 1970). The idea of adaptive utility is that decision makers learn from their experience and modify their expectations and expected utilities of alternatives on the basis of observing differences between their expected and realized returns. Agents are assumed to modify the future expected values of alternatives on the basis of the differences between expected and realized utility, thus learning from prior experience in a way similar to Bayesian updating.

The significant elements in this approach can be summarized in Cyert and DeGroot's own words as follows:

> First, it is assumed that a consumer does not know his or her utility function and must learn about it through experience. Second, the determination of this function is a problem of decision making under uncertainty. Thus, Bayesian theory and methodology are appropriate tools for the analysis. Third, the problem should be perceived as an investment problem in which consumption is an investment in information. Fourth, the problem is a multiperiod problem; the more quickly one learns about his or her actual utility function, the greater will be the utility enjoyed over the remaining periods. (Cyert and DeGroot, 1987, p. 143)

The formulation was explicitly directed to solving an optimization problem under conditions of uncertainty, but in a situation in which a sequential search for the optimum involves learning not only about an uncertain world but also about the decision maker's uncertain desires. The behavioral claim was that the assumptions reflected in the Bayesian structure of the problem were closer than were those of other approaches to the real nature of decision problems, thus were more relevant to such problems.

Cyert and DeGroot contrasted such an approach with two other approaches, game theory and rational expectations theory. They saw the expectational assumptions of the game theory of the time as being particularly weak when compared to actual behavior:

> We are concerned ... that the expectational assumptions of game theory ... have a weak empirical bias. The ongoing development of game theory through the use of more sophisticated mathematical models, we believe, is at best tangential to the actual process of decision making under uncertainty. (Cyert and DeGroot, 1987, p. ix)

And regarding rational expectations, they argued that rational expectations theorists failed to identify the behavioral process by which rational expectations are made 'rational'.

In a bow to the conventions of rational expectations, Cyert and DeGroot accepted the fundamental notion that 'phenomena based on nonrationality ... cannot exist for any period of significant duration' (Cyert and DeGroot, 1987, p. 185). Their acceptance was, however, conditional:

> [W]e have also pointed out that no attention is given to the process by which rational expectations may develop in a market. In particular, the learning process has been ignored and we have attempted to remedy this deficiency by introducing the concept of Bayesian learning. (Cyert and DeGroot, 1987, p. 185)

In the end, in fact, their endorsement of rational expectations was considerably tempered by their showing that though there exist some special cases in which Bayesian learning converges to rational expectations, such convergence is far from the general rule. As a result, they argued, although rational expectation ideas might be imagined to allay concerns about expectations in dynamic models (Sargent, 1995), the behavioral and empirical validity of rational expectation equilibria remained very much in doubt.

University Management

Cyert was passionate about his obligations as an educational leader, believing that universities served society and the individuals they educated. He was committed to higher education in general and Carnegie-Mellon (CMU) in particular. He wanted CMU to be a leading university, but his conception of higher education was populist and utilitarian, not elitist. He never wavered from a view of university education as a vehicle for mobility and economic security for the less favored.

> I always felt we had to have those students prepared so that they could move out into the real world after four years. I think the concept of liberal education as it existed in the past was too much consistent with an upper class notion of education. ... My feelings for us, where our students were middle, lower-middle or upper-middle class, was that we had to worry about how they were going to do when they got out. So I [felt] this notion of having professional education along with liberal education was a way in which we could really meet our obligations. I've often said I want to be able

> to look a parent in the eye and say, 'Your son or daughter will be able to find a job when they get out'. (Cyert, 1990b, p. 22)

Cyert wanted the university to serve its students, but he believed that to do so it had to excel as a center for scholarship. He wanted CMU not only to be the best it could be but also to be the best. Toward that end, he sought to elevate the concept of comparative advantage to the level of gospel in the minds of his deans and department heads.

> My notion from the beginning was that we had to find those ways in which we could have some sort of advantage, to [impress on all units the need to] identify their comparative advantage and to concentrate their resources [on this goal]. These were two principles that I pushed very hard. (Cyert, 1990b, p. 22)

He was always looking for areas in which the university could be first. Recognizing the importance of computers earlier than most and, equally importantly, recognizing that other schools would be inhibited in moving rapidly into this field because of their existing strengths in other fields, Cyert moved decisively to establish computer science and robotics at CMU. He persuaded the Department of Defense to locate its Software Research Institute close to the Carnegie Campus. And he used the computer science initiative as a basis for making the university a leader in the use of computers in on-campus and distance education.

He was entrepreneurial. He proposed that Carnegie generate part-time educational programs for people who were interested in increasing their knowledge without a degree (Cyert, 1990b, p. 24), and he was aggressive in promoting a close relationship between the university and industry, in particular with regard to the problem of transfer of technology. With the assistance of the R.K. Mellon Foundation, he tried to have the university establish a venture capital fund to invest in new businesses.

In 1990 Cyert edited a book on university management, *The Management of Nonprofit Organizations* (Cyert, 1990a), which featured several essays written by him. In the several essays he himself contributed to this book, he summarized his approach to managing universities, drawing both from his training as an economist and from his experience as a dean and university president. A central basis for his writings on management is a distinction between the role of economics as an instrument for improving economic behavior and its role as a description of that behavior. Cyert tried to keep the two aspects of economics separate, though he was not above mixing the two on occasion.

In general, he saw the principles of classical economics as providing much poorer *descriptions* of economic action than *guides* to improving it. The distinction between economic theories of choice as *guides* to intelligent behavior and economic theories of choice as descriptions of observed behavior is, of course, a conventional one. It is, however, not always easy to maintain; and the apparent contrast between Cyert's critiques of economic theory and his utilization of it in his managerial life stimulated at least one wry commentary from a colleague and friend (Dill, 1990). Cyert himself observed that economics required substantial infusion of behavioral elements in order to become fully effective as a prescription for economic action; but he also struggled to educate his administrative colleagues to the possibility and desirability of substituting the principles of rational action for their traditional habits.

As a contributor to management thought, Cyert was a relatively traditional economist. He described his goals as an academic administrator as being to improve the quality of the university and to develop a strategy for doing so within a balanced budget (Cyert, 1990b, p. 21). He enthusiastically endorsed economic principles as guidelines to organizational virtue. He was an advocate of the application of economic analysis and decision theory to the problems of firms and universities. He believed in the possibility of improving the rationality of economic behavior, that is, of making it conform more to the principles of economic theory.

As a result, his visions of the tactics and goals of proper management were almost entirely consistent with conventional economic thinking. He recommended the application of standard economic notions of marginal analysis, comparative advantage, return on investment, alignment of incentives, monitoring through clearly specified performance measures, and attention to competitive position. As William Dill pointed out in a commentary in the same book (Dill, 1990, p. 63), Cyert 'advocates strategic planning, centralized efforts to reach agreement on objectives, commitments and discipline afterwards to manage by objectives, more emphasis on systematic forecasts and budgets, and greater reliance on price and market mechanisms'.

As an administrative theorist, Cyert was an unreconstructed economic and administrative rationalist. In this respect, he differed somewhat from his collaborator on *A Behavioral Theory of the Firm* (Cohen and March, 1974; March, 1988, 1994, 1999) and from some developments stimulated by that book (see below). However, he did not differ from them in his descriptions of the way organizations work. He believed that economic actors often made mistakes and that those proclivities for making mistakes were an important part of an accurate description of economic behavior. Although *The Management of Nonprofit Organizations* can be read as a chorus in praise of the beauty of microeconomics as an ideal and instrument of management, it is also filled with testimony to its unreality as a description. Cyert described universities as deviating significantly from the economic ideal (thus, presumably in need of corrective measures by economizing managers). He portrayed them as filled with conflicts of interest and ambiguity with respect to goals (rather than as having the single, coherent goal to which he aspires). The conflict is exacerbated by the scarcity of resources and the slowing of mobility that stability or contraction induce. Conflict leads to strategic gaming of information, thus biases, and political negotiation over resources. It leads to defensiveness on the part of subunits and professions as they try to protect their own positions.

He pictured universities as responding to problems, that is, through failure, thus as becoming inefficient as a result of continued success and becoming both more efficient and more innovative (as well as more conflictual) when confronted with performance that fails to achieve expectations. At the same time, however, he noted that attendance to short-term performance measures associated with those improvements frequently leads to ignoring long-run effects, particularly where there is relatively rapid turnover of managers. And he observed that universities are resistant to change and profoundly history dependent in their resource allocations, budgets, and procedures. The ordinary processes of institutionalization tend to stabilize arrangements.

As an observer of economic behavior, Cyert saw these features of firms and universities as phenomena to be expected and understood. He considered an economic theory of the firm (or university) as unacceptable insofar as it purported to describe behavior without introducing a detailed awareness of the many ways in which organizations fail to reflect simple, conflict-free rationality. As a manager, however, Cyert clearly saw these features of organizations as defects to be eliminated or overcome. When he spoke as a manager and pushed for clear goals, marginal analysis, and the pursuit of competitive advantage, neoclassical economists cheered. When he spoke as a behavioral economist and detailed the substantial organizational deviations from neoclassical economic ideals, students of organizations cheered.

3 THE LEGACY

Cyert's portrayal of reality was too textured and subtle to be captured easily, but much of it was structured by four relatively simple ideas: bounded rationality, adaptive expectations and utilities, rule-based action, and unresolved conflict. These ideas were not entirely novel, but they were deviant. Writers such as Weber, Coase, Simon, and Marschak anticipated one or more of them, and the ideas were familiar to many others (Weber, 1947; Coase, 1937; Simon, 1947; Marschak, 1955). Nevertheless, they were not part of standard discourse in economics when Cyert began his career. In the early 1950s, the theory of the firm was substantially a theory of autonomous actors pursuing unlimited, calculated, conflict-free rationality. The internal problems of the firm were problems of efficient coordination among cooperating team members. Insofar as behavioral treatments of organizational decision making have made a contribution to economic theories of the firm, it has been by identifying some limitations of such visions and providing clues for alternative formulations. Richard M. Cyert was a pioneer in pursuing and advocating those ideas.

In the years since he first began to articulate his ideas, the interdisciplinary pursuit of the ideas he championed has flowered more than Cyert might reasonably have expected. The core ideas with which he was associated have been elaborated and refined. This is not the place to attempt a comprehensive review of those developments in modern thinking. The chapters in this book provide a sampler of exemplars, and more extended treatments are available elsewhere (Cyert and March, 1992; Day and Sunder, 1996). It may be useful, however, to outline briefly some of the more conspicuous elaborations of his insights.

Bounded Rationality

In Cyert's formulation, intendedly rational actors are constrained by limitations of information and calculation (Simon, 1955, 1956; March and Simon, 1958; Cyert and March, 1963, pp. 44–82; Cyert and DeGroot, 1987; Cyert, 1988). These limitations make determination of optimality prohibitively costly or impossible and expected utility violations common (Camerer, 1995, pp. 626–43). As a result, organizations simplify their decision problems. They set targets and look for alternatives that satisfy those targets, rather than try to find the best imaginable solution. They allocate attention by monitoring performance with respect to targets. They attend to goals sequentially, rather than simultaneously.

Ideas of bounded rationality have entered economics in two significant ways. First, bounded rationality has become a more or less standard characterization of a set of constraints facing rational actors anticipating the uncertain future consequences of current action. The theory of teams developed by Jacob Marschak and Roy Radner in the 1950s and 1960s was an early examination of optimal organization and decision rules, given limited information and a shared preference function (Marschak, 1955; Marschak and Radner, 1972). Elaborations of ideas of bounded rationality in the last half of the twentieth century have led to the present situation in which virtually all areas of microeconomics that consider choice in terms of rational, consequential action are likely to acknowledge the limits imposed on optimization by incomplete information and inadequate capabilities (Conlisk, 1996; Camerer, 1998; Rubinstein, 1998). Theories of decision making have tended to become theories of information (Radner, 2000), and considerable effort has been devoted to imagining economizing bases for the procedures used by individuals and firms in coping with the informational limits on rationality.

Second, ideas of bounded rationality have stimulated what Cyert called 'control' theories of the firm. Where the theory of teams emphasizes calculation of optimal strategies under conditions of bounded rationality, control theories emphasize incremental adaptation through sequences of actions, observations of their consequences, and modification of decision rules (March and Simon, 1958; Cyert and March, 1963, pp. 114–27; Cyert and DeGroot, 1984, 1986, 1987). This cyclic learning process results in a gradual modification of beliefs about the firm and its environment. The process of updating is subject to errors that can be attributed to classical statistical inference problems of specification, measurement, and estimation in dealing with ordinary experience.

Ideas of bounded rationality also made their way into non-economic treatments of organizations (Allison, 1971; Jones, 1999), and they led naturally to a broader concern with observing the subjective factors associated with human judgment in processing information and making decisions (Kahneman et al., 1982; Rabin, 1998). Ideas about the updating of expectations, behavioral biases, sequential attention to targets, search, the temporal sorting of problems and solutions, and the costs and benefits of information have all been folded into a decision-making frame. As a result of these observations, modem theories of choice, particularly outside of economics, are often better characterized as theories of heuristics, attention, search, and learning than of comprehensive anticipatory rationality (March, 1994; Lant and Shapira, 2000). They have been extended to include treatments of the politics of numbers (Alonso and Starr, 1987) and the social construction of accounts (Burchell et al., 1985).

Almost all of these developments emphasize the difficulties of anticipating uncertain future consequences of action, what might be called the 'first guess of rational action'. Students of bounded rationality have devoted less attention to the even more difficult problems of the 'second guess' – anticipating uncertain future preferences (March, 1978; Elster, 1979). Experimental investigations of limits to the preference axioms of rational choice have indicated significant, consistent deviation from the consistency assumptions of standard theory (Schoemaker, 1982; Machina, 1987). Instead of being refined into a coherent, continuous utility function, preferences are often better represented by an inconsistent collection of aspiration levels, or targets. Although a portrait of organizational goals as independent demands (aspirations) of separate groups is frequently reproduced in descriptions of firms, it has not found extensive theoretical development.

Adaptive Expectations and Utilities

In Cyert's view, organizations learn (Cyert and March, 1963, pp. 123–5; Cyert and DeGroot, 1987, Chapter 6; Cyert and Kumar, 1996). They update their understanding of the world and what it might offer, and they update their tastes and aspirations. As a result, theories of the firm need to be attentive to the processes by which expectations and aspirations change and their effects on individual firms and populations of firms.

This set of ideas has found some general support in interest in adaptive economics (Day and Groves, 1975; Kirman and Salmon, 1995) and in efforts to extend notions of Bayesian updating to economic models (El-Gamal and Sundaram, 1993; Chatterji, 1995). All of the major expectational components of decisions – information, alternatives, expectations, organizational forms, ideas, beliefs, and technologies – can be seen as adapting to the direct experience of the decision maker. Ideas about the experiential updating of expectations are now well-represented in economics, though often in a quite stylized form (Chow, 1989; Camerer, 1995; Evans and Honkapohja, 1995). It is also clear that expectations and beliefs spread through populations of organizations (Dutton and Starbuck, 1978; Tolbert and Zucker, 1983; Strang and Soule, 1998). This sharing of expectations, experience, and knowledge makes a difference (Marengo, 1993; Loasby, 1999), poses some problems (Cohen and Levinthal, 1989; Abrahamson, 1991), and depends on the (simultaneously adapting) networks through which diffusion takes place (Greve, 1996; Podolny et al., 1996; Abrahamson and Rosenkopf, 1997).

Attention to adaptive tastes in studies of firms has emphasized the importance of adaptive aspirations. In the satisficing tradition of the behavioral theory of the firm, aspiration levels divide good enough outcomes from those that are not good enough. Aspirations are affected by the past experiences of a particular individual or organization (Revelle and Michaels, 1976; Lant, 1992) and by the past experiences of those individuals and organizations who are perceived as comparable (Brenner, 1983; Bromiley, 1991). If aspirations adapt to history in this way, the evaluation of experience – a fundamental component of adaptive intelligence – contains systematic elements of path-dependent subjectivity.

The rate of aspiration adjustment is critical. It affects *search*. If aspirations adjust to experience rapidly, then slack and search will not adapt rapidly, and vice versa (March, 1994, p. 31). As a result, success contains the seeds of failure, and failure contains the seeds of success (Greve, 1999; Audia et al., 2000). It affects *risk taking*. Risk-taking propensity varies with the relationship between current position and a target or aspiration level, and thus between contexts of success and failure (Tversky and Kahneman, 1974; Payne et al., 1980, 1981; Shapira, 1995). When aspirations are self-referential, rapid adaptation of aspirations to a risk taker's own experience is likely to lead to less risk being taken than slow adaptation, whereas when aspirations are tied to the performance of superior others, fast adaptation is likely to lead to greater risk taking than slow adaptation (Lopes, 1987; March and Shapira, 1992). And it affects *learning*. If aspirations adapt rapidly, the resulting indeterminacy of success and failure reduces the precision of learning and thus reduces short-run returns. However, the same imprecision leads to more frequent subjective failures, thus stimulates search and exploration that may increase longer-run returns (Levinthal and March, 1993; March, 1994, pp. 87–8).

Rule-based Action

In the Cyert conception of organizations, firms follow rules of thumb, routines, and standard operating procedures (March and Simon, 1958; Cyert and March, 1963, pp. 101–13). The logic of choice is a logic of appropriateness rather than a logic of consequences. The immediate problematics of choice lie in the definition of a salient identity and in the recognition of a situation. The longer-run problematics lie in the evolution of rules and identities, the creation of institutions.

Rules, institutions, cultures, and norms have become much more prominent in thinking about economic action since the early speculations of the 1950s and 1960s. It appears to be true empirically that much of the behavior in organizations is shaped by standard operating procedures, professional standards, cultural norms, and institutional structures (Burns and Flam, 1987). The terminology is one of duties, scripts, identities, and roles rather than anticipatory, consequential choice (Stinchcombe, 1974; Turner, 1975; Abelson, 1976; Sen, 1985). It is now frequently argued that action in organizations can be more usefully interpreted as a subtle mixture of intended rationality and rule following than as a consequential calculation alone (North, 1990; Searing, 1991; March, 1994).

Interest in rule-based action leads immediately to interest in the dynamics of rules (March et al., 2000). Three major processes by which rules are created and changed are commonly considered. First, rules can be seen as contracts, chosen and negotiated strategically by rational actors (Chandler, 1962). Second, rules can be seen as developed through direct experiential learning, modified incrementally on the basis of feedback from the environment (Levitt and March, 1988). Third, the population of rules can be seen as evolving through a process of differential survival and diffusion among invariant rules, and the standard operating procedures and other institutionalized features of a firm can be pictured as the 'genes' of an evolutionary theory of economic action (Nelson and Winter, 1982; Carroll, 1984; Hannan and Freeman, 1989).

Although there has been a persistent inclination to assume a kind of crude functionalism that assures intelligence in rule populations that change in any of these ways, that inclination has been buffeted by more careful examinations of the properties of adaptive systems. The mix of rules changes over time, but the sequence of changes that occurs does not lead reliably to a unique equilibrium that is unconditionally optimal (David, 1985; Baumol and Benhabib, 1989; Kreps, 1990, pp. 402–43; Levinthal and March, 1993). These results cast doubt on the possibility of predicting rules and other aspects of the institutional structure of a firm simply from attributes of the current environment in which it is found.

Unresolved Conflict

Cyert saw economic organizations as involving multiple actors with conflicting interests and identities not entirely resolved by employment contracts and organizational rules (March, 1962; Cyert and March, 1963, pp. 26–34). The relation between organizational goals and the interests of subgroups and individuals is continually being negotiated and renegotiated. Consistency among preferences and identities is rarely achieved and difficult to sustain.

The reality and significance of *intrafirm* conflict has become increasingly salient to economic thought, particularly through the impact of transaction cost economics, game theory, and agency theory. Transaction cost economics is largely attributed to Oliver Williamson, who was a student of Richard Cyert in the 1960s (Williamson, 1996). The Williamson (1975) version of transaction costs rests on two behavioral assumptions about 'contracting', as opposed to 'maximizing'. The first assumption is bounded rationality, as above. The second assumption is opportunism, the notion that there is conflict of interest within, as well as among, organizations, that participants in an organization lie, cheat, and steal in their own self-interest if they can. Transaction cost ideas have spread not only through economics (Williamson, 1981) but also into organization studies (Williamson and Ouchi, 1981) and the economics of law (Williamson, 1979).

Game theory has been similarly influential in microeconomics (Kreps, 1990; Gibbons, 1992) and other social sciences (Ordeshook, 1986). Although game theorists have only recently begun to pay attention to problems of bounded rationality (Aumann, 1981, 1985; Rubinstein, 1998), they have long focused on strategic conflict among rational actors. In this sense, game theory is similar in spirit to transaction cost economics and to political visions of organization. Individually rational actors are assumed to act strategically and opportunistically. Alliances involve ambiguous agreements and uncertain expectations across time. As a result, decision making often emphasizes trust and loyalty, in parallel with a widespread belief that they are hard to find and sustain. Echoing these observations, modern research has moved the analysis of repetitive encounters, time horizons, reputations, and trust to central positions in theories of rational bargaining (Kreps and Wilson, 1982; Milgrom and Roberts, 1992).

Game theory slides easily into agency theory (Fama, 1980; Arrow, 1985) with its attention to one of the older problems of political philosophy and economics – understanding the relation between a 'master' who is given socially legitimate control over certain actions and a 'servant' who controls information on which the 'master' acts (Berle and Means, 1932; Burnham, 1941; Cooper, 1951). Modern attention to these problems within economics dates from articles in the 1970s by Alchian and Demsetz (1972) and Jensen and Meckling (1976). Agency theory seeks to identify properties of incentive systems that will lead rational agents, in their own self-interest, to exert full effort on behalf of their principals, rather than their principles (Hart and Holmström, 1987; Levinthal, 1988).

Assumptions of self-conscious rationality and strategic action are also traditional foundations of political treatments of organizational conflict, finding modern expression particularly in various forms of exchange (resource dependence) theories of power (Pfeffer and Salancik, 1978; Pfeffer, 1981; Mintzberg, 1983). Most students of political systems, however, give a somewhat greater role than do economists to the ways in which action stems from coalitions bound together by traditional allegiances and rules (Krasner, 1983; Lipset, 1990), from conflict stimulated by misestimations, misperceptions, and emotions of anger and shame (Flam, 1990a, 1990b), from the happenstance of attention allocation in a world of scarce attention resources (Downs, 1972; Kingdon, 1984; Baumgartner and Jones, 1993), and from the framing of political encounters by the constraints of institutions, ideology, culture, and history (Just, 1992; Rhodes, 1996; March and Olsen, 1998).

4 THE FUTURE

Significant parts of the story of economic theories of the firm over the past forty years can be written as a history of elaboration of the core ideas that Cyert advanced. Ideas of limited rationality, adaptive expectations and utilities, rule following, and unresolved conflict have been accommodated – with some occasional difficulty and even violence – within economic theory. This is not to say that these ideas 'transformed' economic thinking in a straightforward way. Their contribution was part of a gradual reconstruction of the theory of the firm in which the genesis and influence of specific ideas are hard to identify (Holmström and Tirole, 1989; Hart, 1990). Through the mysteries of intellectual development and fashion, economic thought has moved in the direction of the core of Cyert's ideas (Cyert and March, 1992; March, 1992).[21]

At the same time, many elements of the same ideas have been folded into received doctrine in other disciplines concerned with decision making and organizations (Grandori, 1987; Scott, 1987; Hickson, 1995). The ideas that Cyert championed can be seen not only in contemporary thinking about the economics of choice, change, and organization but also in thinking about politics, social groups, and the development of international orders. For the most part, these observations and the associated theoretical developments outside of economics elaborate, rather than contradict, the major themes of Cyert's ideas, though in some of their forms they are probably less compatible with the canons of economics than he might have hoped. The ideas have developed beyond his initial suggestions and perhaps beyond his intentions, but the stimuli he provided to behavioral theories of economic and organizational action have left an enduring legacy.

We have no special crystal ball to foresee where economic theory will wander over the next few decades. Forecasting the future of economics is an exercise in imagination. The very long-run future is clear but uninteresting; the very short-run future is already here; and everything in between is murky. Nevertheless, we think the history of the elaboration of a Cyert tradition in economics and studies of organizations is indicative of the vitality of his vision and his work and of their relevance for the future of economics.

NOTES

* We thank William W. Cooper and Herbert A. Simon for helpful comments and suggestions.

1. 'The Making of a President', Carnegie-Mellon University Archives, Presidential Papers, p. 5.
2. 'The Making of a President', p. 2.
3. Interview with Richard M. Cyert.
4. Interview with Richard M. Cyert.
5. It may be worth noting, however, that John Nash reported later that he first became interested in economics from a course he took in international economics during his years at Carnegie Tech in the 1940s. In 1994, about five decades after his Carnegie experience, Nash was awarded the Nobel Prize in Economics (Nasar, 1998, pp. 39–45).
6. Robert Doherty: 'The First Fifty Years', Speech, October 27, 1950, Carnegie-Mellon University Archives, Presidential Papers.
7. 'The First Fifty Years', p. 4.
8. Bach had already experienced in his study years this interest in real-world economics. As he recalled about one economic lecture, '[t]he professor explain[ed] that, theoretically, there couldn't be a lasting depression in a competitive, capitalist-type economy. I looked out the window at a long line of unemployed men waiting to apply for one of the two WTA jobs the town government had managed to get. There must be a better way for either the economists or the "practical" men who ran the system, I thought' (quoted from Gleeson and Schlossman, 1996, p. 9).
9. 'GSIA History', Carnegie-Mellon University Archives, Presidential Papers, p. 3.
10. See also Cyert (1998, p. 1): 'The early days of planning the program for the Graduate School of Industrial Administration were extremely exciting. I had just taken my first job here, and I can't think of a better place to have started'.
11. In 'The Making of a President', p. 12.
12. In 'The Making of a President', pp. 14–15.
13. In 'The Making of a President', p. 19.
14. Richard M. Cyert: 'Inaugural Speech', Carnegie-Mellon University Archives, Presidential Papers, p. 15.
15. In 'The Making of a President', p. 14.
16. See also Cyert and Hendrick (1972); Cyert and Simon (1983).
17. Interview with Richard M. Cyert.
18. Interview with Richard M. Cyert.
19. Letter from Richard M. Cyert, September 24, 1998.
20. Interview with Richard M. Cyert.
21. The formal rigidity of economic assumptions combined with substantial openness in their interpretation has led students of behavioral economics occasionally to differ in the extent to which they emphasize the consequences of rigidity (Simon, 1999) or the consequences of flexible interpretation (March, 1992).

REFERENCES

Abelson, R.P. (1976), 'Script processing in attitude formation and decision making', in J.S. Carroll and J.W. Payne (eds), *Cognition and Social Behavior*, Hillsdale, NJ: Erlbaum, pp. 33–46.

Abrahamson, E. (1991), 'Managerial fads and fashions: the diffusion and rejection of innovations', *Academy of Management Review*, **16**: 586–612.

Abrahamson, E. and L. Rosenkopf (1997), 'Social network effects on the extent of innovation diffusion: a computer simulation', *Organization Science*, **8**: 289–309.

Alchian, A.A. and H. Demsetz (1972), 'Production, information costs, and economic organization', *American Economic Review*, **62**: 777–95.

Allais, M. (1953), 'Le comportement de l'homme rationelle devant le risque, critique des postulates et axiomes de l'Ecole Americaine', 'The behaviour of the rational man facing risk: a critique of the postulates and axioms of the American school.' *Econometrica*, **21**: 503–46.

Allison, G.T. (1971), *Essence of Decision: Explaining the Cuban Missile Crisis*, Boston, MA: Little, Brown.

Alonso, W. and P. Starr (eds) (1987), *The Politics of Numbers*, New York: Russell Sage.

Arrow, K.J. (1985), 'The economics of agency', in J. Pratt and R. Zeckhauser (eds), *Principals and Agents*, Boston, MA: Harvard Business School Press, pp. 37–51.

Audia, G., E.A. Locke and K.G. Smith (2000), 'The paradox of success: an archival and a laboratory study of strategic persistence following a radical environmental change', *Academy of Management Journal*, **43**: (5), 837–53.

Aumann, R. (1981), 'Survey of repeated games', in R. Henn and O. Moeschlin (eds), *Mathematical Economics and Game Theory: Essays in Honor of Oskar Morgenstern*, Mannheim: Bibliographisches Institut, pp. 11–42.

Aumann, R. (1985), 'What is game theory trying to accomplish?', in K. Arrow and S. Honkapohja (eds), *Frontiers of Economics*, Oxford: Basil Blackwell, pp. 28–76.

Baumgartner, F.R. and B.D. Jones (1993), *Agendas and Instability in American Politics*, Chicago, IL: University of Chicago Press.

Baumol, W.J. and J. Benhabib (1989), 'Chaos: Significance, mechanism, and economic applications', *Journal of Economic Perspectives*, **3**: 77–105.

Berle, A.A. Jr. and G.C. Means (1932), *The Modern Corporation and Private Property*, New York: Macmillan.

Brenner, R. (1983), *History – the Human Gamble*, Chicago, IL: University of Chicago Press.

Bromiley, P. (1991), 'Testing a causal model of corporate risk-taking and performance', *Academy of Management Journal*, **34**: 37–59.

Burchell, S., C. Colin and A.G. Hopwood (1985), 'Accounting in its social context: towards a history of value added in the United Kingdom', *Accounting, Organizations and Society*, **10**: 381–413.

Burnham, J. (1941), *The Managerial Revolution*, New York: John Day.

Burns, T.R. and H. Flam (1987), *The Shaping of Social Organization: Social Rule System Theory with Applications*, Beverly Hills, CA: Sage.

Camerer, C.F. (1995), 'Individual decision making', in J.H. Kagel and A.E. Roth (eds), *The Handbook of Experimental Economics*, Princeton, NJ: Princeton University Press, pp. 587–703.

Camerer, C.F. (1998), 'Behavioral economics and nonrational organizational decision making', in J.J. Halpern and R.N. Stern, (eds), *Debating Rationality: Nonrational Aspects of Organizational Decision Making*, Ithaca, NY: Cornell University Press, pp. 53–77.

Carroll, G.R. (1984), 'Organizational ecology', *Annual Review of Sociology*, **10**: 71–93.

Chandler, A. (1962), *Strategy and Structure*, Cambridge, MA: MIT Press.

Chatterji, S. (1995), 'Temporary equilibrium dynamics with Bayesian learning', *Journal of Economic Theory*, **67**: 590–98.

Chow, G.C. (1989), 'Rational versus adaptive expectations in present value models', *Review of Economics and Statistics*, **71**: 376–84.

Coase, R.H. (1937), 'The nature of the firm', *Economica*, **4** (N.S.): 386–405.

Cohen, M.D. and J.G. March (1974), *Leadership and Ambiguity: The American College President*, New York: McGraw-Hill.

Cohen, W.M. and D.A. Levinthal (1989), 'Innovation and learning: the two faces of R&D', *Economic Journal*, **99**: 569–96.

Conlisk, J. (1996), 'Why bounded rationality?', *Journal of Economic Literature*, **34**: 669–700.

Cooper, W.W. (1951), 'A proposal for extending the theory of the firm', *Quarterly Journal of Economics*, **65**: 87–109.

Cyert, R.M. and M. DeGroot (1971), Interfirm learning and the kinked demand curve, *Journal of Economic Theory*, **3**: 272–87.

Cyert, R.M. (1988), *The Economic Theory of Organization and the Firm*, New York: Harvester.
Cyert, R.M. (ed.) (1990a), *The Management of Nonprofit Organizations*, Lexington, MA: Lexington Books.
Cyert, R.M. (1990b), 'The early days', *Executive Report Magazine*, Special issue in honor of Richard M. Cyert, Pittsburgh, PA: Junior Achievement of Southwest Pennsylvania.
Cyert, R.M. (1998), 'My memories of the early days of GSIA', Unpublished note.
Cyert, R.M. and M.H. DeGroot (1970), 'Bayesian analysis and duopoly theory', *Journal of Political Economy*, **78**: 1168–84.
Cyert, R.M. and M.H. DeGroot (1975), 'Adaptive utility', in Day and Groves (eds), pp. 223–46.
Cyert, R.M. and M.H. DeGroot (1984), 'The maximization process under uncertainty', in L.S. Sproull and P.D. Larkey (eds), *Advances in Information Processing in Organizations*, Greenwich, CT: JAI Press, pp. 47–61.
Cyert, R.M. and M.H. DeGroot (1986), 'Toward a control theory of the firm', in R. Wolff (ed.), *Organizing Industrial Development*, Berlin: Walter deGruyter, pp. 342–86.
Cyert, R.M. and M.H. DeGroot (1987), *Bayesian Analysis and Uncertainty in Economic Theory*, Totowa, NJ: Rowman & Littlefield.
Cyert, R.M., W. Dill and J.G. March (1958), 'The role of expectations in business decision making', *Administrative Science Quarterly*, **3**: 307–40.
Cyert, R.M. and C.L. Hendrick (1972), 'Theory of the firm: past, present and future: an interpretation', *Journal of Economic Literature*, **10**: 398–412.
Cyert, R.M. and P. Kumar (1996), 'Economizing by firms through learning and adaptation', *Journal of Economic Behavior and Organization*, **29**: 211–31.
Cyert, R.M. and J.G. March (1955), 'Organizational structure and pricing behavior in an oligopolistic market', *American Economic Review*, **45**: 129–39.
Cyert, R.M. and J.G. March (1956), 'Organizational factors in the theory of oligopoly', *Quarterly Journal of Economics*, **70**: 44–64.
Cyert, R.M. and J.G. March (1963), *A Behavioral Theory of the Firm*, Englewood Cliffs, NJ: Prentice-Hall.
Cyert, R.M. and J.G. March (1992), *A Behavioral Theory of the Firm*, 2nd edn, Oxford: Blackwell.
Cyert, R.M. and H.A. Simon (1983), 'The behavioral approach: with emphasis on economics', *Behavioral Science*, **28**: 95–108.
David, P.A. (1985), 'Clio and the economics of QWERTY', *American Economic Review*, **75**: 332–7.
Day, R. and T. Groves (eds) (1975), *Adaptive Economic Models*, New York: Academic Press.
Day, R. and S. Sunder (1996), 'Ideas and work of Richard M. Cyert', *Journal of Economic Behavior and Organization*, **31**: 139–48.
Dill, W. (1975), 'From Cyert and March to Cyert vs. March', in R. Cyert (ed.) (1975).
Downs, A. (1972), 'Up and down with ecology: the issue attention cycle', *Public Interest*, **28**: 38–50.
Dutton, J.M. and W.H. Starbuck (1978), 'Diffusion of an intellectual technology', in K. Krippendorff (ed.), *Communication and Control in Society*, New York: Gordon & Breach, pp. 489–511.
Earl, P. (1988), *Behavioral Economics*, Aldershot, UK: Edward Elgar.
Earl, P. (1995), *Microeconomics for Business and Marketing*, Aldershot, UK: Edward Elgar.
El-Gamal, M.A. and R.K. Sundaram (1993), 'Bayesian economists ... Bayesian agents: an alternative approach to optimal learning', *Journal of Economic Dynamics and Control*, **17**: 355–83.
Elster, J. (1979), *Ulysses and the Sirens: Studies in Rationality and Irrationality*, Cambridge: Cambridge University Press.
Evans, G.W. and S. Honkapohja (1995), 'Adaptive learning and expectational stability: an introduction', in Kirman and Salmon (eds), pp. 102–26.
Fama, E.F. (1980), 'Agency problems and the theory of the firm', *Journal of Political Economy*, **88**: 288–307.
Fenton, E. (2000), 'Origins of the Carnegie Plan', *Carnegie Mellon Magazine*, Fall, p. 22.
Flam, H. (1990a), 'Emotional "man" I: The emotional "man" and the problem of collective action', *International Sociology*, **5**: 39–56.
Flam, H. (1990b), 'Emotional "man" II: Corporate actors as emotion-motivated emotion managers', *International Sociology*, **5**: 225–34.
Gibbons, R. (1992), *Game Theory for Applied Economists*, Princeton, NJ: Princeton University Press.

Gleeson, R. and S. Schosselmann (1996), 'George Leland Bach and the rebirth of graduate management education in the United States', *The Magazine of the Graduate Management Admission Council*, pp. 8–46.
Grandori, A. (1987), *Perspectives on Organization Theory*, Cambridge, MA: Ballinger.
Greve, H.R. (1996), 'Patterns of competition: the diffusion of a market position in radio broadcasting', *Administrative Science Quarterly*, **41**: 29–60.
Greve, H.R. (1999), 'The effect of change on performance: inertia and regression toward the mean', *Administrative Science Quarterly*, **44**: 590–614.
Hannan, M.T. and J. Freeman (1989), *Organizational Ecology*, Cambridge, MA: Harvard University Press.
Hart, O. (1990), 'An economist's perspective on the theory of the firm', in O.E. Williamson (ed.), *Organization Theory: From Chester Barnard to the Present and Beyond*, New York: Oxford University Press, pp. 154–71.
Hart, O. and B. Holmström (1987), 'The theory of contracts', in T. Bewley (ed.), *Advances in Economic Theory*, Cambridge: Cambridge University Press, pp. 154–71.
Hickson, D.J. (ed.) (1995), *Managerial Decision Making*, Aldershot: Dartmouth.
Holmström, B.R. and J. Tirole (1989), 'The theory of the firm', in R. Schmalensee and R. D.Willig (eds), *Handbook of Industrial Organization*, Vol. 1, New York: Elsevier Science Publishers, pp. 61–133.
Jensen, M. and W. Meckling (1976), 'Theory of the firm: managerial behavior, agency costs and ownership structure', *Journal of Financial Economics*, **3**: 305–60.
Jones, B.D. (1999), 'Bounded rationality, political institutions, and the analysis of outcomes', in J. Alt, M. Levi and E. Ostrom (eds), *Competition and Cooperation: Conversations with Nobelists about Economics and Political Science*, New York: Russell Sage, pp. 85–111.
Just, P. (1992), 'History, power, ideology, and culture: current directions in the anthropology of law', *Law and Society Review*, **26**: 373–411.
Kahneman, D., P. Slovic and A. Tversky (1982), *Judgment under Uncertainty: Heuristics and Biases*, Cambridge: Cambridge University Press.
Kaplan, F. (1983), *The Wizards of Armageddon*, New York: Simon & Schuster.
Kingdon, J.W. (1984), *Agendas, Alternatives, and Public Policies*, Boston, MA: Little, Brown.
Kirman, A. and M. Salmon (eds) (1995), *Learning and Rationality in Economics*, Oxford: Basil Blackwell.
Krasner, S.D. (1983), 'Regimes and the limits of realism: regimes as autonomous variables', in S.D. Krasner (ed.), *International Regime*, Ithaca, NY: Cornell University Press, pp. 355–68.
Kreps, D.M. (1990), *Game Theory and Economic Modeling*, Oxford: Clarendon Press.
Kreps, D.M. and R. Wilson (1982), 'Reputation and imperfect information', *Journal of Economic Theory*, **27**: 253–79.
Lant, T.K. (1992), 'Aspiration level adaptation: an empirical exploration', *Management Science*, **38**: 623–44.
Lant, T.K. and Z. Shapira (eds) (2000), *Managerial and Organizational Cognition*, Mahwah, NJ: Lawrence Erlbaum Associates.
Levinthal, D.A. (1988), 'A survey of agency models of organizations', *Journal of Economic Behavior and Organization*, **9**: 153–85.
Levinthal, D.A. and J.G. March (1993), 'The myopia of learning', *Strategic Management Journal*, **14**: 95–112.
Levitt B. and J.G. March (1988), 'Organizational learning', *Annual Review of Sociology*, **14**: 319–40.
Lipset, S.M. (1990), *Continental Divide*, New York: Routledge.
Loasby, B. (1999), *Knowledge, Institutions and Evolution in Economics*, London: Routledge.
Lopes, L.L. (1987), 'Between hope and fear: the psychology of risk', *Advances in Social Psychology*, **20**: 255–95.
Machina, M.J. (1987), 'Choice under uncertainty: problems solved and unsolved', *Journal of Economic Perspectives*, **1**: 121–54.
March, J.G. (1962), 'The business firm as a political coalition', *Journal of Politics*, **24**: 662–78.
March, J.G. (1978), 'Bounded rationality, ambiguity, and the engineering of choice', *Bell Journal of Economics*, **9**: 587–608.
March, J.G. (1988), *Decisions and Organizations*, Oxford: Basil Blackwell.
March, J.G. (1992), 'The war is over and the victors have lost', *Journal of Socio-Economics*, **21**: 261–7.

March, J.G. (1994), *A Primer on Decision Making: How Decisions Happen*, New York: Free Press.
March, J.G. (1999), *The Pursuit of Organizational Intelligence*, Oxford: Blackwell.
March, J.G. and J.P. Olsen (1998), 'The institutional dynamics of international political orders', *International Organization*, **52**: 943–69.
March, J.G., M. Schulz and X. Zhou (2000), *The Dynamics of Rules: Change in Written Organizational Codes*, Stanford, CA: Stanford University Press.
March, J.G. and Z. Shapira (1992), 'Variable risk preferences and the focus of attention', *Psychological Review*, **99**: 172–83.
March, J.G. and H.A. Simon (1958), *Organizations*, New York: John Wiley.
Marengo, L. (1993), 'Knowledge distribution and coordination in organizations: on some social aspects of the exploitation vs exploration trade-off', *Revue Internationale de Systémique*, **7**: 553–71.
Marschak, J. (1955), 'Elements for a theory of teams', *Management Science*, **1**: 127–37.
Marschak, J. and R. Radner (1972), *Economic Theory of Teams*, New Haven, CT: Yale University Press.
Milgrom, P. and J. Roberts (1992), *Economics, Organization and Management*, Englewood Cliffs, NJ: Prentice-Hall.
Mintzberg, H. (1983), *Power in and around Organizations*, Englewood Cliffs, NJ: Prentice-Hall.
Nasar, S. (1998), *A Beautiful Mind*, New York: Simon & Schuster.
Nelson, R. and S.G. Winter (1982), *An Evolutionary Theory of Economic Change*, Cambridge, MA: Harvard University Press.
North, D.C. (1990), *Institutions, Institutional Change and Economic Performance*, Cambridge: Cambridge University Press.
Ordeshook, P.C. (1986), *Game Theory and Political Theory: An Introduction*, Cambridge: Cambridge University Press.
Payne, J.W., D.J. Laughhann and R.L. Crum (1980), 'Translation of gambles and aspiration level effects in risky choice behavior', *Management Science*, **26**: 1039–60.
Payne, J.W., D.J. Laughhann and R.L. Crum (1981), 'Further tests of aspiration level effects in risky choice behavior', *Management Science*, **27**: 953–8.
Pfeffer, J. (1981), *Power in Organizations*, Marshfield, MA: Pitman.
Pfeffer, J. and G.R. Salancik (1978), *The External Control of Organizations*, New York: Harper & Row.
Podolny, J., T.E. Stuart and M.T. Hannan (1996), 'Networks, knowledge, and niches: competition in the worldwide semiconductor industry, 1984–1991', *American Journal of Sociology*, **102**: 659–89.
Rabin, M. (1998), 'Psychology and economics', *Journal of Economic Literature*, **36**: 11–46.
Radner, R. (2000), 'Costly and bounded rationality in individual and team decision making', *Industrial and Corporate Change*, **9**(4), 623–58.
Revelle, W. and E. Michaels (1976), 'The theory of achievement motivation revisited: the implications of inertial tendencies', *Psychological Review*, **83**: 394–404.
Rhodes, R.A.W. (1996), 'From institutions to dogma: tradition, eclecticism, and ideology in the study of British public administration', *Public Administration Review*, **56**: 507–16.
Rubinstein, A. (1998), *Models of Bounded Rationality*, Cambridge, MA: MIT Press.
Sargent, T. (1995), *Bounded Rationality in Macroeconomics*, Oxford: Clarendon Press.
Schaefer, L.F. (1992), *Evolution of a National Research University: 1965–1990. The Stever Administration and the Cyert Years at Carnegie Mellon*, Pittsburgh, PA: Carnegie-Mellon University Press.
Schoemaker, P.J.H. (1982), 'The expected utility model: its variants, purposes, evidence and limitations', *Journal of Economic Literature*, **20**: 529–63.
Scott, W.R. (1987), *Organizations: Rational, Natural, and Open Systems*, 2nd edn, Englewood Cliffs, NJ: Prentice-Hall.
Searing, D.D. (1991), 'Roles, rules and rationality in the new institutionalism', *American Political Science Review*, **85**: 1239–60.
Sen, A.K. (1985), 'Goals, commitment, and identity', *Journal of Law, Economics, and Organization*, **1**: 341–55.
Shapira, Z. (1995), *Risk Taking: A Managerial Perspective*, New York: Russell Sage.
Simon, H.A. (1947), *Administrative Behavior*, New York: Macmillan.
Simon, H.A. (1955), 'A behavioral model of rational choice', *Quarterly Journal of Economics*, **69**: 99–118.

Simon, H.A. (1956), 'Rational choice and the structure of the environment', *Psychological Review*, **63**: 129–38.
Simon, H.A. (1999), 'Remarks on the methodology of science: discovery and verification', in J. Alt, M. Levi and E. Ostrom (eds), *Competition and Cooperation: Conversations with Nobelists about Economics and Political Science*, New York: Russell Sage, pp. 326–30.
Stinchcombe, A.L. (1974), *Creating Efficient Industrial Administration*, New York: Academic Press.
Strang, D. and S.A. Soule (1998), 'Diffusion in organizations and social movements: from hybrid corn to poison pills', *Annual Review of Sociology*, **24**: 265–90.
Tolbert, P.S. and L.G. Zucker (1983), 'Institutional forces of change in the formal structure of organizations: the diffusion of civil services reform, 1880–1935', *Administrative Science Quarterly*, **28**: 22–39.
Trueblood, R.M. and R.M. Cyert (1957), *Sampling Techniques in Accounting*, Englewood Cliffs, NJ: Prentice-Hall.
Turner, J.C. (1975), 'Social comparison and social identity: some prospects for intergroup behavior', *European Journal of Social Psychology*, **5**: 5–34.
Tversky, A. and D. Kahneman (1974), 'Judgment under uncertainty: heuristics and biases', *Science*, **185**: 1124–31.
Weber, M. (1947), *The Theory of Social and Economic Organization*, Oxford: Oxford University Press.
Williamson, O.E. (1975), *Markets and Hierarchies*, New York: Free Press.
Williamson, O.E. (1979), 'Transaction-cost economics: the governance of contractual relations', *Journal of Law and Economics*, **22**: 233–61.
Williamson, O.E. (1981), 'The economics of organization: the transaction economics approach', *American Journal of Sociology*, **87**: 548–77.
Williamson, O.E. (1996), 'Transaction cost economics and the Carnegie connection', *Journal of Economic Behavior and Organization*, **31**: 149–55.
Williamson, O.E. and W. Ouchi (1981), 'The market and hierarchies and visible hand perspectives', in A. Van de Ven and W. Joyce (eds), *Perspectives on Organizational Design and Behavior*, New York: Wiley, pp. 347–70.

PART I

Economics of Choice

2. The behavioral theory of the firm in action

Lars Engwall and Rickard Danell

1 INTRODUCTION

Lunches are often considered significant features of business life. They constitute the arenas in which many business deals are prepared and even settled. Less is known about the significance of lunches for research. However, at least one very prominent example exists, and it is the development of *A Behavioral Theory of the Firm* (Cyert and March, 1963). According to its preface it all started 'with a casual conversation over a pair of bag lunches' (Cyert and March, 1963, p. v). This was the beginning of a very successful worldwide crusade for a new perspective on business behavior. For this to happen, however, the lunch bags were not enough. The Graduate School of Industrial Administration (GSIA) at the Carnegie Institute of Technology in Pittsburgh provided a very special academic atmosphere at the time. For Harold J. Leavitt, a faculty member of the school in the 1960s, it had the characteristics of a 'hot group' (Leavitt, 1996, pp. 289–90):

> Carnegie at the time was peopled by young mavericks whom that quiet administrative genius, Lee Bach, had hunted down: Herb Simon, Bill Cooper, Franco Modigliani, Dick Cyert and young Jim March, as well as half a dozen others [like Oliver Williamson, Geoffrey Clarkson, Kalman Cohen, Bill Dill, and Bill Starbuck; cf. the preface of Cyert and March, 1963, p. v]. ... We were proud, certain that we were the best and brightest. ... The search for truth was a core value. The intellectual atmosphere was more than just lively, open, and confrontational.

According to James March this was the result of the joint efforts of Carnegie Tech president Robert Doherty and GSIA dean Lee Bach, along with significant support from the Ford Foundation (see also Simon, 1991, pp. 154–6 and 163–4).

Another significant prerequisite for the book was the continuing struggle to find alternatives to the neoclassical theory of the firm. Already in the 1930s theories had been developed on business behavior modeling markets of imperfect competition (see Chamberlin, 1933; Robinson, 1933; and Sweezy, 1939). Later on in the 1950s the growth of firms attracted the attention of a number of distinguished scholars (see, for example, Baumol, 1959 and Penrose, 1959). An interest in industrial organization was also appearing (see, for example, Bain, 1959). Simultaneously there was the advent of organization theory. In this area one of the GSIA faculty members, Herbert Simon, had followed in the footsteps of his teacher in Chicago, Chester Barnard, who in 1938 had published the classical work *The Functions of the Executive*. Simon's first major contribution to the field was *Administrative Behavior* in 1947, which in 1958 was followed by *Organizations* co-authored with James March. Other classical works published at the time were by Blau (1955), Homans (1950), Selznick (1957), and Whyte (1956).

In addition the development of the field was manifested through the creation of the *Administrative Science Quarterly* in 1956.

These circumstances paved the way for a book that aimed at providing a bridge between economics and the behavioral sciences, thus making the authors hope that it would 'prove relevant both to economic theory and the theory of complex organizations' (Cyert and March, 1963, p. 3). The book also received generally positive reviews in the *American Economic Review*, the *American Journal of Sociology*, *Econometrica*, and the *Economic Journal* (*International Bibliography of the Social Sciences 1964*, 1965, item 2287), but was not reviewed in the *Administrative Science Quarterly* (Lodahl, 1969). In the *American Economic Review*, Sidney G. Winter, at the time at Berkeley, opened his review by describing the book as 'a major blow to the battered but hitherto unshaken intellectual construct, the theory of the profit-maximizing firms' (Winter, 1964, p. 144). And, he concluded by saying (pp. 147–8):

> For the past several years, the research on the theory of the firm conducted at Carnegie Institute of Technology has been distinctive for the boldness of its departure from the accepted modes of economic thought on the subject. Cyert and March and their collaborators have consolidated much of that research, and the result will be impressive to those economists who attended carefully to the fragmentary reports as they came in. Those who have not heard the distant rumblings of the 'behavioral revolution' will be surprised at the momentum it has achieved. The final verdict cannot be predicted, but this book should at least convince most economists that the revolutionaries bear watching.

A similarly positive account was given in *Econometrica* by Richard D. Day, then at the University of Wisconsin (Day, 1964, p. 462):

> The authors provide a convincing argument for giving organizational structure and behavior a prominent place in the theory of the firm. They also display ingenuity in applying their broad framework to several cleverly chosen case studies. The empirical tests of the latter lend considerable support to their views. *For these reasons the book should be read by every serious student of microeconomics* ... It is an achievement of high order to look so closely at mundane events and distill from them theory that is reasonably well defined and still operational! (Day, 1964, pp. 462 and 465; italics added)

Among other positive reviewers was Kenneth E. Boulding, at the time at the University of Michigan, although he described the book as 'an interim report' and concluded by expressing the hope that the authors would 'hole up somewhere and write the book that is implicit in the ore of this rich intellectual mine' (Boulding, 1964, p. 593). In his view 'anyone interested in the general field of the dynamics of organizational behavior [ought to] read it, for it reports some of the most lively and advanced research, and even thought, in this field to date' (p. 592). He also pointed out that it was important to note that the theory was not limited to firms but that 'the moral of the whole approach seems to be that General Motors and the Salvation Army are sisters under the skin'.

Somewhat more skeptical was F. Livesey at Queen's College, Dundee. Although, he acknowledged that the material presented in the book would be helpful in filling gaps in existing theories, he ended by asking two questions: 'how general is this pattern of behavior?', and 'how are the objectives of the firm, here treated as given, determined in practice?' (Livesey, 1964, p. 202).

The positive reviews appear to have reflected the reactions of the wider scientific community. In the words of the now retired marketing professor Hans B. Thorelli of Indiana University: 'It was a case of instant response. Within months of publication of the book, it had been made an obligatory text in scores of capstone, business policy, organization theory etc. courses' (Personal communication in 1999). William H. Starbuck, GSIA alumnus and presently at New York University, even remembers that the book was included in a 'time capsule' arranged by a celebrated magazine. According to Starbuck it was aimed at 'representing the most significant cultural items from the mid-twentieth century'. It also had an apparent impact on the younger generation, such as McGill professor Henry Mintzberg, who at the time was a doctoral student at the Massachusetts Institute of Technology:

> Cyert and March has been an important book for me, and remains so, because of its deep and surprising messages – which sustain themselves even today, I believe. It came along just before I began doctoral studies [and] I was deeply influenced by its spirit of creative insight at least as much as its actual content. (Personal communication in 1999; see also Mintzberg, 1993, pp. 327–8)

There is thus no doubt that *A Behavioral Theory of the Firm* received considerable attention after its publication. However, even today, almost forty years later, the reading of prestigious journals in the management and organization field provides evidence that it is still often cited. To have such a long-term impact on the scientific community does not happen to many publications. As a matter of fact, citation data show that even articles published in top-rank management journals are, on average, only cited at most about three times, and for many the cited half-time is less than ten years (see further Engwall, 1996, Table 1). Thus if a book can survive as a basic source in management and organization research for nearly four decades, it should indeed be considered an achievement. It is a good reason to look more closely at its impact in time and space. We shall therefore in the present chapter provide an analysis of the reception of Cyert and March (1963) in the last two decades.

After a summary of the main arguments of the book in Section 2, we shall, in Section 3, present citation data from the 1981–98 period. In Section 4 we provide evidence from specific regions. Section 5 offers a concluding discussion.

2 THE MAIN ARGUMENTS OF THE BOOK

The focus of *A Behavioral Theory of the Firm* is made quite clear in the first sentence of the book, where the two authors declared that it 'is about the business firm and the way it makes decisions' (p. 1). Dealing with this problem they stressed that firms act in conditions of uncertainty, a circumstance that leads them to 'make decisions by solving a series of problems; each problem is solved as it arises; the organization then waits for another problem to appear' (p. 119). This view of a business organization as a 'fire department' was a result of the authors' perception of an organization as a coalition of different members such as 'managers, workers, stockholders, suppliers, customers, lawyers, tax collectors, regulatory agencies, etc.' (p. 27).

The described organizational view implies that the goals of business firms are not one-dimensional. Instead 'the goals of a business firm are [looked upon as] a series of more or less independent constraints imposed on the organization through a process of bargaining among potential coalition members' (p. 43). In addition, it is argued that the coalition members stay in the organization as long as their rewards are sufficiently large. Thus, employees go on working as long as their wages are high enough, customers go on buying as long as the benefits per dollar spent are large enough, and so on. However, in many cases the rewards obtained by the different organizational participants are larger than the rewards necessary to keep them in the organization. Cyert and March labeled this difference 'organizational slack', which has become a significant concept of the theory. Other important ideas are the four relational concepts: (i) quasi-resolution of conflict, (ii) uncertainty avoidance, (iii) problemistic search, and (iv) organizational learning.

The first concept implies that organizations cannot be expected to exhibit consistent behavior, as many goals prevail in an organization and not all of them can be met at the same time. As a consequence we should, for example, expect a firm 'to resolve conflicting pressures "to smooth production" and "satisfy customers" by first doing one and then the other' (p. 118).

Uncertainty avoidance means that firms try to stabilize their environment in order to make it more predictable. One technique to attain this – which according to the studies of Cyert and March is frequently used – is the formation of a negotiated environment. Examples of such actions are industry practice and agreements on pricing. Within the firm, uncertainty is often avoided by the application of standard operating procedures.

Problemistic search basically implies that one can expect search activities within the firm to be stimulated by problems, and consequently, that the search is most likely to be undertaken in the neighborhood of the problem symptom and the current alternative. In addition, it should be expected that the search would be biased in the sense that it would reflect the characteristics of the organization members (that is, their earlier training and experience).

Organizational learning, finally, simply points to the fact that we can expect organizations to learn from past events. As a result, problems will not only have short-term effects in the form of problemistic search but also have long-term effects on the firm through learning.

In applying the theory the two authors turned to decisions on price and output, the classical problem of microeconomic theory. In so doing they managed to simulate accurately the market share changes in the US can market (pp. 86–99) as well as the pricing behavior in a department store (Chapter 7). Later, the latter was also the focus for a critical examination by Baumol and Stewart (1971) using new data on pricing behavior. They concluded that the behavioral theory had been 'very successful in its attempts to predict simple business decisions on the basis of a careful study of rules of thumb' (p. 119). However, they also considered it to have several deficiencies, namely, not providing any 'theory of the determination of the rules of thumb themselves', or any suggestion as to 'how these rules will vary with changes in the values of exogenous economic variables' (ibid.). Others, like Argyris (1996), with his interest in single- and double-loop learning, make the observation that double-loop learning is missing in the behavioral theory of the firm, while Ansoff (1965, p. 36), with his focus on strategy, pointed to the fact that the theory presented by Cyert and March describes only 'how *some* firms' objective formation processes take place. These happen to be the very types of firms which either refuse to make, or do not have to make, strategic decisions. Therefore, the discussion is limited to the operating rather than the strategic problem of the firm'.

However, there were also a number of researchers who found reason to apply the behavioral theory of the firm. In a review article on behavioral perspectives March and Sevón (1988, pp. 373–4) thus point out quite a few examples starting out with Aharoni (1966), Carter (1971), Swieringa and Waterhouse (1982), and Hopwood (1983). It is also evident from their article that the theory presented in 1963 has links to later works on behavioral decision theory, on attention in decision making, and on adaptation processes in firms. For March's own part the decades after the publication of *A Behavioral Theory of the Firm* were to a large extent devoted to the loose coupling between problems and solutions (see March and Olsen, 1976 and March,

1988, particularly Chapters 12–19) and later to political institutions (March and Olsen, 1995). Cyert, on the other hand, between duties as dean and later on as president of Carnegie-Mellon University, made additional contributions on the pricing behavior of firms (see Cohen and Cyert, 1965; Cyert and DeGroot, 1987; Cyert, 1988, and Cyert et al., 1995), and also on the subject of strategy (Cyert and Williams, 1993; Cyert et al., 1993, and Cyert and Kumar, 1996) and Bayesian statistics and economic theory (Cyert and DeGroot, 1987; see further Day and Sunder, 1996, pp. 142–3). For all these works, *A Behavioral Theory of the Firm*, which is the focus here, provided a point of departure.

3 CITATIONS IN SCIENTIFIC JOURNALS

Introduction

In order to analyse the recent position of Cyert and March (1963) we have downloaded from the Institute for Scientific Information (ISI) database *Web of Science* (that is, Science Citation Index, Social Citation Index, and Art and Humanities Citation Index) all articles between 1986 and 1998 that cited the book, and have classified them according to the National Science Indicator (NSI). It is then apparent that the book has had the greatest impact in the management field, where almost half of all the more than one thousand citations can be found (Table 2.1). The only other field with a share of more than 10 per cent of the citations is economics. However, a closer look at the most influential journals, such as the *American Economic Review* and *Econometrica*, reveals a total absence of citations in the period among their 1,942 and 667 articles, respectively, while the British *Economic Journal* had two citations in its 1,068 articles. It therefore seems fair to conclude that mainstream economists – thus excluding evolutionary economists such as Richard Nelson and Sidney Winter, and transaction economists like Oliver

Table 2.1 Number and percentage of articles citing Cyert and March (1963), 1986–98

Journal classification	Number	Percentage
Management	530	46.8
Economics	200	17.7
Political Science and Public Administration	86	7.6
Sociology and Anthropology	63	5.6
Psychology	40	3.5
Environmental Studies, Geography and Development	25	2.2
Law	24	2.1
Library and Information Sciences	23	2.0
Education	19	1.7
Social Work and Social Policy	16	1.4
Other Fields	107	9.4
Total	1133	100.0

Source: Analysis of data from *Web of Science*.

Williamson – have been less receptive to the offer from Cyert and March for new tools in the microeconomic analysis. Instead we find most of the citations in leading management journals such as the the *Strategic Management Journal*, the *Journal of Management Studies*, and the *Administrative Science Quarterly*. For further studies of the use of Cyert and March (1963) we have therefore chosen to focus on prestigious management journals such as these. In so doing we have analysed nine significant management journals (Table 2.2), namely, the *Academy of Management Journal*, the *Administrative Science Quarterly*, the *Journal of Management*, the *Journal of Management Studies*, *Long Range Planning*, *Management Science*, *Omega*, *Organization Studies*, and the *Strategic Management Journal*. They were chosen with respect to their impact factor and in order to provide a representation of both European and US journals. Citations in the nine journals have been analysed using the *Web of Science*. In this analysis we have also been able to extend the period of analysis to 1981–98.

Table 2.2 Nine management journals selected for the analysis

Journal	Impact	Origin
Administrative Science Quarterly	3.538	USA
Academy of Management Journal	2.449	USA
Strategic Management Journal	1.530	Europe
Organization Studies	1.117	Europe
Management Science	1.056	USA
Journal of Management	1.030	USA
Journal of Management Studies	0.729	Europe
Omega	0.314	Europe
Long Range Planning	0.274	Europe

Note: The impact factor is based on citations from articles published in 1998 to articles published in 1996 and 1997 divided by the total number of articles published in 1996 and 1997.

Citations in Nine Prestigious Management Journals

Our analysis of the selected journals for the 1981–98 period (see Table 2.3) shows that Cyert and March (1963) maintained a front position in the last two decades with 401 citations, a total that is less only than that of Porter (1980), Thompson (1967), and Pfeffer and Salancik (1978), all three more recent publications. In contrast to some other pre-1970 titles (Chandler, 1962; Lawrence and Lorsch, 1967; March and Simon, 1958; and Thompson, 1967), it has a positive trend of 0.36 (see the third column of Table 2.3). In addition to the above-mentioned titles the list contains a number of other well-known books such as those by Williamson (1975), Porter (1985), Weick (1969), Peters and Waterman (1982), Nelson and Winter (1982), Aldrich (1979), and Williamson (1985).

A closer analysis of the development over time (Figure 2.1) reveals that, using a three-year moving window, Cyert and March's (1963) book held a rank of two and three in the early 1980s but that it was losing out to other titles later in the decade. However, even after that decline it held rank ten in the early 1990s. Then it made a comeback in two steps, first to rank five and later on back to rank three. Obviously, this revival of the popularity of the book should

Table 2.3 The most-cited documents in nine management journals, 1981–98

Cited document	Rank	No citations	Slope
Porter (1980)	1	558	1.52
Thompson (1967)	2	514	–0.66
Pfeffer and Salancik (1978)	3	459	0.75
Cyert and March (1963)	*4*	*401*	*0.36*
Lawrence and Lorsch (1967)	5	332	–0.78
Williamson (1975)	6	316	1.18
March and Simon (1958)	7	310	–0.26
Porter (1985)	8	286	1.91
Weick (1969)	9	280	0.05
Chandler (1962)	10	262	–0.39
Rumelt (1974)	11	249	–0.03
Miles and Snow (1978)	12	237	0.26
Peters and Waterman (1982)	13	209	0.16
Nelson and Winter (1982)	14	184	1.53
Burns and Stalker (1961)	15	181	0.09
Aldrich (1979)	16	170	–0.47
DiMaggio and Powell (1983)	17	161	1.22
Hofer and Schendel (1978)	18	158	–0.84
Meyer and Rowan (1977)	19	154	0.43
Williamson (1985)	20	142	1.38

Source: Analysis of data from the Social Science Citation Index (SSCI).

be seen in relation to the publication of the second edition in 1992 by the British publisher Blackwell. Perhaps many of the professors who had grown up academically with Cyert and March (1963) now took the opportunity to introduce the book to their graduate students. They, in turn, embraced the ideas of the book and, like their teachers and supervisors, they started to quote Cyert and March (1963). Such an interpretation seems particularly reasonable in view of the increase in citations after five to six years (that is, the time it may have taken for the doctoral students of the early 1990s to finish their doctoral dissertations and to start publishing articles). Another reason could have been that the late 1990s saw an increased emphasis on lean production (see, for example, Womack and Jones, 1996), which in turn seems to have stimulated the interest in the relationship between slack and learning (see, for example, Nohria and Gulati, 1996).

Variations between Journals

In terms of the variation between the nine journals, four of them (*Strategic Management Journal*, *Journal of Management Studies*, *Administrative Science Quarterly* and *Academy of Management Journal*) account for about two-thirds of the citations (Table 2.4). However, even among the other journals Cyert and March (1963) belongs in the top-ten cited works. In *Management Science* it is the second most-quoted title, and in *Omega* the fourth most quoted.

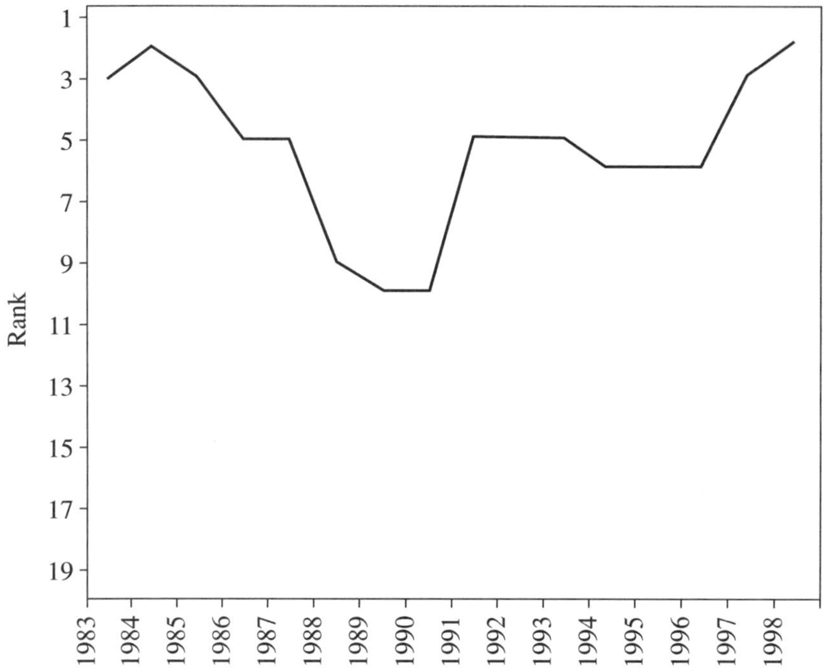

Note: The rank in each period is based on a three-year moving window.

Figure 2.1 Changes in rank of Cyert and March (1963) in all journals

Table 2.4 Citations of Cyert and March (1963) in nine management journals, 1981–98

Citing journal	No citations	Percentage	Rank	Change	R^2
Strategic Management Journal	80	19.9	9	–0.21	0.13
Journal of Management Studies	70	17.5	1	0.05	0.01
Administrative Science Quarterly	60	15.0	6	0.61	0.59
Academy of Management Journal	52	13.0	6	–0.58	0.06
Management Science	49	12.2	2	–0.92	0.34
Organization Studies	33	8.2	10	0.25	0.05
Journal of Management	24	6.0	10	0.46	0.03
Omega	19	4.7	4	–0.50	0.04
Long Range Planning	14	3.5	10	–2.99	0.37
Total	401	100.0	4	–0.01	0.00

Source: Analysis of data from the Social Science Citation Index (SSCI).

The development over time in the nine journals exhibits somewhat varying patterns (fifth column of Table 2.4). In the *Academy of Management Journal*, *Long Range Planning*, *Management Science*, *Omega*, and the *Strategic Management Journal*, the book lost ground, whereas it gained ground in the *Administrative Science Quarterly*, the *Journal of Management*, the *Journal of Management Studies*, and *Organization Studies*. It thus seems that the inclination of scholars oriented toward strategy and normative models to cite the book declined, whereas organization researchers used it more.

The *Administrative Science Quarterly*

It was shown in Table 2.2 above that the *Administrative Science Quarterly* has the highest impact factor of the journals studied. For this reason this journal is particularly appropriate to select for an in-depth study of the issues published during the period under review. This analysis first revealed that the database used for the earlier analysis had somewhat underestimated the number of citations (60 instead of 66). We can also see that the citing articles are relatively well distributed over time, with about ten citations per three-year period (Table 2.5). This means that on average, about every seventh article contained a citation to Cyert and March (1963). In congruence with the earlier results an increase to about one of six can be observed for the last two three-year periods. This is also true for the number of mentions per citing, which rose to about two after a decline in the late 1980s and early 1990s.

Table 2.5 Citations of Cyert and March (1963) in Administrative Science Quarterly, *1981–98*

Period	Citing articles	Percentage of all	Total citations	Average
1981–83	10	10.8	15	1.5
1984–86	12	16.7	25	2.1
1987–89	9	13.0	16	1.8
1990–92	9	12.9	15	1.7
1993–95	12	17.4	24	2.0
1996–98	14	18.7	27	1.9
1981–98	66	14.7	122	1.8

Source: Analysis of all issues of the *Administrative Science Quarterly*, 1981–98.

Among the citations very few provide exact references. This is only true for five of the 66 articles (8 percent): McCaffrey (1982; on standard operating procedures, Cyert and March, 1963, pp. 101–13), Heimer (1985; on uncertainty avoidance and problemistic search, Cyert and March, 1963, pp. 118–21), Friedkin and Simpson (1985; on subjective information, Cyert and March, 1963, p. 83), Kieser (1989; on side payments, Cyert and March, 1963, p. 29), and Uzzi (1997; on slack, Cyert and March, 1992, p. 228). However, although there are a number of general references to Cyert and March (1963) as an important representative of the Carnegie School, there are also a large number of citations that refer to the key concepts of the book (Table 2.6). The three most frequently mentioned concepts are search, coalition, and slack, all of which are mentioned about twenty times. In addition there are references to the discussion of goals, general references to the Carnegie Tech school (that is, Cyert and March, 1963 is mentioned together with March and Simon, 1958 and other works from the group), learning, standard operation procedures (SOP), communication, problem solving, and uncertainty. Over time, between 1981 and 1986, and 1987 and 1992, references to the coalition view, slack, and to the Carnegie Tech school in general increased, although there was a general decline in citations in the same period (see again Table 2.6). From 1993 to 1998 there was a particular increase in the number of mentions of search and goals. Overall, the latter was the six-year period of the three studied that exhibited the largest number of citations.

Table 2.6 References to different concepts from Cyert and March (1963) in Administrative Science Quarterly, *1981–98*

Concept	1981–86	1987–92	1993–98	Total
Search	7	4	12	23
Coalition	5	8	7	20
Slack	4	8	7	19
Goals	6	2	8	16
Carnegie Tech in general	1	5	7	13
Learning	3	2	4	9
Standard operating procedures	2	1	4	7
Communication	5	0	1	6
Problem solving	4	1	0	5
Uncertainty	3	0	1	4
Total	40	31	51	122

Source: Analysis of all issues of the *Administrative Science Quarterly*, 1981–98.

Conclusions

It should be evident from our analysis that Cyert and March (1963) constitutes a survivor in the academic literature. The book has particularly influenced scholars in management and organization, an area that accounts for almost half of all citations in the period from 1986 to 1998. From the early 1980s it has been ranked in the top ten in a selection of prestigious journals and in the early 1990s it returned to the very top ranks. This was the result of organization researchers increasing their citations at the same time as scholars oriented toward strategy and normative models cut down on theirs. It is also evident from the analysis of the *Administrative Science Quarterly* that the citations have been well distributed over time with a more distinct revival in the 1990s. Very few authors make reference to particular pages of the book. Many instead refer to central concepts, such as search, coalition, and slack.

4 THE GEOGRAPHICAL DIFFUSION

Introduction

An analysis of the origin of the citing authors reveals that North American scholars made the majority of the citations – three-quarters of them (see Table 2.7). This is both a reflection of their dominance in the studied journals and their tendency to cite Cyert and March (1963) more frequently than researchers from other areas. More than six articles out of a hundred (see Table 2.7, relative impact) thus contain a reference to the book, whereas the corresponding figure for the other continents is about four. The relative impact is increasing in all areas (fifth column).

Table 2.7 Citations of Cyert and March (1963) by author origin in nine management journals, 1981–98

Region	Number of citations	Number of articles	Citations %	Relative impact (%)	Change in relative impact	R^2
N. America	306.5	4637.5	76.4	6.6	0.47	0.47
Europe	71.7	1657.4	17.9	4.3	0.30	0.27
Asia	18.3	406.4	4.6	4.5	0.51	0.51
Oceania	4.5	113.3	1.1	4.0	0.16	0.16
Total	401.0		100.0			

Note: The change in citations from different regions is based on three-year moving windows.

If we look more closely at the geographical distribution of citations (Table 2.8) we find that the relative impact of Cyert and March among US authors is 6.2 percent. This is somewhat above the average 5.8 percent for all authors. Above average citations of Cyert and March (1963) come from authors from other countries, including Indonesia (although this is an artificial result as it was in only one of two articles); Sweden (15.3 percent); Spain (9.5 percent); Canada (9.1 percent); Finland (9.1 percent); Norway (8.3 percent); New Zealand (7.3 percent); Denmark (6.9 percent); Singapore (6.4 percent); and Israel (6.3 percent). Among them, it is worth noting that the Nordic countries have been particularly influenced by the behavioral theory of the firm. Together they account for 3.5 percent of all citations and have a relative impact factor of 11 percent, almost double that of US authors. It is therefore appropriate to initiate a closer analysis of the diffusion of the behavioural theory of the firm by looking at its reception in the Nordic countries.

The Reception in the Nordic Countries

It is evident from Table 2.8 that among the Nordic scholars, Swedes have been particularly attached to Cyert and March (1963). This state of affairs can be traced to the very close relationships that tended to develop between Swedish researchers in business administration and the Carnegie Institute of Technology in the 1950s and the 1960s. These contacts emerged in the late 1950s as Paulsson Frenckner, then professor at the Stockholm School of Economics, toured the United States (Personal communication from Frenckner). His main interest was in operations research, an area that, to a significant extent, he introduced in Sweden (see Frenckner, 1957, 1958a and 1958b). With this orientation it was natural for him to visit Pittsburgh and the Carnegie Institute of Technology, where he met Abraham Charnes and William W. Cooper, two significant developers of linear programming. However, Frenckner not only met the operations researchers but also scholars more oriented towards organization studies, such as Richard Cyert, James March, and Herbert Simon. In this way he identified a vital research

Table 2.8 Citations of Cyert and March (1963) from different countries in nine management journals, 1981–98

Country	Number of citations	Citations %	Number of articles	Relative impact (%)
USA	271.8	67.7	4403.4	6.2
UK	39.4	9.8	1108.7	3.6
Canada	34.8	8.7	384.4	9.1
Sweden	8.5	2.1	55.7	15.3
Israel	7.8	2.0	123.4	6.3
France	5.3	1.3	101.4	5.2
Netherlands	3.3	0.8	113.5	2.9
Japan	3.0	0.7	79.0	3.8
Germany	2.8	0.7	60.2	4.7
Australia	2.5	0.6	92.5	2.7
Belgium	2.5	0.6	46.7	5.4
Finland	2.0	0.5	22.0	9.1
India	2.0	0.5	52.0	3.8
New Zealand	2.0	0.5	27.3	7.3
Norway	2.0	0.5	24.0	8.3
Singapore	2.0	0.5	31.3	6.4
Denmark	1.5	0.4	21.8	6.9
Hong Kong	1.5	0.4	57.0	2.6
Italy	1.5	0.4	36.0	4.2
Switzerland	1.5	0.4	39.8	3.8
South Korea	1.0	0.2	45.0	2.2
Spain	0.8	0.2	8.4	9.5
Austria	0.5	0.1	10.0	5.0
Indonesia	0.5	0.1	1.0	50.0
Taiwan	0.5	0.1	14.5	3.4
Total	401.0	100.0	6959.0	5.8

Note: The relative impact is the percentage of articles citing Cyert and March (1963) of all articles that included at least one author from the different countries. In international collaborations citations have been split between the different nations of the authors.

Source: Analysis of data from the Social Science Citation Index (SSCI).

environment, which he later recommended that several young colleagues should visit. Among them there were several who would become professors at Swedish institutions for higher business education: Ingemund Hägg, Bertil Näslund, Dick Ramström, and Eric Rhenman. Näslund even presented his doctoral dissertation at Carnegie Tech in 1964 (see Näslund, 1967), while the publications of Hägg, Ramström and Rhenman provide evidence of a strong influence from Cyert and March (1963) (see Hägg, 1966; Ramström, 1967; Rhenman, 1964a and 1964b). Among these works, Rhenman's introduction of the coalition model of organizations to a wider Swedish audience attracted particular attention (see further, Therborn, 1966).

For those who knew about Frenckner's research it probably did not come as a great surprise that he found the reasoning of the Carnegie Tech faculty appealing. Although he focused on issues in managerial accounting control, he retained an interest in administrative problems. He even wrote a piece on industrial democracy and work efficiency (Frenckner, 1947) and an extensive report on the goal function of the firm (Frenckner, 1953). The latter, ten years before Cyert and March (1963), asked the question: 'Do firms aim at maximum profits?'. It was criticized at the time by one of the Swedish senior professors (Sillén, 1954, pp. 11–14) in relation to a promotion to a chair and was therefore not published until 1986 in a concentrated version in a Festschrift (Frenckner, 1986). By then, Cyert and March (1963), among others, had made it uncontroversial.

Another significant introducer of the Carnegie Tech school into Scandinavia was Walter Goldberg, from 1966 professor of administration at the Gothenburg School of Economics and Business. Particularly important was his invitation in the spring of 1969 to Scandinavian business faculty members and doctoral students to a two-week seminar in Lerum, outside Gothenburg, with GSIA faculty. His offer was met with a very positive response from his Scandinavian colleagues and the seminar turned out to be an extremely inspiring experience for the participants. Leader of the Pittsburgh delegation was Richard Cyert, at the time dean of GSIA. He was accompanied by Kalman Cohen, William Cooper, Morris DeGroot, John Farley, Yuji Ijiri, Charles Kriebel, Kenneth MacCrimmon, Herbert Simon, and Victor Vroom. There can be no doubt of the importance of this seminar to the influence of the Carnegie Tech school in Scandinavia (see further, Goldberg, 1970).

Needless to say there were also other Scandinavian management scholars who had paid attention to the ideas coming from Carnegie Tech. The year before the Lerum seminar, Herbert Simon had been awarded an honorary degree at Lund University. For a number of years before that March and Simon (1958) as well as Cyert and March (1963) had already been on the reading lists of a significant number of Scandinavian business departments. The enthusiasm was great both for the perspectives offered by the book and its application of computer simulation techniques. The first was based on earlier frustrations in applying neoclassical economic theory in empirical studies. The latter was linked to the new opportunities to analyse and solve problems through computer programs.

Against the described background it should be no surprise to find a significant influence from the Carnegie school on the thinking of Scandinavian management scholars. An analysis of their citation behavior in the first eight issues of the *Scandinavian Journal of Management*, that is, from 1981 to 1992 (see Table 2.9), thus provides clear evidence that the interest shown in behavioral theory in the late 1960s persisted later on. It turns out that Cyert and March (1963) is the most frequently cited reference, with 20 citations, although it is not cited at all in one of the volumes. The centrality of the book is also clear when the relationship between the top references is analysed (Figure 2.2). Thompson (1967), Pfeffer and Salancik (1978) and Weick (1969) all cite Cyert and March (1963), and Peters and Waterman's *In Search of Excellence* (1982) is indirectly related to Cyert and March (1963) through its citations of Pfeffer and Salancik (1978) and Weick (1969).

Similar patterns to those in the *Scandinavian Journal of Management* were exhibited by Scandinavian management scholars in their publication in 15 prestigious management journals in the period from 1981 to 1992 (Engwall, 1996, Table 5). *A Behavioral Theory of the Firm* (1963) scores second, this time after Pfeffer and Salancik's book (1978), a work that, as shown above, has clear links to the behavioral theory of the firm.

Table 2.9 The most-cited references in the Scandinavian Journal of Management, 1981–92

Rank	Reference	Frequency	Volumes	FM
1	*Cyert and March (1963)*	*20*	*7*	*17.5*
2	Weick (1969)	18	8	18.0
3	Thompson (1967)	18	7	15.8
4	Peters and Waterman (1982)	17	7	14.9
5	Pfeffer and Salancik (1978)	17	7	14.9
6	Glaser and Strauss (1967)	14	7	12.3
7	Porter (1980)	12	7	10.0
8	March and Olsen (1976)	10	7	8.8
9	Brunsson (1985)	10	6	7.5
10	Pfeffer (1981)	10	6	7.5
11	Chandler (1962)	10	5	6.3
12	Berger and Luckmann (1966)	9	6	6.8
13	March and Simon (1958)	9	6	6.8
14	Williamson (1975)	9	6	6.8
15	Burns and Stalker (1961)	9	5	5.6
16	Jönsson and Lundin (1977)	9	5	5.6
17	Mintzberg (1979)	9	5	5.6
18	Williamson (1985)	9	4	4.5
19	Deal and Kennedy (1982)	8	6	6.0
20	Lawrence and Lorsch (1967)	8	5	5.0
21	Mintzberg (1973)	8	5	5.0
22	Aldrich (1979)	8	4	4.0
23	Argyris and Schön (1978)	7	6	5.3
24	Pettigrew (1979)	7	6	5.3
25	Smircich (1983)	7	6	5.3
26	Child (1972)	7	5	4.4
27	Cohen, March and Olsen (1972)	7	5	4.4
28	Mintzberg (1978)	7	5	4.4
29	Pfeffer (1982)	7	5	4.4
30	Porter (1985)	7	5	4.4

Note: FM is the frequency weighted with the share of citing volumes.

Source: Engwall (1995).

Still further support for the popularity of Cyert and March (1963) is provided by an analysis of the 270 Swedish doctoral dissertations in business administration from 1950 to 1985 (Engwall, 1992, Table 6.11). In this material Cyert and March's (1963) book was second only to Thompson's (1967), although it was not cited in two of the six departments. In the same way Tainio and Hänninen (1999, pp. 4–5) in an analysis of 177 dissertations from the two Helsinki business schools concluded that:

> The cumulative influence of the Carnegie school has reached a point in Finland where most of the management students and all organizational students recognize the importance of the Carnegie School and treat its ideas as the first serious attempt to explain organizational outcomes and organizational behavior.

The Reception in Other Countries

Unfortunately, for countries other than the Nordic ones, we do not have much quantitative evidence. The exception is from authors based in France for which data are available from the same database as the one presented above for the Nordic countries (Engwall, 1996). An analysis of their citation behavior (Engwall, 1998) reveals that they made 2,673 citations to 2,226 different publications, that is, every publication was on average cited 1.2 times, with the majority, 1,928, only mentioned once. Here Cyert and March's work (1963) does not belong to the 29 titles mentioned more than three times. It was cited three times, however, by Boisot and Xing (1992), Ruefli and Sarrazin (1981), and Schneider (1989). Of these, the first and third articles appeared in *Organization Studies* and the second in *Management Science*. Nevertheless, the former head of Centre de Recherche en Gestion (CRG) at École Polytechnique in Paris, Michel Berry, points out in a personal communication that the book has had an important influence in France: 'the English version is very often cited, and there has been a

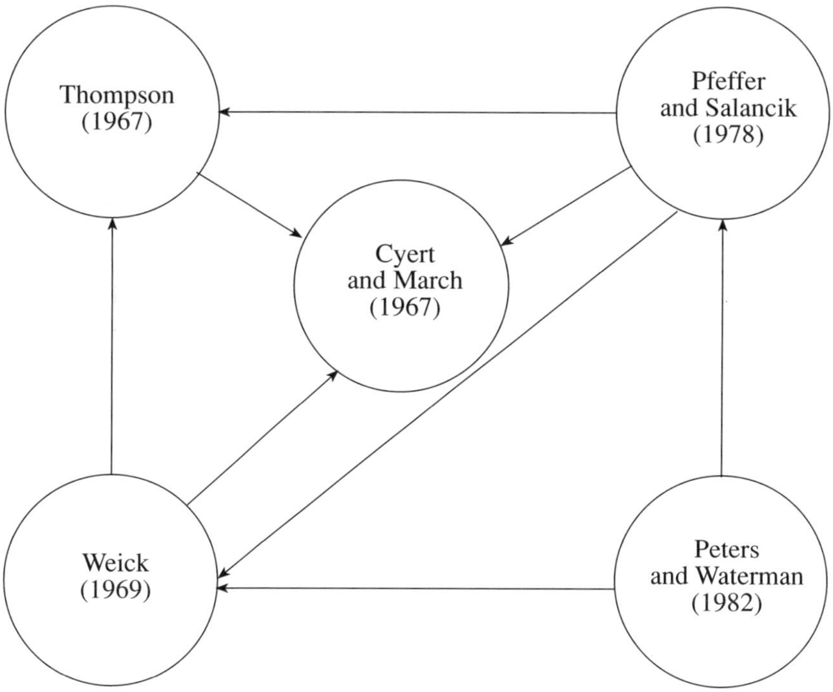

Source: Engwall (1995, Figure 2).

Figure 2.2 Connections between the most frequently cited references in the Scandinavian Journal of Management

French version for many years ... the most important aspects were the critique of rationality that was the basis of operations research [and] the four clinical cases' (our translation from the French). Apparently some of the French scholars, like Jean-Claude Thoenig of INSEAD (the European Institute of Business Administration), were prepared for the ideas in Cyert and March (1963). Thoenig recalls that he first came across the book in the mid-1960s and says that 'Cyert and March's contribution was no real big surprise to me about the content ... but I was fascinated by the elegant style and the argumentation process of their demonstration'. He also expresses his surprise that economists did not draw the implications of the work.

On the other side of the Channel, members of the Aston group (Pugh et al., 1971, p. 80) described the book as 'a notable effort to link classical economics theory to contemporary organization theory', and concluded by stating that it 'is a widely applicable theory'. However, it was also important for representatives of a younger generation like the present editor of *Organization Studies*, David Wilson from Warwick:

> The major influence was that the book was initially cited in connection with a growing interest in power and decision making in organisations. Desperate to get away from the determinism of strategic planning, the book offered a way to conceptualise and explain how organisations faced and coped with uncertainty. ... Together [with James Thompson's 1967 book it] formed the conceptual grounding for a great deal of research on power, influence and decision making (not least a grounding for the Bradford studies on decision making). (Personal communication in 1999)

Wilson also points out that the book survived critical examination by sociologists, such as Peter Bachrach, Morton Baratz, Stuart Clegg, and David Dunkerley. In his view, practitioners were much slower to take up the lessons of Cyert and March, but did so to a certain extent in the late 1970s. The impact was primarily among researchers, however. Wilson continues:

> Scholars in the 1980s began to appropriate the core concepts and began to invent their own concepts based firmly on Cyert and March's work. Initial work on organisational culture and that on handling ambiguity in decision making can be traced directly to Cyert and March. Their work lives on in virtually all aspects of Organization Theory and Strategic Management today. ... In the early seventies in Britain, virtually every Business School and Department of Management was either researching or teaching directly from the work of Cyert and March (over 120 different departments).

However, there are also other views. According to Richard Whitley of the Manchester Business School the book has had less impact in the UK, since 'business and managerial studies in the UK is more of a congery of social scientists than a US-type business school, except LBS [London Business School] and MBS [Manchester Business School]'.

With regard to Germany, Alfred Kieser of Mannheim reports an impression that the book is often quoted in Germany, but adds that it has become 'a ritual to quote Cyert and March in the many articles on organizational learning as the pioneers'. Among Germans working in the Cyert and March tradition, he mentions Werner Kirsch and Niklas Luhmann.

In Southern Europe the book was translated into Italian in 1970 by Alessandra Nennei. It did not become a bestseller but sold 1,042 copies in the period from 1970 to 1992 (Personal communication from Pasquale Gagliardi). Similarly, the reception in Turkey appears to have been limited. Behlül Üsdiken thus only found one citation to Cyert and March (1963) in a data set of Turkish management journals for the period from 1971 to 1991 (Personal communication from Üsdiken).

Conclusions

As a consequence of the dominance of US authors in international management journals, they also account for the lion's share of the citations to Cyert and March (1963): about three-quarters of them. This also means that the book has had an above-average impact (that is, citations per hundred articles) in the United States. However, among nationalities frequently citing *A Behavioral Theory of the Firm*, the Swedes stand out particularly, with a relative impact of about 15 percent. This in turn appears to be the result of long-standing relationships between Swedish institutions and GSIA in Pittsburgh. Seminars and study trips of Swedish scholars seem to have paved the way for the book in Sweden. The reception has also been notable in the other Nordic countries, as well as in some other European countries.

5 CONCLUDING DISCUSSION

In view of the evidence provided in the present chapter it is apparent that the reviewers of *A Behavioral Theory of the Firm*, who welcomed and endorsed it, understood that this was an extraordinary piece of research that would have long-lasting influence. However, those who recommended that economists adopt it were less successful. It seems that it has not had the impact on mainstream economic theory that was expected at the time. Instead, scholars in the growing field of organization studies, evolutionary economics, and transaction cost economics found many of the concepts and the reasoning of the book most useful and relevant.

It is indeed remarkable that this interest in the book is continuing and even increasing after almost forty years. It has been mentioned that the publication of the new edition in 1992 was probably very important for the renaissance of the book. Another factor, which could be of importance, is the increasing interest in stakeholder management, manifested in the 1980s through books by Mitroff (1983) and Freeman (1984). They have been followed by a number of articles, particularly in the prestigious US management journal *Academy of Management Review* (see, for example, Clarkson, 1995; Donaldson and Preston, 1995; Jones, 1995; Mitchell et al., 1997; and Scott and Lane, 2000), and recently a collection of readings by Clarkson (1998). In this way the interest in the coalition model of the firm has received increased attention. Similarly, there has been a growing attention to learning, another key element of the book. Knowledge management inside companies is one of the key elements in modern corporations (see, for example, Edvinsson and Malone, 1997). This in turn has implied that slack resources have been paid increasing attention, even in a time when lean production is widely advocated.

All these circumstances seem to indicate that *A Behavioral Theory of the Firm* has managed to catch some fundamental mechanisms in modem economic life. It has thus succeeded in becoming an evergreen in the academic literature, with a second edition being published in 1992. The interest shown in the book since 1963 appears to be a strong indicator for future editions. Thus there are high hopes that students of management and organization in the future will also look to *A Behavioral Theory of the Firm* as an old indispensable friend and supporter in their research.

REFERENCES

Aharoni, Yair A. (1966), *The Foreign Investment Decision-Process*, Cambridge, MA: Harvard Graduate School of Business Administration.

Aldrich, Howard. E. (1979), *Organizations and Environments*, Englewood Cliffs, NJ: Prentice-Hall.

Ansoff, Igor H. (1965), *Corporate Strategy*, New York: McGraw-Hill.

Argyris, Chris (1996), 'Unrecognized defenses of scholars: impact on theory and research', *Organization Science*, **7** (January–February), 79–87.

Argyris, Chris and Donald Schön (1978), *Organizational Learning: A Theory of Action Perspective*, Reading, MA: Addison-Wesley.

Bain, Joe S. (1959), *Industrial Organization*, New York: Wiley.

Barnard, Chester (1938), *The Functions of the Executive*, Cambridge, MA: Harvard University Press.

Baumol, William J. (1959), *Business Behavior, Value and Growth*, New York: Macmillan.

Baumol, William J. and Maco Stewart (1971), 'On the behavioral theory of the firm', in Robin Marris and Adrian Wood (eds), *The Corporate Economy. Growth, Competition and Innovation Power*, London: Macmillan, pp. 118–43.

Berger, Peter L. and Thomas Luckmann (1966), *The Social Construction of Reality: A Treatise in the Sociology of Knowledge*, Garden City, NY: Doubleday.

Blau, Peter M. (1955), *The Dynamics of Bureaucracy. A Study of Interpersonal Relations in Two Government Agencies*, Chicago, IL: University of Chicago Press.

Boisot, Max and G.L. Ying (1992), 'The nature of managerial work in the Chinese enterprise reforms – a study of six directors', *Organization Studies*, **13** (2), 161–84.

Boulding, Kenneth E. (1964), 'Book Review: *A Behavioral Theory of the Firm*', *American Journal of Sociology*, **29** (August), 592–3.

Brunsson, Nils (1985), *The Irrational Organization*, Chichester: Wiley.

Burns, Tom and George M. Stalker (1961), *The Management of Innovation*, London: Tavistock.

Carter, Eugene E. (1971), 'The behavioral theory of the firm and top level decisions', *Administrative Science Quarterly*, **16** (December), 413–28.

Chamberlin, Edwin (1933), *The Theory of Monopolistic Competition*, Cambridge, MA: Harvard Economic Studies.

Chandler, Alfred D. Jr. (1962), *Strategy and Structure. Chapters in the History of the American Industrial Enterprise*, Cambridge, MA: MIT Press.

Child, John (1972), 'Organizational structure, environment and performance: the role of strategic choice', *Sociology*, **6** (January), 2–22.

Clarkson, Max B.E. (1995), 'A Stakeholder framework for analyzing and evaluating corporate social performance', *Academy of Management Review*, **20** (1), 92–117.

Clarkson, Max B.E. (ed.) (1998), *The Corporation and its Stakeholders. Classic and Contemporary Readings*, Toronto: University of Toronto Press.

Cohen, Kalman J. and Richard M. Cyert (1965), *Theory of the Firm. Resource Allocation in a Market Economy*, Englewood Cliffs, NJ: Prentice-Hall.

Cohen, Michael D., James G. March and Johan P. Olsen (1972), 'A garbage can model of organizational choice', *Administrative Science Quarterly*, **17** (1), 1–25.

Cyert, Richard M. (1988), *The Economic Theory of Organization and the Firm*, New York: Harvester.

Cyert, Richard M. and Morris H. DeGroot (1987), *Bayesian Analysis and Uncertainty in Economic Theory*, London: Chapman & Hall.

Cyert, Richard M. and Praveen Kumar (1996), 'Economizing by firms through learning and adaptation', *Journal of Economic Behavior and Organization*, **29**, 211–31.

Cyert, Richard M., Praveen Kumar and Jeffrey R. Williams (1993), 'Information, market imperfections and strategy', *Strategic Management Journal*, **14** (Winter), 47–58.

Cyert, Richard, Praveen Kumar and Jeffrey R. Williams (1995), 'Impact of organizational structure on oligopolistic pricing', *Journal of Economic Behavior and Organization*, **26**, 1–15.

Cyert, Richard M. and James G. March (1963), *A Behavioral Theory of the Firm*, Englewood Cliffs, NJ: Prentice-Hall (2nd edn published in 1992 by Blackwell, Cambridge, MA and Oxford).

Cyert, Richard M. and Jeffrey R. Williams (1993), 'Organizations, decision making and strategy: overview and comment', *Strategic Management Journal*, **14** (Winter), 5–10.

Day, Richard H. (1964), 'Book Review: *A Behavioral Theory of the Firm*', *Econometrica*, **32** (July), 461–5.

Day, Richard H. and Shyam Sunder (1996), 'Ideas and work of Richard M. Cyert', *Journal of Economic Behavior and Organization*, **31** (2), 139–48.

Deal, Terrence. E. and Allen A. Kennedy (1982), *Corporate Cultures: The Rites and Rituals of Corporate Life*, Reading, MA: Addison-Wesley.

DiMaggio, Paul J. and Walter W. Powell (1983), 'The iron cage revisited: institutional isomorphism and collective rationality in organizational fields', *American Sociology Review*, **48** (April), 147–60.

Donaldson, Tom and Lee E. Preston (1995), 'The stakeholder theory of the corporation concepts, evidence and implications', *Academy of Management Review*, **20** (1), 65–91.

Edvinsson, Leif and M.S. Malone (1997), *Intellectual Capital. Realizing Your Company's True Value: Finding Its Hidden Brain Power*, New York: HarperCollins.

Engwall, Lars (1992), *Mercury Meets Minerva*, Oxford: Pergamon Press.

Engwall, Lars (1995), 'Management studies: a fragmented adhocracy?', *Scandinavian Journal of Management*, **11** (3), 225–35.

Engwall, Lars (1996), 'The Vikings versus the world. An examination of Nordic business research', *Scandinavian Journal of Management*, **12** (4), 425–36.

Engwall, Lars (1998), 'Research Note: Asterix in Disneyland. Management scholars from France on the world stage', *Organization Studies*, **19** (5), 863–81.

Freeman, R.E. (1984), *Strategic Management. A Stakeholder Approach*, Boston, MA: Pitman.

Frenckner, Paulsson (1947), 'Industriell demokrati och arbetseffektivitet' (Industrial Democracy and Work Efficiency), *Svensk linje*, **7** (4), 21–5.

Frenckner, Paulsson (1953), 'Syfta företagen mot högsta möjliga vinst?' ('Do Firms Aim at Maximum Profit?'), Stockholm: Företagsekonomiska forskningsinstitutet vid Handelshögskolan i Stockholm (mimeo).

Frenckner, Paulsson (1957), 'Betriebswirtschaftslehre und Verfahrensforschung' ('Business Administration and Operations Research'), *Zeitschrift far Handelswissenschaftliche Forschung*, **9** (2), 65–102.

Frenckner, Paulsson (1958a), 'Operationsanalys – några egenskaper och metoder' ('Operations Research – Some Characteristics and Methods'), *Ekonomen*, **34** (5), 16–24.

Frenckner, Paulsson (1958b), 'Operationsanalysens betydelse för den företagsekonomiska forskningen' ('The Significance of Operations Research for the Research in Business Administration'), *Ekonomen*, **34** (5), 89–104.

Frenckner, Paulsson (1986), 'Syftar företagen mot högsta möjliga vinst?' ('Do Firms Aim at Maximum Profit?'), in Nils-Göran Olve and Lars Samuelson (eds), *Från kostnadsberäkning till ekonomisk styrning. Fyrtio års kostnads-intäktsanalys med Paulsson Frenckner* (in From Cost Calculations to Economic Control. Forty Years of Management Accounting with Paulsson Frenckner), Stockholm: Sveriges Mekanförbund, pp. 181–206.

Friedkin, Noah H. and Michael J. Simpson (1985), 'Effects of competition on members' identification with their subunits', *Administrative Science Quarterly*, **30** (3), 377–94.

Glaser, Barney G. and Anselm L. Strauss (1967), *The Discovery of Grounded Theory*, Chicago, IL: Aldine.

Goldberg, Walter (ed.) (1970), *Behavioral Approaches to Modern Management I–II*, Gothenburg: Gothenburg Studies in Business Administration, BAS 1970–74.

Hägg, Ingemund (1966), *Företagsekonomisk simulering* (Simulation Studies in Business Administration), Stockholm: EFI.

Heimer, Carol A. (1985), 'Allocating information costs in a negotiated information order: interorganizational constraints on decision making in Norwegian oil insurance', *Administrative Science Quarterly*, **30** (3), 395–417.

Hofer, Charles W. and Dan Schendel (1978), *Strategy Formulation*, St. Paul, MI: West.

Homans, C. George (1950), *The Human Group*, New York: Harcourt, Brace.

Hopwood, Anthony G. (1983), 'On trying to study accounting in the contexts in which it operates', *Accounting, Organizations and Society*, **8**, 287–305.

International Bibliography of the Social Sciences 1964 (1965), London: Tavistock.

Jones, Thomas M. (1995), 'Instrumental stakeholder theory: a synthesis of ethics and economics', *Academy of Management Review*, **20** (2), 404–37.

Jönsson, Sten A. and Rolf A. Lundin (1977), 'Myths and wishful thinking as management tools', in Paul C. Nystrom and William H. Starbuck (eds), *Prescriptive Models of Organizations*, Amsterdam: North-Holland, pp. 157–70.

Kieser, Alfred (1989), 'Organizational, institutional, and societal evolution: medieval craft guilds and the genesis of formal organizations', *Administrative Science Quarterly*, **34** (4), 540–64.

Lawrence, Paul R. and Jay W. Lorsch (1967), *Organization and Environment*, Boston, MA: Graduate School of Business Administration, Harvard University.

Leavitt, Harold J. (1996), 'The old days, hot groups, and managers' lib', *Administrative Science Quarterly*, **41** (June), 23–47.

Livesey, F. (1964), 'Book Review: *A Behavioral Theory of the Firm*: attempts to develop a theory of the firm which is based on empirical studies of decision-making within the firm', *Economic Journal*, **74** (March), 200–202.

Lodahl, Janice Beyer (1969), *Administrative Science Quarterly Index*, Vols 1–12, Ithaca, NY: Graduate School of Business and Public Administration.

March, James G. (1988), *Decisions and Organizations*, Oxford: Basil Blackwell.

March, James G. and Johan P. Olsen (1976), *Ambiguity and Choice in Organizations*, Bergen: Universitetsforlaget.

March, James G. and Johan P. Olsen (1995), *Democratic Governance*, New York: Free Press.

March, James G. and Guje Sevón (1988), 'Behavioral perspectives on theories of the firm', in W.F. Raaij, G.M. van Veldhoven and Karl Erik Wärneryd (eds), *Handbook of Economic Psychology*, Dordrecht: Kluwer, pp. 368–402.

March, James G. and Herbert A. Simon (1958), *Organizations*, New York: Wiley.

McCaffrey, David P. (1982), 'Corporate resources and regulatory pressures: toward explaining a discrepancy', *Administrative Science Quarterly*, **27** (3), 398–419.

Meyer, John W. and Brian Rowan (1977), 'Institutionalized organizations: formal structure as myth and ceremony', *American Journal of Sociology*, **83** (2), 440–63.

Miles, Raymond E. and Charles C. Snow (1978), *Organizational Strategy, Structure and Process*, New York: McGraw-Hill.

Mintzberg, Henry (1973), *The Nature of Managerial Work*, New York: Harper & Row.

Mintzberg, Henry (1978), 'Patterns in strategy formation', *Management Science*, **24** (May), 934–48.

Mintzberg, Henry (1979), *The Structuring of Organizations*, Englewood Cliffs, NJ: Prentice-Hall.

Mintzberg, Henry (1993), 'Twenty-five years later ... the illusive strategy', in Arthur G. Bedeian (ed.), *Management Laureates: A Collection of Autobiographical Essays*, Vol. 2, pp. 321–74.

Mitchell, Ronald K., Bradley R. Agle and Donna J. Wood (1997), 'Toward a theory of stakeholder identification and salience: defining the principle of who and what really counts', *Academy of Management Review*, **22** (4), 853–86.

Mitroff, Ian I. (1983), *Stakeholders of the Organizational Mind*, San Francisco, CA: Jossey-Bass.

Näslund, Bertil (1967), *Decisions Under Risk*, Stockholm: EFI.

Nelson, Richard R. and Sidney G. Winter (1982), *An Evolutionary Theory of Economic Change*, Boston, MA: Belknap Press.

Nohria, Nitin and Ranjay Gulati (1996), 'Is slack good or bad for innovation?', *Academy of Management Journal*, **39** (5), 1245–64.

Penrose, Edith T. (1959), *The Theory of the Growth of the Firm*, Oxford: Basil Blackwell.

Peters, Thomas J. and Robert H. Waterman Jr. (1982), *In Search of Excellence: Lessons from America's Best-run Companies*, New York: Harper & Row.

Pettigrew, Andrew M. (1979), 'On studying organizational cultures', *Administrative Science Quarterly*, **24**, December, pp. 570–81.

Pfeffer, Jeffrey (1981), *Power in Organizations*, Marshfield, MA: Pitman.

Pfeffer, Jeffrey (1982), *Organization and Organization Theory*, Marshfield, MA: Pitman.

Pfeffer, Jeffrey and Gerald R. Salancik (1978), *The External Control of Organizations. A Resource Dependence Perspective*, New York: Harper & Row.

Porter, Michael E. (1980), *Competitive Strategy*, New York: Free Press.

Porter, Michael E. (1985), *Competitive Advantage*, New York: Free Press.

Pugh, Derek S., David J. Hickson and C.R. Hinings (1971), 'Richard M. Cyert and James G. March', in Derek S. Pugh, David J. Hickson and C.R. Hinings (eds), *Writers on Organizations*, Harmondsworth: Penguin, pp. 80–86.

Ramström, Dick (1967), *The Efficiency of Control Strategies. Communication and Decision-making in Organizations*, Stockholm: Almqvist & Wiksell (diss.).

Rhenman, Eric (1964a), *Företaget som styrt system* (The Company as a Controlled System), Stockholm: Norstedts.

Rhenman, Eric (1964b), *Företagsdemokrati och företagsorganisation* (Industrial Democracy and Company Organisation), Stockholm: Norstedts.

Robinson, Joan (1933), *The Economics of Imperfect Competition*, London: Macmillan.

Ruefli, Timothy and J. Sarrazin (198 1), 'Strategic control of corporate development under ambiguous circumstances', *Management Science*, **27** (10), 1158—70.

Rumelt, Rumelt P. (1974), *Strategy, Structure, and Economic Performance*, Boston, MA: Graduate School of Business Administration, Harvard University.

Schneider, Susan C. (1989), 'Strategy formulation – the impact of national culture', *Organization Studies*, **10** (2), 149–68.

Scott, Susanne G. and Vicki R. Lane (2000), 'A stakeholder approach to organizational identity', *Academy of Management Review*, **25** (1), 43–62.

Selznick, Philip (1957), *Leadership in Administration*, New York: Harper & Row.

Sillén, Oskar (1954), 'Sakkunnigutlåtande rörande de sökande till den år 1953 ledigförklarade professuren i företagsekonomi vid Handelshögskolan i Stockholm' (Expert Report regarding the Applicants for the 1953 Vacant Chair in Business Administration at the Stockholm School of Economics), Handelshögskolans i Stockholm arkiv.

Simon, Herbert A. (1947), *Administrative Behavior*, New York: Free Press.

Simon, Herbert A. (1991), *Models of My Life*, New York: Basic Books.

Smircich, Linda (1983), 'Concepts of culture and organizational analysis', *Administrative Science Quarterly*, **28** (September), 339–58.

Sweezy, Paul M. (193 9), 'Demand under conditions of oligopoly', *Journal of Political Economy*, **47** (August), 568–73.

Swieringa, Robert J. and J.H. Waterhouse (1982), 'Organizational views of transfer pricing', *Accounting, Organizations and Society*, **7**, 149–55.

Tainio, Risto and Hannu Hänninen (1999), 'The influence of the Carnegie School on management and organization studies in Finland', Memo, Helsinki School of Economics and Business Administration.

Therborn, Göran (1966), 'Herr Eric Rhenman's omvälvning av vetenskapen' ('Mr Eric Rhenman's Upheaval of the Science'), in Göran Therborn (ed.), *En ny vänster*, Stockholm: Rabén & Sjögren, pp. 169–79.

Thompson, James D. (1967), *Organizations in Action*, New York: McGraw-Hill.

Uzzi, Brian (1997), 'Social structure and competition in interfirm networks: the paradox of embeddedness', *Administrative Science Quarterly*, **42** (March), 35–67.

Weick, Karl E. (1969), *The Social Psychology of Organizing*, Reading, MA: Addison-Wesley.

Whyte, William H. Jr. (1956), *The Organization Man*, New York: Simon & Schuster.

Williamson, Oliver E. (1975), *Markets and Hierarchy: Analysis and Antitrust Implications*, New York: Free Press.

Williamson, Oliver E. (1985), *The Economic Institutions of Capitalism*, New York: Free Press.

Winter, Sidney G. Jr. (1964), 'Book Review: *A Behavioral Theory of the Firm*', *American Economic Review*, **54** (March), 144–8.

Womack, James P. and Daniel T. Jones (1996), *Lean Thinking. Banish Waste and Create Wealth in Your Corporation*, New York: Simon & Schuster.

3. Corporate governance, executive compensation and the theory of the firm

Sok-Hyon Kang and Praveen Kumar*

1 INTRODUCTION

Management compensation is a topic of sustained interest in the theory of the firm. This interest stems, in part, from the potential conflicts of interest that arise from the separation of ownership and control in publicly held firms (Berle and Means, 1932). On account of this separation, corporate executives control vast resources that they do not own. How these resources are allocated, and used in rewarding or compensating top management is, therefore, a central issue in firm behavior. More generally, scholars develop theories of executive compensation determination since any satisfactory framework for understanding decision making in firms must be able to explain salient features of observed compensation behavior.

There are a number of theories in the literature on the determination of top-management compensation (see Section 2). In the economics literature, the neoclassical and agency-theoretic models present powerful and enlightening perspectives on management compensation, while in the organizational behavioral literature Simon (1953) relates top-management compensation levels to the layers of organizational hierarchy. However, the economics and management literature also presents considerable evidence that the received theoretical frameworks do not deal adequately with actual executive compensation determination. For example, Jensen and Murphy (1990) and Kaplan (1994) document a weak-reward-for-performance relationship in the chief executive officer (CEO) compensation of large firms. This finding appears to run counter to the view that top-management compensation is determined in an optimal contracting framework in the presence of agency conflicts. The seemingly *large* levels of CEO compensation, especially the value of equity-based compensation, is also not easily explained by marginal productivity or organizational hierarchy theories.

In this chapter, we present an alternative analytic framework for the determination of executive compensation. This framework is built on a careful consideration of the *process* through which top-management compensation is set in most publicly held firms. We argue that executive compensation in firms is generally set as the outcome of a process that is based on the interaction between the incentives of the CEO and the board of directors (BOD), in a backdrop of implicit monitoring of top-management compensation arrangements by large shareholders. We develop a model of this process that focuses on the most crucial aspects to deliver some refutable predictions regarding the levels of CEO compensation and observable corporate governance- and ownership-related variables.

These predictions are new to the literature to the extent that the existing frameworks do not explicitly accommodate the role of the BOD and the large shareholders in the executive compensation process. Furthermore, our perspective is consistent with the observed weak link between pay and performance and also the 'inordinately' large CEO compensation that is not easily explainable by firm size or organizational characteristics. The refutable predictions of the model are empirically tested on a sample of 1,648 large and small firms. The results indicate a significant role for the distribution of share ownership among the large shareholder(s), the CEO and the BOD, and also for governance characteristics of the BOD, in explaining the observed variations in the *levels* of CEO compensation.

In sum, our analysis demonstrates that a *process-oriented* approach to executive compensation determination (that makes explicit the process through which top-management compensation is determined), rather than the usual normative approach, can be fruitful. In particular, our approach (i) explains seemingly 'anomalous' aspects of observed compensation behavior such as the weak pay–performance link and the large size of top-management compensation, (ii) develops refutable predictions on the relation of executive compensation levels to corporate governance-related variables that are not accommodated by conventional theories, and (iii) provides insights regarding the decision-making process in firms.

The approach adopted in this chapter exemplifies a methodology first set out in *A Behavioral Theory of the Firm* (Cyert and March, 1963). This methodology has proved very useful in understanding the decision-making process in firms. This approach eschews imposing any predetermined objectives and decision-making capabilities on the firm. Instead, it seeks to examine the entire decision-making process, from the formulation of objectives and strategies to the determination of decisions within these strategies. In other words, the process-oriented approach to the theory of the firm attempts to: 'make detailed observations of the procedures by which firms make decisions and to use these observations on a basis for a theory of decision making within business organizations' (Cyert and March, 1992), p. 1).

To date, this approach has been fruitfully applied to studying price and output decisions, and also internal allocation and marketing strategy decisions. This chapter demonstrates the usefulness of this approach in studying another crucial decision in firms: executive compensation determination. The contribution of this approach is crystallized by comparing its ability to address important empirical patterns with that of more conventional approaches in the field.

Another contribution of this chapter is to show that the process-oriented approach adopted by a large literature following the lead of Cyert and March (1963) can be usefully applied by the application of non-cooperative game-theoretic techniques. This modeling approach generates refutable restrictions on the relation of CEO compensation to corporate governance variables. In that sense our chapter complements a recent literature that has fruitfully used game-theoretic techniques to either re-visit or otherwise develop the issues raised by Cyert and March (1963) regarding price and output determination, internal allocation, and product market strategy.[1]

In particular, our approach provides a tractable resolution to the usually thorny issue of specifying the 'appropriate' objective function of the firm. This has been a central issue in the theory of the firm.[2] Our formulation formalizes the outcomes that would arise from bargaining (implicit or explicit) between the CEO, the BOD, and the large shareholder(s). Thus, the polar assumptions, of either total autonomy for a self-interested CEO or the absence of managerial self-interest in maximizing the preferences of a large shareholder, which are sometimes made on a somewhat *ad hoc* basis in the literature, arise endogenously here. In fact, our view of the decision-making process within firms – especially in relation to major decisions such as executive compensation and investment policy – is consistent with the salient aspects of the corporate governance processes observed in practice: the CEO has 'agenda-setting' powers, but is constrained by the self-interested behavior of the BOD, and the monitoring incentives of the large shareholder(s).

The remainder of this chapter is organized as follows. Section 2 provides a brief survey of some of the prominent theories of executive compensation in economics and organizational behavior, and also summarizes the empirical evidence regarding these frameworks. Section 3 then describes salient aspects of the process of top-management executive compensation determination. Sections 4 to 6 present the formal model and analysis. Section 7 presents the empirical analysis. Section 8 relates our approach and results more systematically to the behavioral theory of the firm, and Section 9 concludes.

2 TOP-MANAGEMENT COMPENSATION: THEORIES AND EVIDENCE

Researchers studying top-management compensation use three major theoretical frameworks: human capital theory, agency theory, and organizational behavior theory.[3]

Human capital theory argues that the primary determinant of compensation is the economic value of the worker's skill. Although this theory is successful in explaining the empirically robust relation of education and job training on wages, it does not explain the strong empirical evidence that factors beyond worker productivity affect top-management compensation. For example, the documented impact of accounting or stock performance measures on top-management compensation (Ciscel and Carroll, 1980; Coughlin and Schmidt, 1985) cannot be explained by this theory.

The use of performance-based compensation contracts is consistent with the predictions of agency theory. Although agency theory explains a wide range of observed corporate practices, it is increasingly clear that the strict version of this theory cannot fully explain important aspects of observed management compensation behavior. One reason is that formal empirical testing of the predictions of incentive theory is constrained by the paucity of appropriate data on contracts and performance indicators. Moreover, it is difficult to identify the 'right' level of incentives predicted by the theory, since many of the key variables such as the managerial cost of effort or the subjective beliefs on the relation of production to effort are not identifiable. Nevertheless, authors like Jensen and Murphy (1990) and Kaplan (1994) argue that the observed pay–performance relation is weak, and join in the growing literature that points to the quality of corporate governance as the main problem (Jensen, 1993; Byrne, 1996). But it is also a compelling fact that one would not really observe an active role of the BOD in top-management compensation determination if the predictions of agency theory were *strictly* applicable. This is because top-management compensation would then be *completely* determined by pre-specified contracts based on quantities that are verifiable by third parties.

Similar comments apply to managerial compensation theories based on organizational behavior. These theories emphasize the role of managerial power in setting executive compensation (Simon, 1957; Tosi and Gomez-Mejia, 1989; Finkelstein and Hambrick, 1989).[4] While these theories are illuminating with respect to the forces at play in the determination of top-management compensation, their predictions are also often inconsistent with the evidence. In particular, executive compensation levels, especially equity-based compensation, are not solely driven by organizational hierarchy-related variables. For example, some of the largest stock-option and equity awards to executives are given in the high-technology sectors which are 'flat' organizations *par excellence*. And interestingly, many empirical studies find that CEO ownership is *negatively* related to compensation (Allen, 1981; Lambert et al., 1993; Core et al., 1999). This finding runs counter to the argument (see, for example, Tosi and Gomez-Mejia, 1989) that top-management compensation should be positively related to CEO ownership since CEO power is enhanced with higher ownership.

Motivated by these concerns, we attempt a systematic analysis of the process of top-management compensation determination, focusing on the role of corporate governance (broadly defined) in this process.

3 CORPORATE GOVERNANCE AND CEO COMPENSATION

The first part of this section describes the sequence of behaviors that are central to executive compensation determination in publicly held firms. The second part relates this study to the pertinent literature on corporate governance.

Some Practical Aspects of CEO Compensation Determination: A Behavioral Perspective

The process of compensation determination in firms is usually not based on the neoclassical or the agency theories. Firms do not typically derive the marginal revenue-product maximizing wage or the incentive-efficient wage according to pre-set formulas. While, in principle, the ultimate authority over CEO compensation is vested with the shareholders, in practice, the shareholders delegate the responsibility to a small number of individuals, namely the board of directors. Indeed, the following words taken from the Executive Incentive Plan for a major US corporation are representative of most publicly held firms: 'The board of directors has the right to amend, modify or terminate at any time of their choosing the terms of the compensation structure described herein'.

This vestment of corporate governance to the BOD is, broadly speaking, a reflection of both incomplete contracting (Williamson, 1985; Grossman and Hart, 1986) and the presence of serious transactions costs. Due to bounded rationality, or to the prohibitive costs of writing out all possible contingencies *ex ante*, firms cannot govern CEO conduct entirely through contingent contracting. Meanwhile, there are substantial transaction costs in attempting to continually govern the firm through proxy contests or other vehicles for expressing shareholder preferences. The absence of complete contingent contracting on top-management compensation, and the large costs in shareholder monitoring, often imply that the BOD has considerable leeway in awarding CEO compensation.[5] Thus, the interaction between the CEO and the BOD influences the level of CEO compensation, apart from considerations of marginal factor productivity and incentive provisions.

However, the CEO–BOD nexus cannot operate in an unconstrained fashion. Investors, especially large shareholders, have a self-interest in monitoring the compensation arrangement of the CEO for at least two reasons. First, executive compensation may impact firm performance through well-known incentive effects, and second, executive compensation is costly to the shareholders. Under the appropriate conditions, large shareholders may even pose control challenges to the CEO if the top-management compensation is perceived to be inappropriate. The exact outcome of the compensation determination process then depends on the interplay between self-interests of the CEO and the BOD, and the incentives of the large shareholders to pose control challenges to the CEO and the BOD.

Keeping aside the incentives of large shareholders to protect their interests, the close interaction between the CEO and the BOD over time produces a tendency for an upward drift in the CEO's compensation. Coupled with the fact that there exists considerable public and/or regulatory scrutiny of the CEOs' compensation that effectively imposes a ceiling on CEO compensation *levels* (Jensen and Murphy, 1990), an immediate implication of this tendency is that, over time, the CEO's compensation becomes less and less sensitive to performance. One reason is that the CEO generally has the discretion over the selection and appointment of outside directors. Even if there is a nominating committee for members of the BOD, the CEO exercises considerable influence in the selection of the list of possible nominees. In any case, appointment to the board is extremely difficult, if not impossible, without the approval of the CEO. In sum, outside directors on the compensation committee which implements the BOD's discretion over executive compensation, are quite aware of their obligation to the CEO for their initial appointment to the board and/or its continuance.[6]

On the other hand, a major risk for the BOD in reflexively acquiescing to the CEO's demands is the possibility of low firm performance (especially bankruptcy) and the threat of lawsuits against the directors. Whatever their feeling of obligation to the CEO, most directors would be unwilling to be lenient with a CEO whom they perceive as incapable of keeping the firm in the black over the long run. Conversely, there is also a 'learning' aspect regarding the BOD's preferences and proclivities on the part of the CEO. As he or she gets more experienced with the members of the BOD, the CEO has a better estimate of the kind of strategies that may dilute the negative effect of bad performance periods on his or her compensation.

Existing Literature on Corporate Governance and Executive Compensation

There is a substantial literature that reinforces the issues raised in the preceding paragraphs. Jensen (1993) contends that corporate internal control problems often originate from the BOD itself. He further attributes the BOD's governance failures to factors such as the CEO's informational advantage (the agenda-setting power), low equity ownership of the board members, overcrowding of the board, and a board culture that encourages consent rather than dissent. Compensation experts and the popular press advance similar views.[7] The delegation of fiduciary responsibilities to the BOD can also give rise to other agency problems since the directors have their own private incentives that may not be in the best interest of the shareholders. One reason is that the director-agent's appointment and its continuance are at least in part determined by another agent, namely the CEO (Mace, 1986; Lorsch and MacIver, 1989).

The literature also offers several countervailing forces affect the directors' conciliatory stance toward the CEO. Fama (1980) and Fama and Jensen (1983) emphasize various disciplining devices for the BOD: potential loss of reputation, adverse public scrutiny, or the threat of shareholder lawsuits, particularly in the event of poor performance. Indeed, an increased BOD ownership is often asserted to safeguard against governance failures and CEO overcompensation (Jensen, 1993), although studies are unable to find corroborating evidence (Finkelstein and Hambrick, 1989; Lambert et al., 1993; Core et al., 1999).

Many economists also suggest that blockholders can exert influence on matters such as compensation and monitoring of the executives (Shleifer and Vishny, 1986; Mehran, 1995). The 'managerial power' theory also leads many (Allen, 1981; Finkelstein and Hambrick, 1989; Tosi and Gomez-Mejia, 1989; Boyd, 1994) to predict that large external or internal blockholders (not related to the CEO) decrease the power of the CEO, and thus lower the CEO compensation.[8] However, the empirical literature has not explicitly examined the role of large shareholders on CEO compensation.

The behavioral characteristics of the compensation-setting process motivate further analysis of the interaction between the CEO and the BOD. We now present a formal model of this interaction based on the incomplete contracting approach.

4 THE BASIC MODEL

We model a typical publicly held firm that, over the infinite horizon, may go through a sequence of managerial regimes, each associated with a particular manager or CEO controlling the firm's operational decisions. Our aim in this section is to set out the technology, governance, and decision-making conventions of the firm, and specify how these relate to the CEO's compensation and probability of replacement.

Technology and Firm Governance

We consider a discrete-time model of the firm where decisions are made at (discrete) dates $t = 0, 1, 2, \ldots$, with the time between two adjacent dates being referred to as a period. The firm owns a point input–point output production technology: investment in the production technology today, I_t, stochastically determines the payoffs from the project tomorrow, y_{t+1}, according to:

$$y_{t+1} = F(I_t) + \varepsilon_{t+1}, \qquad t = 0, 1, 2, \ldots \tag{3.1}$$

Here ε is an earnings shock that occurs subsequent to the investment decision. We shall assume that the production function F is non-negative valued, twice continuously differentiable, strictly increasing and strictly concave. The earnings shocks will be assumed to be identically and independently distributed with a density function $p(\varepsilon)$ on the support $[0, +\infty)$.

In each period, the firm may also borrow and lend unrestrictedly for short term at a given one-period rate of return, $r_t > 0$. Thus, the firm in each period faces an investment allocation decision between the production technology and the riskless lending opportunity. We assume that because of technological or business specialization reasons, a CEO is required for the operation of the firm's production technology and for making the investment and financing decisions of the firm. A given CEO can manage the firm for a finite number of periods (T) only.[9]

The economy in which the firm operates comprises two types of agents. There are a continuum of infinitely-lived and risk-neutral consumer-investors, indexed by $i \in Z$. Each agent i's preferences over random consumption streams $(c_1^i, c_2^i, \ldots)$ on dates 1, 2, ... are given by, $E\,[\Sigma_{t=1}^{\infty}\rho^t c_t^i]$, where $0 < \rho < 1$ is a discount factor, and $E[\cdot]$ is the expectations operator. The consumer-investors may, however, differ according to wealth endowments. However, all consumer-investors may also borrow and lend unrestrictedly at the given rate, r_t. Second, there are a continuum of infinitely-lived CEOs for the firm, indexed by $m \in M$, where M is a pre-specified set of managers in the economy. In particular, a CEO, $m \in M$, has preferences over random consumption streams $(c_1^m, c_2^m, ...)$ that are represented by, $E\,[\Sigma_{t=1}^{\infty}\rho^t u^m(c_t^m)]$, where u^m is a strictly increasing and strictly concave von Neumann–Morgenstern expected utility function.[10]

The common stock of the firm is traded in a competitive and frictionless stock market. In any period t, the number of shares of the firm that are outstanding, and the set of shareholders are denoted, respectively, by J_t, and $S_t \subset Z$. It is also convenient to let $\bar{\alpha}_t$ denote the set of equity fractions held in period t.[11] Since the CEO may also be a shareholder, and the fraction of the firm held by the CEO in the beginning of any period t is denoted by, α_t^m. It will also be useful to denote the fraction of the firm held by the largest shareholder other than the CEO as $\alpha_t^L \equiv \sup[\bar{\alpha}_t - \{\alpha_t^m\}]$.

During his or her tenure, the CEO is governed by the BOD. The BOD is composed of the CEO and N outside directors.[12] The set of directors in period t will be denoted as $D_t \subset Z$. Members of the BOD receive a remuneration for every period served, although this remuneration may be individual specific. The identity of these directors, and their remuneration for that period are announced by the CEO in every period.

The BOD performs two major functions. First, it evaluates and approves through a majority vote the investment policy of the firm that is proposed by the CEO in every period. Second, the BOD also plays a significant role in determining the total compensation of the CEO. The CEO compensation in the model has two components: a contractible component wherein the CEO's compensation is determined by the realization of profits through a pre-specified and possibly history contingent sharing rule; and a non-contractible component wherein the BOD has a residual authority in making *ex post* compensation adjustments based on circumstances that cannot be completely contracted on, *ex ante*.

Stockholders can individually and non-cooperatively challenge the control of the CEO either by initiating a proxy contest against specific decisions of the CEO, including the composition of the BOD, or by making a tender offer for the firm's shares. A successful control challenge in a proxy contest requires support from at least 51 percent of the voting stock present, and in the tender offer case requires acquisition of a majority stake in the firm. The outcome of a successful control challenge is the removal of the incumbent CEO, and an option to set up a new BOD.[13]

We shall assume, realistically, that mounting such control challenges involves costs. First, there are fixed costs that have to be borne in order to initiate and administer a proxy contest or a hostile tender offer (see, for example, Shleifer and Vishny, 1986). Furthermore, there are costs involved in attempting to gain the support of a majority stock vote.[14] For any given period t, current stock price, q_t, and a particular shareholder holding, $a_t \in \bar{\alpha}_t$, of the firm, we shall denote as $\kappa_t\,(a_t, q_t)$ the costs to this shareholder of *assuring* a successful control challenge – either in the form of a proxy challenge or through a tender offer.[15]

As noted in Section 3 above, in practice there is another avenue open to the shareholders to influence the behavior of the BOD, namely through personal bankruptcy lawsuits against the directors in the case of demonstrable dereliction of fiduciary responsibility. In our model we shall assume that shareholders can successfully bring these lawsuits with some probability in bankruptcy.

At the beginning of any period t, we take as given the profits of the firm,

$$\pi_t = y_t + \max[0, K_{t-1}(1 + r_{t-1})],$$

where K_{t-1} is the amount lent by the firm in the preceding period. The firm has payout liabilities of $L_t = B_{t-1}(1 + r_{t-1})$, where B_{t-1} are the borrowings in the previous period. We also take as exogenously given the *contractible* component of the current CEO's compensation, s_t; that is, the compensation due to the CEO based on a previously-written and possibly history- and performance- (for example, the realization of π_t) contingent contract. The firm is viewed to be in a normal operational mode if its current profits can meet its payout liabilities (that is, if $\pi_t \geq L_t$); and, in the alternative case, the firm declares bankruptcy.

Even in a normal operational mode, the CEO still has the option of resigning or exiting from the firm. (The reservation utility of the CEO from serving on the firm is normalized to be zero per period.) But if the CEO decides to stay, then he or she first makes changes, if any, in the composition of the BOD; that is, the CEO decides on the composition of D_t, and also effects, through individual negotiations (see below), the remuneration in the period for the directors. The BOD composition decision can be conveniently represented by the non-negative integer, n_t, the number of directors from D_{t-1} replaced in period t. The remuneration for the BOD can be individual specific, and will be denoted as $x_{it} \geq 0$, $i \in D_t$. The selected BOD members for period t, must, of course, have agreed to serve on the BOD at the proposed remuneration.

Once the board is in place, the CEO then proposes, (i) adjustment to the pre-contracted compensation (s_t) by the amount, b_t; that is, the total proposed compensation is $w_t = s_t + b_t$, and (ii) the investment in the productive technology in the current period, I_t. We shall also assume that the firm retains – and lends at the riskless rate – any cash surplus.[16] The CEO's proposals become effective as long as (a) they are not rejected by a majority vote of the BOD, or (b) they are not overridden in a shareholder proxy contest (with at least a majority percentage of the voting stock present), or (c) there is no direct challenge to the CEO's control of the firm through a successful tender offer for the firm by some shareholder. Finally, if the current CEO decides to exit, then the incumbent BOD selects another CEO randomly from the set, M, and the foregoing timing conventions regarding CEO choices apply for the new CEO.

The potential BOD members may have heterogeneous perspectives on service to the firm. Although, by assumption, all BOD members are risk neutral, they may differ in terms of their bankruptcy costs in the event that the firm declares bankruptcy. These bankruptcy costs arise due to (i) the loss in share value if the director has equity in the firm and (ii) future reputational costs (recall that agents are infinitely lived) or bankruptcy exposure in the event of shareholder lawsuits for negligence. These bankruptcy costs will, in general, be heterogeneous. Directors will generally hold a different number of shares, and the liability exposure will be increasing in the personal recoverable assets. We shall thus assume that in a given period t, director i on the BOD has bankruptcy costs of $\mu^i(\alpha_t^i) \geq 0$, where α_t^i is this director's share-ownership fraction in the beginning of the period t. Conditional on the distribution of share-ownership $\bar{\alpha}_t$, the incidence of bankruptcy costs is taken to be random, with a distribution function, $G(\mu^i \mid \bar{\alpha}_t)$.

Since the bankruptcy costs are assumed to be agent specific, potential BOD members will be privately informed of their expected bankruptcy costs. However, the CEO will learn about this characteristic of the directors by observing their behavior. For simplicity, we shall assume that the CEO learns about the type of the directors in at the end of the very first period that they serve on the board.[17] We shall also assume for simplicity that all agents in Z have a common opportunity cost in utility terms of time spent for servicing on the BOD, and set this equal to $\bar{o}$ per period. Thus an agent will agree to serve on the BOD only if the expected utility of remuneration for serving on the BOD net of any potential bankruptcy costs is at least $\bar{o}$ per period. In the event that a candidate board member rejects the CEO's remuneration offer, the CEO proposes alternative selections and the process continues until N agents have agreed to serve on the BOD for the current period.

Finally, following the final investment and governance decisions in the period, the new stock price, q_{t+1}, is set in a stock market equilibrium in the sense of Lucas (1978) or Brock (1982), and remains in effect until the corresponding point in the succeeding period. The timing conventions within a typical period of a firm in normal operational mode is summarized graphically in Figure 3.1.

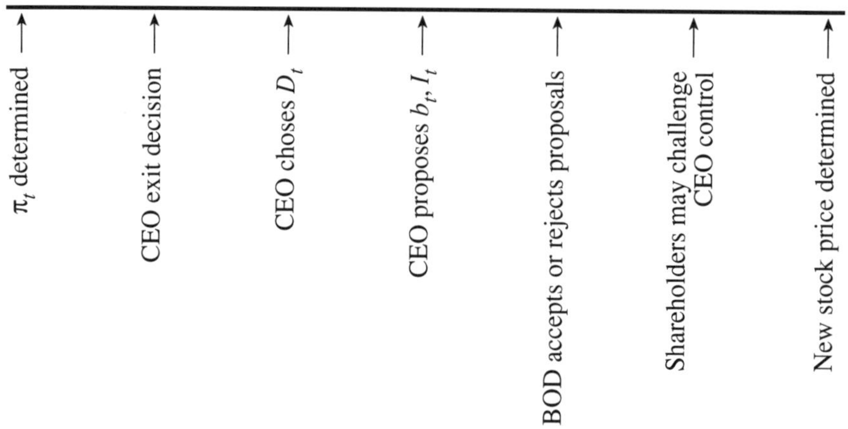

Figure 3.1 Timing conventions for period t

The timing conventions set out in the figure, along with the stated payoffs in various contingencies, can be interpreted to describe an extensive-form game of imperfect information. We shall use the subgame-perfect Bayesian equilibrium concept to study this game.[18]

5 EQUILIBRIUM CHARACTERIZATION

The model described in the previous section is a stylized, but reasonably realistic depiction of the process of corporate governance and its interaction with CEO compensation in public corporations.[19]

Consider then a representative trajectory of the game, with some CEO, $m \in M$, controlling the firm. It is convenient to relabel the first period under this CEO's control as period 0. Then suppose that the firm has not declared bankruptcy by period T, and the CEO is still in control of the firm. By assumption, this is the last period under this CEO's control. We shall now show that the equilibrium outcome in this terminal (for the CEO's control) period can be represented as a solution to a *constrained optimization problem*: the compensation adjustment and investment allocation decision is chosen to maximize the CEO's expected utility subject to two types of governance-related constraints, which are elucidated below.

To express this constrained optimization problem concisely, let γ_T denote the vector of state or exogenously given variables for the firm in period T; that is, $\gamma_T = (\pi_T, L_T, r_T, \bar{\alpha}_T, q_T)$; and let δ_T denote the *future payoff-related* control decisions in period T; that is, $\delta_T = (I_T, b_T, x_T, K_T)$, where $x_T = \Sigma_{I=1}^{N} x_{iT}$, is the total BOD remuneration for the period.[20] The vectors γ_T and δ_T completely determine the probability distribution of the firm's total earnings in the next period. In particular, we let $\psi_{T+1}(\gamma_T, \delta_T)$ denote the transition bankruptcy probability of the firm; that is, $\psi_{T+1} = P\{L_{T+1} - [F(I_T) + K_T(1 + r_T)]\}$, where $K_T = \max[0, \pi_T - (L_T + I_T + s + x_T)]$, and where $P(\cdot)$ is the cumulative distribution function associated with $p(\varepsilon)$. For any agent $i \in Z$, the expected utility from serving on the BOD in period T is, $v_T^i(\gamma_T, \delta_T) \equiv x_{iT} - \rho\psi_{T+1}(\gamma_T, \delta_T)\mu^i(\alpha^i_T)$.

Next, we examine an investor who owns a fraction $a_T \in \bar{\alpha}_T$ of the firm in the beginning of the period and considers holding this fraction until the end of the period. We now compute the maximal value of the firm for this investor. Since the CEO is risk averse, the shareholders are risk neutral, the capital markets are perfect, and there is no moral hazard, the optimal risk-sharing contract between the CEO and the shareholders will specify a fixed cash salary, say s, for the manager (Holmström, 1979). Then let $\hat{\pi}_{T+1} \equiv \max(0, \pi_{T+1} - (L_T + s)]$ denote the cash flow of the firm in period $T + 1$, net of the debt liabilities and the managerial compensation.[21] Next, let $\Pi_{T+1}(\hat{\pi}_{T+1}, \hat{\gamma}_{T+1})$ denote the value of the firm in the beginning of period $(T + 1)$, when the firm's free cash flow is $\hat{\pi}_{T+1}$, and the other elements of the state are, $\hat{\gamma}_{T+1} = (r_{T+1}, \bar{\alpha}_{T+1}, q_{T+1})$. Here we take the view that the elements of $\hat{\gamma}_{T+1}$ are not directly in control of the players (the CEO, the shareholders, and the BOD) in period T.[22] And, by performing a standard many-to-one transformation on the just described probability, we obtain a cumulative probability distribution function of Π_{T+1}, conditional on (γ_T, δ_T), which we denote as $\Phi_{T+1}(\Pi_{T+1} \mid \gamma_T, \delta_T)$. In sum, $E[\Pi_{T+1} \mid \gamma_T, \delta_T] = \int_0^\infty \Pi_{T+1} d\Phi_{T+1}(\Pi_{T+1} \mid \gamma_T, \delta_T)$.

Since the shareholders are all risk neutral, they have common preferences, and since the capital markets are assumed to be frictionless, there is a common optimal investment for the shareholders, given any state γ_T. Similarly, since there is no asymmetric information, the 'first best' for the shareholders involves no additional discretionary compensation for the CEO, and also no rents for the BOD. To see these points, put $\delta^*_T = (I^*_T, b^*_T = 0, x^*_T, K^*_T)$, and taking as given, (γ_T, μ_T), let $I^*_T, x^*_T, i = 1, \ldots, N$, and K^*_T, jointly satisfy,

$$\begin{aligned} &I^*_T \in \operatorname{argmax}\{\rho E[\Pi_{T+1} / \gamma_T, (x^*_T, I_T, K^*_T)] - I_T\}, \\ &x_{iT} - \rho\psi_{T+1}(\gamma_T, (I^*_T, b^*_T = 0, x_T, K_T))\mu^i(\alpha^i_T) = \bar{o}, i = 1, \ldots, N, \\ &K^*_T = \max[0, \pi_T - (L_T + I^*_T + s + x^*_T)]. \end{aligned} \tag{3.2}$$

The solution to the system of equations (3.2) yields the investment that maximizes net expected firm value, subject to the individual rationality constraints for the BOD, and the firm's budget constraint. Since the system of equations in (3.2) is independent of the fraction of the firm held by the shareholders, it is clear that shareholders have a common optimal decision vector for a firm, for any given state and any fixed vector of BOD bankruptcy cost types. It follows, therefore, that shareholders also have a common optimal strategy for reconfiguring the BOD in period T, were they to successfully wrest control from the CEO.

Formally, given γ_T, and information about the liability costs of the BOD, D_T, any shareholder who wrests control of the firm chooses a number, say η_T, of new independent drawings from the director pool Z, to replace the directors chosen by the CEO. This number, η_T, is chosen to maximize the (discounted) expected firm value in period (T+1), taking as given the optimal decision rule, $\delta^*_T\gamma T, \mu_T)$.[23] We can thus compute the indirect expected next-period market value of the firm for the shareholders, given the state γ_T; namely, $E^* [\Pi_{T+1} \mid \gamma_T, \mu_T] \equiv E [\Pi_{T+1} \mid \gamma_T, \delta^*_T (\gamma_T, \mu_T)]$, where the expectations are taken jointly over $Z^{(\eta T)} \times [0, +\infty)$; that is, over the joint probability function of director liability costs and the next-period firm value.

The CEO's optimal strategy in period T can also now be derived. Apart from the decision vector, δ_T, a CEO in control also chooses the members of the incumbent BOD (that is, the BOD in the previous period) who are to be replaced. It turns out that all the optimal decisions of the CEO in period T can be deduced from studying the CEO's optimal control problem for managing the firm with a given BOD. To set up this problem, let A_{T+1}, denote the CEO's net wealth in the beginning of period (T + 1). Also let $V^m_{T+1} (A_{T+1})$ and $\underline{V}^m_{T+1} (A_{T+1})$, respectively, denote the expected utility of the CEO from the period (T + 1) onwards when the firm is solvent or is liquidated in a bankruptcy state, and his or her net wealth is A_{T+1}. The assumption of bankruptcy costs on the CEO implies that $V^m_{T+1}(\cdot) > \underline{V}^m_{T+1}(\cdot)$.

Then consider the CEO's optimization problem which takes *any* BOD with the vector of types, $\mu = (\mu^1, ..., \mu^N)$ as *given*, and chooses investment, discretionary compensation (adjustment) and firm borrowings to maximize his or her expected utility subject to two constraints: (i) the chosen decision vector for the firm leaves the existing shareholders at least weakly indifferent to mounting a successful control challenge, (ii) it also satisfies the (one-period) participation constraint of the chosen BOD. We shall call this problem O_T, which takes the following form:

$$V^m{}_T(A_T, \gamma_T, \mu) = \max_{\delta_T, c^m_T} \{u^m(c^m_T) + \rho[\psi_{T+1}(\gamma_T, \delta_T)\underline{V}^m_{T+1}(\underline{A}_{T+1}) + \int_0^\infty V^m_{T+1}(A_{T+1}(\Pi_{T+1})d\Phi_{T+1}(\Pi_{T+1} \mid \gamma_T, \delta_T)]\} \tag{3.3}$$

subject to,

$$v^i_T(\gamma_T, \delta_T) \geq \bar{o}, i = 1, ..., N \tag{3.4}$$

$$\rho a^j_T E^* [\Pi_{T+1} \mid \gamma_T, \mu_T] - \kappa_T(a^j_T, q_T) \leq \rho a^j_T E [\Pi_{T+1} \mid \gamma_T, \delta_T], \forall_j \in S_T \tag{3.5}$$

$$\underline{A}_{T+1} = (A_T + w_T - c^m_T)(1 + r_T) \tag{3.6}$$

$$A_{T+1}(\Pi_{T+1}) = \underline{A}_{T+1} + s + \alpha^m_{T+1}\Pi_{T+1}. \tag{3.7}$$

Next, the CEO's optimal strategy in terms of BOD replacement can be expressed directly in terms of the indirect value function, V^m_T. Suppose that in the beginning of period T, the incumbent BOD's types are given by the vector, μ_{T-1}. With some abuse of notation, it will be convenient to sort these in ascending order in terms of magnitude, so that $\mu^1_{T-1} < ... < \mu^N_{T-1}$. Since these director types are known to the CEO at the beginning of the period, it is clear from the foregoing that the CEO will replace the directors with the highest bankruptcy costs first. Then let, for any $1 \leq n \leq N$, $\mu_{T-1}(n)$, denote the vector μ_{T-1} with its n-highest values changed. The expected utility gain for the CEO from replacing the n-highest director types may then be written,

$$H^n_T(A_T, \gamma_T, \mu_{T-1}) \equiv \int_{Z^n} V^m_T(A_T, \gamma_T, \mu = \mu_{T-1}(n))dG^n(\mu \mid \bar{\alpha}_T) - V^m_T(A_T, \gamma_T, \mu = \mu_{T-1}), \tag{3.8}$$

where G^n is the n-fold of the distribution $G(\mu)$. The first term in (3.8) represents the expected utility from replacing n incumbent directors by simultaneously and randomly drawing n new directors from the set Z.[24] Thus, replacement of n directors is optimal only if $H^n_T > 0$. But V^m_T is non-increasing in the components of μ_{T-1}. Thus, it is optimal for the CEO to replace a number $n_T(A_T, \gamma_T)$ in period T, where $n_T(A_T, \gamma_T, \mu_{T-1}) \equiv \max\{n \mid H^n_T(A_T, \gamma_T, \mu_{T-1}) > 0\}$. In fact, the replacement rule can be given an alternative characterization that is also useful: there exists a critical value of director bankruptcy costs, say $\mu^c{}_T(A_T, \gamma_T, \mu_{T-1})$, such that a director is replaced if and only if his or her bankruptcy costs exceed this critical value.

The CEO's optimal exit strategy is then straightforwardly derived. At the beginning of the period, the CEO's indirect, expected utility from retaining control of the firm is,

$$\hat{V}^m_T(A_T, \gamma_T, \mu_{T-1}) \equiv \int_{Z^n} V^m_T(A_T, \gamma_T, \mu_{T-1}(N_T)dG^n(\mu \mid \bar{\alpha}_T).$$

It is optimal for the CEO to exit in the beginning of the period if this quantity is negative, and stay on otherwise.

Analysis of the T-period game leads to a general characterization of the equilibrium for any year $1 \le t \le T$ in the CEO's tenure, based on backward induction from the final-period game. Theorem 1 below summarizes equilibrium determination of (i) CEO survival, (ii) CEO compensation, (iii) BOD compensation, and (iv) BOD evolution. (See Appendix 3A for proof of Theorem 1.)

Theorem 1 For every $1 \le t \le T$, given any state, γ_t, the vector of incumbent director types, μ_{t-1}, and the CEO's wealth A_t, there exist functions, $V^m_t(A_t, \gamma_t, \mu_t)$, $\Pi_t(A_t, \gamma_t, \mu_{t-1})$, and $\delta^*_t(\gamma_t, \mu_t)$, such that along the equilibrium path the CEO's period t strategy is described by the triple of functions,

$$X_t(A_t, \gamma_t, \mu_{t-1}),\ n_t(A_t, \gamma_t, \mu_{t-1}), \text{ and } \delta^m_t(A_t, \gamma_t, \mu_{t-1}),$$

where, (*i*) $X_t(A_t, \gamma_t, \mu_{t-1}) = 0$, if and only if $V^m_t < 0$, and is equal to 1 else; (ii) the CEO replaces $n_t(A_t, \gamma_t, \mu_{t-1})$ members of the incumbent BOD with the highest bankruptcy costs, where:

$$n_t(A_t, \gamma_t, \mu_{t-1}) \equiv \max\{n \mid \int_{Z^n} V^m_t[A_t, \gamma_t, \mu_{t-1}(n)]dG^n(\mu\bar{\alpha}_t) - V^m{}_t(A_t, \gamma_t, \mu_{t-1}) > 0\};$$

and, $\delta^m_t(A_t, \gamma_t, \mu_{t-1})$ is a solution to the constrained optimization problem,

$$\begin{aligned} V^m_t(A_t, \gamma_t, \mu_{t-1}) = \max_{\delta_t, c^t_m}\{&u^m(c^m_t) + \rho[\psi_{t+1}(\gamma_t, \delta_t)\underline{V}^m_{t+1},(\underline{A}_{t+1}) + \\ &\int_0^\infty V^m_{t+1}(A_{t+1}(\Pi_{t+1}))\delta\Phi_{t+1}(\Pi_{t+1} \mid \gamma_t, \delta_t)]\} \end{aligned} \tag{3.9}$$

subject to,

$$v^i_t(\gamma_t, \delta_t) = \bar{o},\ i \in D_t \tag{3.10}$$

$$\rho\alpha_t^L \int_0^\infty \Pi_{t+1} d\Phi_{t+1}(\Pi_{t+1} \mid \gamma_t, \delta_t^*) - \kappa_t(\alpha_t^L, q_t) = \rho\alpha_t^L \int_0^\infty \Pi_{t+1} d\Phi_{t+1}(\Pi_{t+1} \mid \gamma_t, \delta_t) \quad (3.11)$$

$$\underline{A}_{t+1} = (A_t + w_t - c_t^m)(1 + r_t) \quad (3.12)$$

$$A_{t+1}(\Pi_{t+1}) = \underline{A}_{t+1} + s + \alpha_{t+1}^m \Pi_{t+1}. \quad (3.13)$$

According to Theorem 1, the participation constraints of the BOD will be binding in equilibrium; that is, the directors will not earn any quasi-rents.[25] The reason for this is that the 'rules of the game' allow the CEO to precommit to *not* bargain with individual directors regarding their remuneration. This precommitment ability allows the CEO to extract the directors' rents. Furthermore, only the non-intervention constraint of the largest shareholder is binding in equilibrium. The reason is that the cost of challenging CEO control, r, is decreasing in the initial ownership of the shareholder. Thus, the largest shareholder faces the lowest cost of challenging the CEO. If the largest shareholder is just indifferent between challenging the CEO and allowing the current management to operate, then it is strictly not in the other shareholders' interest to undertake a control challenge. In sum, in equilibrium, the relatively complex continuum of inequality constraints (for example, (3.4)–(3.5)) are reduced to a tractable finite number of equality constraints (3.10)–(3.13). The resultant simplicity is useful for the characterization of the equilibrium CEO compensation.

Theorem 1 gives a rather complete description of the equilibrium determination of CEO compensation in the model.[26] The CEO uses his or her 'agenda-setting' powers under the assumed governance structure to extract the optimal compensation adjustment from the BOD, subject to the constraints discussed above. CEO compensation may thus be seen as an (efficient) outcome of a bargaining problem where the CEO plays the role of a Stackelberg leader.

Meanwhile, in assessing the desirability of posing a control challenge to the CEO, shareholders essentially follow an 'optimal stopping rule' type of strategy: given the CEO's BOD choice and proposed compensation-investment plans, a typical shareholder compares the net expected utility of a control challenge in the current period versus the expected utility of allowing the CEO to maintain control for another period, along the continuation game. This implies that the CEO cannot choose the compensation-investment policies at will. In particular, the presence of large shareholders, or low transaction costs for proxy contests, can severely limit the CEO's discretion, even to the point of forcing the CEO to exit.

A special situation, which is of considerable empirical interest, is when the CEO is the largest shareholder; that is, $\alpha_t^m > \alpha_t^L$. In that case, the control challenge threat is possibly diluted but not eliminated. For example, take the case where the *second-largest* shareholder has substantial holdings that are close to the fraction of the firm held by the CEO. An interesting implication of the governance constraint (3.11) is also that the CEO has an incentive to increase his or her own shareholdings in the firm.

6 COMPARATIVE STATICS AND DYNAMICS ON CEO COMPENSATION

In this section we perform comparative statics and dynamics on the equilibrium compensation adjustment, $b_t(A_t, \gamma_t, \mu_t)$, $1 \leq t < T$. We derive refutable predictions regarding b_t and empirically measurable variables representing the state of the firm or the characteristics of the BOD.

Theorem 2 In every period $1 \leq t \leq T$, and given any (A_t, γ_t, μ_t), the equilibrium $b_t(A_t, \gamma_t, \mu_t)$, is: (i) decreasing in α_t^L, (ii) increasing in the cost of control challenge, $\kappa(\alpha^L, q)$, (iii) decreasing in the default probability, (iv) increasing in the profits, π_τ, (v) non-increasing in any director's ownership (α_t^i), and (vi) decreasing in the bankruptcy costs of the BOD. Finally, the relation of b_t with the fraction of the firm held by the CEO, α_t^m, is generally ambiguous.

Theorem 2 (see Appendix 3A1 for proof) shows that the discretionary component of CEO compensation is positively (negatively) affected by variation in items that relax (tighten) the governance constraints on the CEO's desired compensation. Take, first, the non-intervention constraint for largest shareholder (compare equation (3.11)). An exogenous increase in this shareholder's ownership (α^L) tightens this constraint in two ways: (i) the value (to the large) shareholder of changing the investment and compensation policy of the firm increases, *ceteris paribus*, and (ii) the cost of control challenge falls. *Both* these factors thus work to deliver the negative relation of CEO compensation to α^L. By the same token, keeping α^L the same, a decrease in the cost of control challenge tightens the constraint (3.11). For example, to the extent that a higher stock price increases the cost of a control challenge, compensation is an increasing function of firm value. Interestingly, this positive relation of CEO compensation to firm value arises even though value is not being taken as a performance measure for agency problems.

In a similar vein, a higher default probability increases the incentives of the large shareholder to intervene or challenge the CEO's control. By contrast, a strong current cash position dilutes the potential threat of future subnormal (from a shareholder point of view) firm performance resulting from the CEO's 'suboptimal' compensation or investment policies.

Turn, next, to the individual rationality constraint for the BOD (compare equation (3.10)). Other things being the same, a higher default probability tightens this constraint and has a negative impact on equilibrium CEO compensation. Furthermore, an increase in a given director's ownership (α_t^i) increases his or her bankruptcy costs, and also tightens the individual rationality constraint, *ceteris paribus*. Similarly, higher bankruptcy costs due to greater reputational costs or legal liability exposure also tighten the individual rationality constraint.

Finally, taking the shareholdings of the CEO as given, the relation of CEO holdings to his or her equilibrium compensation is ambiguous: a higher shareholding increases the CEO's future return from productive investment in the firm, but this wealth effect can also induce greater *current* consumption due to consumption smoothing by the risk-averse CEO (see, for example, Donaldson and Mehra, 1983). On the other hand, α^m can plausibly impact the cost of control challenge as well. If the CEO holds a significant fraction of the firm, for example, then the cost of control challenge is presumably higher, and therefore, α^m would have a positive relation with CEO compensation.

As seen in the previous section, there is an evolution of the BOD along the equilibrium path due to CEO learning. This evolution also leads to interesting comparative dynamics on CEO compensation: under certain conditions there is a positive correlation between CEO total compensation and the length of his or her tenure arising from the CEO's optimal replacement rule for the directors. More precisely, let $\bar{\mu}_t \equiv (\Sigma_{i=1}^N \mu_t^i)/N$, represent the average bankruptcy costs of the BOD in period t. And, let $E_t(\bar{\mu}_{t+k})$ represent the average BOD bankruptcy cost in period $t+k$, $k = 1, 2, \ldots$ as expected in period t.

Proposition 1 (See Appendix 3A1 for proof.) Along the equilibrium path, for any period $1 \le t \le T-1$, $\bar{\mu}_t \ge E(\bar{\mu}_{t+1})$.

The average BOD bankruptcy cost follows a supermartingale process along the equilibrium path. This conclusion follows from the replacement rule followed by the CEO in equilibrium; that is, to replace the directors with bankruptcy costs above a threshold. It is easy to show that due to risk aversion the CEO will only replace those BOD members whose bankruptcy costs are greater than the expected bankruptcy costs of the population of directors. Consequently, *on average* the BOD participation constraints will relax over time.

Indeed, under suitable conditions, one can deduce such a relation between compensation levels and the length of CEO tenure. Suppose that the riskless rate r_t follows a stationary or time-independent process, and the control cost function, rt is also independent of time. Now, take any period $1 \le \tau \le T-2$, fix a state profile, γ, an operational decision leq vector, δ, and a vector of BOD liabilities, μ. Let, for any periods $\tau < t$, $E_{\tau,\mu}[b_t(A_t, \gamma_t)]$, denote the expected value along the equilibrium path in period τ of the discretionary compensation adjustment in period t, given some CEO wealth, A_t, and state γ_t in period t.[27]

Proposition 2 (See Appendix 3A1 for proof.) Under the immediately preceding conditions, for every $1 \le \tau \le T-2$, each $\tau < t$, and any given (A, γ),

$$E_{\tau,\mu}[b_t(A, \gamma)] \ge E_{\tau},\mu[b_{t+1}(A, \gamma)] \tag{3.14}$$

In words, the expected equilibrium compensation adjustment for *a given state and initial wealth* is non-decreasing in the length of the CEO's tenure. This prediction contrasts with relations derived from agency-theoretic viewpoints (Gibbons and Murphy, 1992).

7 EMPIRICAL TESTS

The theoretical analysis above derives cross-sectional restrictions on the relation of CEO compensation to observable attributes relating to the firm, the BOD, and the firm's equity ownership structure. Strictly speaking, these restrictions apply to the component of CEO compensation that is under the discretion of the BOD. From an empirical perspective, however, it is difficult to precisely decompose CEO compensation into discretionary and non-discretionary components. Thus, we use *total* compensation as the dependent variable of primary interest.

As has been made explicit in the theoretical model, total compensation may include components determined on the basis of worker productivity and incentive considerations. The empirical test design must, therefore, control for the influence of productivity- or agency-related variables that are known to be significant in CEO compensation determination (see below). The primary empirical implication of Theorem 2 is then that, controlling for these variables, the identified variables relating to the quality of corporate governance should be significant in the determination of the levels of total CEO compensation.

Empirical Specification

The theoretical analysis motivates the following specification.

$$\begin{aligned}\ln(COMP)_{i,t} = {} & \beta_0 + \beta_1 \ln(SIZE)_{i,t} + \beta_2 \ln(STK.RTN)_{i,t} + \beta_3 \ln(ACCTG.RTN)_{i,t} \\ & + \beta_4 \ln(\alpha^L)_{i,t} + \beta_5 \ln(\alpha^{L,CEO})_{i,t} + \beta_6 \ln(\alpha^m)_{i,t} + \beta_7 \ln(\alpha^{BOD})_{i,t} \\ & + \beta_8 \ln(DEFAULT)_{i,t} + \beta_9 \ln(LEVERAGE)_{i,t} + \beta_{10} \ln(TENURE)_{i,t} \\ & + \text{Control Variables}_{i,t} + \varepsilon_{i,t}, \qquad (3.15)\end{aligned}$$

where i and t denote the firm and time subscripts, and the precise definitions of various variables are provided in Table 3.1.

Some of the equity ownership variables in our theoretical model have a straightforward implementation: for example, the shareholdings of the largest outside shareholder (α^L) and the CEO (α^m).[28] The discussion after Theorem 1 also highlights the role of the CEO as the largest shareholder ($\alpha^{L,CEO}$). As a proxy for the directors' holdings (α^{BOD}), we use the average stockholdings of the compensation committee since this committee is usually given the primary discretion in setting CEO compensation. We shall later show, however, that our results are sustained when we use the average shareholdings of the entire board or of the independent outside directors. We do not provide a separate variable for the bankruptcy costs of the BOD since a suitable proxy is not available.

With respect to the default risk of the firm, we rely on recent evidence by Shumway (1996) that *ex ante* probability of financial distress is best captured by the following three variables: (i) ratio of interest expense to pretax operating profit, (ii) whether or not the firm was a 'loser' during the last three years,[29] and (iii) log market value of the firm. Rather than introducing all three variables in the regression equation, we collapse them into a single factor (denoted *DEFAULT*) using the principal component analysis. However, since firm leverage may be related to the default risk, we also include the firm's debt–equity ratio (*LEVERAGE*).

As elsewhere in the empirical literature, both stock and accounting returns (*STK.RTN*, *ACCTG.RTN*) are jointly used as a proxy for the firm's profits (π). Theorem 2 implies that factors which increase the effective costs of posing successful control challenges to the CEO will be significant in his or her compensation determination. In particular, the role of firm size (*SIZE*) has been implicated above in this light.[30] Furthermore, such challenges may arguably be more difficult to implement, *ceteris paribus*, if the CEO is more entrenched. Thus, corporate governance-related variables that are associated with CEO entrenchment – such as the length of the CEO's tenure (*TENURE*) – can also be included in an empirical model of CEO compensation determination.[31] In addition, Proposition 2 indicates another way in which CEO tenure may be positively correlated with compensation: CEOs with longer tenures will have a greater opportunity to 'select' a more acquiescent BOD. This link between CEO tenure and compensation has not been made in the existing literature.

The *control variables* include a number of variables (apart from firm size) that are motivated by alternative compensation theories, and those that have been shown to be associated with CEO empowerment. In the former class are (i) growth opportunities, (ii) regulated industries, and (iii) firm risk. In the latter class are (i) CEO duality (that is, the CEO also chairs the BOD), (ii) CEO age, (iii) board size, and (iv) the proportion of outside directors.

Smith and Watts (1992) hypothesize that the marginal product of decision-making managers is greater than that of the supervisors, and thus executives of firms with greater growth oppor-

Table 3.1 Variable definitions

$$\begin{aligned}\ln(COMP)_{i,t} = {} & \beta_0 + \beta_1 \ln(SIZE)_{i,t} + \beta_2 \ln(STK.RTN)_{i,t} + \beta_3 \ln(ACCTG.RTN)_{i,t} \\ & + \beta_4 \ln(\alpha^L)_{i,t} + \beta_5 \ln(\alpha^{LCEO})_{i,t} + \beta_6 \ln(\alpha^m)_{i,t} + \beta_7 \ln(\alpha^{BOD})_{i,t} \\ & + \beta_8 \ln(DEFAULT)_{i,t} + \beta_9 \ln(LEVERAGE)_{i,t} + \beta_{10} \ln(TENURE)_{i,t} \\ & + \text{Control Variables} + \varepsilon_{i,t}\end{aligned}$$

Variables	Definition (ln denotes natural logarithm)
COMP (Compensation)	Year *t* CEO compensation, specified as either (i) salary and bonus or (ii) total compensation, all expressed in 1993 dollars
SIZE (Firm size)	Beginning net total assets of year *t* expressed in 1993 dollars
STK.RTN (Stock return)	1+ year *t* common stock return, adjusted for inflation
ACCTG.RTN (Accounting return)	1+ year *t* income before extraordinary items/book value of equity, adjusted for inflation
α^L (Largest ownership, non-CEO)	0.01 + (ownership of the largest stockholder, expressed in percent of total outstanding shares, 0 if the largest holder is the CEO)
$\alpha^{L,CEO}$ (Largest ownership, CEO)	0.01 + (ownership of the largest stockholder, expressed in percent of total outstanding shares if the largest holder is the CEO, 0 otherwise)
α^m (CEO's ownership)	0.01 + stock ownership of the CEO, expressed in percent of total outstanding shares
α^{BOD} (Compensation committee's ownership)	0.01 + compensation committee's stockholdings in percent of total outstanding shares. The committee's holding excludes that of the CEO if the CEO is on the committee
DEFAULT (Default risk)	Principal component of: (i) interest expense/pre-tax operating income, (ii) indicator variable denoting a 'loser' firm (1 if the firm's three-year cumulative equity rate of return belonged to the bottom 5% of all NYSE/AMEX stocks during any of the prior three calendar years, 0 otherwise), (iii) negative of lagged log market value of equity
LEVERAGE (Financial leverage)	0.01 + long-term debt/ (long-term debt + book value of equity) expressed in percent
TENURE (CEO tenure)	Number of years the CEO has served as director

Control variables	
Firm risk	1n [standard deviation (in percent) of the firm's common equity, estimated using the monthly return over the prior 60 months]
Growth opportunity	1n [principal component of (i) the sum of capital expenditures, R&D, and acquisitions scaled by the sum of depreciation expense for the three years $t-2$ though t; (ii) the geometric growth rate of year $t-2$ to t change in the market value of assets; (iii) the year t ratio of R&D to the book value of assets; and (iv) the end of year t ratio of the market value to the book value of assets]
Regulated industry	1 if the firm belongs to utilities (SIC 49) or banking (SIC 602), 0 otherwise
CEO duality	1 if the CEO is the chairman, 0 otherwise
CEO age	ln [age of CEO]
Proportion of outside directors	ln [0.01 + number of outside directors/number of all directors, expressed in percent]
Board size	ln [number of directors on the board]
Internal blockholder	1 if an internal party (directors and officers other than the CEO) owns more than 5%, 0 otherwise
External blockholder	1 if an external party (parties other than the CEO, the CEO's family, directors and officers) owns more than 5%, 0 otherwise.

tunities command higher equilibrium wages than those supervising tangible assets-in-place. We use the measure developed by Baber et al. (1996) as a proxy for future growth opportunities (see Table 3.1). Similarly, Kostiuk (1989) and Smith and Watts (1992) postulate that executives of regulated industries (such as utilities and banks) command lower wages because regulation restricts the managers' discretion, and thus, reduces the marginal product of the managerial decision maker.[32] Finally, agency theory implies that the incentive-efficient pay–performance sensitivity will be related to firm risk (Aggarwal and Samwick, 1999), and Smith and Watts (1992) also provide other reasons for the *size* of executive compensation to be associated with firm risk. We use log of sample standard deviation of stock returns, which encompasses both operating and financial risk, as a proxy for firm risk.

Jensen (1993) recommends that the CEO be separated from the function of the board chairman to have an effective and independent board. From the viewpoint of our theory, CEO chairmanship will lead to larger compensation (other things being the same) since board chairmanship makes it harder for the large shareholders or the BOD to mount a control challenge. The evidence of whether the CEO's compensation increases with the CEO's age is mixed (for example, Kostiuk, 1989), but it is important to control for age because both the CEO's age and tenure are significantly correlated. The proportion of outside directors and board size are also included in the regression since they are considered as useful indicators for the quality of corporate governance.[33]

Finally, an interesting prediction of the theoretical model is that only the equity holdings of the largest (outside) shareholder should be a significant factor in CEO compensation. Other papers in the literature, however, have emphasized the role of other blockholders as well. For this reason, we also control for the influence of blockholders other than the largest shareholder.

Several features of the empirical model specified in equation (3.15) require further elaboration. First, we address two specifications of the CEO compensation (*COMP*), namely (i) cash salary and bonuses, and (ii) total compensation which also includes stock options and other incentive components. Note that the two measures differ primarily in the inclusion of equity-based components that have become increasingly important in recent years (Yermack, 1995). Second, all variables are expressed in natural logs with the exception of 0–1 indicator variables. We use the log specification because the existing literature (Roberts, 1959; Cosh, 1975; Kostiuk, 1989) as well as our own preliminary analysis indicate that firm size is the most influential determinant of the level of CEO compensation and the relation is best described as log-linear.[34] Moreover, given that all forms of compensation will be pegged to some measure of size, the logarithmic form controls for firm size better than the arithmetic form since size interacts multiplicatively rather than additively with other variables. As a result, the regression coefficients in (3.15) have an elasticity interpretation.

Data

Executive compensation and ownership data are taken from 1992 and 1993 proxy statements for 1,648 firms actively traded on the NYSE, AMEX, or NASDAQ National Market System. The sample is selected to reflect considerable diversity in both firm size and industry. Based on the 4-digit SIC classification, 302 industries are represented in the sample (67 on the 2-digit classification), and firm size ranges from $4.2 million to $184 billion in total assets. The financial and stock price data are from COMPUSTAT primary, secondary, tertiary, and full-coverage files and the CRSP (Center for Research in Security Prices) files.

The first panel of Table 3.2 displays the distributions for compensation components. Mean base salary is $366,000, almost 36 percent of mean total compensation of $1,011,000. Cash bonuses ($190,000), awarded in 69 percent of the sample firm years, add about 52 percent to the base salary. Option values are computed as in Jensen and Murphy (1990) – using the Black and Scholes (1973) approach – except that we adjust for early exercise using the algorithm recommended in Hemmer et al. (1994).[35] The mean value of options granted ($310,000) is larger than cash bonuses, and is about 30 percent of mean total compensation. Although almost all firms (91.5 percent) have stock option plans, only about one-half (50.6 percent) granted stock options during 1992–93. When options are granted, however, they constitute about one-half of the total compensation.

The next panel displays summary statistics of the key ownership variables. On average, a typical CEO beneficially holds about 8.07 percent of the firm, while the median stock ownership is substantially lower (2.32 percent). About 26.2 percent of the largest shareholders are the CEO, 18.3 percent are non-CEO inside directors or executives, and the remainder are external parties. The mean ownership of the largest stockholder is about 17.1 percent if it is not the CEO, and 24.2 percent if it is the CEO.[36]

Compensation committees, typically consisting of three to four directors, have mean (median) share ownership of about 4.60 percent (0.48 percent).[37] The middle half of the compensation committees hold somewhere between 0.07 and 3.82 percent of the firm.

Some notable statistics for other governance-related variables are as follows. The CEO is the board chairman for about 70 percent of the sample firms, the CEO is on average 55 years

Table 3.2 Summary statistics

Variables	Mean	Median	Std dev.	Min.	Q1	Q3	Max.
Compensation ($m.)							
Total compensation	1.011	0.552	1.571	0.027	0.311	1.103	23.875
Salary and bonus	0.556	0.398	0.541	0.130	0.256	0.679	7.892
Salary	0.366	0.302	0.241	0.012	0.205	0.456	2.693
Bonus	0.190	0.077	0.392	0.000	0.000	0.223	6.892
Stock options[a]	0.310	0.006	1.119	0.000	0.000	0.219	21.703
Restricted stocks	0.045	0.000	0.306	0.000	0.000	0.000	10.943
Other compensation	0.098	0.012	0.506	0.000	0.002	0.051	16.843
Size and performance							
Total assets ($m.)	2,192.7	220.8	8,941.8	4.2	63.7	1,083.2	184,835.0
STK.RTN	0.197	0.100	0.589	–0.898	–0.103	0.355	8.441
ACCTG.RTN	0.055	0.077	0.376	–0.982	0.009	0.124	13.968
Main variables							
Largest ownership, non-CEO (α^L)[b,c] (%)	17.12	12.10	13.59	5.00	8.72	20.00	82.29
Largest ownership, CEO ($\alpha^{L,CEO}$)[b,c] (%)	24.29	19.80	16.34	5.00	11.70	31.50	93.90
CEO's ownership (α^m)[b,c] (%)	8.07	2.32	12.82	0.00	0.46	10.13	93.90
Comp. committee's ownership (α^{BOD})[b,d] (%)	4.60	0.48	9.97	0.00	0.07	3.82	81.84
DEFAULT[e] (principal component)	2.20	2.12	0.89	0.038	1.66	2.57	8.78
LEVERAGE	0.318	0.238	0.245	0.0	0.082	0.508	0.994
TENURE	14.29	12.0	9.70	1.00	7.0	20.0	50.0
Control variables							
Firm risk	0.116	8.00	0.049	0.023	0.080	0.144	0.453
Growth opportunity[e] (principal component)	1.243	0.932	2.247	0.001	0.752	1.419	14.139
Regulated industry	0.129	0.000	0.335	0.000	0.000	0.000	1.000
CEO duality	0.698	1.000	0.458	0.000	0.000	1.000	1.000
CEO age	55.3	55.0	8.3	33.0	50.0	61.0	87.0
Board size	8.82	8.00	3.22	3.00	6.0	11.00	26.00
Outside directors[f] (%)	67.5	71.4	16.5	0.0	57.14	80.00	100.0
Internal blockholders	0.398	0.000	0.489	0.000	0.000	1.000	1.000
External blockholders	0.742	1.000	0.437	0.000	0.000	1.000	1.000

Notes:

a. Option values are based on the Black–Scholes (1973) method adjusted for early exercise using the algorithm by Hemmer et al. (1994). Some 91.5% of sample firms have option plans.

b. All share ownership data include shares beneficially owned and options that can be exercised within 60 days.

c. Statistics are only for the positive shareholdings. The largest shareholder is the CEO in 26.2% of the sample, non-CEO insider in 18.3%, and external parties in 55.4%.

d. Compensation committee stockholdings exclude those of the CEO when the CEO is on the compensation committee.

e. The principal components are recentered to be a positive number.

f. Outside directors are directors who are neither relatives or family members of the CEO, nor present or former employees of the company.

old, and has held directorship for about 12 years. These numbers are consistent with the statistics of previous studies summarized in Rosen (1992). More than half of the US public firms' board consists of more than eight members, the upper bound recommended by Lipton and Lorsch (1992) and Jensen (1993). On average, about 67 percent of the board is seated by outside directors.

Results

Main results

The primary empirical findings relating to the theoretical analysis are presented in Table 3.3a. Both Pearson and Spearman correlation matrices for the key variables are reported in Table 3.3b. In Table 3.3a, the regression coefficients in the first two columns are for salary and bonuses, and those in the last two columns are for total compensation.[38] For each compensation specification, we report results both with and without the *control variables*, but note that these variables do not change the results materially, with the exception of CEO tenure.[39]

Turning to the variables of our main interest, observe that most of the coefficient estimates support the predictions of Theorem 2 at strong significance levels. First, both salary and bonus and total compensation are negatively related to the largest shareholder's ownership. The point estimate of –0.0792 for total compensation (column 4) suggests that a CEO is expected to receive about 8 percent less in total compensation if the largest shareholder's ownership is twice that of an otherwise similar company. Recall that we control for not only the firm size but also the cases where the CEO is the largest shareholder. Interestingly, the negative impact of the largest share ownership sustains regardless whether the largest shareholder is the CEO or not. The results also show that CEO compensation is generally unaffected by the presence of (other) blockholders *after controlling for* the ownership of the CEO, the BOD, and the largest stockholder.[40]

The effect of the CEO's own shareholdings is also of interest. The positive coefficient on the CEO's ownership for salary and bonuses suggests that the CEO's cash remuneration is increasing in the CEO's ownership, controlling for the case when the CEO is the largest shareholder. Recall that from a theoretical perspective (compare Theorem 2), an increase in the CEO's stockholdings has ambiguous consequences for his or her total compensation. Indeed, past studies have often provided conflicting evidence on the impact of the CEO's shareholding on compensation.[41] Our formal analysis can thus potentially explain why some of the earlier studies have not found a positive relation between CEO compensation and ownership. Finally, the coefficient on the CEO's ownership becomes smaller and its significance weaker when equity-based compensation is included (column 2 versus column 4). This suggests that equity-based incentive bonuses are non-increasing in the CEO's ownership, consistent with the BOD's reluctance to impose excessive risk on the CEO, as argued by Jensen and Murphy (1990).

CEO compensation also has a strong negative association with both the probability of default, and the size of the compensation committee's ownership. From the viewpoint of Theorem 2, this suggests that both the cost of the control challenge and the shareholders' (or the BOD's) incentive to mount a challenge are important factors in determining CEO compensation. As predicted by the theoretical framework (compare Theorem 2), the empirical relationship is negative and robust under different specifications of BOD ownership. Specifically, the coefficient is –0.0270 (t = –3.43) when the ownership is defined as that of the outside directors, and –0.0354 (t = –2.18) when defined as the ownership of the entire board (excluding that of the CEO). Jensen (1993), Elson (1993), and Byrne (1996) have criticized US companies for their alleged governance failure and have argued for an increased BOD ownership. Prior studies, however, have failed to find a relationship between CEO compensation and the board ownership (Finkelstein and Hambrick, 1989); Lambert et al., 1993; Core et al., 1997); and to this extent, this is a significant finding. Moreover, to our knowledge, this is also the first study to document a significant negative impact of default risk to the *levels* of CEO compensation.

The coefficient on CEO tenure is positive and significant at the 10 percent level for salary and bonuses (column 2), but insignificant when equity-based components are included (column 4). The implication is that the CEO's longer tenure leads to higher salary and bonuses, but not necessarily to larger equity-based bonuses. The evidence of decreasing emphasis on equity-based component is inconsistent with Gibbons and Murphy's (1992) argument that, as the CEO nears retirement, the proportion of his or her performance-contingent pay needs to increase to make up for diminishing incentives from career concerns. On the other hand, Proposition 2 suggests an alternative reason. As the CEO serves longer on the BOD, the relationship with the BOD becomes more cooperative, leading to a compensation package that is more preferable to the CEO – relatively larger cash compensation and smaller equity-based compensation.[42]

The coefficients of the control variables are also of interest. First, firm risk is strongly positively related to both salary and bonuses and total compensation. We note that the literature has been unable to document such a robust positive relation between firm risk and CEO compensation. Evidence with respect to the role of growth opportunities is also consistent with the literature (Smith and Watts, 1992; Gaver and Gaver, 1993), as is the finding that CEOs in regulated industries receive lower compensation. Some of the results for other governance characteristics are also in keeping with those of the existing studies. More specifically, (i) the CEO receives higher pay when the CEO is also the board chairman; and (ii) CEO compensation is higher if the board is represented by a greater portion of outside directors. We do not find evidence that CEO compensation is increasing in board size, however. The evidence is more consistent with board size indirectly capturing the strong correlation between firm size and CEO compensation because large firms tend to have a large board.[43]

Corporate governance and cash versus equity compensation

An important issue raised by the theoretical analysis is whether higher equity holdings by the largest shareholder(s) will have a greater (negative) impact on equity rather than cash compensation, and under certain conditions the same will be true for higher BOD ownership. We can infer empirical evidence relating to this prediction by comparing columns 1 and 3 (or 2 and 4) of Table 3.3 since total compensation differs from salary and cash bonus primarily due to the inclusion of stock options. We find that both the size and significance of the coefficient for α^L, α^{BOD}, and the default risk variable are substantially enhanced in column 3 (column 4) relative to column 1 (column 2). In particular, one cannot reject at the 5 percent significance levels the null hypothesis that variations in BOD ownership (or the default risk) are irrelevant for the determination of CEO cash compensation. However, such a hypothesis is rejected at the said significance level when the equity-based compensation is included in CEO compensation. In terms of magnitude of the coefficients, a one percent increase in the compensation committee's ownership decreases salary and bonus by less than one percent, but decreases *total compensation* (which itself is larger than salary and bonuses) by 2 percent.

Table 3.3 Empirical findings

(a) Relation between CEO compensation and ownership and governance characteristics with and without other control variables (t-statistics in parentheses)[a]

	Exp. Sign	Salary and bonus (1)	Salary and bonus (2)	Total comp. (3)	Total comp. (4)
Intercept		7.5422	6.3150	8.8986	6.8553
		(25.27)**	(12.82)**	(21.94)**	(10.55)**
SIZE	(+)	0.2909	0.3093	0.2732	0.3321
(Firm size)		(20.55)**	(19.73)**	(14.20)**	(16.06)**
STK. RTN	(+)	0.1266	0.1204	0.3041	0.3120
(Stock return)		(3.91)**	(3.80)**	(6.92)**	(7.48)**
ACCTG. RTN	(+)	0.6228	0.6892	0.3267	0.5163
(Accounting return)		(7.22)**	(7.88)**	(2.78)**	(4.47)**
α^L	(–)	–0.0412	–0.0554	–0.0779	–0.0792
(Largest stock ownership, non-CEO)		(–2.16)**	(–2.86)**	(–3.00)**	(–3.11)**
$\alpha^{L,CEO}$	(–)	–0.0603	–0.0762	–0.1236	–0.1252
(Largest stock ownership, CEO)		(–3.13)**	(–3.91)**	(–4.71)**	(–4.86)**
α^m	(?)	0.0453	0.0327	0.0521	0.0268
(CEO's stock ownership)		(5.71)**	(4.07)**	(4.83)**	(2.53)**
α^{BOD}	(–)	–0.0114	–0.0090	–0.0262	–0.0200
(Compensation committee's ownership)		(–2.33)**	(–1.78)*	(–3.95)**	(–3.00)**
DEFAULT	(–)	–0.0470	–0.1080	–0.4037	–0.3631
(default risk)		(–0.65)	(–1.33)	(–4.15)**	(–3.39)**
LEVERAGE	(–)	–0.0244	–0.0207	–0.0289	–0.0210
(Financial leverage)		(–3.37)**	(–2.94)**	(–2.94)**	(–2.26)**
TENURE	(+)	–0.0073	0.0342	–0.1146	–0.0018
(CEO tenure)		(–0.44)	(1.89)*	(–5.16)**	(–0.07)
Firm risk	(+)		0.2891		0.5023
			(7.61)**		(10.03)**
Growth opportunities	(+)		–0.0064		0.1096
			(–0.24)		(3.15)**
Regulated industry	(–)		–0.2814		–0.4073
			(–5.40)		(–5.92)**
CEO duality	(+)		0.0614		0.1214
			(2.56)**		(3.83)**
CEO's age	(+)		–0.1105		–0.4377
			(–1.43)		(–4.28)**
Board size	(?)		0.0025		0.0186
			(0.05)		(0.32)
Proportion of outside directors	(?)		0.1329		0.2385
			(3.49)**		(4.75)**

Internal blockholder	(?)		0.0273		0.0020
			(1.20)		(0.06)
External blockholder	(?)		0.0178		0.0837
			(0.63)		(2.24)**
Adjusted R^2		0.50	0.52	0.42	0.48

Notes

** Significant at the 5 percent level, two-tailed.

* Significant at the 10 percent level, two-tailed.

a. The coefficients and standard errors are based on the instrumental variable (IV) estimation where ranks of the regressors are used as instruments. The total sample size is 2,386 firm-years for 1992 and 1993.

(b) Pearson and Spearman correlations

	STK. RTN	ACCTG. RTN	α^L	$\alpha^{L,CEO}$	α^m	α^{BOD}	*DEFAULT*	*LEVERAGE*	*TENURE*
Pearson									
SIZE	0.007	*0.118*	*0.132*	*–0.226*	*–0.442*	*–0.419*	*–0.689*	*0.362*	0.020
STK. RTN		*0.283*	*–0.048*	0.035	0.035	0.010	–0.010	0.036	0.006
ACCTG. RTN			–0.023	0.024	–0.004	–0–036	*–0.309*	–0.009	*0.078*
α^L				*–0.880*	*–0.524*	–0.028	*–0.069*	0.035	*–0.300*
$\alpha^{L,CEO}$					*0.622*	*0.096*	*0.166*	*–0.064*	*0.291*
α^m						*0.248*	*0.346*	*–0.137*	*0.367*
α^{BOD}							*0.345*	*–0.110*	–0.004
DEFAULT								–0.004	0.037
LEVERAGE									–0.009
Spearman									
SIZE	0.031	*0.145*	*0.061*	*–0.233*	*–0.441*	*–0.415*	*–0.723*	*0.416*	0.025
STK. RTN		*0.341*	*–0.056*	0.036	0.038	0.005	–0.012	0.042	0.014
ACCTG. RTN			*–0.073*	0.019	–0.014	*–0.057*	*–0.415*	–0.033	0.028
α^L				*–0.764*	*–0.446*	–0–011	–0.005	0.006	*–0.269*
$\alpha^{L,CEO}$					*0.684*	*0.106*	*0.195*	*–0.047*	*0.291*
α^m						*0.257*	*0.367*	*–0.149*	*0.374*
α^{BOD}							*0.375*	*–0.107*	–0.009
DEFAULT								*–0.048*	–0.027
LEVERAGE									0.024

Note: The italicized numbers indicate significance at the 5 percent level.

These inferences are confirmed by regressing separately cash bonus versus stock options on the covariates of Table 3.3.[44] This analysis shows that the sensitivity of stock options to the equity ownership of the BOD and the largest (non-CEO) shareholder is in each case at least twice the corresponding sensitivity of cash bonus awards.

Sensitivity analysis

Sensitivity analyses establish that relations in Table 3.3 is robust to alternative specifications, performance measures, and outliers. First, we obtain comparable estimates when we control for outliers using the method suggested by Belsley et al. (1980).[45] Next, we also obtain similar results when we use market-model residuals on both equally-weighted and value-weighted CRSP indices, instead of raw stock returns; and when we use return on assets (ROA), instead of return on equity (ROE), as the accounting performance measure. We also investigate industry effects by incorporating industry dummy variables. On balance, the industry variables add little to the explanatory power of the model, nor do they alter the results materially.

Observe that we use current-period CEO's stock ownership as an independent variable. But at least some of the stockholdings represent a reward for the current-period performance, and hence may induce correlations with the dependent variable. In order to assess whether this effect is material, we compare regression estimates from using the lagged CEO stockholdings with those using the current-period CEO stockholdings.[46] These comparisons indicate trivial differences in the estimates as well as the standard errors. Furthermore, the high correlation between 1992 and 1993 CEO stockholdings (0.97) suggests that this is a minor issue.

8 EXECUTIVE COMPENSATION AND THE BEHAVIORAL THEORY OF THE FIRM

An important objective of the research agenda put forth by the behavioral theory of the firm (BTF) was to 'Link models of the firm as closely as possible to empirical observations of both the decision output and the process structure of business organizations' (Cyert and March, 1992, p. 2). The models of decision making and actions were to be explicitly based on the observations of firms and subject to empirical test against the actual behavior of identifiable firms. Indeed, the BTF focused on a specific set of economic decisions (price and output) so that the predictions could be tested with actual data; that is, the object was to go beyond predictions on qualitative aspects of business decisions.

In the BTF, and its many subsequent successful applications, the predictions were tested against data from *individual firms*. Often, these are the only data available for many economic decisions. However, increasingly we have both cross-sectional and panel data available on a large sample of firms, especially relating to the financial and compensation aspects of the firm. These data offer the potential for much greater power in empirical testing. However, generating predictions that are both restrictive (in the sense of imposing empirical content on the model) and applicable across a cross-section of firms requires some methodological innovations.

This chapter provides an example of methodology that develops models based on the decision process structure of firms (regarding the determination of executive compensation) and generates empirical predictions that can be tested against data from a large cross-section of firms. To elaborate somewhat, a systematic examination of the *process* of executive compensation determination has suggested that CEO compensation is determined by (implicit) bargaining between the CEO, the BOD and the large shareholders. The CEO attempts to effect a level of compensation that maximizes his or her expected welfare or utility, subject to the constraints that the CEO's proposals do not motivate the BOD or the large shareholders to pose a management control challenge. Furthermore, we have also argued that due to the CEO's ability to (essentially) choose the BOD, the BOD-related constraints will relax over time as the CEO 'finds' a BOD composition that is least resistant to his or her preferences on matters relating to compensation.

This view of the top-management compensation determination process is markedly different from the existing theories in the field (see Section 2). Unlike the optimal contracting frameworks, our framework is consistent with a weak pay–performance link (if, for example, the corporate governance constraints on the CEO are weak). Moreover, our theory predicts that the pay–performance link will weaken over time in contrast to the agency-theoretic prediction that the pay–performance sensitivity will *strengthen* over time (Gibbons and Murphy, 1992). Furthermore, the theory indicates that the default probability and factors impacting the cost of control challenges will directly impact CEO compensation. Our analysis provides empirical support for these predictions. Finally, in relation to the organizational literature that emphasizes the hierarchical structure or role of CEO ownership, our analysis suggests that the impact of CEO or BOD ownership on CEO compensation will be ambiguous. The interaction between BOD and the size of blockholder ownership is emphasized by our approach.

On the other hand, our approach and the testing of its predictions on large data sets of firm-level business decisions is similar to some recent work in the literature on the behavioral theory of the firm. For example, Cyert et al. (1996) construct a dynamic model of firm dividend policy based on some basic ingredients of the behavioral theory of the firm, in particular, uncertainty avoidance and sequential decision making by self-seeking managers. As in this chapter, comparative statics on the dynamic dividend policy generates refutable predictions on the relation of the likelihood of future dividend changes with respect to current real and financial variables (such as investments and technological parameters that govern the evolution of economic earnings of the firm). These predictions are then tested on time-series data from a large sample of US firms, and (as here) the empirical results are supportive of the predictions of the behavioral model.

9 CONCLUDING REMARKS

We conclude by highlighting some important areas for future research – both empirical and theoretical – that emerge from the foregoing analysis.

Further work on the determinants of the effective cost of control challenges to the CEO appears worthwhile. We have only taken the more obvious determinants, such as size, stock market performance, and blockholder ownership. In practice, the effective costs depend on the possibility of creating shareholder alliances, including forming coalitions between the BOD and certain large shareholders. From a modeling perspective, such strategies are problematic in the non-cooperative framework usually adopted in the agency theory of the firm. Cooperative behavior in shareholder coalitions can be non-cooperatively enforced through credible punishments and so on, but such an analysis would be complex. Nevertheless, a careful analysis of the effective costs of proxy contests in models of corporate governance is an important area for future research.

Our empirical results indicate that there are systematic differences in cash and equity compensation. Analysis that rigorously examines the differences in the process of awarding cash versus equity-based compensation would make important contributions in our understanding of executive compensation.

NOTES

* We thank Rick Antle, Mie Augier, Bill Baber, Agnes Cheng, Richard Day, Jonathan Clover, Yuji Ijiri, Morton Kamien, Jim March, Allan Meltzer, Kimberly Smith, Shyam Sunder, and colleagues and seminar participants at Carnegie-Mellon University, University of Houston, Humboldt University in Berlin, University of Maryland, Yale University, and the American Economic Association meetings for helpful comments and discussions. All shortcomings are, however, our own responsibility.

1. This literature includes papers by Fershtman and Judd (1987) and Cyert and Kumar (1996) and Cyert et al. (1996), which examine price and output determination in oligopolistic competition taking into view a more plausible theory of *internal decision making* compared to the standard oligopoly literature. It also includes papers by Shapiro (1989), Saloner (1991), Cyert et al. (1993), and Cyert and Kumar (1996), which attempt to use decision-theoretic approaches in understanding the strategy formulation process in firms.
2. Cyert and March (1963) were among the first to examine systematically the issue of goal formation in business organizations. The neoclassical theory of the firm has traditionally held expected profit maximization as the appropriate goal. But this objective is not even well-defined in the presence of incomplete markets (see, for example, Duffie, 1995).
3. Excellent surveys of these theories and their empirical relevance have been provided elsewhere (Rosen, 1992; Prendergast, 1996). The discussion here serves only to motivate the role of corporate governance practices on top-management compensation.
4. In Simon (1957), managerial power is related to the number of worker 'hierarchies' controlled by the CEO, whereas in Tosi and Gomez-Mejia (1989) and Finkelstein and Hambrick (1989) managerial power is related to the concentration of ownership.
5. Costs of reliable monitoring of compensation-related circumstances are likely to be large precisely because those circumstances are complex and often vague enough to make complete contracting infeasible. In that sense, the BOD may be considered as a 'body' hired by the shareholders to monitor these circumstances, and decide on total top-management compensation on their behalf.
6. It is also significant that an appointment to the BOD of a large firm is not only lucrative from a pecuniary standpoint but also delivers to the director perquisites and prestige that are highly valued. For example, many of the perquisites for the higher executives of the firm are also available to the members of the BOD. Moreover, membership in the BOD of a large firm increases the likelihood of obtaining an invitation for a BOD membership in other corporations.
7. See Crystal (1991), Lublin (1996), Elson (1993), and Byrne (1996).
8. Allen (1981) provides some evidence that CEO compensation is lower if a non-CEO director controls a large block of shares.
9. The assumption on the presence of a uniform upper bound on a given CEO's tenure is realistic: the length of any CEO's tenure cannot exceed the maximum known human life-span, for instance.
10. As elsewhere in the literature, the managers are assumed to be more risk averse than the shareholders since the former have constraints on their ability to diversify against firm-specific human capital and earnings risk on account of incompleteness of markets and legal restrictions – against shorting, for example.
11. Thus, $\bar{\alpha}_t$ is computed by listing all the different numbers of shares that are being held by the shareholders in period t, and dividing through by J_t. Formally, $\bar{\alpha}_t$ belongs to the Borel sigma algebra on [0, 1], and for $\alpha_i \in \bar{\alpha}_t$, $\int_{\bar{\alpha}t} \alpha_i di = 1$. Thus, in theory, this set can be infinite dimensional. in practice, since a firm's shares can be traded only in some minimum (positive) integer lots, this set will generally be finite.
12. In this model, the CEO is the only manager modeled. Hence, the CEO represents the inside directors. Therefore, for ease of reference, we shall refer to the outside directors simply as directors.
13. Of course, not all successful control challenges in practice end up with the removal of the CEO. But it is usually incumbent upon the CEO to offer to resign upon losing a proxy challenge or a takeover fight, even though the resignation may not be accepted by the shareholders.
14. For tractability reasons, in this chapter we shall not attempt to completely model the determinants of these costs. Instead, we shall take the possibly time-dependent evolution of these costs as given, and attempt to characterize their relation to CEO compensation.
15. 1f there were no price effects in share purchase, then $\kappa_t\,(a_t, q_t) \leq J_t\,(0.5 - a_t)\,q_t$. However, unless a_t is close to one-half, there may in general be infra-marginal price effects on buying the shares for a majority ownership. For notational ease we shall keep implicit other variables that may plausibly determine κ_t, such as the history of variables relevant to firm performance, the fraction of the firm held by the CEO (α^m), and so on.
16. This assumption is without loss of generality since in a competitive stock market equilibrium, an assumption we shall make below regarding the stock price, the opportunity cost to shareholders of not receiving the surplus in the form of dividends is also the riskless rate of return (Lucas, 1978).
17. Allowing the learning to proceed more slowly in the timing framework of the model does not affect the qualitative nature of our results.
18. See Fudenberg and Tirole (1992) for a good exposition on this solution concept.
19. Although the investors are infinitely lived, the fact that a typical CEO only operates for a finite horizon drastically reduces the number of possible economically or behaviorally interesting equilibria. Complex and history-dependent equilibrium paths can only arise if we posit strategic interactions between the investors. Since the focus here is the interaction of the CEO with the BOD and large shareholders, such equilibria are not very interesting. In the following, we shall therefore focus on equilibria where in any period only the history relevant to payoff or economic uncertainty of the firm is relevant.

20. The borrowings, B_T are determined by δ_T according to the firm's budget constraint; that is, $B_T = \min[0, \pi_T - (L_T + I_T + w_T + x_T + K_T)]$.
21. The probability density of $\hat{\pi}_{T+1}$ is easily obtained from a standard transformation of the probability density, $p(\varepsilon)$, of the firm's earning shock; namely, $\hat{p}(\hat{\pi}_{T+1} \mid \gamma_T, \delta_T) = p\{\hat{\pi}_{T+1} + L_T + s - [F(I_T) + K_T(1 + r_T)]\}$.
22. This assumption or view is in keeping with a competitive asset market structure, and the fact that a new CEO will choose his or her own new BOD. If $\hat{\pi}_{T+1}$ affects the choice of the new CEO and so on, then those effects are presumed to be included in the function $\Pi_{T+1}(\hat{\pi}_{T+1})$. Thus, the players take as given, a possibly joint, probability distribution of $(\hat{\pi}_{T+1}, \hat{\gamma}_{T+1})$, conditional on (γ_T, δ_T): Prob.$(\hat{\pi}_{T+1}, \hat{\gamma}_{T+1} \mid \gamma_T, \delta_T)$.
23. Further details regarding the derivation of the optimal director replacement strategy can be obtained below when we explicitly calculate the director replacement strategy of the CEO.
24. Recall that according to the timing conventions set up above, the CEO must effectively wait for at least one period before being able to change the BOD.
25. In equation (3.9) above, $\underline{V}^m_t(\underline{A}_T)$ is the (exogenously given) expected utility of a CEO whose firm declares bankruptcy in the beginning of the period $2 \leq \tau < T + 1$, and whose wealth at that time is $\underline{A}_T$. Meanwhile, $\Pi\tau_{+1}(A_{\tau+1}, \gamma_{\tau+1}, \mu_T)$, is the expected end-of-the-period market value of the firm in the next period, $(\tau + 1)$, in the continuation game represented by the state, $\gamma_{\tau+1}$, incumbent BOD characteristics, μ_τ, and the wealth of the (current) CEO, $A_{\tau+1}$. $\Phi_{\tau+1}(\Pi_{\tau+1} \mid \gamma\tau, \delta_\tau)$ is the transition probability distribution of $\Pi_{\tau+1}$, induced by the transition probability distribution of the next-period state, $\gamma_{\tau+1}$, conditional on $(\gamma_\tau, \delta_\tau)$. Next, $\delta^*_\tau(\gamma_\tau, \mu_\tau)$ has an interpretation analogous to that of δ^*_T defined above, and $v^i_\tau(\gamma_\tau, \delta_\tau) \equiv x_{i\tau} - \rho\psi_{\tau+1}(\gamma_\tau, \delta_\tau)\mu(\bar{\alpha}_\tau)$, is the one-period expected utility of director $i \in D_\tau$.
26. Technically speaking, a complete description of the equilibrium will also require specification of strategies for subgames that are 'off the equilibrium path': for example, the behavior following a defection by a director who rejects an offer satisfying the participation constraint, or that of a shareholder who defects by filing a control challenge even though not optimal to do so. These cases are straightforward to deal with, however, since only uncorrelated defections have to be considered to check subgame perfection (see, for example, Gul et al., 1986).
27. In other words, $E_{\tau,\mu}[b_t(A, \gamma)]$ is the expected compensation adjustment in period t, given some (A, γ) in that period, with respect to the marginal probability distribution of μ_t, conditional on the period τ information set.
28. The share ownership includes 'beneficially' owned shares (for example, shares held by relatives) and options that can be exercised within 60 days, consistent with the treatment in most empirical studies.
29. A firm is operationally defined as a 'loser' if its three-year cumulative equity rate of return belonged to the bottom 5 percent of all NYSE/AMEX stocks during any of the prior three calendar years.
30. Firm size is implicated by a number of alternative theories as well. For example, Baumol (1967) interprets the positive relation of CEO compensation to size as sales maximization by power-hungry managers. Rosen (1981) argues that larger firms attract more talented managers; that is, firm size is a proxy for the worker's productivity or human capital. The positive association between CEO compensation and size is also consistent with Simon's (1957) hypothesis that compensation is increasing in the number of hierarchies controlled by the manager.
31. CEO tenure is measured as the number of years he or she has served as director because this information is available more often than the years served as CEO.
32. An indicator variable that takes a value of one for regulated industry controls for lower CEO compensation in these industries.
33. In keeping with the existing literature (for example, Mayer et al., 1997), we define outside directors as those who are not a direct family member of the CEO or not related to him or her, and not a current or former employee of the firm. While some authors view that outside directors are more independent and thus better represent the owners' interests (Fama, 1980; Fama and Jensen, 1983), others such as Crystal (1991), Mace (1986) and Patton and Baker (1987) suggest that since outside directors are essentially hired by the CEO they are less inclined to be adversarial to the CEO. This, they argue, leads to an overcompensation of the CEO. Lipton and Lorsch (1992) and Jensen (1993) argue that an 'overcrowded' board is less likely to function effectively and is easier for the CEO to control.
34. To permit the log transformation, we add 0.01 percentage point inside the log for all variables that can be zero, but results are unaffected by adding other small numbers ranging from one percent to 0.001 percent. In particular, stock return is defined as the log of one plus raw stock return, as is the accounting return (log of one plus return on equity). Unlike stock returns, however, accounting return can be less than – 100 percent, and therefore, several observations are removed as a result of this log transformation. But the results are similar if we use raw return on equity without excluding the observations with accounting returns of less than – 100 percent.
35. We calculate option values using the stated exercise price and year-end stock prices as in Jensen and Murphy (1990) and adjust for early exercise using the Hemmer et al. (1994) approach. Data required to execute calculations are typically disclosed, but for cases where details are omitted, vesting is assumed to occur two years after the grant, and the exercise period is assumed to be the same. as that for the most recent option where an exercise period is provided. The Hemmer et al. adjustments yield values which, on average, are about 25 percent less than

those obtained from a straightforward application of the Black–Scholes approach used in earlier studies (for example, Murphy, 1985; Jensen and Murphy, 1990). Results are comparable when option values are computed without the early exercise adjustment.

36. We note that the largest stockholder cannot be identified if no single party holds more than 5 percent of the firm because US public firms are not required to report the existence of large blockholders in such a case. Thus the largest shareholder is unidentified for about 9.5 percent of sample firms.
37. The compensation committee stockholdings exclude those of the CEO if the CEO is on the committee because most companies explicitly state that the CEO does not participate when the compensation committee determines the CEO's compensation.
38. Although we start with 1,648 firms for 1992 and 1993, the absence of financial data to calculate all 19 independent variables reduces the maximum number of firm-year observations entering the regression to 2,387.
39. Several estimation details are to be noted. First, although in principle most of the explanatory variables are endogenous, it is infeasible to endogenize all these variables. Following Smith and Watts (1992), we use an instrumental variable estimator for which the instruments are the ranks of the independent variables. Second, we pool the compensation data for fiscal 1992 and 1993. Results are similar when we estimate separate regressions for each year or allow for industry effects (see section on sensitivity analysis, below). Third, we report the results for only the firms with a 5 percent blockholder (90.5 percent of the full sample) since the largest shareholder (α^L and $\alpha^{L,CEO}$) cannot be identified for the remaining firms. Nevertheless, there is no evidence of a selection bias for removing the firms without a 5 percent blockholder: we ran the regression model (3.15) with and without α^L and a $\alpha^{L,CEO}$, using Heckman's (1976) two-step estimator, and found that the difference was immaterial.
40. In fact, the coefficient for internal blockholders does become negative and significant when α^L and $\alpha^{L,CEO}$ are excluded from the regression, but insignificant when they are included.
41. Despite the usual prediction of a positive relation of CEO compensation with ownership (Allen, 1981; Finkelstein, 1992; Finkelstein and Hambrick, 1989), most studies find a *negative* relation (Allen, 1981; Lambert et al., 1993; Core et al., 1997).
42. Observe that when the CEO's age is omitted from the regression, the coefficient for CEO's tenure in salary and bonus regression becomes negative. This is because the CEO's age and tenure are significantly correlated (correlation coefficient = 0.39), and CEO compensation is generally decreasing in CEO's age. This result points out the need to control for both CEO tenure and age.
43. Core et al. (1997) report that CEO compensation is increasing in board size when log of lagged revenue is used to control for firm size. Using log revenues instead of log total assets indeed produces a positive and significant coefficient on board size. The significance vanishes, however, when log assets or both log assets and log revenues are used as regressors. The collineaxity diagnostic (Belsley et al. 1980) does not indicate a significant collinearity problem for introducing both size variables at the same time.
44. These results are not being included for space considerations, but are available from the authors upon request.
45. Specifically, we omit observations with 'dffits' exceeding $2\surd(p/n)$, where p is the number of parameters in the model, and n is the number of observations. We use the full model to identify outliers.
46. We use only the 1993 data for this check since we do not have the ownership data for 1991 needed to estimate the model for 1992.

REFERENCES

Allen, M. (1981), 'Power and privilege in the large corporation: corporate control and managerial compensation', *American Journal of Sociology*, **86**: 1112–23.

Aggarwal, R. and A. Sawick (1999), 'The Other Side of the Trade Off: The Impact of Risk on Executive Compensation', *Journal of Political Economy*, **107**: 65–105.

Baber, W., S. Janakiraman and S. Kang (1996), 'Investment opportunities and the structure of performance-based executive compensation' *Journal of Accounting Economics*, **21**: 297–318.

Baumol, W. (1967), Business Behaviour, Value and Growth', New York: Harcourt, Brace and Jovanovich.

Belsley, D., E. Kuh and R. Welsch (1980), *Regression Diagnostices: Identifying Influential Data and Sources of Collinearity*, New York: Wiley.

Berle, A. and G. Means (1932), *The Modern Corporation and Private Property*, New York: Macmillan,

Black, F. and M. Scholes (1973), 'The pricing of options and corporate liabilities, *Journal of Political Economy*, **81**: 637–54.

Boyd, B. (1994), 'Board control and CEO compensation', *Strategic Management Journal*, **15**: 335–44.

Brock, W. (1982), 'Asset Prices in a Production Economy', in J. McCall (ed.) The Economics of Information and Uncertainty, Chicago: University of Chicago Press, 1–47.

Byrne, J. (1996), 'The best and worst boards', *Business Week*, November 25, pp. 83–91.
Ciscel, D. and T. Carroll (1980), 'The determinants of executive salaries: an econometric survey', *Review of Economics and Statistics*, **62**: 7–13.
Core, J., R. Holthausen and D. Larcker (1999), 'Corporate governance, Chief Executive Officer compensation, and firm performance', *Journal of Financial Economics*, **51**, 371–406.
Cosh, A. (1975), 'The remuneration of chief executives in the United Kingdom', *Economics Journal*, **85**, 75–94.
Coughlin, A. and R. Schmidt (1985), 'Executive compensation, management turnover, and firm performance', *Journal of Accounting and Economics*, **7**: 42–66.
Crystal, G. (1991), *In Search of Excess: The Overcompensation of American Executives*, New York: W.W. Norton.
Cyert, R., S. Kang and P. Kumar (1996), 'Managerial objectives and firm dividend policy: a behavioral theory and empirical evidence', *Journal of Economic Behavior and Organization*, **30**, 8–36.
Cyert, R. and P. Kumar (1996), 'Strategies for technological innovation with learning and adaptation costs', *Journal of Economics and Management Strategy*, **5**, 25–67.
Cyert, R., P. Kumar and J. Williams (1993), 'Information, market imperfections and strategy', *Strategic Management Journal*, **14**, 47–58.
Cyert, R. and J.G. March (1963), *A Behavioural Theory of the Firm*, Englewood Cliffs, NJ: Prentice-Hall (2nd edn published 1992 by Blackwell Cambridge, MA and Oxford).
Donaldson, J., and R. Mehra (1983), 'Stochastic Growth with Correlated Productivity Shocks, *Journal of Economic Theory*, **29**: 282–313.
Duffie, D. (1995), Dynamic Asset Pricing Theory, Princeton, NJ, Princeton University Press.
Elson, C. (1993), 'A broad-based solution to overpaid CEOs', *The Wall Street Journal*, September 27, 1.
Fama, E. (1980), 'Agency problems and the theory of the firm', *Journal of Political Economy*, **88**: 715–32.
Fama, E. and M. Jensen (1983), 'Separation of ownership and control', *Journal of Law and Economics*, **26**: 301–5.
Fershtman, C. and K. Judd (1987), 'Equilibrium Incentives in Oligopoly', *American Economic Review*, **77**: 927–40.
Finkelstein, S. (1992), 'Power in top management team: Dimensions, measurement, and validation', *Academy of Management Journal*, **35**: 505–38.
Finkelstein, S. and D. Hambrick (1989), 'Chief executive compensation: a study of the intersection of markets and political processes', *Strategic Management Journal*, **10**: 121–34.
Fudenberg, D. and J. Tirole (1992), 'Game Theory', Cambridge, MA: MIT Press.
Gaver J. and K. Gaver (1993), 'Additional evidence on the association between the investment opportunity set and corporate financing, dividend, and compensation policies', *Journal of Accounting and Economics*, **16**: 125–60.
Gibbons, R. and K. Murphy (1992), 'Optimal incentive contracts in the presence of career concerns: theory and evidence', *Journal of Political Economy*, **100**: 468–505.
Grossman, S. and O. Hart (1986), 'The costs and benefits of ownership: a theory of vertical and lateral integration', *Journal of Political Economy*, **94**: 691–719.
Gul, F., H. Sonnenschein and R. Wilson (1986), 'Foundations of dynamic monopoly and the Coase conjecture', *Journal of Economic Theory*, **40**, 119–54.
Heckman, J. (1976), 'Sample selection bias as a specification error', *Econometrica*, **47**: 153–61.
Hemmer, T., S. Matsunaga and T. Shevlin (1994), 'Estimating the "fair value" of employee stock options with expected early exercise', *Accounting Horizons*, **8**: 23–42.
Jensen, M. (1993), 'The modern industrial revolution, exit, and failure of internal control systems', *Journal of Finance*, **48**: 35–44.
Jensen, M. and K. Murphy (1990), 'Performance pay and top-management incentives', *Journal of Political Economy*, **98**: 225–64.
Kaplan, S. (1994), 'Top executive rewards and firm performance: a comparison of Japan and the United States', *Journal of Political Economy*, **102**: 510–46.
Kostiuk, P. (1989), 'Firm size and executive compensation', *Journal of Human Resources*, **25**: 90–105.
Lambert, R., D. Larcker and K. Weigelt (1993), 'The structure of organizational incentives', *Academic Science Quarterly*, **38**: 438–61.

Lipton, M., and J. Lorsch (1992), 'A Modest Proposal for Corporate Governance', *Business Lawyer*, **48**, 59–77.
Lorsch, J. and E. MacIver (1989), *Pawns or Potentates: The Reality of America's Corporate Boards*, Boston, MA: Harvard Business School Press.
Lublin, J. (1996), 'Executive pay: the great divide', *The Wall Street Journal*, April 11.
Lucas, R. (1978), 'Asset Prices in an Exchange Economy', *Econometrica*, **46**, 1929–1995.
Mace, M. (1986), *Directors: Myth and Reality*, Boston, MA: Harvard Business School Press.
Mayer, D., A. Shivdasri, and C. Smith (1997), 'Board composition and corporate control: Evidence from the insurance industry', *Journal of Business*, **70**: 33–62.
Mehran, H. (1995), 'Executive compensation structure, ownership, and firm performance', *Journal of Financial Economics*, **38**: 163–84.
Murphy, K. (1985), 'Corporate performance and managerial remuneration: an empirical analysis', *Journal of Accounting and Economics*, **7**: 11–42.
Patton, A., and J. Baker (1987), 'Why do not Directors Rock the Boat?', *Harvard Business Review*, **65**, 10–12.
Prendergast, C. (1996), 'What Happens Within Firms? A Survey of Empirical Evidence on Compensation Policies', NBER Working Paper, Cambridge, MA.
Roberts, D. (1959), 'A general theory of executive compensation based on statistically tested propositions', *Quarterly Journal of Economics*, **74**: 270–94.
Rosen, S. (1981), 'The economics of superstars', *American Economic Review*, **71**: 270–94.
Rosen, S. (1992), 'Contracts and the market for executives', in L. Wernin and H. Wijkander (eds), *Contract Economics*, Oxford: Basil Blackwell.
Saloner, G. (1991), 'Modeling, game theory, and strategic management', *Strategic Management Journal*, **12**, 119–36.
Shapiro, C. (1989), 'The theory of business strategy', *Rand Journal of Economics*, **20**: 332–46.
Shumway, T. (1996), 'Size, overreaction, and book-to-market effects as default premia', University of Michigan working paper.
Simon, H., (1957), 'The Compensation of Executives', *Sociometry*, **11**: 32–35.
Smith, C. and R. Watts (1992), 'The investment opportunity set and corporate financing, dividend, and compensation policies', *Journal of Financial Economics*, **32**: 263–92.
Shleifer, A. and R. Vishny (1986), 'Large shareholders and corporate control', *Journal of Political Economy*, **95**: 461–88.
Tosi, H. and L. Gomez-Mejia (1989), 'The decoupling of CEO pay and performance: an agency theory perspective', *Administrative Science Quarterly*, **35**: 587–603.
Williamson, O. (1985), *The Economic Institutions of Capitalism*, New York: Free Press.
Yermack, D. (1995), 'Do Corporations Award CEO Compensation Effectively?' *Journal of Financial Economics*, **39**, 237–69.
Yermack, D. (1996), 'Higher market valuation for firms with small board of directors', *Journal of Financial Economics*, **40**: 185–211.

APPENDIX 3A1

Proof of Theorem 1 The proof uses a backward induction argument. We first show that the theorem applies for the T-period game, and then use induction to complete the proof. Fix any candidate equilibrium strategy, and $(A_T, \gamma_T, \mu_{T-1})$. Let μ_T be the outcome (in terms of the specification of directors' bankruptcy costs) of the CEO's BOD composition decision in the beginning of period T. Suppose, first, that this equilibrium strategy specifies $v_T^i > 0$, for some $i \in D_T$. Then consider the following defection by the CEO: Set $x'_{iT} = x_{iT} - \varepsilon\ I'_T = I_T + \varepsilon$, for some $\varepsilon > 0$, and leave all other decisions as before. (Here the prime denotes the 'new' strategy.) For ε appropriately small, it is still a subgame perfect strategy for the director i to accept, x_{iT}, since rejection yields the reservation utility of $\bar{o}$, while acceptance is strictly superior. Furthermore, this defection cannot tighten the 'no control challenge' constraint since the investment has increased. For the same reason, the CEO's expected welfare is strictly higher, since the probability of bankruptcy is lower, and the expected wealth in the non-bankrupt state is higher (whenever $\alpha_T^m > 0$). These facts contradict the assumption that the original strategy was a subgame perfect Bayesian equilibrium. An analogous argument applies to show that in any T-period equilibrium, the 'no control challenge' constraint will bind only for the largest shareholder, and in such a case the 'no control challenge' constraint is non-binding for all other shareholders.

In sum, taking as given the (exogenously given) $(T + 1)$-period firm value function, $\Pi_{T+1}(\hat{\pi}_{T+1})$, the theorem is valid for period T, for any given $(A_T, \gamma_T, \mu_{T-1})$. In fact, let $\Pi_T(A_T, \gamma_T, \mu_{T-1})$ denote the expected end-of-period value of the firm with the initial data, $(A_T, \gamma_T, \mu_{T-1})$, taking as given the equilibrium CEO, BOD and shareholder strategies iii this continuation game. Note that for appropriate values of $(A_T, \gamma_T, \mu_{T-1})$, Π_T may take expectations over the random replacement of the CEO and/or the incumbent BOD members. Then fix any $0 \leq t \leq T - 1$, and suppose that the theorem applies for $t + 1 \leq \tau \leq T$. Now take as given a specific CEO, $m \in M$, and his or her BOD choice, μ_t. (The identity of the CEO is determined jointly by the outcome of the CEO strategy, X_t, and the realization of the new CEO choice if the incumbent CEO were to choose to exit.) Put $\delta_t^* = (I_t^*, b^* = 0, x^*_t, K_t^*)$, and for any given, (γ_t, μ_t), let I_t^*, x_{it}^*, $i = 1, \ldots, N$, and K_t^*, jointly satisfy,

$$I_t^* \in \operatorname{argmax}\{\rho E[\Pi_{t+1}^* \mid \gamma_t, (x_t^*, I_t, K_t^*)] - I_t\},$$
$$x_{it} - \rho\psi_{t+1}(\gamma_t, \delta_t^*)\mu^i = \bar{o},\ i = 1, \ldots, N,$$
$$K_t^* = \max[0, \pi_t - (L_t + I_t^* + s + x_t^*)].$$

Then, let $\eta_t(\gamma_t, \mu_t)$ denote the optimal number of directors to be replaced in period t by a typical shareholder, taking as given the optimal decision vector, δ^*_t, and the function $\Pi_{t+1}(A_{t+1}, \gamma_{t+1}, \mu_t)$, the existence of which is given by the induction hypothesis. Clearly, a control challenge for a shareholder planning to hold the fraction, a_t, in the firm into the next period is optimal if and only if,

$$\rho a_t \int_0^\infty \Pi_{t+1} d\Phi_{t+1}(\Pi_{t+1} \mid \gamma_t, \delta^*_t) - \kappa_t(a_t, q_t) > \rho a_t \int_0^\infty \Pi_{t+1} d\Phi_{t+1}(\Pi_{t+1} \mid \gamma_t, \delta_t).$$

It then also follows from a well-known dynamic programming argument that in period t, the choice of the optimal CEO control, δ_t, is the solution to the dynamic programming problem:

$$V_t^m(A_t, \gamma_t, \mu_t) = \max_{\delta_t, c_t^m}\{u^m(c_t^m) + \rho[\psi_{t+1}(\gamma_t, \delta_t)\underline{V}^m{}_{t+1}(\underline{A}_{t+1}) + \int V_{t+1}^m(A_{t+1}(\Pi_{t+1}))d\Phi_{t+1}(\Pi_{t+1} \mid \gamma_t, \delta_t)]\} \quad (3A1.1.)$$

subject to,

$$v_t^i(\gamma_t, \delta_t) \geq \bar{o}, i \in D_t, \quad (3A1.2)$$

$$\rho a_t^j \int_0^\infty \Pi_{t+1} d\Phi_{t+1}(\Pi_{t+1} \mid \gamma_t, \delta_t^*) - \kappa_t(a_t^j, q_t) \leq \rho a_t^j \int_0^\infty \Pi_{t+1} d\Phi_{t+1}(\Pi_{t+1} \mid \gamma_t, \delta_t), \forall_j \in S_t, \quad (3A1.3)$$

$$\underline{A}_{t+1} = (A_t + w_t - c_t^m)(1 + r_t), \quad (3A1.4)$$

$$A_{t+1}(\Pi_{t+1}) = \underline{A}_{t+1} + s + \alpha_t^m \Pi_{t+1}. \quad (3A1.5)$$

Following an argument analogous to that used in the analysis of the T-period game, it is easy to show that along any candidate equilibrium path, $v_t^i = \bar{o}$, for each $i \in D_t$, and for any given (A_t, γ_t). And, similarly, the constraint (3A1.3) will bind only for the largest shareholder, α_t^L. Thus, the theorem is true under the induction hypotheses. The existence of period t optimal CEO, BOD and shareholder strategies, and hence also the function $\Pi_t(A_t, \gamma_t, \mu_{t-1})$ then follows immediately. ■

Proof of Theorem 2 For any given period $0 \leq t \leq T$, we let $\Delta(\gamma_t, \mu_t)$ denote the set of controls, δ_t, that satisfy the constraints (3.10)–(3.13). Parts (i)–(iv) of the proposition follow from the facts that, (i) $\Delta(\alpha_t^{L'}) \subseteq \Delta(\alpha_t^{L'})$, whenever $\alpha_t^{L'} \geq \alpha_t^L$; (ii) $\Delta(\mu') \subseteq \Delta(\mu)$, when $\mu' > \mu$, where $\mu' > \mu$, if there is some i such that $\mu'_i > \mu_i$ and $\mu'_j > \mu_j$, for all other j; (iii) $\Delta(\bar{\kappa}) \subseteq \Delta(\kappa)$, when $\bar{\kappa}(.,.) > \kappa(.,.)$, for every (a, q); (iv) $\Delta(\pi_t') \subseteq \Delta(\pi_t)$, whenever $\pi_t' > \pi_t$.
Next, consider the effect of a small increase in, α_t^m, the fraction of the firm held by the CEO. Examining the form of the CEO's objective function, (3.9), such a perturbation increases both the expectation of the future wealth of the CEO for any given control vector, δ_t. Now, at the optimum point, the marginal expected utility of a higher cash bonus for the CEO is proportional to the marginal utility of current consumption. But it is well known that for a risk-aversive investor, an increase in the expected return on savings has an ambiguous effect on the optimal investment – and hence the optimal consumption (see, for example, Donaldson and Mehra, 1983).

Proof of Proposition 1 The equilibrium replacement rule is such as to exclude, for any t, and *any* given μ_{t-1}, the n_t directors with the highest bankruptcy costs in D_{t-1}. ■

Proof of Proposition 2 Follows immediately from Theorem 2. ■

4. Dynamic capabilities, competence and the behavioral theory of the firm

J. Lamar Pierce, Christopher S. Boerner and David J. Teece

1 INTRODUCTION

Among the scores of articles and books that have helped to shape how economists conceptualize organizations, Richard Cyert and James March's *A Behavioral Theory of the Firm* stands in a class by itself. It is difficult to overstate the influence this work has had on our understanding of the internal organization, operations, and performance of firms. Paramount among Cyert and March's achievements was their effort to open up the world of economics to organization theory. Whereas the economics profession had once viewed itself as somehow removed from other social science disciplines, Cyert and March (along with their colleagues in the Carnegie School) put economics in touch with research in sociology, political science, social psychology and law. In doing so, they distilled new and important insights into the structure and performance of economic organizations, and made internal organization, decision making, and the behavior of firms a subject of serious enquiry. As Oliver Williamson observes, 'The *Behavioral Theory of the Firm* joined economics and organization theory to pry open what had been a black box, in order to examine the business firm in more operationally engaging ways' (Williamson 1996, p. 23).

While the influence of Cyert and March on subsequent work in economics, notably transaction cost and agency theory, is well established, one significant aspect of this work that is frequently overlooked is the role it has played in the development of theories of firm strategy, particularly those relating to the importance of firm competencies and dynamic capabilities. These theories, which focus on the internal characteristics and differential abilities of firms to adapt to and exploit changing environments, draw upon Cyert and March and related literature. While the behavioral theory of the firm provides no proposal for managers seeking to change firm behavior, noting that firms 'solve pressing problems rather than develop long-run strategies' (1963, p. 119), it has unquestionably provided rich insight into business and corporate strategy. This chapter identifies the elements of *A Behavioral Theory* critical in the development of these approaches, and establishes the extent of its influence by showing the epistemological lineage between them.

In the next section we review the key aspects of *A Behavioral Theory of the Firm* that relate to firm strategy. Section 3 traces how these concepts have been applied and extended in various theories of firm strategy. Particular attention is paid to the role Cyert and March's work has played in subsequent work on firm competencies (Section 4) and capabilities (Section 5). The final section provides concluding remarks and directions for future research.

2 THE BEHAVIORAL THEORY OF THE FIRM

When Cyert and March's work appeared in 1963, the utility of conceptualizing the firm as a production function had already been repeatedly challenged in the academic literature. While scholars such as Ronald Coase, Herbert Simon, and Edith Penrose had put forward building blocks for a new approach, the neoclassical view of the firm still predominated. The assumptions of the neoclassical view were that the firm enjoyed perfect information and certainty about environmental outcomes, it suffered no control or adaptability problems, it maximized profit, and it suffered no dysfunctional internal resource allocation problems. Its strategies and performance were predictable, it manufactured and assembled tangible components, and it sold its output in final product markets. These assumptions provided for a very simple and manageable treatment of the firm which could be integrated into neoclassical price theory; but it was not a good abstraction of a firm's internal organization.[1] Indeed, the neoclassical model failed to recognize firm heterogeneity, strategic behavior, and performance.

Meanwhile, early organizational theorists had focused on the internal characteristics that accounted for this diversity of organization. Sociological and social psychological approaches examined the decision-making processes, efficiency of individuals and small groups, and the coordination of effort (Gouldner 1954; Blau 1955; Argyris 1960; Likert 1961). While the work of organizational theorists had yielded insights into the decision processes employed by humans and in organizations, they had failed to relate this understanding specifically to the context of the firm. Their theories did not address the unique environmental and decision variables facing this particular form of organization.

Thus while the work of organizational theorists formed a basis for analysing the structure and actions of organizations, they had by no means developed a theory of the firm. Endeavoring to fill this void, Cyert and March set out to develop a theory that 'takes (1) the firm as its basic unit, (2) the prediction of firm behavior with respect to such decisions as price, output, and resource allocation as its objective, and (3) an explicit emphasis on the actual process of organizational decision making as its basic research commitment' (1963, p. 19). Against these goals, the shortfalls of earlier theories are clear. Although the neoclassical view addresses (1) and (2), it fails to approach the actual processes of condition (3). Likewise, organizational theory satisfies (1) and (3), yet fails to predict the components of firm behavior in (2). Cyert and March sought to create a theory that met all these challenges and, in doing so, develop the language necessary for a robust theoretical discussion of the firm.

Cyert and March argue that a behavioral theory of the firm requires attention to organizational goals, expectations, choice, and control. Only through these characteristics can one truly understand how firms function. Their subtheory on organizational goals focuses on how coalitions of individuals bargain to determine the goals of the greater organization. While the goals of individuals within a coalition may be disparate, so long as the resources available are greater than the demands of the members, the coalition, and thus the organization, will be feasible. At any given time, organizations will have numerous goals pertaining to each of the diverse decision variables facing them. These goals must address a variety of subjects including sales, market share, profit, inventory, and production levels.

Organizational expectations focus on how a firm gathers and interprets information from its environment. Unlike the traditional theory of expectations, Cyert and March do not assume that firms are able to gather all the relevant information and perfectly calculate expected outcomes.

Firms are heterogeneous entities without perfect knowledge of potential costs, returns, and probability distributions. The search for and processing of information is not simply another use for firm resources. Search is initially unsystematic, with commitments to action occurring early in the search process. The intensity of the search increases as the implementation of the action nears. Firms use rather simple computations to process the gathered information, since the gamut of alternative actions is not readily available. Feasibility and improvement on current procedures are the necessary hurdles for the implementation of new procedures. In addition, the analysis of information and the calculation of expectation in the firm is inherently biased, either through the hopes and aspirations of individuals or subunits, or through the bargaining needs of any coalition. Finally, communication is not perfect within the organization. Communication may be biased, and individuals may attempt in their communication to eliminate this bias. Information therefore cannot flow seamlessly through the firm without distortion, manipulation, and misunderstanding.

Cyert and March present the firm as adaptively rational, where its learning and behavior are conditioned by its experience. The adaptive nature of the firm is focused in the firm's learning and memory, which are operationalized in the form of standard operating procedures and decision rules. These standard operating procedures include general choice procedures and specific operating procedures. General choice procedures address three principles: avoid uncertainty, maintain the rules, and use simple rules. These general choice procedures have been learned through the firm's past environmental conditions and internal constraints. Consequently, general choice procedures tend to be extremely stable in the long run and change only with considerable pressure.

Specific standard operating procedures also change slowly, but can be adjusted with concentrated effort. These procedures are the unique characteristics of the firm, which define and determine how the firm reacts to stimuli and situations. Some of these procedures may be codified to achieve consistency in organizational protocol, but other procedures may be tacit in nature. Standard operating procedures can therefore entail everything from the temperature at which coffee is served in a restaurant to the tacit search of applications for basic research. These specific standard operating procedures highly differentiate even those firms producing similar products by creating embedded differences in every common task they perform. Procedures are highly fixed and difficult to change, and therefore represent dissimilarities relatively invulnerable to market transactions.

The four major types of specific standard operating procedures are task performance rules, continuing records and reports, information handling rules, and plans. Task performance rules deal with the specification of methods for accomplishing a variety of tasks, including pricing, and production and accounting procedures. These rules need to be consistent within the organization in order to facilitate coordination between units performing indelibly linked tasks. If units are unable to understand and predict how complementary tasks will be performed, they may hinder one another with conflicting decisions. Task performance rules strictly define the parameters within which one can accomplish a task. This may include production line tasks as well as more complicated engineering and design solutions. These rules are persistent, though they may change as new ideas and rules are brought in with labor movement.

Continuing records and reports concern the documentation and codification of all elements of business operations important to the firm. Records and reports are the way in which a firm controls its procedures and predicts future outcomes and environments. They also control how information is stored and disseminated throughout the firm, an element critical to the firm's ability to monitor adherence to standard procedures. Recording procedures also determine the level of codification of standard operating procedures, a concept extremely important in the replicability and imitability of all procedures. In a related fashion, information handling rules define how the firm absorbs, transmits, and exports information. These procedures dictate what information the firm will perceive in its outside environment, which is critical to its ability to recognize opportunity and potential threats. The transmission of information influences how different components of the firm assimilate outside information, and whether or not this information is analysed and applied within the firm. These procedures have wide-ranging effects for technology adoption and process improvements. Technological spillovers from outside the firm and among intrafirm organizations are dependent on the codified and tacit procedures for information transmission and dissemination. Firms unable to effectively gain outside knowledge and share process improvements will innovate with limited success and will be slow to adapt to a changing environment. These procedures also relate to information leaving the firm, or potentially its protection of intellectual property. Clearly the firm does not want its innovations distributed among its competitors, therefore it will establish strict protocols regarding confidentiality and information releases.

Plan procedures define how resources will be allocated, including both short-run and long-run budgets and expenditures. These procedures have significant influences on the firm's long-run success in that they determine which aspects of the organization will receive priority support. Research and development funding is an integral part of a firm's ability to evolve and grow, and plan procedures dictate the relative support these activities will receive. A firm whose plan procedures do not support innovation is unlikely to survive over long periods of time. More specifically, what types and areas of research and development are supported will tend to determine the firm's potential evolution. Plan procedures can define the firm's intent and ability to innovate and evolve its dynamic capabilities in particular directions.

3 THE BEHAVIORAL THEORY OF THE FIRM AND STRATEGY

While *A Behavioral Theory* provided a revolutionary view of the internal characteristics of the firm, strategic and managerial considerations were not the focus of attention. The goal was not to explain market behavior, but rather to understand decisions and actions inside the firm. Cyert and March believed that organizations were incapable of following specific, unified objectives. Such specific objectives are critical to the establishment of corporate strategy, and without this ability, managers could influence the direction of the firm only marginally. Any objectives agreed upon by a management coalition would inevitably be highly ambiguous goals, enfeebling the ability of a top manager or entrepreneur to truly control the direction of the firm. Cyert and March argued that while 'individuals have goals; collectivities of people do not' (1992, p. 30), and thus the firm could not have well-defined objectives.

Premised on this weak (or the absence of) leadership, *A Behavioral Theory* posits that the firm's strategies and learning processes are short term in focus with adaptations induced by crises. Management is unable to reconfigure internal resources because of the immutability of standard operating procedures and the ambiguity of coalition goals. In his discussion of firm strategy, Oliver Williamson notes that in Cyert and March 'the firm resembles a fire department more than a strategic actor' (1999, p. 14). The firm is focused on finding solutions to immediate problems, not on longer-term strategic options. Although *A Behavioral Theory* 'can not articulate a serious policy proposal for changing the behavior pattern' (Cyert and March 1963, p. 297), it nevertheless provides a greater understanding of the limitations to strategic action. The understanding of how routines and path dependency limit and enable the firm to solve problems was an important step in the development of the strategy literature.

Diverse fields have benefited from *A Behavioral Theory*'s diligent integration of economics and organizational theory. Since the publishing of this book, numerous approaches to understanding the nature of the firm have emerged, most recently theories regarding the importance of various internal firm competencies and capabilities. While this still-emerging literature has helped to reshape our understanding of the nature of the firm, many of its basic insights can be traced to Cyert and March's work in *A Behavioral Theory*.

Perhaps the most basic contribution of Cyert and March to this literature is their recognition of the fundamental importance of firm heterogeneity. Their work presents the firm as a complex organization defined by its unique goals, expectations, and standard operating procedures. Because each firm is uniquely defined by these aspects, firms are heterogeneous and thus not easily modeled. This heterogeneity creates inequalities in both short- and long-term performance, as each firm's unique characteristics make it better or worse suited than its rivals to succeed in a given environment. Cyert and March's analysis of the internal organization of the firm eliminates the possibility of the neoclassical competitive market. A market will never reach equilibrium with identical firms earning the same minimal level of profits. Diversity in firm standard operating procedures within an industry will inevitably produce differential results among competitors, heterogeneity that cannot be explained by industry-level effects. This performance heterogeneity has been subsequently examined and verified by several empirical studies (Jacobson 1988; Hansen and Wernerfelt 1989). Cool and Schendel (1988) have shown that there are systematic and significant differences in performance among firms belonging to the same strategic group within the US pharmaceutical industry. Additionally, Rumelt (1991) found intra-industry profit heterogeneity to be greater than inter-industry differences in profits, suggesting the relative importance of firm-related sources of performance. In a sense, Cyert and March's assertions about the importance of firm characteristics have been verified.

The idea that firms are fundamentally heterogeneous, in terms of their internal knowledge, skills and resources, is at the heart of the field of strategic management. Cyert and March's work in *A Behavioral Theory* was an important step toward understanding this heterogeneity. Their move to develop a complete theory of the firm that explicitly recognized firm differences undercut the prevailing neoclassical assumptions that had so hindered the creation of a useful theory of the firm. Most subsequent economic theories of firm strategy are consequently intellectual descendants of Cyert and March's early efforts.

4 THE BEHAVIORAL THEORY AND FIRM COMPETENCIES

With the aid of Cyert and March's recognition that firms are fundamentally heterogeneous, scholars began working to better understand the nature and origins of this heterogeneity and its implications for firm performance. Early work by Penrose (1959), Rubin (1973), Andrews (1971) and Learned et al. (1969) drew attention to the importance of internal firm resources and skills. Andrews's (1971) classic text on strategy, for example, centered on the resource position of firms. Those internal firm resources, which are unique or superior relative to those of rival firms, may be a source of lasting competitive advantage provided they are matched appropriately to environmental opportunities. Likewise, Learned et al. (1969, p. 179) emphasize the importance of internal firm resources, noting:

> [T]he capability of an organization is its demonstrated and potential ability to accomplish against the opposition of circumstance or competition, whatever it sets out to do. Every organization has actual and potential strengths and weaknesses; it is important to try to determine what they are and to distinguish one from the other.

These ideas serve as the foundation for an important early model of firm strategy, the resource-based view of the firm.

The resource-based approach to firm strategy portrays firms as a collection of tangible and intangible assets, resources or competencies, which are tied to the firm and are difficult for others to imitate. Teece (1988) describes a firm's competencies as a set of differentiated technological skills, complementary assets and organizational routines that provide the basis for a firm's competitive capacities in one or more businesses. Externally, these competencies may be perceived as a firm's skill in a particular product area. However, a competence is the ability of a firm to solve organizational and technical problems, and thus is not limited to a specific set of products.[2] Indeed, firms frequently possess competencies that extend into multiproduct space. Examples of firm-specific competencies include employment of skilled personnel, in-house knowledge of technology, operating routines and trade contacts (Wernerfelt 1984). These resources arise primarily through organizational learning (Nelson and Winter 1982). As a result, they are closely tied to the products and markets in which the firm has historically been active. These resources enable firms to have markedly lower costs or to offer higher-quality products and performance than competitors. To the extent that resource endowments are 'sticky', firms with superior competencies will tend to be more profitable than competitors.

To be considered a source of competitive advantage, an organizational competence must meet three conditions: it must be heterogeneously distributed within an industry; it must be difficult to purchase on the market; and it must be difficult or impossible to imitate. Considerable discussion in the literature suggests that high-technology competencies are particularly likely to meet these conditions since such capabilities are frequently based on tacit knowledge and are subject to considerable uncertainty regarding quality and performance (Dosi 1982; Nelson and Winter 1982). As a result, high-technology competencies are likely to be difficult to acquire through straightforward market transactions or easily transfer internally to new uses (Teece 1982; Mowery 1983). The same features that make the market transfer of technology competencies difficult also limit the ability of other firms to imitate these competencies. The non-replicable nature of many technology competencies is the cornerstone of their strategic importance.

Teece et al. (1994) divide a firm's organizational competence into three components: (i) allocative competence – the decisions involving what to produce and how to price it; (ii) transactional competence – decisions on whether to make or to buy, and whether to do so alone or in a partnership; and (iii) administrative competence – how to design organizational structures and policies to enable efficient performance. Additionally, they define technical competence as the ability to design and develop products and processes, and as the ability to operate facilities effectively. Technical competencies, which also include learning, typically have significant tacit components, making them relatively safe from replication. These competencies reside largely in the organizational routines that contain a firm's collective knowledge. Nelson and Winter (1982) established an extensive discussion of routines in their evolutionary theory of the firm. Routines are patterns of interactions representing solutions to particular problems resident in group behavior, and can only be partially codified, due to their inherently tacit dimension. Routines can be both static and dynamic. Static routines allow the firm to replicate certain previously performed tasks, and although they are generally stable, improvements and mutations will always occur with repetition. Dynamic routines are those that seek new product and process innovations and are generally aimed at learning. These routines are heavily embedded in the research and development a firm pursues. As both Nelson and Winter (1982) and Teece (1982) argue, routines can be highly tacit in nature. This makes replication or imitation of them extremely difficult, and renders them non-contractable in an intermediary market.

Nelson and Winter's work also emphasizes the routine as the organizational memory. They assert that organizations learn by doing, and this knowledge is stored in the routines of the firm. In their view of the firm, information flows into the organization from the external environment. Members interpret this information and react by invoking routines that were successful in the past. Their performance generates information recognized by others, who interpret it and invoke the associated routine. Members of the organization are thus continually reacting to both external and internal information. The routines of the organization are self-sustaining, in that their repetition strengthens their existence in the firm. It is the conformity to these routines that can pose a problem for the organization. As the firm's environment changes, routines will continue to persist even though they may no longer be effective at solving the relevant problems. This persistence is dangerous if it makes the firms unable to adapt to a new environment. Firms will tend to select inputs that are compatible with internal routines rather than alter the routine to fit new alternative inputs.

The resource-based view of firm strategy, as defined above, builds on and extends many core concepts first addressed by Cyert and March in *A Behavioral Theory*. The categorization of competencies by Teece et al. (1997) as allocative, transactional, administrative and technical is directly related to Cyert and March's discussion of standard operating procedures. While Cyert and March do not address the make versus buy decision, the remainder of the competencies discussed in Teece et al. have parallels in the task performance rules, records and reports, information-handling rules, and plans procedures presented in 1963. The allocative competence from Teece would be found in the task performance rules and plans procedures of Cyert and March. Procedures for how to produce the good are task performance rules, while how much of the good to produce is jointly dependent on the budgetary allocation of plans and the more micro-level decisions of task performance rules. Even though the make/buy decision of transactional competence is not discussed in Cyert and March, it could be implicitly included in the allocation of resources to subunits included in plans procedures.[3] Teece's organizational competence cannot be distinctly placed in the procedure categorization of Cyert and March, but rather refers to procedures throughout their specific standard operating procedures. The same can be stated for technical competence, though innovation is not heavily discussed in *A Behavioral Theory*. The ability to accomplish those innovations sparked by problems encountered in production, however, could be specifically placed in task performance and information rules.

Teece et al. (1997) have taken the concept of specific standard operating procedures from Cyert and March and advanced it, placing these procedures in more relevant groupings and adding important specific dimensions such as the make/buy decision, external ties, and technology. They have better clarified the importance of cross-firm differences in these procedures by grouping them in categories of strategic relevance. Most importantly, they have shown the importance of these procedures in the firm's ability to achieve a sustainable competitive advantage. This lays the foundation for the strategic element, missing in *A Behavioral Theory*. However, many of the building blocks can be found in Cyert and March's original work.

In addition, the non-marketable nature of internal firm competencies is hinted at in the early Cyert and March. One aspect of their discussion of standard operating procedures is that these procedures are intimately linked to the firm itself. Indeed, they suggest that these procedures define a given firm by dictating its handling of information, its learning, its operations, and its range of possible actions. The success or failure of a given firm is closely tied to these procedures, as are the directions the firm takes. These procedures are woven into the firm's organizational structure, and thus are not readily transferable or replicable by other firms. Attempts by other firms to develop or adopt new or observed procedures will inevitably be hindered by the entrenchment of existing procedures meant to be replaced. The path-dependent nature of standard operating procedures makes their elimination as difficult as their integration or creation. Competencies that are no longer relevant to the firm's environment are equally as recalcitrant, as they are composed of these entrenched procedures. The extreme embeddedness of competencies therefore makes them unmarketable among organizations.

The concept of organizational routines found in the resource-based view is also directly related to Cyert and March's discussion in 1963. Routines are discussed by Nelson and Winter in much the same way as their predecessors defined procedures, in terms of repetitive patterns of activity in an organization. As in *A Behavioral Theory*, Nelson and Winter present routines as being relatively self-sustaining and static, despite a dynamic environment. Both treatises agree that these routines/procedures define how the firm will treat information and how it will solve observable problems. They also concur that organizational learning is accomplished through and embedded in routines/procedures. The routines/procedures of the firm are therefore deeply rooted in history and difficult to change. They are unique to the firm and inherently simplifying processes. The importance of Cyert and March's examination of standard operating procedures is evident in Nelson and Winter, which in turn greatly influences much of the work in the resource-based view of the firm.

Evidence has shown that routines and internal coordination play a critical role in firm performance. Several papers have sought to document how firm-level competencies, based in routines and procedures, determine differential firm performance. The importance of the integration and coordination of internal activity has been found to be very important to the firm (Aoki 1990). This coordination is also clearly important for relationships with outside suppliers and partners (Shuen 1994). Evidence of the importance of the organization of production is also available. Garvin's (1988) air conditioner plant study found that quality performance was driven by special organizational routines, rather than by capital investment or the level of automation. The importance of coordinating routines is also found by Clark and Fujimoto (1991) in the automobile industry. Differences in the coordinative routines in new model development was responsible for considerable variance in development cost, lead times, and quality. The importance of these routines is evident in studies of Japanese manufacturing by Womack et al. (1991) and Fujimoto (1994). These studies of lean manufacturing indicated not only the importance of these routines but also the difficulty of replicating them. They validate Cyert and March's early assertion of standard operating procedures as key foundations of firm behavior.

5 THE BEHAVIORAL THEORY AND DYNAMIC CAPABILITIES

While the resource-based theory is a relatively static approach toward firm strategy, it does discuss the implications of the nature of firm competencies toward long-run survival and strategy. This long-run view has been further addressed by the dynamic capabilities literature, which studies firms' abilities to adapt to and exploit a changing environment. The dynamic capabilities theory of the firm seeks to explain how firms achieve and sustain competitive advantage despite an ever-changing environment. Building on the resource-based, transaction-cost, and evolutionary theories of the firm, dynamic capabilities argues that a firm gains competitive advantage through internal routines or standard operating procedures that define the firm's processes. Routines, which are patterns of interactions representing successful solutions to specific problems, are deeply conditioned by its history, and not readily changed or developed. They are endemic to the firm, observed in group behavior, and highly subject to path dependency. These routines are defined as how tasks are accomplished, how problems are solved, and how knowledge is learned, and are not tangibly identifiable or necessarily codified. They are the firm's patterns of current practice and its organizational learning.

Dynamic capabilities 'emphasizes the key role of strategic management in appropriately adapting, integrating, and re-configuring internal and external organizational skills, resources, and functional competencies toward a changing environment' (Teece and Pisano 1994, p. 57). The firm's strategic dimensions are constrained by available paths, its current position, and its organizational processes or routines. The available paths represent the firm's opportunities and strategic alternatives. Firms are in part tied to their past and current positions, unable to choose from the infinite array of technologies and markets in existence. Firms typically are only capable of successful learning in areas or ways close to those it currently employs (Teece 1988). The marginal cost of gaining further knowledge in known areas is usually much less than innovating in unrelated fields (Cohen and Levinthal 1990). Thus firms will tend to innovate close in to areas they know well. A firm is not an infinitely malleable entity, but rather is an organization capable of limited change at significant cost. The past and current activities of the firm will powerfully influence the technological paths available to it, in that breakthroughs in related areas will be more readily identifiable and exploitable to the firm (Dosi 1982). The research areas currently focused on as well as the firm's ties to outside innovations will define which technological advances are potentially available for their development and use. Additionally, management's ability to identify and choose among these opportunities will determine the firm's capability in adapting to and exploiting changing technologies.

The firm's current position is defined by its intellectual property, supplier relations, strategic alliances, and endowment of technology. As in the resource-based view, tradable and readily transferable assets represent no concrete competitive advantage. These assets therefore are often tacit knowledge assets, ones deeply embedded in the routines and processes of the firm (Teece 1981). Other assets, such as the firm's location and financial position, can also determine its available strategic options. Those assets that are difficult to replicate or imitate, however, form the key competencies of the firms, and dynamic capabilities are those competencies that allow the firm to respond to and exploit changing market environments.

The organizational processes or routines of the firm can be partly viewed in how efficient the firm is in the integration of its internal activities and its external ties. These routines govern how information is gathered and processed, aspects critical to innovation and problem solving. Routines exist in how the firm relates to its suppliers, and how information is gathered from external sources. The coordination of separate groups within the firm is routinized in the practices of management, as are research and development processes, fields, and goals. The incentives and controls within the firm are critical routines defining its position and future paths.

Some of the most important routines within the firm involve learning. In the dynamic capabilities view, learning in the firm is an inherently organizational process. While individual skills and knowledge can contribute critically to the organization, learning processes are intrinsically social and collective. The coordination of search procedures and communication are necessary for effective learning, and the current routines determine how and what a firm can process. Additionally, the organizational knowledge gained from learning is stored in the new routines and logic of the organization. The existing processes for locating, identifying, and integrating important information into the firm will guide the trajectory of the firm's learning. As discussed in Cyert and March, and Nelson and Winter (1982), learning by the firm is largely determined by these routines and is thus highly path dependent in nature.

Although existing routines are largely determinant of the firm's learning trajectory, the firm may still have difficulty harnessing competencies based in these routines for specific strategic adaptations. The firm may wish to apply its highly successful routines toward other aspects of its organization. Replication of successful routines allows the firm to engage in geographic and product line expansion, and may help it better understand the routines in order to modify and improve them. The capabilities created by routines may be difficult to understand because they involve tacit knowledge and production and research processes not readily observable or codified. The tacit nature of these processes may be impossible to replicate, even by the firm itself, and the firm's ability to replicate its routines may be inevitably hampered by its inability to identify them. Lippman and Rumelt (1982) have argued that some sources of competitive advantage are so transparent that the firm itself cannot identify them. Even if the firm can identify its routines, it may not wholly understand them, or may find them inseparably linked to other specific routines (Teece 1976). Thus attempting to apply these routines in strategic initiative may be improbable.

When the firm is unable to replicate its successful routines, its competitors are even more unlikely to imitate them successfully. When routines are highly tacit, imitation will likely be impossible, as competitors have no ability to observe internal procedures. When competitors are able to observe and imitate competence-forming routines, however, the firm may be able to protect itself with intellectual property rights. Although intellectual property rights, such as patents, are highly observable, they are mostly limited to product technologies. Process technologies, or the routines endemic in the firm's production, are not readily observable, and thus cannot be easily imitated. Such routines may be difficult to replicate as well, but allow no window of observation for the potential imitator.

The critical aspects of dynamic capabilities are the ability of the firm to identify the changing market environment, to sense the opportunity, then to seize it. The ability of the firm to sense the need and the opportunity and then accomplish the necessary transformation is the essence of dynamic capability, and creates significant value (Amit and Schoemaker 1993; Langlois

1994). Part of this ability is dependent on the firm's ability to locate and assimilate information from its environment. The location and integration of this information is grounded in part on the firm's search and information-processing routines, manifested in research and development and the firm's existing ties to the outside environment. Not only must the firm discover new paths through its own and others' research, it must also recognize the importance of these paths. Past experience conditions the feasible alternatives management is likely to perceive (Teece et al. 1997). Firms not only face different costs associated with particular technologies, but they also face different perceived technological choices (Nelson and Winter 1982).

The firm must also be able to reconfigure its organization and assets before its competitors upon recognition of a new opportunity or environmental shift. Despite the assertion of managers, the firm's evolutionary path is rather narrow, and the alternative directions available to the firm are limited by its positions and previous path. The width of the potential path determines the number of options from which a firm can choose. The ability of the firm to follow the chosen path successfully is of equal importance in these capabilities. Key characteristics and routines of the firm will determine its ability to locate opportunities and accomplish the necessary adjustments, and will directly determine the extent of its dynamic capabilities. In particular, the ability to locate and address them is an inherently entrepreneurial function, not an administrative one.

The analysis of relatively static firms in dynamic environments is a key contribution of *A Behavioral Theory*, one which is a starting-point for the development of the dynamic capabilities literature. Cyert and March argue and establish the inherent rigidity of the firm, stating that the alteration and modification of the organization is extremely difficult, even over long periods of time. The standard operating procedures that are critical to the firm's operation cannot be immediately modified. These procedures are built from the entirety of the firm's history, dependent on its previous path and determinant of the future. Even if the firm's information-handling procedures identify an attractive alternative set of goals and expectations, it may be unable to alter standard operating procedures that evolved to serve previous firm goals. A firm's ability to identify alternate choices is intrinsically linked to its past as well. Cyert and March state repeatedly that a firm's search patterns and behavior are heavily biased, such that the information gathered and the opportunities recognized will indelibly be dependent on past and current behavior. The idea that 'history matters' is crucial to the dynamic capabilities literature, which views this history dependence as the driving force in long-run performance heterogeneity.

Dynamic capabilities stresses that the inherently rigid firm is forever challenged with metamorphosing market and technological characteristics. Firms must recognize these changes, identify new opportunities and appropriate adaptations, and successfully mutate toward the new environment. The internal routines or procedures of the firm help determine their ability to identify and accomplish this change. The entrepreneurial capacity of the organization to sense and then seize opportunities is critical to its dynamic capabilities.

A more specific application of Cyert and March in the dynamic capabilities literature is the importance of routines in identifying and exploiting opportunities. Cyert and March intently focus on the critical influence of standard operating procedures in the unique character of the firm, and stress their role in firms' abilities to identify and adapt to changes in their environment. While they portray all firms as sharing the same basic principles of general choice procedure (uncertainty avoidance, rules maintenance, simple rules), they argue that each firm has specific standard operating procedures that define the direction of constantly recurring activities. These procedures provide consistency within the firm and directly influence organizational decisions. Specific standard operating procedures dictate how the firm conducts all of its operations, from the mundane to technologically sophisticated. They also direct how the firm integrates, records, reports, locates, and utilizes the information necessary to identify potential problems and solutions. In addition, they influence the firm's strategic behavior in the allocation of its limited resources among potential alternative uses. Standard operating procedures make a firm unique, both in its static nature and in its dynamic capabilities. They are what define the competencies of the organization, made up of the routines that define its ability to integrate resources and produce products. Routines are also what limit the firm in its ability to adapt to its dynamic environment, for in giving stability to the organization, they limit its flexibility. In the words of Cyert and March, 'these procedures change slowly' (1992, p. 122) and the differential ability to accelerate this rate can determine the survival of the firm.

The dynamic capabilities literature develops the concept of standard operating procedures in discussing the importance of routines in firm performance. A firm's dynamic capabilities depend on two dimensions: its ability to identify opportunities, and its ability to change the firm's organizational structure to accommodate and exploit them. Both of these dimensions are evident in *A Behavioral Theory of the Firm*. The firm's ability to identify opportunities lies in its standard operating procedures for handling and processing information and in innovation realized from its task performance rules. These procedures, deemed routines in later literature, determine in which arenas the firm will be searching. The routines of the firm are its managerial and organizational processes, and search routines will increase the probability of recognizing some opportunities but will eliminate others. Search routines, as in Cyert and March, will depend on the past successes of the firm and its current and future expected problems. Under this acknowledgment of firms' unique search routines, we should expect technological and market strategies to suffer from path dependency. The search routines, founded in past successes and failures, help determine new directions for the firms to take.

Cyert and March also identify firms' differential procedures for processing and evaluating information. This heterogeneity is addressed by the dynamic capabilities literature as critical to the recognition of ripe opportunities. Firms may locate the information necessary to identify a new opportunity, but their processing routines may limit their ability to understand the potential benefits or application of the knowledge. Some firms can be expected to have information-processing routines completely incapable of identifying new directions, while others will be able to know the importance of their discovery immediately. Some firms have the entrepreneurial capacity to respond; some do not. Cyert and March discuss how each firm will have different ways of integrating new knowledge, locating it in different media and locations. The sources of this information will not be uniform across firms, and therefore organizations will have biased and filtered knowledge about their environment and potential opportunities. The firm's task performance procedures will influence its ability to realize learning by doing. Certain manufacturing procedures will tend to produce more innovation in reducing the cost and increasing the speed of production. Heterogeneity in firm task performance procedures will create differential levels of innovation potential from simply performing routines. These firm-specific routines will not only lend certain firms greater potential for efficiency improvements, but will also give them the opportunity for radical innovations. In essence, task performance procedures can provide another mode for identifying potential opportunities, and can thus be determinant of a firm's dynamic capabilities.

Cyert and March's work is also important in the second critical aspect of dynamic capabilities – the ability of the firm to adapt to and exploit opportunities. The path-dependent nature of standard operating procedures is firmly rooted in *A Behavioral Theory*, and is voiced even more loudly in Nelson and Winter (1982). Procedures and routines develop from years of problem-solving behavior in the organization, and are self-reinforcing characteristics. They are extremely difficult to change and determinant of future paths. The inherent heterogeneity of these routines across firms ensures that some firms will be better able to adapt their procedures to changes in their environment, an aspect critical in dynamic capabilities. The basis for the exploitation aspect of dynamic capabilities is firmly established in the work of Cyert and March, and inherited through the evolutionary theory of Nelson and Winter.

6 CONCLUSION

As is shown in this chapter, *A Behavioral Theory of the Firm* has richly contributed to a tradition of literature culminating in theories on firm competence and dynamic capabilities. The focus of Cyert and March on the heterogeneity of firm characteristics was critical to the development of these theories. Less critical but still important was the portrayal of a rigid firm in a dynamic environment. The standard operating procedures detailed in their work formed the basis for the firm routines of Nelson and Winter (1982), which in turn led to the explication of firm competence and dynamic capabilities. The conceptualization of how firms identify opportunities and adapt to exploit them is implicitly tied to procedures explained by Cyert and March.

It is important to note that while *A Behavioral Theory* cannot itself be classified as a study of firm strategy, it is nevertheless the starting point for numerous advances in this field. The literature discussed here by no means adequately summarizes the impact in economics and organization theory. Moreover, *A Behavioral Theory* is by no means the sole contribution of Cyert and March. Both Richard Cyert and James March have provided important later contributions to the theory of the firm, and more specifically to the field of strategy. Yet their 1963 classic remains critical to the modern understanding of the nature and behavior of the firm.

NOTES

1. Economists such as Friedman (1953) argued that whether or not the model accurately represented the firm was irrelevant so long as its predictive value was high.
2. A firm's competencies, as defined by Teece, are typically implicitly or explicitly *assumed* in economic theory. As such, competencies are viewed as widely and freely distributed among firms, thus giving limited insight into heterogeneity, organizational structure or firm performance.
3. The clearly-defined dichotomy of make/buy in the strategy literature, however, should likely be attributed to Williamson's (1975) work and the transaction cost literature that followed it.

REFERENCES

Amit, R. and P. Schoemaker (1993), 'Strategic assets and organizational rent', *Strategic Management Journal*, **14**, 33–46.

Andrews, Kenneth R. (1971), *The Concept of Corporate Strategy*, Homewood, IL: Dow Jones-Irwin.

Aoki, Masahiko (1990), 'Toward an economic model of the Japanese firm', *Journal of Economic Literature*, **28**, 1–27.

Argyris, C. (1960), *Understanding Organizational Behavior*, Homewood, IL: Dorsey.
Blau, P. (1955), *Dynamics of Bureaucracy*, Chicago: University of Chicago Press.
Clark, Kim B. and T. Fujimoto (1991), *Product Development Performance: Strategy, Organization and Management in the World Auto Industries*, Cambridge, MA: Harvard Business School Press.
Cohen, Wesley M. and Daniel A. Levinthal (1990), 'Absorptive capacity: a new perspective on learning and innovation' *Administrative Science Quarterly*, **35**, 569–96.
Cool, K. and D. Schendel (1988), 'Performance differences among strategic group members', *Strategic Management Journal*, **9**, 207–23.
Cyert, Richard M. and James G. March (1963), *A Behavioral Theory of the Firm*, Englewood Cliffs, NJ: Prentice-Hall.
Cyert, Richard M. and James G. March (1992), *A Behavioral Theory of the Firm*, 2nd edn, Cambridge, MA: Blackwell Business.
Dosi, G. (1982), Technological paradigms and technological trajectories: a suggested interpretation of the determinants and directives of technological change', *Research Policy*, **11**, 147–62.
Friedman, Milton (1953), *Essays in Positive Economics*, Chicago: University of Chicago Press.
Fujimoto, T. (1994), *Reinterpreting the Resource-capability View of the Firm: A Case of the Development-production Systems of the Japanese Automakers*, Tokyo: University of Tokyo Press.
Garvin, David A. (1988), *Managing Quality*, New York: Free Press.
Gouldner, A. (1954), *Patterns of Industrial Bureaucracy*, Glencoe, IL: Free Press.
Hansen, G. and B. Wernerfelt (1989), 'Determinants of firm performance: the relative importance of economic and organizational factors', *Strategic Management Journal*, **10**, 399–411.
Jacobson, R. (1988), 'The persistence of abnormal returns', *Strategic Management Journal*, **9**, 415–30.
Langlois, R. (1994), 'Cognition and capabilities: opportunities seized and missed in the history of the computer industry', Conference on Technological Oversights and Foresights, Stern School of Business, New York University.
Learned, E., C. Christensen, K. Andrews and W. Guth (1969), *Business Policy: Text and Cases*, Homewood, IL: Irwin.
Likert, R. (1961), *New Patterns of Management*, New York: McGraw-Hill.
Lippman, S. and R. Rumelt (1982), 'Uncertain imitability: an analysis of interfirm difference in efficiency under competition', *Bell Journal of Economics*, **13**, 413–38.
Mowery, D. (1983), 'The relationship between intrafirm and contractual forms of industrial research in American manufacturing, 1900–1940', *Explorations in Economic History*, **20**, 351–74.
Nelson, R.R. and S.G. Winter (1982), *An Evolutionary Theory of Economic Change*, Cambridge: Belknap Press.
Penrose, Edith T. (1959), *The Theory of the Growth of the Firm*, Oxford: Basil Blackwell.
Peteraf, M. (1993), 'The cornerstones of competitive advantage: a resource-based view', *Strategic Management Journal*, **14**, 179–91.
Rubin, P.H. (1973), 'The expansion of firms', *Journal of Political Economy*, **81**, 936–49.
Rumelt, Richard P. (1991), 'How much does industry matter?', *Strategic Management Journal*, **12**, 167–85.
Shuen, Amy (1994), 'Technology sourcing and learning strategies in the semiconductor industry', PhD Dissertation Walter A. Haas School of Business, University of California, Berkeley.
Teece, D.J. (1976), *The Multinational Corporation and the Resource Cost of International Technology Transfer*, Cambridge, MA: Ballinger.
Teece, David J. (1981), 'The market for know-how and the efficient international transfer of technology', *Annals of the American Association of Political and Social Sciences*, November, 81–6.
Teece, David J. (1982), 'Towards an economic theory of the multiproduct firm, *Journal of Economic Behavior and Organization*, **3**, 39–63.
Teece, David J. (1988), 'Technological change and the nature of the firm', in G. Dosi, C. Freeman, R. Nelson, G. Silverberg and L. Soete (eds), *Technical Change and Economic Theory*, London and New York: Pinter, 256–81.
Teece, D., R. Rumelt, G. Dosi and S. Winter (1994), 'Understanding Corporate Coherence: Theory and Evidence', *Journal of Economic Behavior and Organization*, **23**, (1), pp. 1–30.
Teece, David J. and Gary Pisano (1994), 'The dynamic capabilities of firms: an introduction', *Industrial and Corporate Change*, **3**, 537–56.

Teece, D.J., G. Pisano and A. Shuen (1997),'Dynamic capabilities and strategic management, *Strategic Management Journal*, **18**, 509–33.
Wernerfelt, Birger (1984), 'A resource-based view of the firm', *Strategic Management Journal*, **12**, 75–94.
Williamson, Oliver E. (1975), *Markets and Hierarchies*, New York: Free Press.
Williamson, Oliver E. (1996), *The Mechanisms of Governance*, New York: Oxford University Press.
Williamson, Oliver E. (1999), 'Strategy research: governance and competence perspectives', Working Paper BPP-74, Haas School of Business, University of California, Berkeley.
Womack, J., D. Jones and D. Roos (1991), *The Machine That Changed the World*, New York: Harper-Perennial.

PART II

Information and the Cognitive Basis of Action

5. Auditing and accounting: impacts and aftermaths of R.M. Cyert's research in statistical sampling

William W. Cooper*

1 INTRODUCTION

Other chapters in this volume are devoted to research that has been influenced by Richard Cyert's research. This is entirely proper since Dr Cyert's research has had major (continuing) impacts in both organization theory and economics research. There are, however, other aspects of Cyert's work and other contributions that have resulted from his efforts. One might mention the impact of his educational activity starting with innovative courses he designed, or helped to design, such as the course 'Quantitative Controls in Business'. Taught first at the undergraduate level at the Carnegie Institute of Technology (now Carnegie-Mellon University: CMU), this course was used as a basis for part of the negotiations with William Larimer Mellon that led to the founding of GSIA (Graduate School of Industrial Administration) at Carnegie. This course was only one of many subsequent innovative activities in institution building and curriculum design in which Cyert brought research and education together – first when Cyert was chairman of the undergraduate program and then when he became Dean of GSIA. The results of these innovations were ubiquitously influential in the US, and their impact was felt in more distant locations such as Australia and Europe.

We could also discuss Cyert's administrative activities and accomplishments after he became president of Carnegie-Mellon University. These included 'firsts' such as the first school of computer science as a separate degree granting entity in a university. They also included the first robotology laboratory in a university. Here, too, the organization was designed in a manner that brought industry (represented by Westinghouse, Inc.) and university research together. Finally his efforts as president at CMU also brought government and university research together – as when Cyert persuaded the Department of Defense to locate its Software Research Institute (SRI) on land adjacent to the Carnegie campus in Pittsburgh. The result of all of these (and other) activities by Cyert was to move Carnegie-Mellon into the first rank of research universities. Moreover, these activities in education and research, spearheaded by Cyert, were to become major events leading into the twenty-first century.

There is still another series of activities undertaken by Cyert in the form of the impacts on actual practice that flowed from his activities. Here, too, choices must be made since these activities ranged from his participation on corporate boards to presidencies of scientific–professional societies (such as the Institute of Management Sciences: TIMS) and extended to service on local and national governmental boards as well as services in international institutions –

such as his membership on the advisory board of the International Institute for Applied Systems Analysis (IIASA) located in Laxenburg, Austria.

We bypass all of these different contributions in order to focus on some of Cyert's lesser-known research activities, and to examine their impact on professional accounting and auditing practices. This will allow us to align our presentation with other parts of this book by focusing on research in which Cyert brought (then) new developments in statistical sampling theory and survey design into new (unanticipated) uses in accounting and auditing practice. We shall turn to the history of these areas of Cyert's activities and then track their consequences in a manner that will make it possible to identify their subsequent effects on statistics and statistics research.

2 HISTORY

A good place to begin our discussion is with the historical study by Tucker and Lordi (1997). The announced objectives of this historical study were stated as follows,

> The purpose of this study is twofold. The study first seeks to provide an overview of the issues and conditions that provided the impetus for the U.S. public accounting profession's efforts to investigate the use of statistical sampling [in auditing practice]. Second, the study attempts to provide insight into the initial research effort by the AICPA [American Institute of Certified Public Accountants; earlier known as the American Institute of Accountants: AIA] to determine the feasibility of using statistical sampling to improve the practice of accounting and auditing ... (p.)

The book which Tucker and Lordi cite as the initiating source of these developments is Trueblood and Cyert (1957). For instance, in order to set the stage on the state of the (then) current practice, Tucker and Lordi quote from this volume as follows,

> [It] must be agreed that sample selection techniques are completely based on judgement in present auditing practice. Auditors use their own opinion, checked by whatever experience and facts they may muster for each occasion, in order to determine the size of the sample with which they work, the method of their selection, and the interpretation of sampling results. (1957, p. 58)

Tucker and Lordi (p. 99) then go on to remark:

> Regarding the perceived benefits of statistical sampling, Trueblood and Cyert note that statistical sampling may be used to reduce the area in which purely subjective judgements are required and to improve the quality of, or to serve as a substitute for, the 'judgmental test-check' procedures used so widely in both accounting and auditing.

Tucker and Lordi next note subsequent events in which the same kind of dissatisfaction was expressed. One such example of interest is Kenneth W. Stringer, who conducted what is probably the earliest foray into

> behavioral research [sic][1] in auditing: In 1959, Stringer conducted a laboratory experiment in which 92 senior auditors were asked to determine the sample size they would use in four different cases. The results revealed a very wide distribution of sample size selected by these senior auditors in each of the four cases. When the senior partners of his firm were presented with the results of his experiment, Stringer stated that they were shocked and dismayed at the disparity that the survey showed ... (p. 99)

Other events, many of them related to the activities underlying the Trueblood–Cyert book, are also reported. Thus '[In any event] by November 1956, the accounting profession's interests in statistical sampling had progressed to the point that a special AICPA committee, the Committee on Statistical Sampling (AICPA–CSS) was formed to research the issue. ... The newly appointed special committee was chaired by Robert M. Trueblood' (p. 99).

Finally, we quote from one of the conclusions of this historical study by Tucker and Lordi (p. 112) as follows:

> This study demonstrates the importance of individual leadership in the profession's efforts to adopt new technology. Trueblood was one of the earliest accountants to identify the potential use of statistical sampling. Trueblood coauthored [with R.M. Cyert] one of the earliest books which described applications of statistical sampling to the practice of accounting and auditing. He [Trueblood] then spearheaded the AICPA's initial effort to address the issue by chairing the AICPA–CSS for the first two years (1956 and 1957). The fact that the statistical sampling issue was brought to the attention of the profession by a person of Trueblood's professional stature and credibility lent additional urgency to the issue and increased the visibility of statistical sampling as an issue to be addressed.

3 BACKGROUND

As a member of the project that led to the book by Trueblood and Cyert, I can supply some additions as follows. Bob Trueblood was a first-rate accountant and a highly intelligent and capable person in all respects. He did not possess a background in statistics, however, but rather came to know about these possibilities in the following manner. I first met Bob as a very active, but younger, member of the staff of Touche, Ross, Bailey and Smart (TRBS), CPAs, in Chicago where I was working with E.L. Kohler on his subsequently published book *A Dictionary for Accountants* (Englewood Cliffs, NJ: Prentice-Hall, Inc., 1952).[2] Trueblood was subsequently placed in charge of the TRBS office in Pittsburgh. Fortuitously, this was the same city to which I had moved from my position on the faculty of the University of Chicago in order to accept a position on the faculty of the Carnegie Institute of Technology. Thus we renewed our acquaintance in Pittsburgh.

I earlier mentioned that the Quantitative Controls in Business course involved a novel design intended to educate engineers (especially industrial engineers) in the more sophisticated quantitative tools for use in business and management in a way that would build on (and exploit) the analytical skills these students were acquiring in their engineering education. Replacing a previous requirement of 18 months of accounting and six months of statistics, this new course attempted to package and rearrange these topics in a variety of new combinations that included sample-survey design and econometrics as well as accounting and budgeting.

David Rosenblatt and I, as two of the faculty engaged in this endeavor, had previously been with the US Bureau of the Budget (now the Office of Management and Budget) where we worked in the Division of Statistical Standards (DSS) which had general oversight of the statistical activities of the US government. This brought us into contact with the (then) revolutionary developments in statistical sampling and survey design which were occurring under the leadership of Hansen, Hurwitz and Madow at the US Census Bureau and W. Edwards Deming, who was housed in the same DSS office as Rosenblatt and I. As an aside, this association with Deming also brought us into contact with the important work in statistical quality control which had originated with Shewhart at the Bell Telephone Co. Laboratories in the US – a development which Deming was later to carry to Japan.[3]

Dick Cyert was a third member of the team charged with designing and teaching this course. Fresh from a PhD in economics under George Stigler at Columbia, Dick had also studied with the statistician, Abraham Wald. As a member of the Statistics Research Group at Columbia University, Wald had worked on improving statistical quality control methods, mainly acceptance sampling, for use by the military in the Second World War. This led to Wald's pathbreaking book, *Sequential Analysis* (1947), which added entirely new dimensions and possibilities to acceptance sampling and other parts of statistical quality control. Even more important, and even more revolutionary, was the work that Wald then undertook to give birth to his book (and other writings) on statistical decision functions that laid the foundations for what was to become known as 'statistical decision theory' and subsequently revolutionize theory, practice and research in statistics.

This background of two ongoing revolutions provided part of the ingredients needed for the courses we were supposed to be designing in this two-year sequence of courses. It also provided inspiration and excitement. An additional ingredient was supplied in that these developments had *all* emerged from practical applications which had been accomplished in educational contexts not only by Wald (at Columbia) but also by Deming, Hansen, Hurwitz and Madow – all of whom were involved in designing and teaching innovative courses (arising from their research) at the Graduate School which the US Department of Agriculture maintained for government employees (and others) in Washington during and after the Second World War.

With this background it was probably natural for us – Cyert, Rosenblatt and I – to look to potential applications as opportunities that could improve both our educational and research activities. I happened to locate such a possibility first at a luncheon with Bob Trueblood. National Supply Co., one of his firm's clients, was having trouble with estimating and verifying inventory amounts (and values) which were needed for the tax returns and financial statements that Trueblood's firm was to help prepare. As the (then) largest of all oilfield suppliers, National Supply Co. maintained a huge and varied inventory in many different parts of the world. Complete counts at all sites would have been forbiddingly expensive. I therefore naturally seized on our luncheon conversation as one of the opportunities we had been searching for – after which Trueblood undertook to recommend to the comptroller and top executives at National Supply Co. that they explore the possibilities of statistical sampling.

National Supply Co.[4] being headquartered in Pittsburgh made it fairly easy to agree to participate in the needed statistical study and experiments. I therefore invited Rosenblatt to join me in this new adventure. Confronted with recalcitrant staff in the comptroller's office at National Supply Co., we nevertheless finally won through with the help of Trueblood to a successful application. A new staff under the leadership of Barry M. Rowles (a product of our Quantitative Controls in Business course) was recruited from 3M company in Minnesota and placed in charge.[5] Implementation was undertaken using a new combination of 'cluster' and 'stratified sampling' which Rosenblatt had developed for this purpose as part of our research effort.[6] Next came encounters with the Internal Revenue Service (then known as the Bureau of Internal Revenue) where a lack of experience with such devices aroused apprehensions and concerns about potential manipulative possibilities.[7] With the help of Ed Deming we were again successful. This all led to the final success we were all seeking. Trueblood became sufficiently knowledgeable and sufficiently impressed to initiate a program of research looking toward the uses of such statistical devices and methods to improve auditing practices in his own office and, more generally, in his own firm and in the CPA profession.

4 THE MONONGAHELA PROJECT

At this point Cyert joined Trueblood in a new effort to improve this part of audit practice more generally. He and Trueblood spearheaded this effort in the form of a series of research activities that were to have dramatic effects not only on audit practices in general but also on other practices in accounting and business management.

Preceding sections in the present chapter noted the importance of the Trueblood–Cyert (1957) volume. However, this publication was preceded by much effort, part of which is recorded in the form of chapters in that volume. Since this book is long out of print, and likely to remain so, we record the chapters coauthored by Cyert along with some of the other writings emanating from his research effort as follows,[8]

1. Trueblood, Robert M. and Richard M. Cyert, 'Statistical sampling applied to aging of accounts receivable', *Journal of Accountancy*, **3**/1954, 293–8.
2. Trueblood R.M. and Robert J. Monteverde, 'Bibliography on the application of statistical methods to accounting and auditing', *The Accounting Review*, **4**/1954, 251–4.
3. Buchan, Joseph F. and R.M. Cyert, 'Reduction of clerical costs in the processing of vendors' invoices', in Trueblood and Cyert, 1957, 128–37.
4. Buchan, Joseph F. and R.M. Cyert, 'Substantiation of inventory amounts by sampling of perpetual records', in Trueblood and Cyert, 1957, 85–92.
5. Cyert, R.M. and Robert W. Johnson, 'Acceptance sampling in the inspection of department store billings', in Trueblood and Cyert, 1957, 171–8.
6. Cyert, R.M., Robert Monteverde and Louis N. Teitelbaum, 'Tests of physical inventory quantities of bulk material', in Trueblood and Cyert, 1957, 148–57.
7. Cyert, R.M. and Louis N. Teitelbaum, 'Survey of Air Force internal audit procedures for inventory', in Trueblood and Cyert, 1957, 179–94.
8. Cyert, R.M. and R.M. Trueblood, 'Aging of accounts receivable in a department store', in Trueblood and Cyert, 1957, 108–27.
9. Cyert, R.M. and R.M. Trueblood, 'Statistical sampling techniques in the aging of accounts receivable in a department store', *Management Science*, **1**/1957, 185–95.
10. Cyert, R.M. 'Test-checking and the Poisson distribution – a further comment', *The Accounting Review*, **7**/1957, 395–7.
11. Cyert, R.M. 'Statistical sampling for accountants and auditors', in *Proceedings: Accounting Papers of the Fourteenth Annual Conference of Accountants*, Tulsa, OK: University of Tulsa, 1960, 15–23.
12. Cyert, R.M. and John T. Wheeler, 'Proposal for an integrated course in statistics and accounting', *The Accounting Review*, **1**/1960, 51–9.
13. Cyert, R.M., G.M. Hinckley and R.J. Monteverde, 'Statistical sampling in the audit of the Air Force motor vehicle invertory', *The Accounting Review*, **10**/1960, 667–73.

These efforts, headquartered in Pittsburgh, became known (to us) as the 'Monongahela Project'[9] – after the river by that name which flowed through Pittsburgh next to the offices of Trueblood's firm. All of these papers were based on successful applications and subject to much review prior to publication. In all of them – except for the papers coauthored with Louis Teitelbaum and John Wheeler – the joint authors (with Cyert) had been students in the Quantitative Controls in Business course, and were engaged for this work by Trueblood after their graduation from Carnegie-Mellon University. Moreover, many of these students (and others) were sent from Pittsburgh to other offices of the firm as the use of statistical techniques in auditing began to spread.

There was another interesting feature that Trueblood introduced into the activities of the Monongahela Project. To ensure that none of the standards of good practice in statistics or accounting had been breached, Trueblood arranged periodic reviews by independent statisticians and accountants in joint sessions that were extensive and sometimes lively, since the standards and points of view of the two professions did not always agree. To ensure that the highest standards in both professions were being brought to bear, Trueblood employed for this purpose W. Edwards Deming[10] as an outstanding statistician and E.L. Kohler whose *Dictionary for Accountants* had made him world famous, and whose efforts to improve accounting standards had previously had nationwide impacts on accounting and auditing practices. Again, we may note, both Deming and Kohler had both practical and academic backgrounds and had been involved in extensive research activities. In any case all of the activities of the Monongahela project (including the research accomplishments) were subject to review. In addition, the oral exchanges at these review conferences were followed by written critiques to which written responses were required.

5 IMPACTS AND AFTERMATHS

It is rare for research to have its impacts exhibited, as in this case, even while the research is still ongoing. To summarize: even while the research was continuing, the AICPA accepted the use of statistical sampling as a *bona fide* auditing procedure and so did the stock exchanges and the US Securities & Exchange Commission.

Shortly before this was all accomplished, Trueblood was transferred by his firm to become the partner in charge of their large office in Chicago (in 1960). He then became chairman of the firm's Board of Directors after which he also became president of the AICPA.[11]

After Trueblood left, the activities of the Monongahela Project in Pittsburgh began to wane even while their effects were waxing in other offices – accompanied by the transfer of additional staff from Pittsburgh. Cyert then put his final stamp on all of this work with the successor book by Cyert and Davidson (1962) which is cited in our list of references.[12]

We do not discuss these other aspects of Cyert's uses of statistics, many of which exploit his prior background in 'decision theory' and in 'economics–econometrics'. (See, for example, Cyert et al. 1978 or Cyert and Thompson 1968.) We turn instead to assessing some of the impacts of his work with the Monongahela Project.

The 'impacts' of the Cyert and Trueblood efforts were certainly felt by members of the AICPA, some 75,000 in number at the time. Partly under the influences of Kenneth Stringer (mentioned earlier)[13] there were further 'aftermaths' which continue to have their effects on the (now) 350,000+ members of the AICPA,[14] which we excerpt from American Institute of Certified Public Accountants, Inc. (1989) as follows:

> *Au Section 350*: There are two general approaches to audit sampling: nonstatistical and statistical. Both approaches require that the auditor use professional judgement [to evaluate uncertainty] ... The uncertainty inherent in applying audit procedures is referred to as audit risk. Audit risk consists of (a) the risk (consisting of inherent risk and control risk) that the balance or class and related assertions contain misstatements that could be material ... and (b) the risk (detection risk) that the auditor will not detect such misstatement .... The auditor should apply professional judgement in assessing sampling risk ... [in which] the auditor is concerned with two aspects of sampling risk:
>
> (1) *The risk of incorrect acceptance* is the risk that the sample supports the conclusion that the recorded account balance is not materially misstated when it is materially misstated.
> (2) *The risk of incorrect rejection* is the risk that the sample supports the conclusion that the recorded account balance is materially misstated when it is not materially misstated.

Taken from the *AICPA Professional Standards* (1989), which are binding on the profession, these statements are straightforward adaptations of the Neyman–Pearson Type I–Type II error formulations from statistics. Thus the effects of early efforts undertaken by the Monongahela project continue to evolve and affect many other parts of contemporary accounting and auditing practice.

Another aftermath is the effect on statistics exhibited by articles in the statistics literatures. These aftermath effects on statistics have even assumed the form of a National Research Council, Board of Mathematical Sciences, report entitled *Statistical Models and Analysis in Auditing*, published in 1988 for use in guiding US government support for research.

Finally there was the impact of this research on Richard M. Cyert himself as well as the effects he experienced from his teaching in the Quantitative Controls in Business course. This is best summarized by the following excerpt from his essay 'Does theory help?' published in the 'Manager's Journal Department' of *The Wall Street Journal*, April 7, 1980,

> My training has given me some simple skills that have been useful in obvious ways. Too few university presidents, for example, know how to read and analyze financial statements effectively. With a basic knowledge of cost accounting, I have been able to ease some of my university's financial problems by singling out for corrective measures activities that were running significant deficits or unusual expenses. Several nonacademic activities could be dropped without affecting the academic quality of the university, and others that were 'living too high' had to be curtailed.'

6 CONCLUSION

To summarize, we have here described some lesser-known research activities of R.M. Cyert with an emphasis on their effects in changing important parts of auditing and accounting practice. The significance of these changes was judged to be sufficient to warrant the historical study by Tucker and Lordi (1997) from which we quoted. As can be seen from this history and the AICPA standards manual (from which we also quoted), the initial impacts continue to have aftermaths which extend to the challenges for statistical theory and methodology that we noted in the report of the National Research Council, *Statistical Models and Analysis in Auditing* (1988).

More is involved, however, than we have just described in this summary. In his later years, Dick Cyert became more and more concerned with making theory useful, usable and used. The activities discussed in this chapter helped to provide background for this concern by Cyert as described in his *Wall Street Journal* article from which we quoted. The research strategy followed by Cyert in the Monongahela project provides a way to accomplish what he appeared to have in mind, including the wide-ranging impacts and aftermaths of this research. For those who may be interested in undertaking similar kinds of research we suggest the following for consideration:

1. Be sure you are interested in doing research on ill-structured problems and check your background for the start it can give you in the initial structuring that is likely to be required when dealing with such problems in an analytical manner.
2. Try to work with a Bob Trueblood or some similarly motivated individual who (a) can be critical of your accomplishments and (b) is prepared to carry research results into action when this seems warranted.
3. Be ready to work under severe pressure with tight deadlines and be able to do so without sacrificing your standards for research significance.
4. Beyond the tests of actual use of your results, undertake the added effort to generalize from your research and its applications in order to match your accomplishments with the existing state of knowledge (a) by presenting them, in suitably generalized form, at professional-scientific meetings and (b) by publishing in the scientific-professional literature.

In Cooper and McAlister (1999), the kind of activity we are describing is referred to as 'applications-driven theory' and contrasted with other, more pure, research which is oriented toward 'understanding *per se*'. It can also be contrasted with the 'theory-driven applications' that constitute so much of the research in economics. These contrasts in research strategies do not mean that one or the other of these approaches is wrong and should be abandoned. The promise of research for use and for teaching needs, however, should attend to the times in which it is to be conducted if pertinence is to be attained. For instance, a larger contemporary dose of 'applications-driven theory' would seem to be in order in research on organization design. Such a research strategy would have eliminated or at least ameliorated the lacunae identified by Cooper and Muench (2000) in their search of the literatures for research that could be pertinent to presently occurring problems in organization design. From rule 4, moreover, one might expect further aftermaths in the form of impacts of a research strategy such as the one we have described. This could be manifested in the research activities of others. It could also impact on course content and other aspects of teaching. In any event we believe this could constitute the kinds of research (and teaching) activities and outcomes that would have responded to the concerns expressed by Dick Cyert in his later years. The resulting 'impacts' on use could then be accompanied by further 'aftermaths' with subsequent effects on teaching and research, and so on.

NOTES

* Acknowledgment for support of this research is due to the IC2 Institute of the University of Texas. We also want to express our gratitude to Margaret Cyert for help in securing biographical and other materials on R.M. Cyert.

1. This use of behavioral (laboratory experimental) research techniques may be regarded as another example of Richard Cyert's influence in the development of modern auditing practice. For an extensive review of *A*

Behavioral Theory of the Firm, by Cyert and March, and its relations to accounting problems and practices, see Carl Thomas Devine (1964). (We are indebted to S. Zeff for calling this review to our attention.)
2. See Cooper and Ijiri (1983) for the most recent version.
3. This work also brought us into contact with early uses of electronic computers and mathematical modeling of management problems which were undertaken by George Dantzig (the author of linear programming) at the US Department of the Air Force.
4. National Suppy Co. was subsequently taken over by the AROMCO Steel Co. and lost its separate identity.
5. Rowles subsequently became the president and CEO of the Kentucky Fried Chicken Company.
6. See B.M. Rowles (1953, 1954) where this sampling is referred to as NISS–CL (Non Independent Stratified Sampling–Cluster Equivalent). This novel design also had properties of the 'systematic samples' using a 'random start' which had been developed in Washington in order to avoid disordering files of government agencies that were to be sampled. See Hansen et al. (1953) or Deming (1950) for definitions of these terms.
7. Subsequently IRS, itself, became an extensive user of sampling and other statistical methods.
8. We are indebted to Yuji Ijiri for this compilation.
9. See the discussion of this project on pp. 261 ff. in Bryson (1976).
10. Participation in these activities had further impacts which included a reorientation of Deming's own interests into the potentials of statistical sampling for use by business firms. See, for example, Deming (1960).
11. For a detailed documentation of Trueblood's life and career see Bryson (1976). The firm went through various mergers, acquisitions and changes of name but it still lives on as one of the 'big six' in accounting under the name Deloitte and Touche.
12. A product of the Quantitative Controls in Business course at Carnegie Tech, Justin Davidson was moved from Pittsburgh to Chicago to head the firm's sampling activities. Although possessing only a master's degree in industrial administration, Davidson later became dean of the School of Business at Cornell and then at Ohio State University.
13. Stringer served as chairman of the Committee on Statistical Sampling from 1962 to 1966. See Tucker and Lordi (1997, pp. 114–15). Robert W. Johnson who served as chairman in 1960 and 1965 was also a member of the Monongahela Project and a product of the Quantitative Controls in Business course at Carnegie-Mellon University.
14. We are grateful to S. Zeff for supplying us with this more up-to-date information.

REFERENCES

American Institute of Certified Public Accountants, Inc. (1989), *AICPA Professional Standards*,

Bryson, R.E., Jr. (1976), 'Robert M. Trueblood, CPA: the consummate professional', PhD Thesis, Athens, GA: Georgia State University School of Business Administration.

Cooper, W.W. and Y. Ijiri (1983), *Kohler's Dictionary for Accountants*, 6th edn, Englewood Cliffs, NJ: Prentice-Hall.

Cooper, W.W. and Leigh McAlister (1999), 'Can research be basic and applied? You Bet. It better be for B-schools', *Socio Economic Planning Sciences* **33**, 257–76.

Cooper, W.W. and M.L. Muench (2000), 'Virtual Organizations', *Journal of Organizational Computing and Electronic Commerce* (forthcoming).

Cyert, R.M. and H. Justin Davidson (1962), *Statistical Sampling for Accounting Information*, Englewood Cliffs, NJ: Prentice-Hall.

Cyert, R.M., M.H. DeGroot and C.A. Holt (1978), 'Sequential investment decisions with Bayesian learning', *Management Science* **24**, 712–18.

Cyert, R.M. and Gerald L. Thompson (1968), 'Selecting a portfolio of credit risks by Markov chains', *Journal of Business* **1**, 39–46.

Deming, W.E. (1960), *Sample Design in Business Research*, New York: John Wiley & Sons.

Deming, W.E. (1950), *Some Theory of Sampling*, New York: John Wiley & Sons.

Devine, Carl T. (1964), '*A Behavioral Theory of the Firm*: A review article', *Journal of Accounting Research* **2**, 197–220.

Hansen, M., W. Hurwitz and W.G. Madow (1953), *Sample Survey Methods and Theory*, New York: John Wiley & Sons.

National Research Council, Board of Mathematical Sciences (1988), *Statistical Models and Analysis in Auditing*, Washington, DC: National Academy of Sciences Press.

Rowles, B.M. (1953), 'Auditing uses of statistics – underlying statistical concepts', *Pennsylvania CPA* **24**, 7–10.

Rowles, B.M. (1954), 'Application of statistical sampling techniques to LIFO inventory valuation', *The Accounting Review* **25**, 244–50.

Trueblood, R.M. and R.M. Cyert (1957), *Sampling Techniques in Accounting*, Englewood Cliffs, NJ: Prentice-Hall.

Tucker, James J., III and Frank C. Lordi (1997), 'Early efforts of the U.S. public accounting profession to investigate the use of statistical sampling', *The Accounting Historians Journal* **24**, 93–115.

Wald, A. (1947), *Sequential Analysis*, New York: John Wiley.

Wald, A. (1950), *Statistical Decision Functions*, New York: John Wiley & Sons.

6. Biases in organizational behavior

Massimo Egidi*

1 INTRODUCTION

A large body of experimental results shows that human decisions display systematic deviations from fully rational ones, and that in many cases 'errors' persist even when the rational solution has explicitly been shown to the subjects. This happens both in individual and team decision making. In the case of teams and organizations, systematically erroneous decisions may be made by organizations because – given the bounded rationality of the individuals of which they consist – they may adopt routinized strategies, which are not changed even when they are highly suboptimal.

Levinthal and March (1993) single out a number of 'traps' into which an organization may fall during the process of organizational learning, and among them they analyse the 'failure myopia' and the 'success trap'.

'Failure myopia' consists in the tendency of an organization to ignore or underestimate failures in its activities. The consequence of this form of myopia is the tendency of an organization to overestimate its possibilities of success. A similar phenomenon has been found in the psychology of the individual probabilistic judgment, where it is known as the 'hindsight effect'. As a result of this effect, individuals underestimate past errors in probabilistic assessment and consequently overestimate their evaluative capacities (Fischhoff, 1975).

As regards the 'success trap', the tendency of organizations to focus on success may induce them to persist excessively in the use of procedures and actions that have been associated with successes in the past. Consequently, an organization that falls into this trap tends to anchor its activity in processes of organizational exploitation, to the detriment of research and innovation. Moreover, this tendency may induce organizations not to adapt, or to adapt with difficulty, to changed environmental conditions.

The tendency to extrapolate to inappropriate situations, procedures that in the past have proved efficacious, which is triggered by the emergence of new conditions in a context of routinized behavior, has also been observed at the individual level. In solving repetitive tasks individuals exhibit 'routinized behaviors', that is, they use automatically, and not necessarily deliberately, the procedures they have learned, even in conditions in which they are not efficient.

A key problem is therefore to see whether routinization is created only by the interaction effects among individuals of a team, or whether it is rooted in some features of individual mental activity. There are clues that the second alternative is the right one: the tendency to routinize also exists at the individual level and has been implicitly proved in the studies by Luchins (1942) and Luchins and Luchins (1950). They suggest in fact that individuals, when they cope with repetitive tasks, may 'automatically' use the rules they have learned in a given context even beyond their original domain. This process is called 'mechanization of thought'.

To better clarify this point I have compared the biases emerging in the team activity with those emerging in the activity of individuals facing the same problem. Starting from a previous experiment with Narduzzo (1997), in which, using the game 'Target the Two', we showed that in cooperative contexts team biases may be initiated by a process of routinization, I have run a new experiment in which single individuals were performing the same activities as those teams in the previous experiment. The results of this new experiment suggest that biases emerging when individuals discover a satisficing solution of a problem in a given context, are initiated in the individual's construction of mental models and reinforced and stabilized by the teams' interaction.[1]

As the experiments with Target the Two show, the routinization of the individual's behavior may be a source of biases, because individuals tend to extend the domain of the routine beyond the domain of optimality. The extrapolation of a procedure beyond its domain of validity is the starting-point I shall use to explain how some biases are created by individuals. I shall show that biases in individuals' decision making may result from the process of mental editing by which subjects produce a 'representation' of the decision problem. During this process, individuals make systematic use of default classifications in order to reduce the short-term memory load and the complexity of symbolic manipulation. The result is the construction of an imperfect mental representation of the problem that nevertheless has the advantage of being simple, and yielding 'satisficing' decisions.

Later I shall propose a more detailed definition of 'mental representation'. Briefly, a representation is a way to codify and compress the information on which individuals base their problem-solving activity and construct their strategies. The discovery and the construction of a strategy to solve a problem, especially in the context of repeated games, is a slow and difficult process in which individuals, learning from the experience, build up rules of action, trying to make them as simple and efficient as possible. But there exists a trade-off between the simplicity of representation of a strategy's rules and their efficiency. For simplicity, these rules have to be memorized and represented with some degree of abstraction, so that they are reduced to a manageable number. Raising the level of abstraction with which a strategy's rule is represented, means extending the domain of validity of the rule beyond the field in which it has been tested, thereby leading to the possibility that domains in which the rule is inefficient may be included inadvertently. Therefore an increase in the number of errors in the mental representation of a problem may be the 'natural' effect of the categorization and identification of the building blocks of a strategy. This argument will be discussed in Section 2.

To describe how hidden errors are generated during the categorization of the building blocks of a strategy, we need to understand how individuals build up satisficing solutions, and to compare these solutions with the optimal ones.

One well-known method of problem solving is to decompose a problem recursively into subproblems that can be solved more easily, until elementary solvable subproblems are identified. It is useful to remember that a given problem may be decomposed in a large variety of different ways that also imply different levels of abstraction in the categorization of subproblems. Every decomposition pattern is the result of a different way of codifying information at different levels of abstraction, and gives rise to a different strategy. In Section 2 (third subsection) and Appendix 6A2 we shall compare the optimal decompositions of a problem with other decompositions, which are simpler and more easily learned, but suboptimal. By analysing in full detail a specific puzzle, we shall see that biases emerge from the activity of problem decomposition and extrapolation, in which individuals identify subproblems as building blocks, which do not coincide perfectly with the domain of optimal responses, but also embody suboptimal rules. The formal context in which we shall examine the nature of the 'representations' and the rise of biases during the categorization of subproblems is that of puzzles and finite state machines (automata) (Section 2, first and second subsections).

In Section 3 (fourth subsection) we shall turn our attention to the stability of the representations. The underlying task is to explain the experimental results on the stability of suboptimal strategies. We have to understand why suboptimal strategies, which embody errors, are locally stable, that is, cannot be improved by small changes in the rules.

A very attractive schema to explore the properties of the optimal and suboptimal strategies and their stability, is Kauffman's NK model, because, among other properties, it shows that if there are interdependencies among the rules of a system, then the system admits many suboptimal solutions that are locally stable, that is, cannot be improved by simple mutations.

However, the fitness function in the NK model is a random one. In our context, having identified a strategy with a program (in a world of finite state machines), it is more reasonable to define the fitness of a strategy as efficiency of the program.

The simplest way to define the efficiency of a program is to refer to the number of steps that it requires to achieve the goal. The shorter the path from the starting state to the goal state, the more efficient the strategy. Fitness therefore will be defined in relation to the length of the path connecting the starting and the goal states. This definition is simple and natural if we want to evaluate and compare the efficiency of different programs (strategies).

If we introduce this kind of fitness, then the stability properties of the NK model no longer hold: we shall see, in fact (Section 3, second subsection, and Appendix 6A3) that while the elementary statements of a strategy are interdependent, it is possible to achieve an optimal configuration of the strategy via mutations, and in consequence the suboptimal solutions are not locally stable under mutations.

Therefore a different explanation for the existence and stability of suboptimal strategies has to be found. Here follows a rough sketch of an alternative explanation.

Suppose that an individual has learned a strategy during a sequence of repeated games. Suppose that in a new run he or she encounters a game configuration never previously faced. If the strategy that the individual has adopted is complete, one of the rules of the strategy is applicable by default to the configuration. Suppose that the rule of the strategy that matches with the new configuration is suboptimal in this new context. Then if the individual applies the old rule, the complexity of the strategy is not increased –the list of known rules is still used – but he or she increases the number of inefficient responses, because once more a suboptimal rule is applied.

If on the contrary the individual discovers that a more efficient rule can be activated in response to the new specific condition, he or she must add the new rule to the list, considering it an 'exception' to the rule that was previously used by default. In this case the individual improves the efficiency of the strategy but at the same time increases the complexity of the rule system.

Therefore the trade-off between the simplicity of the strategy's representation and its efficiency emerges once again. I suggest that this trade-off is the driving force that causes the stability of a suboptimal strategy, that is, it prevents individuals from seeking a more efficient strategy when they must cope with only a single or a limited number of 'exceptions' to the known rules.

The problem is that adding one exception to a system of abstract rules does not offer a new, compact representation of the strategy, because if individuals transform a specific exception into a new rule with some degree of generality, the new rule conflicts with many other pre-existing rules of the strategy. Therefore individuals may prefer to maintain the old system, eventually adding a few exceptions, than to rethink new abstract rules, because the mental effort to redefine a subproblem system is higher than the effort to memorize an exception. Therefore a few mutations, even if they improve the system efficiency, are not sufficient to push the system toward a new stable configuration. (The rule system may be characterized by a central core of stable general rules, surrounded by a number of more specific rules that can vary slightly in relation to the different individuals.)

If the number of 'exceptions' becomes too large, and they occur systematically during the game, individuals cannot simply continue to memorize new exceptions, but have to restructure the space of the rules, recodifying information. In other words, they have to change the representation. This change may be highly discontinuous, because it generally requires us to destructure the division of problems and redesign the problem with new building blocks.

Concluding the chapter, I shall use the properties of the representations to suggest an explanation for the discontinuities of the organizational change: a brief comparison of the performances of distributed, parallel organizations, with the hierarchical ones changing their internal rules and escaping from organizational traps, will close the discussion.

2 PUZZLES, AUTOMATA AND PROBLEM SOLVING

To explore problem-solving activity in simplified environments described by systems of rules, it is convenient to choose systems such as puzzles and planned activities.[2]

A puzzle is a game in which a single individual must achieve a given goal, usually by making changes to an initial configuration of the game according to a system of rules and constraints. The rules state what actions may be made for each state of the game, and what their effects will be. A puzzle, therefore, is defined by a system of action rules that operate on configurations or states of the game. Although this type of game has a very simple formal description, it still displays most of the typical properties of general problem-solving models. In fact planning with artificial intelligence (AI) systems, which is one of the most important areas of problem solving, has the same basic definitions as puzzle solving.[3]

There is a second reason for choosing the context of puzzle solving and planning in AI. Because it is a simplified context in which to examine the properties of problems, a puzzle is a good platform to analyse the decomposition in subproblems and therefore to study the solution of a problem as a cooperative process; in fact, if it is possible to decompose the strategy to achieve the goal of the puzzle into a set of independent substrategies, then it is possible to attribute to different individuals the task of discovering and playing the substrategies. A puzzle can therefore be transformed into a game played by numerous cooperating individuals; the game remains formally the same, but with the essential difference that in this case a strategy must be discovered by a team rather than by an individual, so that a process of organizational rather than individual learning takes place.

The first two subsections provide some basic definitions related to problem-solving theory. Readers trained in the field may jump to the third subsection.

A puzzle can be represented very simply by defining the characteristics of the *states* of the game and the *rules* by which they are modified. A well-known puzzle is the Rubik cube – a cube with six faces consisting of nine tiles in six different colors. The rules of the puzzle essentially permit the player to rotate the sections of the cube and rearrange the positions of the tiles. Usually, the final configuration of the game is the one in which each face consists of tiles of the same color. This puzzle, like all others, can therefore be represented as, a condition–action system, or in other words, a list of system-states coupled with the rules to be applied. The system can be depicted as shown in Table 6.1 where S_1, ... S_N are (all) the states of the game and A_1, A_2 ..., A_m are the actions that can be performed. This representation describes the puzzle as an array in which the first column contains the states of the system, and the others contain the actions permitted (in the Rubik cube, $N \cong 3{,}000{,}000{,}000$).

Table 6.1 Condition–action array

Conditions (states)		Actions (rules)		
S_1	A_i	A_s	...	A_p
S_2	A_j	A_r	...	A_g
S_3	A_k	A_h	...	A_1
...	...		...	
S_N	A_g	A_n	...	A_s

Note that if the states of the game are observable, we can know the configuration that is achieved by the puzzle when we apply a given move to a given configuration. In other words, by applying to the state S_i the action (or operator) A_j we get the new state S_{ki}, for all $i, k \in N, j \in m$.[4]

Therefore we can construct a new array that shows the links among the puzzle's configurations, as shown in Table 6.2. In the table, we have codified the configurations (conditions) of the puzzle with progressive numbers 1, 2, 3, ... *N*. The same holds for the 'successors' or 'next configurations' of a given configuration, that is, the configurations that are reached by applying the permissible rules (A_1, A_2 ..., A_m) to a given configuration. In this form the table exhibits the links between every state and its successors but showing not the configurations but only the numbers that denote them. This new table is called the *links array*. Each row of the links array therefore consists of the following elements: the first is the number that denotes the state of the system, that is, the 'state label'; the other elements in the row are the numbers that denote the successors. Thus, if we apply rules A_1, A_2 ..., A_m to the state *k*, we obtain the 'successors', that is, the states n_k, m_k ..., w_k.

In this context a problem is defined by a pair of states, defined as initial state and goal state, and to solve a problem means to achieve the goal state from the initial state through a sequence of rule applications. This sequence is also called a 'plan' in AI planning literature, and together with the definitions I have provided, it fully applies to that field (Yang, 1997). Of course a problem for which there is no sequence connecting the starting configuration with the goal, is a problem for which there is no solution.

As I have, said, in order to devise a strategy to achieve the goal, it is necessary to find a sequence of actions A_{s1}, A_{s2} ..., A_{sn} that, if applied systematically to the starting configuration, leads the system to the goal configuration. This means that a strategy can be described as a subset of the condition–action array of the puzzle (Table 6.1), in which for every condition there corresponds one and only one action. A strategy can therefore be considered as a selection of the condition–action array (Table 6.1), that is, a list of 'instructions' of the condition–action form; of course *effective* strategies must be composed of instructions that allow players to achieve the goal (more or less quickly), but the definition also encompasses strategies that do not achieve a goal.

Table 6.2 Links array

	Actions				
	A_1	A_2	A_3	...	A_m
States	New states				
1	n_1	m_1	r_1	...	w_1
2	n_2	m_2	r_2	...	w_2
3	n_3	m_3	r_3	...	w_3
...					

Note that the definition of *strategy* is equivalent to that of *program* in computation theory. In fact, a strategy as just defined is nothing but a list of instructions of the condition–action type, selected in such a way to achieve the goal, starting from an initial configuration: which is precisely the definition given to 'program' in computation theory.[5] The most important difference with the general definition of a program like a computing machine (Turing machine, Post system, or equivalent mathematical device) is that here the machine is defined as a list of instructions of the condition–action type and therefore is an automaton, which is computationally less powerful than a Post system. Holland's classifiers, which are computationally equivalent to Turing machines, are based on more powerful condition–action systems (Holland et al., 1988).

Abstraction and Categorization

So far, we have considered puzzles in which one starting state and one goal state are defined. But it is useful to drop this restriction, especially if we consider that in the best-known puzzles and games the definitions of the starting and goal states are given with some degree of abstraction, and therefore there are generally many starting states and many goal positions. In chess, for example, the goal configuration is defined in abstract terms, as any configuration in which the king is under attack whatever move he makes; in the Rubik puzzle a state is given by the positions of the colored tiles along the faces, and the moves are rotations that can be applied whatever the game configuration of the puzzle. And so on and so forth.

The simplest way to classify a set of states in a category is by using the symbol # (don't care): a state is in general represented by a set of atomic elements or variables (in the Rubik cube the distribution and the colors of the tiles of the faces, in chess the board positions of the pieces, and so on). Therefore while a specific state S_k may be represented by attributing a value to each of the atomic elements ($S_k = \{v_1\ v_2 \ldots v_n\}$), at a higher level of abstraction we can define states in which some of the atomic elements may assume any of the legal values. For example, by writing $\{v_1 \# v_3 \ldots v_n)\}$ we 'do not care' about the value of the variable v_2, and define a class of states, those that are identical for all variables but v_2. The level of description of a problem, in which all states and rules are specified, is called *ground level.*

In many games there are a large variety of starting configurations, sometimes given at random, an abstract definition of the goal configurations, and the rules of the game are given with some degree of generality. If states, rules, starting and goal configurations are given with some degree of abstraction, problems and subproblems are defined as pairs of sets of states, and to solve a problem means discovering a strategy for achieving one of the goals, for any given starting configuration,

It is easy to recognize that this way of defining states and rules holds in all areas of problem-solving activities: problems, states and rules are defined at some abstraction level. A problem may therefore be defined by a pair of *sets*, the set of starting state and the set of goal states, given the rules that apply to the states.

Subproblems Identification

A classic procedure for decomposing a problem into subproblems is based on the construction of an and/or tree of subproblems (Newell and Simon, 1972; Nilsson, 1971).

Here it is sufficient to outline briefly the procedure's principles. To decompose a problem P we have to identify subproblems and connect with them each other in such a way as to reduce the original problem to a combination of subproblems. Suppose that we split the original problem into N subproblems, $P_1, P_2, \ldots, P_N$; there are two alternative ways in which a problem can be split:

1. In order to solve the original problem P we may have to solve P_1, *and* P_2, ... *and* P_N. This is called an *and* decomposition.
2. In order to solve P we may have to solve *either* P_1, *or* P_2, ... *or* P_N. This is called an *or* decomposition.

An elementary problem is a problem that is immediately solvable by applying one of the rules (actions) of the game.

The decomposition procedure works as follows: suppose that we split the original problem into N subproblems, $P_1, P_2, \ldots, P_M$ (*and/or* decomposition). It may be that P_1 is an elementary problem, otherwise it has to be in turn decomposed into subproblems, $P_{11}, P_{12}, \ldots P_{1M}$ and so on recursively. The same holds for $P_2, \ldots, P_M$; therefore the process of decomposition continues until all subproblems are reduced to elementary subproblems or some subproblem proves unsolvable. The elementary subproblems at which the recursion process stops are also called *terminals.*

Any *solvable* problem can therefore be decomposed into a set of *and/or* subproblems. With the usual conventions of graph theory we can represent the problem as an and/or tree of subproblems.

An example of a decomposition tree is provided in Appendix 6A2.

Once we have successfully decomposed a problem, at the same time we have identified a strategy to solve it. In fact, call $P_{A1}, P_{A2}, \ldots, P_{AN}$ the elementary subproblems (terminals); by definition each of them is represented by a pair $\{S_{Ak}\ S_{Ah}\}$ of states that are connected by an action A: $P = S_{Ak} \rightarrow A \rightarrow S_{Ah}$; therefore instead of using the pair $\{S_k\ S_h\}$, we can represent a terminal state as a pair state–action $S_{Ak} \rightarrow A$.

Here again the states are normally specified at some level of abstraction, that is, they will be described by strings of the type $S_{Ak} = \{v_1\ v_2\# \ldots \#\ v_n\}$, and in consequence the whole set of terminal problems can be represented by an array of the type illustrated in Table 6.3. The array contains all terminal states, and therefore represents the strategy that the players have discovered. The terminal subproblems in fact are all subproblems identified during the problem decomposition that can be solved with an elementary action and therefore, starting from one of the initial configurations, the player can apply sequentially the actions prescribed by the terminals until the goal is achieved.

Table 6.3 A strategy as a set of terminal problems

		Terminal states						Actions
S_1	=	#	*vi*	...	#	*vj*	*vh*	A_i
S_2	=	*vk*	#	...	*vr*	#	*vt*	A_j
S_3	=	*vs*	#	...	*vj*	*vx*	#	A_s
...		...		...				
S_N	=	*vb*	*vx*	...	#	#	#	A_r

Note that many of the terminal subproblems are in some abstract form: should all terminal subproblems be defined at ground level, the list of the statements would be enormous, and the advantage of decomposing the problem would vanish.

A decomposition is therefore a way of building up a hierarchical system of abstractions. The states of the system that are involved in the strategy are classified in categories, according to the decomposition principles, and to each category is attached the action to be performed. Of course the lower the number of categories, the simpler the representation of the problem.

Comparing Optimal Decompositions with Satisficing Ones

Remember that if the starting and goal configurations are unique, individual problem-solving activity consists in a search for a sequence of actions that, applied to the starting configuration, enable the goal to be achieved. Generally there are many starting and goal configurations, and the problem is to determine whether there are classes of starting configurations that lead to classes of goal configurations *with the same sequence of actions.*

But of course this property, which is highly desirable, does not hold in general: it may be impossible to connect all the configurations of a starting class with the configurations of a goal class by using the same sequence of actions. More interestingly, it may be possible to connect the two sets with the same sequence, but the sequence is optimal only for some configurations, not for all of them.

To understand the question better, it is useful to compare a 'natural' decomposition with an optimal one. At the ground level, an optimal solution of a puzzle is a minimal path connecting a starting configuration with the goal. A well-known procedure to find a minimal path between two states is based on the idea of moving back from the goal to the initial configuration. Starting from a state that has been defined as the goal, we can move back to its predecessors, and so on recursively until a starting configuration has been achieved. In this way we can discover the minimal path from a state and the goal, if it exists. In more detail, the backward procedure to identify the minimal paths, works as follows: starting from a goal configuration G, we can find all its 'predecessors', that is, all the states (Table 6.2) that have G as a successor. This can easily be done by selecting the rows of Table 6.2 in which the G state appears. Call X the set of predecessors of G. Next we build up the set X' of configurations that are predecessors of the elements of X (and do not belong to G). Next we continue back including in X'' the predecessors of X' (provided that they do not belong either to X' or to G) and so on until all states of the puzzle are achieved. It is thus possible to reconstruct all the links between the final configuration, its predecessors, the predecessors of the predecessors and so on, and to classify the predecessors for the distance (number of steps) from the goal configuration. In so doing, we build up a tree directed to G. The set $B = XUX'UX''$ ... is the 'basin of attraction' of the goal G. If the problem or the puzzle has been defined at some level of abstraction, we can expect many goal configurations. In this case we can easily extend the backward procedure to all goal configurations, and discover the global basin of attraction. Of course if there are states in the set of starting states that do not belong to the global basin of attraction this means that for these states the problem cannot be solved. For obvious reasons we limit the discussion to solvable puzzles, or to puzzles defined on domains which are solvable.

So far, we have identified a *minimal* tree rooted in the goal G, that is, a tree that connects the starting state S with the goal through the "predecessors" $X, X', \dots X^i \dots$ (where G and S may be nodes or set of nodes, in relation to the definition of the game and its properties). The minimal tree identifies all the possible optimal decompositions of the original problem. In fact, we can decompose the original problem $\{S, G\}$ in many different ways by using elementary sub-problems as for example $\{S, X^k\}$, $\{X^k, X^h\}, \dots$ $\{X^i, G\}$, where X^i is a predecessor of G, X^k a predecessor of X^h, and so on. Therefore by construction for every given sub-problem $\{X^k, X^h\}$, all the elements of X^k are at the same distance from the elements of X^h.

Any decomposition that takes only the X^s as intermediate sub-goals will lead to an optimal solution i.e. to a minimal path from the starting configuration to the final goal. But when an individual decides a decomposition and identifies an intermediate sub-goal X', there are no guaranties that X' belongs to the set of optimal X^s. Therefore a *satisficing* decomposition does not coincide necessarily with an *optimal* one. A clear example in which X' does not coincide with an optimal one, is discussed in Appendix 6A2.

Vice versa, suppose that an individual identifies a specific subproblem, and discovers an optimal action A: if he or she tries to apply the action A to a generalization of the subproblem, obtained by extending by default the original domain of applicability, a systematic error may be introduced. In fact the domain of applicability of the rule A – which was optimal if applied to the original configuration – does not necessarily coincide with the domain of optimality. The rule A may be suboptimal if applied to some configuration that belongs to the extended domain. As a consequence, when individuals try to extend by default generalization a rule that was optimal in a given context, they may introduce hidden errors. In Appendix 6A2 we describe in detail an example of this phenomenon, in the context of a hyper-simplified Rubik cube game.

A further comparison between satisficing and optimal decomposition helps to understand the question better. After a full process of decomposition, by a backward procedure, we create a hierarchy of connected subproblems, at different levels of abstraction. The decomposition is optimal, because it identifies the minimal tree, and therefore the minimal number of actions to be made to achieve the goal. The key point is that we do not have, in general, a 'perfect representation' of the units X_i that we have identified by the optimal decomposition: as we have seen, in general a unit X_i is not described by only one abstract string. But when we decompose a problem, we generally describe and conjecture any terminal subproblem on the basis of *one* abstract string and therefore we may miss some element or include too many elements in the class defined by the string.

This explains why a systematic mismatch exists between the *optimal* subproblems and the *conjectured* subproblems. If we do not create new codifications, for example taking into account the relations among the atomic components, the terminal subproblems that individuals discover do not identify perfectly the optimal subproblems, and induce individuals to make imperfect extrapolations and abstractions.[7] On the other hand a satisficing decomposition may identify rules that are optimal for a relevant part of the domains of applicability.

This happens as a consequence of some features of the learning processes: one of the typical ways to identify a decomposition pattern, mainly for repeated games in which players have to learn a strategy while playing, is the attempt to induce general rules from examples. Induction in this sense (Holland et al., 1988) is the fundamental force that drives, via abstraction, classification and extrapolation, the categorization and the creation of a representation of a strategy.[8]

This process is very powerful, and has some similarities with the process by which children learn language skills: it is astonishing that a three-year-old child is a perfect speaker of his or her native language, without knowing anything of the syntactical and grammatical rules. The child's ability to extrapolate general rules from examples is the key element of his or her growing linguistic skill. But extrapolation may lead to curious errors, which adults systematically correct.

If players learn the rules of action while playing, a similar process occurs: some of the elementary subproblems that players identify locally, may coincide with the optimal ones. Therefore, by abstracting and extrapolating the rules, players do not realize the limits of applicability of the abstract rules. They are not induced to revise these rules until unexpected new configurations arise.

In concluding this section, we note that the level of abstraction with which the strategy's statements are represented, depends upon the way players analyse the problem which in turn depends upon the way the problem is codified. Individuals may try to discover a satisficing or an optimal decomposition, on the grounds of a given representation, or may try to recodify the problem and change the representation itself.

3 APPLYING THE NK MODEL TO PUZZLES AND PROBLEM SOLVING

We have seen that there are many different, both optimal and suboptimal, ways to decompose and represent a problem. The related question is the stability of the representations. From

Target the Two and other experimental contexts we have some evidence of the persistence of suboptimal solutions of given problems. The question is to explain why suboptimal strategies, which embody errors, are locally stable, that is, cannot be improved by small changes, by 'correcting' the specific errors, for example, by mutations of specific strategy rules.

The most important contender for tackling the problem is Kauffman's NK model, which allows us to represent the learning of a strategy as an evolutionary process of rule mutation and selection.

The NK model has the following main features: the evolution of an organism, or in general of a complex biological system, is guided by its 'fitness', that is, by its reproductive success in the environment; the characteristics that determine the fitness of an organism can be represented in a discrete space because they are a list of 'traits' that can assume different values.

In Kauffman's original approach, 'traits' can be proteins or genes, each of which can assume different 'configurations' or 'values' (alleles). An organism is characterized by N traits, each of which assumes a given value. A mutation is nothing other than a change in the value of a trait (allele), and therefore to explore the effect of single mutations on the organism's fitness we have to change the values of the traits, one at a time. A crucial property of the traits is 'epistasis': when a mutation is introduced, the effect on the organism's fitness usually depends on the value of other traits.

> The assumption that each gene contributes to overall fitness independently of all other genes is clearly an idealization. In a genetic system with N genes, the fitness contribution of one or another allele of one gene may often depend upon the alleles of some of the remaining $N - 1$ genes. Such dependencies are called *epistatic interactions*. (Kauffman, 1989, p. 539)

Let K be the average number of genes that contribute to the fitness variation of the organism when a mutation occurs, that is, the average number of epistatic interactions. K may vary from $K = 0$ (total independence) to $K = N - 1$ (total interdependence). In the first case ($K = 0$), the effect of a mutation on the fitness depends solely upon the single gene that is affected by the mutation; therefore by comparing the different effects of different mutations on the same gene, we can discover the allele that produces the higher increase in the fitness. If we sequentially do the same comparison on all the genes, then for every gene we can discover the alleles that make the best contribution to the fitness; therefore we can increase the fitness of the organism to its maximum value, acting on every gene independently. This means that an organism with zero epistatic interactions may achieve an optimal configuration in response to a sequence of random mutations.

Kauffman shows that as the epistatic interaction grows, the number of local optima increase, and an organism that is affected by mutations may remain trapped forever, once it has reached a local optimum.

The NK model can be applied to every complex system, and therefore it can be useful to describe the properties of complex organizations. The only caveat is to remember that in the NK model it is assumed that epistatic interactions are so complex that the statistical features of their consequences are modeled by random fitness functions. With this assumption, Kauffman shows, among other properties, that the basins of attraction of local optima of low-K systems are larger, on average, than the basins of high-K systems. Moreover, the higher their fitness, the larger their basin of attraction. One of the consequences of these properties, as Kauffman suggests, is that systems with a low K value are expected to outperform systems with a high K and therefore are more likely to be selected during evolution.

The most important properties of the NK model concern features deriving from complexity, and in particular from the decomposability of complex systems. Among the recent developments in this field, important contributions have been made by Page (1996); Frenken et al., 1998; Marengo, 1999. Marengo provides a definition of independence among the subsystems of a complex entity, and explores the properties of near-decomposability of the systems. The idea is that to optimize the fitness of a complex system, we can try to optimize parts of it separately. This is possible if the contribution to the fitness of any part is independent of the contribution of the other parts. If the elements of the complex system are K 'epistatically' interdependent, this means that K of them on average jointly contribute to the fitness, and a complex system is therefore decomposable into subsystems of K average size, each of which can be optimized separately.

In the extreme situation, $K = 0$, and then the single elements of the system contribute separately to the fitness: in consequence the discovery of the configuration with optimal fitness may be realized by modifying the alleles independently of each other.

On this basis, we can consider each element of a string of conditions–actions as a genetic trait, and therefore try to apply the NK model to the world of puzzles. Referring to Table 6.1, a condition–action pair can be considered as a gene, and the different possible actions triggered by a 'condition' give rise to different alleles of the same gene.

We may therefore treat a puzzle as an NK model and examine its properties – in particular those that concern the 'ruggedness' of the fitness surface, that is, the distribution of local and global optima in the space of the fitness function. (See also Kauffman, 1989, pp. 680–90.)

The NK model is intended to analyse properties of complex systems and has been used for this purpose in many fields, beyond the specific field of biology in which it has been created (see, for example, Levinthal, 1997). If we drop the assumption, which is typical of the original context, that is, to consider the fitness of the system as a random function, and introduce a measure of efficiency into the system, some of the NK model's properties no longer hold. In Appendix 6.3 it is shown in fact that $K > 0$ in puzzles, that is, that the elementary statements of a strategy are interdependent, because in introducing a different rule of action for a given system configuration (a mutation), the fitness of the system may get better or worse in relation to the other rules adopted for the strategy. But, despite the fact that the epistatic degree K is positive, it is shown that it is possible to achieve an optimal configuration of the strategy via mutations, and in consequence the suboptimal solutions are not locally stable under mutations.

These properties hold if one assumes the fitness as a variable that measures the 'efficiency' of the system. The system here can be identified as a strategy or a program, and it follows that we can measure the efficiency of a program in relation to the number of steps it requires to achieve the goal. Given a starting configuration S_j, the shorter the number k of actions $A_{j1}, A_{j2}, ..., A_{jk}$ with which the goal is achieved using P, the higher the efficiency of the program. When there are many starting configurations it is natural to extend the definition of efficiency of the strategy P in relation to the sum of the lengths of the chains connecting the different starting states with the goal, obtained by applying P. It is obvious that the problem is to find the strategy P^* that minimizes this length. Therefore we can choose as efficient any function $f(P)$ that is monotonically decreasing with the global length of the chains connecting the starting configurations with the goals. A simple example is given by $f(P) = N_s – L$, where L is the global length of the chains and N_s the global length of the network defined by the links array.[9]

Cycles in Random Strategies[10]

Instead of considering a strategy as the result of a conscious process of decomposition of a problem into subproblems, we could investigate whether a strategy can be the result of an unintentional adaptive process through which the system reaches an optimal configuration by way of successive mutations.

In order to deal with this point, it is first necessary to answer the following question: is it possible to determine a strategy by randomly choosing one action for each condition of the matrix that describes the puzzle (Table 6.1)? How can we be certain that we shall successfully reach the final goal of the game through a strategy based only on a random selection of the legal rules?

We have to check whether, once we have randomly chosen a sequence of actions from the game matrix, we obtain a list of conditions–actions that constitute a 'consistent' strategy; that is, a strategy that will allow us to reach the goal regardless of the starting configuration. Here 'consistent ' refers to the player's conduct when he or she decomposes the problem into subproblems. If a rule of the strategy transforms state A to state B and at the same time the strategy comprises a set of rules which transform state B to state A, this creates a 'vicious circle', which denotes that the player has been inconsistent in decomposing the problem. Rules giving rise to cycles must therefore be excluded from a strategy, if strategies are to be effective, that is, to allow players to reach the goal.[11]

The set of condition–action rules that describe a game (Table 6.1), can be represented by an equivalent graph, in which every condition is a node, and every action is an arc connecting two nodes. A more precise definition of the equivalence between graphs and arrays, both with some elementary notions of graph theory are given in Appendix 6A2.

Having considered as *consistent* a strategy that allows us to reach the final stage regardless of the starting configuration, the selection of a consistent strategy means choosing the rules in such a way that from every node there is only one path leading to the goal node; this set of paths directed from the nodes to the root forms a 'directed tree'. In other words, a consistent strategy is a selection, within the graph, of a tree rooted in the final goal and connected with all other configurations.

This kind of tree is usually called a 'spanning tree' of the graph: a spanning tree of a graph, G, is a tree containing all vertices of G. It is well known (Berge, 1985, pp. 22, 24) that if a graph is connected, then it can contain a spanning tree. There are several ways to build up a spanning tree rooted in the goal node from a connected graph. Many of these trees will be highly suboptimal, and in fact the problem of finding an optimal strategy is equivalent to the problem of finding a minimal tree.

By definition, a spanning tree is not directed. To describe an effective strategy, we require something more restrictive than a spanning tree, that is, a spanning tree in which every arc is directed to the root.

Before discussing tree optimization by mutation, we need to see what happens with a random strategy. It is likely that if the action rules are selected at random, then quite often the selected links give rise not to a tree, but to a graph with cycles, and that as a result the strategy will not allow the final objective to be reached from all starting configurations. The graph that represents the random strategy in this case would be made up of disjointed cycles: starting from a node and applying the rules of the strategy, we could enter a cycle without the possibility of achieving the goal.

This is very likely to happen, especially in games where, given an action, a reverse action is also allowed, as in MiniRubik: in this game if condition Y can be attained from condition X through action A, there is also the possibility of moving from Y to X through a symmetric action. In a random selection, both actions could be selected and that would create a cycle (an inconsistent strategy).

It is possible to show that if the randomly chosen strategy does not allow cycles, it is formed by a spanning tree rooted in the goal, in which all nodes are directed toward the goal. This means that by applying a consistent (without cycles) strategy to every starting configuration, after a finite number of steps the goal will be achieved. In terms of finite state machines theory, this means that the finite machine represented by the strategy converges, after a finite number of steps, to a stable point. In terms of graph theory, this means that from every node there exists a path directed to the goal. For a demonstration of this, see Appendix 6A1.

Summing up, to ensure that it is possible to reach the final stage regardless of the initial stage, the graph must be directed and connected. For every node of the graph there must be a directed path connecting it to the goal node. Even though this assumption is restrictive, in relation to general graph properties, it is the mathematical formulation of the idea that the graph represents a problem that allows an attainable solution. Chess is a good example of this situation, because it is a game in which players may be trapped in loops while a large set of attainable goal configurations exist.

Convergence to an Optimal Strategy via Mutations

It is useful at this stage to examine the epistatic properties of puzzles, to understand to what degree strategies can be decomposed into independent components, and what are the properties of the solutions. We shall establish some counterintuitive properties of the solutions: first, we shall see that puzzles allow only stable optimal solutions, while stable suboptimal solutions are not permitted. Second, we shall also show that there is a positive epistatic degree, that is, introducing a mutation on a gene, the effect on the fitness depends upon the alleles of other genes. In terms of problem solving this means that a strategy is not decomposable into independent elementary statements (the genes), but nevertheless, against the prediction of the NK model, it is possible to achieve the optimal solution by optimizing iteratively the elementary statements. In evolutionary terms, this means that a strategy may evolve through mutations starting from a random (consistent) configuration and reaching an optimal configuration. As discussed above, we assume that the fitness function of a condition–action system is defined in relation to the length of the spanning tree of the strategy, in such a way as to measure the efficiency of the strategy.[12]

Assume that a strategy is given, either at random or as the outcome of a learning process, and that it is consistent, that is, it allows an individual to achieve the goal. As usual the strategy is described by a list of condition–action rules, and equivalently by a tree directed to the goal node (or a forest directed to the set of goals). Note that a strategy is a tree extracted by the graph that represents all the possible runs of the game. The graph is equivalent to the links array of the game (Table 6.2), and 'embodies' the strategy tree, exactly as the links array embodies the strategy. Therefore, if we introduce mutations in the strategy, that is, we change some action rules, this implies that we change some nodes and the related links of the strategy, deleting some nodes and including new nodes in the strategy tree. More precisely, suppose we modify a strategy by introducing a mutation in one of its elements, say in the condition N: suppose that in the tree the condition (node) N was linked with the node K by the action A; now we change the action A, and therefore we delete the successor K and link N with a new successor M by the new action A'. In sum, changing a link means changing the successor of the node N. The problem is to verify whether it is possible, starting from a randomly chosen tree, to modify it by mutations until it is transformed into a minimal tree (that is, a tree whose paths from the starting configurations to the goal have minimal length).

Suppose that at a certain stage of the process we improve the fitness of the strategy by removing a link between the node N and its successor K and connecting N to the new node M; this means that *at this stage of the process M* is nearer than K to the goal. But later on, after some mutations on the nodes included in the path between K and the goal, K may become nearer to the goal than M. Therefore we have to remove the link between N and M and link again N to K to increase the fitness. This shows that there is interdependence among the nodes, having defined the fitness in relation to the distance between the starting and the goal configurations: the epistatic degree of the system is positive, because the variation of the fitness when we change a rule depends upon the distances of many nodes from the goal. A more detailed discussion on this point, with an example of epistasis, is reported in Appendix 6A3.

The previous observations on epistatic interdependence show that to reduce a given tree to a minimal one, the order with which mutations are introduced is significant. If, starting for a randomly chosen tree, we introduce mutations in a special order, that is, the order defined by the backward algorithm, the effects of epistasis disappear. In fact, when we start up the backward algorithm, the order with which mutations are introduced is the following: first, mutations are applied to the nodes (genes) that can be directly linked to the root; call these 'nodes of level 1'; next, mutations are applied to the nodes of level 2, that is, nodes that can be directly linked with the nodes of level 1, and so on. At every step, any new node is linked by the algorithm to some node already in the right position, that is, at a minimal distance (level) from the root. For this reason, once a node has been linked by a mutation to some other node, it will never be removed again; the nodes are placed at the minimal distance from the root in a special order so that the links cannot be revised. In general the order is different and epistasis is positive.

Revision of the links among nodes may be needed – as shown in Appendix 6A3 – because the path from a node to the goal has not been selected by moving backward from the goal to the node, and at any step choosing the minimal distance, but moving in some other order that does not ensure, when we select the adjacent node with higher fitness, that the candidates have been put at the minimal distance from the goal.

It is important to note that the backward procedure defines the order with which mutations are introduced: a special order by which it is always possible to build up the minimal tree, provided that the graph is connected. This means, however, that if this strategy is chosen at the beginning of the process of mutation, the optimal strategy can be achieved by introducing mutations in a reverse order. Consequently there are no locally stable suboptimal solutions: in fact the local stability of a configuration means by definition that it is impossible to improve the fitness of the configuration by introducing single mutations.

But for every nonoptimal configuration it is possible to apply the backward procedure, and in consequence to achieve an optimal configuration. This means that suboptimal strategies are not stable, but converge to some optimal one.

Moreover, the optimal configuration can be achieved even if the order of mutations is randomly chosen, provided that all elements of the strategy are submitted to mutations until the fitness can no longer be improved. In fact suppose that we decide to introduce mutations with a random order, say $R = \{7, 2, 12, 34, 1, 5, ...\}$ (the set R must be a random permutation of the set $\{1, 2, 3, ..., N\}$).

After a run, having applied mutations to all genes with the order defined by R, it is possible that the fitness can be improved further; in this case, starting a second run and again selecting the favorable mutations with the same order R, we will improve the fitness once more; we can continue with subsequent runs until there are no more mutations that increase the fitness. We have to show that the process converges.

To this end, suppose that the right order to intervene on genes, defined by the backward procedure, is given by $\{n_1, n_2, n_3, ..., n_N\}$ (n_1 is the first node to be linked to the root, n_2 is the second node to be linked (either to the root or to n_1 and so on).

Suppose now we introduce mutations with a different order. After the first run, at least one node; that is, n_1, will be linked optimally to the goal. In the second run, the same reasoning applies to the nodes that can be linked with $\{n_1\}$, and so on. Therefore the process converges, and in the worst case after N runs all nodes will be placed at their minimal distance.

It follows that whatever order we follow to introduce mutations, the process converges to an optimal solution after no more than N runs.

The results of this section show that the NK model's predictions are no longer valid if we assume a fitness function that measures the efficiency of the strategies: in fact in the NK model, when $K > 0$ and the fitness is random, stable suboptimal solutions emerge. On the contrary, we have now shown that with our fitness, while $K > 0$, only optimal stable solutions exist. These results have curious implications in relation to problem-solving properties: the system (a puzzle) does not allow a perfect division of the problem in elementary subproblems, because the elementary statements are not independent ($K > 0$): but at the same time the system converges to an optimal solution via simple mutations, that is, solving the elementary subproblems separately.

Notes on Near Decomposability

We have seen that because of the epistatic interaction among the nodes, the order with which the mutations are introduced matters. If we label the condition–action statements of a strategy $1, 2, 3, ... N$ and put $L = \{1, 2, 3, ... N\}$, any permutation R of these elements defines a different order, and we have seen that if we analyse the condition–action statements according to the order R^* prescribed by the backward procedure, then the fitness can be optimized finding the optimal value of the fitness separately for any condition–action statement in one iteration (N steps). A different order may require many iterations in the solution process, because of the interaction effects among statements. Moreover we have seen that the list R^* can be considered as composed of subgroups $R_1, R_2, \ldots$ of statements (nodes) in relation to the (minimal) distance 1, 2, ... of the nodes from the goal, and that the subgroups must be optimized sequentially.

This suggests that we should try to identify subsets of L such that it is possible to optimize separately the statements of each subset. A good candidate for the separability of the optimization is the class of the graphs that can be disconnected by the removal of a single node (commonly called *separable* graphs).

For example, let us suppose that the graph of a puzzle is structured as follows: there are a pair of subgraphs, A and B, connected by one link to the goal-state but otherwise mutually independent. It is therefore possible to modify the action rules of the subgraph A without influencing modifications on subgraph B.

In the example (Table 6.4), the player can verify that, as reported in Figure 6.1, two sets $A = \{1, 2, 3, 4\}$ and $B = \{1, 5, 6, 7, 8\}$ are connected with each other only by the goal-state 1. This implies that if the links among the states of the set A are modified by mutations, this part of the strategy contributes to the fitness independently from the part acting on B. The same holds for the set B.

Table 6.4 A decomposable problem

	Adjacency matrix								Links array			
										Actions		
	1	2	3	4	5	6	7	8	State	A	B	C
1			1						1	3	–	–
2	1		1						2	1	–	3
3		1		1					3	–	2	4
4		1							4	2	–	–
5	1					1			5	1	–	6
6					1		1	1	6	–	7	5
7						1			7	6	8	–
8					1		1		8	–	5	7

Here each subgraph contributes separately to the fitness of the system. Note that this property is consistent with the notion of decomposability put forward by Page (1996); Frenken et al., (1998); and Marengo (1999). It is therefore possible to optimize separately the two subtrees that compose the tree: we obtain part of the optimal configuration by acting only on states 2, 3, 4 and not on states 5, 6, 7, 8. The results obtained by acting on one of the subsets need not to be revised later on, when we act on the other subsets to achieve the optimum.

As an exercise, the reader can verify that the optimal strategy exists, and it consists of two sequences that can be computed independently: the substrategy ABA is the optimal substrategy related to the subgraph A, while ABAB is the optimal substrategy related to the subgraph B; the whole strategy is the sequence (ABAABAB) in the links array of Table 6.4.

On the left-hand side of Table 6.4, 1 have reported the adjacency matrix of the graph, that is, the array of the connections among the nodes of the graph. Recalling the properties of the adjacency matrix, we can establish the connection between the approach to decomposability put forward by Simon and Ando, 1961 and that proposed by Page, 1996 and Marengo, 1999.

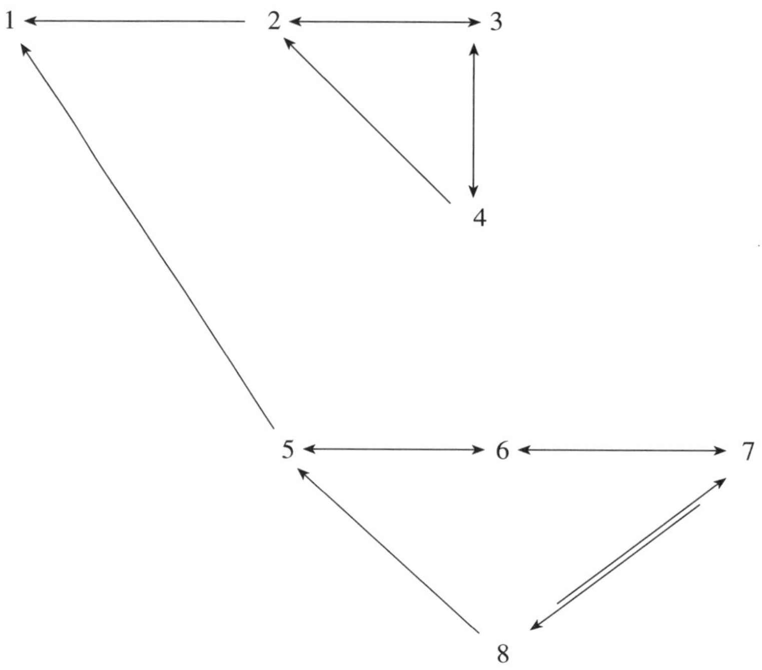

Figure 6.1 A separable graph

Indeed, the property of decomposability can be extended to all *separable* graphs. In conclusion, we can observe that if the graph of the game is separable, then the list of statements that form a solving strategy can be decomposed in subsets that can be separately optimized. This of course gives a more efficient method to find out the best strategy, because it defines independent subsets of genes (that is, an order) that allow us to intervene with mutations only once without being forced to revise the choice during the process. Therefore even though it is true that the optimal solution is achieved whatever the order of mutations, a purely random order would require a huge computation, which humans typically do not make. Note that, by introducing a measure of efficiency based on the length of the game tree, we have 'endogenized' the fitness function: as a consequence, the properties of decomposability of a strategy depend upon the features of the graph of the game.

An Alternative Explanation of Stability of Suboptimal Decompositions

We have seen that any division of a problem into subproblems is based on a structure that is conjectured on the grounds of some decomposition principles; the classifications and abstractions elicited by these principles may embody hidden errors, which cannot be perceived without close inspection. To find them, we would need to examine all the existing condition–action relations in detail. This would be an extremely time-consuming task that would nullify all the advantages of a concise representation. Therefore individuals cannot actively search for exceptions to the rules that they have established to solve the problem. We can see from the

MiniRubik example (Appendix 6A2) that, in order to correct the errors hidden in abstract rules, it is necessary to be guided by emerging exceptions. Any attempt to discover the errors actively would pre-empt the effort to express the strategy simply.

Therefore, the locally optimal solutions in which individuals may remain trapped while analysing a problem are created by the limits of their capacity to *falsify the rules* they have conjectured in all relevant domains, and to discover hidden errors. Because they cannot check the effects of all mutations on the fitness, there is a very low probability that they will discover mutations that improve fitness and therefore they remain trapped in the given representation.

Players do not envisage all possible configurations but in general proceed by generalization on the basis of examples: this means that they try to induce general rules from specific experiences, as, for example, in the process of learning a new language. Therefore whenever possible, players use a generalization–extrapolation by extending as widely as possible the domain of validity of the rules they have discovered.

This procedure allows a complete – even highly suboptimal – preliminary strategy to be created, in which for a large number of configurations the rules of action are defined 'by extension' from similar examples. In general the procedure of extension creates systems of rules described with some degree of abstraction. Therefore the system of rules that form a strategy is complete, that is, for any possible configuration of the game there is a rule that matches it, even if the player does not have direct experience of most of the configurations. Therefore, when a new configuration elicits a new rule as an exception, in general the new configuration gives rise to a new rule that is *more specific* than the default one. There is a difficulty in extending the new specific rule, that is, in extrapolating to larger domains, because this extrapolation will *conflict* with the previous system of rules.

When the players perceive a new example that can be solved more efficiently by activating a new rule rather than the standard rule, there are two possibilities: either they consider the new example as an exception to the previous general rule, or they try to redefine the building blocks of the rule's system, solving the conflicts among rules. This is of course a very demanding mental task, and therefore even though a single mutation can improve the system's performance, it is more likely that it will be seen as an exception and does not lead to a redefinition of abstract subproblems.

Errors that are hidden within the suboptimal representation can be uncovered and corrected mainly by rethinking the representation – that is, reformulating a new division into subproblems – and changing it. Suboptimal solutions are therefore stable under mutations because to change the representation maintaining a limited number of general rules would entail a radical modification of the building blocks – the elementary subproblems – of which a strategy is composed.[13]

4 CONCLUDING REMARKS

Learning and discovering a strategy for solving a problem is a task that humans may tackle with extraordinary speed, but necessarily producing suboptimalities and biases, while an artificial algorithm based on the idea of discovering an optimal solution by trials (mutations) should be successful but would be very slow. For example, a player wishing to tackle Rubik's cube and discover the optimal strategy through trial and error would certainly achieve his or her goal eventually. There are more than three billion configurations, each of which allows six moves (three vertical and three horizontal rotations). The player would not be locked into a suboptimal strategy because he or she could improve by mutation the fitness of every suboptimal configuration and the search would be successful, but only in the long, long run.

Although counterintuitive, this property holds true in the general setting of finite state machines, puzzles and automata problem solving. We have seen in fact that the problems that can be expressed by programs that are computationally equivalent to automata allow a set of optimal stable solutions, each of which may be reached through mutations.

These properties hold, as we have seen provided we define properly a measure of efficiency – or fitness – of the strategy. The fitness for these problems has been defined in relation to the distance between a starting configuration and the final goal, following the principle that the lower the number of actions needed to achieve the goal, the better the fitness. When the fitness function is defined in this way, the NK model predictions are not fulfilled. In fact, the degree of epistatic interdependence is positive because the effect of a mutation on the fitness is affected by the value (the alleles) of some other elements of the system, but at the same time it is possible to modify the strategy via simple mutations, until the optimal configuration is achieved.

This peculiar property has a counterpart in terms of decomposition of problems into subproblems. Here a 'weak' decomposition principle works. In fact if we decompose a strategy into its elementary statements we realize that even though they are not independent, it is possible to optimize each statement separately and achieve an optimal solution (strategy). However this 'possibility' is highly inefficient, because to achieve an optimal configuration by mutations a huge computation would be required.

Players involved in solving a puzzle should in fact remember a huge set of conditions–actions, and could discover the optimal strategy by means of small incremental changes. Because of their limited capacity for calculation and memory, they proceed by constructing compact and simplified representations of the strategies to adopt – representations based on the decomposition of the problem into subproblems and abstractions at various levels. These representations introduce 'errors' into the choice of actions because the subproblems identified are not fully independent, as the subjects believe. These errors are therefore concealed by the representation, and they can be uncovered and corrected only by dispensing with the representation – that is, the division into subproblems – and changing it radically.

This gives stability to non-optimal representations: in fact, to improve a representation it would be possible to modify single statements, so correcting the hidden errors, but it could be incredibly costly, in terms of computation and mental effort, to enumerate and detect the wrong statements of the strategy. Any attempt in this direction would destroy the advantages of a simple and compact – although imperfect – representation.

Therefore it is essential to recodify the problem in such a way as to get closer to an optimal strategy without compromising the simplicity of the representation. As we have shown in the MiniRubik example, there is a trade-off between the simplicity and the efficiency of a decomposition. It follows that simple and compact representations may be locally stable suboptimal solutions.

Let me conclude by suggesting some extensions of the previous analysis of individual problem solving to the context of organizations, mindful that what follows, as with all extensions and extrapolations, may embody hidden errors.

If we want to transfer these properties by analogy to organizations, we should imagine fully fragmented and distributed systems in which organizational learning may occur via random mutations, without any conscious design. Distributed organizations in which there is no conflict in reward allocation may therefore evolve until the optimal configuration is reached. It is difficult to map these types of abstract organizations onto some credible sketch of actual human organizations; a better illustration would be to make a comparison with the organization of ants. The properties we have shown predict that an organization of insects – none of which is able to create complex mental models of the reality (Johnson-Laird, 1983) – may adopt very slowly to an optimal division of tasks, by trial and error. The organization design therefore emerges spontaneously without a plan, as the result of a 'social' computation – a vast, decentralized computation that can be carried out only by a very large society of unaware individuals.

It is reasonable to claim that, within human organizations, the discovery of a strategy is not based on these principles, or at least is not uniquely based on this mechanism. A more powerful mechanism to explain the organizational evolution is based on problem solving and problem representing. We have already discussed many properties related to these processes, and now it is convenient to add further elements to qualify the impact of the representations on organizational problem solving.

Human beings create simplified and incomplete representations of the problems facing them. Some representations may be locally stable for the reasons we have already discussed. We could consider the locally stable representations in some sense as 'ideologies' (Denzau and North, 1994) because they represent the reality in such a simplified way that they are valid only in a certain context and cannot be extended to every condition. These simplified representations allow the evolution of organizational rules to be hugely accelerated, but introduce strong discontinuities in the process. In fact in evolutionary conditions, in which an organization is learning a new division of knowledge and competences, the coordination rules should evolve together with the discovery of a new division of tasks. This process is a very complex one, and may require a vast coordination effort if it is realized in a distributed form. As a consequence, the role of hierarchies becomes relevant as these are leaders of a top-down process of problem solving and planning. The difficulty of coordinating a systemic search for a new organizational form suggests that to escape from a lock-in, small local modifications of the team's strategies can be ineffective, while a dramatic recombination of action rules, planned by a centralized organization, may be successful.

The notion of *representation* may help to reconcile two apparently challenging 'visions' of the evolution of the strategies and of the organizational change. On the one hand is the idea of intelligent planning as a conscious division of a problem into subproblems, in which, despite the limits of individual rationality, a hierarchical organization may improve its efficiency. On the other hand is the idea of the organization's strategy as an evolving system that is transformed by small innovations, mutations, without a conscious plan shared by the individuals; this view considers institutions as the unplanned and unintentional result of human actions, which, as Hayek claims, 'can be understood as if it were made according to a single plan, although nobody has planned it'. (Hayek, F.A. (1980), p. 54)

We may try to go beyond this dichotomy, using the problem-solving approach and the notion of representation. The nature of evolution in human artifacts, institutions and organizations has different features compared to the evolutionary properties of biological systems: in human organizations evolution involves a process of collective learning that is driven by human conscious will, in which, during a rational, intelligent activity of planning, despite the effort of the individuals to be fully rational, nevertheless errors are unintentionally created.

Even though by mutations it is possible to introduce improvements into organizations, and get closer to an optimal configuration, the evolution of an organization based *only* on mutations would require an enormous amount of time. The evolution of organizational structures is, on the contrary, relatively rapid and discontinuous, because it is based on the human ability to represent, design and revise their settings. In keeping with the spirit of Cyert and March's *Behavioral Theory of the Firm* (1992, pp. 117–20), business organizations are characterized by complex hierarchies of rules that change at different rates and with different applicability domains. Plans and strategies therefore are the intentional results of human activities but at the same time they lead individuals and organizations to configurations that are largely different from the original design, because representations – both at the individual and team levels – embody hidden errors systematically.

NOTES

* I am grateful to A. Caranti , F. Giunchiglia, M. Warglien, and L. Marengo for useful discussions on some formal aspects of the chapter. The usual disclaimers hold. During the revision of this chapter, Giunchiglia suggested to me that some of the ideas exposed here are closely related to 'intelligent planning', a classic area of artificial intelligence. A key reference in this regard is Yang (1997).

1. The two experiments with Target the Two, in which individual biases and team traps are compared, are briefly outlined in Bonini and Egidi M. (1999). Having established that, at least in some experimental context, we can consider biases in individual behaviors as the 'seed' of the process of team routinization, in the rest of the chapter I shall focus on the first argument, that is, the emergence of biases in *individual* problem solving and reasoning.
2. See Yang (1997).
3. Of course, a condition–action system as a strategy for solving a puzzle is less powerful than a Post system. While the latter is equivalent to a Turing machine, the former is equivalent to an automaton. However, an automaton is perfectly suited to representing the strategy used to solve a puzzle.
4. If there are covered positions in the game, or more generally not all the conditions of a state are observable, as happens in Target the Two, then players have to consider a non-fully observable state as a class of states, and construct their strategies by considering all possible states with which the non-observable state is compatible. The strategy construction becomes then computationally explosive, even though all propertied of the strategies we have been describing still hold.
5. In this simple form programs are equivalent to automata, not to Turing machines. They are therefore 'weak' in expressive capacity but nevertheless adequate for describing a strategy.
6. It is in some sense a minimal representation of a set. For example, if the atomic components of the strings are binary units, 0–1 The set X = { {000000}, {000001}, {000010}, {000011}, {000100}, {000101}, {000110}, {000111}} can be described by a unique string: X = {000###), while the set X^* = { {1000000}, {000001}, {000010}, {000011}, {000100} }, while composed of a lower number of strings, can be described by a pair of strings: {0000##} U {000100}.
7. The 'representation' of a problem is therefore defined by a decomposition pattern based on a codification of the problem's configuration (see also Marengo, 1999).
8. Holland (Holland et al., 1988) redefines the extrapolation process as 'Q-Morphism'.
9. A very interesting question is if it is possible to know this length a priori: in the case of Turing machines this is a well-known unsolvable problem. In our case, even though machines are automata, the existence of cycles makes it impossible to provide a universal algorithm to verify whether the machine stops.
10. This section contains a few expressions that require some elementary notions in graph theory and semi-group theory. The notions needed to conduct the proofs are briefly defined to allow the reader to follow the reasoning. However, the reader may skip the section and go directly to the next one where the results obtained are discussed.

    Let us synthesize a small lexicon regarding graphs: a graph G(V,E) consists of a finite set V of *vertices* (or *nodes*) , and a set E of *edges* (or *arcs*), joining pairs of distinct nodes. An arc may connect an unordered pair of nodes (A, B) = (B, A) or may connect an ordered pair of nodes (A, B); in the latter case the arc is called a *directed arc*. We write A→B. If all edges are directed, the graph is called a *directed graph*. We say that vertex A is *adjacent* to vertex B if there is an arc from A to B. A *path* is a sequence of adjacent nodes. A *tree* is a graph with a vertex, called a root, such that there is a unique path from the root to any other vertex of the tree. A tree with directed edges is commonly called a *rooted tree*. Suppose we have a tree rooted in vertex A, and all arcs are directed to the root. Choose two adjacent vertices C, D; if C→D then we call C the parent (predecessor) of D and D the child (successor) of C, and vice versa if D→C; vertices with no parents are called *leaves* of the tree or *terminal nodes*. In the present chapter we also use rooted trees in which the orientation is inverted: all the paths starting from the root are directed to the terminal nodes.

11. A *cycle* is a closed path, that is, a path in which the last node coincides with the first. A graph is said to be cyclically connected if any two of its nodes are contained in a cycle.
12. The average number of traits that contribute to the fitness is related to the number of nodes that are linked to the goal by non-minimal paths.
13. Interestingly, the fewer the errors hidden in a representation, the smaller the marginal advantage to restructure the representation. 'Ibis property is similar to the quasi-stability of dynamic biological systems (Kauffman, 1989, pp. 593–7).

BIBLIOGRAPHY

Anderson, J.R. (1983), *The Architecture of Cognition*, Cambridge, MA: Harvard University Press.

Arthur, W.B. (1988), 'Self reinforcing mechanisms in economics', in W.P. Anderson and K.J. Arrow (eds), *The Economy as an Evolving Complex System*, Redwood City, CA: Addison Wesley, pp. 9–31.

Berge, C. (1985), *Graphs*, Amsterdam: North-Holland.

Bonini, N. and M. Egidi (1999), 'Cognitive traps in individual and organizational behavior: some empirical evidence', *Revue d'Economie Industrielle*, **88** (2), pp. 153–85.

Cannon-Bowers, J.A., E. Salas and S. Converse (1993), 'Shared mental models in expert team decision making', in N.J. Castellan, Jr. (ed.), *Individual and Group Decision Making*, Hillsdale, NJ: Erlbaum, pp. 221–46.

Chase, W.G. and H.A. Simon (1973), 'Perception in chess' *Cognitive Psychology*, **4**, 55–81.

Chen, W.K. (1971), *Applied Graph Theory*, Amsterdam: North-Holland.

Clifford, A.H. and G.B. Preston (1961), *The Algebraic Theory of Semigroups*, Vol. I , Providence, RI: American Mathematical Society.

Cohen, M.D. (1991), 'Individual learning and organizational routine: emerging connections', *Organization Science*, **2** (1), 135–9.

Cohen, M.D. and P. Bacdayan (1994), 'Organizational routines are stored as procedural memory: evidence form a laboratory study', *Organization Science*, **5** (4), 554–68.

Cohen, M.D., R. Burkhart, G. Dosi, M. Egidi, L. Marengo, M. Warglien and S. Winter (1996), 'Routines and other recurring action patterns of organizations: contemporary research issues', *Industrial and Corporate Change*, **5** (3), 653–98.

Cyert, R.M. (1988), *The Economic Theory of Organization and the Firm*, New York: Harvester Wheatsheaf.

Cyert, R.M. and J.G. March (1963), *A Behavioral Theory of the Firm*, Englewood Cliffs, NJ: Prentice-Hall, reprinted (1992) by Blackwell, Cambridge, MA.

Denzau, A.T. and D.C. North (1994), 'Shared mental models: ideologies and institutions', *Kyklos*, **47** (1), 3–31.

Egidi, M. (1996), 'Routines, hierarchies of problems, procedural behaviour: some evidence from experiments', in K.J. Arrow, E. Colombatto, M. Perlman (eds), *The Rational Foundations of Economic Behaviour*, IEA Conference Volume 114, New York: St. Martin's Press; London: Macmillan, pp. 303–33.

Egidi, M. and A. Narduzzo (1997), 'The emergence of path dependent behaviors in cooperative contexts', *International Journal of Industrial Organization*, **15** (6), October, 677–709.

Fischhoff, B. (1975), 'Hindsight vs. foresight: the effect of outcome knowledge on judgement under uncertainty', *Journal of Experimental Psychology: Human Perception and Performance*, **1** (3), 288–99.

Frenken, K., L. Marengo and M. Valente (1998), 'Interdependencies, nearly-decomposability and adaptation', CEEL Working Papers, University of Trento, Italy.

Hayek F.A. (1980), 'Economics and Knowledge', in *Individualism and Economic Order*, pp. 33–56, Chicago: University of Chicago Press.

Holland, J.H. (1975), *Adaptation in Natural and Artificial Systems*, Ann Arbor, MI: University of Michigan Press.

Holland, J.H., K.J. Holyoak, R.E. Nisbett and P.R. Thagard (1988), *Induction – Processes of Inference, Learning, and Discovery*, Cambridge, MA: MIT Press.

Johnson-Laird, P.N. (1983), *Mental Models*, Cambridge, MA: Harvard University Press.

Kahneman, D. and A. Tversky (1986), 'Rational choice and the framing of decisions', in R.M. Hogart and M.W. Reder, *Rational Choice: The Contrast between Economics and Psychology*, Chicago: University of Chicago Press, pp. 67–94.

Kauffman, S.A. (1989), 'Adaptation on rugged fitness landscapes', in D.L. Stein (ed.), *Lectures in the Sciences of Complexity*, Santa Fe Institute Studies in the Sciences of Complexity, Vol. 1, Redwood City, CA: Addison-Wesley, pp. 527–712.

Kauffman, S.A. (1993), *The Origins of Order: Self-organization and Selection in Evolution*, Oxford: Oxford University Press.

Kauffman, S.A. and S. Johnsen (1992), 'Co-evolution to the edge of chaos: coupled fitness landscapes, poised states, and co-evolutionary avalanches', in C.G. Langton, L. Taylor, J.D. Farmer and S. Rasmussen (eds), *Artificial Life II*, Redwood City, CA: Addison-Wesley, pp. .

Laird, J.E., A. Newell and P.S. Rosembloom (1987), 'Soar: an architecture for general intelligence', *Artificial Intelligence*, **33**, 1–64.

Levinthal, D. (1997), 'Adaptation on rugged landscapes', *Management Science*, **43** (7), July, pp. 934–50.

Levinthal, D.A. and J.G. March (1993), 'The myopia of learning', *Strategic Management Journal*, **14**, 95–112.

Levitt, B. and J.G. March (1988), 'Organizational learning', *Annual Review of Sociology*, **14**, 319–40.

Loewenstein, G. and J. Elster (eds) (1992), *Choice over Time*, New York: Russell Sage Foundation.

Loewenstein, G. and R.H. Thaler (1989), 'Anomalies: intertemporal choice', *Journal of Economic Perspectives*, **3**, 181–93.

Luchins, A.S. (1942), Mechanization in problem-solving', *Psychological Monograph*, **54**, 1–95.

Luchins, A.S. and E.H Luchins (1950), 'New experimental attempts in preventing mechanization in problem-solving', *Journal of General Psychology*, **42**, 279–91.

March, J.G. (1981), 'Footnotes to organizational change', *Administrative Science Quarterly*, **26**, 563–77.

March, J.G. (1988), *Decisions and Organisations*, Oxford: Basil Blackwell.

March, J.G. (1990), 'Exploration and exploitation in organizational learning', *Organization Science*, **2**, 71–87.

March, J.G. and H.A. Simon (1958), *Organizations* (1993, 2nd edn), New York: John Wiley.

Marengo, L. (1999), 'Decentralisation and market mechanisms in collective problem solving', Working Paper, University of Trento, Italy.

Minsky, M. (1967), *Computation. Finite and Infinite Machines*, Englewood Cliffs,NJ: Prentice-Hall.

Newell, A. and H.A. Simon (1972), *Human Problem Solving*, Englewood Cliffs, NJ: Prentice-Hall.

Nilsson, N.J. (1971), *Problem Solving Methods in Artificial Intelligence*, New York: McGraw-Hill.

North, D.C. (1991), 'Towards a theory of institutional change', *Quarterly Review of Economics and Business*, **31** (4), 3–11.

Page, S.E. (1996), 'Two measures of difficulty', *Economic Theory*, **8**, 321–46.

Simon, H.A. (1971), 'Theories of bounded rationality', in B. McGuire and R. Radner (eds), *Decision and Organisation*, Amsterdam: North-Holland.

Simon, H.A. (1972), 'Theories of bounded rationality', in B. McGuire and R. Radner (eds), *Decision and Organisation*, Amsterdam: North-Holland, pp. 161–76.

Simon, H.A. and A. Ando (1961), 'Aggregation of variables in dynamic systems', *Econometrica*, **29**, 111–38.

Tucker, A. (1984), *Applied Combinatorics*, New York: John Wiley & Sons.

Yang, Q. (1997), *Intelligent Planning: A Decomposition and Abstraction-based Approach*, Berlin: Springer.

APPENDIX 6A1 CYCLES IN RANDOM STRATEGIES

A strategy can be written as a list of pairs of nodes X,Y: in every pair (X,Y), the node X represents the condition and the node Y the new configuration obtained applying the action a to X: X→a→Y. For simplicity we can use integers instead of letters to identify the nodes; if the distinct nodes (statements of the strategy) are N, and we put $A = \{1, 2, 3, ..., N\}$, then a strategy is a set of pairs $(x,y) \in A \times A$ or equivalently, a function $f: A \rightarrow A$.

It is possible to show that f admits a set of disjoint cycles (or fixed points that are cycles of length 1), and that all elements of A not belonging to a cycle, belong to some trees rooted in some cycle. To prove this property, consider all iterations of $f: A \rightarrow A$, and define:

$$f\_1(x) = f(x),$$

$$f\_2(x) = f[f(x)],$$

$$f\_3(x) = f\{f[f(x)]\},$$

...

Define A_i the image of A through f_i, that is, $A\_i = \{f\_i(x) = f(f\{...[f(x]...\}): x \in A\}$. It is clear that the sequence $A\_1, A\_2, ...$ is non-increasing, that is, $A \supseteq A\_1 \supseteq A\_2 \supseteq A\_3 \supseteq ...$ and so on. In fact if, for example, $b \in A\_2$, this means that there is an $a \in A$ for which $b = f[f(a)]$, and at the same time there is a $c \in A$ for which $b = f(c)$ (where $c = f(a)$). Therefore, given that $c \in A, b \in A\_1$.

The set A is finite and not empty, and therefore after a certain number of iterations the sequence of A_i remains constant (and includes at least one element). In other words there must be an index n for which $A\_n = A\_\{n+1\} = A\_\{n+2\} = ...$.

But this implies that $f(A\_n) = A\_n$, that is, that if we restrict ourselves to the domain A_n, the function $f(x)$ for $x \in A\_n$ is surjective, that is, $f(x): A\_n \rightarrow A\_n$. Therefore $f(x)$ is bijective. As a consequence it is a permutation and can be written as a set of disjoint cycles. Furthermore if n is the minimal index i for which $A\_i = A\_\{i+1)$, by applying $f(x)$ iteratively to an $x \in A$ which does *not* belong to A_n we get, after a finite number of steps, one element of A_n. This means that the elements $x \in A$ not belonging to A_n comprise a rooted tree (or a forest) directed on A_n. (For more properties in this regard, see, for example, Clifford and Preston, 1961.)

APPENDIX 6A2 HIDDEN ERRORS SHOWED WITH AN EXAMPLE: MINIRUBIK

In this appendix we shall examine in detail a simple puzzle, by computing the optimal strategy and comparing it with a simple strategy obtained by decomposition of the problem. It will be shown how 'errors' are created during the decomposition analysis.

Let us consider a simple puzzle based on an extreme simplification of Rubik's cube. The player has a square consisting of four differently colored tiles denoted with the letters A, B, C, D (see Figure 6A2.1).

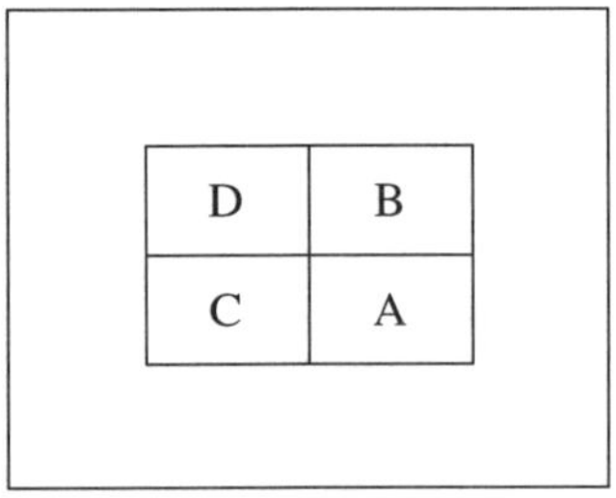

Figure 6A2.1 The MiniRubik puzzle

The tiles can be exchanged horizontally or vertically in the ways shown in Figure 6A2.2.

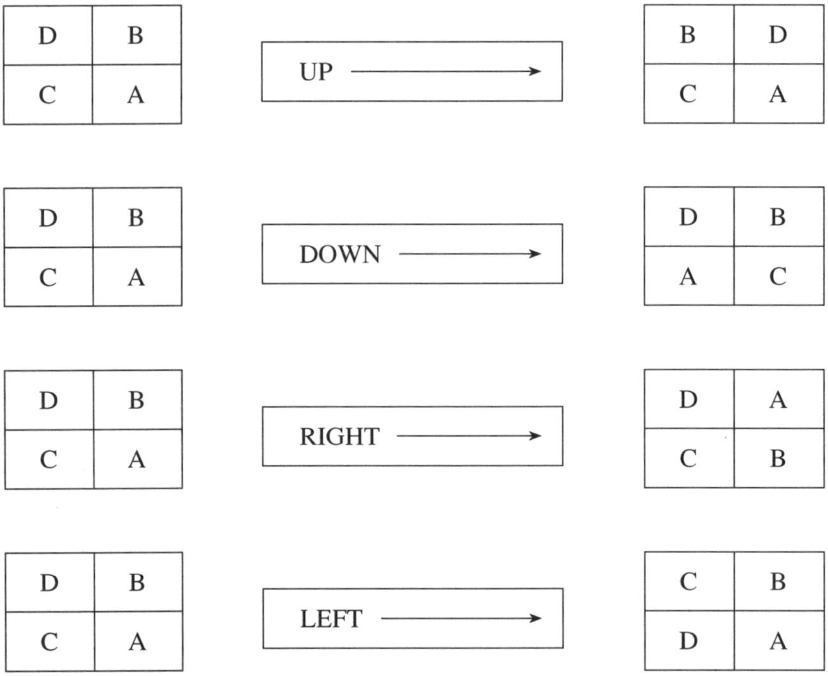

Figure 6A2.2 The repertoire of optimal actions

Let us suppose that a tournament is held in which the initial configuration for every round is selected at random, and for the sake of simplicity let us assume that the final configuration is fixed in the sequence shown in Figure 6A2.3.

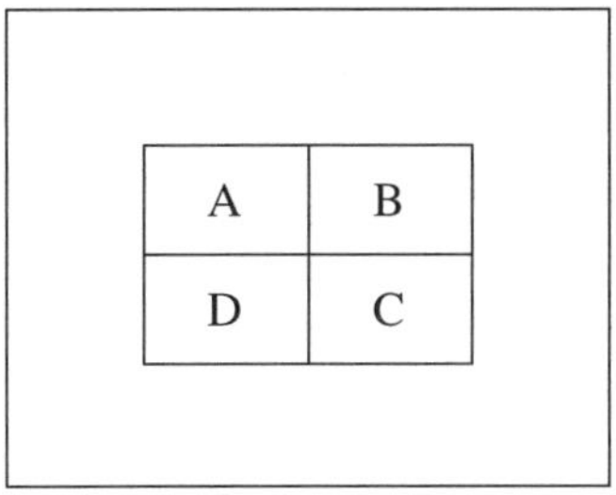

Figure 6A2.3 The final configuration of MiniRubik

The players must exchange the tiles until they have produced this final configuration, and they are rewarded according to the number of moves that they make to achieve it, although a maximum time limit is set for each game. In this context a problem at ground level is defined by a pair of game configurations, the starting one and the goal one, as in Figure 6A2.4.

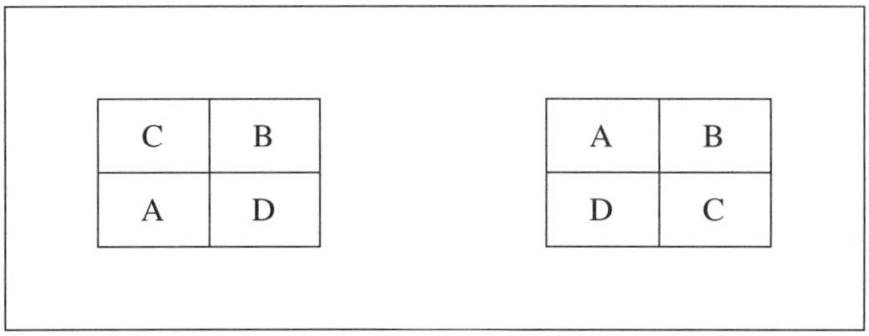

Figure 6A2.4 Representation of a problem

A less natural but more concise representation of the puzzle is shown in Figure 6A2.5. In this formulation, the rules can be recast as exchanges among tiles in horizontal strings and stated as follows:

up: exchange between adjacent tiles in positions 1 and 2;
down: exchange between adjacent tiles in positions 3 and 4;
right: exchange between adjacent tiles in positions 2 and 3;
left: exchange between the tiles on the extreme left and extreme right (positions 1 and 4).

Let us now suppose that we want to expand an initial configuration of the game to create the successors, that is, the new configurations produced by all possible moves applied to the initial configuration. By applying orderly moves U, D, R, L to all 24 different configurations of the game we obtain a list of states, called 'successors' . In Table 6A2.1, listed to the right of every configuration are the four successors; of course, any successor is again a configuration of the game. This table is the *links array* and contains all the links between each state and

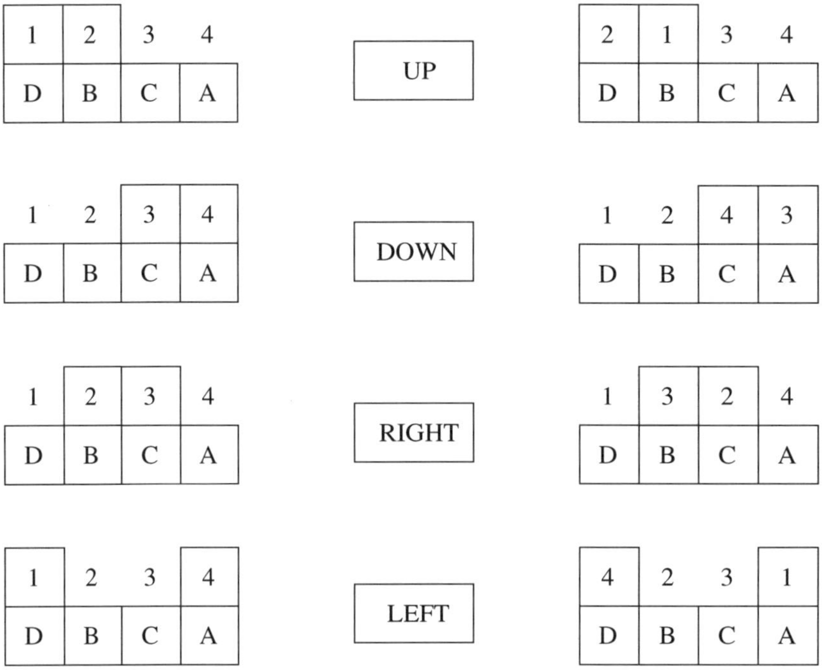

Figure 6A2.5 Minirubik's basic actions

its successors. We can use the links array to discover some of the paths that begin with a given configuration and finish with the target configuration. (There is obviously a countable infinity of such paths.)

Identifying the Optimal Strategies

We have described the backward procedure to identify the minimal paths. Here we apply the procedure. We start by identifying on the array of links (Table 6A2.1) the set of configurations X(l) from which it is possible to achieve the final configuration 1 in one step. To do this, we identify on the right-hand side of the table the rows that contain the number 1: these are rows 2, 3, 7 and 22, and therefore we have the set X(1) = {2, 3, 7, 22}. We then identify the set X(2) of configurations from which it is possible to achieve an element of X(1) in one step. The reader can verify that X(2) = {4, 5, 8, 9, 12, 13, 16, 20, 21, 24}. Repeating this procedure recursively, we obtain X(3) = 16, 10, 11, 14, 15, 18, 19, 23} and finally X(4) = {17}.

Thus we have found all the links that connect all the configurations of the game to the final configuration 1 with a minimal distance; if we rewrite the connections we have identified on the array of links, and cancel the links which have not been involved in the backward procedure, we obtain the section A 'minimal connections' of Table 6A2.2. The table tells us what are the minimal paths between any configuration and the goal configuration, 1.

It is clear from the table of links that there are many minimal paths connecting a state with the goal; for example if we want to find the minimal paths from states 11 and 1, we find the

Table 6A2.1 The array of links among configurations

	1	2	3	4		Links array U	D	L	R
1	A	B	C	D	1	7	2	22	3
2	A	B	D	C	2	8	1	16	5
3	A	C	B	D	3	13	4	24	1
4	A	C	D	B	4	14	3	10	6
5	A	D	B	C	5	19	6	18	2
6	A	D	C	B	6	20	5	12	4
7	B	A	C	D	7	1	8	20	9
8	B	A	D	C	8	2	7	14	11
9	B	C	A	D	9	15	10	23	7
10	B	C	D	A	10	16	9	4	12
11	B	D	A	C	11	21	12	17	8
12	B	D	C	A	12	22	11	6	10
13	C	A	B	D	13	3	14	19	15
14	C	A	D	B	14	4	13	8	17
15	C	B	A	D	15	9	16	21	13
16	C	B	D	A	16	10	15	2	18
17	C	D	A	B	17	23	18	11	14
18	C	D	B	A	18	24	17	5	16
19	D	A	B	C	19	5	20	13	21
20	D	A	C	B	20	6	19	7	23
21	D	B	A	C	21	11	22	15	19
22	D	B	C	A	22	12	21	1	24
23	D	C	A	B	23	17	24	9	20
24	D	C	B	A	24	18	23	3	22

paths 11→21→22→1, 11→12→22→1, 11→8→2→1 and 11→8→7→1, all of which have the same minimal distance from the goal 1.

In the center of Table 6A2.2, I have reported the corresponding optimal actions; so, for example, the path 11→21→22→1 can be followed by applying the actions U, D, L: 11→U→21→D→22→L→1. On the right-hand side of the table, I have selected one optimal strategy, and computed the sequences of actions that lead to the goal applying to every configuration of the optimal strategy.

So far we have formatted the set of optimal (and equivalent) strategies as a condition–action table in which for every condition we have identified one or more optimal actions. We can therefore measure the (minimal) path length for every configuration; the sum of all minimal distances from any configuration and the goal is a measure of the global performance of the strategy. It can be straightforwardly checked that the minimal length is 52 steps. Of course, any strategy obtained by selecting one action for the second column (Actions) of the table is allowed. We can therefore build up a repertoire of many different sets of rules, each of which is a complete optimal solution and requires 52 moves to achieve the goal from all starting

Table 6A2.2 The optimal solution

A Minimal connections									B Optimal action				C Minimal paths		
Conditions					U	D	L	R	Actions				Action	Path	Length
A	B	C	D	1	7	2	22	3							
A	B	D	C	2	8	1	16	5		D			D	D	1
A	C	B	D	3	13	4	24	1				R	R	R	1
A	C	D	B	4	14	3	10	6		D			D	DR	2
A	D	B	C	5	19	6	18	2				R	R	RD	2
A	D	C	B	6	20	5	12	4	U	D	L	R	D	DRD	3
B	A	C	D	7	1	8	20	9	U				U	U	1
B	A	D	C	8	2	7	14	11	U	D			U	UD	2
B	C	A	D	9	15	10	23	7				R	R	RU	2
B	C	D	A	10	16	9	4	12	U	D	L	R	L	LDR	3
B	D	A	C	11	21	12	17	8	U	D		R	R	RUD	3
B	D	C	A	12	22	11	6	10	U				U	UL	2
C	A	B	D	13	3	14	19	15	U				U	UR	2
C	A	D	B	14	4	13	8	17	U	D	L		U	UDR	3
C	B	A	D	15	9	16	21	13	U	D	L	R	D	DLD	3
C	B	D	A	16	10	15	2	18			L		L	LD	2
C	D	A	B	17	23	18	11	14	U	D	L	R	L	LRUD	4
C	D	B	A	18	24	17	5	16	U		L	R	L	LRD	3
D	A	B	C	19	5	20	13	21	U	D	L	R	U	URD	3
D	A	C	B	20	6	19	7	23			L		L	LU	2
D	B	A	C	21	11	22	15	19		D			D	DL	2
D	B	C	A	22	12	21	1	24			L		L	L	1
D	C	A	B	23	17	24	9	20		D	L	R	D	DLR	3
D	C	B	A	24	18	23	3	22			L	R	L	LR	2

configurations. The possible combinations of the optimal actions are 331,776, which means that the game has 331,776 different optimal strategies with the same fitness ($f = 52$).

Representations and Biases. An Example: The 'First A' Strategy

It is obvious that players do not discover the solutions by backward search, and the important point is to understand how they reconstruct a good or optimum strategy, and why they make errors. In some experiments with MiniRubik, a number of players carried out a very simple, 'ingenuous', strategy, based on the attempt to put every square of the board in its right place, disregarding the interferences among the different actions. This strategy can easily be described and formalized via decomposition of the problem into sub-problems.

Assume as before that the goal of the game is to achieve the configuration ABCD, whatever the starting configuration will be. The strategy proposed by players, applied to a randomly chosen configuration, prescribes moving A to the first position, then moving B to the second position and so on until the goal configuration (Figure 6A2.6) has been achieved. This is a 'conjectural' approach to the problem, in the sense that it 'assumes', without any evidence, that it will be possible to move A, B, C and D into their final positions without interfering with any of the sub-goals. In other words, it is assumed (ingenuously) that it is possible to shift a piece to its correct position without moving other pieces away from their correct positions, that is, that the goals can be achieved independently.

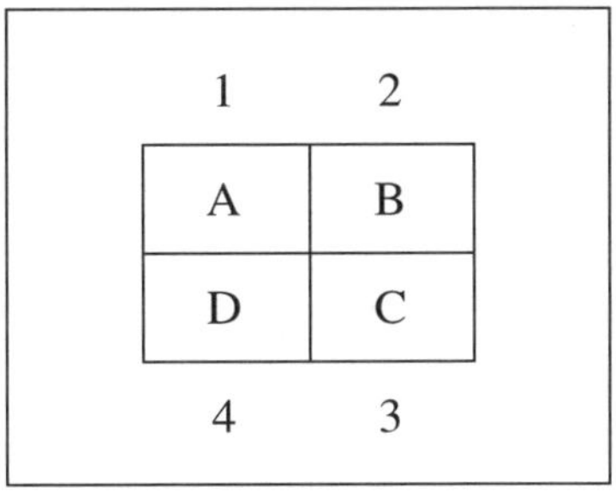

Figure 6A2.6 *The goal configuration*

To write this strategy in the form of instructions (or conditions–actions) we have to decompose the problem into three subproblems:

(P1) Move A from the initial position in the string (whatever it is) to position 1:(####) → (A###).
(P2) Move B from its present position (eventually scrambled after step 1) to position 2 *leaving* A in the first position: (A###) → (AB##).
(P3) If C and D are not in the required positions 3 and 4, exchange them: (AB##) → (ABCD).

The three statements P1, P2 and P3 are a ‘conjectural strategy’, that is, a proposal for a solution of the problem that embodies a decomposition of the problem without proving that the subproblems can be solved independently. Therefore we have to reduce the prescriptions P1, ... P3 to specific elementary actions by decomposing every prescription into more elementary prescriptions recursively until we reduce them to elementary actions.

Starting from statement P1, we may note that the movement of A toward position 1 is a ‘circular’ movement. A reasonable elementary rule consists in moving A to the ‘closest’ distance to position 1; this means that if A is in position 2 it is natural to move it counter-clockwise while it is natural to move it clockwise if it is in position 4. This rule does not apply if A is in position 3, because of course the ‘distance’ between positions 3 and 1 are the same whether if we move clockwise or counterclockwise.

Therefore we can reduce (arbitrarily) P1 to: move A clockwise if it is in position 4, and counterclockwise if it is in positions 2 or 3. Call this specification P11: it is now possible to rewrite this statement as an organized sequence of actions, to be performed for every different position of A in the board.

P11 is therefore rewritten as the sequence of OR actions:

if (#A##) then → U → (A###)
if (###A) then → L → (A###)
if (##A#) then → R → (#A##) →U → (A###).

If we apply the same method to P2 and P3, we obtain the corresponding sequences of conditions–actions. The global problem can therefore be destructured and reduced to a sequence of elementary actions as clarified below.

- (####A) → (ABCD)
  - (####A) → (A###)→
    - (#A##) → U → (A###)
    - (###A) → L → (A###)
    - (##A#) → (A###)→
      - (##A#) → R → (#A##)
      - (#A##) → U → (A###)
  - (A###) → (AB##)→
    - (A#B#) → R → (AB##)
    - (A##B) → (AB##)→
      - (A##B) → D → (A#B#)
      - (A#B#) → R → (AB##)
  - (AB##) → D → (ABCD)

The strategy is now fully described, via a tree that represents the original problem decomposed into a structure, that is, as a set of interconnected elementary sub-problems that are either elementary ones or can be reduced to elementary ones.

A different way of representing the strategy is the array of conditions–actions shown in Table 6A2.3. To build up the array I have simply written a list with the terminal nodes of the previous tree, nodes that are the elementary problems solved.

Table 6A2.3 The conjectural solution: First A strategy

Conditions				Number	Action
A	#	#	B	1	D
#	#	#	A	2	L
A	#	B	#	3	R
#	#	A	#	4	R
#	A	#	#	5	U
A	B	D	C	6	D

Having transformed the three statements P1, ..., P3 into the format of a decision tree, and equivalently in an array of conditions–actions, we can now compare the *conjectural* strategy with the optimal strategies we have previously computed using the backward algorithm.

In the next section we shall see the consequence of designing a decomposition of the problem with a *conjecture* on independence among the subproblems: the optimal solutions of Rubik differ from the one discovered via conjectural decomposition of the problem. The sub-problems identified with the conjecture cannot be connected to one another by a unique optimal action, and embody configurations for which the action is suboptimal.

Optimality and Suboptimality: Hidden Errors

By comparing the conjectural solution (Table 6A2.3), with the optimal one (Table 6A2.2), we can see that the domains of applicability of the conjectured subproblems are not coincident with the domains of the optimal ones (see Table 6A2.4).

Table 6A2.4 Optimal condition–action

Optimal strategy						Configurations involved (Table 6A2.1)
Conditions						
A	#	#	B	1	D	4, 6
#	#	#	A	2	L	10, (12), 16, 18, 22, 24
B	D	C	A	2*	U	
A	#	B	#	3	R	3, 5
#	#	A	#	4	R	9, 11, 15, 17, (21), 23
D	B	A	C	4*	D	
#	A	#	#	5	U	7, 8 13, 14, 19, (20)
D	A	C	B	5*	L	
A	B	D	C	6	D	

In fact the general rules of Table 6A2.3, are not optimal if applied to their entire domains; more precisely, rule 2, which states that if A is in position 4 then move it left, is valid for all conditions in which A is in position 4 *excluding* one special condition, that is, the string BDCA, for which we have to add a new rule (a specification of rule 2), that is, rule 2*. (The same holds for rules 4 and 5.) It follows that the goal 'move A from position 4 to position 1' cannot in every case be separated from the goal 'move B to its position (position 2)', because the action for accomplishing the two goals interferes with the specific condition BDCA: in fact in these conditions if we try to get A into its final (goal) position, at the same time B becomes further from its goal position; so in this particular case the conjecture 'I can first move A to its final position and then move B independently' fails, if we wish to accomplish the goal in an optimal way. Table 6A2.4 is therefore an optimal condition–action table, which differs from the First A strategy (Table 6A2.3) for the three statements 2*, 4* and 5*, which are 'specifications' that conflict with the general rules 2, 4 and 5.

In MiniRubik , most of the combinations allow the player to move each piece towards its correct position without regard to what happens to the other pieces, simply because the interaction exists and is positive, that is, in moving a piece closer to its correct position, the player at the same time gets some other piece closer to its correct position. This positive interaction is violated in two particular situations in which goals are negatively interrelated.

For example CADB is solved by UDR: CADB→U→ACDB→D→ACBD; this action gets D in its correct position and at the same time gets B closer to its correct position.

If on the contrary we attempt to solve BDCA using the First A strategy, we get LDRD: BDCA→L→ADCB→D→ADBC→R→ABDC→D→ABCD, which is of course inefficient, while the game can be solved with only two moves, UL: BDCA→U→DBCA→L→ABCD. The first move prescribed by the First A strategy in fact gets A at the correct place, but B further from its correct position.

The space of the problems generated by Minirubik is fully defined by Table 6A2.2, in which we have reconstructed all minimal paths to achieve a solution. When an individual first starts to play the game he or she has to learn from examples, and any attempt to generalize specific situations may be misleading and prevent from identifying optimal solutions. In a preliminary experiment, some players followed the First A solution, which covers every situation and is perfectly consistent, but unfortunately does not take into account a fundamental property of the game: that is, when players move a piece, getting it closer to its correct position, at the same time they sometimes move some other piece closer to its correct position, but sometimes they move a piece away from its correct position. Therefore a few errors have inadvertently been included in the action rules.

APPENDIX 6A3 EPISTATIC INTERACTIONS

We have already noted that the link matrix of a puzzle can be represented by a graph, whose nodes represent the configurations of the system. (Node A is connected to node B by an oriented arc if and only if by applying a legal rule of action to A we obtain B.) To give a simple example of the equivalence between puzzles, condition–action systems and graphs, consider the links in Table 6A3.1. Here, we have indicated in columns 2 and 3 the states that can be reached by applying, respectively, actions X and Y to the conditions listed in the first column of the array.

Table 6A3.1 The array of links among configurations

Conditions	Actions	
	X	Y
A	–	–
B	A	–
C	–	B
D	C	–
E	H	–
F	D	E
G	–	B
H	A	C
L	F	–
M	–	F

From Table 6A3.1 we build up an equivalent graph, with the simple following convention: if in the matrix we have, for example, F→Y→E, that is, if, by applying the rule Y to configuration F we obtain configuration E, then in the graph we draw a pair F, E connected by an edge oriented from E to F. The graph is called a directed graph, because it is composed of directed edges (arrows). Figure 6A3.1 shows the graph equivalent of the matrix in Table 6A3.1.

Whichever representation we choose for the game, a condition–action system or a graph, a strategy can be described as a selection: in the condition–action system, it is a selection of one among the possible actions corresponding to every condition. In the graph representation, the selection consists of choosing one and only one link between a node (condition) and the adjacent ones (successors).

Now let us try to modify a strategy by introducing mutations. Given a strategy, by introducing a mutation, that is, by changing one action (from A to A') in the condition–action list, we also change one link: suppose that the game is given by the graph in Figure 6A3.1. Let the strategy be defined by the list in Table 6A3.2, or equivalently by the spanning tree represented in Figure 6A3.2, which differs from the graph of the game by the removal of arches FD and HA.

We can now evaluate how the fitness changes when we apply the different available actions (the mutations of a gene) to a given configuration: if, starting from a given strategy (tree), we replace, for example, F→Y→E with F→X→D, this corresponds to removing the link F→E and attaching node F as the parent of D. (See Figure 6A3.2).

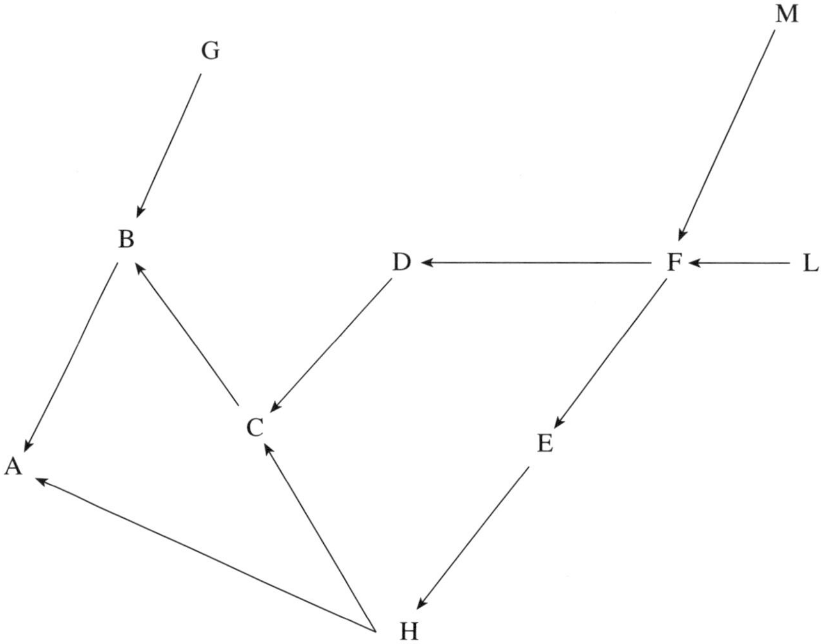

Figure 6A3.1 The graph equivalent to the links array

Table 6A3.2 A strategy described as selection of links

Condition	Actions	
	X	Y
A	–	–
B	A	–
C	–	B
D	C	–
E	H	–
F	–	E
G	–	B
H	–	C
L	F	–
M	–	F

It is obvious that this mutation is convenient if and only if D is nearer than E to the goal, because our fitness measures the distances between the nodes and the goal. In our example (Tables 6A3.1 and Figure 6A3.1), D is nearer than E to the goal; then removing the link F→E and introducing the new link F→D, all the nodes of the tree rooted in F (M and L in the

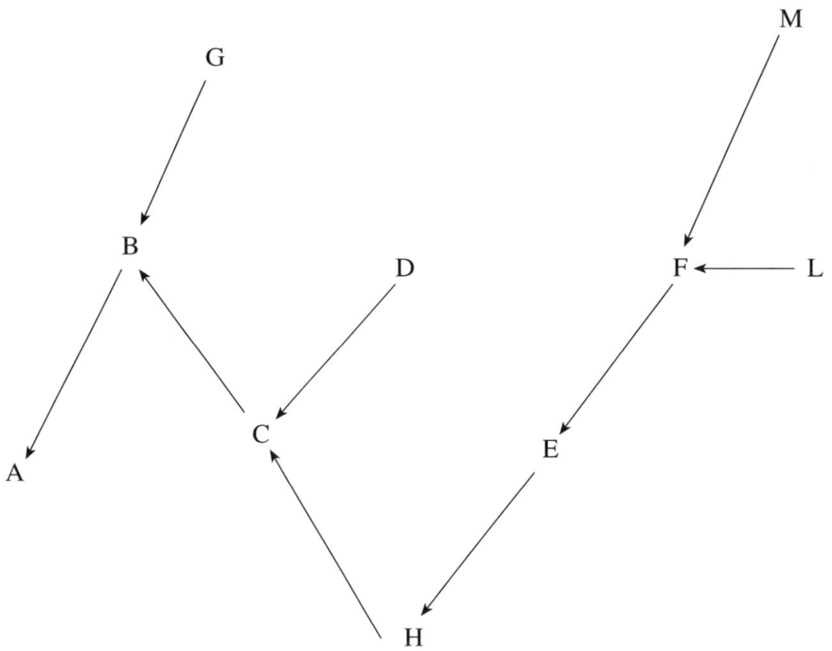

Figure 6A3.2 The graph equivalent to the strategy of table 6A3.2

example) also become closer to the goal. It follows that this mutation increases the fitness value.

More generally it is important to note that if we get node N closer to the root, either this new connection does not have any effect on the positions of the other nodes (when N is terminal) or we have a similar effect: all the nodes rooted in N get closer to the root. The effect of a mutation can therefore vary in strength, in relation to the length of the sub-tree rooted in N (the greater the sub-tree, the higher the improvement of the fitness).

Nevertheless the effects of a mutation depend upon the 'context': in fact by disconnecting node F from E and linking it to D, the fitness function has been increased because node H was connected to C. But if next we introduce a new mutation, by removing the link H→C and linking H to root A, then the fitness associated with the node F changes. Now (Figure 6A3.3) F is nearer to the goal if it is disconnected from D and reconnected again to E: therefore when we compare the value of the fitness function in relation to the different available links between F and its successors, then this value depends upon the length of the paths directed from the successors to the goal: therefore if we modify these paths, by changing some of the links of the nodes involved, the values of the fitness function also change.

In other words, the variation of the fitness that follows a change in a link between node N and its successors depends on how the *other nodes* are linked: this means *by definition* that there is epistatic interaction, that is, K is positive.

The final tree of minimal length (optimal fitness) is shown in Figure 6A3.4.

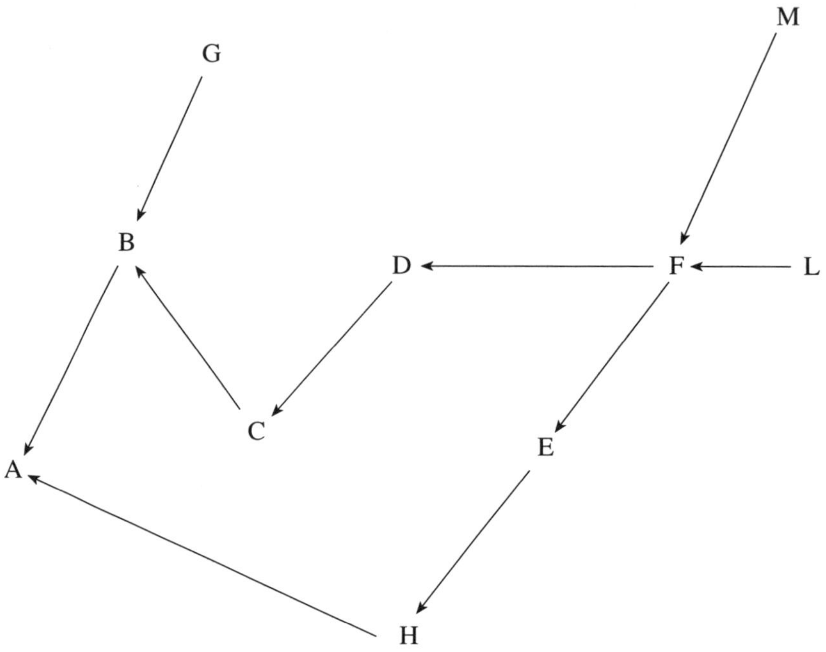

Figure 6A3.3 Epistatic effect

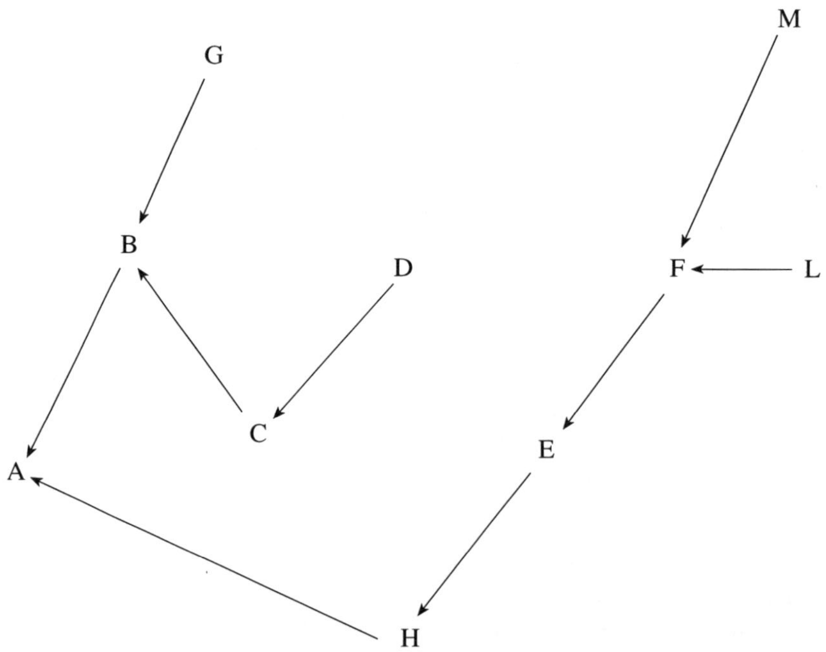

Figure 6A3.4 The graph of minimal length

7. The organizational basis of cognition and the cognitive basis of organization

Brian J. Loasby

1 PROLOGUE

As an undergraduate at Cambridge, I was presented with the theory of imperfect competition as the proven theory of decision making in business. Since I was reasonably certain that few businessmen could often obtain the knowledge that was required to set marginal revenue equal to marginal cost and the marginal revenue product of each input equal to the marginal cost of acquiring that input in imperfect factor markets, it appeared that this logical imperative was impossible to meet. How, then, was business managed? An implicit answer was 'very badly', and it would be much better managed by economists, or by someone following their advice; my own feeling was that there was something very peculiar about the theory of the firm, but I had no idea what could be done about it. A very bright student at my college, Peter Potts, who was a year ahead of me, took a similar view; after a year's postgraduate work as Wrenbury Scholar, he abandoned university for industry, where he subsequently confirmed for me the impossibility of obtaining the apparently indispensable knowledge that was deemed essential in economic theory for good decisions, and concluded that there was a need for developments in the theory of the firm as radical as those introduced by John Maynard Keynes.

I tried to escape into economic history, but the openings were few, and so I found myself as a research fellow at the University of Birmingham making practical studies of location decisions, and discovering that not only was relevant knowledge for decision making often hard to come by but even knowing what issues required decision was problematic. Being less theoretically ambitious than Edith Penrose, I contented myself with a number of generalizations which seemed to me well-supported by the evidence, plausible, and relevant both for businessmen and policy makers; and when *A Behavioral Theory of the Firm* appeared in 1963 I discovered that my generalizations fitted perfectly. The disadvantage of the term 'behavioral' is the danger of confusion with 'behaviorism', which is the exact opposite in denying the possibility of any 'internal explanation' of human actions. Behavioral theory is a theory of mental and organizational models, their creation, development and consequences; and it is a happy coincidence that 1963 was also the year of publication of the shorter version of George Kelly's *Theory of Personality*, which was an assault on behaviorism in psychology but also provided unintended support for the concept of 'administrative man', who turns out to be very like other men and women in cognitive resources and a reliance on interpretative frameworks.

My first substantial book started out as an exposition of behavioral theory linked to my own studies of location decisions, but I became increasingly aware that what seemed to me an obviously helpful way of understanding how firms worked aroused very little interest among economists, and I wanted to know why. Adam Smith would have understood this perfectly, but I had not then heard of his 'History of astronomy' (Smith [1795] 1980). The theme of the book gradually changed into 'an enquiry into economic theory and the practice of decision making' and an explanation of why there was so little connection between the two (Loasby 1976). It resolved, or rather dissolved, my undergraduate puzzle: the theory of imperfect competition was about welfare economics, not business management (though I still believe that a welfare economics that takes no account of business management is liable to be seriously misleading).

The ideas that came out of Carnegie Tech and Carnegie-Mellon are still minority ideas within economics, but among economists who are interested in firms as organizations, in innovation and economic development, and in evolutionary economics they are part of the core, even though their origin is not always acknowledged. As with all good ideas, they have become increasingly interconnected with other ideas, and these connections have improved our understanding of phenomena which some of us think are important; this chapter is devoted to some of these connections. If we look some way back into the history of economics, the improvements are not always as substantial as we might at first think; and the chapter also seeks to remind us of this. But improvements there have been, and some directions for further progress seem reasonably clear. One principle, however, must be asserted: behavior cannot simply be deduced from axiom sets (even neo-Darwinian axiom sets), but must be observed, explored and explained.

2 THE RATIONALE OF THE FIRM

Ronald Coase (1937) is normally credited with the first attempt to explain why firms, as organizations, seem to be so important in modern economic systems. However, Coase (1991, p. 51) tells us that Lionel Robbins, who was the head of his department, after congratulating him on the publication of his now-famous article on 'The nature of the firm' never again referred to it. At the time Coase was both surprised and disappointed; but he later realized that Robbins considered any explanation of the existence and boundaries of firms to be, at best, of peripheral interest and, at worst, that any discussion of such issues might tend to distract attention from the fundamental proposition, as Robbins saw it, of economic theory: that the price system leads to an allocation of resources which reflects the basic facts of resources, preferences, and technology. For Robbins, the choice between firms and markets as allocative instruments was a subsidiary issue, which had no significant consequences for the allocation itself.

It was quite common at the time to refer to money as a 'veil', which tended to conceal the underlying reality of exchanges of goods and services but which – except in times of monetary disorder – had no implications for what exchanges took place or for the terms of exchange. For Robbins, formal organization was also a veil, which might sometimes be preferred to market exchange but which delivered identical results. This has been the standard view within economics; what goes on inside the firm is of no consequence, and so, as Coase (1991, p. 65) has complained, 'economists have tended to neglect the main activity of a firm, running a business'. When it has been thought necessary to give some defense of this standard view, it has been asserted that profit-maximizing businessmen know how to respond optimally to price signals, or alternatively that a market selection process will reject all those who do not. Neither assertion has been substantiated: the former would require an investigation into businessmen's skills as well as their motivation, and the latter an analysis not only of selection mechanisms but also of the ways in which the options for selection are generated. Such investigations and analyses are outwith the range of standard economics; but Dick Cyert recognized their importance and made significant contributions to them. The evolutionary analysis of capabilities is a continuation of his work.

Although Robbins's fundamental proposition about the efficiency of market systems has been disputed, most economists continue to share his view that the subject-matter of 'economic organization' is the coordination of a well-defined set of economic activities; the central question is whether the independent activities of selfish individuals is compatible with an efficient set of outcomes. Although this question has been presented in three forms, the answer always depends on the incentive structures within the system: indeed 'today economists can define their field ... as being about the analysis of incentives in all social institutions' (Myerson 1999, p. 1068). Since, as Myerson (1999, p. 1069) explains, economics is necessarily based on 'a model that assumes that individuals intelligently understand their environment and rationally act to maximise their own welfare', incentive structures are all that is left to analyse. This conception of the individual directs attention to the set of coordinated outcomes and trivializes the process of coordination, implicitly denying the relevance of behavioral economics, and of all topics that involve the extent, dispersion, reliability or growth of knowledge – which might be thought to include most economic problems. But even within Myerson's narrow definition of economics, the concept of incentives is narrowly construed. Agents are driven by their preference functions, but since the satisfaction of all preferences depends on income (the time that is required to satisfy some preferences has to be bought by income forgone) income maximization (with some allowance for leisure) is deemed sufficient for computing optimal behavior. As we shall see, this is not good enough for understanding either the growth of knowledge or the working of organizations; there are powerful motives which cannot be subsumed under income maximization.

The first form of this analysis of self-interested choice began with comparisons of the implications for allocative efficiency of the incentive structures which are provided by competition and monopoly, and culminated in the twin foundation principles of welfare economics: every competitive equilibrium is a Pareto optimum, and every Pareto optimum can be matched to a competitive equilibrium. The model specification that led to these principles also demonstrated that a competitive equilibrium was a decentralized version of central allocation, and since it appeared that a competitive equilibrium might be incompatible with the premises of 'market' models (notably because of economies of scale and the incentives to secure monopoly rents) many economists concluded that in practice decentralization entailed inefficiency. (We should remember that the 'markets' of economic theory are conceptual fictions, without institutional content.) Competition, it was widely believed, was normally imperfect, and therefore undesirable. Since the organizational structures either of firms or of non-market allocative systems had no effects on the real economy, this conclusion was thought sufficient to make the case for government intervention, without any need to analyse the working of either government or markets.

This case was reinforced by presenting the question in the second form, which was addressed to the scope of the market system rather than the degree of perfection within each market. Where significant benefits or costs could not be traded, selfish individuals had no incentive to include them in their calculations, and therefore even a perfectly competitive economy would fail to deliver a social optimum. In the presence of external effects, allocative efficiency always required external intervention. Thus not only could government do anything that perfect markets could do; it could also achieve efficiencies that were beyond the reach even of perfect markets. Coase's (1960) second famous article demonstrated the analytical incoherence of this argument; it implicitly assumed that the potential gains from trade that were the counterpart of unpriced externalities were absolutely unattainable by contract but costlessly achievable by government – even though the standard analysis of markets assumed that the process of making and enforcing market contracts was entirely costless.

Neither of these forms in which the efficiency of an economic system based on independent agents is analysed gives any attention to internal organization, either of firms or governments. This omission eventually provoked the development of what is usually called public choice theory, which applies to bureaucracies and the political process the standard assumptions of rational selfishness which deliver market failure and, not surprisingly, identifies many more failures in these new applications. We shall leave aside this body of theory, though substantial parts of it are also relevant to non-governmental organizations. Instead, we shall note that in the analyses mentioned so far it has generally been assumed that everyone is not only selfish but also honest. People drive hard bargains, but they then keep them. It is apparently only by adding dishonesty to selfishness that economists have been able to present the question of the allocative efficiency of individual incentives in its third form, which allows market contracts to be compared with organizational contracts as efficient solutions to incentive problems.

This third form has resulted in theories of complete contracts governing principal–agent relationships (in which the contracted organization is actually presented as a market), theories of incomplete contracts in which the gaps are filled by the efficient allocation of property rights, and transaction cost theory, as developed essentially by Williamson, which is distinguished by an explicitly hierarchical conception of organizational decision making. Each of these theories is presented as an equilibrium supplement to the equilibrium theory of production, which remains unaffected by them; within the broader scope of economics their purpose is to ensure that appropriate incentives are provided to deliver the efficient productive outcomes which are prescribed by that theory, despite the pervasiveness of opportunism. As Dosi et al. (2001) observe, anyone whose knowledge of firms was derived exclusively from the writings of such economists as Jean Tirole and Oliver Hart would gain the impression that 'firms are places where one confines vicious and cunning people who are made to play extremely sophisticated games according to rules designed to prevent them doing much harm to themselves and to others'. Williamson (1997, p. 130), in particular, has been quite explicit that it is only because people are dishonest as well as selfish that there is any reason for firms to exist.

In addition to opportunism, some deficiencies (and often asymmetries) of knowledge among the contracting parties are required in the specification of these modern theories of organization as a means of securing incentive compatibility; but they are deficiencies which are carefully designed to throw precisely the right kind of spanner in the works, without inhibiting the power of agents to act in ways which constitute a rational equilibrium. As in modern macroeconomics, knowledge is either complete or utterly unobtainable. There is no way that potential victims can discover the private information that makes opportunism possible; nevertheless both parties can calculate accurately the consequences of this irremediable piece of ignorance, and can therefore correctly assess the potential gains from trading away the potential for exploitation, and so conclude the kind of contract that can secure for each party a share of these gains. There is thus no obstacle to 'farsighted contracting' (Williamson 1996, p. 9) which will substantially overcome the barriers to efficiency that are erected by the possibility of opportunism, although principal–agent theory, property-rights theory, and Williamsonian transaction cost theory give different accounts of these farsighted contracts – and it is only Williamson who provides an organizational solution which is more – though not much more – than a special case of a market. It may be worth noting that similarly farsighted contracting could greatly reduce, or even eliminate, the efficiency losses attributable to monopoly or externalities.

Coase has not been notably enthusiastic about these developments. He has reminded us that the argument of his 1937 article (which, like his 1960 paper, though famous, is obviously not well known) does not turn on any systematic superiority of the firm over market exchange in controlling opportunism (Coase 1991, p. 58). We should recall that Coase worked out his explanation of the firm on the basis of his own studies of business behavior, which did not support any such generalization; and there have been spectacular examples of opportunism which have been made possible by the existence of firms. The motivation for the imperfectly specified contracts which constitute Coase's firm does not correspond to the incentives which drive modern theories; it is directly derived from the problems of knowledge, and especially the problems of an economy which, in John Hicks's phrase, is 'in time', considerations that are entirely absent from the kinds of analysis just discussed. Coase's explanation turns on the advantages, in some circumstances, of organized relationships within a continuing group in obtaining and using, over time, the knowledge that is required to make particular kinds of decisions intelligently. Consequently he saw firms as substantively different from markets in their function and modes of operation. That any understanding of organization should be based on knowledge first, and incentives second, is a foundational premise of this chapter; it has been central to the work of Herbert Simon and his colleagues, notably Cyert, as well as that of Coase. Richard Langlois and Nicolai Foss are perhaps the economists who have most actively pursued this theme of the firm as an instrument of knowledge and change.

3 UNCERTAINTY AND ORGANIZATION

It is, however, unfortunate that Coase sufficiently misunderstood Frank Knight's (1921) analysis to miss a major opportunity of developing this theme. He explicitly agreed with Knight that uncertainty was a necessary condition for firms, but he dismissed Knight's claim that the consequences of uncertainty provided sufficient conditions. Knight's analysis is worth revisiting, especially because of the current standard practice of ignoring uncertainty while explicitly claiming to deal with it. We shall also be able to identify precisely why Coase missed his opportunity.

Knight (1921) was the first to examine carefully the conditions that are necessary for competition to be perfect (in the technical sense required for economic theory), and he showed that these conditions were extremely restrictive. They did not, however, include a complete knowledge of future outcomes. Provided, first, that all the possible future states which were relevant to a specific decision could be listed, and second, that the likelihood of each future state could be established, either empirically or by deduction, then the consequences of any available action could be evaluated no less definitively than situations in which the outcome of every action was known for certain. This was Knight's definition of risk, which remains the basis for modem theories of decision making 'under uncertainty'. Knightian uncertainty is unanalysable (Lucas 1981, p. 224), and so is assumed not to exist. That the evaluation might be so complicated as to exceed the bounds of rationality was a possibility that Knight did not consider; it seems to be implicit in Coase's discussion, though in the form of cost rather than feasibility.

Knight's concern was to emphasize the distinction between all such situations and those which were characterized by uncertainty, which he defined as a condition in which there was no assured means of establishing a set of probabilities. Then no definitive evaluation was possible, however 'rational' the evaluators. Except for analytical convenience, the subjective probability distributions which populate economic analyses of 'uncertainty' are not equivalent to the objective distributions that define risk; they are, in Hayek's ([1974] 1978, p. 23) words, 'a pretence of knowledge'. (There are, of course, powerful reasons for such pretences, in economic theorizing and in many other contexts; economists, like other people, cannot bear too much reality.) It was left to Shackle to point out that often – and especially for the more important decisions – there is also no procedure available to produce a definitive list of possible outcomes; this clearly reinforces Knight's argument (as Knight appears to realize) but is not strictly essential to it.

Shackle emphasizes the extent of our ignorance of future possibilities, while Knight's argument only requires the impossibility of distributing probabilities over a set of possibilities in a demonstrably correct manner. However, the two ideas are closely connected, because what frustrates the assignment of probabilities is ultimately our inability to identify all the factors which would tend to permit or prevent the occurrence of each of the outcomes which are, in Shackle's phrase, 'deemed possible', and this is precisely an inability to construct closed sets of future events or of future relationships. We do not know; and often we do not know what it is that we do not know – for example, that inert fluorine compounds, ideal for refrigeration, will damage the ozone layer. There is, in short, no accessible 'correct model of the economy'; but as Shackle repeatedly reminded us, this is what makes discovery possible, in economics as well as in economic systems.

In his very first published article, George Richardson (1953) revisits Knight's distinction between risk and uncertainty, and matches it to a distinction between situations in which there is a procedure of rational calculation which is not merely known but known to be correct, and situations in which no such procedure exists – or can exist as long as the situation is indeed one of uncertainty, whether Shackleian or Knightian. Where there can be no agreed correct procedure, there is no optimum implicit in the data; in such circumstances, Richardson points out, decisions necessarily depend on the particular skills of the decision maker, which are likely to be substantially subjective, tacit, idiosyncratic and experience based. Coase's (1937) claim that Knightian entrepreneurs can trade their distinctive skills rests on an implicit assumption that, despite their non-rational basis, these skills are capable of objective evaluation, thus in effect reducing uncertainty to risk, as economists have so often done. It is because of this implicit assumption, probably resulting from his acceptance of the wide-ranging effectiveness of markets, that Coase missed his opportunity. Richardson (1953) warns us that any appraisal of the efficiency of an economic system which ignores Knight's distinction, the consequent need for skills which cannot be reduced to rationality, and the implications for economic organization and economic policy, is of uncertain value – as Coase (1960) was himself to argue about the neglect of transaction costs. In emphasizing the importance of distinctive skills within an economic system Richardson appears, in retrospect, on the verge of producing in 1953 the analysis of economic organization in terms of capabilities which appeared almost twenty years later (Richardson 1972); and it is noteworthy that he did so in the context not of productive activity but of decision making. This is worth some further consideration.

In exploring the implications of Knight's analysis Richardson (1953, p. 139) refers to Ryle's (1949) distinction between 'knowing that' – knowledge of facts, relationships, historical sequences and theorems – and 'knowing how' – the ability to perform certain operations, a distinction to which Richardson (1972) returns in developing his analysis of the organization of industry. What makes Ryle's discussion particularly appropriate is that he was attacking the privilege that has traditionally been accorded by philosophers to intellectual operations at the expense of practical abilities. Standard economics not only claims to constitute 'knowledge that'; its propositions are formulated in terms of 'knowledge that', and give absolute priority to the intellectual concept of optimization over the practical skills that are required for any productive activity. Preferences, resources and technology are treated as facts (which may include factual probability distributions) from which choices are deduced by procedures which are known to be appropriate. The ability to perform any action that is chosen is never in doubt: input–output relationships may be stochastic, but there is never any question that output will be delivered. Production and consumption skills are never directly addressed; as Robbins desired, production is simply part of equilibrium theory, and economic theory, like most economists, does not venture inside the factory.

However, the neglect of capabilities not only emasculates the notions of productive or consumption activities; it undermines economists' treatment of the intellectual operations which constitute the core of their theoretical apparatus. Decision making is treated as dependent simply on two kinds of 'knowledge that'; relevant facts (where relevance is itself a fact) and logical procedures. Optimization is therefore well defined; anyone can do it – and will have done it long before any economist gets around to analysing the situation. In a theoretical system whose organizing principle is the allocation of scarce resources, the crucial resource of cognition is a free good. It is, however, a matter of common observation that in practice optimization is rarely well-defined: some of the facts are in dispute, some may be unobtainable, we cannot be sure what is relevant, and there is often no obviously correct procedure. Like the production of any good or service, decision making is itself an activity which requires appropriate skills. But to admit diversity into decision-making abilities would be to introduce genuine uncertainty not only into the subject-matter of economics but into economists' methods of theorizing.

In corners of the subject we encounter 'noise traders' and 'trembling hands' as somewhat desperate attempts to resolve difficulties while protecting the formidable but narrow core capabilities of modem economic theory; but these expedients are clearly anomalous and tolerated only because no version of strictly formal rationality can be made to deliver an equilibrium. However, the proliferation of equilibria in game theory has shown that the very notion of rational choice, the supposedly unshakable rock on which modem economic theory has been founded, is itself highly problematic. It may indeed be impossible to have a general theory of choice which does not take into explicit account the capabilities of the chooser, and the process of choosing. Although this may appear a threat to many economists, it opens the prospect of bringing economics much closer to other subjects and to common sense: it does often matter who makes decisions and how they are made, and not only because of the incentives to which they are subject; as Knight (1921, p. 241) noted, some people (and, to anticipate, some organizations) are better than others in coping with particular categories of Knightian (or Shackleian) uncertainty. That would hardly come as news to Cyert; and it explains why behavioral concepts are readily incorporated into evolutionary economics (Nelson and Winter 1982).

It is in these interpersonal differences in decision-making skills that Knight finds the basis of entrepreneurship, and of the possibility of profit which is not just a disguised wage; for neither entrepreneurship nor profit has any basis in conditions where objective, reproducible procedures are available for making every decision. That such procedures, implying no barriers to entry, cannot be a source of assured continuing profit is a useful lesson in first-year economics; it is therefore easier to forgive the Barings' executive who remarked that making money out of derivatives was a simple business than to pardon the elementary error of those Nobel Prizewinning economists who launched Long Term Capital Management as a logically impeccable, and publicly available, instrument for delivering sustainable above-average profits. In practice, before they were able to illustrate this basic proposition of formal economic logic they discovered the reality of Shackleian uncertainty, which makes above-average profits possible but was outside the scope of their well-defined procedures.

Knight goes on to argue that apparently superior skills in coping with a particular category of uncertainty may lead entrepreneurs to create a firm, which others may be very ready to join because of the apparent prospect of continuing employment without the need for decision-making skills which they may not possess. Casson (1982) draws on Knight's argument, and recognizes that entrepreneurs may need to create both an organization and a market in order to profit from such skills, and also that they may have difficulty in funding their enterprise because potential investors and lenders can have no certain means of evaluating it; his examination of the process of creating and running an entrepreneurial business is still unmatched within economics. Knight (1921, p. 259) also draws attention to the inseparability of the management problem and the uncertainty problem, because management is always something more than the automatic application of fully-specified procedures, as Barnard (1938) explains – a realization that should induce some desirable skepticism about the abundant recipes for assured success in business.

Although this link between management and uncertainty may seem to contrast with Schumpeter's vision of entrepreneurship, both Knight and Schumpeter rely on the conceptual distinction between programmed and unprogrammed actions, which has been a theme of Carnegie analyses of organizational behavior. For Schumpeter (1934, p. 80), 'rational choice' is always a fiction; but given sufficient time in a stable environment people may come to act in a fashion which simulates rationality. However, what appears in such an environment to be the result of rational choice is in fact the product of routine, and gives no promise of any ability to respond appropriately to any change; indeed, the origination of change is outside the scope of rational choice or the routines which may mimic its results, though Schumpeter writes of 'imagination' and 'vision' to the neglect of the skills which may be needed to realize entrepreneurial conceptions, and which may indeed help to stimulate them. It is not the least of Penrose's (1959) merits that she places the interaction between skills and imagination at the core of her theory.

If a correct model of the economy were available, then behavior might be fully coordinated, because it could be fully programmed (though necessarily from outside); there would be no function for firms, markets, or any formal organization. Information technology would be sufficient. Organizations, including firms, are a response to uncertainty – not to risk. It is therefore no accident that economists who have taken organization seriously (of whom Cyert and his colleagues are among the most prominent) have not been content with theories which rely on substantive rationality and contractual equilibrium. No complete procedures are available, and tight logical deductions are insufficient: the functions of the executive, as Barnard

(1938) says, are to find effective ways of making decisions that are not dependent on formal logic, and to develop relationships, systems and attitudes that will support the making of such decisions. Knight's specification of entrepreneurship leads directly to specialization in particular kinds of uncertainty-bearing, which, like other kinds of specialization, facilitates the enhancement in real time of the entrepreneur's capabilities for dealing with particular categories of uncertainty; it therefore belongs in a theory of process, the outcomes of which cannot be calculated because some of the data needed for such calculation are products of the process, and in particular of entrepreneurial imagination. However, although an emphasis on entrepreneurs as directors of change is appropriate, entrepreneurship is not confined to those at the head of a business, as both Marshall (1920) and Penrose (1959) remind us. The creation of a firm may, as Coase ([1972] 1988, p. 63) argued, facilitate the development of at least supporting skills, or even help 'to bring out whatever enterprise and power of origination' the employees may possess (Marshall 1920, p. 297). How well this can be done depends, among other things, on the boundaries of the firm and the ways in which its internal activities and external relationships are structured; for, as Marshall (1920, pp. 138–9) notably realized, all these aspects of organization shape the development of knowledge, and all are proper subjects for research into business practice.

The firm is a device for both differentiation and integration; in the economic sphere it is one of the major instruments for the creation of new knowledge through the division of labour, and for the application of that knowledge to new uses. This is the theme of Edith Penrose's (1959) superb book: the firm is 'a pool of resources the utilisation of which is organised in an administrative framework' (Penrose 1959, p. 149). The importance of each firm's pool of resources has recently been quite widely recognized, often with reference to Penrose – though sometimes with incomplete understanding, as Foss (1999) has observed; the administrative framework, however, has been relatively neglected. In Penrose's analysis it has a double role. In prescribing how productive activities are to be decomposed it establishes a particular division of labor within which, as Adam Smith ([1776] 1976b) emphasized, new skills may be developed, and it therefore influences the kinds of productive resources that are developed. It also defines responsibilities for decision making, and the elements, time-horizons, and criteria to be used in making these decisions; it thus not only influences the decisions themselves, but also the non-random sample of experience on the basis of which managerial resources will develop, making possible the provision of new managerial services and the perception of productive opportunities.

The use of present knowledge and the development of fresh knowledge are intimately linked, in organizations as in individuals. It should not, however, be forgotten that the administrative framework may have the effect of diminishing the relevance of managerial resources to new situations – as can be observed in the history of many organizations: substantial organizational redesign has often been necessary to adjust both the use and development of knowledge to new circumstances. Pavitt (1998, p. 447) has emphasized the need 'to improve understanding of the organizational processes of co-ordination and control that make for a successful matching between the development and deployment of bodies of technological knowledge, on the one hand, and commercially successful (or useful) working artefacts, on the other'. But before examining in some detail the importance of the firm as a means of structuring the growth and use of knowledge, it is important to clarify the problem of knowledge, which is either ignored or misrepresented in so much modem economics.

4 THE CONSTRUCTION OF KNOWLEDGE

The concept of rational choice epitomizes the structure of economic theory, which relies on deductive logic to reveal what is implicit in the premises. In other words, economists construct tautologies. As with the tautologies which constitute mathematical theorems, their construction is not necessarily a useless exercise, because the implications of a set of premises are not always obvious, and may indeed be surprising. For example, working out the implications of the premises for a proposed action (for example, by decision analysis or investment appraisal) may prompt a reconsideration which avoids a costly mistake or suggests a profitable modification. But carrying truth values from premises to conclusions does not ensure that the conclusions are applicable to any empirical issue; that requires the premises to be complete and correct in relation to that issue. Shackle (1972, Preface) posed the problem succinctly: 'The economic analyst assumes that men pursue their interest by applying reason to their circumstances. And he does not ask *how they know* what their circumstances are'.

David Hume had given a clear answer – which is also Shackle's answer, independently arrived at – to that question: there is no system of deduction or induction which can yield certain empirical knowledge. Hume had therefore turned from the impossible task of proving empirical truths to a potentially rewarding enquiry into the processes by which people come to accept some empirical propositions as knowledge; and his friend and colleague Adam Smith ([1795] 1980) produced a psychological theory of the growth of science that was based on the human desire to make sense of experience, which stimulated the invention of connecting principles that serve to link phenomena in the imagination. This motivation and its consequences, which are apparent in everyday life, including life in organizations, are hardly less significant for economic development than the incentives to which economists typically restrict themselves. Smith applies his theoretical apparatus to the history of astronomy, and concludes by arguing that Isaac Newton's theories were just such invented principles, while explaining why they had come to be generally perceived as the correct model of reality.

In the course of his exposition, Smith showed how increasing specialization between fields of science led to the identification of anomalies that were not apparent to non-specialists, and thus to the invention of more effective connecting principles. He subsequently applied this principle of problem-driven creativity to the process of economic development, identifying the division of labor as the means of defining problem areas within which new knowledge could be developed – principally in the form of performance skills, but also including the imagination of new combinations, which, as Pavitt (1998, p. 433) notes, is also stimulated by the division of labor (Smith [1776] 1976b, pp. 20–21).

Economics has since contained two incompatible research traditions. One is driven by the search for proofs, primarily for proofs of equilibrium, which necessarily require all change, in the sense of departure from established patterns, to be strictly exogenous; even 'endogenous growth theory' does not encompass the development of an economy 'by its own initiative, from within' (Schumpeter 1934, p. 6). The other tradition seeks to develop accounts of process, and of the structures which facilitate and constrain such processes (Loasby 2002). The invention of non-Euclidean geometry appears to have been decisive in persuading Marshall, before he took up economics, that formal proofs could not deliver empirical truth (Butler 1991); Darwin offered an alternative method of explaining the growth of knowledge, and Marshall (1994) used this to produce a conceptual model of the human brain as a mechanical system interacting with its environment. This now looks like a precursor of a 'classifier system', in which perceptions of specific circumstances are grouped and connected to groups of responses which appear to be effective in those circumstances. Variations in circumstances, in perceptions, and in the sequence in which actions are tried then combine to generate variety of behavior among 'machines' of identical design, thus providing the material for a selection process. A striking feature of Marshall's model is the evolutionary sequence of mental structures; once such a system for connecting perceptions with actions delivers a level of performance which is adequate for survival, but not before, there is scope for the emergence of a higher-level system, which classifies ideas of perception and response, thus moving from reaction to anticipation, and introducing the possibility of consequential reasoning. Moreover the two levels remain intimately linked, since failure at the first level generates problems for the higher level to solve by creating new associations – as in Smith's ([1795] 1980) theory, which Marshall appears never to have read; and success in doing so leads to the installation of new operating systems. (For a fuller account, see Groenewegen 1995.)

That 'rationality', in the standard economic sense of deductive logic, is a relatively late development, and that logical operations rely on, and are typically triggered by, non-logical processes, which may be 'better than rational' (Cosmides and Tooby 1994) is a Marshallian anticipation of modern evolutionary psychology. The high energy demands of the brain (which pose a classic problem of resource allocation) and the importance for survival of rapid assimilation of multiple signals and rapid response were not favorable to the development of intelligence in the form of a general-purpose problem solver. Far more effective and efficient would be an architecture which facilitated the creation of topic-specific patterns, leading to a distributed system of self-organizing networks – a division of labor within the brain. This evolutionary inheritance is the most obvious explanation of the results of the Wason test (named after its originator), which has been extensively replicated by psychologists. When subjects are presented with a simple test of logical reasoning which requires them to identify which of four pieces of evidence is relevant for testing a universal proposition (of the form all A is B) the success rate is very low; but when the equivalent information is presented in a familiar context the success rate rises dramatically – even though, from the logician's perspective, the contextual presentation appears to throw a veil over the stark simplicity of the basic general problem. Although humans have certainly developed logical skills, our cognitive processes still rely much more on pattern making than deductive reasoning. This is what Smith's theory of science tells us; and that would explain why the apparent simplifications of abstract models may impede rather than facilitate the making of effective decisions.

Moreover, this is not necessarily a serious disadvantage. If we were rather better at deductive operations, they might actually lead us astray. Marshall (1920, pp. 770–84) certainly thought so, and warned economists to keep to short chains of reasoning. He pointed out that economic phenomena were often very complex, and that the distant conclusions of a deductive system which was based on simplifications of this complexity were therefore liable to bear rather little resemblance to the conclusions which would be reached by a full specification; but full specifications were beyond human powers, and so limited powerful deductions should be informed and amended by an abundant understanding of the facts. Marshall is known – indeed, for some he is notorious – for his adherence to this principle; no economist has known more about the workings of business in his lifetime, and this knowledge is reflected in both the method and content of his work. His consistent refusal to pursue the apparent logic of his initial simplifying assumptions to their ultimate implications has been repeatedly deplored; but the damage to both understanding and policy that has been inflicted by relentless but unreflective rigor is all too apparent in the record of economics.

We have noted earlier how Coase was guided by his observations of firms and market relationships to an explanation of the firm which is significantly different from those developed by later theorists. Simon was inspired by Barnard's (1938) experience-based analysis of the problems of management to insist on the importance of observation of managerial processes, which is fundamental to behavioral economics; and it has been a persistent argument of behavioral economists that the enterprise of economics should itself be procedurally rather than substantively rational. Andrews (1949) and Penrose (1959, 1995) also resolved to construct theories which respected the facts of business. May it not be significant that none of those mentioned in this paragraph produced theories which closely resemble standard modem economics?

Raffaelli (2001), who is primarily responsible for drawing our attention to Marshall's early intellectual history, plausibly suggests that Marshall's evolutionary model of the human brain may have influenced his account of economic development through an explicit combination of Smith's principle of the division of labor and Charles Darwin's principle of variation; firms in different industries develop knowledge of particular relevance to that industry, and within each industry different firms may develop somewhat different classifier systems out of their different experiences, and devise new experiments in response to anomalies, favorable or unfavorable, which are encountered in the daily management of a business. A more extended account of a similar combination of processes forms the basis of Penrose's (1959) theory; and the interaction between routine and innovation is a central feature of evolutionary economics as conceived by Nelson and Winter (1982). Looking more widely, we can observe similar themes in accounts (broadly Popperian) of the growth of science through the generation and testing of new conjectures in an attempt to resolve the anomalies which result from pursuing the deductive or experimental logic of conjectures which, though established, are permanently unprovable.

Knowledge, except knowledge of implications, cannot be proved, and the empirical relevance of deductive systems is always open to question. It may, however, be more or less reliable (which should not be confused with more or less certain) according to the processes by which it is generated, criticized and tested (Ziman 1978). Scientific claims to credibility depend on process, not proof, although formal proofs may contribute to an effective process, It cannot deliver certainty; Ziman (1978, p. 40) estimates that 90 percent of the contents of the physics journals are false, and that the physics that has survived the process of criticism and testing and been incorporated into the textbooks is no more than 90 percent true. Knowledge grows through the imposition, extension and amendment of structure, and it is falsified by the destruction of previously-accepted structure – as, for example, it is claimed that knowledge of effective retailing is destroyed by the novel structures of e-commerce; in what circumstances, if any, this conjecture is corroborated we shall no doubt discover, by the normal process of trial and error. The organization of economic activity is the organization of a process of generating, criticizing and testing knowledge of how to perform economic activities, of what activities to perform, how to organize them, and how to achieve improvements and innovation. This process relies on the continuous generation of variety through differences between people and firms in the ways that they organize their cognitive activities.

It is implicit in the preceding discussion that the growth of knowledge is a social process; and it is worth pausing to consider why. The underlying reason is to be found in the particular combination of powers and limitations of the evolved human brain. As we have noted, far from being a general-purpose problem solver, which can apply a standard pattern of reasoning to any field, the brain is a network which can be organized in an apparently infinite variety of configurations, each specialized to a particular range of operations; but though any brain is capable of creating and sustaining many such configurations, these are only a very small part of the initial potential. Opportunity costs are therefore inherent in the human situation – indeed in the architecture of the human brain: what any of us can know depends on the way in which our brain becomes organized, and every principle of organization automatically excludes many other possibilities of constructing knowledge. However, within any society, these opportunity costs can be mitigated if its members use different principles of cognitive organization; it is the division of labor that allows us to take advantage of human potential in order to relax the human constraints. That is why the continuing division of labor is the key to the growth of knowledge, and so to economic development. The classic statement of economic development as both cause and effect of changing economic organization is by Young (1928).

The price of increasing the total amount of knowledge within any society is increasing dependence on other people's knowledge. In a market economy, narrowly conceived, we depend on other people's knowledge which is embodied in the goods and services that they supply, and in their contributions to productive systems. Managing this interdependence entails substantial transaction costs, which are basically costs of cognition, and leads to the development of market institutions which mitigate these costs (Loasby 2000). But this dependence is much more pervasive, as Adam Smith realized. We adapt other people's solutions to our problems to save ourselves the trouble of inventing our own, as the acceptance of successive astronomical systems demonstrates; and we look to others for information, ideas, ways of structuring problems, and decision criteria, even within our own areas of special knowledge, as Smith shows in his *Theory of Moral Sentiments* ([1759] 1976a). In this sense knowledge is socially constructed – or, to be more precise, and more informative, some of the principles on which individuals organize their own knowledge, including knowledge of how to make decisions in particular circumstances, are adapted from others.

Choi (1993) has suggested that conventions, procedures and rules of behavior – what we now summarize as institutions – first arose through the search for outside help in solving our own personal problems, and were subsequently found useful for managing interactions; that some shared conventions turned out to be socially as well as individually convenient encouraged the development of institutions with the primary effect of facilitating interactions. Smith's 'History of astronomy' ([1795] 1980) illustrates this sequence. The individual psychological impulse to find some serviceable general explanation of worrying phenomena generates more serviceable ways of organizing knowledge, which are gratefully accepted by others as ways of 'soothing the imagination'; gradually this diffusion of successful methods of sense-making leads to the emergence of scientific communities who develop shared ways of organizing knowledge, though with the variations that are necessary for further development within a 'research programme'.

The discipline of sociology, which explores the influence of groups on individuals, thus has a basis in the psychology of individuals, which leads them to look to others for ways of improving or supplementing their own knowledge. Although this dependence makes opportunism possible, it also often helps to mitigate it; if we are continually treating others as a source of useful knowledge, we may have little time (even if we have the inclination) to develop schemes for exploiting them. Given the dispersion of knowledge and the insistence on extreme self-interest within economic models, we may be surprised that there is not more evidence of opportunism in the economy and society than is readily discernible. Models of repeated games do not seem to provide sufficient explanation; it seems likely that there is often no need for opportunism to be contracted away, because it may simply be crowded out.

Indeed, not only may we not have the spare mental resources to be opportunistic; we often unilaterally accept the authority of others. Barnard (1938, p. 163) insisted that 'the decision as to whether an order has authority or not lies with the persons to whom it is addressed, and does not reside in 'persons of authority' or those who issue these orders'. Of course this decision is influenced by incentives, but often the most powerful incentive is internally generated: the acceptance of authority greatly simplifies our cognitive problems. If Barnard's statement is to be criticized, it should be for its expression solely in terms of communications from superiors to subordinates; for on many occasions every day we accept guidance, and even imperatives, from people who have no claim on our obedience, and who may not even know of our existence. Even in formal organizations, most communications which are treated as authoritative do not come from superiors. Ménard (1994) emphasizes the importance of non-hierarchical authority in formal organizations; and no senior manager can function effectively if s/he is unwilling to accept most of what s/he is told by nominal subordinates. Of course we can reject any source of authority at any time – and sometimes rejection is crucial; but to reject them all would be to deprive ourselves of a great many opportunities to improve the organization of our own knowledge. Like institutions, authority provides an indispensable framework within which we can organize our own cognitive processes. This cognitive dependence provides the psychological basis for the acceptance of formal organization.

These frameworks, and the processes that we organize with their assistance, have no claim to optimality; indeed, from time to time they may lead to unfortunate or even disastrous choices. We may be too susceptible to the advice, information and apparent experience of others (such as management pundits), which may be wrong, or inappropriately applied, just like our home-grown knowledge. Rhetoric, as presented by Smith ([1963] 1983), is necessary for effective communication, and may indeed, as in the scientific practice of reporting experiments in the passive voice to emphasize their claim to reproducibility rather than to celebrate the superior skills of the experimenter, contribute to the effective organization of the process of discovery; nevertheless the familiar negative connotations of the term have abundant justification in human experience. We may be too easily convinced by those who are honestly mistaken; and opportunism is certainly a genuine problem. However, the successes as well as the failures of economic development, and of human civilization, rest on the organization of our cognitive potential, and in particular on a level of organization of our cognitive processes that would not be possible without a very great deal of external assistance.

5 ORGANIZING DECISION PROCESSES AND DEVELOPING CAPABILITIES

Because the remarkable potential of the human brain for making connections so greatly exceeds the number of patterns which any individual can maintain, it is necessarily true that human knowledge grows by division. There can be no single pool of knowledge available to all; efficient allocation cannot in practice be handled as a general problem – and especially not as a problem of defining equilibrium. Everyone must cope with situations which are characterized by Knightian uncertainty. However, the obverse of this problem is the possibility of gaining new knowledge; without uncertainty (whether recognized or not) there can be no innovation. Now our brains are actually rather effective at developing the skills that are necessary to cope with some kinds of uncertainty – that is the cognitive principle which makes Knight's analysis so important for economic analysis; they are also quite effective in extending our individual knowledge in particular directions. Indeed both activities seem to rely on similar skills of pattern-making; making decisions under uncertainty and developing knowledge both require the construction of order.

Knowledge is constructed by imposing organization on phenomena; and any systematic process of creating knowledge, whether in the form of performance skills, codified 'knowledge that', or problem-solving abilities, requires its own forms of organization. The construction of such order may take place at the level of the individual, through the invention of connecting principles and the development of classifier systems, within an academic discipline, which may be thought of as a cluster of institutions which facilitate the development of capabilities by imposing particular kinds of order, within a firm through schemes of decomposition which allow knowledge to be constructed within subdivisions and also by linkages between these subdivisions, and through interfirm alliances and networks which (if they are successful) preserve different schemes of ordering within each member of the alliance or network while facilitating combinations of knowledge which rest on these differences. In this section we shall concentrate on the creation of order within a firm.

Let us recall Penrose's (1959, p. 149) definition of the firm as 'a pool of resources the utilisation of which is organised within an administrative framework'. Her theme is the shaping of cognitive repertoires within an organizational context. The administrative framework defines the space within which new knowledge is created, and by providing a flow of similar experiences it enables an increasing number of activities to be performed by routine, thus releasing cognitive capacity for the making of new patterns; for, as Whitehead ([1911] 1948, pp. 41–2) pointed out, it is only by ceasing to think about old problems that we can develop the capabilities to tackle new problems. We may note also the importance of authority (in Barnard's sense) in creating space for new thoughts. These processes supply the psychological underpinning of Penrose's theory of the growth of the firm, explaining both the development of additional productive skills and the receding managerial limit; and the speed and content of both kinds of development are regulated by the administrative framework which provides an external organization for the individual and interpersonal cognitive processes which deliver new usable knowledge.

The firm is a response to the cognitive limitations of individuals; it is a focusing device, which serves both to allocate the cognitive resources of the firm to its various activities and to facilitate learning within those activities. (Nooteboom 2001, p. 43) The performance of these activities, and the learning that emerges from performance, are both oriented towards sub-objectives, as behavioral theorists have long realized. The importance of the division of labor in fostering the development of productive capabilities has increasingly been recognized; in this section attention is concentrated on skills in decision making, while remembering, as Schumpeter (1934, pp. 20–21) pointed out, that the necessity for making decisions arises, in some form or other, in all activities. The boundaries of the firm limit the field within which decisions have to be made and therefore the potential variety of patterns which might be necessary for making effective decisions: as a notable recent example, the creation of Zeneca as a company separate from ICI was partly justified by the argument that the path and the strength of biological development had accentuated the differences from the more traditional ways of thinking about chemical businesses (which were themselves sufficiently varied) to the point where it was more effective to assign areas of decision making, not just to different divisions but to different companies.

We owe to Richardson (1972) the clear formulation of the principle that dissimilar capabilities, being themselves disparately organized, should be assigned to different formal organizations. This principle is reflected in the title of Neil Kay's recent book, *Pattern in Corporate Evolution* (1997), which signals the importance of matching ways of organizing cognition to corporate activities; extensions of a business into fields where applications and modifications of familiar patterns are appropriate is likely to be more successful than ventures into areas where unfamiliar patterns are more effective, as Penrose (1959) argues, especially when these effective patterns are already familiar to rival firms. However, it is always possible to misjudge the applicability of a firm's productive or managerial resources; the relevance of decision-making capabilities developed in one organizational context to other contexts can never be known before it is tried. Apparent opportunities are always conjectures; they are part of the evolutionary process of variety generation and the winnowing of this variety. What can be expected, and has often been shown, is that ranges of application are always limited, but that these limits vary greatly between individuals – and also vary, though less substantially, between organizations within an industry; and for any individual or organization there is typically much variation between the range of application of different skills. Both Knight and Penrose note this double diversity.

Within their boundaries, firms develop structured procedures for dealing with problems, and for improving their ability to deal with them: organizational design substantially determines not only where problems will be worked on, but how problems are defined, what criteria will guide the acceptability of solutions, and even the ways in which solutions will be sought. Complexity must be simplified, and the process of management, like the process of theory-building, takes place in the space of representations. As Simon (1959, p. 272) observed, 'the perceived world is fantastically different from the "real" world'; it is therefore not a matter of indifference where within this space these processes are located. Decision making is decomposed in ways which are supposed to limit the cognitive demands on individuals by restricting their decision agenda and the kinds of options that they are expected to consider; and these decompositions are also supposed to provide sufficient commonality between decisions to allow appropriate procedures to develop within each sphere of responsibility and to encourage managers to derive improved, and perhaps novel, capabilities from their interpretations of their sample of experience – which, it should not be forgotten, is most unlikely to be random, even within their field of activity.

In an interdependent and open system no decomposition, whether between or within firms, can precisely represent that system. Indeed every decomposition has its characteristic way of failing, as may be observed within firms and every other kind of human organization. (The fallacies of decomposition within firms have been explored by Levinthal 2000.) That decomposition works at all, let alone as effectively as Adam Smith anticipated, indicates that natural systems are usually highly decomposable. Herbert Simon's analysis of organizational behavior has been explicitly based on the presumption of highly decomposable systems, and he has offered an evolutionary argument why this should be so (Simon 1969). However, perhaps because of the attractions of computer logic and the once-seductive potential for developing models of artificial intelligence which emphasize logical systems of information processing, he has not used this evolutionary argument, as some psychologists have done, to extend his criticism of economists' use of rationality beyond the advocacy of the concept of bounded rationality to that of efficient localized neural networks which do not rely on logical processing – even though this conception appears to match Barnard's (1938) emphasis on non-logical reasoning. As a consequence, his emphasis on the importance of decision premises for localized reasoning, premises which are not derived from some basic axiom set but are a subject of specific empirical inquiry, such as economists generally disdain, has been disregarded, and bounded rationality – if not ignored – is interpreted as part of the economics of information, which itself is founded on a false conception of knowledge. The behavioral approach which Cyert both advocated and demonstrated effectively abandons the concept of organization as a means of dividing a single logical problem into subproblems which can then be reassembled into a single argument – which is the general equilibrium view that leads naturally, as we have seen, to the advocacy of centralized decision making – and replaces it by something much closer to the bottom-up perspective that was used by Adam Smith both in his account of the development of scientific knowledge and in his theory of economic development.

The decomposition of objectives entails a decomposition of incentives, which has a number of important consequences, set out in *A Behavioral Theory of the Firm* (Cyert and March 1963). Among these are the superiority of satisficing over optimization as a sensible operating principle, the importance of motivation which is not easily represented or managed in monetary terms, and the notion of an organizational coalition which is preserved, in part, by not drawing attention to issues which might cause controversy – a strategy which is made possible by the cognitive limitations which make a system of efficient contracts impossible. The shared interest in preserving the coalition is a reflection of each member's interest in preserving income and status, but also, and more fundamentally, in preserving individual cognitive systems which draw on the organizational setting. The importance for each individual of substantially preserving an established interpretative framework is the basis of Kelly's (1963) theory of personality; and Kelly's argument that such frameworks are resistant to change, even when outsiders perceive that such change is desirable in order to improve decision making, is directly applicable to the organizational context. It is a familiar observation that the dissolution of a long-established organization can damage the personalities of many long-serving members of that organization.

As in any scientific discipline, the content and quality of knowledge depends on the way that it is generated and tested. (A special case of this relationship is the dependence of substantive rationality on procedural rationality.) The most tightly-organized testing systems within industry are often found, not surprisingly, in research and development departments, and the fallibility of both scientific and commercial conjectures which attempt to construct new knowledge is nowhere better demonstrated than by the success of these departments in rejecting the great majority of ideas that they consider, and in modifying the remainder, often substantially. Even then, success is far from certain. This process, its importance in science and industry, and its significance for economic theory, are all ignored in the standard economic analyses of research and development and, conspicuously, in currently fashionable growth theory.

We should therefore not be surprised to find that economists consistently reduce business projects to probability distributions, and the process of managing a firm to assembling an appropriate portfolio of such projects. For a contrast to this negligence, we may cite the examination by Van de Ven and Grazman (1997) of the contribution of various roles within an organization to the development of knowledge; they identify the division of function between sponsor, critic, leader and mentor as counterbalancing forces which may sustain a kind of creative ambiguity that is beyond the capabilities of most individuals. A similar diversity of cognitive patterns is likely to be important in the construction of action schemes by an iterative process which draws on the distinctive expertise of people who have organized their knowledge in the context of a variety of problem-definitions, each related to distinctive problems; how this process can result in due consideration to all the important relevant elements of a problem situation is powerfully demonstrated by Lane et al. (1996). Action schemes are devised, not deduced; and this is true of all complex decisions.

6 AMBIGUITY, ORGANIZATION AND COMPETITION

Many phenomena are capable of more than one interpretation, each carrying distinctive, and even contradictory, inferences. What Langlois (1984) called structural uncertainty is pervasive. Order must be imposed, and if people are to act, they must, at the least, be willing to suspend their disbelief in the adequacy of that imposed order. In Knight's analysis, entrepreneurs impose their own principles of order on uncertainty; so, on a grand scale, do Schumpeter's, and also, on a smaller scale, the managers of Penrosian firms. Both Knight and Casson explain the creation of a new firm as an instrument for the application and exploitation of entrepreneurial perceptions – in Shackle's (1979, p. 26) phrase, of 'the imagined, deemed possible'. These imaginations may result from the invention of new premises, or of new combinations of familiar premises; they are necessarily fallible conjectures. Martin Fransman (1995) has described the firm as a locus for the construction of beliefs; in this chapter we may prefer to describe it as a cluster of cognitive systems, but since all knowledge – even old knowledge – is fallible, to rely on it requires at least a provisional commitment to believe in these systems. Ulrich Witt (1998) has identified a continuing role for entrepreneurship within a firm in sustaining, and when apparently necessary, modifying beliefs; and as Simon has noted, organization members may be willing to follow this entrepreneurial lead because it helps them to define their own problems, to interpret information, and to work out how to act – to resolve, or at least manage, their own cognitive problems. This conception of the firm is also consistent with Coase's explanation of the firm as an agreement to cooperate in future circumstances, in ways which are left to be decided later.

We all need to make sense of our circumstances, and seek help from others, directly or indirectly through the institutions which are the unintended consequences of many individual actions. In the process we achieve some degree of coordination of independent actions. But many productive activities require the close coordination of differentiated but complementary capabilities. Then something rather more formal is required to provide sufficient coherence of our cognitive frames to produce compatible knowledge and compatible decisions. Firms provide an orientation for our cognitive processes. Of course, any such orientation may prove inappropriate; if so, the firm will fail – as most firms do. Alternatively, and in particular as knowledge develops and circumstances change, some members will become dissatisfied with the orientation; they may leave, perhaps to join a firm which is differently oriented, perhaps to create a new firm which will embody their own preferred ways of constructing knowledge.

Fallacies of decomposition are pathological consequences of the division of knowledge, as Shackle (1972, pp. 353–4) pointed out: 'When the compass of potential knowledge as a whole has been split up into superficially convenient sectors, there is no knowing whether each sector has a natural self-sufficiency. ... Whatever theory is then devised will exist by sufferance of the things which it has excluded'. Our knowledge is always incomplete, and our knowledge of its incompleteness, though capable of being reduced by appropriate investigation, is itself incomplete. (No one that I know has been more insistent on the practical consequences of this principle than Charles Suckling, who grappled with them throughout his career in innovation management, and was extraordinarily imaginative in finding relevant analyses of the issues; see the preface to Loasby 1999.) That is the justification for Marshall's warning against long chains of reasoning, and his own practice of avoiding them. It is also what makes the improvement of knowledge possible, and why both attempts to protect ourselves against the deficiencies of our present knowledge (at the level of individuals, groups, organizations, nations, or the human species) and attempts to create fresh knowledge require attention both to our cognitive systems and to the cognitive implications of our formal organizations, and especially those organizations whose business it is to produce new knowledge and to make better use of what is already available.

If the knowledge available to society is to continue to grow, we need not only a division of labor, but also, as Marshall recognized, variation within each specialism, and some variety in the ways in which specialisms are linked. We must pay attention, as Simon, Cyert and Penrose have done, to the 'insides' of firms, but also to their 'outsides'. A fine specimen of such a study, focused specifically on the role of external relationships on the development of knowledge, has been provided by Andersen (1999); for example, she demonstrates how membership of a large group can have the effect of denying access to relevant knowledge which is located outside that group. We also need the capacity to change the principles on which economic activity, and the knowledge which it both uses and produces, is based. Because our knowledge can never be certain, we cannot rely on procedures which are known to be correct. There is an essential inadequacy in our understanding, and consequently in our decision making. Entrepreneurship is essential because uncertainty is inescapable; but, as Shackle above all has repeatedly told us, it is because of uncertainty that we can hope to improve our knowledge.

REFERENCES

Andersen, Maj M. (1999), 'Trajectory change through interorganisational learning: on the economic organisation of the greening of industry', dissertation presented at Copenhagen Business School, 8 June.

Andrews, Philip W.S. (1949), *Manufacturing Business*, London: Macmillan.

Barnard, Chester I. (1938), *The Functions of the Executive*, Cambridge, MA: Harvard University Press.

Butler, Robert W. (1991), 'The historical content of the early Marshallian work', *Quaderni di storia dell'Economia Politica*, **9** (2–3), 269–88.

Casson, Mark (1982), *The Entrepreneur: An Economic Theory*, Oxford: Martin Robertson.

Choi, Young B. (1993), *Paradigms and Conventions: Uncertainty, Decision Making, and Entrepreneurship*, Ann Arbor, MI: University of Michigan Press.

Coase, Ronald H. (1937), 'The nature of the firm', *Economica*, N.S. **4**, 386–405.

Coase, Ronald H. (1960), 'The problem of social cost', *Journal of Law and Economics*, **3**, 1–46.

Coase, Ronald H. (1972), 'Industrial organization: a proposal for research', in Victor R. Fuchs (ed.), *Policy Issues and Research Opportunities in Industrial Organization*, New York: National Bureau of

Economic Research, pp. 59–73. Reprinted in Ronald H. Coase (1988), *The Firm, The Market and the Law*, Chicago: University of Chicago Press, pp. 57–74.
Coase, Ronald H. (1991), 'The nature of the firm: influence', in Oliver E. Williamson and Sidney G. Winter (eds), *The Nature of the Firm: Origins, Evolution and Development*, Oxford: Oxford University Press, pp. 61–74.
Cosmides, Lena and John Tooby (1994), 'Better than rational: evolutionary psychology and the invisible hand', *American Economic Review*, **84**, 327–32.
Cyert, R.M. and J.G. March (1963), *A Behavioral Theory of the Firm*, Englewood Cliffs, NJ: Prentice-Hall.
Dosi, Giovanni, Daniel Levinthal and Luigi Marengo (2001), 'Bridging contested terrain: linking incentive-based and learning perspectives on organizational evolution', DRUID Nelson and Winter Conference, Aalborg, June 12–15, p. 4.
Foss, Nicolai J. (1999), 'Edith Penrose, economics and strategic management', *Contributions to Political Economy*, **18**, 87–104.
Fransman, Martin (1995), *Japan's Computer and Communications Industry*, Cambridge: Cambridge University Press.
Groenewegen, Peter (1995), *A Soaring Eagle*, Aldershot: Edward Elgar.
Hayek, Friedrich A. (1978), 'The pretence of knowledge' (Nobel Memorial Lecture), in Friedrich A. Hayek, *New Studies in Philosophy, Politics, Economics and the History of Ideas*, London: Routledge & Kegan Paul, pp. 23–34.
Kay, Neil M. (1997), *Pattern in Corporate Evolution*, Oxford: Oxford University Press.
Kelly, George A. (1963), *A Theory of Personality*, New York: W.W. Norton.
Knight, Frank H. (1921), *Risk, Uncertainty and Profit*, Boston, MA: Houghton Mifflin.
Lane, David, Franco Malerba, Robert Maxfield and Luigi Orsenigo (1996), 'Choice and action', *Journal of Evolutionary Economics*, **6** (1), 43–76.
Langlois, Richard N. (1984), 'Internal organization in a dynamic context: some theoretical considerations', in M. Jussawalla and H. Ebenfeld (eds), *Information and Communication Economics: New Perspectives*, Amsterdam: North-Holland, pp. 23–49.
Levinthal, Daniel (2000), 'Organizational capabilities in complex worlds', in Giovanni Dosi, Richard R. Nelson and Sidney G. Winter (eds), *The Nature and Dynamics of Organizational Capabilities*, Oxford: Oxford University Press.
Loasby, Brian J. (1976), *Choice, Complexity and Ignorance: An Enquiry into Economic Theory and the Practice of Decision Making*, Cambridge: Cambridge University Press.
Loasby, Brian J. (1999), *Knowledge. Institutions and Evolution in Economics*, London and New York: Routledge.
Loasby, Brian J. (2000), 'Market institutions and economic evolution', *Journal of Evolutionary Economics*, **10** (3), 297–309.
Loasby, Brian J. (2002), 'Content and method: an epistemic perspective on some historical episodes', *European Journal of the History of Economic Thought* 9(1), 72–95.
Lucas, Robert E. jr (1981), *Studies in Business Cycle Theory*, Cambridge, MA: MIT Press.
Marshall, Alfred (1920), *Principles of Economics*, London: Macmillan.
Marshall, Alfred (1994), 'Ye machine', *Research in the History of Economic Thought and Methodology*, Archival Supplement 4, Greenwich, CT: JAI Press, pp. 116–32.
Ménard, Claude (1994), 'Organizations as co-ordinating devices', *Metroeconomica*, **45**, 224–47.
Myerson, Roger B. (1999), 'Nash equilibrium and the history of economic theory', *Journal of Economic Literature*, **37**, 1067–82.
Nelson, Richard R. and Sidney G. Winter (1982), *An Evolutionary Theory of Economic Change*, Cambridge, MA: Belknap Press.
Nooteboom, Bart (2001), 'From evolution to language and learning', in John Foster and J. Stanley Metcalfe (eds), *Frontiers of Evolutionary Economics: Competition, Self-organization and Innovation Policy*, Cheltenham, UK and Northampton, MA, USA: Edward Elgar, pp. 41–69.
Pavitt, Keith (1998), 'Technologies, products and organization in the innovating firm: what Adam Smith tells us and Joseph Schumpeter doesn't, *Industrial and Corporate Change*, **7**, 433–52.
Penrose, Edith T. (1959), *The Theory of the Growth of the Firm*, Oxford: Basil Blackwell. 3rd edn, Oxford: Oxford University Press, 1995.

Raffaelli, Tiziano (2001), 'Marshall on mind and society: neurophysiological models applied to business and industrial organization', *European Journal of the History of Economic Thought*, **8** (2), 208–29.
Richardson, George B. (1953), 'Imperfect knowledge and economic efficiency', *Oxford Economic Papers*, **5** (2), 136–56; reprinted in George B. Richardson (1998), *The Economics of Imperfect Knowledge*, Cheltenham, UK and Northampton, USA, pp. 1–21.
Richardson, George B. (1972), 'The organisation of industry', *Economic Journal*, **82**, 883–96; reprinted in Richardson (1998), pp. 224–42.
Ryle, Gilbert (1949), *The Concept of Mind*, London: Hutchinson.
Schumpeter, Joseph A. (1934), *The Theory of Economic Development*, Cambridge, MA: Harvard University Press.
Shackle, George L.S. (1972), *Epistemics and Economics*, Cambridge: Cambridge University Press.
Shackle, George L.S. (1979), *Imagination and the Nature of Choice*, Edinburgh: Edinburgh University Press.
Simon, Herbert A. (1959), 'Theories of decision making in economics and behavioral science', *American Economic Review*, **49** (1), 253–83.
Simon, Herbert A. (1969), *The Sciences of the Artificial*, Cambridge, MA: MIT Press.
Smith, Adam (1759), *The Theory of Moral Sentiments*, reprinted in David D. Raphael and Alec L. Macfie (eds) (1976a), *Glasgow Edition of the Works and Correspondence of Adam Smith*, Vol. 1, Oxford: Oxford University Press.
Smith, Adam (1776), *An Inquiry into the Nature and Causes of the Wealth of Nations*, reprinted in Roy H. Campbell, Andrew S. Skinner and W.B. Todd (eds) (1976b), *Glasgow Edition of the Works and Correspondence of Adam Smith*, Vol. 2, Oxford: Oxford University Press.
Smith, Adam (1795), 'The principles which lead and direct philosophical enquiries; illustrated by the history of astronomy', in *Essays on Philosophical Subjects*, reprinted in W.P.D. Wightman and J.C. Bryce (eds) (1980), *Glasgow Edition of the Works and Correspondence of Adam Smith*, Vol. 3, Oxford: Oxford University Press.
Smith, Adam (1963), *Lectures on Rhetoric and Belles Lettres*, reprinted in J.C. Bryce (ed.) (1983), *Glasgow Edition of the* Works and Correspondence *of Adam Smith*, Vol. 4, Oxford: Oxford University Press.
Van de Ven, Andrew and David N. Grazman (1997), 'Technological innovation, learning and leadership', in Raghu Garud, Praveen R. Nayyar and Zur B. Shapira (eds), *Technological Innovation: Foresights and Oversights*, Cambridge: Cambridge University Press, pp. 279–305.
Whitehead, Alfred N. (1911), *An Introduction to Mathematics*, reprinted Oxford: Oxford University Press, 1948.
Williamson, Oliver E. (1996), *The Mechanisms of Governance*, Oxford: Oxford University Press.
Williamson, Oliver E. (1997), 'Review of Harold Demsetz, *The Economics of the Business Firm: Seven Critical Commentaries*', *Journal of Economic Literature*, **35**, 129–30.
Witt, Ulrich (1998), 'Imagination and leadership – the neglected dimension of an (evolutionary) theory of the firm, *Journal of Economic Behavior and Organization*, **35**, 161–77.
Young, Allyn A. (1928) 'Increasing returns and economic progress', *Economic Journal*, **38**, 527–42.
Ziman, John M. (1978), *Reliable Knowledge*, Cambridge: Cambridge University Press.

8. The accuracy of managers' perceptions: a dimension missing from theories about firms

Susan R. Salgado, William H. Starbuck and John M. Mezias

1 INTRODUCTION

This chapter looks at some evidence about the accuracy – or rather the inaccuracy – of managers' perceptions. With few exceptions, academic theorists assume that managers perceive accurately. Some theorists, mainly economists, even assume that managers have precisely correct expectations about future events. But managers often perceive inaccurately. They often make perception errors when they are dealing with phenomena that they run into daily in their jobs; they make larger errors and make them more often when they encounter novel phenomena. Yet academics often base studies on managers' perceptions of phenomena that are unfamiliar to the managers and do not fit into their daily experiences. As a result, academics are generating noisy data that have very different meanings for managers than for academics.

Section 2 reviews debates about the theory of the firm because these debates center on the need for theorists to know what managers perceive, how they reason, and how they make decisions. Some theorists hold that these processes are unimportant, others that they are very important. Thus these debates set a theoretical context for considering the usefulness of understanding managers' perceptions. Section 3 describes some studies that suggest managers make significant perception errors, and it inventories some of the factors affecting the accuracy of managers' perceptions. The final section extracts implications for research about the behavior of firms.

2 HOW REALISTIC SHOULD A THEORY BE?

> Neoclassical economists take the position that 'If the world is not like the model, so much the worse for the world'. (Sir John L. Eatwell, c. 1994, in a speech at the New School for Social Research, New York)

The economic 'theory of the firm' assumes that firms maximize long-run profits. This assumption limits discussion of a firm's decisions about prices and quantities by ruling out almost all of the actions that the firm might consider taking. In fact, economic theorists usually add assumptions that rule out all actions but one. These theorists can then analyse the sensitivity of this unique optimal action to conjectured changes in factors such as costs, market conditions or taxes.

Complaints about the realism of the theory of the firm have a long history. Some of these complaints have emphasized logical problems within the framework of the theory itself. For instance, Tintner (1941) reasoned that a firm could have only a single goal – to maximize profits – only if the firm has perfect knowledge of the future. If a firm has uncertainty about the future, it has to regard the outcomes of its possible actions as probability distributions. But it is not possible to maximize a probability distribution: an evaluation of a distribution must take account of all of the properties of the distribution – its mean, its variance, its skewness and so forth.

However, the most plentiful complaints have concerned the apparent divergence between the assumption of profit maximization and the actions taken by real-life managers. These complaints gained impetus from an empirical study conducted by researchers at Oxford University in 1938–39. They (Hall and Hitch, 1939; Harrod, 1939: 4–5) found that business managers 'were in profound ignorance' concerning the elasticity of demand for their products, that managers had little confidence in their knowledge of marginal costs, and that firms set prices not by optimizing but by applying traditional mark-up rules. Harrod (1939) proposed that economists should pay more attention to what managers actually do rather than to deductions from economic theories.

Complaints escalated in the late 1940s and 1950s. Lester (1946: 72) made an empirical study that echoed the Oxford study; 'most entrepreneurs do not tend to think in tends of marginal variable cost'. Gordon (1948) called for a radically different theory of the firm. He asserted that firms follow accepted maxims that bear no obvious relationships to profit maximization; for example, in the short run, firms seek only to attain satisfactory profits. Andrews (1949) pointed out that, because some costs appear to be 'fixed', firms might expand in pursuit of cost savings that never materialize. Cooper (1949) complained that the theory of the firm did not view firms as organizations. Papandreou (1952) argued that firms develop strategic plans and organization designs and that these plans reflect the interests of different stakeholders. Penrose (1952) pointed out that managers try to alter the environments in which their businesses operate, and thereby to extract success from whatever actions they prefer to take. Simon (1955: 104) contended 'that there is a complete lack of evidence that, in actual human choice situations of any complexity', people make the calculations that would be necessary in order to make optimal choices. People have 'limited' or 'approximate' rationality (1955: 113–14): they do not know all possible outcomes of their potential actions, they engage in limited searches to investigate such outcomes, and they categorize outcomes crudely as satisfactory or unsatisfactory. Making arguments similar to Simon's, Margolis (1958: 189) pointed out that firms use 'non-profit-maximizing goals and business rules' because managers do not have the information they would need to make 'fully rational' decisions. Margolis charged that efforts to apply the theory of the firm to practical problems require 'extra-economic' assumptions.

Of course, the protests against conventional economic theory evoked responses. Machlup (1946) criticized the empirical studies by the Oxford University researchers and by Lester. These researchers, he said, did not allow for the fact that the theory of the firm deals with expectations about the future rather than actual experiences, and they had assumed that entrepreneurs understand concepts such as marginal cost and elasticity of demand. Furthermore, Lester had relied on mailed questionnaires: 'A set formulation of questions will hardly fit any large number of business men in different fields and, hence, questionnaires to be filled out by them will rarely yield useful results' (1946: 537).

Alchian (1950: 217) concurred 'that empirical investigations via questionnaire methods, so far used, are incapable of evaluating the validity of marginal productivity analysis'. However, he argued, economists do not have to look at actual decision processes in order to predict the behaviors that survive in the long run. No matter what decision rules firms might use, they can survive only by earning positive profits; firms that lose money go out of business. Also, firms that behave more optimally have higher probabilities of survival. As a result, an economist 'can state what types of firms or behavior relative to other possible types will be more viable, even though the firms themselves may not know the conditions or even try to achieve them' (1950: 216). However, Alchian (1950: 220) stopped short of the extreme inference that the long-run results would be profit-maximizing: 'The economist may be pushing his luck too far in arguing that actions ... will converge ... toward the optimum action that should have been selected if foresight had been perfect'.

Less cautious than Alchian, Friedman (1953) maintained that evolution would produce profit maximization in the long run. He also opined that economic theory does not have to describe firms' behaviors as long as it helps economists to analyse these behaviors. Thus it is more important for the theory of the firm to meet the intellectual needs of economists than for it to describe firms' behaviors.

Alchian and Friedman framed their defenses around long-run outcomes across populations of competing firms, an orientation that illustrates two differences that have powered and confounded the debates between critics and defenders. One difference is the level of aggregation that the theory of the firm ought to address: is it one firm or a population of competing firms? Although the theory's label speaks of 'the firm' as if the theory deals with a single organization, the theory actually says little about activities within a single organization. Attempts to apply the theory have typically concerned events involving many firms, and very few economists have shown interest in events within a single firm. The second difference is the time period that the theory ought to address. Is it the short run or the long run? The conventional theory does not attempt to describe short-run outcomes; it speaks only of equilibrium states that might be reached in the long run, if ever. By contrast, critics of the conventional theory framed their arguments in terms of short-run activities within a single organization. Proponents of 'a theory of one firm in the short run' were criticizing 'a theory of long-run outcomes across a population of firms'.

The foregoing debates motivated three lines of development during the late 1950s and early 1960s. Focusing on populations of competing firms in the long run, Winter (1964) followed up on Alchian's evolutionary viewpoint, but he expressed much more skepticism about the effectiveness of evolutionary processes in selecting profitable firms. He inferred that there are many reasons why unprofitable firms might survive indefinitely despite evolutionary selection. Since firms mainly compete with similar firms, selection processes are weak. There is no evidence that any firm has discovered and is capable of using decision rules that will maximize profits. Some firms might use suboptimal decision rules that produce profit-maximizing behaviors in their current environments, but as the environments change, the suboptimal rules would become inappropriate. Because stakeholders do not shift their commitments rapidly, a suboptimal firm can survive for a very long time. Stakeholders might erroneously support firms that maximize short-run profits, while withholding support from the long-run profit maximizers, and thereby driving them out of business.

The second and third lines of development focused on a single firm in the short run. Penrose (1959) argued that profitability might come from short-run processes of change rather than from long-run end states achieved through change:

> The growth of firms may be consistent with the most efficient use of society's resources; the result of past growth – the size attained at any time – may have no corresponding advantages. Each successive step in its growth may be profitable to the firm and, if otherwise under-utilized resources are used, advantageous to society. But once any expansion is completed, the original justification for the expansion may fade into insignificance as new opportunities for growth develop and are acted upon. (1959: 103)

Cyert and March (1963) attempted to launch 'a behavioral theory of the firm'. They (1963: 19) wanted to create a theory that would make predictions about the behaviors of a single firm and would base these predictions on 'the actual process of organizational decision making'. To illustrate what they meant by predictions based on 'the actual process of organizational decision making', Cyert and March developed models of decision making about prices and quantities in a department store. These models involved very detailed rules of thumb, and so tests of the models were essentially tests of how closely human beings adhered to the described rules. Although these models were quite accurate, the models described routine, microscopic decisions that occurred over and over again. Only routine, repeated decisions are codified as rules that decision makers can articulate.

Cyert and March championed various generalizations that describe entire organizations macroscopically over long periods. First, organizations pursue conflicting goals; long-run profit maximization is not the sole goal. Second, organizations avoid uncertainty by concentrating on pressing problems, by attempting to control their environments, and by retaining 'organizational slack', meaning resources that are not fully utilized. Third, organizations do not see all alternatives; they have to search for alternatives, and they undertake these searches primarily in response to problems. Fourth, organizations learn: they change their goals and forecasts in reaction to experience; they change their decision rules to suit new circumstances. Finally, organizations' estimates of current and future parameters embody biases. However, Cyert and March's book said little about how these macroscopic properties of organizations do or might relate to the routine, repeated decisions that they actually modeled. The macroscopic properties seem to involve perception of abstract concepts, analysis and debate, whereas the microscopic decision rules seem to act mechanistically in reaction to immediate, concrete events. For example, what is the relation between a long-run pricing strategy and a decision about the price of one specific product right now? Do the routine microscopic behaviors express macroscopic rationales or are people merely repeating programs that they have learned?

Two decades later, Nelson and Winter (1982) produced a second-generation behavioral theory of the firm that partly reconciles the disparity between microscopic current behaviors and macroscopic long-run behaviors. Nelson and Winter described organizational development as an evolutionary process in which standardized behavioral routines survive or disappear; some behavioral routines survive for long periods and others do not. Moreover, a given routine may occur in many organizations, and the entities that develop are populations of organizations that often imitate each other. This view aggregates current, microscopic behaviors, which may apply to very small parts of organizations, into long-run patterns that cross many organizations. However, it also seems to relegate human cognition to very minor roles, as an invisible hand steers development.

Managers and Management Scholars See It Differently

The foregoing theories of the firm reflect their roots in economics and in academe. Economists have emphasized different phenomena than have management scholars. Academics have emphasized different phenomena than managers.

Economists versus management scholars

With the exception of Cyert and March's and Penrose's behavioral theories, the economic theories are not about a firm's behavior in the immediate future, but about industry-level phenomena over the very long run. An aggregate, long-run perspective may have advantages for economists. Behaviors may converge toward consistent patterns over the long run. Firms attend to the actions of their competitors, imitate each other, learn from each other, and form alliances. Also, in the long run, one firm's behaviors may induce changes in the parameters framing an entire industry, such as government policies or resource availability (Miner et al., 1996). However, long-run phenomena must be studied retrospectively, so long-run theories offer little to managers who face immediate problems.

For such reasons, some management scholars, mainly organization theorists, have shifted their attention toward populations of organizations. However, most management scholars are not satisfied to describe or analyse industry-level phenomena over the very long run. They seek theories that address organizational-level issues that exist now. Such theories need to incorporate the kinds of data that are currently available to managers, including the managers' perceptions.

All versions of the economic theory of the firm have a narrow focus on prices and quantities. This narrow focus may have advantages for economists, especially those who like mathematical theories. Simplicity makes theories easier to understand. To exist for long periods, firms must ultimately appear to generate some profits. Prices and quantities may be much more important for generating long-run profits than factors such as advertising, human resources, product quality, or innovation.

By contrast, management theories incorporate many variables because management scholars believe that many factors influence firms' successes in both the short run and the long run. Management prescriptions for organizational design and strategy include abstract variables such as centralization, distinctive competence, environmental dynamism, expertise, formalization and resource munificence. Management scholars regard such variables as relevant because they look upon firms as being complex. For management scholars, firms have many stakeholders, such as employees, customers, suppliers and neighbors, in addition to stockholders. Management scholars also view firms as having diverse legitimate goals in addition to long-run profits, because firms are places to work, to learn, and to pursue careers and they are partners in alliances and citizens in communities.

Academics versus managers

Academic theorists discuss abstract worlds that are strange to managers. The disjunctures between abstract academic perspectives and concrete managerial perspectives become especially large when management scholars ask managers about macroscopic variables such as centralization, environmental dynamism, and resource munificence. Managers work in concrete worlds and they focus on the data about their daily tasks: What do I have to do right now? Do we have enough inventory to fill this order? Boland and his colleagues (2001) concluded that managers make better decisions when they focus on concrete stimuli. Goals with very distant time horizons have little meaning for managers. Indeed, many managers expect to move to another assignment every two or three years, and many of the projects undertaken by firms have similarly short time horizons, so time horizons of two to three years seem realistic to them.

Also, both the theory of the firm and management theories view events macroscopically in comparison with the microscopic worlds in which nearly all managers work. For example, academics classify industries by Standard Industrial Classification codes (SIC codes) and assume that managers see their industries on similarly large scales. Very few managers, however, define their industries in such broad terms; nearly all managers focus on market segments so small that no statistics exist about them. Many managers have little perspective on worlds other than their own. They have had experience in only one work organization and only one functional specialty. When they are asked to compare their organizations with others, their statements are based largely on hearsay or fantasy.

These disparities between the theoretical worlds of management academics and the practical worlds of business managers are both important and difficult to reconcile. The disparities are important because management academics ought to be able to explain how their theories relate to observable phenomena, how managers' actions in microscopic, concrete worlds translate into concepts in macroscopic, abstract theories.

They are also important because they impede communication between academics and managers; the questions academics ask of managers and the responses managers give are often not parallel to one another. The disparities are difficult to reconcile because such explanations do not come easily. For instance, Baumol and Quandt (1964) attempted to study the effectiveness of rules of thumb as ways to approximate optimal behavior; they concluded that this is a 'surprisingly difficult' problem (1964: 41). Winter (1964) showed that we should not rely on evolutionary selection to produce short-run behavior that has long-run benefits. In fact, when organizations imitate each other, there is no reason to believe that any organization can gain a survival advantage by discovering a better way to behave (Starbuck, 1994). But even if evolutionary selection were effective, it would produce long-run consistency between managers' actions and survival conditions, not consistency between managers' actions and the abstract concepts of organizational form or strategic policy that appear in management theories.

In order to reconcile managers' actions with management theories, academics need to understand the disparities that require reconciliation. The arguments above suggest that these disparities have at least four dimensions: (i) long-run versus short-run orientation, (ii) a population of organizations versus one organization, (iii) degree of generality versus specificity, and (iv) degree of abstraction versus concreteness.

This chapter adds a fifth dimension that interacts with the other four: the degree to which managers perceive their worlds accurately. With only a few exceptions, both economic theorists and management theorists have assumed that managers perceive accurately. But quite a lot of evidence indicates that this is simply not so. All people, including managers, make perception errors frequently. They make errors even when perceiving phenomena that they encounter daily. They make bigger errors and make errors more often when they are being asked to perceive unfamiliar phenomena.

If theories are going to be helpful to managers, the theories need to allow for perception errors. Theories are unlikely to provide useful guidance if they make very unrealistic assumptions about the accuracy of the information flowing into decisions. Similarly, researchers who gather data from managers need to allow for perception errors. Researchers have tended to ask managers for their perceptions of unfamiliar phenomena – the long run, the population of firms, the general, the abstract – which are precisely the perceptions that are least likely to be accurate.

The next section reviews some studies that suggest that managers do not perceive accurately and that their perception errors may affect the performance of their firms.

3 HOW ACCURATE ARE MANAGERS' PERCEPTIONS OF THEIR WORLDS?

The literatures on decision making and managerial sense making rely heavily on the assumption that managers are aware of and understand their organizations' environments in terms of the kinds of macroscopic variables that appear in prescriptions for organizational design and strategizing. Almost no research has examined the accuracy of such perceptions (Starbuck and Mezias, 1996). However, a few research studies have compared objective and perceptual data. Disconcertingly, these studies found large errors and biases in managers' perceptions, both of their organizations and of the environments in which the organizations operate. Managers' responses to academics' questions indicate that they live in microscopic, immediate worlds, and have little awareness of long-run issues, of changes from year to year, of comparisons among firms, or of differences among market environments.

In 1967, Lawrence and Lorsch inferred that organizations whose properties match their market environments perform better than firms not aligned with their environments. Their research relied on managers' perceptions of both organizational properties and the environments. The key variable they discussed was environmental uncertainty. However, two later studies presented questions about the accuracy of managerial perceptions of environmental uncertainty. Both studies compared top managers' perceptions of their firms' markets to financial reports and industry statistics. In both studies, the correlations between the two were near zero and were as likely to be negative as positive. Tosi et al. (1973) studied 102 middle and top managers from diverse firms and found correlations from –0.29 to +0.04 between managers' beliefs about environmental uncertainty and stability indices. Similarly, Downey et al. (1975) collected data from 51 heads of the divisions of a large conglomerate and found correlations from –0.17 to +0.11 between managers' beliefs about environmental uncertainty and stability indices.

In their 1975 study, Grinyer and Norburn found that profitability correlated only very weakly with strategic planning ($r = 0.22$). Strategic planning is a double-edged sword that is as likely to reduce profits as to raise them. Strategies that reflect accurate forecasts and assessments of the environment enable organizations to work toward the achievement of appropriate goals, while ignoring irrelevant distractions. But strategies based on inaccurate forecasts and assessments lead to work toward the wrong goals, while overlooking unexpected opportunities. Since negative outcomes occur nearly as often as positive outcomes, strategic planning has negligible effects on the average.

Grinyer and Norburn's study not only suggests that managers misperceive their environments, but also their organizations. They found inconsistent and meaningless correlations between profitability and consensus among executives about their firms' goals or about their personal responsibilities. The correlations ranged from –0.40 to +0.40, indicating that agreement on perceptions did not increase profitability. The fact that there was disagreement implies that some executives misperceived, which highlights the fact that even if consensus is achieved, there is no way of knowing whether or not the consensus is correct. Therefore, achieving consensus on inaccurate perceptions is as likely to lead to unprofitability as not achieving consensus on accurate perceptions. Depending on whether perceptions are accurate, consensus (or lack thereof) can be as harmful as beneficial.

Further evidence about misperceptions of organizational characteristics comes from Payne and Pugh's 1976 review of more than 100 studies. Payne and Pugh examined subjective and objective measures of organizational structures and climates. They drew three conclusions: (a) Employees in the same organization disagree so strongly with each other that it makes no sense to talk about an average perception. 'Perceptual measures of each of the structural and climate variables have varied so much among themselves that mean scores were uninterpretable' (1976: 1168). (b) Except for organizational size, employees' perceptions of organizational properties correlate weakly with objective measures of those properties. (c) Differences among employees' perceptions of organizational properties correspond with employees' jobs and hierarchical statuses. For instance, higher-status employees view their organizations more favorably.

Overall, these early studies showed that perceptual data correlate very weakly with objective data. However, perceptual data seem to be mutually consistent. Lawrence and Lorsch (1967) observed that perceptions of organizations fit logically with perceptions of the organizations' environments. Payne and Pugh (1976) found that perceptions of different organizational characteristics fit together logically. Thus, although people make sense of their organizational environments, the sense that they make seems to have weak correspondence to objective measures of their organizations. The sense that people make may be the result of (i) human brains imposing logic on ambiguous stimuli or (ii) collective sense-making processes within organizations.

Mezias and Starbuck (2002) conjectured that these old studies had to be misleading because managers could not possibly be so far out of touch with their environments. Because the studies had not been designed to access perceptual accuracy, research methodology might have manufactured the inconsistencies between perceptual and objective data: in particular, the 'objective' measures in some of these studies had been rather *ad hoc*.

Therefore Mezias and Starbuck decided to gather data to assess perceptual accuracy, believing that they would find much smaller perception errors. In their first study, they were very disappointed to find large perceptual errors in data collected from managers in several companies. In the best case, 39 percent of managers' perceptions of a given variable were within 50 percent of the objective measure. In the worst case, 31 percent of managers' perceptions exceeded 200 percent of the objective value. Most surprising was that managers' perceptions of variables specifically related to their areas of expertise were no more accurate than other managers' perceptions of those same variables. That is, managers with sales experience were as inaccurate in their estimates of sales-related variables as managers without sales experience.

In a second study, Mezias and Starbuck observed senior managers' perceptions of quality performance in four divisions of a company whose top management says that quality improvement is a top priority. The company has been training all managers in quality, and each business unit has a quality improvement department. The company distributes quality measures to all managers on a regular basis, and managers meet to discuss quality performance in their divisions. Yet 49 to 91 percent of the managers reported 'I don't know' when asked about current levels of quality performance. Although the managers who thought they knew the current levels of quality performance were often fairly accurate, the managers who specialized in quality were no more accurate than the non-specialists.

Because research and managerial prescriptions so often assume that managers perceive accurately, it seems useful to remind people of the many sources of perceptual errors. Indeed, perceptual errors have so many sources that we can list only some of the main ones. We place errors in four categories according to whether they occur during noticing or during sense making, and whether they reflect properties of stimuli or properties of perceivers.

Errors Due to Noticing

> It's not like information comes with a little flag on it that says, 'Look at me; I'm your proactive piece of data.' The people in this world who make money are the people who see things in information that other people don't see. (Leonard M. Fuld, as quoted by Buchanan 1995)

Noticing is a matter of detecting stimuli and distinguishing meaningful information from noise (Starbuck and Milliken, 1988a). Noticing usually exerts strong influence on cognition because it determines whether people even consider responding to events. Noticing also takes precedence over sense making. If events have been noticed, people can try to make sense of them, but if events have not been noticed, they cannot affect sense making.

Some stimuli are more likely to attract attention, and some people are more likely to pay attention to particular stimuli. As a result, errors due to noticing fall into two categories: problems with stimuli and problems with perceivers. Important stimuli may be difficult to perceive; people's biases may lead them to notice the wrong stimuli.

Problems with stimuli

People tend either to ignore changes over time or to underestimate vastly their magnitudes. Changes are more likely to be noticed if they are large or dramatic, less likely to be noticed if they are small or incremental. For example, Microsoft's surprising ignorance of the Internet's emergence and growth illustrates how an industry leader can greatly underestimate changes in the year-to-year growth rate of an important industry segment. Considerable evidence indicates that Microsoft's top managers greatly underestimated the rapid growth and profound implications of the Internet. Rob Glaser, who joined Microsoft in 1983, repeatedly warned Microsoft's top managers not to underestimate the importance of the Internet and to develop a browser immediately. As late as January of 1995, Microsoft had very few people working to develop its own Internet browser (Wallace, 1997).

In unfamiliar circumstances, people feel that they are being inundated with stimuli because the stimuli are difficult to classify. That is, unfamiliar stimuli create the problem of not knowing what to notice because it is difficult to know what is important. After repeated exposure to the same stimuli, some stimuli become familiar and people learn to ignore the stimuli that have had less influence. For example, Gersick and Hackman (1990) discussed how routinized information processing produces insensitivity to unfamiliar stimuli. They examined the crash of a flight that took off from Washington, DC. The Florida-based crew had filtered out unfamiliar stimuli (ice on the wings) when they were going through the all-too-familiar takeoff checklist.

In the US, just three industries – chemicals, petroleum and plastics – account for about half of the forecasts made about manufacturing. Thus managers in these industries receive frequent reminders that they should be thinking about the future. Furthermore, on average, the forecasts made about chemicals and plastics have been distinctly optimistic whereas the forecasts made about other manufacturing industries have been unbiased. Thus managers in the chemicals and plastics industries receive stimuli that encourage overproduction and overinvestment.

Overly abundant stimuli create obstacles in processing information effectively, such that some stimuli are overlooked. Managers often feel that they are drowning in data. Corporate information systems produce reports whether or not the reports are relevant to current issues, so managers learn to ignore nearly all of the data they receive. A study by the Institute For The Future and the Gallup Organization described office workers as being deluged by communications and technology. For example, an average UK office worker receives 48 telephone calls, 23 e-mails, 11 voice mails, 20 letters, 15 internal memos, 11 faxes, 13 Post-it notes and eight mobile phone calls per day. An average US manager in Fortune 1000 companies is sending and receiving about 180–200 documents a day through various media. 'Today's corporate staffs are inundated with so many communications tools – fax, electronic mail, teleconferencing, postal mail, interoffice mail, voice mail – that sometimes they don't know where to turn for the simplest tasks' (Institute For The Future, 1997).

Problems with perceivers

Like other people, managers are prone to seek out data that confirm their beliefs, and analogously, managers' beliefs about what is relevant guide organizational information-gathering operations. Of course, such beliefs have roots in experience, which may be a poor guide to current events. For example, the Facit company was a dominant manufacturer of mechanical calculators in 1969 when electronic calculators first appeared in their market (Starbuck et al., 1978). To assess this threat, Facit's managers instructed sales personnel to ask customers whether they intended to continue purchasing mechanical calculators or whether they intended to switch to electronic calculators. Month after month, the sales personnel reported back that nearly 100 percent of the customers liked mechanical calculators and intended to continue using them. But month after month, there were fewer and fewer customers for the sales personnel to interview.

Involvement in a course of action focuses one's attention. Elaborate strategic planning produces blindness to stimuli that fall outside the plans. This is partly a result of the planners' psychological investments in their plans and partly the result of the information gathering that they set up to implement their plans. For example, Microsoft may have overlooked the development of the Internet because it had all of its resources committed to desktop products such as Office and the Windows operating systems. Similarly, Merrill Lynch fell victim to its commitment to a course of action. To deter insider trading, Merrill required employees to have their brokerage accounts exclusively with the company. But because employees were unable to trade on Internet sites, they were unfamiliar with Internet trading, and ill-equipped to deal with the on-line trading explosion. Spiro (1999: 256) remarked that 'the proud firm earned an unwanted reputation as the case study for Internet anxiety by arriving at the on-line trading party more than two years late'.

Organizational and societal cultures blind people to some stimuli while emphasizing others. To support its effort to be the dominant manufacturer of mechanical calculators, Facit hired the best mechanical engineers and promoted them to senior management positions. The mechanical engineers focused on developments in mechanical design and attached little significance to developments in other fields of engineering. One result was that they greatly underestimated the significance of electronic calculators. Miller (1990) has documented many similar cases in which firms focused so intently on what they perceived as being their strategic strengths that they did not see important developments outside the range of their vision. Cyert and March (1963) asserted that organizations are more likely to respond to threats than to opportunities, which implies that managers should pay more attention to threats. Jackson and Dutton (1988) speculated that managers are indeed more sensitive to threat-consistent information than to opportunity-consistent information, and conversely, that they are less sensitive to threat-discrepant information than to opportunity-discrepant information.

Managers focus on stimuli that they think are immediately relevant to their jobs, and they screen out other stimuli. For example, when Starbuck and Mezias (1996) asked managers to describe their industries, only five of 70 managers gave descriptions that approximated the national industries that appear in government reports. Most managers regarded national industries as too large to be relevant for their business units. Many managers described their business units as competing in local or regional markets, not the entire US. Many other managers described their competitive environments with phrases such as 'Jewish in-ground burial on Long Island', 'entertainment advertising', 'radio air personality', 'alkaline batteries', and 'industrial sorbents for oil-spill clean-up and chemical-spill clean-up'.

Errors Due to Sense Making

> Managers ... must wade into the ocean of events that surround the organization and actively try to make sense of them. (Richard L. Daft and Karl E. Weick, 1984: 286)

Sense making involves placing stimuli into frameworks that reflect habits and beliefs. These frameworks help people to categorize and to interpret data, which often involves filling in missing data and editing out dissonant data (Starbuck and Milliken, 1988a). Ambiguous stimuli are difficult to interpret, and people's biases lead them to interpret stimuli incorrectly. People are also subject to perceptual blind spots that may hinder decision making and that generate self-reinforcing cycles (Watzlawick et al., 1974). Dunbar et al. (1996) advocated that managers should help their organizations to develop effective sense-making frameworks. But, managers' abilities to do this depend on the managers knowing what good sense-making frameworks are.

Starbuck and Milliken (1988a) argued that people possess many sense-making frameworks, and that they can apply several, partially inconsistent frameworks to any specific situation. Furthermore, sense-making frameworks can be evaluated by many, partially inconsistent criteria, which makes it difficult to judge some frameworks as more effective than others except in retrospect.

Like errors in noticing, errors in sense making arise from both problems with stimuli and problems with perceivers. It seems that perceivers present more problems than stimuli. The following sections outline the role of each in sense-making errors.

Problems with stimuli

Managers in different industries make different sense-making errors because either the data change very rapidly or data do not exist. In stable industries, such as furniture or commodity foods, managers develop constricted sense-making frameworks based on long experience, so they have difficulty making sense of surprising developments. In volatile industries, such as capital goods or high-technology industries, managers must keep abreast of changing environmental conditions, so they develop sense-making frameworks that tolerate errors. Horvath (1996) argued that rapid environmental changes and uncertainty about future conditions lead managers to de-emphasize the significance of new data, to refine their knowledge rather than to reformulate it. Because adapting to changes induces people to notice more events and to engage in more sense making, they tend to think they are doing more problem solving and to credit themselves with any good results. Normann (1971) pointed out that managers perceive incremental changes more accurately than dramatic ones. Because incremental changes deviate only slightly from experience, managers can interpret them by modifying existing frameworks. Dramatic changes, on the other hand, force managers to adopt radically different frameworks, so they are prone to err.

Government agencies or trade associations publish data about some industries. In such industries, firms can use published data in their sense making, whereas in other industries, no such data exist. Published data are useful mainly to firms in industries that are changing at moderate rates. In highly stable industries, firms have little need for data that are changing in miniscule increments. In rapidly changing industries, data become obsolete even before they are published, so firms have to develop other ways to gather information (Gulati, 1999).

Top managers receive distorted information from subordinates who tell their bosses what they think the bosses want to hear or who seek to promote their own interests or favored projects. Dunbar and Goldberg (1978) surmised that such distortions play significant roles in top managers' awareness of developing crises. Top managers may also think they have more expertise than their subordinates, causing them to discount the subordinates' input. Thus managers of the space shuttle program thought that their subordinate engineers were exaggerating the significance of burn damage to O-rings in the Solid Rocket Boosters. According to the engineers, damage to O-rings was evidence that the space shuttle was unsafe; but according to the program managers, history had shown that the space shuttle could fly safely despite damage to O-rings. As a result, the managers overruled the engineers and went ahead with the launch of the Challenger (Starbuck and Milliken, 1988b).

Problems with perceivers

Several properties of perceivers may lead to errors in sense making, including biases, vested interests, specialization, culture, and learning. Extensive research has revealed that people do not behave according to prescriptions for rational thought. Bazerman (1997) documented a list of more than a dozen biases that influence cognitive behavior. For instance, Milliken (1990) inferred that managers are less likely to interpret environmental changes as threatening when they perceive their organizations to be performing well than when they perceive their organizations to be performing poorly. Other research shows that people's brains invent memories of events that never occurred (Nisbett and Wilson, 1977), and that people search for confirming evidence of their prior beliefs (Singer and Benassi, 1981). Human cognition tends to edit out dissonant stimuli and to fill in missing stimuli automatically. Thus memories change to fit new information (Kiesler, 1971; Loftus, 1979).

Research on attributions indicates that people tend to overestimate their own impacts on events, and to underestimate the impacts of external forces. That is, people tend to see themselves as causing events. People especially tend to overestimate their own impacts when outcomes are successful. Conversely, people tend to see others' successes as resulting from the situations or environments (Heider, 1958). For example, ambiguous stimuli may cause managers to attribute success to internal strengths of their organizations, and failures to environmental circumstances (Wagner and Gooding, 1997). On the other hand, when interpreting stimuli about others' behaviors, managers are more likely to attribute success to environmental opportunities than to managers' competence, and failures to managers' incompetence than to environmental threats. For instance, Ragins et al. (1998) found that male chief executive officers (CEOs) and female executives hold very different perceptions of work environments in corporations. Whereas the females, all vice presidents or higher, 'were more than twice as likely as the CEOs to consider inhospitable work environments as a barrier to women's advancement' (1998: 35), the male CEOs attributed women's not advancing to a deficiency of general management or line experience.

Managers' sense making also reflects their need to believe that their decisions will turn out to be correct. For example, Jill Barad, Chairwoman and CEO of Mattel demonstrated a need to believe that her purchase of The Learning Company would be profitable. After making the purchase, she repeatedly predicted that profits would rise in the next quarter even though profits had fallen in the previous quarter. After losses had totaled $183 million, shareholders lost faith in her credibility and she resigned her position.

Starbuck (1983) suggested that top managers' sense making is especially prone to errors (see also Glynn et al., 1994). Several factors make it difficult for top managers to interpret events accurately. First, as Payne and Pugh (1976) surmised, the higher up managers are, the more likely they are to perceive their organizations favorably and to perceive problems as benign. Second, because top managers are some distance from customers, first-line workers, and the latest production methods, they may not understand current circumstances. Third, top managers tend to see technological and social changes as threatening to their abilities to control their organizations because new technologies or new markets might require top managers having different expertise. Fourth, because stakeholders typically blame top managers for poor organizational performance, they are less likely to acknowledge that something is wrong (Starbuck et al., 1978).

Just as familiarity makes stimuli easier to process in noticing, familiarity of stimuli facilitates sense-making processes. People are better able to understand and respond to stimuli that resemble those with which they have experience, while they are more likely to misperceive unfamiliar stimuli (Normann, 1971). Managers' experiences in various job assignments give them specific expertise in specific domains. Therefore, someone working in production tends to be better equipped to make sense of production statistics, problems, and issues than someone who works in marketing.

At the same time, organizations cherish illusions of expertise. That is, people in production assume that people in marketing know more about marketing than they actually do. These illusions of expertise influence collective sense making even in situations where experience may not produce expertise. Information systems also create illusions of expertise. Information systems store information that has been historically relevant, but data categories that were relevant in the past may overlook information that is important today. Further, past trends may bias information and cause people to misinterpret important changes in trends.

Social construction makes some stimuli more salient than others. As people talk to each other and share their perceptions, they invent a shared image of reality. Within the same environment, different subgroups of people construct different images of reality. For instance, explaining why men and women view workplaces differently, Ragins et al. (1998: 36) observed:

> The [male] CEOs in this study were logical in their approach and viewed the problem of women's advancement in terms of what they can see and what they can count: the number of women in the pipeline and their years of experience. They have no way of understanding the corporate environment faced by their female employees because it is an environment that they do not currently experience, nor did they face in their rise to the top. As members of the majority, they were in environments designed by and for men.

4 CONCLUSION

While most academics and most managers assume that managers perceive accurately, managers often hold erroneous perceptions. Indeed, research on managerial perceptions has found large errors and biases in managers' perceptions, both of their organizations and of the environments in which they operate.

Perception errors arise during both noticing and sense making. During noticing, stimuli foster errors because they are unfamiliar, changing slowly, or buried in the midst of voluminous data. Managers make errors during noticing because they tend to find data that confirm their prior beliefs, because they become too involved in courses of action to observe stimuli accurately, because their cultures blind them to some stimuli, or because they do not perceive stimuli to be relevant to their jobs. During sense making, stimuli promote errors when data are inaccessible, changing at extreme rates, or distorted by subordinates. Managers make errors during sense making because of their biases, vested interests, hierarchical positions, illusions of expertise, social environments, or strong needs to believe they made correct decisions.

Errors in noticing dominate errors in sense making. Only events that have been noticed can affect sense making. Also, noticing tends to be binary whereas sense making offers many alternatives. People can apply multiple, partially inconsistent sense-making frameworks to any specific situation, and these sense-making frameworks can be evaluated by multiple, partially inconsistent criteria.

Relating Theories to Observations

Efforts to base theories on empirical evidence need to deal with the fact that managers make bigger errors about the phenomena that are most interesting to academics. Managers and academics notice different phenomena and interpret them differently: whereas managers notice and interpret events as participants in a social system, academics perceive these events as observers outside the social system. The most obvious implication of these differences is that academics need to be very careful about relying on managerial informants. Managers are more likely to perceive accurately short-run implications of their behaviors within a single firm than long-run implications of behaviors across a population of firms. Managers are more likely to perceive accurately specific and concrete phenomena than abstract or general concepts. Academics are more likely to ask managers about, or to interpret their responses as being relevant to, long-run behaviors across a population of firms than short-run behaviors within a single firm. Academics also are more likely to ask managers about, or to interpret their responses as being relevant to, abstract or general concepts than specific and concrete phenomena. Hence, literatures relying on managerial perceptions tend to expose managerial misperceptions, but these apparent errors are likely produced by the research methods.

Insofar as one is concerned with theoretically important behaviors, one needs to recognize that managers and academics notice very different phenomena. For example, managers rarely notice competitive behaviors outside the narrowly defined industries that they see as relevant to their jobs. At the same time, academics are unlikely to think that competitive behaviors in these narrowly defined industries are relevant to their theories. Thus, when Porac et al. (1989) asked managers in the Scottish knitwear industry about their competitors, the Scots described themselves as competing solely with other Scottish firms; one manager even represented that his only competitors were other firms in the same city. Consequently, the Scots did not pay attention to the strategic moves of knitwear producers outside of Scotland. Porac et al. (1989: 413) observed that academics define competitive groups very differently from the Scottish managers: '[M]any of the studies measuring strategic group membership have classified firms on the basis of attributes tangentially related to intended strategies. The resulting 'strategic groups' are thus analytical abstractions of the researchers'.

Just as managers and academics notice very different phenomena, they interpret phenomena differently. Whereas managers interpret events as participants inside a social system, academics often interpret managers' behaviors as observers outside the social system. Thus, when Porac et al. (1989) asked managers in the Scottish knitwear industry about their competitors, one manager replied:

> Quite honestly, there is not a lot of competition. The Italian industry is a different industry from ours. The Asian industry is a different industry from ours. ... Basically it's pullovers and cardigans. It's classic type garments. In my opinion, it is quite clearly defined that people expect to buy the best cashmere pullovers from Scotland.

Porac et al. (1989: 414) contrasted such descriptions with the 'analytical abstractions' used by academics who write about strategic groups. Academics regard strategic groups as 'purely economic entities' that are defined in terms of factors such as cross-elasticities of demand, entry and mobility barriers, product differentiation, and pricing. Managers do not perceive 'purely economic entities' but rather 'primary groups' of firms that reflect sociological and psychological factors such as shared perceptions and cognitive models.

Opportunities

Although perception errors add to the yawning gulf between the behaviors of managers and academic theories, they do present some very interesting issues for investigation.

First, to what extent do perception errors introduce randomness into economic activity? The well-known 'random walk down Wall Street' is largely a result of competition between plausible alternative perceptions; some people perceive a stock to be undervalued and others perceive it to be overvalued. Nelson and Winter (1982: 370) pointed out 'that things always are changing in ways that could not have been fully predicted, and that adjustments always are having to be made to accommodate to or exploit those changes. ... [T]hose adjustments and accommodations ... do not lead to tightly predictable outcomes. For better or for worse, economic life is an adventure'. There are other causes of randomness, such as natural disasters and social turmoil, but the uncertainty arising from inaccurate perceptions may be the dominant factor in small-scale, frequent economic change.

Second, to what extent do managers correct for perception errors by turning their visions into reality? Porac and Rosa (1996) argued that any sense-making framework could be effective if a firm is able to impose its framework on its environments. A firm may also be able to elevate the importance of stimuli that its personnel do notice by acting as if these stimuli are important. Such outcomes imply that the firm exercises considerable power in comparison with elements in its environment, and firm size is not the only determinant of such power: a small firm may be powerful if it behaves effectively in its specialized niche. What conditions affect firms' abilities to construct the realities they perceive?

Third, when are perception errors beneficial rather than harmful? Although a rational model says that people will behave more appropriately if they appraise situations accurately, real life holds surprises. In particular, societies may benefit when the faulty perceptions of individuals encourage or deter actions. When does social and economic change depend on some individuals being unusually optimistic or pessimistic? Entrepreneurs often remark that they would never have attempted to innovate if they had foreseen accurately how much difficulty they would have. Yet a classroom experiment induced Jackson and Dutton (1988: 385) to speculate that most managers are 'more likely to perceive an issue as a threat [than as an opportunity] unless there is strong evidence to do otherwise'; most managers must be 'convinced of the presence of opportunities'. The high prevalence of perceived threats might explain Cyert and March's (1963) observation that threats are more likely to induce firms to explore alternative behaviors than are opportunities.

Fourth, are some managers able to operate much more effectively than others in situations that they misperceive? If so, what distinguishes this ability? Many managers are utterly unaware that they are misperceiving, but those who are aware that they may be misperceiving see their environments as ambiguous and uncertain. Baumard (1999) has argued that rational problem solving proves to be more harmful than merely ineffective in ambiguous, uncertain environments, but that some top managers have an ability to operate effectively in such environments. He described this ability as a pragmatic, creative cunning that enables managers to generate new sense-making frameworks. 'Strategy sometimes consists in establishing *temporary articulations* to avoid fossilizing knowledge into restrictive statements, and so as to take tactical advantage of their unfinished or mutable character' (Baumard, 1999: 228). Thus, in addition to the traditional idea of strategizing as a process that appraises the present realistically and forecasts the future accurately, there may be a second mode of strategizing as a creator and exploiter of perception errors.

REFERENCES

Alchian, A. (1950), 'Uncertainty, evolution, and economic theory', *Journal of Political Economy*, **57**, 211–21.

Andrews, P.W.S. (1949), 'A reconsideration of the theory of the individual business', *Oxford Economics Papers*, **1**, 54–89.

Baumard, P. (1999), *Tacit Knowledge in Organizations*, London: Sage.

Baumol, W.J. and R.E. Quandt (1964), 'Rules of thumb and optimally imperfect decision making', *American Economic Review*, **54** (2), 23–46.

Bazerman, M.H. (1997), *Judgment in Managerial Decision Making*, 2nd edn, New York: Wiley.

Boland, R.J., Jr., J. Singh, P. Salipante, J. Aram, S.Y. Fay and P. Kanawattanachai (2001), 'Knowledge representations and knowledge transfer', *Academy of Management Journal*, 44, 393–417.

Buchanan, L. (1995), 'Scavenger Hunt', *CIO Magazine*, July 1, 1995.

Cooper, W.W. (1949), 'Theory of the firm: some suggestions for revision', *American Economic Review*, **39**, 1204–22.

Cyert, R.M. and J.G. March (1963), *A Behavioral Theory of the Firm*, Englewood Cliffs, NJ: Prentice-Hall.

Daft, R.L. and K.E. Weick (1984), 'Toward a model of organizations as interpretation systems', *Academy of Management Review*, **9**, 284–95.

Downey, H.K., D. Hellriegel and J.W. Slocum, Jr. (1975), 'Environmental uncertainty: the construct and its application', *Administrative Science Quarterly*, **20**, 613–29.

Dunbar, R.L.M., R. Garud and S. Raghuram (1996), 'A frame for deframing in strategic analysis', *Journal of Management Inquiry*, **5**, 23–34.

Dunbar, R.L.M. and W.H. Goldberg (1978), 'Crisis development and strategic response in European corporations', *Journal of Business Administration*, **9** (2), 139–49.

Friedman, M. (1953), *Essays in Positive Economics*, Chicago: University of Chicago Press.

Gersick, C.J. and J.R. Hackman (1990), 'Habitual routines in task-performing groups', *Organizational Behavior and Human Decision Processes*, **47**, 65–97.

Glynn, M.A., T.K. Lant and F.J. Milliken (1994), 'Mapping learning processes in organizations', *Advances in Managerial Cognition and Organizational Information Processing*, **5**, 43–93.

Gordon, R.A. (1948), 'Short period price determination in theory and practice', *American Economic Review*, **38**, 265–88.

Grinyer, P.H. and D. Norburn (1975), 'Planning for existing markets: perceptions of executives and financial performance', *Journal of the Royal Statistical Society*, Series A, 138819, 70–79.

Gulati, R. (1999), 'Network location and learning: the influence of network resources and firm capabilities on alliance formation', *Strategic Management Journal*, **20**, 397–420.

Hall, R.L. and C.J. Hitch (1939), 'Price theory and business behavior', *Oxford Economic Papers*, **2**, 12–45.

Harrod, R.F. (1939), 'Price and cost in entrepreneurs' policy', *Oxford Economic Papers*, **2**, 1–11.

Heider, F. (1958), *The Psychology of Interpersonal Relations*, New York: Wiley.

Horvath, J.A. (1996), *Managerial Learning: An Inductive Systems Perspective*, New Haven, CT: Yale University Press, Department of Psychology.

Institute For The Future (1997), *Managing Corporate Communications in the Information Age*, Menlo Park, CA: Institute For The Future, SR-619.

Jackson, S.E. and J.E. Dutton (1988), 'Discerning threats and opportunities', *Administrative Science Quarterly*, **33**, 370–87.

Kiesler, C.A. (1971), *The Psychology of Commitment*, New York: Academic Press.

Lawrence, P.R. and J.W. Lorsch (1967), *Organization and Environment*, Boston, MA: Graduate School of Business Administration, Harvard University.

Lester, R.A. (1946), 'Shortcomings of marginal analysis for wage–employment problems', *American Economic Review*, **36**, 62–82.

Loftus, E.F. (1979), 'The malleability of human memory', *American Scientist*, **67**, 312–20.

Machlup, F. (1946), 'Marginal analysis and empirical research', *American Economic Review*, **36**, 519–54.

Margolis, J. (1958), 'The analysis of the firm: rationalism, conventionalism, and behaviorism', *Journal of Business*, **31**, 187–99.

Mezias, J.M. and W.H. Starbuck (2002), 'Studying the accuracy of managers' perceptions: A research odyssey', *British Journal of Management*, forthcoming.

Miller, D. (1990), *The Icarus Paradox: How Exceptional Companies Bring About Their Own Downfall*, New York: Harper Collins.

Milliken, F.J. (1990), 'Perceiving and interpreting environmental change: an examination of college administrators' interpretations of changing demographics', *Academy of Management Journal*, **33**, 42–63.

Miner, A.S., J.-Y. Kim, L.W. Holzinger and P. Haunschild (1996), 'Fruits of failure: organizational failure and population level learning', *Best Papers Proceedings, Academy of Management*, 239–43.

Nelson, R.R. and S.G. Winter, Jr. (1982), *An Evolutionary Theory of Economic Change*, Cambridge, MA: Belknap Press.

Nisbett, R.E. and T.D. Wilson (1977), 'Telling more than we can know: verbal reports on mental processes', *Psychological Review*, **84**, 231–59.

Normann, R. (197 1), 'Organizational innovativeness: product variation and reorientation', *Administrative Science Quarterly*, **16**, 203–15.

Papandreou, A.G. (1952), 'Some basic problems in the theory of the firm', in B.F. Haley (ed.), *A Survey of Contemporary Economics*, Vol. II, Homewood, IL: Irwin, pp. 183–219.

Payne, R.L. and D.S. Pugh (1976), 'Organizational structure and climate', in M.D. Dunnette (ed.), *Handbook of Industrial and Organizational Psychology*, Chicago: Rand McNally, pp. 1125–73.

Penrose, E.T. (1952), 'Biological analogies in the theory of the firm', *American Economic Review*, **42**, 804–19.

Penrose, E.T. (1959), *The Theory of the Growth of the Firm*, Oxford: Basil Blackwell.

Porac, J.F. and J.A. Rosa (1996), 'In praise of managerial narrow-mindedness', *Journal of Management Inquiry*, **5**, 35–42.

Porac, J.F., H. Thomas and C. Baden-Fuller (1989), 'Competitive groups as cognitive communities: the case of Scottish knitwear manufacturers', *Journal of Management Studies*, **26**, 397–416.

Ragins, B.R., B. Townsend and M. Mattis (1998), 'Gender disparity in the executive suite: CEOs and female executives report on breaking the glass ceiling', *Academy of Management Executive*, **12** (1), 28–42.

Simon, H.A. (1955), 'A behavioral model of rational choice', *Quarterly Journal of Economics*, **69**, 99–118.

Singer, B. and V.A. Benassi (1981), 'Occult Beliefs', *American Scientist*, **69**, pp. 49–55.

Spiro, L.N. (1999), 'Merrill's e-battle', *Business Week*, November 15, 256–68.

Starbuck, W.H. (1983), 'Organizations as action generators', *American Sociological Review*, **48**, 91–102.

Starbuck, W.H. (1994), 'On behalf of naïveté', in J.A.C. Baum and J.V. Singh (eds), *Evolutionary Dynamics of Organizations*, London: Oxford University Press, pp. 205–20.

Starbuck, W.H., A. Greve and B.L.T. Hedberg (1978), 'Responding to crises', *Journal of Business Administration*, **9** (2), 111–37.

Starbuck, W.H. and J.M. Mezias (1996), 'Opening Pandora's box: studying the accuracy of managers' perceptions', *Journal of Organizational Behavior*, **17** (2), 99–117.

Starbuck, W.H. and F.J. Milliken (1988a), 'Executives' perceptual filters: what they notice and how they make sense', in D.C. Hambrick (ed.), *The Executive Effect: Concepts and Methods for Studying Top Managers*, Greenwich, CT: JAI Press, pp. 35–65.

Starbuck, W.H. and F.J. Milliken (1988b), 'Challenger: changing the odds until something breaks', *Journal of Management Studies*, **25**, 319–40.

Tintner, G. (1941), 'The theory of choice under subjective risk and uncertainty', *Econometrica*, **9** (3/4, July–October), 298–304.

Tosi, H., R. Aldag and R. Storey (1973), 'On the measurement of the environment: an assessment of the Lawrence and Lorsch environmental uncertainty subscale', *Administrative Science Quarterly*, **18**, 27–36.

Wagner, J.A. III and R.Z. Gooding (1997), 'Equivocal information and attribution: an investigation of patterns of managerial sensemaking', *Strategic Management Journal*, **18**, 275–86.

Wallace, J. (1997), *Overdrive: Bill Gates and the Race to Control Cyberspace*, New York: Wiley.

Watzlawick, P., J.H. Weakland and R. Fisch (1974), *Change*, New York: Norton.

Winter, S.G., Jr. (1964), 'Economic "natural selection" and the theory of the firm', *Yale Economic Essays*, **4**, 225–72.

PART III

Economics of Change

Section A

Learning

9. Interorganizational learning and network organization: toward a behavioral theory of the interfirm

Joel A.C. Baum and Paul Ingram*

1 INTRODUCTION

The behavioral theory of the firm rests on empirical observation of economic behavior in organizations, and was motivated by the 'disconnect' between that observation and prevailing economic theory. March and Simon (1958) and Cyert and March (1963) disputed the claim of prevailing economic theory that organizational decision outcomes were uniquely determined by environmental constraints, and developed a behavioral theory in which firms were conceived as complex, adaptive systems whose behavior was only loosely coupled to environmental constraints. The behavioral theory revealed a tension between two images of adaptation. On the one hand, firms' behavior was seen as directed toward performance improvement, compatible with rationalistic assumptions of economics theories. On the other hand, firms' behavior tended to be complex, slow and sensitive to organizational conditions, characteristic of bounded rationality (Simon 1957). Thus, while intendedly adaptive, firms' behavior might not necessarily result in performance improvement.

We believe that there is a comparable tension between reality and theory with regard to the persistent, systematic relationships between organizations. Observation belies the traditional view that organizations are distinct and autonomous units of action. Instead, it appears that they are very often embedded in organizational groups comprising close, robust and multidimensional ties that blur hierarchical boundaries (Granovetter 1994; Gulati and Gargiulo 1999; Powell and Smith-Doerr 1994). These groups, which we call interfirms, demand analysis. Why do they exist at all? What processes cause them to take the forms that they do? Under what circumstances are they more or less useful for their constituents?

In this chapter we offer answers to these questions. Our approach to explaining interfirms builds on earlier cognitive and behavioral arguments regarding the existence, structure and behavior of firms. First, we explain the existence of interfirms as a response to the transaction costs that emerge under conditions of bounded rationality. This argument locates the interfirm within broader justifications for institutions, which build on Coase's ([1937] 1988) transaction cost and March and Simon's (1958) and Cyert and March's (1963) behavioral explanations for the firm. Next, we offer an *evolutionary process model* of the emergence of one type of interfirm, the network organization – a production network based on strategic alliances (Powell and Smith-Doerr 1994).

Our goal is to outline the processes that give interfirms their specific characteristics. We chose the network organization as the basis for the model because network organizations arise in a decentralized manner and are therefore particularly illustrative of the information-processing requirements that are central in the structuring of interfirms (as with firms, Cyert and March 1963). We advance interorganizational learning as a theory of organizational action to explain how organizational groups choose strategic and operational paths given bounded rationality, providing a positive alternative to rational choice assumptions (Cohen and Sproull 1991; Weick and Westley 1996).

Finally, we consider competitive and economic factors that combine to determine which interfirms will persist and grow, and which will fail. Even here, however, we challenge neoclassical arguments, as we look to the social content of interfirm ties, and their structure, as key determinants of success. Ties within the interfirm may create the interorganizational equivalents of empathy, trust and even altruism (Uzzi 1996, 1997). These ties enable mechanisms of social control to operate, creating, within the interfirm, a 'moral economy' that leverages social and political interests to achieve economic ends (Granovetter 1994).

Our theoretical model builds on behavioral theories of the firm in several basic ways. First, our explanation for the emergence and dynamics of interfirms is grounded firmly in learning ideas that are core to the behavioral theory of the firm – that organizations are complex, intendedly adaptive systems, which change behavior in response to changing environmental demands by following standard operating procedures that led to beneficial outcomes in the past. We conceive organizational learning as a complex, multilevel process. At the organization level, learning is strongly shaped by past choices as boundedly rational decision makers' reliance on attention and search routines that conserve cognitive resources binds their search for alternatives to past choices reinforced by increasing returns to experience and the absence of immediately negative outcomes. At the interorganizational level, the same boundedly rational decision makers, faced with insufficient information to learn from their own experience, attempt to reduce uncertainty by attending to easily observed and comparable competitors' actions for clues about how to interpret their own situation and act.

Second, through the notion of embedded organizational action (Granovetter 1985), we connect the organization-level standard operating procedures of the behavioral theory of the firm to their interorganizational analogs – collective social representations such as industry models (Porac and Rosa 1996) and conceptions of control (Fligstein 1996) that grow out of interactions among boundedly rational industry participants to provide a basis for describing, selecting, and interpreting organizations' actions (White 1981).

Third, our perspective on interfirms contributes to the emerging theory of organizational attention (March 1994a; March and Shapira 1992; Ocasio 1997). March and Olsen (1976) proposed that a key component of a theory of organizations is a theory of how organizational decision makers' attention is shaped by context and how this, in turn, influences organizational search processes. Interorganizational learning is an important vehicle for developing such a theory of attention because organizations are highly selective in their observation and imitation of other organizations, and because diffusion of routines among organizations can be used to document the patterns of attention guiding organizational decisions.

Fourth, we make an explicit link between interorganizational learning and organizational decision making. The behavioral theory of the firm and neoinstitutional theory share an emphasis on uncertainty and attention allocation and a cognitively based theory of action, By concentrating on decision making, however, the behavioral theory of the firm lacks neoinstitutional theory's attention to organizational environments. Conversely, neoinstitutionalists' theory of environmental effects on organizations based on individual cognition lacks the behavioral theory of the firm's attention to organizational decision making. By connecting theories of interorganizational learning and decision making, we take a step toward integrating these theoretical perspectives, which are so similar in their underlying assumptions and interests (DiMaggio and Powell 1991; Levitt and March 1988).

2 INTRODUCING THE INTERFIRM

Interfirms are collections of organizations joined by ties which may vary in formality, but which are stable and significant enough to create a reasonably persistent interorganizational structure. The emergent, interorganizational characteristics of interfirms may not exist in dyadic relationships (which may be dominated by one organization), so our operational definition requires at least three organizational participants (Ingram and Baum 1997). Interfirms may be categorized into two broad classes. Vertical interfirms span differentiated organizations that combine symbiotically to achieve collective ends. Examples include business groups such as the Japanese *keiretsu*, Latin American *grupos*, Indian *business houses*, and South Korean *chaebol* (Khanna and Palepu 1997; Lincoln et al. 1996), production networks based on family, regional or ethnic cohesion (Dutta 1997; Lazerson 1995; Uzzi 1996), or network organizations structured by strategic alliances (Baum et al. 2000a; Powell and Smith-Doerr 1994). Horizontal interfirms span similar organizations that combine commensalistically to achieve collective ends. Examples include service chains (Ingram and Baum 1997), multi-location manufacturers (Sorenson and Audia 2000), research consortia (Aldrich and Sasaki 1994; Grindley et al. 1994), and trade associations (Aldrich et al. 1994).

At the most basic level, the interfirm can be seen as an institutional arrangement for managing interdependence between organizations. Under conditions of bounded rationality (namely limited human cognitive capacity and costly information), exchange is inhibited by the inability to foresee contingencies, and observe all of the actions of exchange partners (Coase [1937] 1988; Simon 1957; Williamson 1975). Like the firm, the interfirm may smooth exchange by providing a set of rules and understandings, which limit the costs and uncertainty that might otherwise prevent exchange. This account of the institutional role of the interfirm raises two questions. The first concerns the interdependencies that require organizational exchange in the first place. We argue that interfirms are structured around a broad set of economic and non-economic interdependencies, facilitating organizational cooperation in pursuit of many different interests. The second question concerns the theoretical boundary between the firm and the interfirm. Transaction costs emerging from bounded rationality open an opportunity for institutional structures such as firms and interfirms, but when should we expect to see large firms, and when smaller firms joined in an interfirm? Our answer builds on the recognition that different institutional arrangements have costs of their own, and may be more or less suited to govern any particular form of interdependence. Further, history and inertia combine to create an influence on institutions that goes beyond the minimization of transaction costs.

In broad terms, interdependence focuses on two considerations: resource procurement and uncertainty reduction (Pfeffer and Salancik 1978). Organizations form interorganizational relations to access resources that are essential to pursuing their goals but are at least in part controlled by other organizations. *Competitive* interdependence arises between organizations occupying similar domains, and may motivate the formation of alliances to dampen competition between them (Pfeffer and Salancik 1978) or to promote interorganizational learning (Gulati 1995; Powell et al. 1996). *Symbiotic* interdependence arises between organizations occupying different domains, which may motivate partnerships to take advantage of complementary differences (Hawley 1950).

Oliver (1990) summarized the literature on six exogenous drivers of interorganizational relations. The first, necessity (for example, regulatory requirement), involves mandated ties, but the other five – asymmetry, reciprocity, efficiency, stability, and legitimacy – lead to voluntary cooperative ties based on specific needs resulting from external interdependencies. From this perspective, firms build relationships with other firms for a variety of reasons, including the need to share the costs and risks of undertaking large-scale projects, to develop existing markets or enter new ones, to pursue resource specialization, or to mitigate or otherwise control competition. Such objectives make organizations behaviorally interdependent with other organizations that possess the capital, complementary assets, and technical capabilities that can help them to achieve their ambitions. Although transaction cost economics originally viewed such 'bilateral dependence' as creating hazardous conditions for exchange (Williamson 1975), research indicating that bilateral dependence is more stable than unilateral dependence (for example, Monteverde and Teece 1982) has increased transaction cost economists' appreciation for the value of credible commitments in supporting exchange. Williamson (1983), for example, suggests that one way to support an exchange relationship that requires specific investments by one firm is to increase the level of specific investment made by the other.

Thus, interfirm (re)formation is initiated by exogenous factors, such as the distribution of capital and technological resources and the pattern of resource dependence. Organizations create ties with organizations that have resources and capabilities that can help them cope with uncertain environments and satisfy their resource needs.

Although the set of interdependencies that may seed interfirms is large, the possibility of knowledge sharing deserves particular attention as it is often cited as a primary benefit of interfirms (Darr et al. 1995; Ingram and Baum 1997; Ingram and Simons 1999). Some accounts, for example, point to learning benefits of thick interorganizational ties as the foundation for the rapid diffusion of the network organizational form (Powell et al. 1996). By bringing members of organizations together for both task-oriented and social purposes, interfirms facilitate interorganizational transfer of experience by increasing opportunity and motivation for transfer, and the ability of organizations to successfully apply experience transferred from other organizations.

The role of interfirms in smoothing the transfer of knowledge also serves to illustrate why interfirms may sometimes be an effective institutional arrangement. In our study of organizational learning in the Manhattan hotel industry, we found evidence of knowledge transfer within hotel chains, but not between unrelated hotels (Baum and Ingram 1998). It is not surprising that knowledge does not transfer easily between organizations in the 'open market' as the difficulties in measuring and valuing knowledge are obvious. The tacit quality that useful knowledge often has may also necessitate empathy and familiarity between parties as a minimum condition for communication sufficient for knowledge transfer, Such circumstances, where relationship-specific investments are required for coordinated exchange, are particularly difficult without some form of institutional governance (Teece 1982, 1986; Williamson 1975). Between market and hierarchy exist a range of intermediate, interfirm governance forms such as long-term contracts, franchises, and alliances. Interfirms provide the necessary ongoing collaborative interaction required to effectively transfer knowledge, thereby providing a means of overcoming knowledge-based market failures in discrete resource exchange. But why should the chosen governance mechanism be the interfirm rather than *within* firm?

According to Williamson (1991), interfirms are characterized by semi-strong incentives, an intermediate degree of administrative control, and semi-strong autonomous and coordinated adaptation. This characterization locates this 'hybrid' governance mode between market and hierarchy with respect to incentives, bureaucratic costs, and adaptability: compared with a market, the interfirm sacrifices incentives in favor of superior coordination, and compared to hierarchy, the interfirm sacrifices cooperativeness in favor of more intense incentives. Because of their greater adaptive capabilities than hierarchies and stronger administrative control than markets, interfirm modes of governance are conceived as particularly well-suited organizations (that is, 'efficient') for transactions requiring a mix of autonomous and coordinated adaptation, particularly at moderate levels of asset specificity.

Sometimes knowledge is best applied in various, discrete places in the organizational landscape – in the Manhattan hotel industry those places are the physical locations of various hotels. Sometimes also, it is costly to stretch a firm to encompass disparate locations (in multidimensional organizational space) that are interdependent. This is clear in the hotel industry, where it is the overwhelming choice to establish self-contained local organizations to operate each hotel, and to link those organizations in an interfirm, rather than build firms that encompass multiple hotels in one organizational structure.[1]

It is also sometimes difficult to discern the appropriate boundaries for bureaucratic rules in a firm that spans diverse locations and activities. For example, small firms in an interfirm can exercise local expertise to make better decisions regarding which knowledge is useful for them, while large firms sometimes establish bureaucratic rules which result in knowledge being applied where it is not useful, or even harmful (Baum and Ingram 1998; Greve 1999). Similarly, interfirms may be more flexible and so better able to supply consumer markets where differentiated products are valued (Piore and Sabel 1984).

Other interfirm advantages concern strategic interaction in specific situations. Hadfield (1991) showed that a chain-type interfirm that delegates pricing authority to its components has strategic advantages over one that centralizes pricing authority in a bureaucratic center. Strategic interaction was also a key justification for the spinoff of GM's Delphi auto-parts division (Howes and Vlasic 1998). Since GM planned to maintain a close relationship with Delphi, the spinoff could be characterized as a transformation from a firm to an interfirm arrangement. In other circumstances, exogenous factors inhibit large firms, and favor interfirms. For example, Israeli kibbutzim, whose ideological value of organizational democracy prohibits a large firm, manage interdependence with a federation interfirm (Simons and Ingram 1997, 2000). Consider also competing Sydney hotels, which are prevented by anti-trust law from being part of the same bureaucratic structure, but which use friendship groups to mitigate competition (Ingram and Roberts 2000).

More generally, the trade-off between firms and interfirms for managing interdependencies may be understood in similar terms to the departmentalization decision within a firm. Thompson's (1967) seminal work on organizational design advocated a matching of the intensity of interdependence between organizational participants, and the level of coordination between them. This position is based on recognition both of the need to coordinate between interdependent actors, and that coordination comes with a cost. The most interdependent participants deserve the highest coordination, and should normally be organized together in a single department. Less interdependent participants might be organized in separate departments, and connected by less intense coordination mechanisms. Analogously, we would argue that more interdependent actors are better organized into a single firm. But as the interdependence between actors decreases, and as the costs of coordinating between them increases (due to, for example, physical separation) interfirm organization becomes more attractive.

3 DYNAMICS OF NETWORK ORGANIZATIONS

To this point we have emphasized the efficiencies (albeit in the face of bounded rationality) produced by the interfirm as an institutional mechanism. Our understanding of the interfirm goes beyond simple efficiency, however. As Granovetter (1994, p. 454) observes, there are many instances where profitable organizational structures fail to be established. In light of this observation, he suggests the question 'What makes possible the agglomeration of firms into some more-or-less coherent social structure, and what determines the kind of structure that results?'. In this section we develop a process model that describes how interfirms come to be. Our starting-point is the recognition that economic behavior is embedded in non-economic institutions (Polanyi et al. [1957] 1971).

The concept of embeddedness, which is central to contemporary research in economic sociology (Smelser and Swedberg 1994), is typically treated as synonymous with the notion that organizations and the economy are part of a larger institutional structure, and that the context of organizational action shapes rational choice. In particular, we see the *structural* and *cognitive* embeddedness of organizations as influential to the processes through which interfirms emerge and persist. *Structural embeddedness* refers to contextualization of economic exchange in patterns of ongoing interpersonal relations. Non-economic interests are apparent in market dynamics to the extent that factors such as friendship ties, kinship relations, and social or ethnic group membership influence market behavior (Granovetter 1985, 1994). *Cognitive embeddedness* refers to the importance of organizational performance programs (March and Simon 1958), standard operating procedures (Cyert and March 1963) and routines (Nelson and Winter 1982) and social representations such as market reputations, mental models, and conceptions of control (Fligstein 1996; Porac and Rosa 1996). These firm- and industry-specific collective representations grow out of the problem-solving and cognitive activity of the industry's participants and provide the social knowledge that resolves market ambiguities, and languages for describing, defining, and interpreting firms' activities (Porac and Rosa 1996; White 1981).

So, while interdependencies in the face of transaction costs set the stage for the interfirm, the dynamics of interfirms are driven by embeddedness processes – structural and cognitive – that help them determine with whom to build relationships, and reinforced through imitation fostered by the institutionalization of an interfirm mental model. The performance of the interfirms that emerge from these dynamics feed back into the system, shaping and refining the interfirm mental model. In the sections that follow, we outline in more detail our model in three phases: *firm-level embedding*, *network-level embedding*, and *network performance feedback*. We elaborate this model with specific reference to one type of interfirm, the *network organization*.[2]

Network organizations are a form of production network based on strategic alliances (Gulati 1995; Powell and Smith-Doerr 1994). We chose them as the focus of our dynamic model because they are more clearly emergent than other interfirms which may rely more on a natural source of cohesion (for example, family business groups), or on growth through explicit strategy (for example, chain organizations). Strategic alliances are typically short-term arrangements designed for specific purposes (for example, produce a component, establish a joint venture, enter a new market). In such settings, trust is not easily engendered (Axelrod 1984); fear of potential opportunism and uncertainty must be overcome before information can be shared openly. Because strategic alliances lack a natural basis for trust that other network forms (for example, business groups, industrial districts) possess, they typically rely on contractual agreements to curb potential opportunism, and monitoring tends to be formally structured (Powell and Smith-Doerr 1994). But, once a strategic alliance is successfully pursued, further cooperation between the same partners becomes easier and more likely (Gulati 1995). The level of trust and cooperation increases with each further agreement between the same partners, and individual partners become more skilled at partnering and develop their reputations as reliable, trustworthy partners (Baker 1990; Gulati 1995).

Phase 1 Firm-level Embedding

The interdependence-in-the-face-of-transaction-costs perspective provides useful explanations of factors influencing the propensity of firms to form ties in the first place, but it does not provide insight into the particular organizations with which they will build relations (Gulati and Gargiulo 1999). This difficulty stems from the challenges associated with obtaining information about the competencies, needs, and resources of potential partners. Thus, while interorganizational relations can be a valuable means of managing environmental uncertainty and interdependence, there is considerable uncertainty associated with entering cooperative ties (Gulati and Gargiulo 1999). Imperfect information about potential partners raises search costs and the risk of exposure to opportunistic behavior. So, how do firms choose partners?

Through previous direct ties, partners' partners, and status positions of potential partners, information about the quality and trustworthiness of firms diffuses (albeit unevenly). In turn this first- and second-hand information about potential partners reduces the cost and risk of establishing relationships (Li and Rowley 1999).

Firm-level structural embedding: relational and third-party embedding

Relational embeddedness highlights effects of dyadic ties between firms on subsequent cooperation between them (Gulati and Gargiulo 1999). To reduce search costs and alleviate risks of opportunism associated with interfirm relationships, firms tend to create stable, preferential relationships characterized by trust and rich information exchange with specific partners. Prior direct ties provide channels through which each partner can learn about the competencies and reliability of the other, amplifying trust and diminishing uncertainty associated with future ties (Chung et al. 2000; Gulati 1995).

Third-party embeddedness incorporates the local structure of partners' relations around firms on their tendency to cooperate with one another (Granovetter 1985). The frame of reference shifts from direct ties and communication to indirect channels of information, reputation, and referral. Firms tied to a common partner can utilize reliable information about each other from that partner (Baker 1990). When two firms share common ties it signals that both are regarded as trustworthy partners by the same organization. Third-party ties can also promote good behavior by fostering a concern for local reputation (Burt and Knez 1995).

Thus a history of direct and indirect cooperative experience becomes a unique source of information about various potential partners' capabilities and reliability that affects the likelihood of two firms partnering in the future by shaping firms' local search for partners (Chung et al. 2000; Gulati 1995). For example, syndication of investment is crucial to venture capital (VC) firms' performance. The search for business ideas to fund requires substantial time and is riddled with uncertainty. VCs must assess many projects before identifying one or a few that might provide high returns. Coinvesting with other VCs permits pooling of evaluations and judgments, reducing the risk in screening, as well as minimizing the winner's curse (Lerner 1994). Moreover, investments require extensive monitoring and active management involvement by VCs to appraise the venture's value for future investment rounds. So, joining syndicates can reduce VCs' search as well as monitoring costs. Despite these benefits, the VC syndication process is fraught with uncertainties and market failures. In particular, syndication is subject to *adverse selection* (VCs in prior funding rounds have superior information on the investment's value) and *moral hazard* (free riding on the search and monitoring efforts of other syndicate members) problems associated with entry of new VCs into an existing syndicate. As Anand and Piskaski (2000) show, however, past direct ties and partners in common help VCs overcome these information asymmetries and free-rider incentives, making syndication systematically more likely among VCs with dyadic and triadic ties.

Firm-level cognitive embedding: routinization

Learning by firms from their own experience is widely held to be a major source of improved performance. For more than 40 years, organizational learning theorists have characterized firms as routine-based, path-dependent systems that adapt incrementally to their past experience (Cyert and March 1963; Levinthal and March 1993; Levitt and March 1988; March and Simon 1958). Organizational routines are socially constructed programs of action that embody the knowledge, capabilities, beliefs, values, and memory of the organization and its decision makers. They are products of a process of incremental updating of routines based on the interpretation of experience, and the short-run focus of organizational decision making and action. Organizational routines both enable and constrain organizational action by conserving the cognitive capabilities of decision makers and by limiting and channeling political conflict. Actions encoded in routines are thus more likely to be attended to and accepted by organizational decision makers.

Individual organizations face the question of how to divide attention and resources to exploring new knowledge and *exploiting* existing knowledge. *Exploitation* refers to learning gained via the refinement and selection of existing routines. *Exploration* refers to learning gained through processes of search, concerted variation, planned experimentation and play. March (1991; Levinthal and March 1993) advocates that organizations endeavor to strike a balance between exploitation and exploration. Too much emphasis on exploitation can lead to the adoption of suboptimal routines, while too much emphasis on exploration can lead to incurring the high costs of experimentation without realizing its benefits. In practice, achieving this balance is elusive. The sure short-run rewards of exploitation distract organizations from exploration, where returns are far less certain. Even if the expected value of exploration is greater than that of exploitation, loss aversion might still lead to a preference for exploitation (Kahneman and Tversky 1979). The short-run rewards of exploiting organizational routines learned in the past thus typically quickly drive out exploration of novel – potentially superior – behaviors.

Experiential organizational learning processes are thus highly localized and strongly path dependent (that is, sensitive to initial conditions). For example, each time an organization engages a particular partner, its members increase their competency at working with it and their familiarity with it, which increases the likelihood of obtaining rewards for partnering with it, while making rewards from other partnerships increasingly uncertain (Levitt and March 1988; March 1991). Thus, considerations that are close in cognitive, organizational, and strategic distance come to dominate those that are more distant. This self-reinforcing bias creates *organizational momentum*, the tendency to maintain the direction and emphasis of prior actions in current behavior (Amburgey and Miner 1992; Miller and Friesen 1980). Consequently, early partnering experiences are likely to prove especially fateful as organizations commit to partnering routines shaped more by early, sometimes arbitrary, conditions, experiences and actions than by information gained from later learning situations (Hedberg et al. 1976; Levitt and March 1988; Stinchcombe 1965). This path dependency limits the scope of the firm, reducing exploratory search and learning activities despite the fact that new opportunities and threats are present, and leading organizations to repeatedly engage partners from the past – possibly beyond their point of usefulness.

An emphasis on exploiting partnering routines refined through feedback from experience may significantly enhance performance by reducing variability in the quality of decision making or efficiency of collaborative task performance. An emphasis on routine operation can also prevent firms from adjusting too quickly and detrimentally to idiosyncratic events and from engaging in costly explorations into uncertain domains. Moreover, in the face of production pressures and the need for reliability and consistency of action, exploitation may significantly enhance performance by reducing variability in the quality of decision making or efficiency of task performance (Hannan and Freeman 1984). Routinization of partnering also creates competitive advantages that make imitation difficult because the ability of firms to acquire, develop and exploit routines often depends on their location in space and time (Arthur 1989; Barney 1991; Peteraf 1993). Once history passes, firms that do not have history-dependent routines face a significant disadvantage in developing them. Firms that exploit experience-based routines may therefore enjoy a sustained competitive advantage (Barney 1991).

Nevertheless, gains from exploiting partnering routines will be short-lived if success criteria change after a firm has routinized its partnering behavior. Then, a firm's past investment in routines is rendered obsolete, and the lack of exploration that results from a focus on routines of the past beyond their point of usefulness can inhibit adaptation and hasten failure (Baum and Ingram 1998; Ingram and Baum 1997). Indeed, even doing extremely well what it learned in the past, the firm may perform poorly and even fail; it may suffer the so-called *competency trap* (Levitt and March 1988).

Phase 2 Network-level Embedding

The world of organizational decision makers is fundamentally uncertain; as a result, they can rarely (if ever) tell if they are 'doing the right thing'. They have too much information to process about their markets and firms to be sure if their actions have positive or negative outcomes. Decision makers scan the information environment to gain insight into firms and their behaviors as well as their own competitive position *vis-à-vis* others (Porac et al. 1995). Over time, interfirm relationships accumulate into a network that becomes a growing repository of information on the availability, competencies, and reliability of prospective partners (Gulati

1995). The more the network internalizes information about potential partners the more firms resort to the network for cues about future partnerships and the more firms' access to capable partners depends on their own prior alliances and reputation for successful cooperation (Ahuja 2000; Chung et al. 2000; Gulati 1995; Walker et al. 1997). The network also shapes decision makers' cognitive representations, or mental models, of how a market is bounded and works, enabling them to interpret the actions of others and act themselves (Porac and Rosa 1996).

Network-level structural embedding: position and clique

In building new alliances, firms contribute to the formation of the network structure that shapes future relationships. Interfirm networks are thus the evolutionary outcome of structurally and cognitively embedded organizational action in which new relations are increasingly embedded in the very same network that shaped the organizational decisions to create them. This dynamic between embedded organizational action and network structure that results from that action drives a progressive *structural differentiation* of the interfirm network (Gulati and Gargiulo 1999). Structural differentiation refers to the extent to which firms in a network occupy an identifiable set of self-reproducing network positions characterized by distinct relational profiles. *Positional embeddedness* captures the impact of the positions firms occupy in the overall structure of the network on their decisions about cooperative ties.

These self-reproducing network positions can be represented as a status order in which access to rewards in the market (for example, higher revenues, higher prices, greater market share) is mediated by the centrality of the network position one occupies (Bonacich 1987; Borgatti and Everett 1992; Podolny 1993). Central firms have greater access to more fine-grained information about competencies, needs, and reliability of potential partners, as well as a better comprehension of the existing network (Krackhardt 1990; Powell et al. 1996). Central firms are also more visible, and represent more attractive, high-status partners. The signaling property of central network positions is particularly important in uncertain environments because it introduces systemic status differences among firms that can travel well beyond their immediate circle of direct and indirect ties (Podolny 1993). If a firm is uncertain of the quality of the partners available, or is unable to bear the search costs of investigating all the different alternatives, then the regard other market participants display for a given firm provides a strong indication of the quality of the firm's performance.

Status flows through interconnections between firms. Ties to higher-status firms enhance one's own status, while ties to lower-status firms detract from it (Faulkner 1983; Stuart and Podolny 1996; Stuart et al. 1999). Thus, a firm's relations with others in the market mediates the relationship between status and quality, creating inertial tendencies in the formation of exchange relations and biasing evaluation in the direction of the status of those to whom the firm is tied. This encourages low-status firms to try to enhance their own position by engaging in strategic behavior, including bargaining, exchange, and coercion (Brager and Holloway 1978; Willer and Anderson 1981), or co-sponsorship and cooptation (Sharpe 1985), to establish and maintain ties with higher-status firms (Leik 1992). Central firms may not, however, have any incentive to accept advances of peripheral firms since they add little – and may damage the central firm's own attractiveness (Gulati & Gargiulo 1999; Podolny 1993). Thus, consistent with the tendency toward homophily under conditions of uncertainty (Podolny 1994), in a structurally differentiated network, the likelihood of partnering increases with similarity in status (for example, Anand and Piskorski 2000; Chung et al. 2000).

In addition to self-reproducing firms' positions, self-reproducing cliques of repeatedly cooperating sets of firms – network organizations – also emerge as embedded organizational action increasingly reinforces repeated ties among firms. Studies of established interfirm networks suggest that structural differentiation proceeds rapidly as ties accumulate at first, but slows over time, ultimately stabilizing at a set of differentiated, self-reproducing positions occupied by organizations with similar network profiles (Gulati and Gargiulo 1999). These durable patterns of relations among firms tend to lock them in place, constraining their possible strategies, and segmenting an industry into distinct, semi-detached network organizations (Walker et al. 1997).

Network-level cognitive embedding: mental models and interorganizational imitation
Under uncertain and ambiguous conditions, decision makers must rely on social comparison of firm-level traits and actions with other similar firms to obtain information about their own capabilities, competitive position and identity, and to select and evaluate their own actions (DiMaggio and Powell 1983). Faced with insufficient information to learn from their own experience, firms' decision makers turn to the actions of their competitors for clues about how to interpret their situation. By observing competitors, firms' decision makers can potentially learn the multiplicity of strategies, administrative practices, and technologies employed by other successful organizations (Levitt and March 1988; Levinthal and March 1993). Since other firms presumably act on strategic options that they have positive opinions of, their actions are informative to strategists without strong opinions on the strategic options.[3]

To effectively interpret and make use of available information about other firms and their behavior, firms' decision makers must construct a worldview – a mental model – that reduces market ambiguity and gives meaning to available environmental information (Porac and Rosa 1996). Mental models refer to decision makers' cognitive representations that structure their perceptions of how a market is bounded and works, enabling them to interpret the actions of others and act themselves. A mental model reflects locally viable market-specific agreements between firms' decision makers on principles of organizational structure and boundaries, tactics for competition or cooperation, and status ordering of firms in a given market. Fligstein (1996) interprets such mental models as incumbents' attempts to impose stability on markets and to control potentially destabilizing competitive situations.

For example, a key element of the mental model of US venture capital firms (VCs) is an 'equity norm' that makes it very rare for a VC to obtain shares in a coinvestment syndicate that are not directly proportional to the investment it makes.[4] This norm about how the VC market works serves both to stabilize and to control competition. By definition, the equity norm all but eliminates price competition for coinvestment partners. This norm also increases the tendency of 'like' VCs to partner by forcing higher status or capability VCs in a syndicate to provide their services to its coinvestors at a lower price. In combination, the normative press away from price competition and tendency for likes to partner fosters preservation of the status quo by reinforcing central firms' positions and denying new and peripheral players admission to core syndicates by paying a premium to participate.

Mental models develop over time, as cognitive representations of competing firms' decision makers converge as they become reciprocally intertwined through their strategic choices and interaction in a competitive arena, and increasingly take place within the context of many shared beliefs about how and with whom to compete (Porac et al. 1995). As shared definitions of competitors and market boundaries stabilize, firms' key competencies become identifiable, their strategies decipherable, and rules-of-the-game playable. When a particular mental model becomes shared by decision makers from several firms, the joint focus of these firms' decision makers on each other creates a market in which firms are engaged in reciprocal monitoring and mutual adjustments (White 1981). Thus, to the extent that a mental model is shared across a set of firms, the market space implied by the consensus stabilizes as firms' decision makers enact the market defined by the collective representation. In this way, mental models are defined by firms' decision makers and are sustained through a self-reinforcing reciprocal process of cognition and enactment through which firms' decision makers both respond to and create their environments (Porac and Thomas 1994; Weick 1979).

Decision makers' convergence on a 'network organization' mental model is fostered as progressive structural differentiation of an interorganizational network reveals an increasingly ordered set of self-reproducing network positions, and reinforced by the emergence of distinct self-reproducing cliques of repeatedly cooperating sets of firms – network organizations.

Convergence on a shared mental model institutionalizes behavior among competing firms by creating common beliefs about the meaning and appropriateness of organizational structures, practices, strategies, actions, and networks of relations (Zucker 1977). This facilitates interorganizational imitation by enabling firms' decision makers to interpret and give meaning to information about other firms and their behavior. Interorganizational imitation takes two basic forms: *frequency* based and *trait* based (Miner and Haunschild 1995).

Frequency-based imitation Since under conditions of uncertainty a firm's strategists are often not privy to the value of particular practices used by others, they frequently rely on prevalence as a proxy for value. More frequent use provides more information that others find a practice/action valuable, which, in turn, increases its likelihood of adoption (DiMaggio and Powell 1983). Finns may thus wait until others have proven a particular strategy or practice viable. Neoinstitutional theorists explain such frequency-based imitation by noting that the prevalence of a practice increases its legitimacy, and that firms' desire for legitimacy leads them to imitate (DiMaggio and Powell 1983). Prevalence also increases taken-for-grantedness and unthinking adoption (Zucker 1977).

Trait-based imitation Firms are sometimes selective, however, in their imitation of other firms and select firms to serve as role models based upon their traits (DiMaggio and Powell 1983; Haunschild and Miner 1997). High-status firms, which occupy central network positions, or are large and successful, are particularly likely targets of imitation because their success signals that they have done something right to gain access to resources and to satisfy constituents (for a review, see Miner and Haunschild 1995). Imitation of firms with superior access to information and resources may also satisfy firms' desire for legitimacy (DiMaggio and Powell 1983).

Phase 3 Network Organization Performance Feedback

Over time, as durable patterns of relations emerge among firms, the overall network is segmented into distinct network organizations that vary in their degree of functional integration. As interfirm relationships stabilize, competition may shift from the firm to the network organization level. What was once competition between firms becomes rivalry between network organizations. Thus, in a network organization, the outcomes for firms may be fundamentally intertwined with other firms that belong to the same network organization.

The concept of 'shared fates' is thus central to network organizations. The activities of a firm can affect its performance relative to other firms in the same and different network organization, but they can also affect the abundance of all firms in its network organization as a unit. When multiple network organizations exist that vary in their composition, patterns of interaction, beliefs and customs, and social–organizational structures, those that function better as a unit will outcompete those that do not function as well. If between-network organization competition is sufficiently intense, over time network organizations become functionally organized to maximize their contribution to future local organizational communities. Under such conditions, the functional form of network organizations can be seen as adaptations that have evolved because those expressing them outcompete other groups.

Of course, all of this requires an appropriate network structure. Competition at any level of organization requires variation. If the network does not become sufficiently differentiated into varied self-reproducing cliques, then intergroup competition will not emerge. Organizational networks frequently consist of a mosaic of semi-isolated network organizations (Gulati and Gargiulo 1999), however, and the variations among them promote a process of competition at the network organization level. Moreover, the positive feedback inherent in experiential learning driven by relational and third-party structural embeddedness implies that small differences in initial partner choices will be intensified, reinforcing small early variations between emergent network organizations. Thus, the sensitive dependence of firm-level structural and cognitive embedding on initial conditions can magnify initially random variation among partnerships.

Although differences between network organizations need not be interpreted solely as products of competition (they may, for example, result from innovative firm-level adaptations), they do, however, provide a basis for 'group selection'. The network organization whose composition, set of beliefs, and social organization are most group-beneficial will have a higher global fitness and tend to outcompete those with less-adaptive beliefs and constitutions. In this context, 'beneficial' implies beliefs and relationships that promote a synergetic pattern of interaction within the network organization. The more network organizations vary in fitness the stronger such group selection becomes (Baum and Rao 2002).

Consider, for example, the returns to research activity in a network organization, which depend on the richness of the pool of research activity in partner firms. If other firms in the network organization invest in a high level of research and development (R&D) activity, the pool of new knowledge into which the firms can tap will be quite rich. And, since research performs the dual role of both generating new knowledge as well as absorbing new knowledge generated by other firms (Cohen and Levinthal 1990), network members will find it attractive to invest in R&D as well. Of course, low-level R&D equilibria are also possible in which the level of new knowledge is too limited to motivate individual firms to invest. Thus, at the network organization level, there are increasing returns to investment in R&D, and network organizations that settle at high-level equilibria will tend to outcompete those that settle at low-level equilibria.

Once performance differentials appear around network organizations and become salient, these differentials may provoke firms' decision makers to rethink and alter their pattern of interfirm relationships. Decision makers *may* revise or refine their network organization mental models, altering their understanding of how their market works (and what it is), and giving new meaning to the actions and relationships of other firms (and which firms to attend to). All of which *may* imply a need to alter patterns of relations to model interfirm arrangements of similar firms in other, higher-performing network organizations. Other decision makers *may* alter their patterns of ties as poor group performance renews the salience of firm-specific interdependencies. Still others *may* defect from their network organization, and attempt to join another, more successful group. Here, the emphasis is on 'may' since multilevel embedded interaction patterns among firms may be very difficult to dislodge – and so selection among network organizations may account for a good deal of change in the structure and composition of network organizations over time.

Synopsis

Figure 9.1 summarizes the dynamic relationships implied by our account of the evolution of network organizations. Patterns of interdependence among firms initiate patterns of relational and third-party embeddedness among firms. If patterns of interfirm interdependence remain stable, relational and third-party embeddedness take over as dynamics, driving a progressive structural differentiation that shapes positional embeddedness, the status of the firms occupying the positions, and the formation of repeatedly cooperative cliques, or network organizations. As interorganizational relations proliferate, interorganizational knowledge created through firms' mutual monitoring and interaction institutionalizes the network organizational form as a shared mental model, and provides a further impetus for imitative partnering. The emergent structure of the network, positions of firms, and network organizations within it will tend to

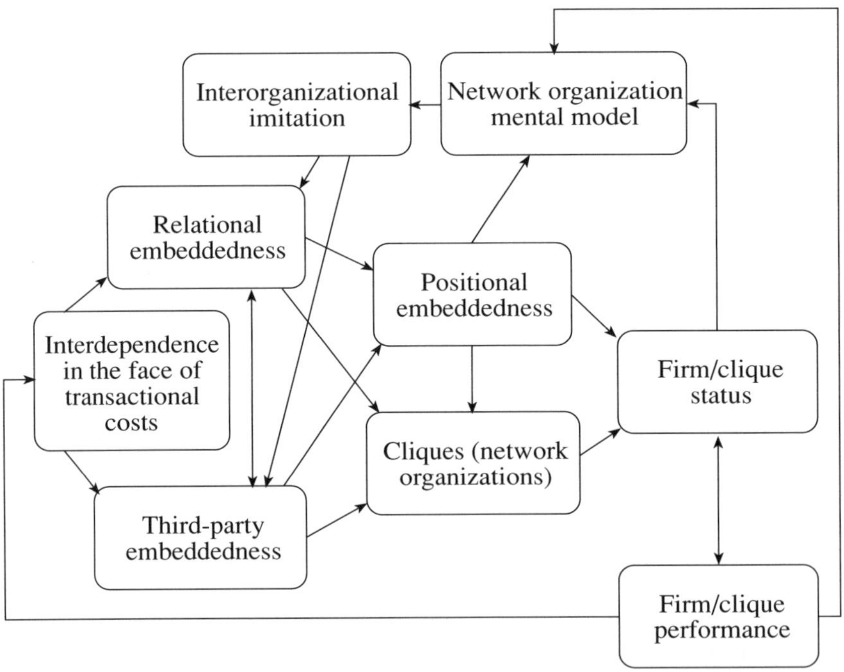

Figure 9.1 Dynamics of network organizations: Relationships among key processes and outcomes

remain stable, reproduced over time through embedded interfirm interactions unless salient performance differences emerge among competing network organizations. Then, decision makers may revisit their network organization mental models, renewing their focus on interdependence considerations, engendering firm-level efforts to reconfigure interorganizational networks, and a reshaping of network organizations.

Figure 9.2 presents our model in a slightly different way, illustrating how the relative influences of the model's core processes vary over time.[5] Initially, interdependence drives network formation, but its influence declines as firm-level structural embeddedness, followed by firm-level cognitive embeddedness, increasingly take over as dynamics. Firm-level embedded partnering drives structural differentiation, giving rise to increasing influences first of network-level structural and then cognitive embeddedness. Once firm- and network-level embeddedness processes stabilize the network, network organization performance outcomes begin increasingly to shape interfirm behavior, and intergroup competition. This cycle is repeated each time the network restablizes at an embedded configuration.

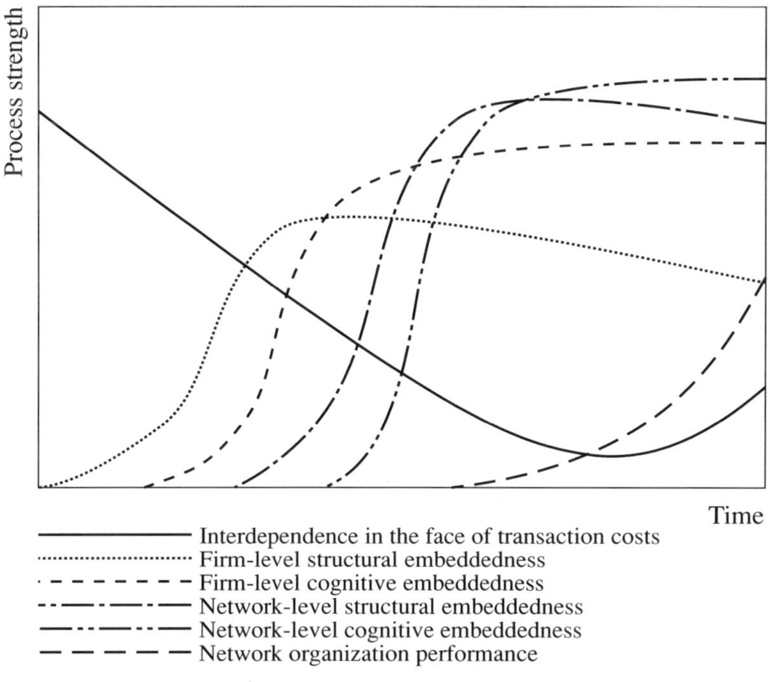

Figure 9.2 Dynamics of network organizations: Relative influences of core processes over time

4 STRUCTURING NETWORK ORGANIZATIONS

Now that we have explored the dynamics underlying the emergence, spread, and institutionalization of network organizations, we are ready to turn to the more normative question, how *should* network organizations be structured?

The literature offers conflicting views on this question. For example, in terms of relational embeddedness, both strong ties steeped in trust and fine-grained information exchanges between partners (Larson 1992; Uzzi 1997) and weak ties that access novel information (Burt 1992; Granovetter 1973; Hansen 1999), are argued to be performance enhancing. Similarly, in terms of positional embeddedness, Burt's (1992) theory of structural holes predicts firms embedded in sparsely connected networks realize efficiency and brokering advantages from non-redundant information exchanges, while Coleman's (1988) theory of network closure predicts benefits of a dense network that promotes trust and cooperation among members.

Several recent efforts have been made to reconcile these contradictions. Burt (1998), for example, suggests that structural holes and network closure are not necessarily contradictory, but rather play different roles, which are useful for different aims. Building on Burt's contingency view, Rowley et al. (2000) argue that relational and positional embeddedness are not independent, but interdependent, and that whether a network organization should be built on strong or weak relational ties depends on the structure of its interorganizational network. We build on these recent observations.

Weak and Strong Ties: Firm-level Embeddedness

Granovetter defines tie strength based on a 'combination of the amount of time, the emotional intensity, the intimacy (mutual confiding), and the reciprocal services which characterize the tie' (1973, p. 1361). Weak interfirm ties, characterized by infrequent and distant relationships, are conduits to unfamiliar firms possessing novel, potentially unique information. A weak tie is beneficial, because it embeds a firm in (or provides its access to) distant regions of the interorganizational network rather than to a densely interconnected set of firms. However, they may be limited to transfer of knowledge that is relatively simple and codified (Hansen 1999). A collection of weak interfirm ties is thus more likely to be a sparse structure reaching disparate regions of the broader interorganizational network.

Strong interfirm ties include equity arrangements, manufacturing joint ventures and joint R&D projects that are 'broader and deeper' in terms of investment and interaction than joint marketing ventures and technology licenses that require only minimal coordination, information sharing, or partner understanding (Powell 1990, p. 314). Strong ties yield two primary advantages. In developing strong ties, partners learn about each other, become more dependent on one another and develop relational trust (Larson 1992). Based on their deeper mutual understanding, high-quality information and uncodified, tacit knowledge is more readily shared and transferred across organizational boundaries, which are blurred by close contact (Hansen 1999; Powell et al. 1996; Uzzi 1996). Uzzi (1996, p. 678), for example, describes information exchange as one of the principal advantages of interorganizational ties that are embedded in social relationships: 'Information exchange in embedded ties is more proprietary and more tacit than the information exchanged at arm's length'.

Strong ties also serve a social control function, governing partner behavior. Firms enter partnerships with potential competitors to gain access to external resources, share information, risks and cost, or pool complementary skills (Kogut 1988). But, interfirm collaborations do not possess the control and coordination mechanisms governing hierarchies or markets (Powell 1990). They are inherently incomplete contracts in which the property rights associated with alliance output and profits may not be well defined. As a result, collaborators risk opportunistic exploitation by their partners, including leaking proprietary knowledge to partners or otherwise losing control of important assets (Williamson 1991). Although appropriate use of governance structures might ameliorate these concerns (Oxley 1997), intra-alliance rivalry retains the potential to severely disrupt interfirm collaboration, and to harm a participating firm. Strong ties produce and are governed by relational trust and norms of mutual gain and goodwill between partners based on interdependence and a history of reciprocity and mutual forbearance (Larson 1992; Powell 1990).

The operation of strong ties to create social control occurs by creating a 'normative capacity' and enabling social sanctions. To see this, first consider the process of norm enforcement among groups of individuals (Coleman 1990). When relationships between individuals are close, and imbued with positive affect and sentiment, they take on a life of their own apart from any instrumental implications they may have. Such relationships are valued for their own sake, and individuals will forgo some amount of economic gain to maintain them. Therefore, the relationship itself becomes a mechanism of influence. Groups form norms, which are rules of expected behavior. Violators of the norms are punished by a reduction in their social relationships with others in the group. Those that are particularly observant of norms may enjoy an improvement of their relationships (Homans 1950). Similar processes may occur when strong ties between organizations in an interfirm create social relations among their individual participants. For example, Ingram and Roberts (2000) show that chain ties between hotels in Sydney contribute to the creation of interpersonal friendships between the hotels' managers. They further argue that friendships between managers create a social-sanctioning mechanism that supports norms of cooperation among the hotels. It can also be seen that there is sometimes an interorganizational equivalent of the interpersonal social sanction. Of course, it would be silly to talk of 'affect' and 'sentiment' between organizations. But there may be analogous relational assets among organizations that are strongly tied. Ingram and Simons (1999), for example, demonstrate the equivalent of social norms operating within federations of Israeli kibbutzim. The basis of sanctioning in those interfirms was the sharing of experience. When a kibbutz violated its interfirm's norms (the norms were in support of ideological ideas about appropriate practices), it suffered a reduction in the sharing of experience from others in the federation.

Closure and Holes: Network-level Embeddedness

Dense interconnections govern actions in a group and lead to cooperative behavior (Coleman 1988). Interfirm ties facilitate the diffusion of norms across the network and, as a result, firms embedded in highly interconnected, 'closed' networks develop shared behavioral expectations (Meyer and Rowan 1977; Oliver 1991; Rowley 1997). Dense ties also produce a reputation effect: a firm is less likely to cheat a partner, who is tied to the same third parties, because these mutual contacts will be aware of their actions (Burt and Knez 1995; Kreps 1990). Competitive firms within a dense network organization thus quickly establish norms of cooperation because firms trust that the well-organized network will facilitate collective monitoring and sanctioning, producing an effective incentive for cooperation (Coleman 1988). Thus, as Walker et al. (1997, p. 111) suggest: 'If all firms in an industry had relationships with each other, interfirm information flows would lead quickly to established norms of cooperation. In such a dense network, information on deviant behavior would be readily disseminated and the behavior sanctioned'.

Burt's (1992) structural hole argument, which directs firms in certain circumstances to embed themselves in sparse networks of disconnected partners, prescribes the opposite to Coleman's (1988) network closure argument (without denying the benefits of closure that Coleman describes). Firms occupying many structural holes – the positions between other firms that are not themselves directly linked – gain efficiency and control benefits. A firm occupying many structural holes has a network that contains few redundant ties and economizes on the number of ties required to access unique information. Firms situated in structural holes also earn control benefits because they act as brokers between disconnected partners, who rely on the firm to facilitate exchange flows across the network. A firm occupying many structural holes thus has an advantage over firms who rely on it to send and receive information and resources in the network organization.

In contrast to the cooperative orientation fostered by network closure, an emphasis on structural holes fosters a more competitive orientation as firms attempt to segregate information to produce a distribution of information within the network organization that leaves information brokers in a privileged position *vis-à-vis* recipients of the information (Burt 1992). Finns in a broker mode thus attempt to create information (and other) asymmetries between themselves and other firms, as well as between the other firms, in such a way as to increase others' dependence on them and their centrality to the network organization. By selectively building – as well as undermining – trust among recipient organizations such brokering behavior controls, in part, the formation (and demise) of interfirm coalitions.

Embedded Interactions across Firm and Network Levels

The comparison of the structural holes and closure arguments indicates a tension in the prescriptions for network organization that can be derived from a theory of the interfirm. Rowley et al. (2000) argue that to understand how firms can secure competitive advantages through firm- and network-level embeddedness, we need to consider conditions under which firms are better off possessing the distinct benefits of different strength ties and network densities.

Dense networks are advantageous for developing trust and cooperation through collective monitoring and sanctioning, but often provide redundant information from multiple sources. In contrast, a sparse network provides a firm with the ability to efficiently obtain and broker information and resources, but the structure does not generate a governance mechanism to impede opportunism.[6]

Holes and weak ties for exploration – closure and strong ties for exploitation

The appropriate type of network organization for firms to embed themselves within is influenced by the diverging information requirements between exploitation and exploration learning modes (March 1991). For exploratory network organizations, the focus is on gathering new information on many different alternatives. Information is relatively broad and general in nature, because the emphasis is on identifying viable alternatives rather than fully understanding how to develop any one innovation. Thus, explorers concentrate on broad searches. This task does not have a well-defined solution space so firms perform broad searches of their environments in order to identify a variety of future options. Because explorers place a premium on timely access to new and more general information, they are willing to tolerate some information noise in order to access a wider breadth of sources.

For exploitative network organizations, by contrast, the emphasis is on refining an existing innovation by gathering specific information that will provide deeper knowledge in that particular area. In other words, the solution space is well defined, and search is highly localized. As a result, exploiters perform deep searches of this limited solution space. Compared with exploration, exploitation requires a deeper understanding of specific information rather than a wider grasp of general information. Partners must work closely together to facilitate the creation and noise-free transfer of complex and tacit knowledge and experiences that enables full exploitation its core technology and routines.

According to Burt's (1992) structural hole argument, the ideal network organization for gaining access to unique information occurs when network members are not connected to one another or similar others. Network members gain unique information and perspectives from each of its partners by occupying structural holes. Thus, for exploratory purposes, low-density network organization structures are preferred.

For exploration, dense connections are constraining. As norms diffuse across a dense network, deviant behavior, regardless of its value to network members, is curtailed and, as a result, innovation is suppressed (Coleman 1988). Dense coupling can thus limit network members' openness to information and to alternative ways of doing things, producing forms of collective blindness (Rowley et al. 2000). Moreover, connections to groups of partners who are connected to one another provide redundant information and limit the networks access to divergent perspectives and distant, less familiar relationships. Table 9.1 summarizes these ideas.

Table 9.1 Network organization structure

Embeddedness	Behavior mode	
	Exploration	Exploitation
Firm level	Weak ties	Strong ties
Network level	Structural holes	Closure

Holes for vertical relations – closure for horizontal relations

In addition to learning mode, the preferred structure of network organization relations also depends on the type of interorganizational relations being governed (Ingram and Roberts 2000). Horizontal network organizations are made up of commensals – organizations that are similar – and therefore, potential competitors. This has implications for both the informational and social control functions of interorganizational ties. In both cases, horizontal relations favor denser ties and network closure in an interfirm.

When the source of information is a competitor, there is added uncertainty because competitive advantages may be gained by misinforming a competitor, opportunistically exploiting proprietary knowledge, or engaging in learning races to extract as much knowledge as possible while divulging as little as possible (Baum et al. 2000b; Khanna et al. 1998). Reinforcing this point, research highlights appropriability as a key attribute of exchanges, particularly transactions related to innovation (Teece 1986; Oxley 1997). A weak 'appropriability regime' increases the risk that proprietary technological knowledge will leak from one partner to another during the course of an exchange. Of course, a strong tie to the competitor may add an element of trust, but there is no certainty, particularly when stakes are high. When the veracity of information and partner motives are in question, dense networks, with many ties between organizations in an interfirm, are useful because they provide an opportunity to check the information against multiple sources (Coleman 1988). When there is less concern with veracity and motives, as when the source of information is not a competitor, sparse ties in an interfirm may be more efficient in the sense of connecting organizations (directly or indirectly) with a minimum of ties. Assuming that there is some capacity on the number of ties an organization can effectively manage, such a sparse structure maximizes the number of organizations, and therefore the information, that a given organization can access (Granovetter 1973).

As for social control, Burt (1992, 1998) contends that structural holes – the absence of a tie between two others to which an actor is tied – confer powerful advantages. With a structural hole, a firm can play others off against one another. For example, a seller facing two buyers is in a stronger position if the buyers do not know each other, and cannot compare the seller's different price quotes. Similarly, structural holes give an actor valuable autonomy from others' attempts to control it. As Burt recognizes, however, the effect of a structural hole between actors depends on whether the actors are different (vertically related) or similar (horizontally related). 'Structural holes among people who are similar allow outsiders to play the people against one another, which erodes the value of whatever social capital they hold' (1992, p. 345). Burt provides evidence of this by showing that more-concentrated industries (presumably those with fewer structural holes between competitors) are more profitable. In vertical interfirms, an organization that spans structural holes will enjoy power and autonomy over those in the interfirm. In a horizontal interfirm, by comparison, structural holes between organizations reduce their exposure to organizational power plays from beyond the interfirm.

5 NETWORK DYNAMICS AND NETWORK ORGANIZATION STRUCTURE

One question remains unanswered: How are the dynamics of network organizations related to their structure? Our answer is that network organizations' structures are shaped by the *relative* strengths of firm- and network-level embedding processes. An emphasis on firm-level embeddedness will produce network organizations characterized by strong ties and closure. And, in particular, the more interorganizational ties are formed in response to relational embeddedness, the greater the *strength* of the ties, while the more ties are formed in response to third-party embeddedness, the greater the *closure* of the network organization.

In contrast, the more partnering decisions are shaped by network-level positional embeddedness, the weaker and sparser network organizations are likely to become. If firms' partnering decisions are driven either by central firms using their status positions and fine-grained information about other firms' competencies and reliability for information arbitrage, or by a more general focus on the signaling property of central positions, firms may choose to partner with firms in different regions of the network. An emphasis on frequency- and trait-based interorganizational imitation may, similarly, produce novel and divergent ties. Such behavior does not reinforce a strengthening and closure of network organizations, but instead a weakening and opening of them.

For example, Anand and Piskorski (2000) show how US VCs' decisions to coinvest are shaped by their attention to each other's 'network centrality' and, in addition, that central VC firms (especially cash-strapped ones) are much more likely to coinvest with non-central *but* financially well-endowed venture firms. Central firms thus have greater flexibility than more peripheral firms in choosing partners that meet their current needs than more peripheral firms, for example, trading their 'perceived quality' for access to peripheral firms' resources, innovative technologies, or other special capabilities. Central firms may also be in a position to engage in information arbitrage – competitive partnering strategies based on producing and taking advantage of information asymmetries that create dependence on them (Burt 1992). Figure 9.3 modifies our original framework to capture this idea. In the figure, the shaded area maps the range of emphasis that central firms may place on addressing current resource needs and dependencies. When such flexibility results in new firms entering the network organization, central firms' partnering can create 'mobility' in the network positions of individual firms, and 'turbulence' for the overall configurations of interfirms.

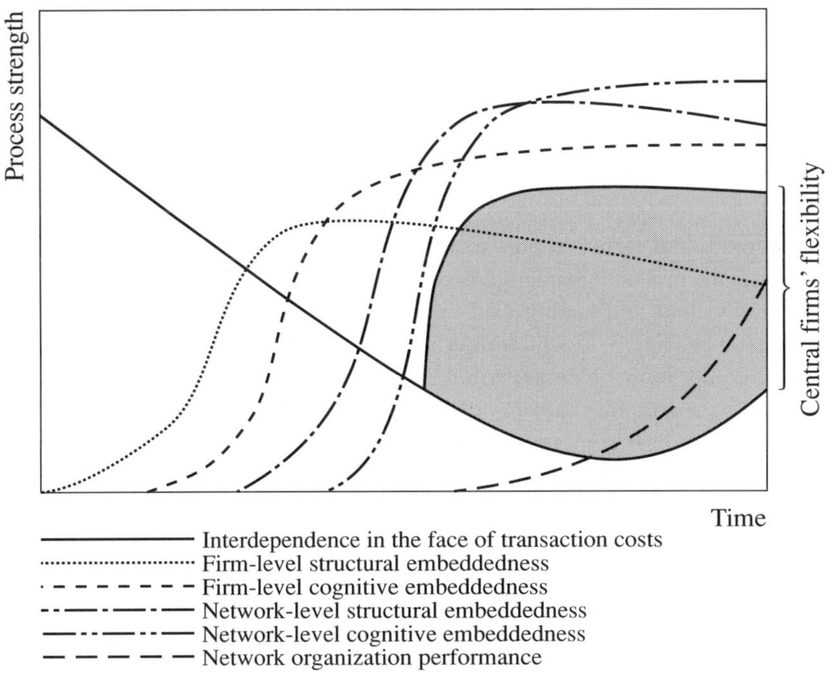

Figure 9.3 Dynamics of network organizations

Thus, we expect network organizations whose dynamics are dominated by firm-level embeddedness to be characterized by strong ties and closure, and weak ties and structural holes to characterize network organizations whose dynamics are dominated by network-level embeddedness. These observations have two broader implications for implications for the dynamics of network organization structuring. One is that network organization structures may often follow a common evolutionary path, with emergent network organizations tending toward strong ties and closure as firm-level embedding takes hold, and a subsequent shift toward weak ties and structural holes as network-level embeddedness increases. Accompanying such a transformation is likely to be a metamorphosis from a more cooperative to a more competitive orientation as firms central to network organizations (and broader networks) use their status and positional advantages to selectively build and undermine trust among other network organization members for their own advantage. Although, as noted, such a configuration is likely to be more turbulent, the selective trust that disconnected firms develop with central firms can still create a self-reinforcing logic of cooperation that sustains the topology of the network.

The other is that the common uneven structure of mature interorganizational networks composed of regions that are more and less densely connected by relationships (Nohria and Garcia-Pont 1991; Walker et al. 1997) is consistent with the simultaneous operation of firm- and network-level embeddedness processes. In complex interorganizational networks, structurally differentiated network organizations are thus likely to emerge in different regions of the global network. In some regions, ties are increasingly reinforced, closed, and stabilized by firm-level embeddedness. In others, where relationship formation is driven more by network-level embeddedness, weak ties and structural holes predominate, and networks are more prone to reshaping and blurring.

6 CONCLUSION

Observation belies the traditional view that organizations are distinct and autonomous units of action. As a consequence, the image of exchange between organizations as comprising arm's-length transactions across clear and meaningful organizational boundaries is fast fading. Increasingly, it is replaced by a view in which interorganizational exchange is embedded in organizational groups comprising of close, robust, multiplex ties that blur hierarchical boundaries. These ties also enable mechanisms of social control to operate, creating within the organizational group a 'moral economy' that combines instrumental and sentimental influences to encourage collective action (Granovetter 1994).

To close the gap between reality and theory with regard to the persistent, systematic relationships between organizations, we sketched the outline of a 'behavioral theory of the interfirm'. We located interfirms within broader forms of institutions and conceptualized their existence as a response to dependence in the face of transaction costs that arise under conditions of bounded rationality. But, rather than the *economics* of interfirm governance, we emphasized the behavioral and cognitive processes that explain how firms choose interorganizational paths given bounded rationality. Because organizations prefer to transact with others of known reputation, and tend to mimic one another, particularly when environmental uncertainty is high, convergence around an 'interfirm' institutional arrangement can reflect social and cultural agreement, as well as (or rather than) competitive or economic processes.

Our main goal was to introduce an evolutionary model to account for the dynamics of one specific type of interfirm, the network organization, and its specific characteristics. Our 'behavioral theory of the interfirm' attempts to lay a foundation for comprehending the evolutionary dynamics of interfirms by focusing on the distribution of information and resources among firms, and derives explanations for interfirm dynamics based on a conception of firms as resource-dependent, uncertainty-reducing entities. In our model firms act on information embedded in the current network structure, and particularly in the idiosyncrasies of interorganizational ties and network topology.

Operationally, our model specifies interfirm dynamics in terms of embeddedness – structural and cognitive – that develops at firm and network levels as a result of interorganizational learning process. Interdependence drives relationship formation initially, but its influence declines as firm-level structural embeddedness, and then firm-level cognitive embeddedness, increasingly take over as dynamics. Firm-level embeddedness, in turn, drives a structural differentiation, giving rise to increasing influences of first network-level structural and then cognitive embeddedness. Thus, as interfirm dynamics unfold, our model specifies shifts from reductionist (upward causation) to contextualist (downward causation) causal mechanisms, and from behavioral to cognitive to institutional processes. Once firm- and network-level embedding stabilize the network, network-level organization outcomes increasingly shape interfirm behavior, and intergroup competition, which can destabilize the network and restart the evolutionary cycle. Key determinants of interfirm success include the social content of interfirm ties, and their structure, which may create the interorganizational equivalents of empathy, trust and even altruism.

Our behavioral theory of the interfirm is, of course, incomplete. Two limitations, in particular, stand out to us. Although our model offers insight into the dependence of interfirms on what firms know and how they know it, it does not link interfirm dynamics to firm-level information-processing and uncertainty-reduction strategies. Nor do we consider the influence of environmental context on firm-level choices and partnering strategies or interfirm topologies. Incorporating behaviorally realistic firm-specific information-gathering and -processing strategies would increase the realism of our intertemporal model of network evolution (Moldoveanu and Baum 2000a). So too would consideration of how the information environment (for example, the distribution and commonality of information among firms) interacts with firm-level information strategies to shape the evolution of interfirm topologies (Moldoveanu, Baum, and Rowley 2002).

Two distinctive features characterize evolutionary process models such as ours (March 1994b). First, part of the explanation for current conditions is historical contingency – early events (that is, particular interfirm relations) are consequential for the subsequent evolution and to some degree arbitrary. Second, the mechanisms of evolution – variation, selection, and retention (Campbell 1965) – are systematic and consequential, predictably shaping beliefs and practices among firms. This balance between specific contingencies and general mechanisms distinguishes evolutionary theory from pure description on the one hand and 'just-so' explanations for why the current conditions are efficient on the other (Aldrich 1999). Some advocates of static efficiency as a primary mode of explanation invoke evolution as a mechanism for making *efficient* things happen while ignoring the historical contingency of evolutionary arguments (for example, Williamson 1975). It is perhaps a reaction to such past static analyses that has increasingly led organizational scholars to specify sophisticated evolutionary process models (for example, Baum and McKelvey 1999). We hope such efforts continue.

NOTES

* We are grateful to Tim Rowley for conversations that influenced and improved our ideas on interfirms. The second author was greatly influenced by discussions with Dick Cyert about organization.

1. The preference of hotel chains for the interfirm model is not because the alternative of including multiple hotels in one organizational structure is impossible. That practice, called 'complexing', has existed to a small degree

since the beginning of the twentieth century. Complexing has become slightly more common in recent years, probably because of advances in the information technologies that support large organizations.
2. Ingram and Baum (2001), Baum et al. (2000b) and Greve (2000) present dynamic models of multiunit chain interfirms.
3. Such a strategy seems at odds with resource-based theory, which suggests that common capabilities and routines are sources of competitive parity not competitive advantage for any one of them (Barney 1991; Peteraf 1993). In dynamic competitive environments, however, the stickiness and uncertain value of firms' capabilities means that firms will often look to others' successes to gauge the value of their own and each other's capabilities. The identification of 'best practices' and the practice of 'benchmarking' both typify this reality.
4. One rare exception to this norm occurs in first-round financings when a VC joins a syndicate with a small investment just before the round closes to get, essentially, 'founder stock'.
5. The details in Figure 9.2 are premised on several assumptions that are speculative on our part and open to empirical testing. One is that cognitive embeddedness at firm and network levels follows structural embeddedness (that is, routinization follows repeated action). A second is that cognitive embeddedness influences interfirm behavior more strongly than structural embeddedness, and that the strength of structural embeddedness diminishes with increasing cognitive embeddedness (that is, once established, routines and mental models shape organizational action more than contemporaneous environmental conditions). And, finally, we assume that network-level embeddeness has a greater impact on interfirm behavior than firm-level embeddedness (that is, once established, mental models and status orderings shape organizational action more than firm-specific routines and relations).
6. Interconnectedness and strong ties lead firms to trust different aspects of their networks, but both serve as governance mechanisms in interfirm relations. In this sense, interconnectedness and strong ties are 'substitutes' for each other (Rowley et al. 2000). Because a firm already benefits from the governance mechanisms supplied via the dense network, the firm will gain much less from dyadic trust fostered by strong ties in a dense network than when its partners are sparsely connected. By accessing a dense network predominately through strong ties, the firm is overembedded for the purpose of governing the exchange. This does not imply, however, that a firm's set of opportunities and constraints are the same whether it is surrounded by densely connected partners or has strong ties with its partners – interconnectedness involves norm creation at the network level, strong ties creates trust at the dyadic level.

REFERENCES

Ahuja, G. (2000), 'The duality of collaboration: inducements and opportunities in the formation of interfirm linkages', *Strategic Management Journal*, **21** (Special Issue), 317–44.

Aldrich, H.E. (1999), *Organizations Evolving*, London: Sage.

Aldrich, H.E. and T. Sasaki (1994), 'R&D consortia in the United States and Japan', *Research Policy*, **24**, 301–16.

Aldrich, H.E., C.R. Zimmer, U.H. Staber and J.J. Beggs (1994), 'Minimalism, mutualism and maturity: the evolution of the American trade association population in the 20th Century', in J.A.C. Baum and J.V. Singh (eds), *Evolutionary Dynamics of Organizations*, New York: Oxford University Press, pp. 223–39.

Amburgey, T.L. and A.S. Miner (1992), 'Strategic momentum: the effects of repetitive, positional, and contextual momentum on merger activity', *Strategic Management Journal*, **13**, 335–48.

Anand, B.N. and M.J. Piskorski (2000), '(Why) are networks important?', Working paper, Harvard Business School.

Arthur, W.B. (1989), 'Competing technologies, increasing returns, and lock-in by historical events', *Economic Journal*, **99** (March), 116–31.

Axelrod, R. (1984), *The Evolution of Cooperation*, New York: Basic Books.

Baker, W.E. (1990), 'Market networks and corporate behavior', *American Journal of Sociology*, **96**, 589–625.

Barney, J.B. (1991), 'Firm resources and sustained competitive advantage', *Journal of Management*, **17**, 99–120.

Baum, J.A.C., T. Calabrese and B.S. Silverman (2000a),'Don't go it alone: alliance networks and startups' performance in Canadian biotechnology, 1991–97', *Strategic Management Journal*, **21** (Special Issue), 267–94.

Baum, J.A.C. and P. Ingram (1998), 'Survival-enhancing learning in the Manhattan hotel industry, 1898–1980', *Management Science*, **44**, 996–1016.

Baum, J., S.X. Li and J.M. Usher (2000b), 'Making the next move: How experiential and vicarious learning shape the location of chains' acquisitions', *Administrative Science Quarterly*, **45**: 766–801.

Baum, J.A.C. and B. McKelvey (1999), *Variations in Organization Science: In Honor of Donald T. Campbell*, Thousand Oaks, CA: Sage.

Baum, J.A.C. and H. Rao (2002), 'Evolutionary dynamics of organizational populations and communities', in M.S. Poole and A.H. Van de Ven (eds), *Handbook of Organizational Development and Change*, New York: Oxford University Press, forthcoming.

Bonacich, P. (1987), 'Power and centrality: a family of measures', *American Journal of Sociology*, **92**, 1170–83.

Borgatti, S.P. and M.G. Everett (1992), 'Notions of position in social network analysis', in P.V. Marsden (ed.), *Sociological Methodology*, **22**, 1–37, San Francisco: Jossey Bass.

Brager, G. and S. Holloway (1978), *Changing Human Service Organizations: Politics and Practice*, New York: Free Press.

Burt, R.S. (1992), *Structural Holes: The Social Structure of Competition*, Cambridge, MA: Harvard University Press.

Burt, R.S. (1998), 'The network structure of social capital', Presented at the Social Network and Social Capital Conference, Duke University, Durham, NC.

Burt, R. S. and M. Knez (1995), 'Kinds of third-party effects on trust', *Rationality and Society*, **7**, 225–92.

Campbell, D.T. (1965), 'Variation and selective retention in socio-cultural evolution', in H.R. Barringer, G.I. Blanksten and R.W. Mack (eds), *Social Change in Developing Areas: A Reinterpretation of Evolutionary Theory*, Cambridge, MA: Schenkman, pp. 19–48.

Chung, S., H. Singh and K. Lee (2000), 'Complementarity, status similarity, and social capital and drivers of alliance formation', *Strategic Management Journal*, **21**, 1–22.

Coase, R.H. ([1937] 1988), *The Firm, the Market, and the Law*, Chicago: University of Chicago Press.

Cohen, M.D. and L.S. Sproull (1991), 'Editors' introduction', *Organization Science*, **2** (1), i–iii.

Cohen, W.M. and D.A. Levinthal (1990), 'Absorptive capacity: a new perspective on organizational learning and innovation', *Administrative Science Quarterly*, **35**, 128–52.

Coleman, J.S. (1988),'Social capital in the creation of human capital', *American Journal of Sociology*, **94**, 95–120.

Coleman, J. S. (1990), *Foundations of Social Theory*, Cambridge, MA: Belknap Press of Harvard University Press.

Cyert, R.M. and J.G. March (1963), *A Behavioral Theory of the Firm*, Englewood Cliffs, NJ: Prentice-Hall.

Darr, E.D., L. Argote and D. Epple (1995),'The acquisition, transfer and depreciation of knowledge in service organizations: productivity in franchises', *Management Science*, **42**, 1750–62.

DiMaggio, P.J. and W.W. Powell (1983), 'The iron cage revisited: institutional isomorphism and collective rationality in organizational fields', *American Sociological Review*, **48**, 148–60.

DiMaggio, P.J. and W.W. Powell (1991), 'Introduction', in W.W. Powell and P.J. DiMaggio (eds), *The New Institutionalism in Organizational Analysis*, Chicago: University of Chicago Press, pp. 1–38.

Dutta, S. (1997), *Family Business in India*, New Delhi: Response Books, Sage Publications.

Faulkner, R.R. (1983), *Music on Demand: Composers and Careers in the Hollywood Film Industry*, London: Transaction.

Fligstein, N. (1996), 'Markets as politics: a political–cultural approach to market institutions', *American Sociological Review*, **61**, 656–73.

Granovetter, M.S. (1973),'The strength of weak ties', *American Journal of Sociology*, **78**, 1360–80.

Granovetter, M.S. (1985), 'Economic action and social structure: the problem of embeddedness', *American Journal of Sociology*, **91**, 481–510.

Granovetter, M.S. (1994), 'Business groups', in N.J. Smelser and R. Swedberg (eds), *Handbook of Economic Sociology*, Princeton NJ: Princeton University Press, pp. 453–75.

Greve, H.R. (1999), 'Branch systems and nonlocal learning in organizational populations', in A.S. Miner and P.C. Anderson (eds), *Advances in Strategic Management*, **16**, 57–80, Stamford, CT: JAI Press.

Greve, H.R. (2000), 'Market niche entry decisions: competition, learning, and strategy in Tokyo banking, 1894–1936, *Academy of Management Journal*, 43, 837–53.

Grindley, P., D.C. Mowery and B. Silverman (1994), 'SEMATECH and collaborative research: lessons in the design of high-technology consortia', *Journal of Policy Analysis and Management*, **13**, 723–58.

Gulati, R. (1995), 'Social structure and alliance formation patterns: a longitudinal analysis', *Administrative Science Quarterly*, **40**, 619–52.

Gulati, R. and M. Gargiulo (1999), 'Where do interorganizational networks come from?', *American Journal of Sociology*, **104**, 1439–93.

Hadfield, G. (1991), 'Credible spatial preemption through franchising', *Rand Journal of Economics*, **22**, 531–43.

Hannan, M.T. and J. Freeman (1984), 'Structural inertia and organizational change', *American Sociological Review*, **49**, 149–64.

Hansen, M.T. (1999), 'The search-transfer problem: the role of weak ties in sharing knowledge across organizational subunits', *Administrative Science Quarterly*, **44**, 82–111.

Haunschild, P.R. and A.S. Miner (1997), 'Modes of interorganizational imitation: the effects of outcome salience and uncertainty', *Administrative Science Quarterly*, **42**, 472–500.

Hawley, A.H. (1950), *Human Ecology*, New York: Rowland Press.

Hedberg, B., P.C. Nystrom and W.H. Starbuck (1976), 'Camping on seesaws: prescriptions for a self-designing organization', *Administrative Science Quarterly* , **21**, 41–65.

Homans, G.C. (1950), *The Human Group*, New York: Harcourt, Brace.

Howes, D. and B. Vlasic (1998), 'Spinoff of Delphi alters GM course: carmaker moves out of parts-making business', *Detroit News*, August 4, A1.

Ingram, P. and J.A.C. Baum (1997), 'Chain affiliation and the failure of Manhattan hotels, 1898–1980', *Administrative Science Quarterly*, **42**, 68–102.

Ingram, P. and J.A.C. Baum (2001), 'Interorganizational learning and the dynamics of chain relationships', in J.A.C. Baum and H.R. Greve (eds), *Advances in Strategic Management*, 18, 103–39, Oxford UK: JAI Press, Elsevier.

Ingram, P. and P. Roberts (2000), 'Friendships among competitors in the Sydney hotel industry, *American Journal of Sociology*, 106, 387–423.

Ingram, P. and T. Simons (1999), 'The exchange of experience in a moral economy: embedded ties and vicarious learning in kibbutz agriculture', *Best Paper Proceedings of the Academy of Management* (CD-ROM).

Kahneman, D. and A. Tversky (1979), 'Prospect theory: an analysis of decision under risk', *Econometrica*, **47**, 263–91.

Khanna, T., R. Gulati and N. Nohria (1998), 'The dynamics of learning alliances: competition, cooperation and relative scope', *Strategic Management Journal*, **19**, 193–210.

Khanna, T. and K. Palepu (1997), 'Why focused strategies may be wrong for emerging markets', *Harvard Business Review*, July–August, 41–51.

Kogut, B. (1988), 'Joint ventures: theoretical and empirical perspectives', *Strategic Management Journal*, **9**, 319–32.

Krackhardt, D. (1990), 'Assessing the political landscape: structure, cognition and power in organizations', *Administrative Science Quarterly*, **35**, 342–69.

Kreps, D.M. (1990), 'Corporate culture and economic theory', in J.E. Alt and K.A. Shepsle (eds), *Perspectives on Positive Political Economy*, New York: Cambridge University Press, pp. 90–143.

Larson, A. (1992), 'Network dyads in entrepreneurial settings: a study of governance of exchange relationships', *Administrative Science Quarterly*, **37**, 76–104.

Lazerson, M. (1995), 'A new phoenix: modern putting-out in the Modena knitwear industry', *Administrative Science Quarterly*, **40**, 34–59.

Leik, R.K. (1992), 'New directions for network exchange theory: strategic manipulation of network linkages', *Social Networks*, **14**, 309–23.

Lerner, J. (1994), 'The syndication of venture capital investments', *Financial Management*, **23** (3), 16–27.

Levinthal, D.A. and J.G. March (1993), 'The myopia of learning', *Strategic Management Journal*, **14**, 94–112.

Levitt, B. and J.G. March (1988), 'Organizational learning', *Annual Review of Sociology*, **14**, 319–40.

Li, S.X. and T.J. Rowley (1999), 'Locating capable and reliable allies: the role of experiential and non-experiential information in interorganizational partner selection', Academy of Management Meetings, Chicago, August.

Lincoln, J.R., M.L. Gerlach and C.L. Ahamdijian (1996), '*Keiretsu* networks and corporate performance in Japan', *American Sociological Review*, **61**, 67–88.

March, J.G. (1991), 'Exploration and exploitation in organizational learning', *Organization Science*, **2**, 71–87.

March, J.G. (1994a), *A Primer on Decision Making: How Decisions Happen*, New York: Free Press.

March, J.G. (1994b),'The evolution of evolution', in J.A.C. Baum and J.V. Singh (eds) *Evolutionary Dynamics of Organizations*, New York: Oxford University Press, pp. 39–49.

March, J.G. and J.P. Olsen (1976), *Ambiguity and Choice in Organizations*, Bergen, Norway: Universitesforlaget.

March, J.G. and Z. Shapira (1992), 'Variable risk preferences and the focus of attention', *Psychological Review*, **99**, 172–83.

March, J.G. and H.A. Simon (1958), *Organizations*, New York: Wiley.

Meyer, J. W. and B. Rowan (1977), 'Institutional organizations: formal structures as myth and ceremony', *American Journal of Sociology*, **80**, 340–63.

Miller, D. and P.H. Friesen (1980), 'Momentum and revolution in organizational adaptation', *Academy of Management Journal*, **4**, 591–614.

Miner, Anne S. and Pamela R. Haunschild (1995), 'Population level learning', in B. Staw and L. Cummings (eds), *Research in Organizational Behavior*, **17**, 115–66.

Moldoveanu, M.C. and J.A.C. Baum (2000),'An inter-temporal computational model of firm network dynamics', Academy of Management Meetings, Toronto, August.

Moldoveanu, M.C. and J.A.C. Baum (2000b), 'Stars and cliques: the effects of distributed and common information on the topology of interfirm networks', International Sunbelt Social Network Conference, Vancouver, April.

Moldoveanu, M.C., J.A.C. Baum and T.J. Rowley (2002), 'Information Regimes, Information strategies and the evolution of network typologies', in F. Dansereau and F.J. Yammarino (eds), Research in Multilevel Issues, Oxford: JAI Press/Elsevier. Forthcoming.

Monteverde, K. and D.J. Teece (1982), 'Appropriable rents and quasi-vertical integration', *Journal of Law and Economics*, **25**, 321–8.

Nelson, R.R. and S.G. Winter (1982), *An Evolutionary Theory of Economics Change*, Cambridge, MA: Harvard University Press.

Nohria, N. and C. Garcia-Pont (1991), 'Global strategic linkages and industry structure', *Strategic Management Journal*, **12**, 105–24.

Ocasio, W. (1997), 'Towards an attention-based view of the firm', *Strategic Management Journal*, **18** (Summer Special Issue), 187–206.

Oliver, C. (1990), 'Determinants of inter-organizational relationships: integration and future direction', *Academy of Management Review*, **15**, 241–65.

Oliver, C. (1991), 'Strategic responses to institutional processes, *Academy of Management Review*, **16**, 145–79.

Oxley, J.E. (1997), 'Appropriability hazards and governance in strategic alliances: a transaction cost approach', *Journal of Law, Economics and Organization*, **13**, 387–409.

Peteraf, M.A. (1993), 'The cornerstones of competitive advantage: a resource-based view', *Strategic Management Journal*, **14**, 179–91.

Pfeffer, J. and G.R. Salancik (1978), *The External Control of Organizations*, New York: Harper & Row.

Piore, M. and C. Sabel (1984), *The Second Industrial Divide: Possibilities for Prosperity*, New York: Basic Books.

Podolny, J.M. (1993), 'A status-based model of market competition', *American Journal of Sociology*, **98**, 829–72.

Podolny, J.M. (1994), 'Market uncertainty and the character of economic exchange', *Administrative Science Quarterly*, **39**, 458–83.

Polanyi, K., C. Arensberg, and H. Pearson (eds) ([1957] 1971), *Trade and Market in the Early Empires: Economies in History and Theory*, Chicago: Henry Regnery Company.

Porac, J.F., and J.A. Rosa (1996), 'Rivalry, industry models, and the cognitive embeddedness of the comparable firm', in J.A.C. Baum and J.E. Dutton (eds), *Advances in Strategic Management*, **13**, 363–88, Stamford, CT: JAI Press.

Porac, J. and H. Thomas (1994), 'Cognitive categorization and subjective rivalry among retailers in a small city', *Journal of Applied Psychology*, **79**, 54–66.

Porac, J.F., H. Thomas, F. Wilson, D. Paton and A. Kanfer (1995), 'Rivalry and the industry model of Scottish knitwear producers', *Administrative Science Quarterly*, **40**, 203–27.

Powell, W.W. (1990), 'Neither market nor hierarchy: network forms of organization', in B. Staw and L. Cummings (eds), *Research in Organizational Behavior*, **12**, 295–336. Stamford, CT: JAI Press.
Powell, W.W., K.W. Koput and L. Smith-Doerr (1996),'Interorganizational collaboration and the locus of innovation: networks of learning in biotechnology', *Administrative Science Quarterly*, **41**, 116–45.
Powell, W.W. and L. Smith-Doerr (1994),'Networks and economic life, in N.J. Smelser and R. Swedberg (eds), *Handbook of Economic Sociology*, Princeton, NJ: Princeton University Press, pp. 363–402.
Rowley, T.J. (1997), 'Moving beyond dyadic ties: a network theory of stakeholder influences', *Academy of Management Review*, **22**, 887–910.
Rowley, T.J., D. Behrens and D. Krackhardt (2000), 'Redundant governance structures: an analysis of structural and relational embeddedness in the steel and semiconductor industries', *Strategic Management Journal*, **21** (Special Issue), 369–86.
Sharpe, L.J. (1985), 'Interorganizational policy-making: the limits of subnational autonomy', in F.X. Kaufmann, G. Majone and V. Ostrom (eds), *Guidance, Control and Evaluation in the Public Sector: The Bielefeld Interdisciplinary Project*, Berlin: De Gruyter, pp. 159–81.
Simon, H.A. (1957), *Models of Man*, New York: Wiley.
Simons, T. and P. Ingram (1997), 'Organization and ideology: kibbutzim and hired labor, 1951–1965', *Administrative Science Quarterly*, **42**, 784–813.
Simons, T. and P. Ingram (2000), 'The kibbutz for organizational behavior', in B.M. Staw and R.I. Sutton (eds), *Research in Organizational Behavior*, Stamford CT: JAI Press, Forthcoming.
Smelser, N.J. and R. Swedberg (eds), *Handbook of Economic Sociology*, Princeton, NJ: Princeton University Press.
Sorenson, 0. and P.G. Audia (2000), 'The social structure of entrepreneurial activity: geographic concentration of footwear production in the U.S., 1940–1989', *American Journal of Sociology*, 106, 424–62.
Stinchcombe, A.L. (1965), 'Social structure and organizations', in J.G. March (ed.), *Handbook of Organizations*, Chicago, IL: Rand McNally, pp. 153–93.
Stuart, T.E., H. Hoang and R.C. Hybels (1999), 'Interorganizational endorsements and the performance of entrepreneurial ventures', *Administrative Science Quarterly*, **44**, 315–49.
Stuart, T.E. and J.M. Podolny (1996), 'Local search and the evolution of technological capabilities', *Strategic Management Journal* (Summer Special Issue), **17**, 21–38.
Teece, D.J. (1982), 'Towards an economic theory of the multi-product firm', *Journal of Economic Behavior and Organization*, **3**, 39–63.
Teece, D.J. (1986), 'Profiting from technological innovation: implications for integration, collaboration, licensing, and public policy', *Research Policy*, **16**, 285–305.
Thompson, J.D. (1967), *Organizations in Action*, New York: McGraw-Hill.
Uzzi, B. (1996), 'The sources and consequences of embeddedness for the economic performance of organizations: the network effect', *American Sociological Review*, **61**, 674–98.
Uzzi, B. (1997), 'Social structure and competition in interfirm networks: the paradox of embeddedness', *Administrative Science Quarterly*, **42**, 35–67.
Walker, G., B. Kogut and W.J. Shan (1997), 'Social capital, structural holes and the formation of an industry network', *Organization Science*, **8**, 109–25.
Weick, K.E. (1979), *The Social Psychology of Organizing*, 2nd edn, Reading, MA: Addison-Wesley.
Weick, K.E. and F. Westley (1996), 'Organizational learning: affirming an oxymoron', in S. Clegg, C. Hardy and W. Nord (eds), *Handbook of Organization Studies*, London: Sage, pp. 440–58.
White, H.C. (1981), 'Where do markets come from?', *American Journal of Sociology*, **87**, 517–47.
Willer, D. and B. Anderson (eds) (1981), *Network, Exchange and Coercion*, New York: Elsevier.
Williamson, O.E. (1975), *Markets and Hierarchies*, New York: Free Press.
Williamson, O.E. (1983), 'Credible commitments: using hostages to support exchange', *American Economic Review*, **73**, 519–40.
Williamson, O.E. (1991), 'Comparative economic organization: the analysis of discrete structural alternatives', *Administrative Science Quarterly*, **36**, 269–96.
Zucker, L.G. (1977), 'The role of institutionalization in cultural persistence', *American Sociological Review*, **42**, 726–42.

10. Adapting, learning, economizing and economic evolution*

Richard H. Day

So long as the environment is predictably unstable, the heart of the theory must be the process of short-run adaptive reactions. (Cyert and March, *A Behavioral Theory of the Firm*, p. 100)

1 INTRODUCTION

It is not always recognized that adaptation, learning, and evolution are integral parts of the classical and neoclassical economic heritage. These concepts run through the discipline's development, implicitly or explicitly, and in varying ways from Adam Smith, Thomas Malthus, and John Stuart Mill, through Alfred Marshall and Léon Walras, Joseph Schumpeter, John Maynard Keynes, and Friedrich von Hayek and on into the present. In the third quarter of the twentieth century the channel through which the adaptive stream of economic ideas flowed ran quite deep. In the hands of James Duesenberry, Lawrence Klein, Franco Modigliani, and their various collaborators around the world, mechanisms of partial adjustment and adaptive anticipation played prominent roles in macroeconomic model building. In the 1960s, contributions aimed at the microeconomic level appeared, among them Cyert and March's *A Behavioral Theory of the Firm*, which set out to develop 'a theory connected to empirical observation of what happens inside firms' and based on the characterization of businesses as 'adaptively rational' rather than as 'omnisciently rational'. A number of principles were identified that constituted a coherent, computable, empirically realistic theory, as demonstrated in computer simulations of three manufacturing and retail enterprises. It was perhaps the first – and still one of the few – microeconomic studies based directly on actual behavioral rules and decision-making procedures.

Of course, theoretical work of the mathematical type flourished in the equilibrium stream, extending the concepts of agent optimality, perfect interagent coordination, and social efficiency to incorporate uncertainty and intertemporal structure. Meanwhile, adaptive economic research continued to swell in volume so that by now it is quite appropriate to think of it as another mainstream of economic work. I see it, not as a substitute or alternative way of thinking, but as a complement, dual to the other.

In any case, this book in celebration of Richard Cyert's life is an especially appropriate venue to consider developments in adaptive economics. To do so is the purpose of this chapter. In Section 2 the basic concepts of adaptation, learning, economizing, and evolution are defined and the distinction among them identified; in Section 3 their past use in the discipline is sketched; in Section 4 some key works of the third quarter of the twentieth century are briefly summarized; Section 5 is devoted to a more detailed look at one particular mode of adaptation, that of trial-and-error search or experimentation. This mechanism illustrates several of the important properties of adaptive processes in general. Moreover, most models of adaptation and evolution are, in effect, an elaboration of this basic mechanism. Section 6 then presents a brief survey of recent developments of the last several decades; Section 7 presents reflections for both micro- and macroeconomics of the behavioral, adaptive point of view. A personal epilog concludes the chapter.

2 DEFINITIONS

Adaptation is a process by which living things, organisms or organizations (or agents) adjust to their environment. Changes in conditions in the environment may stimulate a response, that is, they may impel behavior. Response is successful if the agent's chance for survival (its 'fitness') is improved over what it would have been without adjustment. Successful responses are called adaptive; an agent that exhibits successful responses is called well-adapted (or just adapted) to its environment.

In general, however, an adaptive process need not imply success. It implies only the interactive adjustment of behavior to environment. To avoid confusion, perhaps it would be helpful to refer to the general process of interaction as an 'adapting process' and use the term 'adaptive' to connote improving or successful adjustment. This distinction is not generally made in the literature but is usually clear from the context.

Adaptation in the sense defined so far does not involve all behavior because an organism may also be impelled to action by its internal conditions, that is to say, behavior can change even in the absence of any external stimulus.[1] Indeed, it is this possibility that gives an agent the ability to initiate action and establish an identity separable from its environment. But this can be thought of as the adjustment of behavior to internal conditions. So, in general,

- by *adaptation* we shall mean the process by which an agent's behavior adjusts to and interacts with its external environment and internal conditions.

In studying the behavior of an agent–environment system, therefore, one must take account of the internal dynamics of the agent in a constant environment, how it responds to changes in the environment, and to close the system, how the environment changes as a result of action taken by the agent.[2]

Learning is a closely related idea:

- *Learning* is the acquisition or process of acquiring information or competence useful for the performance of some action or task.

It takes time and energy so necessarily involves investment. Thus, useful economic information and competence are rightly referred to as 'human capital'. Since it enhances the capacity for adjustment, learning can be a form of adaptation.

In equilibrium theory economic behavior is characterized by sufficient conditions for a constrained optimum. In behavioral terms, however, economic behavior is a process:

- *Economizing* is the adjustment of behavior in an attempt to improve income, wealth, or the satisfaction of needs and wants now and in the future.

Economizing behavior is economic if it is successful, that is, if it does improve or maximize satisfaction. Thus, to be 'economical' is to have succeeded in economizing; to be uneconomical is to have failed.

Learning to economize involves accumulating information about the alternatives that are available for choice, and the relative benefits and costs associated with them. It includes the acquisition of competence to use these data in economizing calculations including (but not confined to) explicit knowledge of decision-making models and the computational algorithms for utilizing them.

Adapting, learning and economizing are closely related but not identical. One can economize well or poorly, and one can learn to do so more or less effectively. To learn to economize well certainly involves adapting, but it need not be adaptive. Thus, behavior that seems economical may not improve fitness or survival. This is because economical behavior is determined by a *subjective* measure of satisfaction which is an internal state of the agent; whereas, adaptive or well-adapted behavior is determined by an *objective* state of the agent, its chance of survival, which depends on external states of the environment.

In all three concepts there is both the aspect of *process*: the adjustment of behavior and the aspect of *evaluation*: the success of behavior in terms of a criterion: survival, competence or satisfaction. One has to discern which of these aspects (processual or evaluative) is meant in context.

Explicit or conscious economizing behavior is characteristic of humans and, assuming that we are the product of biological evolution, one may argue – in spite of what has been said above – that economizing may sometimes have a biologically adaptive quality and, indeed, to have been responsible for the state of development from which humans have come to dominate the earth.

But fitness is a relative term: what is fit under one set of circumstances may not be fit under another. It is said that far more species have existed than now exist; each extinct example had to have had a competitive advantage for some time to have left a geological trace, but each extinct example must also have lost that relative advantage to other forms of life.

Likewise, successful economic development requires the exploitation of resources whose potential exhaustion can remove the basis for further development and establish the conditions for decline and even demise if a successful adaptation to such endogenously generated environmental change is not achieved. Learning, therefore, plays a two-edged role in economic development. It is both a process by which economies can adapt to changing scarcities and, ironically, it is a process of development that contributes to the emergence of new survival-threatening scarcities.[3]

At this point it is appropriate to introduce the concept of evolution, for among the implications of adapting and learning behavior is that economic behavior in general takes place out of equilibrium, that is, when economic conditions motivate attempts to gain more knowledge, to form new plans, to develop new ways of learning and planning, or to find a way to modify the environment itself.

The term evolution has various specific meanings in different scientific contexts. These, however, can be boiled down to two cases:

- *evolution in the broad sense* means change in form and complexity of structures as various parts of the world self-organize and react or adapt to one another; *evolution in the narrow or Darwinian sense* means the process of changing structures mediated through populations by means of variation, inheritance, and selection.

Returning to the previous observation about the role of economic development in creating survival threatening scarcities, we infer how human activity is driven not only by the desire to satisfy needs and wants, but also by a *creative potential* that in effect anticipates future needs and wants by inventing new ways for satisfying them when old ways become too costly or infeasible. Thus,

- *invention* and *innovation* are adaptations to conjectures about the future: *human adaptation* induces economic evolution.

With this background we are now ready to summarize how these concepts have been used.

3 THE CLASSICAL AND NEOCLASSICAL HERITAGE

As noted above, adaptive, evolutionary thinking in economics seems to have originated with Adam Smith and Thomas Malthus, who in turn had a great influence on its subsequent development in biology.[4] The idea was that economic competition led to the abandonment of uneconomic practices and to growth in economically advantageous ones. Individual discretion in the pursuit of private advantage led (in the Darwinian terms developed later) to variation. Market forces led to selection of activities most suited to current conditions. Individuals and organizations evolved through a process of increasing specialization of activity and increasingly indirect exchange through elaborating institutions of mediation. Costly technologies fell by the wayside as more economic alternatives were adopted, entrepreneurs and financiers investing as profits directed, and prices adjusting to imbalances in supply and demand with supply and demand adjusting in turn to changes in prices.

The subsequent formalization of classical theory focused on general, competitive equilibrium which every economist – to go by name – must understand at some level. In terms of the definitions of Section 2, a general competitive equilibrium is a state in which all the agents' behaviors are *economic*, one in which the agents are *perfectly adapted* to one another and have nothing to learn that they can exploit in their self-interest without disrupting the distribution of wealth or without modifying the coalition structures among themselves.

However, neoclassical economists who produced the formal theory understood that equilibrium implies its dual, disequilibrium: a state in which not all individual behavior has achieved optimality at stated prices, some agents' plans are inconsistent with one another, or some reorganization of agents can be carried out to the benefit of some and the detriment of none. In terms of the definitions in Section 2, out-of-equilibrium behavior is not economic; agents are not adapted; they have something to learn. In disequilibrium, a process of adjustment must occur unless it is prevented by coercion or inertia, that is,

- disequilibrium drives adaptation.

To Walras, supplies and demands for consumer goods adapt to prices that adjust to the excesses in supplies or demands in a recursive scheme while outputs of producer goods and capital adapt to profits or losses (which in turn depend on prices, supplies, and demands). To Marshall, individual economizing behavior takes place at the margin, that is, in the neighborhood of experience, and through a sequence of marginal adjustments; business investment takes place through an adjustment of capacity to current quasi-rents above normal profits that accrue when shortages of capacity yield temporary scarcity rents.

Schumpeter, like Walras and Marshall before him, had in mind a dynamic, out-of-equilibrium conception of the market economy. In his seminal *Theory of Economic Development* (1938) he argued that decentralized agents achieve individual equilibria (if they do so at all) because experience 'teaches them what to do'. They might, in principle, arrive at an economywide equilibrium, not by making elaborate computations that would generate optimal equilibrium responses, but by adapting gradually to market conditions. An equilibrium, once achieved, could be perpetuated, not by perfect rationality, but by inertia, habit, and tradition. Before one is ever reached, however, innovations, financed by credit, perturb the menu of products and techniques and set the process off in a new direction and away from the old equilibrium toward that which it might have been heading.

Keynes's investment theory is a variation of Marshall's quasi-rent theory. He emphasized the role of cumulative interactions that lead to speculative waves, a form of social adaptation typical of human behavior in many other economic settings. Moreover, he saw outputs adjusting to demand and prices adjusting – or failing to adjust – out of equilibrium.

4 ADAPTIVE ECONOMICS AND THE BEHAVIORAL HERITAGE

The work of Schumpeter and Keynes bring us to mid-century when the *equilibrium* mainstream received a tremendous boost in the reformulation of general competitive equilibrium theory in topological terms by Arrow and Debreu (1954). The mathematical conditions for existence, the number and character of equilibria, the extension to intertemporal exchange, and exchange with uncertainty continued to attract much of the attention of mathematical economists, so much so that to some economists general equilibrium is the defining subject matter of the discipline: other concepts may be interesting and useful, but they are not *economics*.

Nonetheless, virtually all of the major mathematical economists at mid-century, including Kenneth Arrow, Frank Hahn, Leonid Hurwicz, Michio Morishima, Hukukare Nikaido, Herbert Scarf, and Hirofumi Uzawa, contributed analyses of Walras's excess demand/supply/price adjustment process and the conditions under which it converged. This would seem to have given the *adaptive* mainstream a big boost. Regrettably, many micro, macro, and applied economists seem to have lost touch with this stream entirely, so that by now the term 'neoclassical economics' is most frequently used as a synonym for 'equilibrium economics', but the latter is a more accurate appellation.

The work on tâtonnement, however, is not the only line of investigation that incorporated adaptive processes and learning explicitly. As mentioned above, macroeconometric models incorporated mechanisms of partial adjustment. The basic idea is the following. What appears to be the optimal action on the basis of the data (and on the basis of how one thinks) at a given time will quite often eventually prove to be incorrect; yet, at the time, the agent has no better rational basis for action, given his or her knowledge and level of competence. As a hedge against uncertainty, a partial adjustment is taken from the agent's current behavior in the direction of the currently conceived best action. Behavior at any one time is therefore a weighted average of past behavior and the current plan. The idea, which reflected thinking of the Stockholm School, for example, Gunnar Myrdal and Erik Lundberg, and of John Hicks, Hart, Cohen, and Modigliani, and so on, was a close relative of Goodwin's flexible accelerator, and was incorporated in virtually all econometric models of macroeconomic behavior through roughly 1975.

A variant of the idea was the derivation of the adjustment parameter from an economizing calculation based on the cost of adjustment. This line of work, to which Robert Lucas was an early contributor, was a forerunner of his more general specification of the economy as a set of agents behaving according to optimal equilibrium strategies but without any learning required to reach such a state. It should be recognized that the rationalization of partial adjustment on the basis of cost is an additional explanation of partial adjustment, the original one being a behavioral hedging strategy not explicitly derived from a risk program. Certainly, both uncertainty and costs are involved in actuality.

Cyert and March's book, which built on Simon (1957) and March and Simon (1958), incorporated adaptation and learning explicitly into models of the business firm based on observed rules of thumb, standard operating procedures, and empirically grounded adjustment procedures. Central to their theory is the conception of the firm as a coalition of agents with a multiplicity of goals arrived at through a negotiational process, and whose decision making involves sequences of standard operating procedures that are adjusted in response to unsatisfactory performance.

In 1963, my book, *Recursive Programming and Production Response*, appeared. It was based on the idea that producers behave as if they solve an explicit optimization model, but one that is highly simplified relative to the true complexity of the problem that they face. They are constrained not only by resources and financial limitations, but by self-imposed behavioral constraints. The latter form a *zone of flexible response* which limits search to an adapting neighborhood of recent experience. The resource, financial and behavioral constraints and the profit expectations are updated each period in response to past performance and feedback from the economic environment (market prices, labor supplies, and so on). In a closed model this feedback depends recursively on the aggregate of the agents' actions so that behavior over time is represented by a sequence of optimizations in which the parameters or decision data at any one time depend recursively on experience. Thus, from a mathematical point of view, the model is one of recursive programming; from a behavioral point of view, it is one of 'sequential planning with evolving knowledge' or 'adaptive economizing'. One could show in specific examples that aggregate behavior could converge to competitive equilibrium. In general, however, the best that can be expected is that behavior will eventually come to fluctuate around an equilibrium. Learning and adaptation occur, and the 'market' serves as a teacher, but its lesson need not be learned perfectly. My initial study involved agriculture but subsequent models were constructed for steel, coal, and petroleum industries. Like Cyert and March's work, the models were designed to mimic explicit empirical settings using actual data.[5]

A closely related line of work was initiated by Sidney Winter (1964) who, building on early essays by Alchian (1950) and Papandreou (1952), considered the role of variation and selection of decision-making rules as a means by which firms learn to cope with changing economic conditions by adopting new technologies. This work, continued in collaboration with Richard

Nelson in a series of papers in the 1970s and 1980s, culminated in their book, *Toward an Evolutionary Theory of the Firm* (1982).

In Cyert and March and Nelson and Winter economic experience drives the selection of rules, in the former in response to the satisfaction of multiple goals, in the latter in response to a profit criterion. In both, evolution consists in the changing structure of operating procedures that determine behavior. In my recursive programming models, the adaptive economizing drives selection from the menu of production activities at each point in time with the result that the various species of technology grow or decline, as the case may be, depending on the direction that market forces, operating through profits, give.

Another line of research was taken by Peter Diamond, Dale Mortenson, Robert Lucas, Edward Prescott and others who developed search models for consumers in product markets and workers in markets for labor. In these models agents are thought of by their modelers as solving stochastic control models, deciding in a sequential process whether or not to search for a better bargain or to terminate search and execute the best deal at hand. Equilibrium, or at least stochastic equilibria of some kind, can emerge from such a process. A more explicitly adaptive, boundedly rational view of search was taken by Porter (1975) in a model of adjustment by agents on both sides of the labor market.[6]

Nelson and Winter introduced into economics the philosopher Michael Polanyi's concept of *tacit knowledge*: the capacity to perform a task without conscious understanding, clearly a factor of great importance in business where worldly acumen often takes the form of hunches, which if taken, lead to successful economizing actions, but which cannot be completely explained in explicitly rational terms.

Although individuals may be endowed with varied levels of tacit knowledge as a part of their mental make-up, learning is probably essential in its development. This no doubt explains why successful decision makers often evolve 'through the ranks' and emerge into top managerial positions relatively late in their careers after they have acquired unusual competence and after their capacity has been recognized by others who are in a position and possess the desire to promote them.

In the context of economic growth, Arrow developed a model of learning by doing on the basis of a previous empirical study of production efficiency in the airplane industry. It would seem that 'learning by doing' is a quantifiable variant of tacit knowledge. That is to say, the capacity to perform production efficiently improves with experience in a way that has no visible embodiment in terms of labor or material input but which nonetheless needs to be taken into account in calculating the future benefits that may be expected to flow from costs expended in the present. It provides an endogenous explanation of shifts over time in the aggregate production function. It would seem to be a good example of the manner in which managers and workers adapt to their own internal states where the latter includes the stock of accumulated technical experience.

The role that tacit knowledge in the form of managerial and entrepreneurial competence plays in the modern complex business firm and its implications for ownership, corporate control and the market system, has been given an insightful treatments by Pelikan (1989) and Eliasson (1990). The latter's use of the concept is a natural extension of his earlier study (1975) of corporate strategic planning and of his attempt to simulate the macroeconomic consequences of microeconomic decision making based on simple adaptive rules of adjustment.

5 EXPERIMENTATION, TRIAL-AND-ERROR SEARCH OR STIMULUS/RESPONSE (S/R) LEARNING

Perhaps the most basic form of learning and adaptation is that which occurs in 'trial-and-error search' or more generally in experimentation. Experimentation involves taking a 'real-world' action, observing the outcome in terms of a criterion of that action, comparing it with previous action/outcome pairs and choosing a new action on the basis of this comparison. Each such experiment is a trial. If the criterion is improved over the preceding trial, the latest trial is (at least locally) a success; if the criterion has worsened, it is on the face of it a failure and the choice an error. Success reinforces a given direction of search; error has the opposite effect, motivating search in a new direction.

This mode of learning frequently guides action in economic as in other situations and is the basis for several important psychological theories of behavior including Frederic Skinner's behaviorism. It is the basis of stochastic stimulus–response or S/R models of learning in which random directions for search are chosen at each trial and in which the *probability* of selecting a given direction is increased as a result of success. Such models were described very early on in papers by Atkinson, Bush, Estes and Luce in Arrow et al. (1960). Trial-and-error search in one form or another is also the basis for virtually all algorithms for finding optima and equilibria in decision and game-theoretic models.

I developed a deterministic version of this approach inspired by Cyert and March's explicit espousal of the adaptive point of view. The model, which was set forth in two papers (1967, 1968) (the latter with Herb Tinney), was later tested experimentally by Kevin O'Connor (in an unpublished term paper, 1973) and with market data for individual firms by Crain et al. (1984). It provides an instructive format for illustrating the nature of learning in situations where the knowledge available at each stage is very small relative to that which would be required to describe accurately the environment within which acts must be chosen.

Imagine that a given agent sets a single control variable, an action which can be expressed as a positive real number. The agent's environment generates a real-valued payoff in response to each action through a continuous payoff function which is not known to the agent. The relevance of this state of ignorance is far greater than usually recognized. No one person in a typical business firm actually knows or comprehends completely its production function, a fact recognized by the famous statistician George Box (1957) in his award-winning development of the Evolutionary Operations Procedure (EVOP) for production control in the chemical-processing industry.

The agent uses the past two action/payoff pairs to estimate the marginal benefit of his last change in action. Successive action is based on the principles that:

A. successful behavior should be repeated; and
B. behavior should become more cautious in response to failure.

The choice is between increasing or decreasing the control variable. The strategy table that gives the response to possible payoff/action pairs is shown in Table 10.1.

The decision parameters include:

1. *initial daring parameters*, expansion and contraction coefficients that give the percentage increase and decrease in the control that the agent is initially willing to contemplate; these describe the state of *initial caution*;
2. *failure response parameters*, the fraction by which the expansion or contraction coefficients are reduced in response to error;
3. *satisficing parameters* and *cost of adjustment* that determine when behavior modification or search is discontinued.

The strategy table must be augmented to allow for mistaken convergence; for evidently, the agent could, in 'passing over' an optimum, achieve a marginal payoff less than or only slightly greater than the cost of adjustment and mistakenly conclude that he or she is doing as well as can be expected. In this case, the past decision would be repeated. The jump to a mistaken conclusion can be avoided, however, by introducing a perturbation, an experimental change taken *in the absence of any motivating reward.*

Table 10.1 A strategy table

Past action	Consequences	
	Improvement	Disimprovement
Expanded	Expand again	Contract Increase caution
Contracted	Contract again	Expand Increase caution

One kind of unmotivated search, the one used here, is to act *as if* a mistake has been made, become more cautious and continue to learn. (In optimization algorithms something similar is sometimes done by simply halving the step length and continuing the algorithm.) In any event, to A and B should be added a third principle:

C. behavior should be perturbed even when no motivation exists, or to put it in evolutionary terms, *unmotivated experimentation has adaptive value because it induces environmental response*.

This learning process was initially investigated in the context of the monopolistic and monopsonistic, profit-maximizing firm first, where output was decided on the basis of given revenue and cost functions, then, in the article with Tinney, when both output level and input mix had to be determined. The latter application involves the firm as an adaptive team with two agents, each of whom determines an action independently according to the strategy table already given. The 'sales manager' decides on the output level and the 'production manager' decides on the input mix. A certain degree of coordination is important, however. This is because convergence can occur away from a maximum if, in the course of time, a step in a given direction crosses the payoff 'hill' in such a way as to produce a satisficing change in payoff as described above. It can also happen if by chance through a sequence of trials and error, a local maximum *in a given direction of search* is approximated. If this should happen, learning ceases, perhaps far from the optimum. To prevent this possible occurrence, one or both agents must strike off in a new direction *without motivation*. A possible way this could occur is if learning is suspended by one agent while another one continues until convergence occurs. Then the first agent resumes experimentation while the second 'relaxes'. This is what was done in the original study.

Still another possibility is *phased learning* in which the behavioral variables are not altered simultaneously and independently but rather one after another in decreasing frequency. Thus, one variable might be altered each period, the second every third period, and so on. This is the analog of actual business practice. For example, in supermarkets some items are ordered each day, prices might be altered weekly, brand choices made monthly or quarterly, and investment decisions in building and equipment made annually. The effect is to introduce an element of experimental control which aids in identifying the source of success or failure that results from the combined actions of all the agents involved.

Two illustrative cases were considered by Tinney (1969); one in which the managers shared a common profit goal and one in which the sales manager uses a profit criterion but the production manager uses a unit cost criterion. For each case numerical experiments were performed for several sets of common parameter values representing weak, moderate and strong initial daring and moderate and strong failure response. Figures 10.1 and 10.2 present the results of these two sets of simulations. (Note that the parameters are the same for 1a and 2a, 1b and 2b, and so on.)

A study of these examples and the learning process that generated them suggests a number of noteworthy implications:

1. Error plays a fundamental role in learning.
2. With strong initial daring and mild failure response, learning is highly unstable.
3. Strong failure response can stymie learning.
4. Performance would appear to perform well robustly with moderate daring and moderate failure response.
5. 'Relaxed' or 'phased' learning plays the role of experimental control, in effect partially alleviating the identification problem.
6. 'Unmotivated search' plays a crucial role in preventing erroneous convergence or convergence to suboptima.
7. With uncommon goals, independent learning can wander more widely than with common goals (not surprisingly) because identification mistakes can occur more easily.

To these may be added the sobering observation that learning can be distressfully slow *even* when the environment is passive, benign and well behaved (that is, single peaked) as in the example for which the numerical experiments were calculated. It is for this reason that more sophisticated control-theoretic methods of learning might be justified, but their superiority can scarcely be taken for granted. Any control, or dynamic programming model, must incorporate simplifying assumptions about both organizational structure and environmental feedback. Theoretical convergence to optimal behavior in such hypothetical environments *may* but *need not* produce truly optimal behavior in the real environment. No matter how sophisticated, each such model is just another boundedly rational strategy to be considered along with many others, including the simple, economical methods of trial and error search.[7]

A stochastic model of trial-and-error was studied by Arthur (1990) in which asymptotic optimality in a simple stochastic environment is established. Arthur also estimates the algorithm's parameters, using published psychological experiments, and finds that the S/R

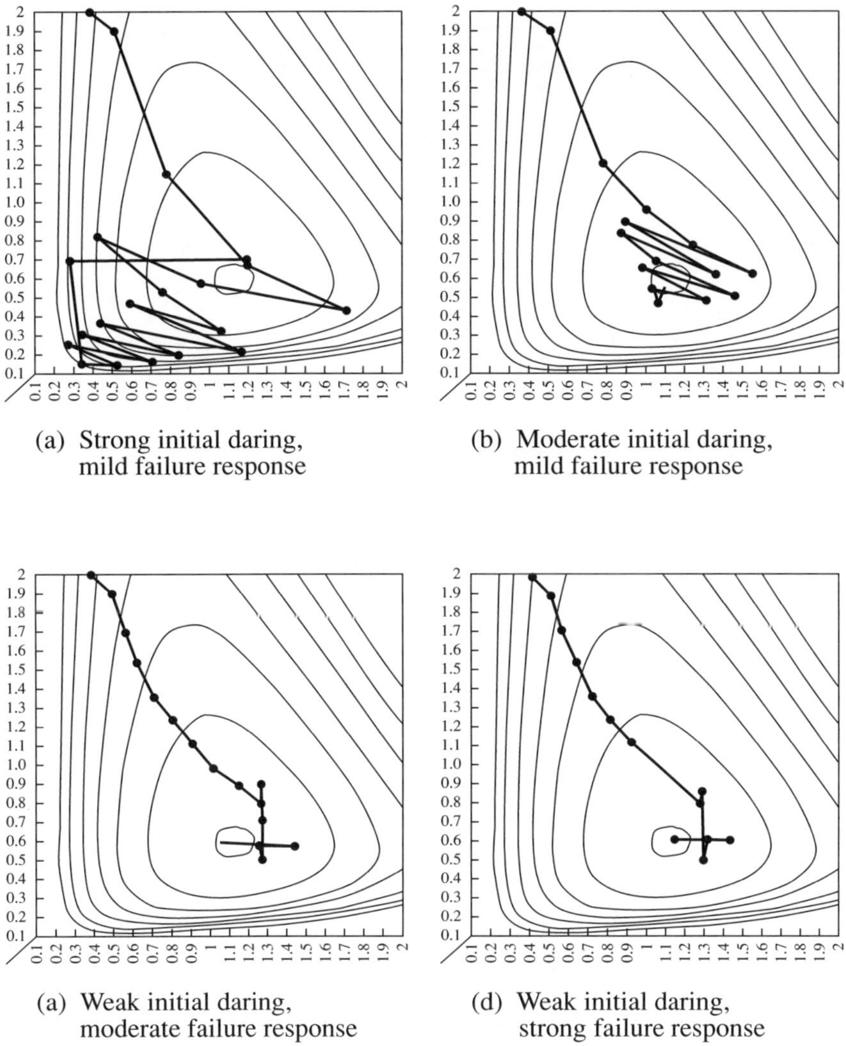

(a) Strong initial daring, mild failure response

(b) Moderate initial daring, mild failure response

(a) Weak initial daring, moderate failure response

(d) Weak initial daring, strong failure response

Figure 10.1 Team learning with a common profit goal

model performs in a manner qualitatively like that of the original human subjects, including environments in which (unlike the ones assumed for his optimality theorems) the distribution of payoffs depend on past actions.

Evans (1990) applies the stochastic S/R learning model to an adaptive game, showing that play will converge to pure strategy equilibria if they exist, thus fulfilling Hahn's (1972) conjecture.

An experimental study by Pingle (1990) of costly decision making in a deterministic environment indicates that trial-and-error type search procedure appears to be used by most subjects, but with great variation in daring and failure response. He also found evidence that a few

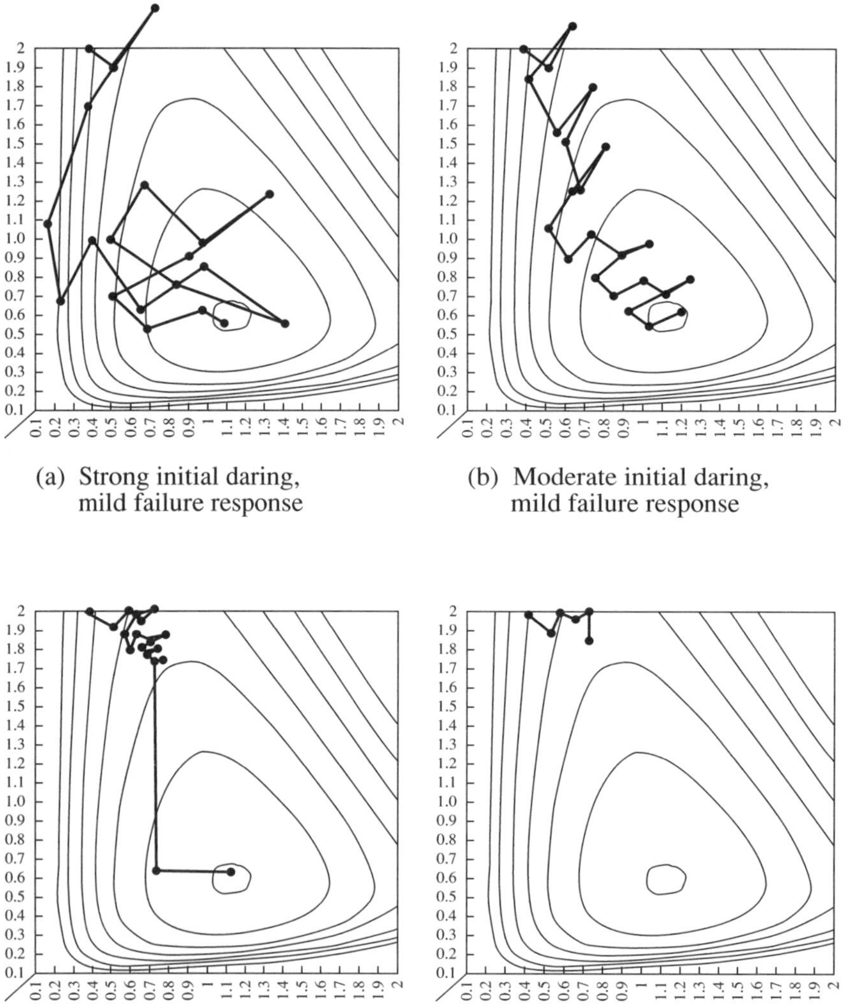

(a) Strong initial daring, mild failure response

(b) Moderate initial daring, mild failure response

(a) Weak initial daring, moderate failure response

(d) Weak initial daring, strong failure response

Figure 10.2 Team learning with profit and cost goals

agents persist in making 'unmotivated' perturbations in behavior at more-or-less periodic intervals, even when they are close to the optimum and even when they are punished by reduced payoff for doing so. The rationale for this has been hinted at above in our discussion of deterministic S/R learning.

Because of the great variation in individual behavior in most psychological learning experiments, the stochastic S/R version of experimentation would appear to be a natural hypothesis. It seems to me unlikely, however, that it is a good model of actual learning. That would be tantamount to a hypothesis that agents have a mechanism for storing and updating a number of probability distributions and for generating random drawings based on them – a hypothesis of doubtful validity on the face of it. Rather, it seems to me agents use much simpler deterministic schemes – akin to the non-stochastic S/R model discussed above and that seem suggested in O'Connor's and Pingle's findings – and that the variability of agent behavior rests primarily on the variation in the parameters of the learning algorithm. It would be nice if these were equivalent formulations, but it seems unlikely. Indeed, the biases suggested by Kahneman and Tversky's classic work on framing and the 'ameliorating' behavior of Richard Herrnstein seem to me very likely to be due to the character of practical, deterministic decision rules. If that is the case, it would reduce in empirical relevance the kind of stochastic convergence to equilibria results that are the object of so much research in this field. Here is an area that deserves more close experimental and theoretical study.

6 FURTHER DEVELOPMENTS

The work reviewed in Sections 4 and 5 is, of course, but an arbitrary sample of the early work in adaptive economics. The volume of work in the last decade has become so vast that an adequate review, even of the major contributions, is impossible in the brief space one is allotted in a volume such as this. It would perhaps be useful, however, to outline a few of the distinct approaches that have emerged in the last two decades.

The stochastic learning procedure that models the dynamics of probabilities over the space of actions in response to success or failure of past actions has been augmented by substituting a strategy space for the action space as the basic instrument of adaptation. That is, actions are replaced by action strategies each of which offers an alternative way of adjusting actions to information and experience. Thus, learning is modeled as an adjustment of the probability distribution over strategies. This yields randomly determined rules at any one time with the selection of better-performing rules becoming more probable and lesser-performing rules less probable. These are known in the literature as *classifier systems*. Their range of application in economics has become quite wide, but I believe they are subject to the reservation made at the close of Section 5.

The theory of neural nets originated by Warren McCulloch and Walter Pitts and developed by John von Neumann and Stephen Kleene, involves the flow of input signals among discrete entities. Input signals are accumulated and, when a threshold is exceeded, induce an output signal. A good review is Baum (1988).

Various examples of such models were described in papers by Baum, Kauffman and Packard in the volume edited by Anderson et al. (1988). They are examples of a *system of switches and rules* which I defined as one of the canonical forms of adaptive behavior (1975), but augmented by the assumption that an essential part of the process is stochastic and that the probability distributions themselves depend on the past behavior of the system.

The genetic algorithms developed by John Holland and others allow for the construction of rules by stochastic recombination of potential components in a manner analogous to genetic inheritance. A substantial application and development of this approach has appeared in Dawid's recent book (1999).

Many models of learning and adaptive adjustment are carried out in a game-like setting of interactive agents often with neighborhood effects. Augustin Cournot offered the first of these with his 'best response' strategy in a context of two competitors who understand their environment but not each other. There are now many sorts of variants with multiple strategies and multiple agents who may learn according to more or less sophisticated rules and/or by imitation, often using classifier-like representations. An early pioneer of this approach is Peter Albin who eventually teamed with Duncan Foley to produce a substantial investigation with economic content.

Experimentalists study behavior in economic-like contexts in some cases focused on the degree to which subjects' behaviors satisfy equilibrium properties or converge to them, but in a growing number of examples are aimed at identifying the specific rules or strategies individuals actually follow, as in Pingle's paper mentioned earlier.

Progress in the adaptive, evolutionary approach was greatly stimulated by a series of conferences over the years that led to useful proceedings volumes. Among these is the 1975 Conference on Adaptive Economic Models (Day and Groves, 1975) sponsored by the University of Wisconsin's Mathematics Research Center, and a series of conferences initiated by Ilya Prigogine at the Bruxelles Solvay Institute and the Institute for Statistical Mechanics at the University of Texas at Austin, one of which led to the essays by Prigogine and others in Day and Chen (1993). Gunnar Eliasson of Sweden's Royal Institute of Technology and formerly the Research Director of Sweden's Institute for Industrial and Economic Research (IUI), likewise sponsored a series of conferences with similar objectives, several jointly with the *Journal of Economic Behavior and Organization*, Day and Eliasson (1986), and Day et al. (1993). A significant milestone was also reached with the establishment of the Santa Fe Institute in 1984 with its research agenda focused on complex adaptive systems and with the publication of the proceedings volume edited by Anderson et al. (1988) which contains papers by Arthur, Baum, Boldrin, Holland, Kauffman, Packard, Palmer, and others.

In addition to these more or less *ad hoc* conferences, the adaptive, evolutionary paradigm has been institutionalized in the Schumpeter Society with its series of biannual conferences and proceedings volumes (for example, by those edited by Horst Hanusch, Arnold Heertje and Mark Perlman, and by Eliasson, Green and McCann 1998), and with the establishment of a number of journals devoted in part to the encouragement of the adaptive evolutionary approaches: *Journal of Economic Behavior and Organization*, established in 1981, *Journal of Structural Change and Economic Dynamics*, established in 1990, and *Journal of Evolutionary Economics*, established in 1991.

7 IMPLICATIONS

The implications of developments in adaptive economics are clear, learning is often slow and normally fraught with error. For some purposes it may do relatively little harm and may yield positive insight to assume equilibrium as a first crude approximation, for a system might under some circumstances fluctuate around such a state, as Walras and Keynes supposed. In those cases comparative statics (for large 'parametric' changes) could in principle indicate directions and rough magnitudes of change. In general, however, the economy needs to be thought of as a complex adaptive system working out of equilibrium.

As seen above, the volume of work in this 'dual mainstream' has grown in magnitude and exhibits great variability in techniques and model structures. Most of the work is theoretical in nature with rare attempts to base models on *observed* rules or test models with empirical data.

Microeconomists need to formulate stylized models of business organization, and study their behavior in response to various 'outside' disturbances. In this way, the efficacy and robustness of alternative planning procedures and learning processes might be identified. Work of this kind was implemented by Cyert, March, Simon, and their students long ago. Forrester (1961) and his intellectual descendants, for example, Sterman (2000), have emphasized such a program. Similar work, spread across the discipline, could greatly enhance the practical relevance of economic research for improving business and government practice.

For macroeconomics, the implications are also clear. Adaptive processes, such as partial adjustment and adaptive expectation mechanisms, need to be restored to economywide modeling, taking advantage of computational power to explore the efficacy and robustness of alternative fiscal, monetary, welfare, and regulatory policies. By constructing explicitly adaptive representation of aggregate supply and demand, the hypotheses of equilibria existence and stability can be tested under differing policy scenarios. Basic work in this direction is underway primarily by Europeans (see Flaschel et al. 1997 and Amendola and Gaffard 1998). Further developments are urgently needed to anticipate and prepare for the problems that will arise as economic development, population growth, and resource depletion continue in the coming decades and, as the integration of the world economy further complexifies production, exchange, and finance.

8 EPILOG

Very early in my professional life, I was given the opportunity to review Cyert and March's book for *Econometrica* (1964). Although I was 'full of' my own ideas at the time, I was excited to recognize a kindred approach to economics. I followed the advice of a young colleague, Ed Greenberg, to assign the book in the second semester graduate micro theory course that I was to teach. Thus, for a decade or so every Wisconsin PhD was exposed – along with Robert Dorfman, Paul Samuelson, and Robert Solow and various works of Arrow, Tjalling Koopmans, Wassily Leontief, and so on to Cyert and March. To show how Carnegie ideas were related to standard ideas of equilibrium, I used the learning model described in Section 5. A year or two later I found myself next to Dick Cyert in the hotel lounge after arriving for a conference organized by Emile Grunberg on behavioral economics. I saw Dick as much my senior (though he was still quite young himself), but he was friendly and absolutely without affectation. I was immediately at ease and was able to enjoy a long conversation about mutual interests. We had only occasional contacts after that, but his generosity of spirit stayed with me.

The triumvirate of Simon, March, and Cyert produced an impressive flow of research and students. Their work securely established the adaptive and organizational aspects of behavior in the economics discipline and paved the way for those working in the field now. One cannot deny that adaptive economics is maturing as more and more mathematical concepts and techniques are being introduced in its development. Not all of it, however, has the same basis in observable behavior that characterized the Carnegie School. Perhaps this volume will remind current researchers of their intellectual heritage and inspire some to follow the scientific objective that these three exemplified.

NOTES

* An early version of this chapter was presented at the Workshop on Expectations and Learning at the University of Siena, Certosa Pontignano, June 20–30, 1990, subsequently published in Dopfer (2001). It was revised and augmented for this occasion but incorporates material in the earlier paper with permission of Kluwer Academic Publishers.

1. See Lorenze and Leyhauser (1973).
2. Formal models or frameworks embodying this general concept are found in various places including my own 1975 and 1995 papers.
3. On this aspect of development, see Day (2000, Chapters 21–25). An example is thought to be the Maya. See Fash (1988) or Sablov (1990). Certainly, the decline and disappearance of many cultures and civilizations are related to, if not exclusively caused by, their own past economic expansion; a fact already noticed by Thucydides who remarked on the decline of Greek timber and the consequent rise in the cost of maintaining fleets and commerce.
4. See, for example, Geoffrey Hodgson (1993).
5. For a general discussion and various examples, see Day and Cigno (1978). This work is quite similar in spirit to Cohen and Modigliani (1961). For other examples, see Powers and Rudd in Day and Groves (1975). For a general discussion of rationality and adaptive economizing within zones of flexible response, see Day (1971).
6. For those early examples of adaptive search, see Porter (1975) and the references there.
7. A similar conclusion was reached by Hadar (1976), who noted 'the disturbing fact that in some circumstances it may be just as well for the decision-maker to ignore information available to him, and to adopt a fairly simple trial and error formula'.

REFERENCES

Albin, Peter S. (1998), *Barriers and Bounds to Rationality: Essays on Economic Complexity and Dynamics in Interactive Systems*, Princeton University Press.

Alchian, Armen (1950), 'Uncertainty, evolution and economic theory', *Journal of Political Economy*, **58**, 211–21.

Amendola, Mario and Jean-Luc Gaffard (1998), *Out of Equilibrium*, Oxford: Clarendon Press.

Anderson, P.W., Kenneth Arrow and David Pines (eds) (1988), *The Economy as an Evolving Complex System*, Redwood City, CA: Addison–Wesley.

Arrow, K, and G. Debreu (1954), 'Existence of an Equilibrium for a Competitive Economy', *Econometrica*, **22**, 265–90.

Arrow, Kenneth (1962), 'The economic implications of learning by doing', *Review of Economic Studies*, **29**, 155–73.

Arrow, Kenneth, Samuel Karlin and Patrick Suppes (1960), *Mathematical Methods in the Social Sciences*, Stanford, CA: Stanford University Press.

Arthur, B. (1990), 'Positive Feedbacks in the Economy', *Scientific American*, Feb. 1990.

Baum, Eric B. (1988), 'Neural nets for economists', in Anderson, Arrow and Pines (eds), pp. 33–48.

Box, George E.P. (1957), 'Evolutionary operation: a method for increasing industrial productivity', *Applied Statistics*, **6**, 3–23.

Brousseau, V. and Alan P. Kirman (1990), 'The dynamics of learning in mis-specified models', presented to Workshop on Expectations and Learning at Certosa di Pontignano, Siena: University of Siena.

Chrystal, Donald, Thomas G. Guenther and Eldo C. Koenig (1962), 'Allis–Chalmers manufacturing company: applying control concepts to an organization', in A.D. Meacham and V.B. Thompson (eds), *Total System*, Detroit: American Data Processing, Inc., pp. 110–29.

Cohen, Kolman J. and Franco Modigliani (1961), 'The role of anticipations and plans in economic behavior and their use in economic analysis and forecasting', *Studies in Business Expectations and Planning*, No. 4, Urbana: University of Illinois.

Crain, W. Mark, William F. Shugart and Robert D. Tollison (1984), 'The convergence of satisficing to marginalism: an empirical test', *Journal of Economic Behavior and Organization*, **5**, 375–86.

Cyert, Richard and James G. March (1963), *A Behavioral Theory of the Firm*, Englewood Cliffs, NJ: Prentice-Hall.

Dawid, Herbert (1999), *Adaptive Learning by Genetic Algorithms*, Berlin: Springer-Verlag.

Day, R.H. (1963), *Recursive Programming and Production Response*, Amsterdam: North-Holland.
Day, Richard H. (1967), 'Profits, learning and the convergence of satisficing to marginalism', *Quarterly Journal of Economics*, **81**, 302–11.
Day, Richard H. and Herbert J. Tinney (1968), How to cooperate in business without really trying: a learning model of decentralized decision-making', *Journal of Political Economy*, July/August, pp. 583–600.
Day, Richard H. (1971), 'Rational choice and economic behavior', *Theory and Decision*, **1**, 229–51.
Day, Richard H. (1975), 'Adaptive processes and economic theory', in Day and Groves (eds), pp. 1–38.
Day, R.H. and P. Chen (1993), *Nonlinear Dynamics and Evolutionary Economics*, Oxford: Oxford University Press.
Day, R.H., G. Eliasson and C. Wihlborg (eds) (1993), *The Market in Ownership, Innovation and Control*, Amsterdam: North-Holland.
Day, Richard H. (1995), 'L'économie hors de l'équilibre', (Existence out of equilibrium), *Revue Économique*, **46** (6), 1461–71.
Day, Richard H. (2000), *Complex Economic Dynamics, Volume II, An Introduction to Macroeconomic Dynamics*, Cambridge, MA: MIT Press.
Day, Richard H. and Alessandro Cigno (1978), *Modelling Economic Change: The Recursive Programming Approach*, Amsterdam: North-Holland.
Day, Richard H. and T. Groves (eds) (1975), *Adaptive Economic Models*, New York: Academic Press.
Dopfer, Kurt (2001), *Evolutionary Economics: Progress and Scope*, Boston, MA: Kluwer Academic.
Eliasson, Gunnar (1975), *Business Economic Planning*, New York: John Wiley & Sons.
Eliasson, Gunnar (1990), 'The firm as a competent team', *Journal of Economic Behavior and Organization*, **13**, 275–98.
Eliasson, G., C. Green and C. McCann (eds) (1998), Microfoundations of Economic Growth: (1986) A Schumpeterian Perspective, Ann Arbor: The University of Michigan Press.
Evans, Robert A. (1990), 'Out-of-equilibrium learning: analyses based on cognitive-scientific models', presented at Workshop on Expectations and Learning, Certosa di Pontignano, Siena: University of Siena.
Fash, William L., Jr. (1988), A new look at Maya statecraft from Copán, Honduras', *Antiquity*, **62**, 157–69.
Flaschel, Peter, Reiner Franke and Willi Semmler (1997), *Nonlinear Dynamics and Economic Theory*, Cambridge, MA: MIT Press.
Forrester, J. (1961), *Industrial Dynamics*, Waltham, MA: Pegasus Communications.
Hadar, Josef (1976), 'Learning with deterministic decision rules', *Decision Sciences*, **7**, 18–28.
Hahn, Frank (1972), 'On the notion of equilibrium in Economics', *Econometrica*, Cambridge: Cambridge University Press.
Hahn, Frank (1990), 'On learning', lecture presented at Workshop on Expectations and Learning, Certosa di Pontignano, Siena: University of Siena.
Hodgson, Geoffrey (1993), *Economics and Evolution*, Ann Arbor, MI: University of Michigan Press.
Holland, John H. (1988), 'The global economy as an adaptive process', in Anderson, Arrow and Pines (eds), pp. 117–24.
Kauffman, Stuart A. (1988), 'The evolution of economic webs', in Anderson, Arrow and Pines (eds), pp. 125–46.
Lindh, Thomas (1990), 'Lessons from learning about rational expectations', Working Paper, Department of Economics, Uppsala: Uppsala University.
Lorenze, Konrad and Paul Leyhauser (1973), *Motivation of Human and Animal Behavior*, New York: Van Nortrand.
March, James G. and Herbert Simon (1958), *Organizations*, New York: John Wiley & Sons.
Nelson, Richard and Sidney Winter (1982), *Toward an Evolutionary Theory of the Firm*, Cambridge, MA: Harvard University Press.
O'Connor, Kevin (1973), 'Rate and nature of convergence to an optimum performance point as a function of learning under varying degrees of environmental stability', *Social Systems Research Institute*, No. 7303, Madison, WI: University of Wisconsin.
Packard, Norman (1988), 'A simple model for dynamics away from attractors', in Anderson, Arrow and Pines (eds), pp. 169–76.

Papandreou, Andrus G. (1952), 'Some basic problems in the theory of the firm', in B.F. Haley (ed.), *A Survey of Contemporary Economics*, Vol. II, Homewood, IL: Richard D. Irwin, pp. 183–219.
Pelikan, Pavel (1989), 'Evolution, economic competence and the market for corporate control', *Journal of Economic Behavior and Organization*, **12**, 279–304.
Pingle, Mark (1990), 'Cost of optimization: a controlled experiment', Working Paper, Reno: University of Nevada.
Porter, William R. (1975), 'Market adjustment with adaptive supply and pricing decisions', in Day and Groves (eds), pp. 309–25.
Sablov, Jeremy A. (1990), *The New Archeology and the Ancient Maya*, New York: W.H. Freeman & Company.
Schumpeter, Joseph (1938), *Theory of Economic Development* (Translation, Rudgers Oppie: Original in German), Cambridge, MA: Harvard University Press.
Simon, Herbert A. (1957), *Administrative Behavior*, 2nd edn, New York: Free Press.
Sterman (2000), *Business Dynamics: Systems Thinking for a Complex World*, Irwin/McGraw-Hill.
Tinney, Herbert (1969), 'Analysis and Simulation of Dynamic Microeconomic Models', PhD Dissertation, Madison, WI: University of Wisconsin.
Tversky, A., and D. Kahneman (1982), 'Judgment under uncertainty: Heuristics and biases', in D. Kahneman, P. Slovic and A. Tversky (eds), *Judgment under uncertainty: Heuristics and biases*, Cambridge: Cambridge University Press, pp. 3–20.
Winter, Sidney (1964), 'Economic "natural selection" and the theory of the firm', *Yale Economic Essays*, **4**, 225–72.

11. Organizational learning through rule adaptation: from the behavioral theory to transactive organizational learning

Alfred Kieser and Ulrich Koch*

1 ORGANIZATIONAL LEARNING IN THE BEHAVIORAL THEORY – THE EVOLUTION OF RULES

The behavioral theory modeled the firm as an adaptively rational system (Cyert and March 1963). Adaptive rationality of organizations follows from bounded rationality which, in contrast to classical concepts of omniscient rationality, encompasses search processes and satisficing by individuals (Simon 1979). Thus, the adaptively rational firm is characterized by the following properties (Cyert and March 1963: 99):

1. There exist a number of states of the system. At any point in time, the system in some sense 'prefers' some of these states to others.
2. There exists an external source of disturbance or shock to the system. These shocks cannot be controlled.
3. There exist a number of decision variables internal to the system. These variables are manipulated according to some decision rules.
4. Each combination of external shocks and decision variables in the system changes the state of the system. Thus, given an existing state, an external shock, and a decision, the next state is determined.
5. Any decision rule that leads to a preferred state at one point is more likely to be used in the future than it was in the past; any decision rule that leads to a non-preferred state at one point is less likely to be used in the future than it was in the past.

Adaptive rationality implies that the organization learns from experience. In this view organizations act predominantly by applying standard operation procedures and they learn by changing existing standard operating procedures, if necessary several times, and through retaining those that improve the performance of the firm. Standard operating procedures provide guidelines for organizational members on how to deal with problems of information processing, decision making, and evaluating the outcomes of decisions.

If the solutions that are achieved by applying the existing standard operating procedures are no longer regarded as satisfactory, which is indicated by the non-achievement of goals, a search for more satisfying problem solutions is initiated. Initially this search tends to be 'local', that is it concentrates on solutions within the department to which this problem was initially attributed. If this search is unsuccessful, it is expanded – more dramatic deviations from the proven courses of action are taken into consideration which usually involve a number of departments. If a solution appears satisfying, it is programmed into the form of a new standard operating procedure. Not only are the procedures for decision making programmed into standard operating procedures, but procedures for search and performance evaluation (attention rules) are as well.

Since organizational members record solutions that have proved successful in the past, rules 'permit the transfer of past learning' (Cyert and March 1963: 104). With the help of standard operating procedures organizational members of large organizations who are only in command of limited rationality are able to make numerous more or less routinized decisions every day, and the decisions that are made within the various departments only loosely connected are miraculously compatible – in the majority of cases at least. This coordination, according to Cyert and March, is a result of organizational evolution or, as they label it, adaptive rationality. If coordination problems arise in everyday processes between departments, rules and routines are changed on a trial-and-error basis, if necessary several times, until a satisfactory coordination is achieved. In this way, rules or the standard operating procedures provide solutions for decision makers who typically were not involved in their construction. By serving as organizational memories, standard operating procedures or rules prove to be powerful instruments for the 'reduction of complexity' (Luhmann 1972, 1973). The knowledge that is provided by rules brings about a great deal of organizational coordination. Thus, the amount of knowledge individual organizational members would have to learn may well be quite moderate while organizations as a whole can learn on the level of procedures that connect these individuals (Dosi 1988: 1133).

March and Olsen (1975) point out that organizational learning on the basis of standard operating procedures is a bit more problematic than originally conceptualized by the behavioral theory. A fundamental problem which lies within this early model is that it defines whole organizations or organizational subunits as the units of analysis and, thereby, neglects the link between individual learning and organizational learning. March and Olsen overcome this problem by explicitly taking into consideration the roles of individuals in processes of organizational learning. They conceptualize a complete learning cycle and identify barriers able to interrupt learning at different points in this cycle. The complete cycle consists of four stages: (i) individual actions are based on certain individual beliefs; (ii) these actions lead to organizational actions that produce certain outcomes; (iii) these outcomes are interpreted in terms of environmental response, with success being distinguished from failure, and links being drawn between actions and perceived outcomes; and (iv) this reasoning leads to beliefs.

The creation or modification of rules that lead to actions are the results of experimentation. In this respect, organizational learning consists of three steps: variation through experimentation, selection based on inferences drawn from experiments, and retention through the formulation of rules that produce successful actions and that thus can be passed on to other organizational members.

2 RESULTS OF AN EXPLORATORY STUDY ON ORGANIZATIONAL LEARNING

In this section we report findings from an exploratory study of rule-change processes. The research questions that guided this study were derived from an understanding of organizational learning as an evolution of rules. As described above, from this perspective, organizations are seen as learning by accumulating experiential knowledge in rules and by making decisions on the basis of these rules (Cyert and March 1963; Levitt and March 1988; March 1991; Nelson and Winter 1982; Schulz 1993). However if one assumes that only individuals are able to both make and interpret experiences (Hedberg 1981: 7; Simon 1991: 125), then the question arises as to how organizations actually manage to transfer individual experiences into organizational rules. In other words: a mechanism is needed that transfers individual learning into organizational learning. To identify and to describe such a mechanism was the aim of our exploratory study.

Our analysis is based on data from 25 semi-structured interviews which have been conducted in several branches and the headquarters of a large German bank.[1] The interviews lasted between 60 and 90 minutes. Twenty rule users and five rule authors were among the interviewees. The questionnaires included items on the general perception of standard operating procedures by the interviewee and on the ways in which organizational members learn and interpret standard operating procedures. Rule users were asked when and how they try to change standard operating procedures that they perceive as in need of improvement. Finally and most important for this study, questions were asked how organizational members come to the conclusion that a rule change is necessary and how the content of a new or changed rule is determined. In the following we concentrate on the question how new rules or new rule versions are designed.

All interviews except one have been tape-recorded and completely transcribed. Transcripts were coded with a coding scheme that was derived in part from the literature on organizational learning and in part from the data itself (Araujo 1995: 96; Coffey and Atkinson 1996: 31; Miles and Huberman 1984; Tesch 1995: 139).[2] For the following short summary, quotations were chosen from the transcripts that could be classified as 'typical' for certain aspects of rule-change processes in the bank.

Findings

Processes during which a rule is designed or redesigned appear highly diffuse at first glance. This impression is mainly due to the fact that, generally, a multitude of organizational members participate in these processes. However, none of these individuals is able to accurately describe a rule change in its entirety. That is, in most cases, s/he is not able to identify the organizational members who initiated the change or all the other organizational members who became involved in the formulation of a new rule. In other words, the involved actors' understanding of rule-change processes is always restricted by their specialized and bound perspectives. In the following quotation the interviewee describes the course of a rule change. It seems as if the process has no clear beginning and end. The process is brought to an end when a number of organizational members have commented on the rule version in question. The interviewee also indicates that it is important that all organizational members likely to be affected by the planned rule change are involved.[3]

> I1: ... Then, OK, the rule is changed. The author formulates it [the first version of a new rule] ... in writing and then it is negotiated with, perhaps with other departments, especially with those departments that will be more strongly affected. You coordinate yourself with the others, you get opinions and, perhaps, suggestions for improvements and critique, I find this very important and appropriate.

> And then you can say: 'OK, someday this so-called corpus of law is done and is duplicated [that is, issued and copied for all subunits for which the rule is relevant] for the entire bank'.

Some organizational members are officially in charge of writing or changing certain categories of rules. Formal responsibilities, however, do not determine exclusively who gets involved in the change process. What appears diffuse at first glance does not resemble a garbage-can process, however, insofar as those who have access to the process cannot dump all sorts of problems into the decision-making situation. Rather, only those organizational members who are assumed to have relevant knowledge are consulted. The rule-change processes that we have observed are handled by organizational members with specialized knowledge. In the following quotation one such rule author describes how suggested rule versions are passed back and forth several times between several groups and departments for comments and reformulation. In this case, the suggested rule version was first submitted to a committee that is in charge of evaluating improvement proposals. The interviewed rule author is a member of a team that is responsible for the optimization of work processes.

> Q: Are there formal channels to which that [a suggested rule version] is passed on?
> I22: Very creative. Depends lastly on what the issue is. When they [the suggestion program committee] reach an opinion it is passed on to our team, which is asked to review the whole thing.
> By the way, a huge part of the proposals for rule changes in the whole organizational, technical area [that is, the interviewee's area] comes from the bookkeeping corner. These issues are incorporated into people's daily jobs in a very concrete manner.
> These suggestions end up with Mr Smith.[4] That's where this is settled. And then he divides the suggestions up, according to special areas, for example to my team [team that is responsible for the optimization of work processes]. Then we pass it on to our groups, to the employees, wherever we think the expert is. [S]he [the expert] should take a look at the proposal. If the proposal is recommended [that is, judged to be reasonable by this expert], then it goes back to that committee [the suggestion program committee].
> Q: From this single person [expert]?
> I22: From that one single person. And the manager who is responsible also signs. Then this expert's opinion goes back to the committee, to this suggestion program. And if they end up approving it statewide [that is, for the entire bank], then a rule change mostly occurs [that is, is released/implemented].

The organizational members who get involved in rule-change processes are expected to comment on the respective rule versions only from the perspective of their specialized knowledge. Those who get involved come from different hierarchical levels and from different departments. They are regarded as specialists in their respective task environments. However, their expertise on other organizational task environments also effected by the rule change is limited. At best a specialist can tell which other departments have a stake in the ongoing change process and which members of these departments are likely to have relevant knowledge to contribute. In the following quotation a rule author states that he passes on proposals for rule changes to those organizational members whom he assumes have relevant knowledge with regard to the rule change at hand.

> Q: How do you pass these [proposals for rule change] on, the ones you cannot comment on yourself?
> I23: Well, I just know people I can turn to. For example I just know there is a member of the department for the optimization of work processes who is knowledgeable at cash transactions, who deals with

cash procedures, and there are people who deal with other processes. I just know which of my colleagues are highly specialized in which areas. ...
Q: But those people are not necessarily responsible to do something like that?
I25: No, looking at it from a formal perspective it is my job to comment on the thing and to send it back. Well, but the discussion or the decision is not made at my desk. Rather it is made where life actually takes place, namely in the affected group [the network of organizational members who are likely to be affected by the rule change], for example, the administration department.

The interviewed persons listed several criteria that guide them in their evaluations of rule versions. Of course the costs of a rule change are an important factor. However as the expenses and, even more, the benefits of changes in a rule book are extremely difficult to calculate, other criteria are more salient. Besides the question of assessing whether a suggestion for change 'makes sense', the 'feasibility' of the suggested changes is mentioned as an important criterion for evaluation of rule versions. These criteria seem to be elements of the organizational members' routinized experiential knowledge, that is knowledge that is stored in mental scripts and schemas. Explaining why a certain rule version is acceptable or what a rule has to look like is not necessary for an evaluation, though, as the following statement of a rule author indicates:

Q: How do you then decide if it [a suggested rule change] makes sense, or not? Are there criteria for this, or ... ?
I25: ... I get it in, pass it on to one of the people I can address who is an expert in this area with the request that they check 'Does it make sense – yes, no', without him worrying about how we will carry out the whole thing, but rather from the viewpoint 'Does it make sense, can we put that into practice in this way?' If the answer is yes, we will report back a positive answer, if for important and urgent reasons the answer is no, we will feed back a negative answer.

The aim of the rule-change process is to minimize necessary corrections after the new rule version has been officially issued. In order to ensure the appropriateness of a new rule, it seems that two conditions have to be met. First, specialists of all the affected departments need to be consulted before the new rule is implemented. Second, the involved specialists have to be experienced enough to be able to judge the feasibility of a rule version from the perspective of their respective departments. Sometimes, however, it occurs that a revised rule proves inadequate after it has been officially released. A rule user describes such a case which he attributes to a lack of experience among the involved organizational members:

Q: Have you ever been confronted with a rule that was impossible to apply as it was written?
I20: That happens, yes.
Q: What could be the reason for this?
I20: Well the reason for this could be, and please don't get me wrong, that the wrong people were in this particular work group [that is, the organizational members who were involved in the rule-change process], that this particular work group, for example, was made up of people whose experiences were not appropriate. Those persons made recommendations based on only three, four, five experiences [that is, they had gone through the process that was up for revision only a limited number of times] that were not suited for an implementation [of the rule] in the entire bank.

Summary of the Findings

In short, the findings of this study indicate that changes of standard operating procedures are based on the specialized and therefore limited experiential knowledge of organizational members who get involved in the change process. Knowledge from different departments is required in order to change standard operating procedures successfully. Organizational members who are responsible for the coordination of change processes of standard operating procedures have to be able to locate those organizational members who, since they have collected relevant experience, have knowledge that is relevant for the reformulation of the rule. These 'specialists', in turn, have to be experienced enough to be able to decide whether the solution that is programmed into a suggested rule version is feasible for the rule users. Since work processes are highly interconnected, several specialists from different departments have to cooperate. For those organizational members who cooperate in a process of rule change it is neither necessary nor possible to gain a shared in-depth understanding of the problem at hand, or to learn the knowledge of other cooperating organizational specialties.

3 THE MISLEADING NOTION THAT ORGANIZATIONAL MEMBERS LEARN AS MUCH AS POSSIBLE FROM ONE ANOTHER IS A PRECONDITION FOR ORGANIZATIONAL LEARNING

In the preceding section we have presented results of an exploratory study in which we have tried to find out how the experiential knowledge of individual organizational members informs the formulation of formal rules. This question is highly important with respect to organizational learning because only individuals possess the capability to interpret experience. However, as we have seen in the discussion of March and Olsen's (1975) model of learning cycles, organizational learning requires more than the acquisition of new knowledge by organizational members.

Our results suggest that the knowledge from several specialized knowledge bases has to be recombined during the process of designing a new formal rule. If the rule affects several departments, individual organizational members in these departments cannot be expected to hold all the knowledge relevant to formulate or change such a rule. Our question, therefore, can now be stated more precisely: how is the experiential knowledge of organizational members whose knowledge is specialized in different fields incorporated into the design of a rule if none of these specialists possesses all the relevant knowledge alone?

Some authors maintain (more or less explicitly) that the transfer of the experiential knowledge of several organizational members into an organizational knowledge base such as a new product or a new organizational rule requires that these organizational members share a good deal of or even all their specialized individual knowledge. From this perspective, organizational learning presupposes that individual organizational members substantially learn from other organizational members. With regard to formal rules this assumption means that a rule designer has to learn the specialized knowledge of different departments in order to be able to take into consideration the specific requirements of these other departments when formulating or reformulating a rule. Only through acquiring all the relevant knowledge him- or herself can a rule designer guarantee that all relevant knowledge is contained in the new rule.

Such a process of in-depth mutual learning is, as our case study suggests, not required in any case. In the rule-change processes we observed, it did not seem necessary for the rule designers to acquire additional knowledge, to a large extent, from other organizational members in order to formulate a new rule. For a transfer of the required knowledge into the new rule it was sufficient that the specialists evaluated a suggested rule version from their specific perspectives and, if they considered it necessary, to make suggestions for improvement.

However, before we develop our own concept, we want to demonstrate how deeply engrained in theories of organizational learning the assumption that in-depth mutual learning is a necessary precondition for organizational learning is. Thereby it is not our aim to reject the approaches which we are about to criticize altogether. Rather our criticism is aimed at a tendency in these approaches to overestimate the potential of cognitive efforts for the transfer and integration of individual knowledge and to underestimate the condition of bounded rationality and limited cognitive capacities in the context of organizational learning. Accordingly we argue that scholars of organizational learning and knowledge integration tend to be overly optimistic with regard to the abilities of individual organizational members, when applying concepts such as organizationally shared reality constructions, cross-functional knowledge, or shared interpretations of problems in trying to describe the link between individual and organizational knowledge. In contrast to these approaches, we suggest that concepts that take into account bounded rationality and organization-specific learning conditions like the division of labor (and, more crucially: the division of the respective knowledge), seem to be much more promising when applied in analyses of organizational learning and knowledge management.

Authors like Nonaka (1994), Kim (1993), Fiol (1994), and Argyris and Schön (1978) derive their conceptions of a link between individual and organizational learning from the assumption that, in order to change an organizational knowledge base, organizational members need to change their shared constructions of reality. From this perspective, organizational members combine their individual experiences by mutually adapting their conceptions of reality through communication processes. At this point, the question arises as to just how suitable terms such as 'organizationally shared reality constructions' are for analysing changes in an organizational knowledge base. By no means, however, do we question the existence of such 'mental models' that are held on the level of groups and organizations. Rather the key question is whether it is necessary that these mental models should be perceived as central elements in analyses of organizational learning.

Argyris and Schön, for example, conceptualize organizational learning as an exchange of knowledge between organizational members. 'Organizational maps', one of their key concepts, denote the 'shared descriptions of organization which individuals *jointly construct* and use to guide their own inquiry' (Argyris and Schön 1978: 17). Organizational maps are, according to the authors, the 'media of organizational learning' (ibid.). They contain the 'organizational theory-in-use' which is 'encoded in private images and in public maps' (ibid.).

In his 'A dynamic theory of organizational knowledge creation', Nonaka (1994, see also 1991) starts from the assumption that in order to transfer their knowledge to an organization, organizational members need to 'construct "social reality"' ... within teams that are 'made of several members coming from a *variety of functional departments*' (Nonaka 1994: 23, emphasis added). According to Nonaka, the creation of common perspectives within such cross-functional teams is facilitated through shared experiences: 'Direct understanding of other individuals relies on shared experience that enables team members to "indwell" into others and to grasp their world from "inside". Shared experience also facilitates the creation of "common perspectives" which can be shared by team members as a part of their respective bodies of tacit knowledge' (ibid.: 24).

Kim (1993) likewise builds his understanding of the link between individual and organizational knowledge on the notion of shared reality constructions. In his model, organizational learning takes place when individual mental models are changed in response to experiences, made explicit and, finally, merged into shared mental models: 'Individual frameworks become embedded in the organization's *weltanschauung*. The organization's view of the world slowly evolves to encompass the current thinking of the individuals within' (Kim 1993: 45). However Kim does not provide a detailed description of the transformation process itself.

The integration of knowledge through individual learning is not only formulated as a requirement in approaches to organizational learning; it is also seen as a success factor in approaches to strategy formulation and, sometimes, even as a general requirement that follows naturally from the division of work. A case in point is the management of product or process innovations. Authors who discuss how to increase the frequency, effectiveness and efficiency of organizational innovations stress that integration of specialized knowledge is the way to achieve these goals (Hoopes and Postrel 1999). Complex innovations require, as does the design of new rules, the cooperation of several specialized organizational members. Authors who deal with organizational innovations agree that the solution to these problems requires more than the transfer of knowledge between departments. Rather the problem is similar to the one we have discussed above: how to combine the knowledge of organizational members who are specialized in different fields when none of these members is alone able to completely overlook and evaluate possible combinations of knowledge.

We shall try to show how different mechanisms that have been promoted for a solution of this problem contain the same problematic aspects that the concepts of organizational shared mental models do: these mechanisms require a great deal of mutual learning or they tend to imply that individual organizational members are able to absorb all the relevant knowledge from the different specialized fields. Thus, we argue that these approaches to knowledge integration appear unrealistic when analysed from a behavioral theory perspective. In particular they appear overly optimistic with respect to the required cognitive capabilities of the organizational members.

Brown and Duguid (1998) place the evolution of new organizational knowledge into 'communities of practice' in which organizational members collectively work and jointly collect experiences. The exchange of knowledge within these communities is not problematic, it is an automatic side product of everyday communication (Brown and Duguid 1991). However the transfer of knowledge between different specialized communities of practice presents a number of difficulties: 'Beyond communities, locally developed knowledge is difficult to organize. The hard work of organizing knowledge is a critical aspect of what firms and other organizations do' (Brown and Duguid 1998: 91). In order to facilitate the integration of knowledge across the borders of communities of practice Brown and Duguid (ibid: 103) suggest the application of three mechanisms: 'translation', 'procuring' and 'boundary objects'. However these mechanisms require, as we hasten to demonstrate, that some organizational members are capable of placing themselves into the perspectives of a number of different communities.

Organizational translators, according to the authors, 'are individuals who can frame the interests of one community in terms of another community's perspective. The role of translator can be quite complex and the *translator must be sufficiently knowledgeable about the work of both communities* to be able to translate' (ibid.: 103, emphasis added). *In-firm brokers*, in turn, need to be able to '*truly participate in both worlds*' (ibid.: 103, emphasis added). *Boundary objects*, finally, are suggested by Brown and Duguid as mechanisms that '*help to clarify attitudes of other communities*' (ibid.: 104, emphasis added). Contracts are an example of boundary objects: 'They develop as different *groups converge*, through negotiation, on an agreed meaning that has significance for both' (ibid.: 104, emphasis added). Brown and Duguid argue that the groups within organizations are subject to a '*compelling need to share an interpretation of these important documents*' (ibid.: 104, emphasis added).

Leonard (1998) pursues the question of how organizations should combine strategic competencies. With respect to different specializations, Leonard (1998: 65) argues: 'Specialization leads to expertise, of course, and therefore the availability of deep knowledge to apply to problems. However the resulting distinct "thought worlds" rarely intersect, unless purposely driven to do so'. For this reason, she argues, it is necessary to overcome conflict or to make constructive use of tensions between organizational units in order to generate innovations: 'Groups comprising individuals who operate from a base of deeply specialized knowledge need mechanisms to translate across the different "languages" and encourage the depersonalization of conflicting perspectives' (ibid.: 65).

Leonard proposes to impart to organizational members T-shaped skills which they need for the integration of knowledge. Organizational members with T-shaped skills have, on the one side, deep specialized knowledge – this is represented by the trunk of the T – and, at the same time, wide, possibly theoretical knowledge – as represented by its crossbeam:

> As individuals grow in experience, some begin to embody apparently opposing signature skills, especially a combination of both deep theoretical knowledge and practice. Such people are extremely valuable for managing the integration of very diverse knowledge sets since they speak two or more professional 'languages' and can see the world from two or more different perspectives. They have T-shaped skill sets. ... The need for T-shaped skills surfaces anywhere problem solving is required across different deep functional knowledge bases or at the juncture of such deep knowledge with an application area. ... Given their [the organizational members' with T-shaped skills] wide experience in applying functional knowledge, they are capable of convergent, synergistic thinking. (ibid.: 75)

Boland and Tenkasi (1995) label organizational units with different specializations 'communities of knowing'. They argue that communication is equally important within such units as between them: 'Knowledge production involves communication within and between a firm's multiple communities of knowing. We refer to communication that strengthens the unique knowledge of a community as perspective making, and communication that improves its ability to take the knowledge of other communities into account as perspective taking' (Boland and Tenkasi 1995: 351).

Two of Boland and Tenkasi's arguments in the quotation above are decisive: First they argue that knowledge of other communities has to be taken into account when new knowledge is produced. Second only through communication is this process of knowledge acquisition across the borders of units possible. However, we believe that the meaning ascribed to these expressions by Boland and Tenkasi is problematic in two regards. First, the ability to take the existence of different perspectives into consideration is equated with the ability to place oneself in the position of other units, that is with the ability of perspective taking. In addition this capability of perspective taking is postulated as being the essence of any organizational communication. Consequently Boland and Tenkasi maintain with reference to Mead (1934): 'The fundamental importance of taking the other's point of view into account is seen in Mead (1934) who referred to it as taking the attitude of the other and equated our ability to be fully human with our ability to maintain an inner conversation with a generalized other' (Boland and Tenkasi 1995: 358).

However, we question whether it can simply be assumed that organizational members possess the ability of perspective taking. Moreover a transfer of knowledge does not depend on perspective taking. Perhaps Boland and Tenkasi (as well as other authors) make the assumption that mechanisms like 'perspective taking' are required because they bear in mind models of communication which focus on the analysis of interaction between individuals or even between a generalized alter ego and ego akin to symbolic interaction as conceived by Mead. Mead (1934) was concerned with the process through which individuals construct a common definition of the situation from which they then infer what kind of behavior is expected in the further course of this interaction. However, processes which combine knowledge pertaining to specialized perspectives involves input from organizational members who are first of all representatives of different knowledge domains. As experts of different knowledge domains, it would not be functional for organizational members to start with the aim of constructing a common definition of the situation. All-encompassing, widely shared definitions of the situation would be too extensive to be handled by single individuals. A more appropriate approach is to generate knowledge that is compatible with the specific situations of the actors. In the case of rule changes this means that, from the perspectives of the affected units, a suggested rule version makes sense and appears implementable for all the affected departments. A more profound understanding of the input of other units is not required. Perspective taking is not necessary in order to be able to take the existence of other knowledge domains into account to a sufficient degree.

In contrast to the reviewed conceptions of a link between individual and organizational knowledge, our findings within a German bank suggest that the formation of significant amounts of shared knowledge is not a prerequisite for the transformation of individual knowledge into an organizational knowledge base. On the contrary, exactly because members of an organization specialize in their various fields they can produce rules that represent more experiential knowledge than individual organizational members could possibly grasp. The organizational members involved in the rule-change process get involved in the design process because they are specialists in their respective departments. It is due to their capacity as bearers of different specialized knowledge that they become valuable for the successful implementation of a rule change. None of these organizational members, however, has enough knowledge in different areas to be able to formulate a rule change without the advice of other specialists. In order to set up a rule which is practicable for all affected organizational members, it is not necessary, however, to develop either a mutual perspective and 'shared meanings' or a substantial amount of overlapping knowledge. It is sufficient that members of affected departments examine a suggested rule version. When these specialists assess a proposed rule they ask themselves whether it will be compatible with other rules and routines in their respective departments and suggest corrections that they consider necessary. In this way they add their specialized experiential knowledge to the new rule.

4 ORGANIZATIONAL LEARNING UNDER CONDITIONS OF BOUNDED RATIONALITY AND SPECIALIZATION: ELEMENTS OF A CONCEPT

Specialization as an Indissoluble Organizational Condition for Learning

In our review, we have tried to show that a number of approaches to organizational learning and knowledge integration tend to neglect elementary organizational conditions like specialization of organizational units and members as well as bounded rationality. We argue that these approaches therefore create problematic recommendations on how to achieve organizational learning and knowledge integration. The recommendations appear problematic because they are based on a conceptualization of knowledge integration that relies on knowledge sharing instead of framing the problem as one of recombining knowledge from different knowledge bases into a new knowledge base. However, when organizational members are specialized and are characterized by limited rationality, only a recombination of specialized individual knowledge is possible.

In the following we shall analyse the implications of bounded rationality for processes of organizational learning. Building upon the results of this analysis, we shall carve out some antecedents of a model which describes how individual experiential learning is transformed into an organizational knowledge base.

From a behavioral theory perspective, complex problems of organizational design are split into subproblems so that they become manageable for organizational members with limited rationality. A consequence of this specialization of organizational units is, however, that the knowledge required to bring about complex organizational outputs is dispersed among different actors. And in order to achieve organizational learning, knowledge which has been accumulated in different organizational units has to be recombined in a goal-directed fashion that does not require that the advantage of specialization is given up. This problem is universal insofar as it concerns societies as well as organizations, as Tsoukas (1996: 12) points out: 'there is a similarity between a society and a firm: both face the problem of how to use widely dispersed knowledge and, therefore, how to extend the span of utilization of resources in a way that exceeds the span of control of any one mind'. This means that we need to develop a model of organizational learning that describes a combination of knowledge (and its transfer into an organizational knowledge base) without assuming a high degree of knowledge sharing.

A combination of specialized knowledge is also central to the knowledge-based view, which takes the knowledge of organizational members as the most important strategic assets of organizations (Grant 1996a, 1996b; Kogut and Zander 1992, 1996; Zander and Kogut 1995). Since this knowledge is highly dispersed the question arises as to 'how to communicate from highly specialized bases of expertise to provide instructions and tools that are employable by large numbers of people' (Kogut and Zander 1996: 509). Or, in Grant's (1996a: 375) words: 'If the strategically most important resource of the firm is *knowledge*, and if knowledge resides in specialized form among individual organizational members, then the essence of organizational capability is the integration of individuals' specialized knowledge'. Consequently the proponents of this approach concentrate on the 'combinative capabilities' (Kogut and Zander 1992) that come into operation within organizations.

Such a mechanism cannot simply consist of organizational members learning as much as possible from one another so that, in the end, everyone possesses the knowledge that is required for solving a complex problem. There is a trade-off between specialization and knowledge sharing: 'Due to the cognitive limits of the human brain, knowledge is acquired in a highly specialized form: an increase in depth of knowledge implies reduction in breadth. Advances in knowledge tend to be associated with increased specialization' (Grant 1996a: 377). Demsetz (1991: 172) makes a similar observation: 'Although knowledge can be learned more effectively in a specialized fashion, its use to achieve high living standards requires that a specialist somehow use the knowledge of other specialists. This cannot be done only by *learning* what others know, for that would undermine gains from specialized learning'. An integration mechanism that minimizes the degree of mutual learning is required. 'But *transferring* knowledge is not an efficient approach to *integrating* knowledge. If production requires the integration of many people's specialist knowledge, the key to efficiency is to achieve effective integration while minimizing knowledge transfer through cross-learning by organizational members' (Grant 1996b: 114).

Our provisional conclusion is that sharing a certain amount of general knowledge is a necessary but not a sufficient condition for the integration of specialized knowledge in organizations which rely on the division of work. What is needed is an integration mechanism which does not rely on cross-learning.

Shared knowledge provides a basis for mutual understanding between 'departmental thought worlds' (Dougherty 1992: 182). For example, a common language or code facilitates communication between different specialized units that are characterized by different frames of thinking (Marengo 1996). The musical notation or the techniques for analysing workflows are examples of such languages. However, a common language only allows communication about specialized knowledge; it does not incorporate this knowledge. 'The importance of common knowledge is that it permits individuals to share and integrate aspects of knowledge which are *not* common between them' (Grant 1996b: 115–16). Those knowledge elements that are required for the design of a new rule version extend far beyond common knowledge.

In the following we concentrate on organizational mechanisms that enable organizational learning without presupposing a high degree of mutual learning of organizational members. We try to show that, even with very limited capabilities and in spite of maintaining a division of labor, a significant amount of learning can be achieved. By no means do we intend to design a comprehensive model of organizational learning, however. Rather our aim is to focus on possibilities of learning that are neglected in the literature reviewed above. This discussion is guided by three questions:

1. How is the knowledge that has to be recombined with respect to a specific problem identified within an organization, and how are organizational members who possess this knowledge identified?
2. To what extent are organizational rules an appropriate medium for storing knowledge that exceeds the memory capacity of individual organizational members?
3. Which are the mechanisms through which dispersed specialized knowledge is transferred and stored in a non-human medium like organizational rules?

The answers to these questions are finally integrated into a model of transactive organizational learning.

Transactive Memory in Organizations

If we try to solve a specific design problem that requires the recombination of specialized knowledge, the question arises as to which of the individual knowledge bases should be considered in the recombination process. If we overlook a relevant knowledge base a bad solution or even a non-workable solution may result (Hoopes and Postrel 1999). On the other hand it would be wasteful to consider a lot of knowledge that, in the end, turns out irrelevant. The recombination process should be efficient. But how can one identify the organizational members who have knowledge that is relevant for the problem at hand? Our model of organizational learning requires a mechanism that coordinates search in dispersed specialized memories.

The transactive memory concept (Liang et al. 1995; Wegner 1995; Wegner et al. 1991) proves helpful in identifying such a mechanism. From the perspective of this approach, groups manage to coordinate and to retrieve knowledge that is stored by different members of a group by simulating a shared memory. For example, the individual members of a family can specialize in storing different categories of knowledge. They, as a group, thereby manage to store more knowledge than individual members of the family could. In order to find out where a certain tool is located or what the status of the family budget is, it is sufficient to know which family member is specialized in storing the respective knowledge and to ask this person. For the individual family member it is not necessary to share the total knowledge that is available with the family but only a directory of this knowledge: 'Our directories for memories held by others can be thought of as metamemories. That is, they are memories about memories' (Wegner 1995: 326).

We hold that this concept of meta-knowledge or directory-knowledge can also be applied in descriptions of the connections between the knowledge bases of different specialists. The existence of this kind of knowledge could be observed in our case study. The first steps in processes that lead to a recombination of knowledge in organizational rules consisted in identifying the organizational units which would be affected by the intended rule change and, within these units, the persons who were the best informed to handle the problem at hand. This search could only be carried out with the help of meta- or directory-knowledge. However this directory-knowledge was not really shared in the organization of our case study. Rather, some organizational members in central staff positions turned out to be 'directory specialists' (ibid.: 328). They knew best which departments would be affected by a rule change and who could be considered a specialist in these departments. In contrast, organizational members on lower hierarchical levels could best evaluate whether a suggested rule version was implementable. Thus, in organizations we find several hierarchical levels of transactive memories (De Boer et al. 1999; Grant 1996a). One need not even know someone who knows something, it suffices to know someone who knows someone who knows something ...

For the solution of problems that only affect single subunits of an organization, our model of organizational learning based on rule changes would already be complete. With the help of the existing directory-knowledge (perhaps involving a directory specialist) the problem could be delegated to the organizational members who are specialists on the respective relevant knowledge. However, for design problems that involve complex processes across a number of specialized units, a recombination of specialized knowledge that is dispersed across different organizational units is required. The transactive memory concept can help to describe storage and retrieval among specialized organizational members. Additional concepts are needed, however, to understand how knowledge is recombined when rules are made and revised.

Rules as Media for Organizational Learning

Rules help individuals to learn by providing knowledge that enables them to solve problems fast and in a highly flexible fashion:

> Thousands of observations are summarized in the rules of physics and economics and transferred to novices who do not know and cannot reproduce that experimental and evidential base for the rules.

> Similarly, experience with technologies or marketing strategies are transferred to new technicians and new product managers in the form of rules that reflect but do not reproduce the experiences on which they are based. (March 1994: 33)

However individuals who know little beyond the text of formal rules cannot behave appropriately in changing situations and they cannot learn. It is necessary that they have some background knowledge about the interdependencies on which the rules are built and about the situations to which they have to be applied.

This also applies to organizational rules. They should not be regarded as fixed programs that are always executed in the same way every time a stimulus occurs. Rather they facilitate the development of organizational routines which support the work of organizational members (Kieser et al. 2001). Routines reside in the individuals' head and contain information on how to behave when certain rules apply. Thus as Pentland and Rueter (1994) point out with reference to Giddens (1984), even organizational interactions that are commonly held to be highly routinized are not automatic responses, but exhibit a considerable amount of variety and require effort from the participants to proceed successfully. Consequently they conceptualize routines as 'grammars of action' (Pentland and Rueter 1994: 489): just as the grammar of a language enables individuals to engage in conversations with changing contents, so the grammar of rules or routines enables individuals to perform complex tasks under changing conditions.

Formalized organizational rules can now be interpreted as a kind of protocol through which organizational members who are entitled to formulate those rules can effectively communicate the behavior they expect from organizational members in certain situations. A codification of rules, even if it is detailed, can only provide a limited description of the behavior that is considered appropriate by major actors. Since the designers of formal rules can never foresee all eventualities, they themselves have only limited ideas of how the actual behavior that is triggered by the rule will look like (Johnson 1977).

When a new rule is officially announced, the organizational members whose work is affected by it interpret it from their specific perspective, either as soon as they receive it or when they apply it in their work for the first time. The rule users are likely to simulate the work process according to the new rule in their imagination. Perhaps it is impossible to detect bugs in the rule before its application to work processes. Nevertheless, those for whom the rule is designed are also specialists who test the rule from their specific perspective, either in a thought experiment or during the first implementations. As long as they feel that problems can be dealt with within the range of possible interpretations of the rule text, they will not initiate changes in its formulation. However, if they think that the rule, as it was formulated will not work, or, in the light of experience they can see that it does not work, they will probably contact the rule designers – in the bank of our case study their telephone number is listed for this purpose next to the newly published rule – who then either suggest an interpretation of the rule that the rule user was not aware of or they will initiate a new round of expert evaluations and reformulation on the basis of the information that was provided by the rule user. Thus, the rule is exposed to the rule users as specialists just as earlier versions were exposed to the experts of the first group. Therefore, the exposure of rules to experts can be conceptualized as a multilevel process.

Simulated Prototyping as an Organizational Learning Mechanism

The transactive memory concept provides a mechanism for the coordination between specialized memories or, more precisely, for locating relevant knowledge bases in organizations.

Rules are a medium for which such a mechanism for identifying relevant knowledge can be utilized. The remaining question is what the mechanism for the recombination of knowledge looks like, and in particular, how does specialized knowledge find its way into a new rule?

As already mentioned, from the viewpoint of the behavioral theory, the answer is essentially a trial-and-error process: rules which do not produce the desired outcomes or do not prove to be feasible are changed, several times if necessary, or are replaced by new rules (Beck and Kieser 1997; Nelson and Winter 1982). This explanation, however, is not completely satisfactory. Failures that are due to faulty rules are costly. It therefore makes sense to ask whether organizations have developed a mechanism to avoid these costs. With the notion of 'inferential learning', Miner and Mezias give a clue as to the existence of such a mechanism:

> Inferential learning can be distinguished from pure trial and error learning, which does not require deductions about why particular behaviors have specific outcomes. Inferential learning can arise from informed observation of natural variation but also from active experimentation. ... Surprisingly, there is almost no research explicitly addressing organizational *experimentation* in pursuit of inferential learning. (1996: 92–3)

Miner and Mezias point to March et al.'s (1991) concept of simulating experience as an example of inferential learning. In this concept, March et al. describe various possibilities for organizations to learn effectively from rare experiences. One of these possibilities is simulating hypothetical events. This technique involves, for example, the application of fictitious 'near-histories': we try to learn from accidents which actually only almost occurred. 'Hypothetical histories' are a second possibility: we should try to use the little experience we have to construct a new theory, which, in turn, helps to produce hypothetical scenarios (March et al. 1991: 4–5).

Following this line of theorizing, we suggest a further possibility for simulating experience: to conduct concerted thought experiments. A proposal for a new rule or a rule revision is presented to organizational members from different departments who possess experiential knowledge. The organization learns by submitting a rule version for evaluation by organizational members from different subunits who have relevant experience. When organization members discuss the feasibility of suggested rule versions and make suggestions for improvement, these reflect their experiential knowledge. This procedure resembles the simulation of a trial-and-error process: feedback on rules is not provided on the basis of actual experiences with a new rule or rule version but through – if necessary repeated – assessments by experienced organizational members from their specific perspective. When the assessment of the rule version no longer triggers suggestions for correction, that is, it passes all the required 'trials' (each assessment representing one trial), then the rule becomes official. Each 'error' (each feedback that a suggested rule version is not feasible, is interpreted as an error) necessitates a reformulation.

We suggest that recurrent exposure of alternative rule drafts to the specialized knowledge of relevant experts represents a mechanism for recombining knowledge. This view also suggests a comparison of rule versions with prototypes. The expression prototype usually denotes the first exemplars of product innovations. We hold, however, that the 'prototype' is an appropriate metaphor for the description of the rule-change processes that we have observed in our case study. This comparison underlines the experimental character of the process for the recombination of knowledge that we have conceptualized. A rule version is presented to different specialists for approval, just as a prototype serves to trigger feedback from experts.

Leonard (1998), for example, explicitly compares the process of prototyping to the simulation of changing environmental conditions: 'Companies gain an inherent advantage in learning when employees can simulate an outside market – in effect, prototyping the conditions that the new product will face when launched' (Leonard 1998: 125). She also points out that the aim of such a process is 'to execute a design on a small scale as a knowledge-generating experiment' (ibid.: 127).

5 A CONCEPT OF TRANSACTIVE ORGANIZATIONAL LEARNING

How can organizations learn when they depend on the division of labor and when their members are equipped only with limited rationality? This was the guiding question of our discussions in the preceding sections. More specifically we dealt with three problems:

1. How can relevant specialized knowledge be identified and incorporated in rules?
2. What is a possible medium for a recombination of specialized knowledge?
2. How could the knowledge get into this medium and what could the process of recombination look like?

The mechanisms that we have conceptualized in order to answer these questions had been triggered by our observation of the rule-change processes within a German bank. In this section, we try to integrate these mechanisms into a framework of transactive organizational learning.

The transactive memory concept describes how organizational members can specialize in numerous separate disciplines of knowledge and at the same time simulate a joint memory. In this way it is possible to identify the relevant knowledge and to localize it in organizations without having to share it between organizational members. 'Just as we can separate knowing something from knowing that we know it, we may know that others know something without knowing it ourselves' (Wegner 1995: 326). Formal organizational rules, just like new products or prototypes, provide a medium on the basis of which specialized knowledge can be recombined. More knowledge can be considered in the design of such a medium than a single human memory can possibly store. From this perspective the recombination of specialized knowledge bases does not take place in the minds of individual organizational members but is achieved through the application of these knowledge bases to an organization-specific medium.

Prototyping represents a possible mechanism by which specialists can contribute their specialized knowledge to organizational rules without having to overextend their limited cognitive capabilities. Drafts of new rule versions are presented to a number of organizational members with different specialized knowledge for examination and, possibly, correction. In this view rules 'learn' through exposure to experts. Several rounds are possibly necessary before each specialist lets the latest draft pass without further correction. The cognitive requirements for such a process should be much lower than for intensive mutual learning and sharing of a number of extended knowledge bases. Furthermore it is much easier for an expert to judge whether a proposed rule version will function well than having to specify, from his or her perspective, all requirements this organizational rule has to fulfill.

However, how rational are processes of organizational learning that make only modest demands on the rationality of the actors involved? As we have shown in the introduction, the behavioral theory conceptualizes the learning of organizations as adaptively rational. Rules that appear as problematic, that is which no longer guarantee goal achievement, are replaced by more effective ones. The selection of rule versions can be seen as experimentation. Organizations experiment with revised rules. From this perspective the processes of rule change that we have explored also represent a form of adaptively rational organizational learning. A rule version that is submitted to an expert for evaluation also represents a kind of experiment. However, in contrast to what behavioral theory seems to suggest, the experiments that we have described are only thought experiments or simulations of real experiments. Organizational learning in this phase is not based on experiencing but uses experience of organizational members prospectively. A new rule-version is not (only) tested by implementing it and evaluating how it subsequently affects organizational performance. Rather the experience of organizational members is used as much as possible before a new rule is officially implemented. From this perspective new knowledge that broadens the action potential of an organization results not only from new experiences but also from recombining existing experiential knowledge. These insights add to the conceptualization of adaptive rationality of behavioral theory.

Of course, cycles of repeated tests of consistency with local conditions can be interrupted in several ways. It is not clear what happens, for example, when some powerful areas are overrepresented or if the experts have incompatible requirements. In addition, even without such interruptions, it is not difficult to point out potential misdirections of organizational learning processes that are restricted to mechanisms of the kind we have suggested. A permanent focus on consistency between activities of different departments maximizes the implementability of solutions. At the same time, however, there is a danger of growing inertia with regard to fundamental change.

We never intended to build a comprehensive model that ensures global optima, though. On the contrary our aim was to draw a deliberately one-sided picture of organizational learning in order to point out how, even with very limited capabilities, a substantial amount of learning can be achieved. Therefore in the following, we concentrate on the question of how organizational learning mechanisms that rely on past experiences and are subjected to bounded rationality allow for a flexible and dynamic adaptation of rules. Drawing on Teece et al. (1997: 516), who define dynamic capabilities as 'the firm's ability to integrate, build and reconfigure internal and external competencies to address rapidly changing environments', we can also talk of an organization's dynamic capability for the adaptation of organizational rules. In the following we explore aspects of our framework that might be regarded as dynamic capabilities.

To begin with, we suggest that a minimal overlapping of specialized knowledge domains allows a flexible recombination. 'Modularity is especially important in organizing highly complex capabilities which involve broad-scope knowledge integration' (Grant 1996a: 381). Similar to modular systems in computer or car production, knowledge bases can be developed separately and recombined in a goal-directed fashion (Sanchez and Mahoney 1996). Modules of specialized knowledge can be recombined faster and more flexibly than cumulated experiences of specialists and their cognitive patterns can be altered, and this is what dynamic capabilities are based on. Besides, a strong overlapping between knowledge domains would have to be restricted to a limited number of subunits, and this would restrict search in areas outside the respective clusters (Granovetter 1973; Hansen 1999).

Moreover, the idea that a great deal of experiential knowledge is routinized, that is, it is stored in mental scripts and schemas, does not necessarily reduce the dynamics and flexibility of organizational learning. On the contrary: while scripts and schemas – routines – in isolation from each other may only produce a foreseeable reaction to a stimulus (Nelson and Winter 1982), routines in combination with other experiences enable organizational members to generate highly flexible responses (Narduzzo et al. 1997). On the basis of their routines, the specialized actors can imagine which effects a hitherto unknown stimulus can have; they can imagine whether a suggested rule version is likely to work properly. From this perspective, routines can take the role of experimental conditions in a simulation model. Thus, an assessment of whether a suggested rule version makes sense or requires improvement can be reached much faster than by a process in which actors try to design a rule rationally in a one-shot process by taking into consideration all relevant aspects. In this view, prototyping has the potential to be faster than intended rational design, in spite of, or because, loops occur. In many cases, a great number of thought experiments or 'design iterations' (Eisenhardt and Tabrizi 1995), perhaps allow more dynamic adaptation than intendedly rational one-shot design processes, which require a lot of cognitive effort.

6 CONCLUSION

Organizational learning has become a buzzword within the arena of popular management concepts (for example, Senge 1990) as well as within academic circles. More recently, this field has been absorbed by concepts of knowledge management and associated themes of effective storage, identification, and retrieval of knowledge (Nonaka and Takeuchi 1995). As we have attempted to show in this chapter, the behavioral theory which was founded by Dick Cyert and his students in the early 1960s still proves to be a most fruitful theoretical basis for the development of concepts of organizational learning and knowledge management. Original formulations of the behavioral theory provided rough descriptions of rule-creation processes and established a conceptual foundation for explorations of how feedback from the environment leads to improvements of rules. In this study, we have attempted to build on to that theory and submit that feedback from thought experiments conducted by specialized organizational experts can increase the effectiveness of new rules before they are implemented and exposed to their environment. This involves a kind of variation that is not 'blind', and which stands in contrast to notions prevalent in the population ecology approach (Hannan and Freeman 1984: 151). Rather, in the context of organizational learning, organizational variation is informed by specialized knowledge that is recombined during the process of designing a new rule or a rule revision. Nevertheless organizational learning remains an evolutionary adaptively rational process since the specialists' rationality remains limited. However, evolutionary mechanisms are themselves subject to an evolutionary process. Organizations improve their capabilities for storing relevant knowledge, for localizing relevant knowledge, and for bringing it to bear on the generation of rule variations. That way, organizations also learn to improve internal selection before 'external' selection takes place.

It is amazing that so many concepts of organizational learning and knowledge management concentrate their analysis on the question of how organizational members can learn as much as possible from one another. Under the conditions of limited rationality and specialization it seems at least equally appropriate to ask how new knowledge can be created when mutual learning is minimized. We can give only a very tentative answer: the vision of intelligent people who build teams or communities in which they exchange their knowledge and jointly struggle for the most creative solutions is obviously a highly attractive one. Of course the team members may make use of the internet and intranet in order to retrieve relevant knowledge, but, in any case, they should form teams or communities in which creativity blossoms. It has become commonplace that modern managers or leaders have to fight bureaucracy, and organizational rules are part of bureaucracy. Yet the enabling features of rules (Adler and Borys 1996) are more and more lost from sight.

Of course the empirical data which triggered our analysis was extremely limited. It would be desirable to collect more extensive data based on observations of ongoing processes of rule changes and on the factors that inhibit or facilitate the assessment of suggested rules by specialized organizational experts. An analysis of the different versions of rules that are generated during rule-change processes and a reconstruction of these processes in interviews with the organizational members involved on the basis of these documents might prove a helpful research strategy in this context.

Much needs to be done, and can be done, for extending the concept of organizational learning that was originally developed by Dick Cyert and his students as a part of the behavioral theory.

A Concluding Personal Note by Alfred Kieser

As a student of organizational behavior in Germany who had earned his Diploma, an equivalent to an MBA, in 1967, I had become thoroughly impressed by three books: Simon (1958), March and Simon (1958) and Cyert and March (1963). These books fascinated me through their 'real science' content. Namely, they contained testable hypotheses. Such an approach contrasted sharply with the organizational rules of thumb and 'proverbs' (March and Simon 1958: xxxiii) or principles of organizational design *à la* Fayol (1930) or Gulick and Urwick (1937) that were still in vogue in the German textbooks on organizations of this time.

The knowledge that I was able to gain from these three books proved to be highly influential in the first step of my career as a student of organizations. Still a graduate student, I became an expert on the Carnegie-Mellon approach (at this time still a Carnegie approach) to organizational analysis and a dedicated advocate for the replacement of 'organizational proverbs' through scientific analyses. My co-students and professors who had not read these three books with the same intensity were impressed with my arguments. So I decided to continue my studies with a PhD in organization theory. I won a scholarship which allowed me to spend a year as a special student at the Graduate School of Industrial Administration (GSIA) at the Carnegie Institute of Technology (which was later to become Carnegie-Mellon University). In my dissertation I constructed and analysed a simulation model of the firm, using the simulation models of Cyert and March (1963) and Bonini (1963) as examples. Dick Cyert agreed to set up a research seminar which would meet weekly with me as the only student. I was overwhelmed. In Germany, experience had shown that it was difficult to attract a professor's attention for 15 minutes in order to discuss various ideas (there was not a single female professor in the department at this time) with a professor who still taught organizational 'proverbs' – and now I could hold a 90-minute discussion each week with the co-author of one of my three most admired books. I was also able to attend two of Herb Simon's classes. Thanks to this intensive supervision and the fantastic working conditions at GSIA, my dissertation on the Growth of Firms (Kieser 1970) was completed within two years and submitted to the Faculty of Business Administration at the University of Cologne, Germany. Although I also used other theories after completing my dissertation, I always took a profound interest in the development of the behavioral theory. Some years ago I started a research program on decision rules as a media of organizational learning which is mainly based on this theory. Some preliminary results from this research program have been presented in this chapter. Without having experienced Dick Cyert as a most creative researcher, inspiring teacher, and extremely supportive person my present attitude towards organization theory and towards my students would certainly be a different one.

NOTES

* We are grateful to John Meyer, Martin Schulz and Peter Walgenbach for valuable comments to earlier versions of this chapter.

1. The study is part of the research project 'Standard operating procedures, decisions in organizations, and organizational learning' of the Sonderforschungsbereich 504 at the University of Mannheim. Support by the German Research Foundation is gratefully acknowledged.
2. The qualitative software tool ATLAS/ti was used to support the coding procedure and the analysis.
3. 'Q' stands for the interviewer. 'I' and the respective number stands for the interviewed person.
4. The name has been changed.

REFERENCES

Adler, P.S. and B. Borys (1996), Two types of bureaucracy: enabling and coercive', *Administrative Science Quarterly*, **41**, 61–89.

Araujo, L. (1995), 'Designing and refining hierarchical coding frames', in U. Kelle, G. Prein and K. Bird (eds), *Computer-aided Qualitative Data Analysis. Theory, Methods and Practice*, London: Sage, pp. 96–104.

Argyris, C. and D.A. Schön (1978), *Organizational Learning: A Theory of Action Perspective*, Reading, MA: Addison-Wesley.

Beck, N. and A. Kieser (1997), 'Standard operating procedures and organizational learning', University of Mannheim, SFB 504 Discussion Paper 97-34.

Boland, R.J. and R.V. Tenkasi (1995), 'Perspective making and perspective taking in communities of knowing', *Organization Science*, **6**, 350–72.

Bonini, C.P. (1963), *Simulation of Information and Decision Systems in the Firm*, Englewood Cliffs, NJ: Wiley.

Brown, J.S. and P. Duguid (1991), 'Organizational learning and communities-of-practice: toward a unified view of working, learning, and innovation'. *Organization Science*, **2**, 40–57.

Brown, J.S. and P. Duguid (1998), 'Organizing knowledge', *California Management Review*, **40**, 90–111.

Coffey, A. and P. Atkinson (1996), *Making Sense of Qualitative Data: Complementary Research Strategies*, Thousand Oaks, CA: Sage.

Cyert, R.M. and J.G. March (1963), *A Behavioral Theory of the Firm*, Englewood Cliffs, NJ: Prentice-Hall.

De Boer, M., F.A.J. Van Den Bosch and H.W. Volberda (1999), 'Managing organizational knowledge integration in the emerging multimedia complex', *Journal of Management Studies*, **36**, 379–98.

Demsetz, H. (1991), 'The theory of the firm revisited', in O.E. Williamson and S.G. Winter (eds), *The Nature of the Firm*, Oxford: Oxford University Press, pp. 159–78.

Dosi, G. (1988), 'Sources, procedures, and microeconomic effects of innovation', *Journal of Economic Literature*, **26**, 1120–71.

Dougherty, D. (1992), 'Interpretive barriers to successful product innovation in large firms', *Organization Science*, **3**, 179–202.

Eisenhardt, K.M. and B.N. Tabrizi (1995), 'Accelerating adaptive processes: product innovation in the global computer industry', *Administrative Science Quarterly*, **40**, 84–110.

Fayol, H. (1930), *Administration Industrielle et Générale* (Industrial and General Administration) London: Pitman & Sons.

Fiol, Mariene C. (1994), 'Consensus, diversity, and learning in organizations', *Organization Science*, **5**, 403–20.

Giddens, A. (1984), *The Constitution of Society: Outline of the 'Theory of Structuration*, Berkeley, CA: University of California Press.

Granovetter, M.S. (1973), The strength of weak ties', *American Journal of Sociology*, **6**, 1360–80.

Grant, Robert M. (1996a), 'Prospering in dynamically-competitive environments: organizational capability as knowledge integration', *Organization Science*, **7**, 375–87.

Grant, Robert M. (1996b), Toward a knowledge-based theory of the firm', *Strategic Management Journal*, **17** (Winter Special Issue), 109–22.

Gulick, L.H. and L.F.H. Urwick (1937), *Papers on the Science of Administration*, New York: Augustin M. Kelley.

Hannan, M.T. and J. Freeman (1984), 'Structural inertia and organizational change', *American Sociological Review*, **49**, 149–64.

Hansen, M.T. (1999), 'The search-transfer problem: the role of weak ties in sharing knowledge across organization subunits', *Administrative Science Quarterly*, **44**, 82–111.

Hedberg, B. (1981), 'How organizations learn and unlearn', in P. C. Nystrom and W.H. Starbuck (eds). *Handbook of Organizational Design. Volume 1: Adapting Organizations to Their Environments*, Oxford: Oxford University Press, pp. 3–27.

Hoopes, D.G. and S. Postrel (1999), 'Shared knowledge, "glitches", and product development performance', *Strategic Management Journal*, **20**, 837–65.

Johnson, B.M. (1977), *Communication: The Process of Organizing*, Boston, MA: Allyn & Bacon.

Kieser, A. (1970), *Untemehmungswachstum und Produktinnovation* (Growth of organizations and product innovation), Berlin: Duncker & Humblot.

Kieser, A., N. Beck and R. Tainio (2001), 'Rules and organizational learning: the behavioural theory approach', in M. Dierkes, J. Child and I. Nonaka (eds), *Handbook of Organizational Learning*, Oxford: Oxford University Press, pp. 598–623.

Kim, D.H. (1993), 'The link between individual and organizational learning', *Sloan Management Review*, **35**, 37–50.

Kogut, B. and U. Zander (1992), 'Knowledge of the firm, combinative capabilities, and the replication of technology', *Organization Science*, **3**, 383–97.

Kogut, B. and U. Zander (1996), 'What firms do? Coordination, identity, and learning', *Organization Science*, **7**, 502–18.

Leonard, D. (1998), *Wellsprings of Knowledge: Building and Sustaining the Sources of Innovation*, Boston, MA: Harvard Business School Press.

Levitt, B. and J.G. March (1988), 'Organizational learning', *Annual Review of Sociology*, **14**, 319–40.

Liang, D.W., R. Moreland and L. Argote (1995), 'Group versus individual training and group performance: the mediating role of transactive memory', *Personality and Social Psychology Bulletin*, **21**, 384–93.

Luhmann, N. (1972), *Funktionen und Folgen formaler Organisation* (Functions and Consequences of Formal Organization), 2nd edn, Berlin: Duncker & Humblot.

Luhmann, N. (1973), *Zweckbegriff und Systemrationalität* (Purpose and System Rationality), Frankfurt a. M.: Suhrkamp.

March, J.G. (1991), 'Exploration and exploitation in organizational learning', *Organizational Science*, **1**, 71–87.

March, J.G. (1994), *Three Lectures on Efficiency and Adaptiveness in Organizations*, Helsingfors: Swedish School of Economics and Business Administration.

March, J.G. and J.P. Olsen (1975), 'The uncertainty of the past: organizational learning under ambiguity', *European Journal of Political Research*, **3**, 147–71.

March, J.G. and H.A. Simon (1958), *Organizations*, New York: Wiley.

March, J.G., J.L. Sproull and M. Tamuz (1991), 'Learning from samples of one or fewer', *Organization Science*, **2**, 1–13.

Marengo, L. (1996), 'Structure, competence and learning in an adaptive model of the firm', in G. Dosi and F. Malerba (eds), *Organization and Strategy in the Evolution of the Enterprise*, London: Macmillan, pp. 124–54.
Mead, G.H. (1934), *Mind, Self and Society*, Chicago, IL: University of Chicago Press.
Miles, M.B. and A.M. Huberman (1984), *Qualitative Data Analysis: A Sourcebook of New Methods*, Beverly Hills, CA: Sage.
Miner, A.S. and S. Mezias (1996), 'Ugly duckling no more: pasts and futures of organizational learning research', *Organization Science*, **7**, 88–99.
Narduzzo, A., E. Rocco and M. Warglien (1997), 'Talking about routines in the field: the emergence of organizational capabilities in a new cellular phone network company', University of Trent, Computable and Experimental Economics Laboratory (CEEL), Working Paper 6-97.
Nelson, R.R. and S.G. Winter (1982), *An Evolutionary Theory of Economic Change*, Cambridge, MA: Harvard University Press.
Nonaka. I. (1991), 'The knowledge-creating company', *Harvard Business Review*, **69**, (November–December), 96–104.
Nonaka, I. (1994), 'A dynamic theory of organizational knowledge creation', *Organization Science*, **5**, 15–37.
Nonaka, I. and H. Takeuchi (1995), *The Knowledge-creating Company: How Japanese Companies Create the Dynamics of Innovation*, New York: Oxford University Press.
Pentland, B.T. and H.H. Rueter (1994), 'Organizational routines as grammars of action', *Administrative Science Quarterly*, **39**, 484–510.
Sanchez, R. and J.T. Mahoney (1996), 'Modularity, flexibility, and knowledge management in product and organization design', *Strategic Management Journal*, **17** (Winter Special Issue), 63–76.
Schulz, M. (1993), 'Learning, institutionalization and obsolescence in organizational rule histories', Dissertation Stanford University.
Senge, P.M. (1990), *The Fifth Discipline: The Art and Practice of the Learning* Organization, New York: Currency/Doubleday.
Simon, H.A. (1958), *Administrative Behavior*, 2nd edn, New York: Macmillan.
Simon, H.A. (1979), 'Rational decision making in business organizations', *American Economic Review*, **69**, 493–513.
Simon, H.A. (1991), 'Bounded rationality and organizational learning', *Organization Science*, **2**, 125–34.
Teece, D.J., G. Pisano and A. Schuen (1997), 'Dynamic capabilities and strategic management', *Strategic Management Journal*, **18**, 509–33.
Tesch, R. (1995), *Qualitative Research: Analysis Types & Software Tools*, 3rd edn, New York: Falmer Press.
Tsoukas, H. (1996). 'The firm as a distributed knowledge system: a constructionist approach', *Strategic Management Journal*, **17**, 11–25.
Wegner, D.M. (1995), 'A computer network model of human transactive memory', *Social Cognition*, **13**, 319–39.
Wegner, D.M., P. Raymond and R. Erber (1991), 'Transactive memory in close relationships', *Journal of Personality and Social Psychology*, **61**, 923–9.
Zander, U. and B. Kogut (1995), 'Knowledge and the speed of the transfer and imitation of organizational capabilities: an empirical test', *Organization Science*, **6**, 76–92.

12. Cognition and models of adaptive learning

Daniel A. Levinthal*

1 INTRODUCTION

A fundamental element of any social science model is how one is to characterize choice processes. Indeed, beliefs as to the appropriate starting-point for modeling individual decision making is a primary source of the great divide between the high-church of the neoclassical theory of the firm of microeconomics and deviant reform movements, such as the behavioral theory of the firm and evolutionary economics. My suspicion, though possibly false, is that readers of this volume are for the most part a self-selected group of believers in the truth and wisdom of a behavioral approach to understanding firms and therefore will dispense with efforts at convincing readers of its virtues.

Rather, I want to focus on some of the important challenges and difficulties that this intellectual tradition faces. In particular, I want to consider the uncomfortable role that free will and intentionality play in evolutionary theory. This is a natural problem for the evolutionary program, for it is an issue that biologists with wonderful models of genetic drift and selection have not faced. However, if Charles Darwin, one forefather of evolutionary thinking has little to offer on this issue, Herbert Simon, a different sort of forefather does have something to say.

For those who come to evolutionary theory via some prior training and unsuccessful socialization efforts within the economics profession (where unsuccessful is with respect to the established beliefs and norms of that profession), Simon is a critical way-station. Simon's suggestion to economists in 1955 was that they might which to reconsider the basic primitives of their models. Individuals do not optimize over a global set of latent alternatives, but satisificed – stopping their investigation of possible alternatives when a possible action is identified that is 'good enough'.

It is useful to return to this source document and observe the issues that it highlighted and those that remained in the background, which in turn gives us insight as to the subsequent path-dependent development of evolutionary models in economics and management.

Two points are focal in Simon's argument and they have served as central building blocks of behavioral economics since then. One is that only a subset of the entire space of alternatives is considered in a given choice setting. Furthermore, decision makers may be confronted with a sequential unfolding of these possible alternatives, even among the limited set considered. Second, he postulated that these alternatives are evaluated by a simple discrete value function that distinguished between satisfactory and unsatisfactory outcomes. In this sense, Simon substituted for the usual objective function of economic theory an additional constraint of what constitutes a feasible solution to the choice problem. The value function becomes no different than the requirement that, say in the context of the decision to purchase a home, the home has the requisite number of bedrooms.

What is less salient, though considered, in the original discussion is how actors are to evaluate the proposed solutions or alternatives. How do we know whether the various feasibility constraints are satisfied or not? Simon notes that there may be uncertainty as to whether a particular alternative may yield a state of nature that is in the satisfactory set or not, but the text suggests that this indeterminacy may be resolved by identifying a new alternative that does not suffer this risk. This discussion of the mapping of actions to outcomes (at least a discrete representation of the outcome space) points to an important lacuna in this early expression of behavioral economics and to its subsequent development as well.

While ideas of search are central in behavioral theories of the firm, the mechanisms by which these alternatives are evaluated are less clearly developed. Typical models of adaptive search have the following characteristics. Some space of possible alternatives is sampled. The realization from this 'draw' is then compared either to the current status quo action or in other cases to an aspiration level. When the space of alternatives constitute attributes such as prices, the model does not seem to require any elaboration. However, consider other possible spaces of alternatives, such as the space of possible spouses or the set of possible new production technologies for a factory. When presented with a new alternative from one of these sorts of 'spaces', how are we to recognize a satisfactory solution when we are confronted with one?

Quick inspection of a possible spouse or a production plan may reveal certain proposed alternatives to be unsatisfactory. Surface features of the proposed solution may violate one or more feasibility constraints. However, the satisfaction of other constraints, particularly the constraint associated with the value function, may not be so self-evident. Will this proposed spouse prove to be an enjoyable companion upon repeated dining experiences? Will he or she prove to be reasonably tolerant of your array of annoying habits? Similarly, how will the workforce respond to the production process? How reliable will the process prove?

The evaluation of proposed alternatives is a relatively undeveloped facet of the behavioral theory of the firm. To provide some structure with which to consider such issues, it is useful to distinguish between two sorts of evaluation mechanisms – 'on-line' and 'off-line' evaluation. On-line evaluation refers to those setting in which evaluation can only take place by actual trial of the proposed alternative, whereas off-line evaluation indicates the ability to assess value in the absence of such a trial. As with many dichotomies, this one is both informative and misleading. The distinction is clearly important. Some possibilities are evaluated by thinking, by imagining possible futures should that alternative (spouse, production process, car, and so on) be adopted. Sometimes this thinking is supported with various tools of analytical reasoning such as spreadsheets and yellow-pads.

However, the dichotomy is also quite misleading. There is an enormous gray area between these two poles and most evaluation processes occur somewhere in this intermediate zone. New production processes need not require shutting down the firm's entire operations and substituting the proposed process. One plant may serve as a test, while the prior technology is exploited in the remaining plants. In cases of more incremental changes, only a single line or shift of the production process may serve to provide an experiential basis on which to evaluate the proposal.

In other cases, an 'artificial' environment is created in order to evaluate a proposed alternative that does not introduce the risk associated with a full commitment. The natural examples of this in the spousal problem are first-dates, weekends in the country, and living together in an unmarried state. In the case of production processes, a pilot plant may be established. The pilot plant operates at a smaller scale than the ultimate substantiation of the alternative would imply, but again it allows a detailed examination of feasibility at lower cost and lower risk than full adoption.

A particular type of artificial environment, wind-tunnels, to test the performance of new aircraft, offers some additional insights as the boundaries of on- and off-line evaluation. Wind-tunnels allow engineers to test loft and drag in a variety of conditions of a possible airframe. However, wind-tunnels have substitute modes of evaluation. One of course is to engage in the enormous financial commitment of the full development of a working prototype and the human risk posed to the pilot of such craft. The other route is cognitive: to build computer models that simulate the performance of proposed designs. As knowledge of the underlying material and aeronautical engineering improves, off-line evaluation can substitute for more on-line forms of evaluation. But note that this is really a matter of degree. The computer simulator in some form creates its own kind of experience base. It is simply a lower-cost artificial world than ones that involve bending metal, such as wind-tunnels, or pouring concrete, such as pilot plants.

A different sort of experience is the experience of others (March et al., 1991; Miner and Haunschild, 1995). This sort of experience has the virtue that trial does not require the disruption of one's own activities and, furthermore, that the set of alternatives that are being explored at a given time are vast. Its weakness lies, of course, in the inferential difficulties that it poses. How much do I learn, by watching a woman with another man about what she would be like as a wife? Or, perhaps less daunting, how much does some other plant's experience tell me about my likely success with a new production technology? We are probably more comfortable with generalizing in the latter case, but that may in part stem from the fact that more of us have experience in being spouses than in being plant managers and are more keenly aware of the idiosyncratic features of such relationships than that of production processes.

In some sense, the issue of on- or off-line search becomes less a categorical distinction than factors that influence the cost, risk, and possibly accuracy of the evaluation process. On-line search often entails a particular sort of cost, that of the opportunity cost of not making use of established options. It is this opportunity cost that underlies the tension in the now oft-cited exploration–exploitation trade-off. In turn, the degree to which current operations are disrupted by the need to evaluate a proposed alternative influences how painful that trade-off is. Even learning from the experience of others entails a disruption cost as time devoted to intelligent inference is taken away from other potential uses.

These issues of the nature of evaluation processes are closely tied to the extensiveness and range of alternatives that are considered in a choice process. If alternatives can only be evaluated on the basis of a full and complete trial, then obviously search will be quite limited in terms of the number of alternatives that are considered. In the limit, for choices such as what a different chief executive might be like, an organization can only experience one alternative at any moment in time. To the extent that simulated trails can be held, what is this person like when he or she runs a division of the company, then multiple alternatives can be explored simultaneously. As one moves towards pure off-line evaluation of alternatives, a vast set of possible futures can be considered. Of course, the off-line evaluation of alternatives does not imply that these possible futures can be known with any degree of certainty; nor, for that matter, is on-line, experiential evaluation a sure guide to the future consequences of the sampled alternative.

Figure 12.1 characterizes search processes along three dimensions: the degree to which evaluation is on- or off-line, the extensiveness of the set of alternatives considered at one time, and the degree to which the alternatives considered are similar to or relatively distant from the present actions. Given this framing, we can locate a number different characterizations of choice processes. The classic model of rational choice can be positioned in this space as corresponding to the off-line evaluation of the whole set of alternatives, both local and distant. One might imagine, and cognitive psychology strongly suggests, a more limited form of off-line search. Individuals cannot imagine all possibilities but adopt mental frames that provide a particular perspective on the world that both constrains the set of alternatives that they consider as well as possibly distorts their evaluation of these alternatives. In contrast, processes of local experimentation (Cyert and March, 1963; Nelson and Winter, 1982) are examples of on-line evaluation. The alternative is explored through actual experience, rather than putatively in the form of a mental model. The process of logical incrementalism (Quinn, 1980), while also focused on a small set of alternatives in the near-neighborhood of current action, suggests the off-line evaluation of these alternatives.

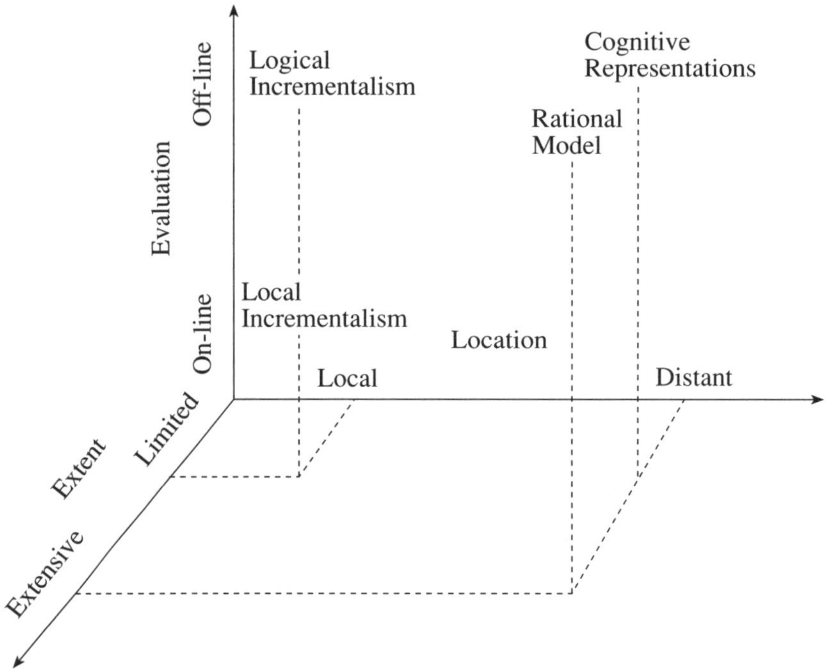

Note: From Gavetti and Levinthal (2000)

Figure 12.1 Choice processes

The localness of search under logical incrementalism is driven by the reduced demands on actors' power of off-line evaluation that alternatives that are not too different from current actions pose. Current actions provide a controlled base-line from which possible deviations can be judged. Both incremental search in the context of neighborhood search and logical incrementalism also have the virtue that the demands on implementing a new alternative are limited by its proximity to current action.

Neighborhood search in the context of experiential, or on-line, evaluation of alternatives, however, has additional virtue. Neighborhood search provides an effective, though not necessarily optimal, balance for the need to explore alternative bases of action at the same time that one exploits current wisdom about the world. The need for this balance between exploration and exploitation depends entirely on whether the evaluation process of proposed alternatives is on- or off-line. Thus, the wisdom of a particular sampling strategy is intimately connected to the form of evaluation of those samples that is possible. Many of our discussions of search processes have suffered by not sufficiently disentangling these two features of search processes.

To make this point clearer, a formal model of search processes is developed. The basis of this model structure is Kauffman's (1993) NK fitness landscape, which has proved to be a useful starting-point to consider issues of organizational adaptation (Levinthal, 1997; Gavetti and Levinthal, 2000; Rivkin, 2000). Section 2 introduces the basic structure of fitness landscapes and Section 3 provides the analysis of alternative search processes on these surfaces.

2 FITNESS LANDSCAPES

What might be a useful structure with which to consider these issues of search processes? One minimal criterion is that the search problem be fairly complex. Issues of appropriate sampling strategies and evaluation mechanism are germane to the extent that the decision problem exceeds the capacity of the decision-making agent. Of course, to some extent this criterion can be satisfied by the modeler sufficiently tuning down the assumed capacity of the agent being modeled.

A different sort of criteria has to do with the specific search process of neighborhood search. For this to be a meaningful notion, we must be able to characterize a sense in which there is localness in the search space – one alternative being more proximate than another. In particular, the notion of neighborhood search (Cyert and March, 1963) suggests that proximity implies a high degree of similarity in the actual behaviors and in the payoff associated with these behaviors.

An analytical structure that captures these notions of proximity is Kauffman's (1993) framework of NK fitness landscapes. This framework builds on Wright's (1931 and 1932) notion of a fitness landscape. Wright, a biologist interested in the evolution of organisms, considered the mapping of the attributes of organisms (genes) to the fitness level of the overall organism (that is, the phenotype). The variable N refers to the number of distinct attributes in an overall policy choice. For instance, in a choice of a firm's business strategy, a number of decisions must be made, including decisions about how the product or service is to be marketed, such as issues of brand name and distribution channels, and how it is to be produced, such as the degree to which activities will be done within the firm versus out-sourced. The variable K refers to the extent to which the payoff associated with one policy choice depends on other policy choices.

The degree of interrelationship among policy choices has a somewhat counterintuitive implication for the topography of a fitness landscape and, in turn, the similarity of adjacent points on the landscape's surface. The fitness landscape is the mapping from the N policy choices to a payoff value. When the value of K is low and there is little interaction among policy choices, then the fitness landscape is smooth or highly correlated. With a low value of K, a change in one policy has little impact on the fitness contribution of other choices. As a result, incremental changes in the vector of N policy variables have a relatively modest impact on overall performance. In contrast, with a high K value, a change in one policy, such as distribution strategy, has implications for the payoff contribution of a large number (K) of other policy choices. In such a setting, even an incremental change in the vector of N policy variables may substantially change the overall payoff level. As a result, the fitness landscape becomes less correlated, or equivalently, more rugged, with a high K value.

Figure 12.2 depicts a smooth fitness landscape. Adjacent locations within the landscape tend to have similar fitness values. This landscape has a further, and related, property in that there is only one peak in the landscape. The term 'peak' is defined as a point within the landscape such that any incremental movement from that location will diminish performance.

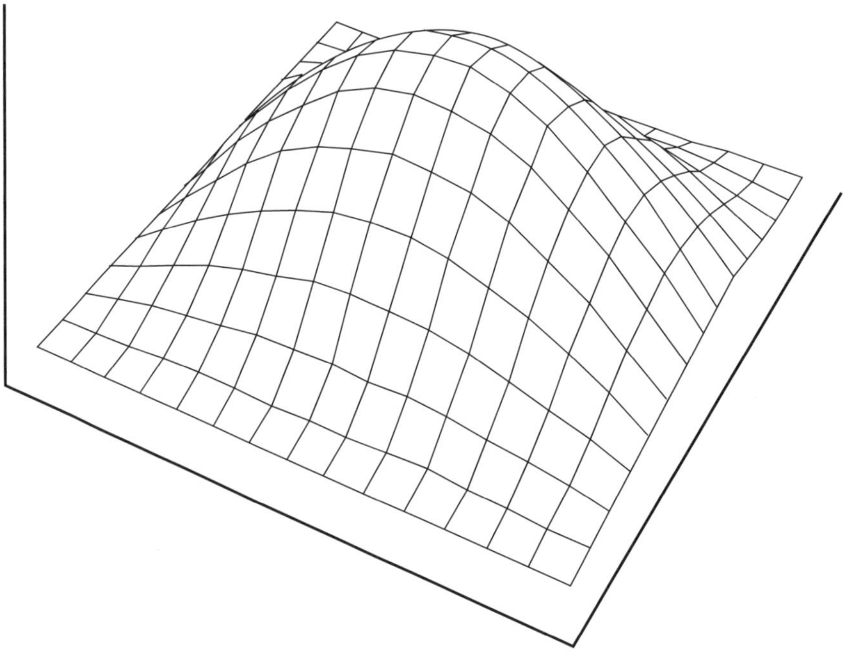

Figure 12.2 Smooth fitness landscape

However, when there are significant interaction effects among policy variables, there may be a number of local peaks. Figure 12.3 depicts such a landscape. Each peak can be viewed as comprising a consistent set of practices – a configuration in the language of Miller and Friesen (1984). With no interaction effects, the landscape has a single peak and one can identify superior policies or 'best practices', whose superiority is independent of the other characteristics of the firm. With substantial interaction effects, the notion of universal best practice is not valid.

More formally, the fitness landscape is modeled as follows.[1] A policy is characterized as consisting of N attributes where each attribute can take on two possible values. Thus, the fitness

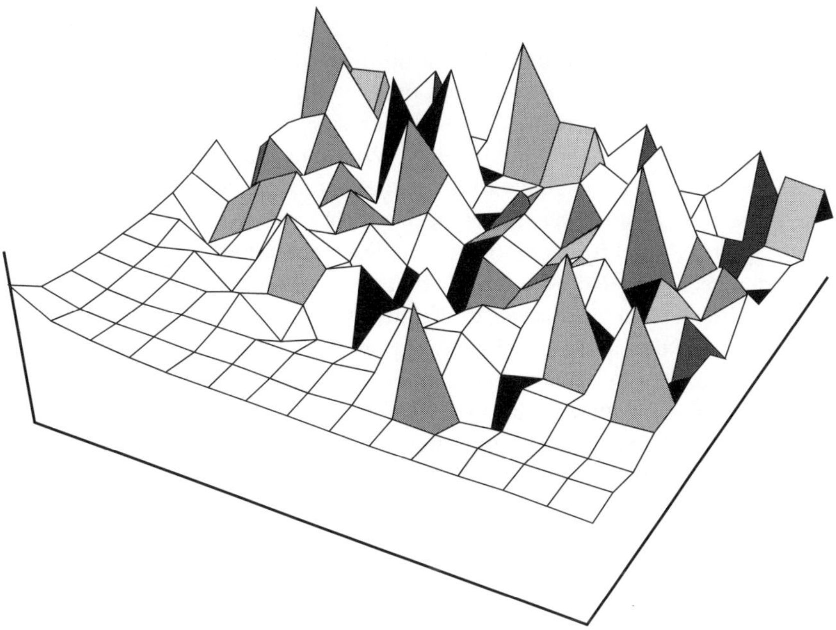

Figure 12.3 Rugged landscape

landscape consists of 2^N possible policy choices, with the overall behavior of the organization characterized by a vector $\{x_1, x_2, ..., x_N)$, where each x_i takes on the value of 0 or 1.

The contribution of a given attribute, x_i, of the policy vector to the overall payoff is influenced by K other attributes. As a result, the payoff to a particular choice, x_i, can be represented by the following expression: $f(x_i \mid x_{i1}, x_{i2},..., x_{iK})$. The K variables with which a given element x_i interacts is specified as being the K adjacent elements $(x_{i+1}, x_{i+2}, ..., x_{i+K})$.[2] Therefore, each attribute can take on 2^{K+1} different values, depending on the value of the attribute itself (either 1 or 0) and the value of the K other attributes with which it interacts (each of these K values also taking on a value of 1 or 0).

A random number drawn from the uniform distribution from zero to one is assigned to each possible $f(x_i \mid x_{i1}, x_{i2}, ..., x_{iK})$ combination. Thus, the framework specifies the intensity of interaction effects via the parameter K, but provides no restrictions on the particular functional form of the interaction effect. The overall fitness value associated with the full vector of N values, $F(x_1, x_2, ..., x_N)$, is simply the sum of these individual contributions divided by N:

$$F(x_1, x_2, ..., x_N)N = \Sigma_{i=1} f(x_i \mid x_{i1}, x_{i2}, ..., x_{i\mathrm{K}})/N.$$

3 SEARCH ON RUGGED LANDSCAPES

How can an organization move with some intelligence over a rugged landscape? There are a number of possibilities. Perhaps the most self-evident is for the organization simply to choose the global peak on the landscape. But how is a decision maker to be aware of the full surface of this, potentially complex space? Another possibility, explored with *NK* landscapes by Rivkin (2000), is some form of population learning. By examining and attempting to imitate the position of a successful organization, the organization may intelligently adapt.

The focus here is on processes of search by the focal organization. One possibility is local search (March and Simon, 1958; Cyert and March, 1963). Within the context of the *NK* model a neighborhood is defined as those forms that vary from the current organization by only one attribute. Therefore, if there are *N* attributes that comprise an organization, then each organization has *N* different organizational forms in its immediate neighborhood.

In contrast, radical change is modeled by assuming that each period, an organization draws at random a new organizational form in the space of 2^N alternatives. Kauffman (1993) uses the term 'long-jump' to indicate such a change. Following the terminology of Tushman and Romanelli (1985), such a change can be thought of as a reorientation.

Local and distant search are, however, simply characterizations of the sampling strategy of the search. While the literature has tended to suppress the mode of evaluation of these alternatives, it is a distinct and important issue. For instance, in his model of the evolution of proteins, Kauffman assumes that proteins identify superior alternatives in their immediate neighborhood and in that manner 'climb' the fitness landscape to a local peak in the fitness landscape. While sampling the fitness landscape via one-element mutations from the existing state seems sensible, the assumptions regarding the evaluation of the sampled alternative are not so obvious.

Although not expressed in this manner, the proteins in Kauffman's model (as in earlier work by Smith, 1970) are engaged in the off-line evaluation of the proposed new structure. That is, prior to the adoption of the new form, the new form is evaluated and is only adopted if it yields a higher fitness value than the current form. Proteins have many extraordinary properties, but the *ex ante* evaluation of possible new forms is unlikely to be one of them.

This *ex ante*, off-line evaluation of sampled alternatives is a mainstay of models of organizational adaptation that build on March and Simon (1958) and Cyert and March (1963). For instance, firms in Nelson and Winter (1982) draw from a set of possible alternatives and adopt the proposed alternative if in fact it is superior to the current technology – again, a form of off-line evaluation in the language developed here.

Certainly, the possibility of off-line evaluation seems much more compelling in the case of business firms than for proteins. However, we must take more explicit account of evaluation mechanisms in our models of search. One of the cornerstones of the notion of bounded rationality is that the set of possible actions is now known to the decision maker a priori, but must be 'discovered'. However, we need to fully acknowledge another truth. The evaluation of these alternatives subsequent to their identification is imperfect. The ability to make such evaluations depends on the quality of the decision maker's mental model of his or her decision environment and his or her ability to anticipate the consequences of the proposed actions. Thus, we need to balance our models of search processes with models of the evaluation of the proposed alternatives.

Local Search and the Exploration–Exploitation Trade-off

While an intuitive sense of these issues has been provided, it is helpful to put these issues more forcefully in the context of a formal model. I draw on the idea of the framework of fitness landscapes previously introduced. The following analysis contrasts the effect of alternative assumptions regarding the means by which alternatives are evaluated, on- or off-line, under two sampling strategies – local and distant search.

Figure 12.4 portrays the change in fitness level over time when the evaluation of alternatives corresponds to the perfect off-line evaluation typically postulated in such models. We see the pronounced increase in fitness with local search. However, somewhat surprisingly, we see an essentially equivalent rate of progress for sampling based on distant search. Indeed, at high K values the distant sampling strategy generates slightly higher asymptotic performance levels. How can this be? Local search has an inherent intelligence in its sampling behavior. If the current action yields a high level of fitness, then it is likely that actions in the neighborhood of the current state also will yield a high performance, possibly even higher than the current initiative. However, the long-jump search strategy consists of randomly trying alternatives out of the enormous space of 2^N possibilities. There is no intelligence in the search process. Poor-performing alternatives are as likely to be identified as are superior ones.

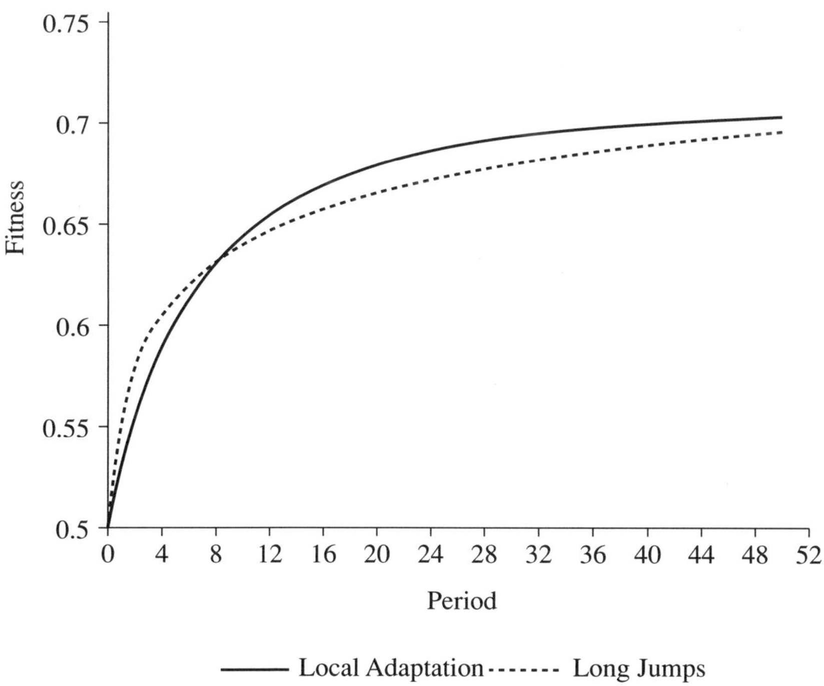

*Figure 12.4 Off-line search on a rugged landscape (*N *= 10,* K *= 3)*

The resolution of this puzzle lies in recognizing that the power underlying the adaptive capabilities of the two search processes characterized in Figure 12.4 stems from the assumed evaluation mechanism and is not dependent upon the sampling strategy. This is demonstrated by the stark contrast between Figure 12.4 and Figure 12.5, which models the same two sampling strategies of local and distant search under the assumption that alternatives can only be evaluated on-line through actual trial. If an action results in a lower level of fitness than the prior one, after this initial trial the alternative is rejected and the organization is assumed to return to its prior action. Alternatively, if the sampled alternative proves superior through trial, it is adopted and becomes the new starting-point for subsequent search efforts.

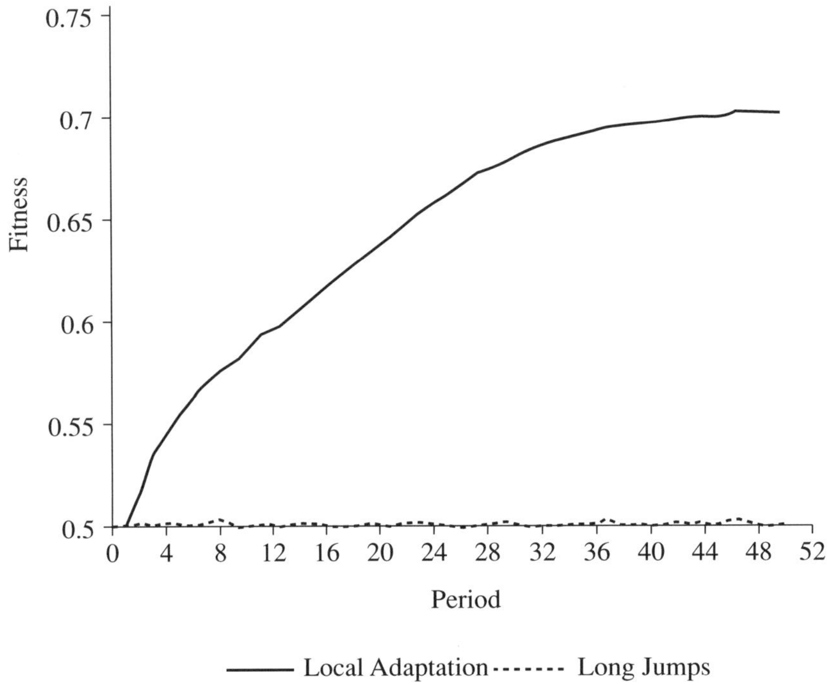

*Figure 12.5 On-line search with local and distant sampling (*N = *10,* K = *3)*

Neighborhood search has two important virtues in this context. First, and most important for our purposes, the sampling strategy of neighborhood search substantially reduces the risk associated with on-line search processes. Due to the correlated nature of the fitness landscape, as the organization improves its fitness level, it also, on average, improves the value of the alternatives that may be identified by neighborhood search. This 'boot-strapping' of organizational performance has a corresponding effect on the possible sample. This is not an artifact of fitness landscapes. Indeed, the appeal of fitness landscapes for this analysis is that it captures well the notion of a neighborhood of related, both in behavior and performance terms, alternatives.

The other relevant property of neighborhood search is that it has a built-in stopping rule of some intelligence. If the organization has a memory of prior alternatives that had been sampled and chooses not to revisit inferior actions, then neighborhood search will cease when the organization has identified a local peak in its neighborhood and the organization has convinced itself through trial of all adjacent points that its current action is indeed a local peak.

However, this property of a stopping rule is not critical to the power of neighborhood search. Figure 12.6 carries out the same analysis as in Figure 12.4, with the only difference being that organizations are assumed to have memory of only their most recent experience – only enough memory to return to the prior status quo if that proves to be superior to the most recent alternative sampled. It is striking how little both curves are affected by this shift in assumption. In the absence of memory, search continues indefinitely under both local and distant search. With local search, however, the organization wanders around a local peak in the landscape. In the case of distant search, the organization continues its series of random draws as long as the space of possible alternatives, 2^N, exceeds the time horizon considered. In such settings, the only impact of memory under distant search is whether sampling takes place with or without replacement.

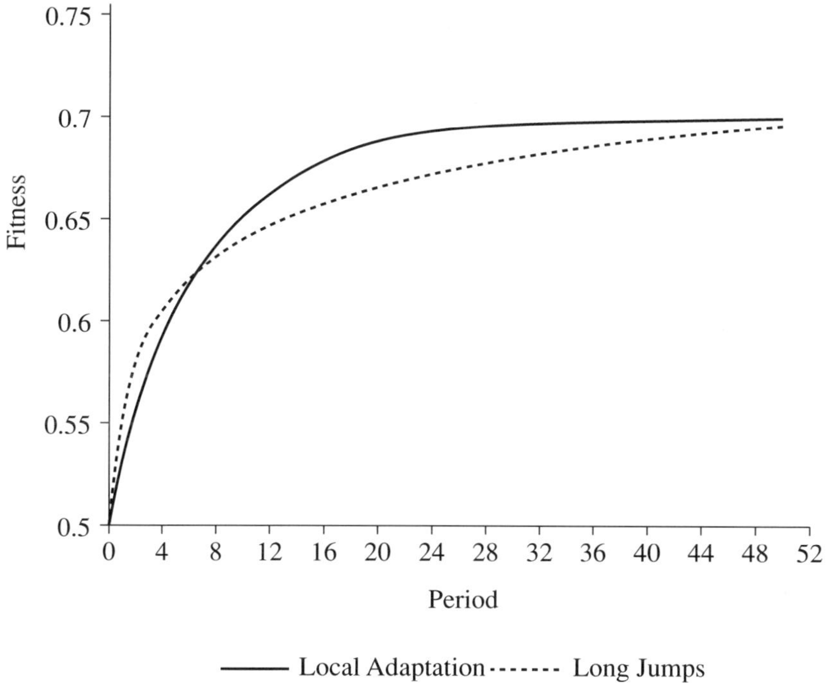

*Figure 12.6 Off-line search on a rugged landscape with memory (*N = *10,* K = *3)*

Of course, one might postulate a more sophisticated stopping rule for distant search. Figure 12.7 illustrates the performance of distant search under a variety of aspiration levels or stopping rules such that search ceases when the specified fitness level is obtained. As illustrated by Figure 12.8, a higher value of the stopping rule raises the asymptotic level of performance but tends to slow the rate at which the asymptote is approached.

While the stopping rule can be specified such that the asymptotic value of fitness is similar to that achieved under neighborhood search, distant search still suffers from a substantial difficulty. Until that point at which the aspiration level is reached, the organization's performance will vary in a random manner and have an average payoff corresponding to the average of the fitness landscape as a whole. Figure 12.9 provides an illustrative example of this phenomenon from a single run of the simulation. Therefore, in a competitive context, such organizations are likely to be killed off by competitors using a sampling strategy of local search. In a competitive context, parity in the asymptote offers little solace.

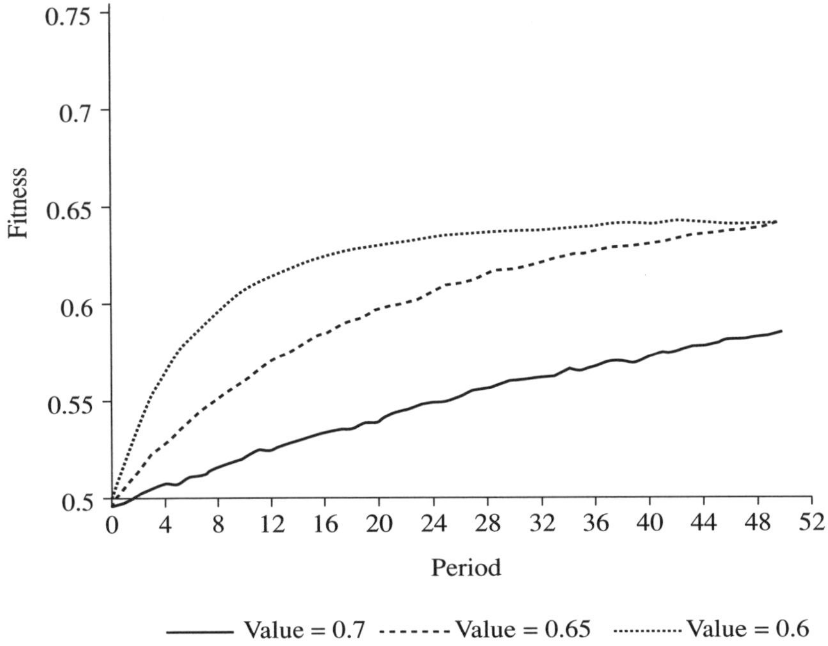

*Figure 12.7 On-line distant search with stopping rules (*N = *10,* K = *3)*

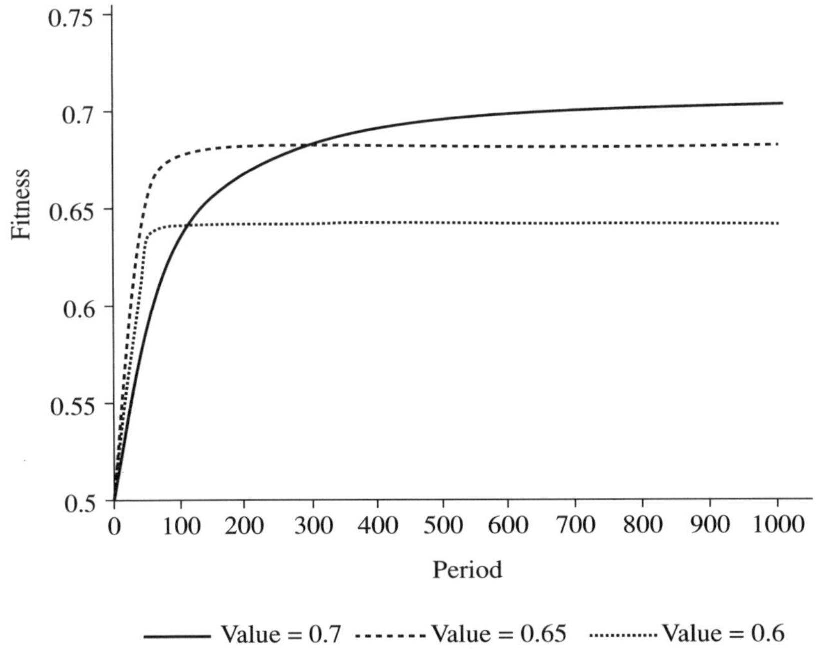

*Figure 12.8 Asymptotic performance under on-line distant search with stopping rules (*N = *10,* K = *3)*

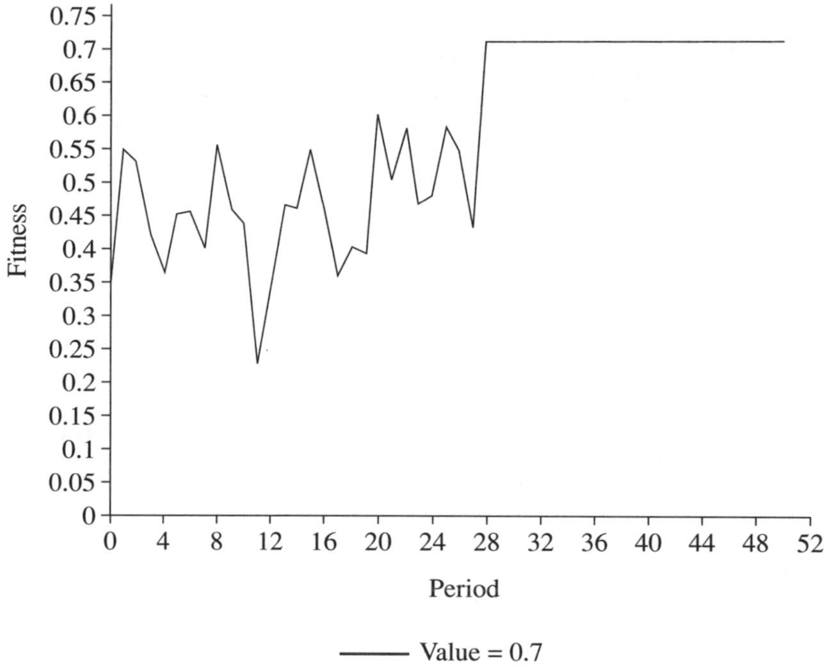

Figure 12.9 Organizational level performance under on-line distant search with stopping rules (N = *10*, K = *3)*

Mental Models and Adaptive Search

The behavioral economic research program has made considerable progress and has engendered a subfield that its pioneers should view with enormous pride. However, in the effort to contrast the strong rationality assumptions of traditional economic models, this research tradition may have overshot the middle ground that the notion of bounded rationality attempted to capture. Experiential trial and reinforcement learning is clearly an important form of adaptation. In addition, adaptation takes place at the population level in the form of differential growth rates (Nelson and Winter, 1982) and differential selection (Hannan and Freeman, 1989). However, behavioral models should incorporate not only such backward-looking forms of rationality (Gavetti and Levinthal, 2000) but also the logic of consequences (March, 1994). Consequential reasoning is hidden or absent in most of our behavioral models. As we address the consequential reasoning implicit in our models of search and develop more explicit representations of cognition, we return to and enrich the original agenda of the behavioral economic research program.

NOTES

* I thank Giovanni Gavetti and Sid Winter for many stimulating discussions of these issues and Jim March for comments on a prior draft.

1. Figures 12.2 and 12.3 provide an intuitive sense of smooth and rugged landscapes; however, these graphs do not directly correspond to the formal model. The formal model constitutes a hyper-cube, a multidimensional discrete space, rather than the three-dimensional continuous curve depicted in the figures.
2. The vector is treated as circular for the purposes of determining fitness values. For instance, if $N = 10$ and $K = 3$, then the fitness contribution of the ninth element in the vector will depend on the value of the tenth, first, and second elements in the vector. An alternative formulation of the model is to postulate that the interaction effects are with K randomly chosen other elements of the vector. This alternative formulation results in a similar fitness landscape (Kauffman, 1989).

REFERENCES

Cyert, Richard and James G. March (1963), *A Behavioral Theory of the Firm*, Englewood Cliffs, NJ: Prentice-Hall.
Gavetti, Giovanni and Daniel Levinthal (2000), 'Looking forward and looking backward: cognitive and experiential search', *Administrative Science Quarterly*, **45**, 113–37.
Hannan, M. and J. Freeman (1989), *Organizational Ecology*, Cambridge, MA: Harvard University Press.
Kauffman, Stewart (1989), 'Adaptation on rugged fitness landscapes', in D. Stein (ed.), *Lectures in the Sciences of Complexity*, Reading, MA: Addison-Wesley, 517–618.
Kauffman, Stewart (1993), *The Origins of Order*, New York: Oxford University Press.
Levinthal, Daniel (1997), 'Adaptation on rugged landscapes', *Management Science*, **43**, 934–50.
March, James G. (1994), *A Primer on Decision Making*, New York: John Wiley & Co.
March, James G. and Herbert A. Simon (1958), *Organizations*, New York: John Wiley & Co.
March, J.G., L.S. Sproull, and M. Tamuz (1991), 'Learning from samples of one and fewer', *Organization Science*, **2**, 1–13.
Miller, D. and P. Friesen (1984), *Organizations: A Quantum View*, Englewood Cliffs, NJ: Prentice-Hall.
Miner, Anne and Pam Haunschild (1995), 'Population level learning', in L.L. Cummings and B.M. Staw (eds), *Research in Organizational Behavior*, Greenwich, CT: JAI Press, 115–66.
Nelson, Richard and Sidney Winter (1982), *An Evolutionary Theory of the Firm*, Cambridge, MA: Harvard University Press.
Quinn, J.B. (1980), *Strategies for Change: Logical Incrementalism*, Homewood, IL: Irwin.
Rivkin, J. (2000), 'Imitation of complex strategies', *Management Science*, **46**, 824–44.
Simon, Herbert A. (1955), 'A behavioral model of rational choice', *American Economic Review*, **69**, 99–118.
Smith, J.M. (1970), 'Natural selection and the concept of a protein space', *Nature*, **225**, 563.
Tushman, M. and E. Romanelli (1985), 'Organization evolution: a metamorphosis model of convergence and reorientation', in L.L. Cummings and B.M. Staw (eds), *Research in Organizational Behavior*, Greenwich, CT: JAI Press, 171–22.
Wright, S. (1931), 'Evolution in Mendelian populations', *Genetics*, **16**, 97–159.
Wright, S. (1932), 'The role of mutation, inbreeding, cross-breeding and selection in evolution', *Proceedings XI International Congress of Genetics*, **1**, 356–66.

13. The relative standing of routines: some jobs are more equal than others

Thekla Rura-Polley and Anne S. Miner*

ALL ANIMALS ARE EQUAL
BUT SOME ANIMALS ARE MORE
EQUAL THAN OTHERS
(George Orwell 1945)

1 INTRODUCTION

Organizational routines frequently guide organizational activity (Cyert and March 1992 [1963]; Nelson and Winter 1982; Barley 1986; Amburgey and Miner 1992). However, anecdotal and systematic qualitative evidence suggest that not all routines 'are created equal' – in the sense that they are equally embedded in the normal workings of organizations (Rogers 1995, p. 399). Some routines are deeply entrenched in the normal workings of their organizations – as when naval blockade procedures, developed in the age of pirates, guided actions in the 1964 Missile Crisis (Allison 1971). Other routines gain formal standing but may remain marginal to the regular activities of an organization – as when a longstanding procedure in an administrative handbook is rarely followed.

In Cyert and March's (1992 [1963]) classic behavioral model of the firm, creating, following, and maintaining routines turns an organization into 'an *adaptively rational* system rather than an *omnisciently rational* system' (1992, p. 117). Adaptation occurs at many levels; some new routines are created while existing routines sustain continuity (Cyert and March 1992 [1963], p. 122). In this chapter we argue that routines differ in the degree to which they are seen as part of the normal workings of an organization (Cyert and March 1992 [1963]; Argote and Epple 1990; Epple et al. 1996; Argote 1999). Moreover, we propose that organizational learning processes will influence a routine's relative standing, or in other terms, its degree of routinization. We further contend that social factors and processes influence the degree of such routinization and ultimately, that social factors moderate the learning processes (Berger and Luckman 1967; Barley 1986; Scott 1987; Zucker 1977; Mezias 1990; Mezias and Scarselletta 1994; Miner 1994). We test these ideas using data on 210 individual formalized jobs in 43 departments in a large, decentralized organization over a seven-year period – defining the jobs as a special type of organizational routine (Miner 1991).

Our results indeed show that learning processes affect the relative standing or degree of routinization of jobs. Furthermore, person–job links and organizational uncertainty and ambiguity also influence the level of the routinization. of jobs. Finally, the data suggest that social features moderate learning effects, but only for jobs assessed as making a moderate contribution. This is consistent with the notion that social processes have more explanatory power when technical contributions are difficult to assess (Salancik and Pfeffer 1978; Haunschild and Miner 1997; March and Olsen 1989). Our findings reaffirm in many ways the invigorating and enduring richness of Richard Cyert's insights into organizational processes.

We also believe that findings about the relative standing of routines are ultimately important for broader theories of organizational action. March and Olsen (1989) distinguish two forms of logic that are commonly used to explain action. In the logic of consequences, actions are driven by expectations of their consequences, as assumed in many instrumental models of rational choice and political action. In the logic of appropriateness, actions are driven by enacting identities, roles, and rules. We think that the degree to which a given routine is seen as part of the normal organizational workings affects the nature and strength of appropriate action and may consequently influence the nature of organizational action. Although our study does not examine such potential consequences of the relative standing of routines, this potential linkage forms an important backdrop for our investigation.

In the next section, we briefly review the literature on organizational routines and routinization to clarify the framing of our empirical study. We then develop our argument about how learning and social processes affect the degree of routinization (Section 3), and proceed to methodological issues (Section 4). Results (Section 5), discussion and implications (Section 6) follow. Section 7 concludes.

2 ORGANIZATIONAL ROUTINES, JOBS, AND ROUTINIZATION

Organizational Routines

In their original work, Cyert and March (1992 [1963]) emphasized four types of procedures which generated both stability and de facto decisions: task performance rules, continuing records and reports, information-handling rules, and plans. Theorists have built on the intuition behind this description of standard operating procedures to develop more general notions of organizational routines. In the process of developing the concept of routines further, researchers have used a number of distinct definitions of routines. For instance, routines have been contrasted with non-routine practices or decisions (March and Simon 1958; Perrow 1986 [1972]), compared with genes in biological sciences (Nelson and Winter 1982), and called sets of functionally similar patterns (Pentland and Rueter 1994) (see review by Bodewes 1998).

These widely varying views on and definitions of routines may have slowed down the development of overarching theories, although they also reflect varying theoretical concerns with the creation, negotiation or impact of routines. For example, Berger and Luckmann (1967) contended that stable behavior unfolds over time through several distinct phases. Neoinstitutional theorists highlight the powerful role of 'taken-for-granted' stable practices (Zucker 1977; Scott 1987; Jepperson 1991) in guiding immediate action. Evolutionary and learning theorists have explicated models of organizational routines and their role in long-term organizational inertia and change (Nelson and Winter 1982; Miner 1990, 1991; Baum and Singh 1994; Cohen and Bacdayan 1994). However, on close inspection, these insights sometimes draw upon substantially different notions of what a routine is.

When we reviewed varied threads of extant theory, we found three implicit but distinguishable themes in defining routines themselves, as shown in Table 13.1. Some definitions evoke consistency or stability of action while others evoke codification of potential action, the latter being the core of our own approach. Within those themes, some work emphasizes routines as executable, consistent performance capabilities, emphasizing execution. Other work envisages organizational routines as habituated action, defined as a repeatedly recurring action which acquires an automatic status. The accumulation of knowledge on routines will be facilitated by explicating the underlying notion of routine in a particular study. Our research is rooted in the general definition of routines as consistent, repetitive action or codes for action. In this particular study, we sought to examine routines that represent executable, consistent performance capabilities.

Table 13.1 Definitions of routines

Source	Text
(a) Routines as repetitive consistent activity or codes	
Nelson and Winter (1982, p. 97)	'We use "routine" in a highly flexible way ... *It may refer to a repetitive pattern of activity in an entire organization*, to an individual skill, or as an adjective, to the smooth uneventful effectiveness of such an organizational or individual performance.'
Levitt and March (1996 [1988], p. 320)	'The generic term "routines" includes the *forms, rules, procedures. conventions, strategies, and technologies around which organizations are constructed and through which they operate*. It also includes *the structure of beliefs, frameworks, paradigms, codes, cultures, and knowledge* that buttress, elaborate, and contradict the formal routines.'
Feldman (1989, p. 136)	Organizational routines are 'complex *sets of interlocking behaviors* held in place through common agreement on the relevant roles and expectations.'
Miner (1991, p. 773)	'I define an organizational routine as a coordinated, *repetitive set of organizational activities*.'
Pentland and Rueter (1994, p. 484)	'A set of functionally similar *patterns*.'
Cohen and Bacdayan (1996 [1994], p. 406)	'By "organizational routines" we mean *patterned sequences of learned behavior* involving multiple actors who are linked by relations of communication and/or authority.'
Feldman (2000)	'[R]outines are *repeated patterns of behavior* that are bound by rules and customs and that do not change very much from one interaction to another.'
(b) Routines as performance capabilities	
Pentland and Rueter (1994, pp. 490–91)	'The set of possible performances for a particular task, described in part by a grammar ... An organizational routine is not a single pattern but, rather, set of possible patterns – enabled and constrained by a variety of organizational, social, physical, and cognitive structures – from which organizational members enact particular performances.'

Table 13.1 continued

Source	Text
Cohen et al. (1996, p. 683)	'A routine is an executable capability for repeated performance in some context that has been learned by an organization in response to selective pressures.'
(c) Routines as habituated action	
Winter (1986, p. 165)	'A relatively complex pattern of behavior (or the theoretical representation of such a pattern) *triggered by a relatively small number of initiating signals* or choices and functioning as a recognizable unit in a relatively automatic fashion.'
Gersick and Hackman (1990, p. 69)	'A habitual routine exists when a group repeatedly exhibits a functionally *similar pattern of behavior in a given stimulus situation without explicitly selecting it over alternative ways of behaving*.'
Weick (1993, p. 632)	'The crew at Mann Gulch have routine, *habituated action patterns, they come together from a common pool of people*, and while this set of individual smokejumpers had not come together at the same places of times, they did come together around the same episodes of fire.'
Weick (1996 [1991], p. 165)	'Organizational response systems which emphasize *relatively constant responding* are called organizational routines. These basic building blocks represent efficient tools designed to transform variable inputs into less variable outputs through a standardized sequence of operations.'
Scott (1995, p. 54)	'Routines are carriers that rely on patterned actions that reflect the tacit knowledge of actors – *deeply ingrained habits and procedures* based on inarticulated [*sic*] knowledge and beliefs.'

Note: Emphasis added by authors.

Jobs as Routines

We argue that *formalized* jobs represent a special type of organizational routine. Formalized jobs are those for which written job descriptions exist; they are executable performance capabilities enacted in a specific way by incumbents, a view that is consistent with Miner (1991). In essence, formalized jobs define a range of possible enactments of a particular task. There is an underlying grammar, in the form of a formal job description and behavioral expectations, that structures performance of a job and helps lead to functionally similar patterns of behavior. For this study we are interested in the behavioral routine: the sets of actions carried out in the job, not the formal representation of the job in writing. It is what organizational members would be referring to when describing their behavior when 'doing their job'.

Our view of jobs as routines is consistent with Pentland and Rueter's (1994) research on service interactions, which examined the grammar of organizational routines that structured the performance of a specific encounter. For example, a receptionist's job entails tasks such as answering the phone, giving information, setting up appointments, and acting as gatekeeper for the organization. Each of these tasks may be done in a variety of ways. The receptionist may smile when answering questions, conscientiously keep the office calendar, or be friendly with some, but not others, who try to contact the chief executive officer. If the receptionist is sick and somebody else fills the position temporarily, the new incumbent will also answer the phone, give out information, and act as a gatekeeper. The micro behaviors may not be identical across incumbents or time, but there is a restricted menu of activities that creates a boundary around the behaviors which are viewed as being part of the job.

Routinization

Similar to the different connotations of routine found in the literature, we also found distinguishable conceptualizations of routinization. While research has substantially extended Cyert and March's discourse on the importance of standard operating procedures, routines and the routinization of action, routinization can denote varied constructs. From work on the diffusion of innovations, we know that routines differ in the extent to which they have been incorporated into the regular activities of an organization (for example, Rogers 1995). In such work, routinization refers to incorporation into the regular activities of an organization.

Other organizational behavior literature sees routinization as occurring when actions are frequently repeated and the performer of the routine does them automatically, often without conscious thought about the routine. Here routinization refers to the automation of behavior (for example, Weiss and Ilgen 1985). Berger and Luckmann (1967), and researchers following their conceptualization, view routinization as a process by which action becomes typified and objectified – that is, internalized and separated from individual human beings (Zucker 1977; Tolbert and Zucker 1983). Here, routinization refers to the process of objectification. Often these conceptualizations of routinization are implicit rather than explicit within the particular research streams. Applying findings from one set of studies to another can therefore be difficult. To help in the interpretation of our results, we briefly describe two main distinctions that we have found in the literature and then delineate into which category our study fits.

The first group of definitions views routinization as a process of variance reduction in action or cognition over time. During the process of routinization, varied activities converge on a narrower set of options. Table 13.2 (a) presents language in prior work that is consistent with this conceptualization of routinization. The second set of definitions (b) emphasizes the increasing normalization of an action as it becomes routinized. This connotation implies that the *degree* of routinization reveals the extent to which an action is viewed as normal and as part of the regular activities within an organization.

This second set comes closer to our interest: the standing of existing standardized routines relative to one another. Theories of organizational learning and social interaction, we argue, imply different degrees of routinization even for clusters of activities that have already been narrowed through a variance reduction process. For our study, then, we define routinization as the process by which an activity becomes incorporated into the regular workings of the organization (Rogers 1995). The degree of routinization then assesses the *extent* to which a routine has been incorporated.

Table 13.2 Approaches to routinization

Source	Text
(a) Routinization as a variance reduction process	
March and Simon (1958, p. 142)	A set of activities is regarded as 'routinized, then, to the degree that choice has been simplified by *the development of a fixed response* to defined stimuli. If search has been eliminated, but choice remains in the form of clearly defined and systematic computing routine, we will say that the activities are routinized.'
Berger and Luckmann (1967, p. 53)	Repeated actions are habitualized by being cast into patterns that can be 'reproduced with an economy of effort ... Habitualization carries with it the important psychological claim that *choices are narrowed. While in theory there may be a hundred ways to go about the project of building a canoe out of matchsticks, habitualization narrows these down to one.*'
Kraft (1977, pp. 20–21)	Creating '*any sort of routine, repetitive activity* that can be standardized and then *done in a standard, i.e., machine-controlled, manner.*'
Cohen and Bacdayan (1996 [1994], p. 405)	'Routines arise in repetitive situations where the recurring cost of careful deliberation can become a heavy burden; *they store organizational experience in a form that allows the organizations to rapidly transfer that experience to new situations.*'
Weiss and Ilgen (1985, p. 59)	'The *development of routines* is a function of repetition and task success.'
Weiss and Ilgen (1985, p. 64)	'Organizations *develop typical patterns of behavior which stabilize and habituate* as a result of repetition and initial utility.'
(b) Routinization as a normalizing process	
Giddens (1984, p. 376)	'The habitual, taken-for-granted character of the vast bulk of activities of day-to-day social life; *the prevalence of familiar styles and forms of conduct, both supporting and supported by a sense of ontological security.*'
Ashforth and Fried (1988, p. 321)	'The outcomes of exchanges tend to become formalized in goals and policies, budgets and long-term contracts, departmental functions, appointments ... In short, *the process ... becomes somewhat routinized in organizations, and the outcomes institutionalized. Once an issue is resolved it becomes taken for granted and effectively forgotten.*'
Tyre and Orlikowski (1993, p. 13)	'*In effect, the technology, as well as the habits and assumptions surrounding it tend to become "taken for granted" and built into standard operating procedures.* This initiates a period of stability in which users focus attention more on regular production tasks than on further adaptation.'
Tyre and Orlikowski (1993, p. 18)	'Successful implementation means that, *over time, the technology becomes increasingly integrated into the production process.* The new technology gets physically interconnected with the rest of production process, and users learn to rely on it for production needs.'

Rogers (1995, p. 399)	'*Routinization occurs when the innovation has become incorporated into the regular activities of the organization*, and the innovation loses its separate identity ... Organizational members no longer think of the innovation as a new idea. It has been completely absorbed into the organization's on-going activities.'
Starbuck (1996 [1992], p. 502)	'Routinization helps to make knowledge intensity unstable. As with physical capital, converting expertise to routines is risky. Routines may become targets of imitation, spread, and *gradually lose the character of being esoteric and advantageous.*'
Winter (1996 [1994], p. 476)	'Routines emerge ... through a protracted process of organizational learning ... The initial learning phase ends ... when performance that is deemed satisfactory is achieved ... *when the improvement of the routine is an issue that no longer successfully competes for attention of the kind that is actually needed to produce improvement.*'

Note: Emphasis added by authors.

3 THE IMPACT OF LEARNING AND SOCIAL PROCESSES ON ROUTINIZATION

Some studies have contrasted learning and institutional or social models as competing theories of social action (for example, Lant 1992; Lant and Mezias 1990, 1992). In this study, similar to the spirit of the behavioral theory of the firm, we explore how learning and institutional processes may complement and interact with each other to influence organizational action. We begin with basic predictions from learning theories, considering trial and error, innovation-based learning (learning through the adoption of novel routines), and practice learning (learning through repeating a behavior) (Levitt and March 1988; Argote 1999).

We follow the broad learning tradition that defines learning as *a change in behavior or knowledge informed by experience* (Levitt and March 1988; Argote 1999). In this view, learning can involve changes in behavior, cognition or both (Glynn et al. 1994). Although early work on organizational learning tended to address it as a single process (for example, Cyert and March, 1963 [1992]), contemporary research envisages multiple authentic learning processes. These later conceptualizations add depth to learning process research by acknowledging both knowledge generation and forgetting, learning from an organization's own experience and learning from others, experimentation and trial-and-error learning, as well as refinement and exploration (Huber 1991; March 1991; Van de Ven and Polley 1992; Glynn et al. 1994, Argote 1999) – setting the stage for our exploration of different types of learning.

We then draw on a variety of institutional and other theories that highlight social processes to examine how person–job factors and context influence the degree to which a job is seen as part of the normal workings of its department. We argue that the social and contextual processes actually moderate learning, rather than working simply as additional, independent effects.

The Impact of Job Traits on Job Routinization

Job contribution to the department: trial-and-error learning

Cyert and March (1992 [1963], p. 119) argued that '[s]tandard operating procedures are the memory of an organization. Like any other memory or learned behavior, standard operating procedures change over time at varying rates'. Although Cyert and March emphasized that organizations learn higher-level procedures such as decision rules, aspiration levels, attention rules, and goals, their arguments often imply that simple trial-and-error learning of lower-level routines plays an important role as well. We define trial-and-error learning as occurring when an organization carries out an action, and the outcome of that action then determines the strength of that activity in the future (Miner et al. 2000). Thus, routines with positive outcomes may be seen as more valuable and become more easily part of the standard set of procedures in an organization. When trial-and-error learning occurs, what appears to work at one time period becomes more influential at a later time period (Knicely 1983; Weiss and Ilgen 1985).

Trial-and-error learning may involve explicit observation of outcomes and deliberate strengthening (or weakening) of a routine, or may occur as a result of less self-aware organizational reinforcement processes (Burgelman 1994). We think that, consistent with a simple reinforcement model, organizational trial-and-error learning processes will strengthen the degree to which routines making strong contributions are seen as part of the normal workings of an organization. A growing body of research which has found that the ultimate standing of a routine is influenced by its apparent outcome (Nelson and Winter 1982; Burgelman 1983; Miner 1990; Lant and Mezias 1992; Lant 1992; Miner et al. 2000) gives credence to this argument.

Hypothesis 1 The higher the level of a job's contribution to its department, the higher its degree of routinization.

Job novelty: innovation learning and practice learning

Innovation learning Trial-and-error learning theories stress that the retention or lack of retention of prior bundles of activities is based on their perceived outcomes (March and Olsen 1976; Van de Ven and Polley 1992; Cheng and Van de Ven 1996). Organizational learning may also involve the acquisition of new practices or routines that did not previously exist in the organization (Levitt and March 1988; Miner 1990; Huber 1991; March 1991). In our case, such learning would involve the addition of novel sets of job duties to a department's existing set of jobs. Innovation-based learning arises through the creation of novel sets of job duties for a given department. A novel job refers to a job with a new set of duties and tasks that had not been part of the departmental workings previously (Miner 1991).

In the *Behavioral Theory of the Firm*, Cyert and March (1992 [1963]) underscore the potential importance of such innovative learning through their exploration of different types of organizational search procedures. In the same vein, Weiss and Ilgen (1985) claimed that failures to reach one's goals lead to a reassessment of existing routines and ultimately to new ones. When environments change, previously stated goals may no longer be achievable with the existing routines. If novel jobs, however, reflected crucial changes in organizational priorities or external demands, they would represent adaptation to changing environments or goals (March 1981). In this case we would expect that novel jobs are more likely be seen as part of the regular workings of the department, because they would be associated with crucial contingencies and central objectives. In periods of major exogenous turbulence or change in organizational strategies, we might expect then that novel jobs would actually have higher levels of routinization than pre-existing jobs. The organization from which we gathered our data faced a rapidly changing environment in the period of our study, making plausible:

Hypothesis 2a Novel jobs will show higher levels of routinization than pre-existing jobs.

Practice learning Individuals and organizations also learn through practice and repetition to make a particular activity more consistent over time and to make it seem more normal. For example, an individual practices a sports move until that move becomes a natural extension of the person. NASA's astronauts, charged with repairing the Hubble Space Telescope, practised their moves for many months until a particular routine was so embodied in the person it seemed the normal thing to do in the situation (Story Musgrave 2000, personal communication). Similarly, organizations repeat and practise processes either in order to reduce variance or to make them seem normal. Such practice effects are thought to generate increased productivity indicated by the organizational learning curve literature (Yelle 1979; Argote 1999). In addition, prior repetitions of a routine may create linkages with other routines in the department. Rogers (1995) linked the adoption rate of innovations to their compatibility with existing technologies and procedures. Tyre and Orlikowski (1993, p. 18) describe how novel technological routines become 'physically interconnected with the rest of the production process, and users learn to rely on [them] for production needs'. These observations imply that novel actions which have not previously been part of the organization are probably less likely to be viewed as part of regular activities, that is, have lower degrees of routinization.

Several social process frameworks make the same prediction, of course. Berger and Luckmann (1967, p. 53) claim that social and cognitive processes generate habitualization (automatic replication) and sometimes the objectification (separation from the person performing the actions) of activities by an individual. Their observations imply that novel routines are much less likely to be perceived as regular activities because they are still in the early stages of moving towards habitualization. Barley's (1986) description of the evolution of new interactions and job patterns by technicians and doctors using new CT scanning equipment is consistent with this prediction.

Hypothesis 2b Novel jobs will have lower levels of routinization than pre-existing jobs.

The Impact of Person–Job Links on Job Routinization

Familiarity of first incumbent

Linkages between the familiarity of a *situation* and routinization of related activities have long been suggested in the routines literature. Weiss and Ilgen (1985) argue that if a situation is perceived as familiar, previously memorized responses will be followed, indirectly contributing to the further reinforcement of this response. In this study, we consider a different question: we explore the effect of the *familiarity of the person implementing a routine* and the degree of routinization of the routine itself. Specifically, we distinguish between jobs where the first observed incumbent was a person who had already worked in the department (that is, who got the job through promotion or transfer) and jobs where the incumbents had not worked in the department before. We ask whether having *a familiar original incumbent of a job* affects the degree to which that job is seen as part of the regular workings of the organization.

Social interaction theories clearly imply that the nature of a job's incumbent can influence the standing of a routine (Strauss 1978; Barley 1986). Social theories primarily imply that if someone already working in a department fills a job, the departmental embeddedness of that person may foster the embeddedness of the job itself. It may be seen as part of the regular workings of the department because the person linked to it is part of normal departmental life (Berger and Luckmann 1967). In addition, incumbents may possess political skills and insider information, allowing them to manipulate perceptions of the centrality of a job (Cyert and March 1992 [1963]; Thompson 1967; Miner 1991). Miner (1991) found that familiarity of the incumbent did enhance the chances that a job would survive over time. We reason it will also enhance the chances that the job will be seen as part of regular organizational activities.

We note that some institutional reasoning suggests that the familiarity of the incumbent could jeopardize the degree to which a job is seen as an objective entity (Berger and Luckmann 1967; Tolbert and Zucker 1996). In a formalized organization, this could make a job seem less normal, reducing its level of routinization. On balance, however, we expect:

Hypothesis 3 Jobs with familiar first incumbents will have higher levels of routinization than other jobs.

Job idiosyncrasy

An idiosyncratic job is one whose duties are designed around the abilities and interests of a particular person (Miner 1987), rather than being preplanned in advance by management. An example of an idiosyncratic job would be the following. A talented head technician in a laboratory proposes new training programs for other technicians, based on his or her personal interests, prior training activities, and perceived laboratory needs. The laboratory manager has no plan to create such a job, but nonetheless creates a new full-time administrative training position for the head technician – in part to keep the latter in the lab and in part because the manager anticipates the programs would have value (for additional examples, see Miner 1987).

The creation of idiosyncratic jobs may unfold in varied ways. They may unfold over time as employees accrue duties and later formalize these activities. They may be created as an organizational experiment prompted by a particular person's interests, or opportunistic use of individual talents. They may be created to bind specific persons and their specific skills more closely to their departments (Miner and Estler 1985). In some cases, the idiosyncratic job may disappear from the organizational chart as soon as the incumbent leaves the job. Yet in other cases, an idiosyncratic job can end up adding unplanned but sustained new activities to a department.

Idiosyncratic jobs, then, represent the outcome of joint specialization of a person and organization and may provide the potential for serendipitous learning. As Miner (1990) pointed out, selecting and retaining idiosyncratic jobs was one way in which the organization that she studied acquired new competencies. Some idiosyncratic jobs were incorporated into the organizational memory and lasted well past their original incumbents. To the degree that such jobs represented rewards to valuable or powerful current employees, we expect that incumbents of such jobs should have unusually high influence – which in turn will permit them to influence the status of the job itself (March and Simon 1958; Thompson 1967). They will be able to influence managers and others so that their peers and superiors tend to perceive their jobs as part of regular departmental activities. In this case:

Hypothesis 4a Idiosyncratic jobs will show higher degrees of routinization than non-idiosyncratic jobs.

When we look at idiosyncratic jobs through a traditional institutional lens, however, we would expect idiosyncratic jobs to be *less routinized* than non-idiosyncratic jobs. According to institutional theories, the routinization of action implies objectification, or the detachment of the action from any particular actor (Berger and Luckmann 1967; Zucker 1977; Nelson and Winter 1982; Tolbert and Zucker 1996). Since idiosyncratic jobs are by definition created around specific actors, the actual bundle of activities is linked intrinsically to a person rather than to the department. If this alternative form of routinization increases the chance that an activity will be seen as part of the organization's normal routines, the lack of objectification should decrease routinization as we define it. Moreover, the original 'non-objective' status of an idiosyncratic job may make the job more vulnerable to social intervention, that is, to being questioned rather than being taken for granted as part of the department. These factors predict a negative relationship between job idiosyncrasy and routinization, all else being equal.

Hypothesis 4b Idiosyncratic jobs will show lower degrees of routinization than non-idiosyncratic jobs.

The Impact of Organizational Context

Social interaction theories imply that the *context* in which a job exists also affects the degree to which it is seen as part of the normal workings of an organization (Giddens 1979). We consider two contextual variables that have been shown to influence organizational action (March and Olsen 1976): change in mission ambiguity and change in resource uncertainty. These variables are especially relevant for examining the impact of social interaction processes on the relative standing of routines. Both have been theoretically linked to the creation and meaning of routines themselves. For instance, data from prior studies showed that these variables were linked to the creation of some types of jobs (Miner 1987). Furthermore, Weiss and Ilgen (1985) claim that when a particular action is repeated without damage, uncertainty about the situation is reduced and individuals become more confident. In addition, theories of negotiated order, political models of organizations and social information processes all imply that changes in resource uncertainty and mission ambiguity will generate both greater struggle for material resources and more contested meanings (Cyert and March 1992 [1963]; Strauss et al. 1963; March and Simon 1958; Salancik and Pfeffer 1978; Barley 1986).

Change in mission ambiguity

March and Olsen (1976) stated that under ambiguity of intention, organizational preferences may be diffuse or conflicting. Ambiguity refers to indeterminacy in the *meaning* of what happens, or what should happen (Miner 1987, p. 335). This makes the evaluation of actions and outcomes problematic. *Mission* ambiguity refers specifically to indeterminacy in the goals and objectives of a department (ibid.). This indeterminacy may translate into vagueness and diffuse ideas about performance standards for organizational routines as well as for members of the organization.

Social theories that emphasize political struggle imply that jobs will have a lower probability of being seen as part of the normal workings of their departments. Such models of organizational action point to ongoing struggle for both material resources and control of rules and decisions in organizations (March and Simon 1958; Strauss 1978). Changing mission ambiguity, by increasing complexity and making it harder to anticipate how different actions will be valued, increases both the motivation for and feasibility of such political conflict (March and Simon 1958 p. 119). If it is harder to evaluate an outcome or task, as is true when a department's goals are ambiguous, it is easier to contest any given routine's value and centrality. Increased levels of such conflict should reduce the chances that a focal job in this context will be seen as part of the regular workings of the department.

Hypothesis 5a Jobs in contexts with higher levels of change in mission ambiguity will have lower degrees of routinization than other jobs.

On the other hand, social theories that stress collective interpretation and constant creation of meaning imply that change in mission ambiguity will generate higher levels of routinization because it will be easier to create favorable meanings for jobs in such a context. Thus, theories that stress the centrality of meaning over instrumentality raise an intriguing alternative possibility: changing mission ambiguity may increase the chances for a job to be seen as part of the regular workings of the organization. An increasingly ambiguous mission may be seen as providing a more generous or varied filter through which routines – in this case jobs – must pass before they are seen as normal or regular (Weick 1979). Mission ambiguity implies that multiple and even conflicting goals may exist at one time. There are more contexts in which the same activity may have meaning or be perceived as normal (Feldman 1989). This permits many different bundles of duties to be considered as potential solutions to central organizational problems and thereby, as regular departmental workings.

Hypothesis 5b Jobs in contexts with higher levels of change in mission ambiguity will have higher degrees of routinization than other jobs.

Change in resource uncertainty

Uncertainty refers to indeterminacy about *what* will happen (Miner 1987, p. 335). In this study, we focus on change in uncertainty about the availability of resources, which we argue will strengthen the impact of political processes. Resource uncertainty refers to the lack of predictability of the stream of resources in the future, that is, a department is not certain about the levels and sources of funding that it will receive (Hickson et al. 1971; Miner 1987). In the research setting for this study, departments could gain resources from multiple distinct sources including the organization's regular operating budget, gifts, federal research grants, special tuition funds, and research contracts. High levels of change in resource uncertainty represent increased unpredictability about such future resources. Political models of organizations imply that changing resource uncertainty should provoke higher conflict over resources and roles related to them (Cyert and March 1992 [1963]). Jobs seen as part of normal departmental workings presumably have higher chances of remaining funded. This in turn will create increased conflict over job standing, making any particular job more subject to a contested standing (March and Simon 1958; Thompson 1967).

Hypothesis 6a Jobs in contexts with changing resource uncertainty will have lower degrees of routinization than jobs in other contexts.

Less obviously, changing resource uncertainty may create an organizational landscape with varied criteria by which routines and thus jobs may be evaluated. Anticipating different resource constraints may generate ambiguity in evaluation criteria which in turn permits more jobs to be constructed as part of the normal workings of a department (Strauss 1978). In essence, we argue that changing resource uncertainty, like changing mission ambiguity, may generate ambiguity of meaning. This in turn creates a broader net of value within which a given routine may stand a higher chance of being perceived as part of the normal workings of the department.

Hypothesis 6b Jobs in contexts with changing resource uncertainty will have higher degrees of routinization than jobs in other contexts.

The Interaction of Social Processes and Organizational Learning

Our first two hypotheses considered three different learning processes – trial-and-error learning, innovation-based learning, and practice learning – all of which we have claimed would influence the degree to which a job is seen as part of the regular workings of a department. We also hypothesized that social interaction processes and context would influence a job's degree of routinization. We now propose that traditional learning and social processes not only co-exist, but that they intertwine to affect the relative standing of different organizational routines. In short, social process and context variables should moderate the impact of learning effects.

Trial-and-error learning, person–job links and job context

As described earlier, many theories argue that the outcome of an action affects its standing. Actions with perceived positive outcomes will be strengthened in their relative standing as part of the regular procedures in an organization, others will be weakened (Van de Ven and Polley 1992; Cheng and Van de Ven 1996). Thus, the instrumentality affects the standing of an action and its perceived contribution level should affect the relative standing of 'a formalized job. Social information-processing theories amend this sensible picture, based on the degree to which actions and outcomes can be easily evaluated (Pfeffer et al. 1976). If well-defined – instrumental standards for evaluating an action are available, those will be used; if shared criteria are lacking, social factors will become more salient (Pfeffer et al. 1976; Haunschild and Miner 1997; March and Olsen 1989).

In the simplest case, observers may use social frequency as a factor to guide action under uncertainty. Pfeffer and his colleagues (1976, p. 230) observed that 'when you don't know what to do because there are no clear standards to guide your behavior, you look around and observe what others like you are doing'. Perrow (1986 [1972], p. 11) argued that 'competence is hard to judge, so we rely upon familiarity'. Thus, where instrumentality does not provide sufficient information, other factors will become more salient in determining the standing of a routine in its department. Related research indicates that copying the most common practice is just one of many social processes that may influence action under ambiguity or uncertainty

(Miner and Raghavan 1999). Organizations may use varied imitation rules, may be affected by political struggle, and may be influenced by different interpretation modes when the instrumental value of a given activity is especially hard to evaluate (Weick 1979; Haunschild and Miner 1997).

This line of reasoning implies that social factors matter not only when the standards and criteria for evaluating jobs are unclear, but also when the outcome of a particular routine is intermediate – neither clearly high nor clearly low. A job that is perceived as making a very high contribution to the department will more likely be seen as part of the regular departmental workings; a job seen as making a very low contribution would be much less likely to be seen that way. The standing of a job seen as making a moderate contribution would more likely be influenced by additional factors. Empirical support for this idea can be found in Haunschild and Miner (1997) who examined how prior acquisition premia in past deals influenced the choice of investment bankers. In cases of extreme positive or negative performance, the choice was largely driven by prior performance. However, in the moderate performance category, social and contextual factors moderated the effect of prior performance. These findings are consistent with the broad assumption that the logic of consequences and the logic of appropriateness may hold different sway under varying conditions (March and Olsen 1989).

Specifically, we expect that the person–job linkage (that is, familiarity of the first incumbent and the job idiosyncrasy) will play a larger role in the standing of medium-contribution jobs than in low- or high-contribution jobs. Medium-contribution jobs should be more susceptible to political processes generated by either job incumbents or other departmental members. They should also be more influenced by the existence of multiple ways to interpret the value of a job.

Hypothesis 7a The effect of having a familiar first incumbent will be stronger for medium-contribution jobs.

Hypothesis 7b The effect of job idiosyncrasy will be stronger for medium-contribution jobs. Similarly, changing mission ambiguity and changing resource uncertainty should have a stronger impact on jobs making medium contributions in contrast to those making very high or low contributions. As noted previously, ambiguity and uncertainty facilitate political struggles over the value of activities including routines and jobs (Strauss 1978) and offer more complex landscapes of value, which – regardless of conflict – offer participants a larger number of metrics to use in evaluating routines.

Hypothesis 7c The effect of change in mission ambiguity will be stronger for medium-contribution jobs.

Hypothesis 7d The effect of change in resource uncertainty ambiguity will be stronger for medium-contribution jobs.

4 METHODS AND ANALYSIS

To examine our hypotheses we needed assessment of: (i) the traits of the jobs themselves (for example, had they been created around a particular person and were thus idiosyncratic?); (ii) the traits of the departments in which these jobs were created; (iii) the perceived effects of the jobs on their departments at some later time; and (iv) the degree to which the jobs were seen as part of regular departmental workings. The full longitudinal research program spanned seven years. We interviewed senior officers, collected and coded archival data, included participant observation and obtained informant ratings of jobs and departments. Our research design for this segment involved two main data collection waves and several data sources, including three different informant groups. One group of raters assessed job traits at the time of job birth. A second, independent group assessed the characteristics of the pertinent departments in the same data collection wave. Finally, several years after job birth, a third group assessed the contribution and degree of routinization of those jobs.

Setting

Data collection occurred in a private research university during an era of substantial change that specifically affected administrative goals and activities. As an active leader and observer of universities, Cyert (1975) argued that 'private universities must manage themselves more effectively ... Steps in this direction are already being taken, and I predict that within a five-year period private universities will become models of efficient use of resources'. While observers would contest the level of efficiency achieved in the late 1970s and early 1980s, these universities did indeed engage in major structural and administrative changes. All jobs included in this study were those of non-faculty employees. Each employee was assigned to one of about 250 job titles which were attached to established compensation groups and formalized, that is, they had written job descriptions. Departments were free to reorganize and redesign such positions within budget limits.

Sample

We began with 479 jobs – new positions created between April 1980 and December 1982 as well as a stratified random sample of old jobs located in the same departments as the newly created jobs. During the second data gathering, we were able to obtain complete ratings of 210 jobs, 44 percent of those identified in earlier studies. We assessed potential sample bias by comparing rated and non-rated jobs on several characteristics using *t*-tests. The results showed no significant differences in departmental characteristics of rated jobs, job type, or occupation. Thus, we concluded that the likelihood of major bias in the final sample was small.

Measures

Dependent variable

Our examination of routinization used Rogers' used (1995, p. 399) definition: 'routinization occurs when the innovation has become incorporated into the regular activities of the organization'. The dependent variable, Degree of Routinization (ROUT), was assessed by asking informants, 'To what extent was the job actually incorporated into the regular department workings and routines?' – with information gathered at least five years after a job was created or reclassified, since we expected that this time span would allow for an accurate assessment. A group of 34 raters evaluated incorporation into a department on a seven-point, Likert-type scale: a response of 1 indicated 'minimally'; a score of 7 indicated 'completely' (see Appendix 13A1).

These 34 informants had responsibility for personnel administration within the university, working for line officers. They were picked by senior officers as the informants best capable of assessing the history and effects of jobs in the pertinent departments, and were seasoned observers with detailed knowledge of the local setting but no political stake in the fate of particular jobs. They were also aware neither of the specific purpose of this research nor of the original job trait ratings obtained at job birth from a different group of raters (see Appendix 13A2).

Independent variables

The theoretical independent variables consisted of Contribution to Department (*CONTR*), Job Idiosyncrasy (*IDIOS*), Novel Job (*NOVEL*), Familiarity of First Incumbent (*FAMIL*), Change in Mission Ambiguity (*MISAM*), and Change in Resource Uncertainly (*RESUN*). Most characteristics of the jobs (Novel Job, Familiarity of First Incumbent, Job Idiosyncrasy) derive from the original study (Miner 1987, 1991) where each job was typically evaluated by two informed, independent raters (inter-rater reliability 0.78 to 0.97 (1987, pp. 338ff)).

The first independent variable, Contribution to Department, was measured with a seven-point, Likert-type scale involving the same raters who were used to measure the degree of routinization. Two traits defined the second, Idiosyncratic Jobs: '(1) the existence of the jobholder prompted the creation of the position in its current form; and (2) the combination of job activities was designed to match the perceived abilities, interests, or priorities of the person around whom the position was created' (Miner 1987, p. 327). We supplemented the original idiosyncrasy ratings with ratings by the 34 second-panel informants (see Appendix 13A1).

We used Miner's (1991) definition and measures for the Novel Job variable. The procedure is summarized in Appendix A1. Measuring Familiarity of First Incumbent also followed Miner's (1991) procedures (brief summary in Appendix 13A1) with one difference, as information that was more accurate became available during the second data collection wave. Planned novel jobs were coded 1 when the job had been filled by someone within the department, and coded 0 in all other cases. This information had not been available on publication of earlier studies; after carefully checking archival records, we were able to improve Miner's (1991) coding accuracy with respect to Familiarity of First Incumbent.

The measures for Change in Mission Ambiguity and Change in Resource Uncertainty were taken from Miner (1987) who asked ten senior informants to assess the characteristics of the departments. These informants had a general overview of the total internal environment which permitted them to compare departments, a significant working knowledge of the departments they rated, and knowledge of the history of the departments. They differed from the 34 second panel informants in that they were dealing with, and had experience in, many different departments.

Control variable

We reasoned that departmental size may affect the routinization of a job, since it affected job creation (Miner 1987) and retention (1991), and may also create noise affecting the accuracy of the departmental ratings. It also serves to control for the effects of other unmeasured department traits with which size is correlated. Therefore, we included Department Size (*SIZE*) as a control variable. We measured Department Size by the number of employees at the beginning of the study period with data taken from organizational computer records.

Note that the dependent variable stemmed from job rating evaluation sheets, the ambiguity and financial information from a separate set of informants' rating departments, and the job characteristics from classifications obtained in earlier, separate studies based on archival information and earlier informants. Thus, our design eliminated a substantial part of the danger arising from common method variance or from implicit theories held by informants about the relationships among these variables.

Analyses

We examined correlation coefficients for collinearity and used multiple regression to estimate the association between dependent and independent variables. We first regressed the dependent variable on the main effect variables and then assessed the interaction effects by running different regression models for jobs that had made low, medium, or high contributions to their departments. We used separate regression models for each of the contribution groups rather than adding one interaction variable to the regression model, because we did not expect a linear relationship between the main and the interaction effects. To test the robustness of the models, we estimated both additive and multiplicative models. The results were not substantively different, but the R^2 coefficients were higher for the additive model. We report those models.

5 RESULTS

Examining the correlation matrix of all variables, we concluded that collinearity was not a major concern for interpreting the results (see Table 13.3). None of the correlation coefficients was greater than 0.54 and only three of 36 correlation coefficients were greater than 0.3.

Table 13.3 Descriptive statistics and correlation coefficients among variables

	MEAN	SD	*CONTR*	*NOVEL*	*FAMIL*	*IDIOS*	*RESUN*	*MISAM*	*SIZE*
ROUT	5.43	2.00	0.53*	–0.07	0.16	–0.07	0.06	0.18*	0.13
CONTR	4.60	1.47	—	–0.01	0.06	–0.01	–0.03	–0.05	–0.03
NOVEL	0.56	0.50		—	–0.50*	0.54*	0.04	–0.08	–0.07
FAMIL	0.76	0.43			—	–0.03	–0.14	0.08	0.01
IDIOS	1.54	0.66				—	–0.05	0.00	–0.09
RESUN	4.51	0.69					—	–0.28*	0.29*
MISAM	4.06	0.71						—	0.19*
SIZE	68.82	54.53							—

Note: * significant at 0.01, $n = 210$.

Table 13.4 provides results for the multiple regression models. The first column shows the coefficients for the basic, main effect model. This model was significant at the 0.05 level (F = 18.368) and had an R^2 adj. of 0.368.

The Impact of Job Traits

Hypothesis 1 proposed that a job's perceived contribution to its department increased its degree of routinization. The data show a positive coefficient of 0.765 which is significant at the 0.05 level, consistent with the occurrence of trial-and-error learning. Jobs that are perceived as creating positive outcomes are more likely to become part of the normal workings of a department.

Table 13.4 Predictors of degrees of routinization (degree to which a job is seen as part of regular workings of department)

	Main effects	Interaction effects (by contribution)		
		Low	Medium	High
Contribution	0.756^{***}			
	(0.075)			
Novelty	0.649^{*}	0.180	0.638	0.579
	(0.322)	(2.396)	(0.423)	(0.546)
Familiarity	0.919^{*}	–0.246	1.214^{*}	0.332
	(0.317)	(1.723)	(0.412)	(0.577)
Idiosyncrasy	-0.617^{*}	0.909	-0.620^{*}	–0.360
	(0.211)	(1.246)	(0.287)	(0.347)
Resource	0.379^{*}	–0.858	$0.456^{\dagger}$	0.282
Uncertainty	(0.179)	(1.193)	(0.263)	(0.262)
Mission	0.665^{**}	1.752	0.591^{*}	0.185
Ambiguity	(0.169)	(1.014)	(0.247)	(0.263)
Number of	0.002	–0.008	0.003	–0.002
Employees	(0.002)	(0.011)	(0.003)	(0.004)
Constant	-2.699^{*}	–1.308	0.281	4.572^{*}
R^2	0.389	0.424	0.175	0.056
R^2 adj	0.368	0.079	0.136	–0.046
F	18.378^{**}	1.228	4.424^{**}	0.549
n	210	17	132	63

Note: $^{\dagger} = p < 0.1$; $^{*} = p < 0.05$; $^{**} = p < 0.001$.

We predicted that novel jobs are more likely to become part of the regular workings if an innovation learning process underlies the routinization. If, on the other hand, practice learning dominates the routinization process, pre-existing jobs will have higher degrees of routinization. Our results support the innovation learning process. Being a novel job *increased* the degree of routinization significantly ($b = 0.649, p < 0.05$). In the rapidly changing environment of the organization, innovation learning dominated practice learning.

The Impact of Person–Job Links

Based on prior routines research, we proposed (Hypothesis 3) that jobs with familiar first incumbents should show higher degrees of routinization, because the person would already be embedded in the department and people familiar with the department could exploit insider information. The positive coefficient of 0.919 ($p < 0.05$) supports this prediction.

Following a similar logic, we predicted that idiosyncratic jobs should have higher degrees of routinization. However, we also noted that idiosyncratic jobs may be perceived as belonging to a particular person rather than to the department, thereby making them appear less part of the regular activities of the department (Hypotheses 4a and 4b). The results in Table 13.4 show that Job Idiosyncrasy had a *negative* effect on routinization ($p < 0.05$). Apparently, idiosyncratic jobs are not viewed as objectified routines that have a standing apart from the person around whom they were created.

The Impact of Organizational Context

In Hypotheses 5 and 6, we predicted that changes in mission ambiguity and resource uncertainty would affect the relative standing of a job. Both change in mission ambiguity (0.665, $p < 0.05$) and change in resource uncertainty (0.379, $p < 0.05$) had a positive impact on the degree to which a job is seen as part of the regular workings of its department, consistent with Hypotheses 5b and 6b. This finding supports the idea that the presence of multiple criteria or evaluation contexts will increase the chances that a routine will be seen as part of the regular organizational activities.

The Interaction of Social Processes and Organizational Learning

Hypotheses 7a and 7b predicted that familiar first incumbents and idiosyncratic jobs would have larger effects in medium-contribution jobs because they would provide additional information beyond the contribution itself. Hypotheses 7c and 7d predicted change in mission ambiguity and resource uncertainty would be stronger on medium-contribution jobs because they would be more subject to social processes. The pattern of results indicates these 'social process' variables do indeed have their strongest effects on *medium-contribution* jobs. The only statistically significant effects below the 0.05 level occur for the medium-contribution jobs.

We considered whether this finding may be an artifact of the sample size, but believe there is reasonable evidence that it represents a substantive finding. For example, the coefficient and standard error for the effect of familiar first incumbent on medium-contribution jobs are 1.214 (0.412), while the coefficients for low- and high-contribution jobs are –0.246 (1.723) and 0.332 (0.577), suggesting a substantively larger effect for the medium-contribution jobs, even though the large standard error for the low-contribution jobs clearly reflects its small sample size. Moreover, when we ran a regression for medium- versus non-medium-contribution jobs, that is, putting low- and high-contribution jobs into one group and medium-contribution jobs into the other, the significant effects within the medium-contribution jobs remained. Thus, the overall pattern of findings here suggests that when jobs make a clear contribution – either high or low – social processes are less likely to moderate learning processes.

6 DISCUSSION AND IMPLICATIONS

Cyert and March (1992 [1963], p. 119) claimed that '[s]tandard operating procedures are the memory of an organization'. We began this chapter by claiming that this fundamental insight has informed several literatures emphasizing the creation, turnover, and impact of organizational routines and inertia. Some work emphasizes routines as executable performance capabilities of the organization; other work emphasizes routines as habituated action. For the most part, literatures that study organizational routines tend to regard them – once created – as similar in strength and organizational impact. Closer inspection, however, reveals that routines may have different standing or different degrees of normalization within the organization, which we refer to as differences in their degree of routinization.

We examined formalized jobs as instances of specific routines, and asked informants about the relative standing of jobs in their departments. Following Cyert and March's (1992 [1963]) lead in several ways, we found support for the overall notion that both innovation learning and trial-and-error learning processes, as well as varied social interaction and interpretative processes, can influence the degree to which jobs are seen as part of the regular workings of their departments. We also found evidence that social and interpretative factors may moderate the impact of these learning processes. We shall briefly outline the limitations of our findings before we develop implications for theories of organizational learning, evolution and social interaction processes. We close by arguing that our results reinforce Cyert and March's implicit vision of organizations as ecologies of standard operating procedures or routines that unfold on interpretative and social landscapes.

Limitations

A strength of the study is that most measures of the job traits were constructed from archival sources combined with assessments from different informants about the departments several years prior to this study. We also had three different sets of informants assess jobs and departments at different times. However, the contribution to the department and the degree to which a job was seen as part of regular routines were both obtained in the same rating instrument. This means that the strong association between contribution and routinization could reflect some level of common methods variance. However, the entire study spanned seven years so that the informants who produced the final ratings were able to assess the contribution to and the incorporation into the department over a long time, independent from the current situation. In addition, the fact that the other variables seemed to have the predicted effect primarily on 'moderate'-contribution jobs suggests that the contribution–routinization link does not reflect a simple linear cognitive association between the constructs in the minds of our informants.

While the findings in our study are robust, the dependent variable and the measures of the context variables each consisted of a single, global assessment of the core characteristic by senior informants. Moreover, we studied the perception of the relative standing of one type of routine – jobs. We think that additional work could link the perception of job contributions to actual behavioral measures such as contributions to innovation, resources or productivity and to the job's impact on other observable outcomes. Future research could also fruitfully include multiple and archival measures of these variables, examine varied types of routines, and link perceptions of relative standing to behavioral outcomes.

Organizational Learning Implications

The behavioral theory of the firm laid the foundation for models of behavioral learning in organizations, which has represented a distinct theoretical focus for over 40 years in organizational theory. Behavioral learning theories focus on the birth and death of standard operating procedures or organizational routines, as well as on their impact and – in this chapter – relative standing. Behavioral theories contrast with but do not necessarily conflict with cognitive learning theories, which emphasize inference, cognitive memory and mental processes (Miner and Mezias 1996). Our results advance behavioral learning theories in three ways.

Our most intriguing finding related to the learning process, which we termed innovation learning. Perhaps surprisingly, novel sets of duties were *more* likely, rather than less likely, to be seen as part of the regular workings of the department. We argued that this would occur when the novel routines are set in place as part of major changes in aspirations or external conditions that are accepted or seen as important to the organization. This finding contrasts with a more intuitive notion of practice learning which says that, all else being equal, *pre-existing sets* of duties should be seen as more normal or regular. We expect that innovation learning is more likely to occur when an organization is dealing with substantive external shocks or altered goals. During the period of this study, the entire university adopted a series of major change initiatives, many of which specifically involved the employees who filled the jobs in this study.

This somewhat unexpected finding is consistent with a simple version of Cyert and March's (1992 [1963]) original vision of organizations as adaptive systems in which standard operating procedures change over time (Miner 1990). Further work could test this hypothesis by contrasting degrees of routinization in organizations with varying levels of major change.

The finding that high-contribution jobs are more likely to be seen as part of the regular workings of a department confirms the intuitive notion that the perceived outcome of a routine influences its standing relative to other routines. This is consistent with trial-and-error learning or simple reinforcement strengthening the standing of a focal routine. Finally, we found that factors other than contribution – the presence or absence of a familiar first incumbent, job idiosyncrasy, change in mission ambiguity and change in resource uncertainty – also influenced the degree of routinization of formalized jobs. We believe our data also imply that these factors had the greatest impact when jobs were seen as making a moderate contribution. This pattern implies that social processes not only complement, but directly intertwine with learning processes in the normalization of organizational routines. These findings are consistent with prior work on social information processing (Pfeffer et al. 1976; Haunschild and Miner 1997) and with some theoretical approaches to the relationship of the logic of consequences to the logic of appropriateness (March and Olsen 1989). Further research could fruitfully investigate whether these findings are replicated in larger sample sizes, with different types of routines and in different cultural or organizational contexts.

Our findings contribute to the organizational learning literature by linking learning to normalization, highlighting three potential, related forms of learning (trial-and-error/reinforcement, innovative, and practice learning), and underscoring how social processes may not only complement but directly moderate organization-level learning.

Evolutionary Theory Implications

Our study also extends the research tradition that envisages organizations as bundles of nested routines. Organizations change through variation, selection, and retention cycles (Burgelman 1983; Miner 1990, 1994; Baum and Singh 1994). Our study contributes in part by highlighting two different types of routines that previously have not been distinguished. On the one hand are routines that represent organizational performance capabilities; on the other are routines that develop out of previously repeated performance of an action and therefore represent habituated or automatic action.

While we started out saying that formalized jobs fall into the executable performance capability classification, some of our results seem to indicate that typification and objectification manifest in traditional views on habitualization nonetheless matter. For instance, idiosyncratic jobs had lower degrees of routinization. Thus, we now believe that many routines, including some of the formalized jobs studied here, embody both forms of prior definitions of routines. This important possibility suggests to us the value of retaining a basic definition of the construct of routines that does not restrict them to certain types of regularities, or certain origins, for their existence. In some cases routines may involve performance capabilities, in others not; in some cases routines may have become automatic through repeated enactment, in others not. This interpretation is also consistent with Nelson and Winter's (1982) suggestion that some standardized routines represent performance capabilities but have not evolved through a gradual habitualization or repetition processes, while other organizational routines have unfolded through habitualization but do not represent performance capabilities (for example, organizational routines such as informal traditions about recreation, holiday traditions, and some social hierarchies).

Some evolutionary theories of change assume that routines are disembodied bundles of activities. Our findings that job–person links, uncertainty and ambiguity influence the fate of routines point to the importance of including both competitive and interpretative social processes in considering organizational change through the variation, selection, and retention of routines (Miner 1994). Our findings actually point to a fairly complex evolutionary process. While novel duties and sets of activities were less likely to survive in Miner's (1991) previous study, they were more likely seen as part of the regular workings of the department in our study. Thus, when compared to Miner's (1991) study of factors that influence the survival of formalized jobs (in contrast to their relative standing), our current study shows that different factors may influence these two outcomes. Further research could fruitfully explore whether factors that increase routinization in the sense of normalization, are different from factors that encourage routinization in the sense of variance reduction within a given set of activities (as described in Table 13.2b).

We also propose that both behavioral learning and evolutionary theories may find it useful to conceptualize specific individuals as a type of routine. Each person represents a menu of likely activities and performance capabilities. As Perrow (1986 [1972], p. 22) noted, professionals are basically people 'who have complex rules built into them'. From this perspective, an important question about the fate of a performance routine is to see whether it is also attached to a 'person' routine already in the organization. The relative standing of a job filled by a familiar incumbent, from this viewpoint, would be affected by the fact that this represents two pre-existing organizational routines linked together.

Implications for Social and Neoinstitutional Theories of Change

We have drawn on several lines of theorizing about social processes, including frameworks that stress political, interpretative and emergent processes. Our results not only give credence to concerns that learning and evolutionary theories may be 'undersocialized,' but also allow specific predictions on how social processes may moderate learning. In that way, our work extends early theorizing by Berger and Luckmann (1967) by distinguishing not only different ways in which routines may be created, but also normalization from reduction in variance.

Neoinstitutional theory has increasingly argued that instrumentality has complex relationships with legitimacy (Orrú et al. 1991). Our work supports such an approach while highlighting some specific connections. Early neoinstitutional theory argued that instrumentality matters in the early existence of an action (DiMaggio and Powell 1983; Tolbert and Zucker 1983). More recent work has emphasized that the instrumental and non-instrumental should both independently influence action (Orrú et al. 1991). Yet other work indicates that the impact of instrumental criteria will vary by context (Westphal et al. 1997). We found main effects for the contribution of social processes as well as robust interaction patterns between social and learning processes for medium-contribution jobs, consistent with emphases on contingency approaches to the impact of instrumental and other factors. Future research should try to examine the detailed processes involving either trade-offs or intertwining more directly.

Our study also contributes to fine-grained work on structuration of organizations in which routines have different levels of influence on persistence behavior (Giddens 1979; Barley 1986). Several of our hypotheses posited that political processes (Strauss 1978) would affect the chance that jobs would be seen as part of the regular workings of a department. Others claimed that the possibility of multiple interpretations (Weick 1979) would increase the chances for higher degrees of routinization. We found that changes in mission ambiguity and in resource uncertainty *increased* the chances that a job would be seen as part of the regular workings of a department. These effects were particularly important for medium-contribution jobs. If we are right in our line of reasoning, our findings predict that a higher number of frameworks for interpretation or evaluation increases the odds that a given routine will obtain a higher degree of routinization. Thus, future studies on structuration may be enhanced by examining the effects of multiple frameworks more explicitly.

Returning to March and Olsen's (1989) distinction between the logic of consequences and the logic of appropriateness in organizational action, we think our results endorse the suspicion that both forms of logic may not only occur, but also interact within organizations. The relative standing of routines was influenced by both outcomes and by variables we believe reflect interpretative and social forms of logic. Perhaps even more importantly, we anticipate that the degree to which particular jobs are seen as part of the regular workings of their departments probably influences the organizational impact of the job activities and higher-level organizational action. Further research could usefully examine this prediction.

7 CONCLUSION

Richard Cyert remains an architect of the behavioral theory of the firm, from which many different literatures have drawn insight and lines of empirical research. Our study follows in the tradition of the behavioral theory of the firm by emphasizing links between organizational routines and standard operating procedures, organizational learning and social processes. Richard Cyert also served as president of a private major research university in the United States, the institutional context examined in this study, and no doubt could have anticipated the substantive as well as theoretical focus of our work.

Our study builds on and extends Cyert's original insights and desire for a more nuanced and realistic theory of organizational action. It supports the vision of intentionally adaptive institutions that change through variation – including deliberate variation – selection, and retention of routines. It supports a vision of an interactive landscape of interpretation and evaluation that influences the relative standing of routines already created. It begins to reveal factors that create the status of different routines, which in turn may play a key role in organizational action. Importantly, our findings point to the intricate links between, and intertwining of, learning and social processes that can change the relative standing of organizational routines in organizations.

NOTE

* The authors thank Joel Baum, Cristina Gibson, Jim March, Todd Saxton, Mary Waller, Lynne Zucker, and three anonymous reviewers of the Academy of Management OMT Division for their valuable and constructive comments. We appreciate the help in data collection provided by Judy Jewison, Charles Lehner, and Robert Shaver. We are grateful for the editorial assistance provided by Margaret Wilkins. An early version of this chapter was presented at the Academy of Management Meetings in Dallas, TX, in August 1994. We thank Richard M. Cyert for helping create the discourse to which this contributes.

REFERENCES

Allison, Graham T. (1971), *Essence of Decisions: Explaining the Cuban Missile Crisis*, Boston, MA: Little, Brown.

Amburgey, Terry L. and Anne S. Miner (1992), 'Strategic momentum: the effects of repetitive, positional and contextual momentum on merger activity', *Strategic Management Journal*, **13**, 335–49.

Argote, Linda (1999), *Organizational Learning: Creating, Retaining and Transferring Knowledge*, Boston, MA: Kluwer.

Argote, Linda and Dennis Epple (1990), 'Learning curves in manufacturing', *Science*, **247**, 920–24.

Ashforth, Blake E. and Yitzhak Fried (1988), 'The mindlessness of organizational behaviors', *Human Relations*, **41**, 305–29.

Barley, Stephen R. (1986), 'Technology as an occasion for structuring: evidence from observations of CT scanners and the social order of radiology departments', *Administrative Science Quarterly*, **31**, 78–108.

Baum, Joel A.C. and Jitendra V. Singh (1994), *Evolutionary Dynamics of Organizations*, New York: Oxford University Press.

Berger, Peter L. and Thomas Luckmann (1967), *The Social Construction of Reality*, New York: Doubleday.

Bodewes, Wynand E.J. (1998), 'Codified routines and innovation: formalization's role in organizational evolution', Working Paper, Rotterdam School of Management, Rotterdam.

Burgelman, Robert A. (1983), 'A process model of internal corporate venturing in the diversified major firm', *Administrative Science Quarterly*, **28**, 223–44.

Burgelman, Robert A. (1994), 'Fading memories: a process theory of strategic business exit in dynamic environments', *Administrative Science Quarterly*, **39**, 24–56.

Cheng, Yu-Ting and Andrew H. Van de Ven (1996), 'Learning the innovation journey: order out of chaos?', *Organization Science*, **7**: 593–619.

Cohen, Michael D. and Paul Bacdayan (1994), 'Organizational routines are stored as procedural memory: evidence from a laboratory study', reprinted in Michael D. Cohen and Lee Sproull (eds) (1996), *Organizational Learning*, Thousand Oaks, CA: Sage, 403–29.

Cohen, Michael D., Roger Burkhart, Giovanni Dosi, Massimo Egidi, Luigi Marengo, Massimo Warglien and Sidney Winter (1996), 'Routines and other recurring action patterns of organizations: contemporary research issues,' *Industrial and Corporate Change*, **5** (3), 653–98.

Cyert, Richard M. (1975), *The Management of Non-profit Organizations: With Emphasis on Universities*, Lexington, MA: Lexington Books.

Cyert, Richard M. and James G. March (1992 [1963]), *A Behavioral Theory of the Firm*, Englewood-Cliffs, NJ: Prentice-Hall.

DiMaggio, Paul J. and Walter W. Powell (1983), The iron cage revisited: institutional isomorphism and collective rationality in organizational fields', *American Sociological Review*, **48**, 147–60.

Epple, Dennis, Linda Argote and Kenneth Murphy (1996), 'An empirical investigation of the microstructure of knowledge acquisition and transfer through learning by doing', *Operations Research*, **44**, 77–86.

Feldman, Martha (1989), *Order without Design. Information Production and Policy Making*. Stanford, CA: Stanford University Press.

Feldman, Martha (2000), 'Organizational routines as a source of continuous change', *Organization Science*, **11**, 611–29.

Gersick, Connie J.G. and J. Richard Hackmann (1990), 'Habitual routines in task-performing groups'. *Organizational Behavior and Human Decision Processes*, **47**, 65–97.

Giddens, Anthony (1979), *Central Problems in Social Theory*, Berkeley, CA: University of California Press.

Giddens, Anthony (1984), *The Constitution of Society*, Berkeley, CA: University of California Press.

Glynn, Mary Ann, Theresa K. Lant and Frances J. Milliken (1994), 'Mapping learning processes in organizations: a multi-level framework linking learning and organizing', pp. 43–83 in *Advances in Managerial Cognition and Organizational Information Processing*, **5**, Greenwich, CT: JAI Press.

Haunschild, Pamela and Anne S. Miner (1997), 'Modes of interorganizational imitation: the effects of outcome salience and uncertainty', *Administrative Science Quarterly*, **42**, 472–99.

Hickson, David J., C. Robert Hinings, C.A. Lee, R.E. Schneck and Johannes M. Pennings (1971), 'A strategic contingencies theory of intra-organizational power', *Administrative Science Quarterly*, **16**, 216–29.

Huber, George (1991), 'Organizational learning: the contributing processes and a review of the literatures', *Organization Science*, **2**, 88–115.

Jepperson, Ronald L. (1991), 'Institutions, institutional effects, and institutionalism', reprinted in Walter W. Powell and Paul J. DiMaggio (eds), *The New Institutionalism in Organizational Analysis*, Chicago, IL: University of Chicago Press, 143–63.

Knicely, A.S. (1983), 'A study of the effect of job change in simulated organizations of work habits', Unpublished Master's Thesis, Purdue University.

Kraft, Philip (1977), *Programmers and Managers: The Routinization of Computer Programming in the United States*, New York: Springer Verlag.

Lant, Theresa K. (1992), 'Aspiration level updating: an empirical exploration', *Management Science*, **38**, 623–44.

Lant, Theresa K. and Stephen J. Mezias (1990), 'Managing discontinuous change: a simulation study of organizational learning and entrepreneurship', *Strategic Management Journal*, **11**, 147–79.

Lant, Theresa K. and Stephen J. Mezias (1992), 'An organizational learning model of convergence and reorientation', *Organization Science*, **3**, 47–71.

Levitt, Barbara and James G. March (1988), 'Organizational learning', *Annual Review of Sociology*, **14**, 319–40.

March, James G. (1981), 'Footnotes to organizational change', *Administrative Science Quarterly*, **26**, 563–77.

March, James G. (1991), 'Exploration and exploitation in organizational learning', *Organization Science*, **2**, 71–87.

March, James G. and Johan P. Olsen (1976), *Ambiguity and Choice in Organizations*, Bergen, Norway: Universitetsforlaget.

March, James G. and Herb A. Simon (1958), *Organizations*, New York: Wiley.

March, James G. and Johan P. Olsen (1989), *Rediscovering institutions: the organizational basis of politics*, New York: Free Press.

Mezias, Stephen J. (1990), 'Institutional sources of organizational practice: financial reporting at the Fortune 200', *Administrative Science Quarterly*, **35**, 431–57.

Mezias, Stephen J. and Mario Scarselletta (1994), 'Resolving financial reporting problems: an institutional analysis of the process', *Administrative Science Quarterly*, **39**, 654–78.

Miner, Anne S. (1987), 'Idiosyncratic jobs in formalized organizations', *Administrative Science Quarterly*, **32**, 327–51.

Miner, Anne S. (1990), 'Structural evolution through idiosyncratic jobs: the potential for unplanned learning', *Organization Science*, **1**, 195–210.

Miner, Anne S. (1991), 'Organizational evolution and the social ecology of jobs', *American Sociological Review*, **56**, 772–85.

Miner, Anne S. (1994), 'Seeking adaptive advantage: evolutionary theory and managerial action', in Jitendra V. Singh and Joel A. Baum (eds), *Evolutionary Dynamics of Organizations*, New York: Oxford University Press, 76–89.

Miner, Anne S., Paula Bassoff and Christine Moorman (2000), 'Contours of organizational improvisation and learning', University of Wisconsin Working Paper 2005, Madison, WI, USA.

Miner, Anne S. and Suzanne E. Estler (1985), 'Accrual mobility: Job mobility in higher education through responsibility accrual', *Journal of Higher Education*, **56** (1), 121–43.

Miner, Anne S. and Stephen J. Mezias (1996), 'Ugly duckling no more: pasts and futures of organizational learning research', *Organization Science*, **7**, 88–99.

Miner, Anne S. and Sri Raghavan (1999), 'Interorganizational imitation: a hidden engine of selection', in Joel A.C. Baum and William McKelvey (eds), *Variations in Organization Science: In Honor of Donald T. Campbell*, Thousand Oaks, CA: Sage, 5–62.

Nelson, Richard R. and Sidney G. Winter (1982), *An Evolutionary Theory of Economic Change*, Cambridge, MA: Harvard University Press.

Orrú, Marco, Nicole Woolsey Biggart and Gary G. Hamilton (1991), 'Organizational isomorphism in East Asia', in Walter W. Powell and Paul J. DiMaggio (eds), *The New Institutionalism in Organizational Analysis*, Chicago, IL: University of Chicago Press, 361–89.

Orwell, George (1983 [1945]), *Animal Farm*, Essex, UK: Longman Group.

Pentland, Brian T. and Henry H. Rueter (1994), 'Organizational routines as grammars of action', *Administrative Science Quarterly*, **39**, 484–510.

Perrow, Charles (1986 [1972]), *Complex Organizations: A Critical Essay*, 3rd edn, New York: Random House.

Pfeffer, Jerry A., Gerald R. Salancik and Huseyin Leblebici (1976), 'The effect of uncertainty on the use of social influence in organizational decision making', *Administrative Science Quarterly*, **21**, 227–45.

Rogers, Everett M. (1995), *Diffusion of Innovations*, 4th edn, New York: Free Press.

Salancik, Gerald R. and Jerry A. Pfeffer (1978), 'A social information processing approach to job attitudes and task design', *Administrative Science Quarterly*, **23**, 224–53.

Scott, W. Richard (1987), 'The adolescence of institutional theory', *Administrative Science Quarterly*, **32**, 493–511.

Scott, W. Richard (1995), *Institutions and Organizations*, Thousand Oaks, CA: Sage.

Starbuck, William H. (1992), 'Learning by knowledge-intensive firms', reprinted in Michael D. Cohen and Lee S. Sproull (eds) (1996), *Organizational Learning*, Thousand Oaks, CA: Sage, 484–515.

Strauss, Anselm (1978), *Negotiations*, San Francisco, CA: Jossey-Bass.

Strauss, Anselm, Leonard Schatzman, Danuta Ehrlich, Rue Bucher and Melvin Sabshin (1963), 'The hospital and its negotiated order', in Eliot Freidson (ed.), *The Hospital in Modern Society*, New York: Free Press, 147–69.

Thompson, James D. (1967), *Organizations in Action*, New York: McGraw-Hill.

Tolbert, Pamela S. and Lynne G. Zucker (1983), 'Institutional sources of change in the formal structure of organizations: the diffusion of civil service reform, 1880–1935', *Administrative Science Quarterly*, **28**, 22–39.

Tolbert, Pamela S. and Lynne G. Zucker (1996), 'The institutionalization of institutional theory', in Stewart R. Clegg, Cynthia Hardy and Walter Nord (eds), *Handbook of Organization Studies*, London: Sage Publications, 175–90.

Tyre, Marcie J. and Wanda J. Orlikowski (1993), 'Exploiting opportunities for technological improvement in organizations', *Sloan Management Review*, **35** (1), 13–26.

Van de Ven, Andrew and Douglas Polley (1992), 'Learning while innovating', *Organization Science*, **3**, 92–116.

Weick, Karl E. (1979), *The Social Psychology of Organizing*, Reading. MA: Addison-Wesley.

Weick, Karl E. (1991), 'The non-traditional quality of organizational learning', reprinted in Michael D. Cohen and Lee Sproull (eds) (1996), *Organizational Learning*, Thousand Oaks, CA: Sage, 163–74.

Weick, Karl E. (1993), 'The collapse of sensemaking in organizations: the Mann Gulch disaster', *Administrative Science Quarterly*, **38**, 628–52.

Weiss, Howard M. and Daniel R. Ilgen (1985), 'Routinized behavior in organizations', *Journal of Behavioral Economics*, **14** (Winter), 57–67.

Westphal, James D., Ranjay Gulati and Stephen M. Shortell (1997), 'Customization or conformity: an institutional and network perspective on the content and consequences of TQM adoption', *Administrative Science Quarterly*, **42**, 366–94.

Winter, Sidney G. (1986), 'The research program of the behavioral theory of the firm: orthodox critique and evolutionary perspective', in Benjamin Gilad and Stanley Kaish (eds), *Handbook of Behavioral Economics*, Volume A: Behavioral Macroeconomics, Greenwich, CT: JAI Press, 151–88.

Winter, Sidney G. (1994), 'Organizing for continuous improvement: evolutionary theory meets the quality revolution', reprinted in Michael D. Cohen and Lee S. Sproull (eds) (1996), *Organizational Learning*, Thousand Oaks, CA: Sage, 460–83.

Yelle, Louis E. (1979), 'The learning curve: historical review and comprehensive survey', *Decision Sciences*, **10**, 302–27.

Zucker, Lynne G. (1977), 'The role of institutionalization in cultural persistence', *American Sociological Review*, **42**, 726–43.

APPENDIX 13A1 PROCEDURES AND QUESTIONNAIRE ITEMS FOR RATING JOBS AND DEPARTMENTS

Degree of Routinization (Rated in Second Data Collection Wave)

To what extent was the job actually incorporated in the regular department workings and routines?

1 2 3 4 5 6 7
Minimally Completely

Contribution to the Department (Rated in Second Data Collection Wave)

The informants were asked to assess, 'In retrospect, compared to other ways in which the department might have used the same resources, how much did this job *actually* contribute to the department?'

1 2 3 4 5 6 7
Very *Un*favorable Contribution Very Favorable Contribution

During the training session, the raters were given specific anchors for each value of the scale and were also prompted to think specifically about *actual* positive effects that a job had on a department and not about expectations that the departments might have had about the job.

Job Types (Summary of Procedure Used in Miner 1991)

Planned novel jobs were planned in advance by management and then filled either from internal or external candidates. *Reclassifications* were existing jobs sufficiently expanded to receive new titles without altering their basic duties while *old jobs* did not change in duties or titles. Data on these three job types were drawn from archival computer sources. The duties of *evolved jobs* formed around the skills or interests of particular individuals *within* the organization and *opportunistic hires* formed around the skills or interests of particular individuals previously *outside* the organization. These job features were rated in the original study of idiosyncratic jobs.

Novel Jobs (Summary of Procedure used in Miner 1991)

All evolved jobs, opportunistic hires, and planned novel jobs were coded as 1 on Novel Job, all reclassifications and old jobs were coded as 0.

Familiarity of First Incumbent (Summary of Procedure used in Miner 1991)

Familiarity of First Incumbent was constructed by assigning a value of 1 to each evolved job, each reclassification, and each old job, since by definition all of these jobs were held by insiders to their departments. Opportunistic hires, by definition, involved people from outside the department and were given a value of 0. Each planned new job was coded based on whether it was filled from outside or inside the department.

Idiosyncrasy

At both first-wave and second-wave assessments informants answered, 'To what degree did the content of the job develop around the skills and/or interests of the person?' on a five-point scale.

1. job content did not develop around this person to an unusual extent
2. job content developed somewhat around the person
3. job content developed quite a bit around the person, but major components did not develop around the person
4. job content developed largely around the person
5. job content developed nearly completely around the skills and/or interests of the person.

Following Miner's (1987) rationale, we then reasoned that the degree of idiosyncrasy was very high (3) when observers at both times gave the job a rating of four or higher on this question, of middle strength (2) when only one observer rated the job as four or higher, and low (1) when neither rater ever rated it over 4 on that scale.

Change in Mission Ambiguity (Rated During First Data Collection Wave)

Our informants were given the following instruction to assess their department's change in mission ambiguity.

We want to know how much ambiguity there is in the mission of this department or unit. A unit has high ambiguity if it is difficult to specify its main mission. This can be because it has multiple goals, there is conflict over the goals, or because there is something inherently difficult to pin down about its goals. In contrast, a unit has high clarity if it is relatively easy to specify its mission.

Pattern of change since 79/80:

Ambiguity

1 2 3 4 5 6 7
Rapid Decline Stable Rapid Increase

Change in Resource Uncertainty (Rated During First Data Collection Wave)

Our informants were given the following instruction to assess their department's change in resource uncertainty.

This question asks about the degree of uncertainty in total resources. A department with a very stable base in the operating budget that does not change from year to year except to reflect inflation, for example, would be scored a 1. A department with a single source of income, but which suffered an unexpected reduction of 30 percent in funds in a one-year period would be scored a 7.

Pattern of change since 79/80:

1 2 3 4 5 6 7
Rapid Decline Stable Rapid Increase

Raters were asked to assess the changes in mission ambiguity and resource uncertainty since the beginning of the longitudinal study (April 1980) using the above scale. A special sheet reminded raters of highly charged university events during that period (for example, resignation of president) and helped them ground themselves in time for the ratings. Ninety percent of the departmental ratings were returned and usable. Most departments were rated by two independent raters whose inter-rater reliability ranged from 0.69 to 0.85.

APPENDIX 13A2 PREPARATION OF INFORMANTS FOR SECOND DATA WAVE

Evaluation sheets and coding rules were pilot tested with an initial panel of managers and personnel professionals within the organization to assure validity and feasibility. All 34 raters attended a two-hour training and job evaluation session. They were told that the research commenced as a broad project on organizational decision making and organizational inertia. In the second phase they, as the 'richest' source of organizational history, were being asked to provide global evaluations of job outcomes and influences on departments. The investigator asked each rater to rate three fictitious job examples to become familiar with the job evaluation sheet.

While retrospective perceptual measures can be problematic when assessing characteristics, we used several strategies to diminish this difficulty. Every informant was provided with a standard stimulus for each job, including initial employee name, initial job classification, initial job title, changes in classification, if any, changes in formal title, and dates of any transitions between incumbents. In addition, raters were provided with a list of key visible events in the university community for the time period covered by the study to help them recollect the period of time involved.

For our analyses, we used the ratings provided by the primary informant. However, we also recruited a second rater for a subset of jobs to probe the nature of our measures. These additional raters varied in the degree to which they were familiar with the focal departments and jobs. We estimated the inter-rater reliability using correlation coefficients based on questions used in this study as well as other questions and found that more than 50 percent of the coefficients were greater than 0.7. The overall inter-rater reliability across all departments was 0.63, but the true reliability may well be higher because pooling the ratings may have deflated the true inter-rater reliability. These assessments increased our confidence in the primary ratings by the key informants.

14. The role of adaptation and targets in organizational learning

Sridhar Seshadri and Zur Shapira

1 INTRODUCTION

Organizational learning became a salient topic in the organizational literature in the 1990s. It has been linked to research on innovation (Brown and Dugoid, 1991), entrepreneurship (Lant and Mezias, 1990), corporate renewal (Brown, 1990) and productivity (Argote, 1999). Two major approaches to organizational learning have been advanced: the adaptive learning paradigm and the knowledge development perspective (see Glynn et al., 1994). The adaptive learning paradigm views organizations as target-oriented, routine-based systems which respond to experience by repeating successful behaviors and avoiding those which have failed (Levitt and March, 1988; March, 1991). In contrast, the knowledge development approach emphasizes the content produced by the learning process, such as the pattern of cognitive associations (see, Argyris and Schön, 1978; Duncan and Weiss, 1979), as well as the processes by which these causal beliefs are communicated and institutionalized within and among organizations (see, Glynn, et al., 1994).

Research in the adaptive learning paradigm emphasizes search processes and decision making under uncertainty where managers attempt to uncover the nature of cause–effect relationships by adjusting their aspirations and behavior in response to experience (Cyert and March, 1963; Levinthal and March, 1981; Levitt and March, 1988; Lant, 1992). Other studies have examined the implications of incremental adaptation for search strategies and innovative behavior (Lant and Mezias, 1990; March, 1991).

2 LEARNING AND RATIONAL CHOICE BEHAVIOR

The ideas of choice and learning are intimately related in some respects but may be contrasted in others. For instance, it is perfectly sensible to assume that choice is informed by learning, as is the case with the notion of adaptive utility (see, for example, Cyert and DeGroot, 1987). On the other hand, experiential learning can be considered an alternative to choice in explaining behavior. In a recent article, March (1996) suggests that the behavioral pattern that is defined as risk aversion, may not characterize individual decision makers' specific traits (as is assumed under theories of rational choice), but be conceptualized as a result of the process of experiential learning. March (1996) used three different models as a vehicle to demonstrate the relationship between choice and learning. In his paper, a simulated learner is presented with the decision of choosing between two projects. The criterion used to select the project, and the method of updating these criteria based on the observed outcome constitute a learning model. We use the same models to examine their role in organizational learning, to understand the power of these models for distinguishing between alternatives, and to examine how targets and adaptation can be incorporated within the context of these learning models.

3 ORGANIZATIONAL LEARNING CHOICE AND RISK TAKING

To couch the discussion of learning and risk taking in an organizational context, consider the claim of Kahneman and Lovallo (1993) that decision makers display excessive risk aversion in organizations. They suggest that decision makers consider problems in isolation which may lead to overcaution in risk taking. The seemingly cautious attitude might actually be due to lack of statistical aggregation when evaluating projects. Thus, if decision makers evaluate projects in isolation (and possibly as a sequential decision-making process in which each project evaluated is either recommended for funding or not), the beneficial effects of statistical aggregation are neglected. What can be said for learning in this context? Two aspects appear relevant in answering this question:

1. What is the decision problem faced by a learner? Is it improvement in decision making over time so that each decision is taken in a better manner? Or is it taking a sequence of decisions correctly, in other words, is the sequence of decisions viewed as a single collective decision?
2. The second aspect is whether learning implies only gaining an understanding of the risk return trade-off associated with certain classes of projects?

In answering these questions, it may be worthwhile to revisit the paradox devised by Samuelson (1963). In the problem fashioned by Samuelson, a decision maker is given the option of selecting a single play of a gamble in which he or she has equal chances of winning of $200 or losing $100. Persons who rejected this gamble offered by Samuelson said that they would accept multiple plays of the same gamble. The paradox arises in part because under certain conditions accepting the single gamble can be shown to be equivalent to accepting multiple plays of the same gamble (see Tversky and Bar-Hillel, 1983). Kahneman and Lovallo (1993) argue that narrow framing could lead to such apparently contradictory behavior, that is if the decision maker instead of evaluating the single gamble changes to a framework in which the same gamble is offered again and again, then the decision could be different.

This provides a partial answer to (1), namely that narrow framing leads to isolated evaluation of individual decisions even though each decision might be part of the same sequence of decisions. In the models to follow, the learner is assumed to use one of three mechanistic rules that is oriented more towards making the correct decision than toward taking a set of decisions correctly. This might pose problems in organizational contexts. As to (2), the mechanistic rules examined below deal with situations in which there is a richness of information that is difficult to describe or to embed in a 'many-to-one' mapping. (A rule might be generally construed to be a many-to-one mapping or many-to-many mapping.) Thus, in general a rule that cannot evaluate different payoff structures may prove to be adequate in responding to variations. The outcome from applying such rules might look like risk aversion but the causal factor might not be risk aversion but could simply be the use of rules without comprehending the limitations and potential dangers associated with incorrect or inappropriate framing (at least from the organizational perspective).

This viewpoint could also be exacerbated by focus on survival (see, March and Shapira, 1992). To a certain extent, emphasis on survival leads to decision makers seeking strategies that improve the chances of survival rather than evaluating a decision using the full richness of information. On the other hand, Kahneman and Lovallo (1993) suggest that decision makers could be overly optimistic due to various factors contributing to overconfidence in one or more of their beliefs, their confidence in their own capabilities and capacity for controlling the outcome (see also Shapira, 1995). Once again, focus on high returns that blank out low ones could result in a sequence of decisions that appear to be overly optimistic or overconfident.

As March (1996, p. 309) notes, 'Two of the grandest theoretical traditions for understanding human choices are found in theories of rational choice and theories of experiential learning'. As expressed above, it is rather difficult even to set out the objectives of learning, yet there have been numerous popular books on learning in organizations.

March (1996) looks to models of experiential learning to provide insights into 'risk taking as a propensity, that is, in part, learned' (p. 310). We revisit these models, and extend them so that we can examine what can additionally be said about the following:

1. Can the experiential models accommodate the concept of focus?
2. Can becoming more adept at undertaking a project from experience be incorporated into these models?
3. Are the 'learning powers' of the three models different?
4. Can the models distinguish subtle differences between alternative projects? In particular, can they properly distinguish between clearly better and clearly worse alternatives? Can they distinguish between more risky and less risky alternatives?

Questions 1 and 2 pertain to the modeling issues. Questions 3 and 4 to whether the learning models examined in this chapter are sufficiently discriminating. Following March (1996), we consider the same class of models of experiential learning. In each model:

1. There is a learner. The learner has an initial probability vector of choices among alternatives. After each learning trial, this probability vector is updated according to a learning rule.
2. The learner has a decision rule. In each trial, the learner chooses an alternative using the probability vector of choices. The choice is among two or more alternatives with probabilistic or deterministic outcomes. The choice is probabilistically determined using a random draw based on the probability vector of choices. The actual outcome depends on an outcome rule.
3. The outcome rule is invoked once the learner chooses an alternative. The actual outcome is based on a probabilistic draw from the distribution of returns for that alternative.
4. The learning rule is used to update the probability vector of choices between alternatives. Thus, if $p_{i,t}$ is the probability of choosing alternative i on the t-th trial, and alternative j is actually chosen on this trial, then the learning rule uses the knowledge that alternative j was chosen as well as the knowledge of the outcome on the t-th trial to update the probability vector, $(p_{i,t})$ to $(p_{i,t+1})$.

The class of models that accommodate 1–4 above is very rich. We first describe the three models considered by March (1996), then make some minor modifications to incorporate focus and experience. The three models are: a *fractional adjustment* model that is a variation of the Bush–Mosteller–Estes model (Bush and Mosteller, 1955; Estes, 1959), an *average adjustment* model that is based on the Herrnstein, matching model (Herrnstein, 1961, 1970; Staddon, 1977), and a *weighted return adjustment* model that is based on exponential updating. The second and third models employ techniques for updating that are often used to generate a forecast based on time-series data. The first model is rather unique in this regard, and does not bear any resemblance to time-series forecasting rules.

The Fractional Adjustment Model

The fractional adjustment model updates the probabilities ($p_{i,t}$) to ($p_{i,t+1}$) based on the most recent outcome. If alternative j was chosen and the outcome was favorable then $p_{j,t+1}$ is increased; else it is decreased. The learning rule uses a parameter α to update the probability vector. The parameter α can take any value between 0 and 1. We only consider two alternatives in our experiments, thus the updating rule takes a simple form. (In the case where there are more than two alternatives the probability vector will have to be re-normalized after the update.) If alternative j is chosen on the t-th trial and yields a reward of $k \geq 0$ then:

$$p_{j,t+1} = 1 - (1 - \alpha)^{\kappa} (1 - p_{i,t}). \tag{14.1}$$

$$p_{3-j,t+1} = 1 - p_{j,t+1}. \tag{14.2}$$

In equation (14.2), note that when $j = 1$, $3 - j = 2$, and vice versa. Thus, equation (14.2) states that an increase (or decrease) in the probability of selecting alternative j results in a corresponding decrease (or increase) in the probability of choosing the other alternative. If the reward k is negative then:

$$p_{j,t+1} = (1 - \alpha)^{\kappa} p_{i,t}. \tag{14.3}$$

$$p_{3-j,t+1} = 1 - p_{j,t+1}. \tag{14.4}$$

Thus, positive rewards increase the probability of choosing the alternative and negative rewards decrease it. The probability vector has to be initialized at time zero. This can be done in any convenient fashion. We set the probability of choosing an alternative equal to 0.5. As mentioned by March (1996), setting the learning rule parameter to be the same for positive and negative rewards is a simplification, as is also the setting the learning limits in the model between 0 and 1. Moreover, the manner of dealing with varying amounts of reward (that is, using the exponent form $(1 - \alpha)^{\kappa}$ is only one way of modeling the problem.

In order to include focus in this model, define a target level λ that the decision maker desires. Then, before applying the rule the reward is truncated using the target level as follows:

$$k_{\lambda} = \max \{0, k - \lambda\}. \tag{14.5}$$

The truncated value k_λ is used instead of the actual reward k in (14.1)–(14.4). The value of λ is the second parameter in the model. To include experience effects in the model, we use a third parameter ε (≥ 0) and modify the reward as a function of the number of times prior to trial t that the alternative was chosen. Let alternative j be chosen at trial t and the number of times the alternative was chosen prior to this trial be $N_{j,t-1}$. Then,

$$k_1 = \max\ \{0, ke^{\varepsilon N_{j,t-1}} - \lambda\}. \tag{14.6}$$

We only consider alternatives with all outcomes greater than or equal to zero. Thus, with increasing experience, the expected reward grows 'with the growing experience. The greater the value of ε the greater is the effect of experience. This model is consistent with the learning curve model (Argote, 1999).

It is of interest to observe what happens when the learner (without his or her knowledge) is faced with two deterministic alternatives. Let λ and ε be equal to zero. Let the alternatives $i = 1, 2$ yield the deterministic return of a and b, respectively. Define a steady state to be one in which the probability vector does not change from one trial to another. In a steady state, which exists in this case, the probability of choosing alternative i are denoted as p_i. The probability p_1 has to satisfy equation (14.7). In this equation, the first term on the right-hand side represents the probability of choosing alternative 1 and then updating p_1 according to (14.1). Similarly, the second term represents the probability of choosing alternative 2 and then updating p_1 according to (14.2). The sum total should equal p_1 is steady state. Obviously, both $p_1 = 0$ and $p_1 = 1$ are feasible solutions to (14.7). If p_1 is not equal to zero, then dividing both sides of equation (14.7) by p_1 we obtain (14.7a) which is true when $a \neq b$ only if $p_1 = 1$. Thus unless the two alternatives yield the same return ($a = b$) (and we begin with non-zero probability of choosing the alternative with the higher return) it can be established that the probability of choosing the alternative with the higher return will eventually go to one:

$$p_1 = p_1(1 - (1 - \alpha)^a (1 - p_1)) + (1 - p_1) ((1 - \alpha)^b p_1) \tag{14.7}$$

$$1 = 1 - (1 - \alpha)^a (1 - p_1) + (1 - p_1)(1 - \alpha)^b \tag{14.7a}$$

In summary, for deterministic alternatives the fractional adjustment rule eventually selects the outcome with the highest return. For later reference, let $a = 1$, $b = 2$, and label the two alternatives as D_1 and D_2, respectively. The case when the returns are random is examined later in this section.

Average Return Model

In this model, the probabilities are adjusted to be proportional to the average reward received from choosing the alternative. To compute the average reward define the following quantities:

$S_{j,t}$ = Sum of return from choosing alternative j during periods 1 through t
$N_{j't}$ = Number of times alternative j was chosen during periods 1 through t.

Then the average return obtained from alternative j is defined as:

$$A_{j,t} := S_{j't} / N_{j,t}. \tag{14.8}$$

We shall ensure that the returns are always non-negative, thus avoiding any ambiguity in the calculations below. The probability of choosing alternative j in period (t+1) is given by:

$$P_{j,t+1} = A_{j,t} / \Sigma_i A_{i,t}. \tag{14.9}$$

Note that the probabilities are automatically normalized to sum up to unity. The initial values of the probabilities are set proportional to the expected value of the two alternatives, the values of $N_{j,0}$ to one, and the values of $S_{j,0}$ to the expected value of the alternatives. The initial choice does not matter as long as none of the initial probabilities is equal to zero. As summarized by March (1996), this model is a simplification as well as a fundamental modification of the matching models. The model presented above assumes infinitely long memory of results whereas the matching models normally truncate the length of experience. The fundamental deviation is that this model relates to a sequential trial-based choice of probabilities, whereas matching models relate to response rates.

In order to include focus in this model, define as before a target level λ that the decision maker desires. Then, the reward is truncated using the target level as previously to $k_\lambda = \max\{0, k - \lambda\}$. The truncated value k_λ is used instead of the actual reward k in computing the sum $S_{j,t}$. To include experience effects in the model, we use the third parameter ε and modify the reward as a function of the number of times prior to trial t that the alternative was chosen. Let alternative j be chosen at trial t. The number of times the alternative was chosen prior to this trial is $N_{j,t-1}$. Then,

$$k_e = \max\{0, ke^{\varepsilon N_{j,t-1}} - \lambda\}. \tag{14.10}$$

The k_λ's are used to compute the sum's $S_{j,t}$'s. (see equation 14.8).

Consider the two deterministic alternatives described previously. Let λ and ε, be equal to zero. In a steady state and with any starting condition that has a probability vector strictly greater than zero, the steady-state probability of choosing alternative i, namely, p_i, is given by:

$$p_1 = a/(a+b), \text{ and } p_2 = b/(a+b). \tag{14.11}$$

In other words, this model does *not* eventually choose the alternative that has the greater reward. The veracity of this claim follows from the fact that the average return equals the deterministic return, which is a and b for the two alternatives. In particular, since we set a = 1 and b = 2, the probability of choosing D_1 is 1/3 and the probability of choosing D_2 is 2/3.

Weighted Return Model

In this model, the average returns are updated using the most recent history and the current outcome. If alternative i is not chosen at trial t then $A_{i,t}$ is not changed. If alternative j was chosen at trial t and the return was k from choosing this alternative, then:

$$A_{j,t+1} = \beta k + (1 - \beta)A_{j,t}. \tag{14.12}$$

In this model, β is a parameter that takes a value in the interval (0,1). A larger value of β places greater weight on more recent outcomes. This model is similar to the exponential smoothing technique for generating a forecast. This model removes some of the drawbacks of the average return model by requiring the decision maker to store just the average returns. In the average return model the decision maker stores both the average return as well as the number of trials conducted of each particular alternative.

In order to include focus in this model, define as before a target level λ that the decision-maker desires. Then, the reward is truncated using the target level as previously to $k_\lambda = \max\{0, k - \lambda\}$. The truncated value k_λ is used instead of the actual reward k in updating the average. To include experience effects in the model, we use the third parameter ε and modify the reward as a function of the number of times prior to trial t that the alternative was chosen. Let alternative j be chosen at trial t. The number of times the alternative was chosen prior to this trial is $N_{j,t-1}$. Then,

$$k_e = \max\ \{(0, ke^{\varepsilon N_{j,t-1}} - \lambda\}. \tag{14.13}$$

The k_e's are used to update the averages. The starting values in this method are identical to those used in the average return model.

Consider the two deterministic alternatives described previously. Let λ and ε be equal to zero. In a steady state and with any starting condition that has a probability vector strictly greater than zero, the steady-state probability of choosing alternative i, namely p_i, is given by:

$$p_1 = a/(a+b), \text{ and } p_2 = b/(a+b). \tag{14.14}$$

In other words, this model does *not* eventually choose the alternative that has the greater reward. The veracity of this claim follows from the fact that the average return equals the deterministic return, which is a and b for the two alternatives. Thus, even exponential smoothing fails to differentiate between the two alternatives. Once again the probability of choosing D_1 is 1/3 and the probability of choosing D_2 is 2/3.

4 COMPARISON AMONG THE MODELS

March (1996) used these models as a vehicle to demonstrate how choice and learning are related. He simulated a learner who is presented with the decision of choosing between two projects. The criterion used to select a project and the method of updating these criteria based on the observed outcome was formulated as a learning model. We make comparisons among the same models to understand the power of these models for distinguishing between alternatives.

In particular, we introduce the concept of stochastic dominance, and ask whether the three models differ in their ability to distinguish between projects, when the payoffs from undertaking one project stochastically dominate the payoffs from the other in a variety of ways. We consider two types of stochastic dominance, one in which the payoffs from one alternative are greater in probability than the payoffs from the other; and the other in which the expected value of the payoffs are the same but the payoffs from one alternative are less 'risky' compared to the payoffs from the other. These concepts are described in detail below.

Finally, two aspects of organizational learning, the experience curve and the setting of targets are integrated. The experience curve stipulates that the organization gets more efficient at carrying out a task the more times the task is repeated. The setting of targets develops a focal target for the persons within an organization to maintain while choosing among alternatives or executing a task. We show that these can be added to the models of learning. The effects of adaptation and targets on outcomes produced by the three modified models are discussed. We compare how the three models deal with deterministic as well as stochastic dominance, and we show that the outcomes from applying the models differ sharply when these aspects are incorporated into the models.

Comparison of Alternatives: Stochastic Dominance

An alternative A is said to stochastically dominate another alternative B, if the probability that alternative A yields a return that is greater than or equal to any given number x is not less than the probability that alternative B yields a return greater than or equal to x. A 'rational' decision maker is expected to prefer A over B if A stochastically dominates B. Consider the alternatives shown in Table 14.1.

Table 14.1 Stochastic dominance

Alternative	Probability				
	0.2	0.2	0.2	0.2	0.2
A_1	\$0.5	\$1.0	\$1.5	\$2.0	\$2.5
A_2	\$1.0	\$2.0	\$3.0	\$4.0	\$5.0

In this example, alternative A_2 yields twice the return of alternative A_1. However, because the outcome is stochastic, there is a non-zero probability that A_1 gives a higher return than A_2. We say that alternative A_2 stochastically dominates alternative A_1. Let λ and ε be equal to zero. Let α and β be equal to 0.1. We obtain the results shown in Table 14.2 after simulating 8000 trials[1] of each of the three models.

Table 14.2 Comparison of models under stochastic dominance

	Fractional adjustment model	Average return model	Weighted return model
Steady-state probability of choosing alternative A_1	0.076000	0.333331	0.334180

Thus, similar to the deterministic case, the fractional adjustment model is better able to detect the superior alternative A_2 when compared to the other two models. It is more discriminating because the steady-state probability of choosing A_2 is higher but the fractional adjustment model is not perfect. It does not eventually *always* choose the better alternative.

Comparison of Alternatives: Concave Order Stochastic Dominance

An alternative A is said to stochastically dominate another alternative B in the concave order sense, if the expected returns of the two alternatives are identical and the graph of the distribution function of A crosses the graph of the distribution function of alternative B once and from below (see Shaked and Shanthikumar, 1994). Intuitively, B's return is more spread out. Therefore, a 'risk-averse' decision maker prefers alternative A over alternative B. Consider the alternatives shown in Table 14.3.

Table 14.3 Stochastic dominance in the concave sense

Alternative	Probability				
	0.2	0.2	0.2	0.2	0.2
B_1	\$0.5	\$1.0	\$2.0	\$5.0	\$7.0
B_2	\$1.5	\$2.0	\$4.0	\$4.0	\$4.0

Both alternatives, B_1 and B_2 yield the same expected return of \$3.10. However, alternative B_2 is less risky because it stochastically dominates alternative B_1 in the concave order sense. To see this, observe that the $\Pr\{B_1 \leq x\}$ is larger than the $\Pr\{B_2 \leq x\}$ for values of x less than or equal to \$2.00 but smaller for larger values of x. Let λ and ε be equal to zero. Let α and β be equal to 0.1. We obtain the results shown in Table 14.4 after simulating 8000 trials of each of the three models. We again see that the fractional adjustment model has better discriminating power with regard to detecting stochastic dominance in the concave sense.

Table 14.4 Comparison of models under stochastic dominance in the concave sense

	Functional adjustment model	Average return model	Weighted return model
Steady-state probability of choosing alternative B_1	0.446000	0.499949	0.491957

Comparison of Alternatives: Focus and Experience

Focus

We shall revisit the examples discussed above but with the addition of focus first, and then with the experience effect incorporated into the three models. Let the focus equal one. The decision maker ignores all returns that are less than or equal to one. Thus, $\lambda = 1$ and ε is equal to zero. Let α and β be equal to 0.1. We obtain the results shown in Table 14.5 after simulating 8000 trials of each of the three models. Recall that D_1 has half the return of D_2, similarly, A_1 has half the expected return of A_2, and B_1 is the 'riskier' alternative. The results without 'focus' are shown in parentheses.

The main inference from these results is that adding the focus variable in any of the three models leads to the desired direction of change for two cases: the deterministic case when the return from an alternative is higher than the return from another and the stochastic dominance case in which the probability of obtaining a return larger than any given value is equal or higher for one alternative when compared to another. However, only the fractional adjustment model gives the desired shift for stochastic dominance in the concave order. The reason is that the 'riskier' alternative looks more attractive in the other two models when the focus is on high returns. (Mathematically, the ratio of the expected values increases.) The fractional adjustment model discounts infrequent but large returns, thus reducing the effect of significant deviations from influencing future decisions. In particular, this result is in marked contrast to the results reported by March (1996), where all models produced similar results. These results can also be established analytically without recourse to simulation.

Table 14.5 Comparison of models with focus added

Criterion for discrimination	Fractional adjustment model	Average return model	Weighted return model
Steady-state probability of choosing alternative D_1	0.000000 (0.000000)	0.0079221 (0.333333)	0.0012001 (0.333333)
Steady-state probability of choosing alternative A_1	0.0030000 (0.076000)	0.230907 (0.333331)	0.227005 (0.334180)
Steady-state probability of choosing alternative B_1	0.432000 (0.446000)	0.511494 (0.499949)	0.497145 (0.491957)

Note: Results without 'focus' shown in parentheses.

Extreme focus

It is evident that if we let focus equal four, then the decision maker ignores all returns that are less than or equal to four. Thus, when comparing alternatives B_1 and B_2 all three models will eventually choose B_1.

Now, we add the final dimension of learning to the models. We do this in two stages: adding learning without focus, and then adding both.

Learning

The parameters used are: $\lambda = 0$ and $\varepsilon = 0.01$. Let α and β be equal to 0.1. The results after 8000 trials are shown in Table 14.6.

Table 14.6 Comparison of models with learning added

Criterion for discrimination	Fractional adjustment model	Average return model	Weighted return model
Steady-state probability of choosing alternative D_1	0.000000 (0.000000)	0.000000 (0.333333)	0.000000 (0.333333)
Steady-state probability of choosing alternative A_1	0.089000 (0.076000)	0.000000 (0.333331)	0.000000 (0.334180)
Steady-state probability of choosing alternative B_1	0.449000 (0.446000)	0.451000 (0.499949)	0.396000 (0.491957)

Note: Results without 'focus' shown in parentheses.

We can see that in startling contrast to the case when 'focus' is added to the models, experience shifts the choice in the desired direction for the average returns and the weighted returns model. The reason is that these two models are significantly influenced by the growing returns of alternatives that are chosen more often. In particular, the weighted returns model places greater weight on more recent returns. Thus, the alternative that has been chosen more often looks even more attractive.

Focus and experience

Now we let $\lambda = 1$ and $\varepsilon = 0.01$. Let α and β be equal to 0.1. The results after 8000 trials are shown in Table 14.7. As expected, combining the two variables yields a mix of the earlier results.

Table 14.7 Comparison of models with focus and learning added

Criterion for discrimination	Fractional adjustment model	Average return model	Weighted return model
Steady-state probability of choosing alternative D_1	0.000000 (0.000000)	0.000000 (0.333333)	0.000000 (0.333333)
Steady-state probability of choosing alternative A_1	0.012000 (0.076000)	0.000000 (0.333331)	0.000000 (0.334180)
Steady-state probability of choosing alternative B_1	0.455000 (0.446000)	0.487000 (0.499949)	0.404000 (0.491957)

Note: Results without 'focus' shown in parentheses.

5 DISCUSSION AND CONCLUSIONS

Our findings suggest that the three models can be classified into two classes: those that are influenced by recent results and those that are not.

The fractional adjustment model (and less so the weighted return model if β is low) belongs to the latter class. Focus is a key variable for influencing the decision maker to choose alternatives that are stochastically or deterministically dominant in the fractional adjustment model. Focus reduces the risk-taking tendencies when it is set to a moderate value but extreme focus can result in very risky decision making.

The average returns model belongs to the former class. In addition, if the value of β were low (0.1 is low), the weighted returns model also belongs to the former class. In these models, experience is a key variable. Thus, as the decision makers learn to execute better they tend to make the 'right' choices – to choose alternatives that are stochastically or deterministically dominant. Focus actually reduces the power of these two learning models to discriminate between alternatives. However, extreme focus can result in very risky decision making.

These results extend March's (1996) findings. They also raise some issues with regard to experiential versus latent learning. In these models the learner is changing the probabilities of choosing among alternatives based on outcomes by focusing on more recent outcomes or by looking at a weighted average of the outcomes' history. There are situations where feedback is not available (at least not immediately) and where the outcomes depend on exogenous forces rather than the learner's responses (see Einhorn, 1980), so inference based on outcomes may be erroneous. It is therefore of interest to examine situations in which feedback is limited, or where the learner does not respond to all choice alternatives. Such conditions may give rise to studying the notion of latent learning, an idea that was salient during the era of 'cognitive' (rather than 'incentive') interpretation of learning and may shed more light on the process of knowledge development. Both perspectives are needed for a better understanding of the phenomena underlying organizational learning.

While our discussion extends March's (1996) treatment, it bears relevance to the behavioral theory of the firm's focus on organizational learning (see, for example, Cyert and March, 1992, pp. 171–4). As noted by Glynn et al. (1994) current perspectives on organizational learning follow either the 'adaptive learning' approach or the 'knowledge development' approach. The former is associated with the work of researchers like Argyris and Schön (1978), while the latter follows the behavioral theory of the firm, which emphasizes behavioral aspects such as changes in organizational routines, goals and structure.

Our formulation is also related to Cyert and DeGroot's (1975) notion of *adaptive utility* which conceives the multiperiod problem from a normative perspective. The motivation for their study is that a decision maker might envisage in her/his mind the expected utility from performing a certain action. However, upon actually undertaking it, he/she experiences a different level of utility. For example, in trying out a new product the prior expectation might not be realized. In order to formalize this decision-making problem Cyert and DeGroot observe that, 'It is our belief that the concept of learning can be applied to utilities as well as to probabilities' (1975, p. 223). Thus, in their model instead of the decision maker updating the probabilities based on the history of outcomes, the decision maker updates his or her utility function. The premise is that there are two utility functions. The first is represented by the expected utility. The second is the actual utility derived from choosing an action. Decisions are based on the expected utility, but there can be a gap between the expected and the actual utility. Based on this gap, the decision maker applies a rule to update the expected utility function. This idea is formalized by Cyert and DeGroot (1975). Based on a mathematical model, they show that the multiperiod decision-making problem can be solved by using dynamic programming. In some instances, dependent on the rule used to discern the gap between the expected and the actual utility, the myopic but optimal solution is to maximize the expected utility in each period. However, in other circumstances, the myopic solution is not optimal because it pays to learn about the utility function by taking a different decision. Apart from the obvious connection between their use of learning models and the models studied by us and by March, the deeper connection is to understand the role of learning in resolving dual levels of uncertainties, namely, in both the utility function as well as the probability distribution of an outcome. Future research should examine whether adaptive utility and adaptive probability can be studied in a unified manner.

NOTE

1. The number of trials should be sufficiently large so that the probability vector of choices attains a value that is close to the steady-state value. In all our experiments, 8000 trials were adequate for this purpose.

REFERENCES

Argote, L. (1999), *Organizational Learning: Creating, Retaining and Transferring Knowledge*, Boston, MA: Kluwer.

Argyris, C. and D. Schön (1978), *Organizational Learning*, Reading, MA: Addison-Wesley.

Brown, J. (1990), 'Research that reinvents the corporation', *Harvard Business Review*, (January–February), 102–11.

Brown, J. and P. Dugoid (1991), 'Organizational learning and communities of practice: toward a unified view of working, learning and innovation', *Organization Science*, **2**, 40–57.

Bush, R.R. and F. Mosteller (1955), *Stochastic Models for Learning*, New York: Wiley.

Cyert, R.M. and M.H. DeGroot (1975), 'Adaptive utility', in R.H. Day and T. Groves (eds), *Adaptive Economic Models*, New York: Academic Press, pp. 223–46.

Cyert, R.M. and M. DeGroot (1987), *Bayesian Analysis and Uncertainty in Economic Theory*, Totowa, NJ: Rowman & Littlefield.

Cyert, R. and J.G. March ([1963] 1992), *A Behavioral Theory of the Firm*, 2nd edn, Cambridge, MA: Blackwell.

Duncan, R. and A. Weiss (1979), 'Organizational learning: implications for organizational design', *Research in Organizational Behavior*, **1**, 75–123.

Einhorn, H. (1980), 'Learning from experience and sub-optimal rules in decision making', in T. Wallsten (ed.), *Cognitive Processes in Choice and Decision Behavior*, Hillsdale, NJ: Erlbaum, pp. 1–20.

Estes, W.K. (1959), 'The statistical approach to learning', in S. Koch (ed.), *Psychology: A Study of Science*, Vol. 2, New York: McGraw-Hill, pp. 380–491.

Glynn, M., T. Lant and F. Milliken (1994), 'Mapping learning processes in organizations: a multi-level framework linking learning and organizing', *Advances in Managerial Cognition and Organizational Information Processing*, **5**, 43–84.

Herrenstein, R. J. (1961), 'Relative and absolute strength of response as a function of frequency of reinforcement', *Journal of Experimental Analysis of Behavior*, **4**, 267–72.

Herrenstein, R.J. (1970), 'On the law of effect', *Journal of Experimental Analysis of Behavior*, **13**, 244–66.

Kahneman, D. and D. Lovallo (1993), 'Timid choices and bold forecasts: a cognitive perspective on risk taking', *Management Science*, **39** (1), 17–31.

Lant, T. (1992), 'Aspiration level adaptation: an empirical exploration', *Management Science*, **38**, 623–44.

Lant, T. and S. Mezias (1990), 'Managing discontinuous change: a simulation study of organizational learning and entrepreneurial search', *Strategic Management Journal*, **11**, 147–79.

Levinthal, D. and J. March (1981), 'A model of adaptive organizational search', *Journal of Economic Behavior and Organization*, **2**, 307–33.

Levitt, B. and J. March (1988), 'Organizational learning', *Annual Review of Sociology*, **14**, 319–40.

March, J. (1991), 'Exploration and exploitation in organizational learning', *Organization Science*, **2**, 71–87.

March, J.G. (1996), 'Learning to be risk averse', *Psychological Review*, **103** (2), 309–19.

March, J. and Z. Shapira (1992), 'Variable risk preferences and the focus of attention', *Psychological Review*, **99**, 172–83.

Samuelson, P.A. (1963), 'Risk and uncertainty: a fallacy of large numbers', *Scientia*, **98**, 108–13.

Shaked, M. and J.G. Shanthikumar (1994), *Stochastic Orders and Their Applications*, San Diego, CA: Academic Press.

Shapira, Z. (1995), '*Risk Taking: A Managerial Perspective*', New York: Russell Sage Foundation.

Staddon, J.E.R. (1977), 'On Herrnstein's equation and related forms', *Journal of Experimental Analysis of Behavior*, **13**, 163–70.

Tversky, A. and M. Bar-Hillel (1983), 'Risk: the long and the short', *Journal of Experimental Psychology: Learning, Memory, and Cognition*, **9**, 293–315.

Section B

Evolution

15. The resource-based view of strategy: a behaviorist critique

Philip Bromiley and Lee Fleming*

1 INTRODUCTION

Researchers in strategic management use a variety of paradigms and approaches. Researchers favoring industry organization economics emphasize the impact of industry structure on firm strategy and performance (Porter 1980). Transactions cost economists emphasize the importance of fit between structure and strategy (Williamson 1985; Chandler 1990). Population ecologists examine how intensity of competition and age influence firm survival (Carroll and Hannan 1995; Barnett 1997). In recent years, however, the 'resource-based view' (RBV) has come to dominate many areas of strategy research. This chapter offers a critique of the RBV as a theory of firm strategy and proposes an alternative approach, based on the behavioral and evolutionary views of the firm (Cyert and March 1963; Nelson and Winter 1982).[1]

The RBV argues that firms within a given industry vary due to differences in 'resources'. The definition of resources includes capital and labor but also a wide variety of other firm characteristics such as reputation, organizational coordination, and tacit knowledge. Scholars in the RBV tradition look for differences across firms in such resources as the cause of sustained competitive advantage. While the RBV has contributed to our understanding of firm heterogeneity and imitation, it is plagued by contradictory assumptions, unclear constructs, and poorly articulated causal processes.

Our analysis assumes that strategic management theories should pass the same logical and scholarly tests as theories of empirical social science. While empirical work may fruitfully invoke multiple theories to explain and test different aspects of a phenomenon, a theory should strive for a parsimonious and consistent view that generates predictions which differentiate it from other theories. To evaluate the RBV as social science, we emphasize Barney's (1991) article because it presents one of the most rigorous presentations of the theory, or what some have called the 'high church' presentations of the RBV. We begin by considering what problem the RBV attempts to solve (Section 2). We then clarify our criteria for a good theory and proceed to evaluate the RBV by these criteria (Sections 3–8). The conclusion acknowledges the contributions of the RBV and offers an alternative framework for future work in strategic management theory (Sections 9–12).

2 WHAT PROBLEM DOES THE RBV SOLVE?

Scholarly paradigms attempt to solve some set of empirical or theoretical problems. For example, agency theory attempts to explain the relations between superior and subordinate with regard to the alignment of objectives. Population ecology attempts to explain birth and death rates for firms. So in considering the RBV, we first ask: 'What problem does RBV attempt to solve?'.

Traditional strategy scholars clearly assumed that firms differ (see, Andrews 1971; Ansoff 1965), but some strategy scholars have interpreted microeconomics as implying firm homogeneity.[2] Under perfect information, with no transactions or adjustment costs, models exist where firms do not differ. Information about best practices diffuses easily and competitors quickly move to the optimum production function. Consequently, all firms produce at the same cost. Given such a view, the question arises: 'Why do firms differ?'[3]

This line of reasoning seems to motivate the original RBV work; early discussions of the RBV express an underlying concern with firm heterogeneity. For example, Lippman and Rumelt (1982) explicitly attack the problem of developing a model that includes performance differentials in a competitive market at equilibrium. Wernerfelt (1984) and Peteraf (1993) both allude to Andrews (1971) and his discussion of strengths and weaknesses of the firm, which implicitly assumes that firms differ in strengths and weaknesses. Peteraf notes that 'a major contribution of the resource-based model is that it explains long-lived differences in firm profitability that cannot be attributed to differences in industry condition' (Peteraf 1993, p. 186). RBV scholars seek to explain persistent differences in firm profitability as a function of firm heterogeneity.

From a strategy perspective, however, this appears unnecessary. Indeed, other perspectives start by asking the opposite question. DiMaggio and Powell begin their famous institutional paper by literally asking, 'What makes organizations so similar?' (DiMaggio and Powell 1983). In population ecology, Hannan and Freeman ask, 'Why are there so many (or so few) kinds of organizations?' (Hannan and Freeman 1989). As Porter (1991, p. 108) notes, 'the role of internal resources is an important insight for economic modelers, though less novel a notion for strategy researchers'. As a less academic and more applied exercise, we would challenge those who are troubled by the issue to identify two identical firms!

We agree completely with the RBV positions that firms differ and that industry membership alone provides a poor explanation of firm performance (Rumelt 1991; Roquebert et al. 1996; Brush et al. 1999). However, we reject the RBV response. We reject the RBV response for its inconsistent theoretical assumptions, poorly defined constructs, lack of causal arguments, and lack of testable empirical implications.

3 CRITERIA FOR A GOOD THEORY

Strategy is, or at least should be, an empirical science. Strategic management scholars define their tasks as explaining differences in firm performance and (perhaps) developing strategies to improve firm performance, both of which clearly call for a realist, empirical approach. Such an empirical framework imposes a variety of demands upon theorizing, mainly that a good theory should (see, Popper 1959, p. 32, Bacharach 1989; and Pfeffer 1982):

1. Demonstrate internal and logical consistency – its assumptions and implications should not contradict one another.
2. Define clear and parsimonious constructs that relate and differ in sensible ways.

3. Present a clear explanation of the process by which the constructs interact.
4. Avoid tautology.
5. Be refutable, that is, have empirical implications that can be falsified by data.
6. Lead to predictions that differ from other theories.

We proceed from these criteria in our critique of the RBV and possible alternatives for a theory of the firm. We emphasize Barney (1991) as the statement of the RBV primarily because it most clearly attempts to develop a coherent and theoretical statement of the RBV.

4 THE RBV MAKES INCONSISTENT ASSUMPTIONS

The RBV implicitly adopts many assumptions from traditional economics, most importantly, optimal decision making and equilibrium analysis. These assumptions, however, clash with the RBVs liberal use of assumptions of bounded rationality.

Barney (1991) states that the RBV tries to explain variation in firm performance at equilibrium with rational decision makers. Levinthal (1995, p. 23) also notes that Barney's extensive work on RBV often assumes both rationality (meaning optimal decision making) and equilibrium. Wernerfelt implicitly makes the same assumption when he argues that, 'by specifying a resource profile for a firm, it is possible to find the optimal product-market activities' (Wernerfelt 1984, p. 171). Peteraf (1993) presents a simple traditional microeconomic model (derived under assumptions of both rationality and equilibrium) and discusses Ricardian and monopoly rents from a conventional (equilibrium) economics standpoint.

These assumptions of rationality and equilibrium let RBV theorists tie resources directly to performance. Given rational decision makers and markets in equilibrium, there exists a clear relation between a firm's resources and profits. Without these assumptions, however, resources have no unique relation to performance. If decision makers differ in their quality of decisions, then some will use resources well and some will squander them; the tie between resources and performance becomes unclear.[4] Similarly, for markets in disequilibrium, the association between resources and performance may reflect transient happenstance rather than the true value of resources. Consider, for example, two competing teams. We can only be sure that the quality of the players (resources) determines the winner if we assume perfect coaching. Furthermore, we need to assume a sufficiently long game to ensure that true quality wins out over happenstance.

Traditional research in industrial organization economics (IO economics) used a similar logical structure to conclude that industry structure alone drives profitability. In theories where all firms make optimal decisions, the decision or management process of the firm cannot influence performance. This allows IO economists to argue that industry structure determines firm conduct and, consequently, performance. If all firms make optimal decisions, then differences in firm behavior and performance must reflect prior conditions rather than firm choices (Amit and Schoemaker 1993). The RBV implicitly accepts this logic, even while rejecting the IO argument that industry structure alone drives profitability.

In justifying their rejection of the strict IO model, RBV scholars often adopt aspects of bounded rationality. They emphasize routines, while ignoring that the theoretical justification for routines lies in bounded rationality (March and Simon 1958). Most importantly, RBV proponents argue that the most important resources are those that reflect bounded rationality – the ambiguous, tacit, hard to imitate, and so on. If firms and their managers operate under bounded rationality, however, then the tie between resources and performance becomes unclear. Under bounded rationality, given the same resources, firms and managers will differ widely in behavior and outcomes. If dealt the same hand, all firms would not play it the same way.

These inconsistent assumptions generate theoretical difficulties. Under optimal decision making, management skill and strategic management have no meaning or value. Clearly, if we assume that managers make optimal decisions, then scholars cannot hope to improve such decisions. Assumptions of bounded rationality make the problem more interesting, but as argued above, eliminate the tight relationship between resources and performance. As an example of these contrasting assumptions, Barney (1991, p. 117) argues that all firms within an industry will adopt the optimal strategy if they possess the necessary resources. On the other hand, he also argues that, 'managers are important in this model, for it is managers that are able to understand and describe the economic performance potential of a firm's endowments'.

Scholars, including some in the RBV tradition, have recognized this potentially devastating critique of strategic management theory: if we assume rationality and equilibrium, then systematic patterns cannot lead to high performance. In other words, there can be 'no rules for riches'[5] (Mosakowski 1998; Dierickx and Cool 1989; Barney 1986). The assumptions rule out the phenomenon of interest.

Let us examine the same problem in a different context: chess. If we assume perfect rationality, then everyone will make the optimal moves at chess. As von Neumann and Morgenstern's classic *Theory of Games and Economic Behavior* (1944, p. 125) points out:

> [I]f the theory of Chess were really fully known there would be nothing left to play. The theory would show which of the three possibilities ['white wins', 'tie', or 'black wins'] actually holds and accordingly the play would be decided before it starts ... human difficulty necessitates the use of those incomplete, heuristic methods of playing, which constitute 'good' Chess; and without it there would be no element of 'struggle' and 'surprise' in that game.

Rationality assumes the ability to solve well-specified problems like chess. The initial resources (that is, whether you start with white or black) would fully determine the outcome. Furthermore, no one would read or write books on how to play chess well, for everyone would already make optimal moves.

Yet, in fact, people differ widely in their ability to play chess and many find that studying books on chess (yes, 'rules' for winning chess) improves their play. In a boundedly rational world, people cannot make optimal choices and so rely on heuristics and search to aid their decisions. Such individuals can learn better heuristics and search patterns from books and can improve their performance.[6]

In other words, if we assume that everyone does not know all the 'rules', then there can exist rules for riches that benefit many participants. Indeed, half the firms in any industry would improve their status by becoming average. If everyone knows all the rules, then knowing the rules will not differentiate winners from losers. We suspect, however, that many do not know all the rules, nor can they apply them correctly. This conforms with our knowledge of sophisticated games like chess, bridge, and poker, but also the existence of consultants, business schools, and strategic management scholars.

5 ASSUMPTIONS OF EQUILIBRIUM CREATE ADDITIONAL DIFFICULTIES

RBV assumptions of equilibrium create additional difficulties, especially with regard to the identification and acquisition of resources. First, such assumptions imply that actors will not attempt to improve their position. For example, in finance, an investor who believes that the market is in equilibrium will neither pay for new information nor spend funds seeking new investments. As an additional example, in most definitions of market equilibrium, firm behavior will not change if the external factors around the market do not change. While short-term price equilibrium may be common, we suspect higher-level product or market structure equilibria are somewhat less common. If we were in equilibrium, we could not take actions to improve our position, so we would not try. Yet, managers do try.

Second, equilibrium misleads if we apply it to adapting systems. Suppose that advantage is fleeting but comes from happening upon the right products? The temporarily wealthy in the Internet business world often have no fancy intangible resources. Just ahead of the crowd, they happened on an idea that the capital market liked. As an additional example, poorly performing but large and diversified firms do not immediately exit the market – they can hang on for many years. In rapidly fluctuating systems, today's relation between firm characteristics and performance may have little or no relation to the equilibrium relations.

Most importantly with regard to the RBV, equilibrium arguments have inherent difficulties in handling the creation or purchase of resources. If useful resources have such elusive and tacit characteristics, then managers cannot rationally create, value, or purchase such resources (Amit and Schoemaker 1993). The RBV solution in many ways mimics the approach of traditional economics to technological change, assuming it is either exogenous or a resource itself. Neither approach tells us much about managing change.

Some might argue that the equilibrium analysis still provides a useful definition of where the competitive system will go. This argument reflects a very old debate in economics concerning the utility of equilibrium analyses (Herbert Simon and others contributed to the debate, see Stinchcombe (1999) for a recent version of the argument). If we admit that markets may not be in equilibrium, but still wish to apply equilibrium analyses, then we need to address two issues: how close the markets are to equilibrium and whether the characteristics of the equilibrium tell us about the dynamic process of reaching equilibrium.

Consider a system (for example, a group of firms) or an organism adapting to its environment. Whether the organism adapts completely to the environment depends on the relative rate of change of the organism and the environment. If the organism changes much more quickly than the environment, then it will tend to be close to fully adapted to the environment. But if the environment changes more quickly than the organism, then the organism can be far from adapted to the environment. Some characteristics of economic systems appear to adapt quickly (for example, pricing in markets with good information), but others adapt slowly to their environments. Consider the industry structure of financial services. Continuing changes in regulation and international competition have meant that the structure of the financial services industry has not been in equilibrium for decades. If regulatory changes stopped, we would still see changes in the structure of the financial services industries for some time. Indeed, we doubt that many managers (today or ever) would perceive their market to be stable. Furthermore, such unstable markets are exactly those for which strategic insight is most needed.

Once we allow a market to be out of equilibrium, the equilibrium analysis becomes moot. Some economists justify the discussion of equilibrium because they believe it informs us concerning firm behavior even when industries are not in equilibrium. However, the dynamics of moving toward X may have no relation to the circumstances of being at X. Mountain climbing and survival atop the mountain differ greatly. Being (staying) rich and getting rich differ. Models exist that have stable equilibria if firms reach their equilibrium positions, but where firms will not move to such positions if they ever get out of equilibrium (see, for example, March's (1991) work on local maxima). Just as the theory of the second best in welfare economics showed that one cannot casually generalize from a model when the model's assumptions are violated (Henderson and Quandt 1971), one cannot generalize from a model that assumes the industry is in equilibrium to an industry that is not in equilibrium. An equilibrium argument that tells us that resources determine performance does not tell us what happens out of equilibrium.

6 THE RBV'S PRIMARY CONSTRUCT REMAINS UNCLEAR

Sutton and Staw (1995) remind us that clear and independently defined variables are necessary but insufficient for the development of a strong theory. Unfortunately, the central RBV construct of 'resources' remains ill defined, inconsistent (Foss et al. 1995), and contradictory across researchers. For example, Barney (1991), defines resources as untradable. In contrast, Amit and Schoemaker (1993, p. 35) define resources as 'stocks of available factors ... *Resources* consist *inter alia*, of know how that can be traded (e.g., patents and licenses), financial or physicals assets (e.g., property, plant and equipment), human capital, etc'. Wernerfelt avoids explicit comment on tradability when he defines a resource as 'anything which could be thought of as a strength or weakness of a given firm' or 'those (tangible and intangible) assets which are tied semi-permanently to the firm' (Wernerfelt 1984, p. 172).

Contradictions among researchers aside, individual definitions also remain problematic. Wernerfelt's expression 'anything which could be thought of' makes his first definition subjective and vague, because individuals can differ in what characteristics they think of as a 'strength' or 'weakness'. Furthermore, the assumption of optimal decision making should rule out subjectivity in decision making. If we allow managerial perceptions to differ from reality in ways that influence behavior, then we lose optimal decision making. Wernerfelt's latter quotation defines a resource as an 'asset', which only substitutes the problem of defining an 'asset' for the problem of defining a 'resource'. Particularly if we take an expansive view of assets, the second definition implies that all firm characteristics are resources. If so, why refer to them as 'resources'?

Even more troubling, many RBV papers restrict the definition of 'resources' to firm characteristics that give above average profits (see Foss et al. 1995). Barney notes (1991, pp. 102) that:

> [N]ot all aspects of a firm's physical capital, human capital, and organizational capital are strategically relevant resources. Some of these firm attributes may prevent a firm from conceiving of and implementing valuable strategies (Barney, 1986b). Others may lead a firm to conceive of and implement strategies that reduce its effectiveness and efficiency. Still others may have no impact on a firm's strategizing processes. However, those attributes of a firm's physical, human, and organizational capital that do enable a firm to conceive of and implement strategies that improve its efficiency and effectiveness are, for purposes of this discussion, firm resources ....

Barney's definition implies that resources can only improve firm performance: 'attributes only become resources when they exploit opportunities or neutralize threats in a firm's environment' (Barney 1991). Consider the case, however, where a firm analyses its attributes and acts to 'improve its efficiency'. According to Barney (1991), if those acts fail, the firm lacked resources. If they succeed, the firm possessed resources. Yet the failure might come from influences totally unrelated to the considered characteristics (for example, a fire in the warehouse) and which seem totally implausible as firm resources. The logic of the theory ascribes outcomes to causes that may be obviously incorrect.

The definitions also suffer from circularity. As Foss et al. noted (1995, pp. 1–17), defining 'resources' as things that give above-average performance is to state a tautology. If we want to understand how firms increase performance, resources must have a definition independent of performance. This does not mean that performance may not influence resources, but they must stand as separate constructs.[7] Focusing on success also makes empirical work prone to sampling on the dependent variable (Montgomery 1995).

In addition to structural difficulties with the definition of resource, the term itself gives a misleading appearance of concreteness or tangibility. The things a firm can do (capabilities) do not have the clear existence or valuation that 'resource' suggests. The terminology of resources and rents-from-resources conjures up a tangible image where a resource exists as a distinct thing that earns rents. Instead, we have complex organizational and market processes that translate things a firm can do into earnings. As Levinthal (1995) notes, capabilities come from a complex and interdependent organization and often do not exist as independent entities. Suppose that a firm can do A and B well. We might call A and B the firm's 'resources'. However, the same underlying organizational process may actually generate both. Alternatively, the process that generates positive A and B may also generate negative C and D, and the impact of all four will depend on where and how the firm competes. Labeling these independently as the fundamental constructs or units in one's view of the firm makes it difficult to understand how the firm actually generates them and what the firm can do with them.

7 RBV DOES NOT SPECIFY THE PROCESS WHEREBY FIRMS GENERATE PROFITS

These confusing definitions also make it difficult to develop a strong explanation of how a firm generates profits. A good theory explains a process (Lave and March 1993). Unfortunately, many RBV authors do not clearly explain the process by which resources generate profits (Poppo and Wiegelt 1999). This difficulty in articulating the process stems partly from the issues described above, including the vague definition of 'resources' and inconsistent assumptions. It also stems from the innate complexity of a firm's capabilities, choices, and interaction with other firms and the market. As Miller and Shamsie (1995, p. 60) note, 'It is meaningless to attempt to define resources independent of the tasks they are to serve and the environment within which they must function'.

Describing a firm as a 'bundle of resources' (Wernerfelt 1984) does not enable us to understand how firms behave. If we can specify the resources *and* the decision rules, then we have a model of the firm. Without them, a 'bundle of resources' does not provide a model of the firm. For example, Peteraf (1993) argues that resources provide a firm with the ability to either have lower production costs than others (Ricardian rents) or create monopoly rents. Along with the usual assumptions of rationality and equilibrium, this argument rests on an implicit assumption of a homogeneous product market. But most applications of the RBV involve markets with differentiated products where the tie from resource to cost to performance is not clear. Furthermore, resources have been ascribed to many kinds of activities where cost may be secondary (for example, in explaining research and development productivity, or network effects in currency trading).

In other words, an effective model of the process by which firms generate profits within an RBV approach would need to explain *how* firm resources translate into market-related behaviors and *how* such market-related behaviors translate into profits within non-commodity markets (see also Porter 1991). Even theories that do not attempt to explain process need to explicate the process by which they operate to provide a coherent argument (see, for instance, the Walrasian auctioneer's role in microeconomic theory). A process explanation of the RBV would require greater clarity on the constructs (for example, resources), the decision rules, and the market mechanisms. Such clarity would result in models that predict a number of intermediate outcomes that researchers could then use to test their causal arguments. Instead, the literature often moves from resources to performance without a clear intermediate mechanism (see also Poppo and Wiegelt 1999). The 'resources generate rents' model oversimplifies an often complex and challenging process.

Furthermore, tying specific resources to performance outcomes poses challenges (Poppo and Weigelt 1999). Even within a conventional economic framework, ascription of returns or rents to a particular resource requires numerous assumptions. We can clearly discuss returns to capital or returns to labor based on the market process that provides payments to the providers of these resources. Without such mechanisms, however, we have difficulty determining which 'resource' earned which returns. Barney's (1991) resources by definition cannot have market prices. Karl Marx's labor theory of value (that all real value comes from labor rather than capital) suffers from a similar problem – in general, we cannot ascribe returns to particular resources.

Our position on the RBV as a theory stands in opposition to Conner (1991), who concludes that the RBV constitutes a theory of the firm. We partially attribute this to Conner using different criteria than we do for a theory of the firm. Conner claims that 'the primary requirements of a theory of the firm are to explain the reasons for existence of the firm, and what limits its size and scope' (Conner, 1991, p. 139). She adds another 'test' in that a theory should explain 'why a particular firm exists, as opposed to its assets being distributed among other firms'.

However, we do not think that the RBV meets Conner's criterion of predicting a limit on the size and scope of firms. Consider, for example, a firm without resources (in the Barney sense), which the RBV predicts will earn normal returns. Such a firm can grow without limit without lowering those returns – it can acquire other firms and expect to earn normal returns on those acquisitions. The firm's profitability remains the same. Thus, optimizing returns makes no prediction concerning the size of this firm. We need to impose an assumption of transaction costs (traditionally not part of the RBV) to limit the size of firms (see Foss 1996a; and related papers by Conner and Prahalad 1996; Kogut and Zander 1996; and Foss 1996b). Likewise, the RBV provides a poor explanation of the creation of firms since it would require that the new firm somehow have these intangible, imitable, and so on, resources. If resources are very hard to understand and create, a new firm could not predict their existence *ex ante* (that is, that the firm will have them if formed).

A theory of the firm needs to explain much more than the existence and limits on size and scope of the firm. A theory of the firm for strategic management needs to explain firm behavior and the potential impact of various behaviors on firm performance. Indeed, most RBV advocates clearly claim much more for the RBV. To explain size and scope does not imply explaining variation in firm performance below the limits on size and scope. Yet such variation constitutes the central feature RBV scholars claim the theory handles. Indeed, mainstream RBV work almost always focuses on explaining performance differentials, not size and scope limits.

8 THE RBV'S EMPIRICAL IMPLICATIONS ARE NEITHER UNIQUE NOR TESTABLE

Because the RBV lacks strong causal and process arguments, it has difficulty making unique and empirically testable predictions. Popper (1959) and Pfeffer (1982) remind us that good empirical science should lead to refutable predictions. Without refutable predictions, a theory or a model is essentially a good story. Such stories can explain everything – Lave and March (1993) call them 'magic theories': they explain a great deal but predict very little.

Furthermore, a theory only adds unique value and becomes testable if it makes some predictions that differ from other theories. Research can only differentiate between explanations A and B if they imply different and testable outcomes. The RBV's main implications appear to be that firms and firm performances differ, and firm behavior will be serially correlated over time. But these 'predictions' agree with almost any reasonable model (population ecology, behavioral theory of the firm, evolutionary theories, power, and so on) and so do not allow real testing of the RBV.

While the lack of testable predictions results partially from the inconsistent assumptions and definitions discussed above, the RBV may face even greater fundamental challenges to empirical validation. Barney argues that the link between resources and sustained advantage must remain causally ambiguous:

> Ironically, in order for causal ambiguity to be a source of sustained competitive advantage, *all* competing firms must have an imperfect understanding of the link between resources controlled by a firm and a firm's competitive advantages ... Although managers may have numerous hypotheses about which resources generate their firm's advantages, it is rarely possible to rigorously test these hypotheses. (Barney 1991, pp. 109 and 110, italics original)

That managers cannot understand resources raises two major problems. First, how could they hope to create or manage things they cannot understand? Second, if resources must be so ambiguous that managers cannot understand them, how could external scholars study them? If resources are truly idiosyncratic, most research methodologies have little to tell us about them. In some sense, this resembles the same problem that researchers had with the Harvard policy view as stated in Andrews (1971). Andrews provides a complex statement of how managers should do strategy. His arguments may be correct, but they remain largely untestable.

Poppo and Weigelt (1999) express similar concerns. They attempt to test whether resources acquired in an inefficient market lead to competitive advantage. They conclude that the resource examined (baseball free agents) trades in an inefficient market, but also that they cannot demonstrate the causal ties from inefficient market to managerial actions and advantage. They note, 'the theory needs to erect more clarity of how market imperfections, based on incomplete information, will actually deliver competitive advantage. Is it luck or managerial foresight that generates advantage?' (Poppo and Weigelt 1999, p. 30).

Perhaps the most problematic use of RBV is its citation in any empirical paper that addresses interfirm differences. These papers often begin with a story about resources and RBV but then proceed to use some other theoretical approach to justify a particular model of performance. The theoretical approach justifying the actual model often conflicts with the RBV's assumptions. The accompanying references to RBV only confuse the theoretical issues. Rather than developing clearer ideas of how firm activities, choices, and markets interact, the RBV overview gives a false appearance of commonality among papers where none exists.

9 A SUMMARY OF CONCERNS

The RBV attempts to achieve an extremely difficult objective: to develop a theory of firm strategy driven by imperfect information within an optimizing model. While other such efforts have been undertaken in agency theory and transaction cost economics, they all share some serious difficulties and create apparent inconsistencies. For example, most agency theory applications assume the agent knows the correct (principal wealth-maximizing) thing to do. Furthermore, agency theorists generally assume that everyone knows everything, *except* the principal, who does not know how hard the agent is working. Transaction cost economics assumes much greater bounds on rationality, except that firms know the optimal organizational structure. These differences in where managers do and do not know things arise from theoretical convenience rather than empirical or logical analysis. Neither theory deals well with either learning or information transfer.

Oddly enough, in the high-bastion of rational economics, finance theory, strong attacks have been mounted against such rationality assumptions. Black (1986) notes that you cannot really tell the individuals who trade on good information from those who trade on bad information. He argues stock price should be within a factor of two of value most of the time – if the true value is one, the traded value will fluctuate between one-half and two, most of the time. Related critiques come from Shiller (1981), DeBondt and Thaler (1986) and others who show that fads and other factors influence the market as well. Most basically, if most traders really believed the market was fundamentally efficient, they would not pay for information and would seldom trade.

Optimizing models (that assume individuals know everything or almost everything) provide poor bases for studying learning and ignorance. Yet, if we believe managers really optimize, then we risk finding ourselves back in the industrial organizations economics trap: if everyone optimizes, then firm strategy *per se* has no reason to exist. Prior conditions (industry structure in IO economics and resources in the RBV) determine everything. The study of strategy only has meaning where firms do not know what to do. However, the RBV has difficulty giving up the optimizing assumption, because without it, the tie between resources and performance becomes questionable.

Thus, our concerns may be summarized as:

1. To tie resources directly to outcomes, RBV must assume optimizing decision makers. But with optimizing decision makers, companies cannot gain from improvements in decision processes.[8]
2. Assumptions of equilibrium provide a poor basis for predicting the creation or purchase of resources and imply that actors will not move to improve their position.
3. The underlying construct of a resource remains unclear and internally inconsistent. Some define a resource as any characteristic of the firm – in which case saying 'resources impact performance' is equivalent to saying 'firm characteristics impact performance'. Other definitions verge on tautology by defining resources as characteristics of the firm that determine performance or that provide above-average returns.
4. The RBV lacks a model of the process whereby a firm generates profits.
5. The empirical predictions of RBV are few in number and do not distinguish it from other theories.

10 YES BUT PRIOR TO THE RBV ...

While accepting some of these criticisms, many of our colleagues attempt to justify the RBV by allusion to what strategic management research did prior to the RBV. By focusing on the economically based work, they propose that strategic management previously focused on product market positions and industry as determinants of firm performance. In other words, strategy ignored firm differences, prior to the RBV (for example, Priem and Butler 2001; Dierickx and Cool 1989). The RBV has therefore provided the opportunity to explain firm differences below the industry group.

We propose, however, that strategic management researchers have always looked at within-firm factors and their influence on performance. Examining the first two issues of the *Strategic Management Journal* of 1985, we find the following papers:

1. A theory paper advocating deductive theory.
2. An empirical paper on the impact of managers' personal views on firm performance.
3. An empirical paper on managing the new venture division.
4. An empirical paper on competitors' responses to easily imitated new products.
5. A note on multiple point competition.
6. An empirical paper on models of strategic decision making.
7. A theoretical paper on corporate control systems.
8. An empirical paper on political strategies of regulated organizations.
9. An empirical study of acquisitions.
10. A non-empirical note on retrospective reports of managers.
11. A non-empirical note on 'intrapreneurship strategy for internal markets'.

We list the papers to make the point quite clear: strategic management research before the RBV's influence already focused primarily on interfirm differences. Later issues of the *Strategic Management Journal* present a very similar pattern. Interfirm differences such as managerial compensation, process innovation, and managerial controls still dominate in the first and second issues of the 1990 volume.

In other words, while some late entrants to the field may have gained the impression that industry analysis dominated research in strategic management, at no time in the history of the field did such models dominate scholarly work or instruction. Almost all popular strategic management textbooks of the 1980s and 1990s included Porter and industry issues as just one of numerous topics. To summarize, while some scholars view RBV as saving them from relying solely on industry factors, the bulk of strategic management research has always assumed firms differed and has attempted to explain differences in firm-level performance using firm-level (or lower) variables.

11 WHAT SHOULD WE DO?

We realize that those who criticize bear the onus of offering a better solution. What should characterize a theory that would help strategic management researchers? If strategic management researchers want to explain variation in firm performance with an eye to advising management on how to increase performance, then strategic management must do empirical science. In this sense, strategic management resembles engineering. Thus, we take a clearly empiricist approach in proposing the following criteria:

1. The theory must include the firm, firm behavior, markets, and the interaction of firms in markets. A theory of firms competing in a market economy can hardly ignore firms, markets, or competition.
2. The theory must allow for market disequilibrium and equilibrium. If strategic management centers on managing to improve the corporation's position, then a theory that only deals with positions where no one can act to improve their position (that is, an equilibrium) misses the point. While disequilibrium market models often can naturally evolve to lower and lower levels of disequilibrium thus at the limit reaching equilibrium (see Stinchcome 1999), most equilibrium market models impose the equilibrium assumption. In other words, an equilibrium market may be seen as a special case of a set of disequilibrium market models, but not vice versa.
3. The theory must satisfy the criteria previously discussed: it must have well-motivated and defined basic constructs, the relations among the constructs need to be clear and justified by an explicit process explanation, and the testable implications of the theory should differ from other theories.

Amit and Schoemaker (1993) proposed a starting-point for such a theory, namely an integration of IO economics (to emphasize industrial forces), RBV (to emphasize firm heterogeneity), and a behavioral view of the firm (to emphasize the reality of bounded rationality). Oliver (1997) offers another approach in a model that combines RBV and institutional views. While ecumenical movements have emotional appeal, they suffer severe problems as scientific theories (Pfeffer 1993). These different traditions have different core assumptions making efforts to integrate them exceedingly difficult. When one theory assumes optimal decision making and another assumes optimal decision making is impossible, consistent theoretical integration seems unlikely.

This is not to reject the factual basis of findings in other traditions, but rather to argue against *ad hoc* theoretical integration. A good theory of strategy must make some predictions consistent with IO economics; for example, monopolists should make high profits. A good theory of strategy must allow firms with special capabilities to make high profits in specific circumstances. A good theory should account for these previously well-established facts. But this does not imply that the theory itself must be subsumed within other theories.

We have not developed a definitive and complete solution but believe that a modified representation of Nelson and Winter's evolutionary theory (N&W) (1982) offers a starting-point. Evolutionary theory can encompass Amit and Schoemaker's (1993) issues because evolutionary theory looks at a market or industry, intrinsically considers variation and differences across firms, and is fundamentally grounded in a behavioral theory of the firm. Furthermore, evolutionary theory already has the potential for normative comment because it explicitly models firm behavior and then allows the firm models to interact within markets.

Let us briefly consider an evolutionary theory with respect to our criteria. Beneath N&W lies the behavioral theory of the firm (Cyert and March 1963). Firms constitute large combinations of routines, dissatisfaction drives search and search affords opportunities for change. N&Ws major breakthrough comes from putting such simple firms into markets and allowing market interaction. The markets can be in equilibrium or disequilibrium. As N&W show, the theory leads to models that have testable predictions, including both short- and long-term performance differences. Finally, the models rest on logically consistent assumptions of bounded rationality.

On the other hand, N&W need substantial development and modification for strategic purposes. Given their interests, N&W emphasized technological change, but their general approach is not wedded to technological change. Basically, N&W model boundedly rational firms that search for better ways to do things. For strategic management purposes, N&W need two extensions. N&W's models used very simple firm submodels that searched solely for technological advances. For strategic management purposes, the models need to be extended along numerous differing dimensions – products, customers, geography, efficiency, and so on. In addition, whereas N&W modeled homogeneous commodity markets, strategic management needs models of the heterogeneous product markets that characterize much of economic activity.

Within such models, firm strategies reflect different firm decision rules. The original behavioral theory of the firm (Cyert and March 1963) showed one such simulation; a duopoly simulation where the smaller firm makes more aggressive quantity decisions than the larger firm. The major breakthrough of N&W was to combine multiple firms within industries and to enable each firm to compete on a given basis. Thus, while Cyert and March provide the first simple but relevant example, N&W elaborated it as a template for further research.

Unfortunately, this approach may not generate the superficially neat strategic implications that other approaches might offer. The approach will not tell us what strategies always work best: the quality of a strategy must be discovered within the complex interactions of the models. Ideas from prior strategic research and behavioral theories may guide such a search. One would also expect that the quality of a given strategy probably depends on the strategies of competitors.

Building a normative framework on assumptions of bounded rationality will not be easy. Such assumptions make search and uncertainty central tenets of any resulting theory. Causality is far more difficult to trace in such a world, for example, while dissatisfaction may drive search, the outcome of search is fundamentally unpredictable. Theories of the firm, whether explanatory or normative, should explicitly incorporate such uncertainty. Firm actors should be modeled as making decisions that depend on the results of their search outcomes. Unfortunately, all of these activities – aspiration, search, interpretation of search results, and decisions – are intimately and unavoidably interdependent for boundedly rational actors. On top of this, such actors and their firms then need to interact in a market, in a way that the best strategies become apparent. N&W offer us a confusing world, unfortunately, but a more realistic and ultimately more interesting world for strategic management scholars to study.

12 THE CONTRIBUTIONS OF THE RBV

Much of the RBV literature can contribute substantial value within our proposed research agenda. RBV scholars have advanced understanding of interfirm imitation and the difficulties of imitation. Studying processes of imitation makes more sense, however, within bounded rationality models of firms and industries than it does in optimizing models. Likewise, work on the creation of new skills and capabilities fits a bounded rationality perspective better than the RBV approach.

Some scholars might argue that the RBV can be part of an evolutionary model. Certainly not in Barney (1991) – evolutionary models are inherently disequilibria models within the 'high church' view. More specifically, the two differ substantially in the following ways:

1. RBV assumes equilibrium while evolutionary theories allow for both equilibrium and disequilibrium models.
2. Whereas RBV sees resources as the only explanation for firm heterogeneity, evolutionary models provide a variety of explanations. In evolutionary models, firms differ due to differences in resources but also due to path dependence, randomness, managerial attention and skill, environmental change, and so on.
3. Whereas RBV assumes valuable resources must be 'rare' and 'inimitable', evolutionary models do not necessarily do so. While some equilibrium models require such characteristics for resources to generate rents, in an evolutionary world lots of less 'special' resources can generate rents. You do not have to be a great marketer to make money from marketing – just a better marketer than your competition. You do not have to be producing at minimal cost to make money from a low-cost strategy – just lower cost than some of your competitors.
4. RBV generally assumes easy technology transfer from an innovating firm to competitors – only the hardest-to-steal skills stay in the firm. But evolutionary models can accommodate a variety of different technology transfer assumptions. In reality some kinds of technology transfer readily but others do not. In addition, some environments encourage technology transfer and others do not.

To give a military analogy, if we assume that officers make optimal decisions, then resources determine the outcome of battles (excluding luck). If we assume that officers do not make optimal decisions, then strategy matters – different generals use their armies differently. While the second may be labeled 'bounded rationality' and some might see this as akin to 'rationality', the difference is massive. In the optimal world, no one needs to study strategy – prior conditions determine all. In the bounded rationality world, prior conditions matter along with management, organization, and numerous other factors.

We suspect that the RBV reflects an attempt to make strategy palatable for economically trained scholars. Given its emphasis on rationality, economics seldom assumes that well-motivated decision makers differ in the quality of their decisions. Such differences, however, constitute the core of strategic management – some firms make better strategic and other choices than others. The RBV simply labels all the unknown things with a term that economists knew (resources). Rather than illuminating the issues, however, this conflation of disparate constructs has confused them.

Overall, we believe that a N&W perspective offers much to strategic management. We need a perspective that recognizes that managers often do not know what to do, that managers try things and learn from experiments, that much of the learning comes from interaction with markets, and that most interesting markets have substantial imperfections. In short, our real managers operate firms they do not fully understand (see the comments by John Reed, Citicorp Chairman (Reed 2000)), and compete in complex, often imperfect markets that, again, they do not fully understand. Strategic management needs to keep both these in mind and in its models.

NOTES

* We wish to thank Xavier Canstaner, Connie Helfat, Connie James, Sue McEvily, Kent Miller, Margie Peteraf, Richard Priem, and Aks Zaheer for comments on previous drafts and Laurie Calhoun for outstanding editorial assistance. Of course, we retain responsibility for all limitations of this chapter.

1. Prior to completion of this chapter, we became aware of related forthcoming work by Priem and Butler (2001) and Barney (2001). We have chosen to comment briefly on their debate rather than enter into it fully. We commend the reader to the original works.
2. As Lieberman and Montgomery (1988, p. 52) note in the context of first-mover advantage research, 'models from the economics literature typically make only the most rudimentary distinctions among firms – indeed firms are usually assumed identical along all dimensions except timing and size. The strategic management field has traditionally emphasized a wider set of inter-firm differences'.
3. While often phrased this way, scholars also attend to two other, closely related questions: why do firm differ in performance, and why are firm rents not competed away?
4. Barney (1989, p. 1513) tries to solve this problem by arguing that 'the managerial skill needed to exploit opportunities is simply another strategic asset whose acquisition (or development) has a cost'. If management constitutes just another asset to acquire, what body or individual remains to make these acquisition decisions? Porter (1991, p. 109) raises a similar issue by questioning how valuable resources can be created.
5. Mosakowski (1998) responds to the criticism that managerial choices cannot systematically create value within the RBV. She assumes that there can be no 'rules for riches', that is, rules that provide benefits in the long run. Consequently, she argues that 'managerial prescription must alter the firm's performance distribution in a risk-adjusted mean-preserving way' (Mosakowki 1991, p. 1171). She follows Lippman and Rumelt's (1982) argument and generates variance in firm returns by having risk-neutral firms randomly draw from a distribution of production functions. Firms appear to have one choice: to draw a production function and have the potential for higher or lower returns, or to not draw a production function and have guaranteed returns. Such a model can lead to variation in returns. But it seems extremely unlikely that all options would provide identical *ex ante* risk-adjusted returns. Furthermore, if all options did provide identical *ex ante* returns, why would a risk-neutral manager choose one over another? Finally, the model implies that managerial skill has little influence on fundamental strategic choices.
6 While we claim such research helps many players, we do not claim it will help the very top players. The very top players may have found better heuristics than have been found by others, may have assimilated experience more effectively than others, and may simply be smarter (able to process information more effectively) than others. But for the other 99 percent of players, coaching and studying probably helps.
7. The exchange between Priem and Butler (2001) and Barney (2001) rests heavily on this point. Priem and Butler argue that the RBV presents a tautology because substituting definitions for resources and performance results in the same terminology on both sides of the 'resources determine performance' equation. Barney argues by analogy to Porter's competitive analysis work that RBV does not create a tautology. We agree with Priem and Butler's

argument. If one can define resources or valuable resources independently of the 'resources influence performance' relation, then no tautology would exist. Furthermore, the value of resources can only be determined by their usage within a given market context. Barney, for example, mentions a 'valuable culture' as a resource, but one only has a valuable culture if that culture leads to performance. If, independent of the performance relationship, you can determine the value of resources, then you can eliminate the tautology. For example, size could be considered a resource and we can measure size independently of performance. Many of the intangible and complex resources proposed by Barney do not have such independent valuation.

8. The critical issue is tying resources *directly* to outcomes. Resources can influence outcomes in non-optimizing models, but the connections require specification of the process by which firm actors use resources to influence outcomes. Yet such specification weakens the ties between resources and outcomes.

REFERENCES

Amit, R. and P. Schoemaker (1993), 'Strategic assets and organizational rent', *Strategic Management Journal*, **14**: 33–46.

Andrews, K.R. (1971), *The Concept of Corporate Strategy*, Homewood, IL: Irwin.

Ansoff, H. I. (1965), 'Checklist for competitive and competence profiles', *Corporate Strategy*, New York: McGraw-Hill.

Bacharach, S.B. (1989), 'Organizational Theories: Some Criteria for Evaluation', *Academy of Management Review*, **14** (4), 496–515.

Barnett, W. (1997), 'The dynamics of competitive intensity', *Administrative Science Quarterly*, **42** (1):128–60.

Barney, J. B. (1986), 'Strategic factor markets: expectations, luck, and business strategy', *Management Science*, **32** (10): 1231–41.

Barney, J.B. (1989), 'Asset stocks and sustained competitive advantage: a comment', *Management Science*, **35** (12): 1511–13.

Barney, J.B. (1991), 'Firm resources and sustained competitive advantage', *Journal of Management*, **17**: 99–120.

Barney, J.B. (2001), 'Is the resource-based "view" a useful perspective for strategic management research? Yes', *Academy of Management Review*, **26** (1): 41–56.

Black, F. (1986), 'Noise', *Journal of Finance*, **41** (3): 529–43.

Brush, T.H., P. Bromiley and M. Hendrickx (1999), 'The relative influence of industry and corporation on business unit performance: an alternative estimate', *Strategic Management Journal*, **20** (6): 519–47.

Carroll, G. and M. Hannan (1995), *Organizations in Industry: Strategy, Structure, and Selection*, New York: Oxford University Press.

Chandler, A. (1990), *Scale and Scope: The Dynamics of Industrial Capitalism*, Cambridge, MA: Belknap Press of Harvard University.

Conner, K.R. (1991), 'A historical comparison of resource-based theory and five schools of thought within industrial organization economics: do we have a new theory of the firm', *Journal of Management*, **17** (1): 121–54.

Conner, K.R. and C.K. Prahalad (1996), A resource-based theory of the firm: knowledge versus opportunism', *Organization Science*, **7** (5): 519–32.

Cyert, R.M. and J.G. March (1963), *A Behavioral Theory of the Firm*, Englewood Cliffs, NJ: Prentice-Hall.

DeBondt, W.F.M. and R.H. Thaler (1986), 'Does the stock market overreact?', *Journal of Finance*, **40** (3): 793–807.

Dierickx, I. and K. Cool (1989), 'Asset stock accumulation and sustainability of competitive advantage', *Management Science*, **35** (12) 1504–11.

DiMaggio, P. and W. Powell (1983), 'The iron cage revisited: institutional isomorphism and collective rationality in organizational fields', *American Sociological Review*, **48**: 147–60.

Foss, J.J., C. Knudsen and C.A. Montgomery (1995), 'An exploration of common ground: integrating evolutionary and strategic theories of the firm', in Montgomery (ed.), *Resource-based and Evolutionary Theories of the Firm: Towards a Synthesis*, Norwell, MA: Kluwer, pp. 1–17.

Foss, N.J. (1996a), 'Knowledge-based approaches to the theory of the firm: some critical comments', *Organization Science*, **7** (5): 470–76.

Foss, N.J. (1996b), 'More critical comments on knowledge-based theories of the firm', *Organization Science*, **7** (5): 519–23.

Hannan, M. and J. Freeman (1989), *Organizational Ecology*, Cambridge, MA: Harvard University Press.

Henderson, J.M. and R.E. Quandt (1971), *Microeconomic Theory: A Mathematical Approach*, (2nd edn) New York: McGraw-Hill.

Kogut, B. and U. Zander (1996) 'What firms do? Coordination, identity, and learning', *Organization Science*, **7** (5): 502–18.

Lave, C. and J. March (1993), *An Introduction to Models in the Social Sciences*, New York: University Press of America.

Levinthal, D. (1995), 'Strategic management and exploration of diversity', in C.A. Montgomery (ed.), *Resource-based and Evolutionary Theories of the Firm: Towards a Synthesis*, Norwell, MA: Kluwer, pp. 19–42.

Lieberman, M.B., and D.B. Montgomery (1988), 'First-mover advantages', *Strategic Management Journal*, **9**, 41–58.

Lippman, S. and R. Rumelt (1982), 'Uncertain imitability: an analysis of interfirm differences in efficiency under competition', *Bell Journal of Economics*, **13**, 418–38.

March, J.G. and Simon, H.A. (1958), *Organizations*, New York: Wiley.

March, J. (1991), 'Exploration and exploitation in organizational learning', *Organization Science*, **2**: 71–87.

Miller, D. and J. Shamsie (1995), 'A contingent application of the resource-based view of the firm: the Hollywood film studios from 1939 to 1965', *Academy of Management Best Papers Proceedings 1995*, 57–61.

Montgomery, C. (1995), 'Of diamonds and rust: a new look at resources', in Montgomery (ed.), *Resource-based and Evolutionary Theories of the Firm: Towards a Synthesis*, Norwell, MA: Kluwer, pp. 251–67.

Mosakowski, E. (1998), 'Managerial prescriptions under the resource-based view of strategy: the example of motivational techniques', *Strategic Management Journal*, **19** (12): 1169–83.

Nelson, R. R. and S.G. Winter (1982), *An Evolutionary Theory of Economic Change*, Cambridge, MA: Harvard University Press.

Oliver, E. (1997), 'Sustainable competitive advantage: combining institutional and resource-based views', *Strategic Management Journal*, **18** (9), 697–713.

Peteraf, M.A. (1993), 'The cornerstones of competitive advantage: a resource-based view', *Strategic Management Journal*, **14** (2): 179–91.

Pfeffer, J. (1982), *Organizations and Organization Theory*, Cambridge, MA: Ballinger.

Pfeffer, J. (1993), 'Barriers to the advancement of organizational science: paradigm development as a dependent variable', *Academy of Management Review*, **18**: 599–620.

Popper, K. (1959), *The Logic of Scientific Discovery*, New York: Routledge.

Poppo, L. and K. Weigelt (1999), 'The immunogenic nature of the resource-based view of the firm: an empirical example using baseball free agents', paper presented at the Academy of Management.

Porter, M. (1980), *Competitive Strategy*, New York, Free Press.

Porter, M. E. (1991), 'Towards a dynamic theory of strategy', *Strategic Management Journal*, **12** (Winter special issue): 95–118.

Priem, R.L. and J.E. Butler (2001), 'Is the resource-based "view" a useful perspective for strategic management research?', *Academic of Management Review*, **26** (1): 22–40.

Roquebert, J.A., R.L. Phillips and P.A. Westfall (1996), 'Markets vs. management: what "drives" profitability?', *Strategic Management Journal*, **17** (8), pp. 653–64.

Reed, J.S. (2000) 'A practitioner's view of management', *Academy of Management Executive*, **14** (1): 56–64.

Rumelt, R.P. (1991). 'How much does industry matter?', *Strategic Management Journal*, **12** (3): 167–85.

Shiller, R.J. (1981), 'Do stock prices move too much to be justified by subsequent changes in dividends?', *American Economic Review*, **71** (3): 421–36.

Stinchcombe, A.L. (1999), 'On equilibrium, organizational form, and competitive strategy: a comment on Barney's firm resources and sustained competitive advantage', Working paper, Northwestern University.

Sutton, R. and B. Staw (1995), 'What theory is not', *Administrative Science Quarterly*, **40** (3): 371–85.
Von Neumann, J. and O. Morgenstern (1944), *The Theory of Games and Economic Behavior*, Princeton, NJ: Princeton University Press.
Wernerfelt, B. (1984), 'A resource-based view of the firm', *Strategic Management Journal*, **5** (2): 171–80.
Williamson, O. (1985), *The Economic Institutions of Capitalism*, New York: Free Press.

16. Interpreting economic change: evolution, structures and games

Giovanni Dosi and Sidney G. Winter

1 INTRODUCTION

A century after Veblen's famous article complaining about the lack of evolutionary foundations of the economics discipline (Veblen 1898) the notion of evolution features as a central concept in several current analytical perspectives, although with different interpretations and uses. Sometimes it is barely distinguishable from the very notion of dynamics itself, cum some non-linearities and phase transitions. Elsewhere, it takes a meaning much nearer to that in biological theories involving selection, inheritance and variation. In yet other perspectives, it borrows only part of the biological view, significantly modified to suit the distinctive features of socioeconomic processes.

It would be a futile exercise to try to review here what is actually meant by evolution in these different theories. Rather, in the following, we shall, first, sketch out what we consider to be the main results achieved so far by a few different approaches that invoke, one way or another, evolutionary explanations of economic phenomena, and second, map some overlaps and some differences among them that hint, in our view, at some major unresolved issues ahead. More specifically, we shall concisely consider (a) models and empirical studies broadly in a *post-Schumpeterian* perspective of the genre often ascribed to Nelson and Winter (1982); (b) *evolutionary game* theories; (c) *organizational ecology* approaches; (d) *artificial economies*; and (e) part of that expanding literature on *adaptive learning* which is based on some evolutionary argument.

To set some sort of benchmark for the discussion below, let us start from what we deem to be a 'maximalist' vision of an evolutionary research programme.

2 EVOLUTIONARY THEORIES: SOME BUILDING BLOCKS[1]

For the purposes of this work, let us confine ourselves to some basic features of evolutionary theories of *economic* change. First, notwithstanding possible differences in other more substantive hypotheses, evolutionary theories share the methodological imperative '*dynamics first!*'. That is, the explanation for why something exists, or why a variable takes the value it does, ought to rest on a process account of how it became what it is. Loosely speaking, that amounts to the theoretical imperative: provide the process story either by formally writing down some dynamical system, or by telling a good qualitative historical reconstruction (or, much better *both*). Putting it in terms of negative prescriptions: be extremely wary of any interpretation of what is observed that runs just in terms of *ex post* equilibrium rationalizations ('it has to be like that, given rationality'). Never take as a good 'explanation' either an existence theorem or a purely functionalist claim (entity x exists because it performs function y ...). [Note, in this perspective that, Milton Friedman's old 'as ... if' interpretation of the properties of equilibrium behaviors (Friedman 1953) should be taken as a (daring!) conjecture on the limit properties of some unspecified dynamics; and so should be notions such as that of evolutionary stable strategies (ESS) as originally put forward in biology by John Maynard Smith (1982), although the dynamical intuitions are more understandable in the latter case.]

Given this general epistemological prescription (admittedly not an obvious one or even generally accepted among economists), the following substantive building blocks give shape to a fully-fledged evolutionary research programme.

1. *Theories* ought to be *microfounded*, in the sense that they ought to be grounded explicitly (though perhaps indirectly) in a plausible account of what typical agents do and why they do it.[2]
2. *Realism* is a virtue and in certain respects a necessity. Although theories are necessarily abstract and admit less of reality than they omit, there are some broad features of reality that are omitted at the theorist's peril – in the sense that the conclusions are unreliable guides to the interpretation of reality, though perhaps instructive regarding important mechanisms or otherwise useful.
3. Among these features is the fact that agents have at best *imperfect understanding* of the environment they live in, and, even more so, of what the future will deliver. Hence, 'bounded rationality' is generally assumed, with its specific content varying with context.
4. Also, imperfect understanding and imperfect, path-dependent, learning entails persistent *heterogeneity* among agents, even when facing identical information and identical notional opportunities. Capturing heterogeneity is crucial to the representation of aggregate dynamics; a model without heterogeneity is like a flower garden without color.
5. The knowledge margin is always active: agents are always capable of discovering new technologies and ways of organizing, and adopting new behavioral patterns. Allowing for the *immanent possibility of novelty* in the system is a major theoretical and modeling challenge that cannot safely be ignored.
6. While (imperfect) adaptation and discovery generate variety (often in a seemingly random fashion), collective interactions within and outside markets operate as *selection mechanisms*, generating differential growth (and possibly also different survival probabilities) of different entities that are the 'carriers' of diverse technologies, routines, strategies, and so on.
7. As a result of all this, aggregate phenomena (for example, regularities in the growth process or in industrial structures, and so on) are often captured theoretically as *emergent properties* – the collective and largely unintentional outcome of *far-from-equilibrium micro interactions and heterogeneous learning*. Such properties often have a *metastable* nature, in the sense that while persisting on a time scale longer than the processes generating them, they disappear ultimately with probability one.[3]
8. A similar style of representation and interpretation should apply to the emergence and self-maintenance of *organizational forms and institutions*: they are partly the result of directed (purposeful) action by the agents but also, partly, the unintentional outcome of the interplay of agent learning and collective interactions.

9. The relation of the 'higher-level' regularities manifested in institutions, rules and organizational forms to 'lower-level' evolutionary processes is a complex one of *co-evolution* across *levels of analysis* and *time scales* – and ought properly to be modeled as such. While the former are emergent phenomena of the latter, they may be considered as relatively invariant structures which constrain and shape the latter on shorter time scales. Modeling approaches that take these higher-level quasi-invariants as given have the same provisional legitimacy granted more generally to models that exclude, in the imperative spirit of dividing the difficulties, significant forms of novelty.

This is the grand programme, as we see it. It is obviously impossible to review here the rapidly growing literature of contributions that share some or all of the foregoing theoretical 'building blocks'.[4] We review here some of the major lines of research, achievements and distinctive features.

3 EVOLUTIONARY LINES OF RESEARCH AND MAIN RESULTS: A BRIEF OVERVIEW

Above we called one of the evolutionary-inspired research perspectives 'post-Schumpeterian', lacking a better word. In the following we shall refer to it, with some imperialism, as 'evolutionary theories of economic change' (ETEC), borrowing from the title of Nelson and Winter (1982). ETEC do indeed share most of the foregoing 'building blocks', and on that ground aim at the interpretation of economic phenomena at different levels of aggregation – including industrial dynamics and macroeconomic growth.

For the sake of illustration, consider, in a nutshell, the ETEC story on the economic growth process. The story crucially involves a multitude of (heterogeneous) firms searching for more efficient techniques of production and better-performing products, and competing in the markets for products, inputs and finance. Differential success in search, together with different behavioral and strategies (concerning, for example, pricing, investment, and so on) determine their differential revealed performances (in terms of, for example, their profitability, market shares, and survival probabilities) and hence their ability to grow. Aggregate growth, in this view, is – in a first approximation – driven by (partly endogenous and idiosyncratic) technological advances. Thus, the eye of the analyst is naturally drawn to the origins, nature and accessibility of technological *opportunities*; the ease with which firms can imitate each other (affecting *diffusion* and *appropriability* conditions); the ways firms are able to store and augment their knowledge (that is, affecting *organizational routines* and their relationship to *competences*); and the mechanisms and speed of *market selection*. Finally, note that such an evolutionary programme demands a complementary explanation of the key features of the environment faced by firms and individuals, especially the technological opportunities tapped by private agents; the legal framework shaping appropriability conditions; the origins of particular sets of corporate routines; the nature of product market interactions among rivals; the ways wages react to the changes in the demand for labor induced by technical change and growth; and so on. In all of these respects, economic institutions play a key role: consider, respectively, university and government laboratories, patent laws and courts, trade associations and business schools, antitrust and regulatory authorities, labor laws and unions. It must be admitted, however, that the detailed exploration of these linkages has barely begun: for a discussion of the relationship between institutions and evolutionary processes, see Coriat and Dosi 1998a).

There is indeed a flourishing family of formal models and historical interpretations constructed along these lines, construing economic growth as an evolutionary process propelled by technical change. After Nelson and Winter (1982), see among others Dosi et al. (1988), Day and Eliasson (1986), Silverberg and Verspagen (1994), Conlisk (1989), Chiaromonte and Dosi (1993), Silverberg and Soete (1993), Fagerberg (1994), and the discussion in Nelson (1995) and Silverberg and Verspagen (1995).

Relatedly, the diffusion of innovation has been analysed, from different angles, as a process highlighting at least some of the evolutionary, path-dependent, features outlined above (see, among others, David 1985 and 1992; Silverberg et al. 1988; Arthur et al. 1987; Nakicenovic and Grübler 1992; Metcalfe 1992 and 1995).

The development of an evolutionary perspective has been deeply intertwined with the historical analysis of the processes by which technical change is generated, ranging from the microeconomic level all the way to 'national systems of innovation' (within an enormous literature, see Freeman 1982; Dosi 1982; David 1975, Rosenberg 1976 and 1982; Basalla 1988; Mokyr 1990; Grandstrand 1994; Vincenti 1990, Nelson 1993; Lundvall 1992; and the reviews in Dosi 1988 and Freeman 1994).

Finally, a growing number of industrial case studies and models of industrial change fits quite well the evolutionary conjectures outlined above (again, just as examples, see Pavitt 1984; Utterback and Suarez 1992; Klepper 1993; Malerba and Orsenigo 1994; Winter 1984; Dosi et al. 1995).

The properties of industrial dynamics have been addressed also from a partly overlapping perspective, namely the *ecology of organizational populations* (EOP), a literature stream based in sociology that has emphasized the processes of entry, social legitimization and mortality as drivers of industrial evolution, operating on changing populations of heterogeneous firms characterized by highly inertial organizational and behavioral traits (Hannan and Freeman 1989; Hannan and Carroll 1997; Carroll 1997).

Notwithstanding the great variety in the objects of analysis, styles and hypotheses, it is still fair to say that most of the foregoing contributions share a distinct 'phenomenological' flavour. They typically identify the empirical phenomena to be interpreted and then proceed with that task by telling a microfounded dynamic story, wherein the assumptions on the microentities (principally the structures and behaviors of firms) and on their interactions draw a lot from empirical generalizations or reasonable conjectures specific to the problem at hand. So, for example, most of the ETEC and EOP works entail 'boundedly rational' agents; but, given that, the specification of what agents actually do – whether they are characterized by behavioral routines, and, if so which ones and so on – is highly context dependent, and often behaviorally quite rich (for example, the Nelson-Winter model(s) specify rules for technological search, investment, pricing, and so on). We shall come back below to some problems involved in this style of analysis.

A related but contrasting methodology inspires work in so-called *artificial economies* (AEs) (Axtell and Epstein (1996) is an archetypical example) and is common to the broader class of *artificial worlds* (AW) models. In an insightful discussion, Lane characterizes such models as follows:

> Artificial worlds ... are computer-implementable stochastic models, which consist of a set of 'microlevel entities' that interact with each other and an 'environment' in prescribed ways. The aim of AW modeling is to discover whether (and under what conditions) histories [that is, sample paths under well-specified interaction rules and initial conditions] exhibit interesting *emergent properties*. An emergent property is a feature of a history that (1) can be described in terms of aggregate-level constructs, without reference to the attributes of specific microentities; (2) persists for time periods much greater than the time scale appropriate for describing the underlying micro-interactions; and (3) defies explanation by reduction to the superposition of 'built in' micro-properties of the AW. (Lane 1993, pp. 90–91)

Lane (1993) reviews some examples from different disciplines, including Walter Fontana's Function–Object Gas (Fontana 1992) from chemistry,[5] Christian Lindgren's evolutionary prisoner's dilemma (Lindgren 1992) and a would-be Chiaromonte–Dosi–Lane–Lippi–Pelkey–Tayler model of economic dynamics, of which a preliminary version was developed in the early 1990s at the Santa Fe Institute.

These and others models – some of which building upon Kauffman's models of evolution and self-organization (see Kauffman 1993; Kauffman and MacReady 1995; Levinthal 1997; Frenken et al. 1999; Westhoff et al. 1996) – ambitiously begin to explore some possible *generic* conditions under which aggregate statistical regularities, or organized structures emerge, most often under far-from equilibrium conditions.[6]

In the simplest cases, these regularities concern emerging patterns of behaviors and/or location in some spatial dimension (see Axtell and Epstein (1996), and for a presentation of some results in a language familiar to economists, Krugman (1996)), in others, they refer to properties of stylized ecologies or organizational forms (Kauffman 1993; Frenken et al. 1999; Levinthal 1997). In terms of the 'grand' evolutionary research programme outlined earlier, the AE perspective emphasizes – and indeed has contributed path-breaking insights into – the notion of emergence in complex evolving systems. Moreover, it builds upon appropriate evolutionary microfoundations in that agents have, at best, a 'local' knowledge of the environment in which they operate, and endogenously learn, or at least adjust, in ways possibly marked by systematic mistakes (from a hypothetical observer's standpoint).

Growing out of quite different theoretical origins, a wide class of models of *evolutionary games* (EGs) also share the general assumption of boundedly rational agents and a commitment to some underlying collective dynamics as a basic explanatory process, often driven by a selection mechanism at the population level. The focal reference is Maynard Smith's notion of an evolutionary stable strategy (ESS) – in fact a refinement of Nash equilibrium – developed with respect to the static properties of population ecologies in biology (Maynard Smith 1982). Since then, that analytical perspective has been enriched by diverse dynamic developments which have began to explore the limit properties of selection/ adaptation processes – both in deterministic and stochastic settings – and have also tried to reflect upon some abstract mutation-generating mechanisms. For comprehensive presentations of the state of the art at various dates, together with a few key advances (see Hofbauer and Sigmund (1988); D. Friedman (1991); Vega-Redondo (1996); Weibull (1995); Samuelson (1997); Young (1998).

Unlike the ETEC and EOP approaches, the broad evolutionary game modeling enterprise – at least within the economic discipline – has been largely theory driven, with comparatively low 'phenomenological' discipline. Loosely speaking, EG appears to be the symmetric opposite (but sometimes a useful complement) to canonic game theory, at least in three respects. First, it swings the microfoundations of strategic analysis the opposite way from the increasingly incredible forward-looking rationality postulated by what one could call the '*ex ante* consistency view' of strategic interactions. Second, it tries to tackle the multiplicity-of-equilibria issue. This is a general unresolved problem for the '*ex ante*' rationalists, but it is particularly acute in the plausible circumstances of repeated strategic interactions that lack any termination point well perceived by the agents. In that respect, EG theorists attempt to identify some broadly plausible selection mechanism that picks out equilibria. Third, and relatedly, EGs address the issue of the stability of particular equilibrium concepts, in principle allowing for seemingly 'irrational' micro perturbations or 'mutations'.

The foregoing bird's-eye appreciation of the diverse perspectives that share some of our evolutionary building blocks might give the (misleading) impression of a comfortable convergence toward an increasingly coherent *weltanschauung* centered on common evolutionary ideas. This, however, is too optimistic a view. A more fruitful dialogue among the perspectives sketched above requires facing quite a few difficult and controversial issues concerning the basic nature of evolutionary dynamics in the socioeconomic domain.

Let us briefly flag some of them.

4 SOME OPEN QUESTIONS ON STRUCTURES, LEARNING, GAMES AND OTHER INTERACTION PATTERNS[7]

Small Worlds versus Open-ended Dynamics

Evolutionary processes, in biology as well as in the social domain, clearly involve the emergence of novelty of various kinds along the evolutionary path. Although novelties are constrained to some extent by past history, there is still ample room for unexpected emergent phenomena and surprises. But capturing this in models presents tricky modeling challenges.

We believe that a fully-fledged evolutionary dynamics would most likely entail an endogenous explosion of the dimensionality of the state space explored by the system. As the complexity of functions and traits increases in biological evolution from unicellular entities to mammals, so it happens also in the socioeconomic arena.

One possible modeling strategy is to allow for a notionally infinite-dimensional space of search,[8] without being able to fully specify the 'law of motion' over that space, except locally. But what might be the analytical objectives in studying such a system? Clearly, there is by intended construction hardly any hope of finding some particular limit state where the system might end up – such a result would indeed spell the failure of the attempt to capture the persistent emergence of novelty. Under such open-ended dynamics, one might aim at best to find some emergent regularities in the process itself, concerning, for example, the properties of emerging, metastable structures, the temporal patterns of events – such as the 'punctuation' of (quasi) equilibria and major structural discontinuities[9] – average dynamic properties such as rates of growth of some variables, and so on. This is indeed the philosophy of many AEs and is shared by a few ETEC models.

However, EGs are in this respect located at the opposite extreme: they generally assume some closed and well-defined domain of exploration given from the start, allowing a rigorous characterization of the limit states of dynamical systems that represent mechanisms of adaptation and selection over a given fitness landscape.[10]

Ultimately, the appropriateness of the theoretical representation depends on the nature of the phenomena to be explained. The 'small world 'methodology is best suited to the interpretation of those properties of environments where the rates of adjustment to given 'fundamentals' – for example, technologies, organizational forms, and so on (that is, to a given evolutionary landscape) – are of orders of magnitude greater than the rates of change in the fundamentals themselves (and thus in the selective environment). Given the rate of technological and organizational innovation in modern economies, suitable targets would seem to be rare.

Limit versus 'Transient' Properties

Given an evolving system, what are the properties we primarily wish to study? This issue overlaps with the previous point. Whenever we are pretty sure that adaptation is 'fast' compared to innovation, we may assume that most empirical observations of the phenomenon at hand are close-to-equilibrium outcomes of the underlying adaptive dynamics: hence it should be *descriptively* fruitful to study the properties of the limit states of the dynamical system in the model. Conversely, when the foregoing condition does not apply it might be of greater interest to study the *transient* ('disequilibrium') properties of the system, recognizing that in the reality to which the model relates, the fundamental parameters will be shocked well before the system reaches anything approaching an equilibrium. This indeed is what most ETEC and AE modelers do.[11]

It seems to us that typical EG methodology too often subscribes cavalierly to the former assumption. And sometimes it does worse than that: it starts from some equilibrium notions which have 'nice' properties from the point of view of economic theory (for example, because they correspond to microbehaviors that can be supported by standard 'rationality' assumptions) and then searches for dynamical processes able to generate them. If the point is to understand reality, this style of intellectual production seems to us to be too roundabout. And, at bottom, it rests on unquestioning faith in the view that economic rationality is the only viable approach to understanding behavior in the specific case – as distinguished from the less doctrinaire view that the rationality assumption is sometimes a fruitful approach.

More to the point, however, a general issue concerns what we can learn about a system's finite-time behaviors from the characterization of its asymptotic properties. In some cases, empirically interesting propositions may be derived from the rates-of-convergence properties,[12] since the latter allow us to infer, loosely speaking, how quickly the finite time (disequilibrium) observations should be expected to converge to something resembling the limit predictions. However, even assuming a qualitatively correct dynamic model, empirically relevant conclusions on this point cannot be derived from purely analytical studies of convergence: the quantitative magnitudes always matter. It is a point in favor of simulation modeling in that it offers the opportunity to explore the quantitative convergence behavior of the model experimentally, drawing on rough evidence or intuitions concerning parameter magnitudes.

Interaction Dynamics and Selection

A minimal requirement, common to different genres of the evolutionary approach, and shared with a vast class of models of decentralized economies,[13] is microfoundations involving a large number of interacting agents. This requires the specification of (a) the *levels* at which interaction occurs (for example, does it concern product-market competition? behavioral imitation?

mutual technological learning? and so on); (b) the *mechanism of interaction* (who can do what to whom, when, and under what types of rules ...); and, possibly, (c) some *topology* over which agents are distributed, which may also shape the actual interaction process (for example, by making interaction probabilities dependent upon some distance in an appropriately defined space), as mentioned earlier, complete evolutionary models of economic change ought to account explicitly for the joint dynamics of learning and selection. Ideally, one should specify the 'physics' of interaction in both domains together with the ways they are dynamically coupled. Actual practice typically remains well short of that ideal. In many models, either learning or selection is bracketed – which is not necessarily a bad intellectual strategy since it allows the exploration of the properties of single dynamic processes, holding the rest constant. So, for example, several models of stochastic, decentralized, adaptive economic agents – but without explicit market competition (see note 14) – offer very useful insights into the collective outcomes of mutual adjustments by boundedly rational agents. In a similar spirit, so do various models of innovation diffusion with heterogeneous agents, increasing returns and/or network externalities, and sequential adoptions.[14] Within a distinctly different modeling style, most AE models also focus upon the collective properties of adaptive interactions (for example, in the simplest cases some rudimentary forms of local learning). Nearer the ETEC philosophy, Dosi and Fagiolo (1998) study the properties of a reduced-form evolutionary model wherein, without any form of market competition, the whole dynamics is driven by decentralized activities of technological exploration, learning and imitation over a notionally unbounded opportunity space.

At the opposite extreme, quite a few models explore the properties of selection dynamics driven by competitive interactions in the absence of any explicit microlearning: compare most EOP models. Within the ETEC perspective, among others, Metcalfe (1992, 1995) refines the Fisher Law, originally developed with reference to populations in biology,[15] and insightfully applies it to industrial dynamics, while Winter et al. (1997) study generic properties of market selection fed by the persistent arrival of technologically heterogeneous entrants.

EGs rely extensively upon selection dynamics of some sort. However, many models in this perspective appear to fold together properties of population dynamics and properties involving, at least implicitly, some form of adaptive learning at the level of microentities: we shall come back to this shortly.

As we see it, the basic shortcoming of most current modeling of interaction mechanisms does *not* concern the *ceteris paribus* assumptions typically made (to repeat, a possibly healthy style of preliminary exploration). Rather, our concerns primarily relate to the general lack of any disciplined mapping between the theoretical constructs on interaction processes and empirical 'stylized facts' on those very processes.

Consider competitive selection dynamics. (We shall discuss learning processes below.) Most of us have utilized on several occasions some 'blackboxed' representation of an aggregate interaction law – be it an aggregate demand curve or a replicator dynamics of some sort. So, for example, in Nelson and Winter (1982) interactions in the product markets are compressed into an unmodeled market-clearing process involving a standard demand curve. In turn, the outcome of that collective interaction feeds back upon the growth possibilities of each individual entity (and thus operates as a selection mechanism) via the gross surplus each entity is able to invest – determined by the difference between the industry-wide price and firm-specific unit costs. Similarly, in models such as Silverberg et al. (1988), selection is explicitly modeled via a replicator dynamics, defining the 'law of change' in market shares as a function of the 'competitiveness' of each firm as compared to the industry average.

The point that we want to emphasize here is that it might be time to go beyond such 'blackbox' assumptions and reconstruct the collective dynamics starting from an explicit account of the 'microphysics' of market interactions.[16] This would imply taking much more seriously the question of *how markets work*:[17] for example, what are the effects of the specific institutional architectures of particular markets upon the ensuing collective dynamics? How do they affect selection processes? In what circumstances is something like a replicator dynamics a good approximation of collective selection patterns? A simulation environment for financial markets designed in this spirit is presented in Chiaromonte and Dosi (1998) and will soon be available on the Net at the Laboratory of Economics and Management, www.sssup.il.

A distinct, albeit overlapping, issue concerns the dimensions over which selection occurs. In the economic arena an obviously fundamental one has to do with output prices, but what about the non-price dimensions of competition?[18] This is another domain where evolutionary modeling can be substantially enriched by empirical investigations into the actual determinants of competitiveness in different industries and under different institutional settings.

More generally, as argued at greater length in Dosi and Nelson (1994) and Tordjman (1998), analyses of selection in the social arena – and their relationship to some notion of 'fitness' – must confront the question of the endogeneity of the selection criteria themselves. As in biological evolution, what is selected is likely to be determined in some complicated and non-linear way by the distributions of actual populations present at a point in time and by their history. However, in biological systems we might reasonably hold that the selection *criteria* (for example, the reproduction abilities or the food-processing efficiencies) remain relatively invariant. This might not be so in many socioeconomic circumstances: that is, not only are we likely to find 'dancing' fitness landscapes, but also the dimensions of the space over which such landscapes are defined are likely to change, too.[19]

On the Usefulness of the Phenotype/Genotype Distinction in the Social Domain

A general feature of evolutionary interpretations of change (in biology but also in economics) is that selection ultimately operates upon a pool of 'fundamental traits' of some kind, determining also their probabilities of transmission over time. The common biological story is known: the 'fundamental units' of selection are the genes which (together with the environment) shape the phenotypic characteristics of the individual entities upon which selection operates; inheritance is the mechanism of transmission; and selection acts by 'weeding out' phenotypic distributions, affecting over time the frequencies in the underlying genetic pool.

In fact, the real story is not so simple even in biology, and it is even less so in the social domain. For example, there might not exist a clear one-to-one mapping between the genes and their phenotypic manifestations affecting fitness (for example, due to fitness-neutral genetic drifts). Or, there might be *epistatic correlation* (for an in-depth discussion, see Kauffman 1993), so that different traits combine non-linearly to yield a particular phenotypic fitness.

Further peculiarities are specific to the socioeconomic domain (see also Dosi and Nelson 1994; Winter 1984 and 1988). First there is, *rightly*, much more ambiguity in the identification of what the 'fundamental units' are. Good candidates – depending on the problem at hand – are routines, technologies, organizational forms, behavioral patterns, or even 'mental models'.

Second, technologies, behavioral patterns, and so on can be improved and modified over time in 'Lamarkian' fashions. Third, 'inheritance' takes diverse meanings. In some circumstances, the biological metaphor on intergenerational transmission is not too much off the mark. In others, inheritance should be understood mainly as 'social imitation'. Yet, in others, there is no generation-to-generation 'inheritance' but rather the indefinite perpetuation (and possibly growth over time) of the 'phenotypic' expression of the underlying traits: this is the case of industrial evolution, where, at least in part, the frequency of particular technologies or organizational forms grow, shrink or die together with the organizational entities embodying them (see Winter 1990 for discussion).

Finally note that, in biology and even more so in economics, the objects over which selection is exerted are not single elementary traits but structures of much higher dimension in which traits are nested. So, for example, markets choose relatively complex products or technological systems – not individual elements of technological knowledge or organizational routines. Therefore, even after assuming some underlying space of technological and organizational traits as the appropriate 'primitive' dimension of evolution, we still need some interpretation of organizational development in order to relate 'evolution' and 'selection'. Putting it another way, we need a much better grasp of the relationships between the 'genotypic' and 'phenotypic' level: we understand this is so in biology and it is certainly a priority in economics. This is also a major area of complementarity between evolutionary theories on the one hand, and business economics and experimental psychology, on the other. (See also below.)

Here let us just mention two points. First, studies focused on 'organizational routines' and 'capabilities' begin to forge that link, building on an ETEC perspective and exploring, for example, the ways organizational knowledge is stored and reproduced within organizations (see Dosi et al. 2000), the nature and origins of routines themselves (Cohen et al. 1996, among others), and so on. Second, note also that the genotype /phenotype problem has been largely neglected within the EG perspective, at least so far. In fact the straightforward biological interpretation of an EG is as population dynamics at the genetic level. Economic applications are more ambiguous, but one may reasonably understand them as defining dynamics on some metaphorically equivalent space of strategies (the 'fundamental units of selection'). Here 'selection', which has – at least in principle – a clear meaning in biology as an environmental pressure toward/against the reproduction of particular traits, is taken to be equivalent to some payoff-driven pressure on the adaptive learning of boundedly rational agents (as Samuelson puts it, 'I describe the forces guiding agents' strategy choice as "selection" or "learning". I use these terms interchangeably, though the former has a more biological flavor, while the latter is commonly used in economic contexts' (Samuelson 1997, p. 22). But in a way the 'learning' interpretation is like saying that there is some set of given strategies, and that agents 'climb' through them by means of some unspecified algorithm operating internally in each agent – which, however, yields, at least on the average in the population, results identical to genuine environmental selection operating upon different pure strategy types.[20] Ultimately this boils down to an assumption that, one way or another, the 'selection landscape' in the heads of the agents is isomorphic to the 'true' selective ecology in which the whole population lives.

By contrast, the distinction between selection and learning is highlighted within the ETEC perspective. Selection, to repeat, has to do with what actually happens to agents (that is, at the *phenotypic* level) in terms of markets shares, profitability, survival probability, and so on. Learning, on the other hand, concerns what 'goes on in their minds'. Once we abandon the idea that the latter accurately mirrors the former, then the obvious question is: what and how do agents learn?

Learning in Evolutionary Environments

This issue is clearly too broad to be adequately handled in these short notes: see Dosi et al. (1996) for a much more extensive discussion. The question here concerns how agents (individuals and organizations) make sense of complex and changing environments and how they act in them. Different strands of 'evolutionary' thinking certainly have in common the hypothesis of some 'bounds' on agents' rationality. Generally, this should be taken just to mean that they are less omniscient than God (or than the local gods, the creators of the model at hand) Beyond that, there is not much agreement on where the 'bounds' are and what they imply.

Indeed, in Dosi et al. (1996), it is argued first, that agents (including of course ourselves) are not only characterized by information-processing and memory limitations, but more fundamentally, by an intrinsic *competence-gap* concerning (a) the representation of the environment; (b) the problem-solving repertoire; (c) the detection and assessment of payoffs; and (d) the very nature of goals and preferences. Learning affects all four domains, and their co-evolution.

Second, one is likely to obtain precious clues on such learning mechanisms by the observation of cognitive and behavioral patterns in circumstances that are not at all 'evolutionary' – the context is stationary and relatively simple, the payoffs are straightforward and the action menu is trivial – wherein agents nevertheless display systematic biases *vis-à-vis* the prescriptions of 'rational' decision making, as experiments have shown.

More generally, third, the evidence both on individual patterns of cognition/ decision behaviors and on regularities in organizational adjustments and learning should be considered as fundamental disciplining criteria for the microfoundations of evolutionary models.

At this level, the difference among alternative perspectives is striking. At one extreme, ETEC models have attempted to represent agents reflecting certain 'phenomenological' regularities – for example, on pricing, research and development investment, and so on. At the other extreme, EG modelers, while congenial to heroic simplifying assumptions in other respects, have almost entirely eschewed the incorporation of stylized reflections of empirical considerations reported from experimental economics and cognitive sciences. Indeed, Camerer's remark that 'when game theory does aim to describe behavior, it often proceeds with a disturbingly low ratio of careful observation to theorizing' (Camerer 1997, p. 167) applies equally to its EG version. As a case in point, compare Fudenberg and Levine (1998) and Samuelson (1997), on the one hand, with the experimental evidence discussed in Camerer (1995 and 1997), on the other. And even more striking is the contrast between what modelers of industrial organization theorize (or prescribe?) and the evidence on actual corporate behaviors.[21]

As an illustration, consider the suggestive examples of interactions involving a strategic dimension presented in the pathbreaking work of Schelling (1978). Certainly, the environments defining most of these 'games' are *not* evolutionary in any specific sense: there is no dynamics in the 'fundamentals'; the menu of actions is fixed, given from the start and fairly understandable to the agents; there is no replicator dynamics. If there is an evolutionary part to them, it is in the way people come to understand such environments and develop their action repertoires. Since Schelling's contribution, what have we learned in terms of *descriptive* theories? (Agreed, we have learned a lot about the logic of structures and incentives of the interactions by restating them in formal game-theoretic terms.) What descriptive gains derive from postulating some variety of dynamics in the EG style? In fact, those dynamics point toward an implicit theory of adaptive learning. Whether it is a sound descriptive theory is indicated, presumably, by the empirical check from the behavioral and cognitive disciplines. For example, do people actually learn via mechanisms that entail the self-seeking reinforcements postulated by most EGs? Roughly speaking, the experimental answer seems to be negative. Rather, as is argued at greater length in Dosi et al. (1996), a more promising avenue of research appears to be an explicit account of the nature and dynamics of *mental models* and *interpretative categories* through which agents make sense of the environment they are facing and adjust to it. *A fortiori*, we suggest, this applies to evolutionary environments with the characteristics described earlier. But all that, in turn, demands descriptive theories of economic behaviors resting on empirically disciplined 'nanofoundations', taking on board the evidence from the growing literature on the dynamics of cognition, 'reasoning', 'sentiments', and so on – on the individual level – and organizational behaviors – at collective levels.

5 CONCLUSION

In sum, there are multiple dimensions over which the different perspectives invoking evolutionary arguments may be evaluated.

A *first* one is the degree of 'rational,' forward-looking, understanding of their decision environments that agents are assumed to possess, as compared to the objective complexity of their cognitive and problem-solving tasks.

A *second* relates to the nature of the evolutionary environments analysed, and in particular whether the focus is upon 'small-world' setups versus an 'open-ended' dynamics allowing for various forms of endogenously generated novelty.

Third, at a methodological level, a crucial issue concerns the degree of phenomenological discipline to which models subscribe in such significant respects as agents' cognitive abilities, learning mechanisms, behavioral rules, interaction format, and so on.

And, *finally*, there is the question of what the various models are meant to interpret, and what testing criteria they set for themselves.

It is clear from this brief assessment of the state of the art that wide differences persist across all these dimensions. The hopeful message is that, at the least, all the reviewed perspectives subscribe to the 'dynamics first' commitments discussed above: interpreting change means telling, in one way or another, a process story rather than a 'rationalization' of how what exist may coherently be accounted for. But this is certainly not enough to yield a consistent evolutionary interpretation of economic dynamics. The challenge ahead, as we see it, involves a painstaking reassessment of the microfoundations characterizing what agents do, how they learn, their interactions and the ways all that is embedded into institutional structures and 'habits of thought' that shape the possible worlds achievable at any point in time. Certainly, for economists, that reassessment requires more attention to the wealth of evidence from other disciplines, from psychology to political science. The upside of such inquiry might be that the descriptive analysis of observed courses of individual and collective behavior is freed (at last) from the conceptual prison of a deductive, prescriptive, theory of action.

NOTES

1. This section draws upon Coriat and Dosi (1998a). More detailed discussion in germane perspectives are in Hodgson (1993), Dosi and Nelson (1994), Nelson (1995), Silverberg (1988), Silverberg and Verspagen (1995), Metcalfe (1992), Anderson (1988), Witt (1993), Dosi et al. (1996), Lesourne (1991) and Lesourne and Orléan (1998).
2. Note, however, that quite a few 'aggregate' (that is, non-microfounded) dynamic models are nonetheless consistent with an evolutionary interpretation (some of them are surveyed in Silverberg and Verspagen (1995) and in Coriat and Dosi (1998a); see also the survey in a different perspective, by Boldrin (1988)).
3. On the notions of the 'emergence' and 'metastability', cf. the suggestive discussion in Lane (1993); see also below.
4. Note that, given the above broad definition of an 'evolutionary research programme', it may well also partly cover contributions of authors who could not call themselves 'evolutionist' in any strict sense.
5. Further challenging developments are presented in Fontana and Buss (1994a and b).
6. The debt to the works of Ilya Prigogine as a fundamental source of inspiration along this line of research ought to be more widely acknowledged: see, among the others, Nicolis and Prigogine (1977).
7. For broad discussions along similar lines, see Winter (1988), Dosi and Nelson (1994), Nelson (1995), Metcalfe (1992), Coriat and Dosi (1998a), Dosi et al. (1996), Tordjman (1998).
8. Or, for computer-implementable models, finite for obvious technical reasons, but with a dimensionality high enough to practically simulate the absence of dimensionality limits.
9. For example, Eldredge and Gould (1972). See also Casti (1992) and the remarks in Lane (1993).
10. But also some 'reduced'-form models developed in the ETEC spirit: see Winter et al. (1997).
11. Without, however, any religious commitments to the methodology. So, for example, the ETEC perspective draws fully from those works on innovation diffusion where suggestive empirical implications may be derived from the limit properties of dynamics cum heterogeneous agents and increasing returns (see, among others, David 1988; Arthur et al. 1987; Bassanini and Dosi 1998).
12. An example concerning the patterns of innovation diffusion is explored in Bassanini and Dosi (1998); convergence properties in stochastic EG are discussed in Vega-Redondo (1996).
13. See the critical surveys in Kirman and Weisbuch (1998) and Fagiolo (1998), and the references therein.
14. More on them in David (1992) and Bassanini and Dosi (1998).
15. In brief, the Fisher Law establishes the *law of motion* of average 'fitness' – and, thus, of the relative frequencies of the related traits – as a function of the higher moments of the distribution of the latter in the appropriate fitness space. In particular, the rate of increase of average fitness is proportional to its variance. Setting aside some important technical qualifications, one may regard it as a typical implication of the standard replicator dynamics common to theoretical biology, EGs applied to economics and many ETEC models: relative frequencies change with monotonic dependence upon the relative 'fitness' of particular trait(s) as compared to the overall population's averages. Nelson and Winter (1982, pp. 240–43) establish a dynamic analogue of the standard comparative statics result for a price change in the in the context of the Fisher Law type of replicator dynamics. (For a germane critical discussion of these issues, see Silverberg 1988.)
16. This indeed is a challenge that has been powerfully brought to evolutionary modeling by the AE methodology, with its abhorrence of pre-defined 'laws of motion' and its emphasis on explicit rules for 'local' interactions among microentities; see also Fagiolo (1998).
17. One of the few notable works in this spirit is Kirman and Vignes (1991) on the Marseilles fish market.
18. Here we are primarily talking about real markets (that is, markets for commodities and services): financial markets are likely to embody quite different selection criteria, much more related to speculative phenomena: more on this in Marengo and Tordjman (1996).
19. Note incidentally that all this casts serious doubts on the monotonicity in the effects of selection forces generally assumed in EGs.
20. 'The agents in biological application of evolutionary game theory never choose strategic and never change their strategies. Instead, they are "hard-wired" to play a particular strategy, which they do until they die. Variations in the mix of strategies within a population are caused by differing rates of reproduction. In economic applications, we have a different process in mind. The players in the game are people, who choose and may change their strategies. An evolutionary approach in economics begins with a model of this strategy adjustment process' (Samuelson 1997, p. 18).
21. For some insightful remarks, see the reviews by Loasby (1995) and Metcalfe (1995) of Milgrom and Roberts (1992).

REFERENCES

Anderson, P., K. Arrow and D. Pines (eds) (1988), *The Economy as an Evolving Complex System*, Redwood City, CA: Addison-Wesley.

Arthur, B., Y. Ermoliev and Y. Kaniovski (1987), 'Path-dependent processes and the emergence of macrostructure', *European Journal of Operations Research*, **30**, 294–303.

Axtell, R. and J. Epstein (1996), *Growing Artificial Societies: Social Science from the Bottom Up*, Washington, DC: The Brookings Institution.

Basalla, G. (1988), *The Evolution of Technology*, Cambridge: Cambridge University Press.

Bassanini, A. and G. Dosi (1998), 'Competing technologies, international diffusion and the role of convergence to a stable market structure', International Institute for Applied Systems Analysis (IIASA), Laxenburg, Austria, IR-98–012.

Boldrin, M. (1988), 'Persistent oscillation and chaos in economic models: notes for a survey', in Anderson et al.(eds), (1988).

Camerer, C. (1995), 'Individual decision making', in J.H. Kagel and A.E. Roth (eds), *The Handbook of Experimental Economics*, Princeton, NJ: Princeton University Press.

Camerer, C. (1997), 'Progress in behavioral game theory', *Journal of Economic Perspectives*, **11**, 167–88.

Camerer, C. and T.H. Ho (1997), 'Learning in games', in Plott and Smith (eds), (1997).

Carroll, G.R. (1997), 'Long term evolutionary change in organizational populations: theory, models and empirical findings in industrial demography', *Industrial and Corporate Change*, **6**, 119–43.

Casti, J.L. (1992), *Reality Rules*, New York: Wiley.

Chandler, A., P. Hägstrom and Ö. Sölvell (eds), (1998), *The Dynamic Firm*, Oxford: Oxford University Press.

Chiaromonte, F. and G. Dosi (1993), 'Heterogeneity, competition and macroeconomic dynamics', *Structural Change and Economic Dynamics*, **4**, 39–46.

Chiaromonte, F. and G. Dosi (1998), 'Modeling a decentralized asset market: an introduction to the Financial "Toy-Room"', Interim Report, IIASA, Laxenburg, Austria.

Cohen, M., Egidi M. Bekhart R., G. Dosi, L. Marengo, M. Warglin and S. Winter (1996), 'Routines and other recurring action patterns of organizations: contemporary research issues', *Industrial and Corporate Change*, **5**, 653–98.

Conlisk, J. (1989), 'An aggregate model of technical change', *Quarterly Journal of Economics*, **104**, 787–821.

Coriat, B. and G. Dosi (1998a), 'The institutional embeddedness of economic change: an appraisal of the "evolutionary" and "regulationist" research programmes', in Nielsen and Johnson (eds), (1988).

Coriat, B. and G. Dosi (1998b), 'Learning how to govern and learning how to solve problems: on the co-evolution of competences, conflicts and organizational routines', in Chandler et al. (eds), (1988).

Cyert, R.M. and J. March (1963), *A Behavioral Theory of the Firm*, Englewood Cliffs, NJ: Prentice-Hall.

David, P.A. (1975), *Technical Choice, Innovation and Economic Growth*, Cambridge: Cambridge University Press.

David, P.A. (1985), 'Clio and the economics of QWERTY', *American Economic Review*, *Papers and Proceedings*, **75**, 332–7.

David, P.A. (1988), 'Path-dependence: putting the past into the future of economics', Stanford: Institute for Mathematical Studies in Social Sciences, Technical Report, 533.

David, P.A. (1992), 'Heroes, herds and hysteresis in technological change: Thomas Edison and the battle of the systems', *Industrial and Corporate Change*, **1**, 139–80.

Day, R. and G. Eliasson (eds) (1986), *The Dynamics of Market Economies*, Amsterdam: North-Holland.

Dosi, G. (1982), 'Technological paradigms and technological trajectories, *Research Policy*, **11**, 147–62.

Dosi, G. (1988), 'Sources, procedures and microeconomic effects of innovation', *Journal of Economic Literature*, **26**, 126–73.

Dosi, G. and Fagiolo, G. (1998), 'Exploring the unknown: on entrepreneurship, coordination and innovation-driven growth', in Lesourne and Orléan (eds), pp. 309–50.

Dosi, G., C. Freeman, R.R. Nelson, G. Silverberg and L. Soete (eds) (1988), *Technical Change and Economic Theory*, London: Francis Pinter, New York: Columbia University Press.

Dosi, G., O. Marsili, L. Orsenigo and R. Salvatore (1995), 'Learning, market selection and the evolution of industrial structures', *Small Business Economics*, **7**, 411–36.

Dosi, G., L. Marengo and Fagiolo, G. (1996), 'Learning in evolutionary environments', Laxenburg, Austria: IIASA Working Paper.

Dosi, G. and R.R. Nelson (1994), 'An introduction to evolutionary theories in economics', *Journal of Evolutionary Economics*, **4**, 153–72.

Eldredge, N. and S. Gould (1972), 'Puntuacted equilibria: an alternative to phyletic gradualism', in T.J.M. Schopf (ed.), *Models in Paleobiology*, San Francisco, CA: Freeman, Cooper & Co., 82–115.

Fagerberg, J. (1994), 'Technology and international differences in growth rates', *Journal of Economic Literature*, **32**, 1147–75.

Fagiolo, G. (1998), 'Spatial interaction in dynamic decentralized economies: a review', in P. Cohendet, P. Llerena, H. Stalin and G. Umbhauer (eds), *The Economic of Networks*, Berlin/New York: Springer Verlag, pp. 53–91.

Fontana, W. (1992), 'Algorithmic chemistry', in C.G. Langton, C. Taylor, J.D. Farmer and S. Rasmussen (eds), *Artificial Life II*, pp. 159–209, Redwood City, CA: Addison-Wesley.

Fontana, W. and L. Buss (1994a), '"The arrival of the fittest": toward a theory of biological organization', *Bulletin of Mathematical Biology*, **56**, 1–64.

Fontana, W. and L. Buss (1994b), 'What would be conserved if the "tape were run twice"?', *Proceedings of the National Academy of Science*, **91**, 757–61.

Freeman, C. (1982), *The Economics of Industrial Innovation*, 2nd edn, London: Francis Pinter.

Freeman, C. (1994), 'The economics of technical change', *Cambridge Journal of Economics*, **14**, 463–514.

Frenken, K., L. Marengo and M. Valente (1999), 'Interdependencies, near-decomposability and adaptation', in Th. Brennen (ed.), *Computational Techniques for Modeling Learning in Economics*, Boston, MA/ Dordrecht: Kluwer, 145–65.

Friedman, D. (1991), 'Evolutionary games in economics', *Econometrica*, **59**, 637–66.

Friedman M. (1953), 'The methodology of positive economics', in *Essays in Positive Economics*, Chicago: University of Chicago Press, 3–43.

Fudenberg, D. and D.K. Levine (1998), *The Theory of Learning in Games*, Cambridge, MA: MIT Press.

Grandstrand, O. (ed.), (1994), *The Economics of Technology*, Amsterdam: Elsevier/North-Holland.

Hannan, M.T. and G. R. Carroll (1992), *Dynamics of Organizational Populations*, New York/Oxford: Oxford University Press.

Hannan, M.T. and J. Freeman (1989), *Organizational Ecology*, Cambridge, MA: Harvard University Press.

Hodgson, G. (1993), *Economics and Evolution*, Cambridge: Polity Press; Ann Arbor, MI: University of Michigan Press.

Hufbauer, J. and K. Sigmund (1988), *The Theory of Evolution and Dynamical Systems*, Cambridge: Cambridge University Press.

Kauffman, S.A. (1993), *The Origins of Order: Self-Organization and Selection in Evolution*, New York/Oxford: Oxford University Press.

Kauffman, S.A. and MacReady (1995), 'Technological evolution and adaptive organizations', *Complexity*, **2**, 26–43.

Kirman, A.P. and A. Vignes (1991), 'Price dispersion: theoretical considerations and empirical evidence from the Marseilles fish market', in K. Arrow (ed.), *Issues in Contemporary Economics*, London: Macmillan, 160–85.

Kirman, A.P. and G. Weisbuch (1998), 'Market organization', in Lesourne and Orléan (eds), pp. .

Klepper, S. (1996), 'Entry, exit, growth and innovation over the product life cycle', *American Economic Review*, **86**, 562–83.

Klepper, S. (1997), 'Industry life cycles', *Industrial and Corporate Change*, **6**, 145–81.

Kreps, D.M. (1996), 'Markets, hierarchies and mathematical economic theory', *Industrial and Corporate Change*, **5**, 561–96.

Krugman, P. (1996), *The Self-Organizing Economy*, Oxford /New York: Blackwell.

Lane, D. (1993), 'Artificial worlds and economics', Parts I and II, *Journal of Evolutionary Economics*, **3**, 89–107 and 177–97.

Lesourne, J. (1991), *L'Economie de l'Ordre et du Désordre* (The Economics of Order and Disorder), Paris: Economica.

Lesourne, J. and A. Orléan (eds) (1998), *Advances on Self-Organization and Evolutionary Processes*, Paris: Economica.

Levinthal, D. (1997), 'Adaptation on rugged landscapes, *Management Science*, **43**, 934–50.

Lindgren, R. (1992), 'Evolutionary phenomena in simple dynamics', in C.G. Langton (ed.), *Artificial Life II. Proceedings of the Interdisciplinary Workshop on the Synthesis and Simulation of Living Systems*, Redwood City, CA: Addison-Wesley, pp. 295–312.

Loasby, B.J. (1995), 'Running a business: an appraisal of *Economics, Organization and Management* by Paul Milgrom and John Roberts', *Industrial and Corporate Change*, **4**, 471–90.

Lundvall, B.-Å. (ed.) (1992), *National Systems of Innovation*, London: Francis Pinter.

Malerba, F. and L. Orsenigo (1996), 'The dynamics and evolution of industry', *Industrial and Corporate Change*, **5**, 51–87.

Malerba, F. and L. Orsenigo (1997), 'The dynamics and evolution of industries', *Industrial and Corporate Change*, **6**, 51–87.

March, J. and H. Simon (1958), *Organizations*, New York: Wiley.

Marengo, L. and H. Tordjman (1996), 'Speculation, heterogeneity and learning: a model of exchange rate dynamics', *Kyklos*, **47**, 407–38.

Maynard Smith, J. (1982), *'Evolution and the theory of games'*, *American Scientist*, Cambridge: Cambridge University Press.

Metcalfe, S. (1992), 'Variety, structure and change: an evolutionary perspective on the competitive process', *Revue d'Economie Industrielle*, **65**, 46–61.

Metcalfe, S. (1995), 'Economics, Organizations and Management: a review of Milgrom and Roberts', *Industrial and Corporate Change*, **4**, 491–7.

Milgrom, P. and J. Roberts (1992), *Economics, Organization and Management*, Englewood Cliffs, NJ: Prentice-Hall.

Mokyr, J. (1990), *The Lever of Riches*, Oxford: Oxford University Press.

Nadal, J.P., G. Weisbuch, O. Chenevez and A. Kirman (1998), 'A formal approach to market organization: choice functions, mean field approximation and maximum entropy principle', in J. Lesourne and A. Orléan (eds), 149–59.

Nakicenovic, N. and A. Grübler (eds) (1992), *Diffusion of Technologies and Social Behaviour*, Berlin/Heidelberg/ New York: Springer Verlag.

Nelson, R.R. (ed.), (1993), *National Innovation Systems: A Comparative Study*, Oxford/New York: Oxford University Press.

Nelson, R.R. (1995), 'Recent evolutionary theorizing about economic change', *Journal of Economic Literature*, **33**, 48–90.

Nelson, R. and S. Winter (1982), *An Evolutionary Theory of Economic Change*, Cambridge, MA: Belknap Press of Harvard University Press.

Nicolis, G. and I. Prigogine (1977), *Self-organization in Non-Equilibrium Systems*, New York: Wiley.

Nielsen, K. and B. Johnson (eds) (1988), *Institution and Economic Change*, Aldershot: Edward Elgar.

Pavitt, K. (1984), 'Sectoral patterns of innovation: toward a taxonomy and a theory', *Research Policy*, **13**, 343–75.

Plott, C.R. and V.L. Smith (eds) (1997), *Handbook of Experimental Economics Results*, Amsterdam/New York: North-Holland.

Rosenberg, N. (1976), *Perspectives on Technology*, Cambridge: Cambridge University Press.

Rosenberg, N. (1982), *Inside the Black Box*, Cambridge: Cambridge University Press.

Samuelson, L. (1997), *Evolutionary Games and Equilibrium Selection*, Cambridge, MA: MIT Press.

Schelling, T.C. (1978), *Micro Motives and Macro Behaviors*, New York: Norton.

Silverberg, G., G. Dosi and L. Orsenigo (1988), 'Innovation, diversity and diffusion. A self-organization model', *Economic Journal*, **98**, 1032–54.

Silverberg, G. (1988), 'Modeling economic dynamics and technical change: mathematical approaches to self-organization and evolution', in G. Dosi et al. (eds), (1988), 531–59.

Silverberg, G. and L. Soete (eds) (1993), *The Economics of Growth and Technical Change: Technologies, Nations, Agents*, Aldershot: Edward Elgar.

Silverberg, G. and B. Verspagen (1994), 'Learning, innovation and economic growth: a long-run model of industrial dynamics', *Industrial and Corporate Change*, **3**, 199–223.

Silverberg, G. and B. Verspagen (1995), 'Evolutionary theorizing on economic growth', IIASA Working Paper WP-95-78, forthcoming in K. Dopfer (ed.), *Evolutionary Principles of Economics*, Norwell, MA: Kluwer.

Tordjman, H. (1998), 'Evolution: history, change and progress', in Lesourne and Orléan, (eds), 9–36.

Utterback, J. and F. Suarez (1992), 'Innovation, competition and market structure', *Research Policy*, **21**, 1–21.

Veblen, T. (1898), 'Why is economics not an evolutionary science?', *Quarterly Journal of Economics*, **12**, 373–97.

Vega-Redondo, F. (1996), *Evolution, Games and Economic Behaviours*, Oxford/New York: Oxford University Press.

Vincenti, W.A. (1990), *What Engineers Know and How They Know It: Analytical Studies from Aeronautical History*, Baltimore, MD: Johns Hopkins University Press.

Weibull, J.W. (1995), *Evolutionary Game Theory*, Cambridge, MA: MIT Press.

Weisbuch, G., A.P. Kirman and D. Herreiner (1998), 'Market organization', in Lesourne and Orléan (eds), 221–40.

Westhoff, F.H., B.V. Yabrourgh and R.M. Yabrourgh (1996), 'Complexity, organization, and Stuart Kauffman's *The Origins of Order*', *Journal of Economic Behavior and Organization*, **29**, 1–25.

Winter, S.G. (1984), 'Schumpeterian competition under alternative technological regimes', *Journal of Economic Behaviour and Organisation*, **5**, 287–320.

Winter, S.G. (1986), 'The research program of the behavioral theory of the firm': orthodox critique and evolutionary perspective', in B. Gilad and S. Kaish (eds), *Handbook of Behavioral Economics* Greenwich, CT: JAI Press, 155–88.

Winter, S.G. (1988), 'Economic natural selection and the theory of the firm, in P.E. Earl (ed.), *Behavioural Economics*, Vol. 1, Aldershot: Edward Elgar.

Winter, S.G. (1990), 'Survival, selection and inheritance in evolutionary theories of organization', in J.V. Singh (ed.), *Organizational Evolution: New Directions*, Newbury Park, CA: Sage, 269–97.

Winter, S.G., Y.M. Kaniovski and G. Dosi (1997), *A Baseline Model of Industry Evolution*, Laxenburg: IR-97-013, IIASA.

Winter, S.G., Y. Kaniovski and G. Dosi (1997b), 'A baseline model of industrial evolution', Interim Report, Laxenburg, Austria: IIASA.

Winter, S.G., Y.M. Kaniovski and G. Dosi (2000), 'Modeling industrial dynamics with innovative entrants', *Structural Change and Economic Dynamics*, **11**, 255–366.

Witt, U. (ed.) (1993), *Evolutionary Economics*, Aldershot: Edward Elgar.

Young, P. (1998), *Individual Strategy and Social Structure*, Princeton, NJ: Princeton University Press.

17. A behavioral and evolutionary model of the dynamics of the computer industry

Franco Malerba, Richard Nelson, Luigi Orsenigo and Sidney G. Winter*

1 INTRODUCTION

This chapter introduces a new generation of evolutionary economic models. We call these models 'history friendly' because they are intended to explain the observed patterns of historical outcomes and behaviors associated with important economic episodes. The particular model presented here is designed to explore the factors that explain how the structure of the computer industry evolved in the United States. The focus is on the following phenomena: the rise of a single firm (IBM) to dominance in the production and sale of mainframe computers, the ability of IBM to maintain its dominance in the mainframe market even in the face of technological advances which might have been 'competence destroying', but its inability to maintain similar dominance in new segments of the computer market that were enabled by new technologies. We seek to explain and explore these phenomena with the aid of a special-purpose simulation model grounded in evolutionary economic theory.

Our criteria for a successful 'history-friendly' model are twofold. First, the model must be broadly consistent with the important empirical phenomena of the episode in question. But second, and less conventionally, we think it important that the 'explanation' built into the model attempt to capture the beliefs of knowledgeable people regarding what happened and why. We aspire to create a model whose central causal propositions will be endorsed by such people (after reflecting on a careful explication) as basically correct.

We believe that the causal arguments used by knowledgeable people to explain the phenomena they have lived with, or studied, should be taken seriously as 'theory', even when they are not advertised as theory, or presented with the formal trappings that economists and other social scientists have come to associate with the concept of theory. We have called this informed but relatively informal kind of causal argument 'appreciative theory'. In our view, one of the most important roles of formal theory in economics and social science is to engage in dialogue with appreciative theory. Appreciative theory is real causal theory, and in many cases reflects the best attempt of people who know the phenomena in detail to express what they think really is going on. When it is deeply informed by contact with rich empirical sources, such appreciative theory deserves to be taken very seriously. However, appreciative theory generally is not well suited for logical exploration of whether its causal arguments are internally consistent, and if consistent whether they are sufficient to provide an explanation – or, alternatively, whether they need to be modified in certain ways so that they are consistent, or need to be augmented to be able to explain the subject matter.

In contrast, formal theory is more distant from the empirical subject matter, more abstract, but also more amenable to logical examination. Economists who know the empirical subject matter seldom take formal theory seriously as the explanation they believe. But on the other hand, formal theory can be of great help in thinking through the appreciative theory. It can identify gaps in the logic, and lead the analyst to consider mechanisms and factors that were missing, or muted, in the informal account. This is a key role we see for 'history-friendly' modeling. Also, it often happens that there is less than a full consensus among the different informed observers, and even an interpretation supported by a strong consensus may conceivably be quite wrong. Here also, the attempt to model formally the main elements of the leading appreciative theory is a key step toward sorting out the differences at a more detailed level, and constitutes a sort of audit of the logic of the dominant view.

In our usage, the term 'formal' means that all of the logic that drives model outcomes is explicit and at least potentially on display, a characteristic shared by simulation models and analytical models. The virtues and uses ascribed to formal models above apply to both categories, but not, by any means, to all models in either category. For both types of models, an important hazard is that complexity may render the model opaque, producing obfuscation rather than clarification of the issues of causal structure. The complexity risks are of a different character in the two categories, however.

In the present context, there is a definite tension in between the objective of 'getting close to the appreciative theoretic story', and having a model whose mechanisms are not opaque. To be useful in the role we describe, the formal model must be capable of faithful representation of the verbal argument, at least in stylized form. In general that verbal argument is sufficiently complicated that a simulation model is the only way that its gist can be captured formally. But if the central purpose of developing a formal model is to check or firm up the logical consistency of the appreciative theory, it is important to be able to understand just how the model works. Particularly if early versions of the model do not work as expected, suggesting that there are gaps or flaws in the appreciative theory or its formal counterpart, it is important that the mechanisms built into the formal model be transparent enough so that the analyst can figure out just what is wrong about, or incomplete in, the appreciative theoretic account and/or its formal representation. The process of developing and analysing a formal model may itself bring to light mechanisms, factors, and constraints that were missing in the initial appreciative account, but, again, this can happen only if the model is understandable. The creation of formal representations that serve these purposes and satisfy these criteria is a difficult challenge.

Our objectives here are not simply to develop a set of particular models aimed at separate empirical episodes, although major episodes like the evolution of the computer industry certainly are important to understand in their own right. Rather, we intend to develop a class of models that have a common basis in the central propositions of evolutionary theory, but with different episode-specific features, capable of 'explaining' (in the sense above) a wide range of empirical phenomena and, in particular, highlighting the factors behind the significantly different patterns of evolution in different industries.

Our particular philosophy seems basically consistent with that behind much of the work of Richard Cyert, and certainly his work with James March which resulted in their magisterial *A Behavioral Theory of the Firm* (Cyert and March 1963). It is clear that the intent behind much of the theorizing in *A Behavioral Theory of the Firm* was as much to get the process modeled right, as to explain particular outcomes. In common with Cyert and March, we distrust economic models that propose that individuals and organizations behave 'as if they were doing something or other when, in fact, both available evidence and common sense indicate that they were doing no such thing. And for us, as for them, a good part of the satisfaction of developing a model that provides a process explanation of the relevant empirical phenomena derives from the affirmation of the unity of truth: the result confirms that the specified process characterization, which seems to be correct based on other evidence, indeed is capable of generating those phenomena.

Of course, this consonance of ontological and epistemological views is no coincidence. *An Evolutionary Theory of Economic Change* (Nelson and Winter 1982) was profoundly influenced not only by *A Behavioral Theory of the Firm*, but also by the earlier volume. *Organizations* by James March and Herbert Simon (March and Simon 1958). In addition to a basic methodological outlook, we have drawn from these works, first, an appreciation that much of organizational behavior derives from 'programmed behavior', 'standard operating procedures' or 'routines'; the notion of a routine has been a fundamental building block in our evolutionary theory. And we drew from this work, second, an understanding of the value of simulation as a technique for modeling complex dynamic phenomena. Both of these elements will show up sharply when we set forth our model of the computer industry.

However, before doing this, we need to sketch out the empirical episodes that the model is designed to explain. This we do in Section 2. In Section 3 we present the model. In Sections 4 and 5 we report some history replicating and history divergent simulations, and discuss the major factors affecting the specific historical patterns the model has addressed. In Sections 6 and 7 we return to the discussion of useful theorizing in economics and social science more generally, and to the connections between evolutionary economic theory and behavioral theory.

2 THE EVOLUTION OF COMPUTER TECHNOLOGY AND THE COMPUTER INDUSTRY

Given space constraints, we can recount only a stylized history of computer technology and the computer industry. The story draws heavily from more detailed analytic historical accounts by Flamm (1988); Langlois (1990); Bresnahan and Greenstein (1999); and especially Bresnahan and Malerba (1999).

An essential element of the story involves the pattern of technological change. The history of the computer shows continuous improvements in machines that serve particular groups of users, punctuated from time to time by the introduction of significant new component technologies. These not only permit the needs of existing users to be met better, but also open up the possibility of designing machines that serve new classes of users whose needs could not be met using older technology. In the United States these punctuations were associated with the entry into the industry of new firms, and these new firms almost always were the first to venture into the new market. However, this happened to a significantly lesser degree in Europe, and hardly at all in Japan.

A Stylized History

The evolution of the industry divides rather naturally into four eras. The first began with the early experimentation with computers, which culminated in designs sufficiently attractive to induce their purchase by large firms with massive computation tasks, as well as by scientific laboratories. This opened the era of the *mainframe computer*. The second era began with the introduction of integrated circuits and the development of *minicomputers*. The third era is that of the *personal computer* (PC), made possible by the invention of the *microprocessor*. We now are in the era of *networked PCs* and the increasing use of the Internet.

During the Second World War and the years just after, governments in several countries funded a number of projects with the aim of developing computers useful for governmental purposes. In the late 1940s and early 1950s a number of companies, in Europe as well as in the United States, began investing their own funds hoping to develop a computer sufficiently attractive to win the market of scientific laboratories, large firms, and other organizations who had large-scale computation needs. The early 1950s saw the entry into the industry of IBM – then a major punched-card and tabulating machinery company, but with significant capabilities in electronic computing derived in good part from government research and development (R&D) contracts – and the rest of the 'Bunch' (Burrows, Univac Rand, NCR, Control Data, Honeywell), as well as GE and RCA. These companies differed in the strategies they pursued, and in their success in developing machines that would sell at a profit. By 1954, with the introduction of the 650, IBM began to pull ahead of the Bunch. With the introduction of the 1401 in 1960, it came to dominate the world market for accounting machines.

IBM dominated not only in the American market, but also in Europe and Japan. A small-scale domestic industry was able to hold on in Europe, and later in Japan, only by virtue of a combination of government subsidy, a guaranteed government market, and protection.

Component technology improved greatly over what we are calling the mainframe era, and transistors gradually replaced vacuum tubes as the basic circuit elements. These developments enabled significant improvements in mainframe performance, and some reduction in cost. In the early 1960s, IBM introduced its 360 family of models, and seized an even larger share of the mainframe market.

The invention and development of the integrated circuit enabled even further improvements in mainframe computers and also reduced barriers to entry in the mainframe industry, thus stimulating the entry of new competitors to IBM. However, integrated circuits not only permitted the development of even more powerful large computers. They opened the possibility of designing smaller computers that had a considerable amount of power, but could be produced at a much lower cost than mainframes. DEC's PDP8, the first minicomputer, was produced in 1965. Minicomputers opened up a new demand class which had not been tapped by mainframes, which included medium-sized research laboratories, manufacturing firms, and some small businesses.

In the United States, new firms like DEC were the first into the new minicomputer market; these new firms seized and held a significant share of that market. IBM lagged in getting into minicomputers, and never achieved there the dominance it achieved in the mainframe market. While the availability of integrated circuits provided an opportunity for European and Japanese firms to get into the minicomputer market, these firms lagged just as in the earlier case with mainframes. American firms took a considerable fraction of the minicomputer market in Europe and Japan, and domestic firms held on there only through a combination of subsidy and protection.

The introduction of the microprocessor marked another punctuation in the history of the industry. Microprocessors enabled significant improvements in mainframe and minicomputer designs. However, their most important impact was to permit the design of reasonably powerful computers that could be produced at quite low costs. Personal computers opened up a new demand segment that had not been touched by mainframes and minicomputers: small firms, and personal users.

As in the case of minicomputers, in the United States new firms entered the industry aiming to serve the new personal computer (PC) market: these included prominently some specialized PC design and manufacturing firms (such as Apple, Commodore, Tandy, and Compaq). Established mainframe and minicomputer producers were slow in seeing the new market and the needs of users in that market. Interestingly, when IBM did get into PCs, it did so with external alliances: Microsoft for operating systems software, and Intel for microprocessors. IBM did manage to seize a significant fraction of the personal computer market, but never was as dominant there as it had been in mainframes. And, of course, in recent years IBM's share in PCs has eroded significantly.

A striking characteristic of the firms producing PCs is that they are primarily assemblers, buying most of their components on the open market. Also, most of the software for PCs is developed and supplied by software specialists. This is in sharp contrast with mainframe production, particularly in the early and middle stages of the industry. IBM not only designed and produced most of the critical components for its mainframes, but also wrote most of the basic software. For a time, IBM also designed and produced a significant fraction of the integrated circuits that were employed in its mainframes. In minicomputers there was, from the beginning, more vertical specialization than in mainframe production, with most minicomputer companies buying their integrated circuits, and a number of other key components, on the open market. But PCs have seen even more vertical disintegration.

As noted, the advent of PCs led, in the United States, to the birth of a number of new firms, several of which turned out to be very successful. In contrast, just as in the case of minicomputers, few European and Japanese firms entered. And, except where there was heavy government protection or subsidy, American firms have come to dominate foreign markets for PCs.

These technological and market characteristics are even more emphasized in the new era – the one of *networked PCs and the Internet* – in which specialized firms compete in horizontal market layers (microprocessors, other components, printers, computer disks, operating software, application software, and so on) connected through open standards and interfaces. In this period, technological and market leadership is divided among several firms, each of which may be a prominent actor in a specific market segment.

Challenges for History-friendly Modeling

There are at least three interesting challenges for history-friendly modeling in the history recounted above. One is the explanation of the characteristics and the changes in the structure of the industry structure over time, in particular as new technologies were introduced and new markets emerged. The evolution of market structure has been marked by the following elements. A dominant firm emerged relatively early in the history of the industry, and that firm held its grip on the market share in the segment of the market it first seized in the face of several 'competence destroying' (Tushman and Anderson 1986; Henderson and Clark 1990) technological changes. On the other hand, new firms (and not the established ones) have been the vehicles through which the new technology opened up new market segments. The old established leaders have also entered the new market but have been unable to rout the newcomers from the new markets. A second challenge is provided by the progressive vertical disintegration of the computer industry, and in particular by the sharp increase in specialization that has marked the era of personal computers. Still a third challenge is to explain the significant differences between the characteristics, changes and performance of the industry in the United States on the one hand, and Europe and Japan on the other, particularly with respect to the role of incumbents and the ability of new firms to take advantage of new technological and market opportunities.

In this chapter we focus only on the first challenge. The verbal histories of the industry provide a sketch of a theory of why incumbent firms have been able to hold off newcomers with new technology in their traditional market, but have not been able to seize the new market opportunities. In the model we present below we have tried to present some of that verbal argument in stylized form.

3 THE MODEL

In this section we lay out the basic model. Given the nature of complex simulation models, it is impossible to present all the details of all the equations, without befuddling the reader and obscuring the basic logic of the model. We have tried, therefore, to lay out in transparent form what we regard as the gist of the model. Interested readers may obtain a full copy of the simulation model by writing to the authors.

The Topography

The model represents a single stylized episode of the sort under consideration. At the start of the episode, there is a single component technology, which we shall call 'transistor' technology, which has the promise of enabling useful computers. Later, a new component technology, which we shall call 'microprocessors', comes into existence. The potential purchasers of computers value two attributes. One is the 'performance' of the computer. The other is its price, which we represent inversely as the desirable attribute 'cheapness'. The desirability of any computer design can be summarized in terms of how it rates in those two dimensions of Lancaster attribute space. By a 'useful' computer we mean one that meets threshold requirements of potential purchasers. More on this shortly.

Each of the component technologies is associated with outer limits on what computers incorporating them can achieve in the two relevant dimensions. For analytic convenience, we have treated those technological constraints as defining a rectangular box. Thus in Figure 17.1 the two boxes depict the set of technological characteristics that potentially can be achieved in computers designed around transistor (TR), and microprocessor (MP), component technologies. Note that the use of microprocessors permits computers to be designed that are better than transistor-based computers regarding both performance and cheapness. However, the most dramatic improvement that is permitted by the incorporation of microprocessors lies in the cheapness direction.

Those outer limits of what is feasible under the two technologies are 'potentials'. The potential is not achievable, however, without significant investment of resources in research and development, and requires learning from experience. The first efforts of a new firm trying

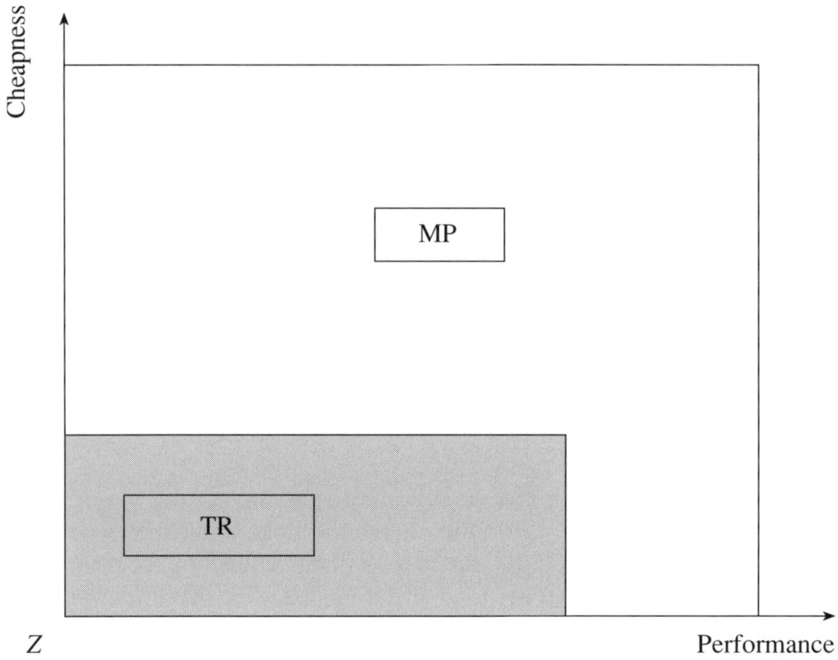

Figure 17.1 Technological potentials

to design a computer using transistors, or (later) microprocessors, will only be able to achieve a design characterized by point *Z* (for zero experience). We shall specify the dynamics of design improvement built into the model in the next subsection, 'Innovation Dynamics'.

On the demand side, there are two separate groups of potential customers. One group, which we shall call 'large firms' greatly values 'performance' and wants to buy 'mainframes'. The second group, which we shall call 'individuals' or 'small users', has less need for high performance but values 'cheapness'. They provide a potential market for 'personal computers', or PCs.

Each of our two user groups requires a minimum level of performance, and cheapness, before they can be enticed to buy any computers at all. Once threshold requirements are satisfied, the merit that customers perceive in a computer design is an increasing function of its performance and its cheapness. In Figure 17.2 we depict the preferences of 'big firms' and 'small users', respectively. The difference in the demands of the two user groups, is reflected both in the difference in threshold requirements and in the indifference curves.

If we overlay Figure 17.2 onto Figure 17.1, we can note that even if computers achieve the outer limits permitted by transistor technology, the threshold requirements of small users will not be met. Thus the design of computers that can successfully enter the PC market depends on the availability of microprocessors.

The 'indifference curves' of Figure 17.2 depict designs of equal value or 'merit' in the eyes of the two customer groups. We assume that higher computer merit translates into more

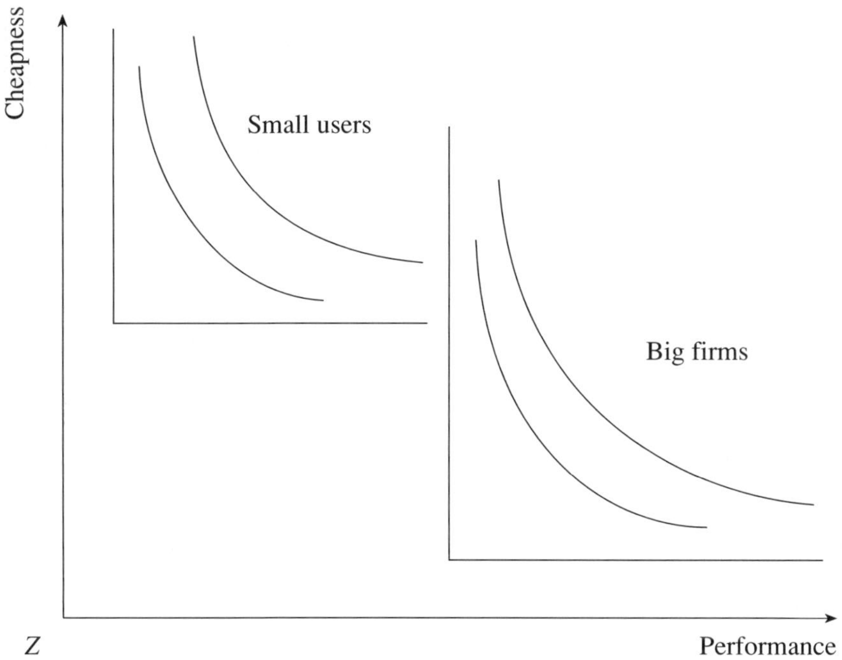

Figure 17.2 Customer preferences

computers bought by customers. We shall develop the details in the third subsection, 'Market Dynamics'.

The above discussion indicates clearly some of the broad outlines of what we would expect to see in a simulated industry history, and also points to some of the matters that need to be treated in specification of the dynamics. Assuming that there is some way that firms can obtain funds, computer technology will start out at *Z*. Over time, and with R&D spending, computer designs will improve until ultimately they crack through the threshold requirements of the 'mainframe market'. Then firms that have achieved threshold-meeting designs will begin to make sales. As computers improve, sales will grow. The introduction of microprocessors will open the potential of meeting mainframe demands even better, and of designing machines that will sell on the PC market. Firms that try to pursue those possibilities will need some funding in order to do that because, initially at least, no one will buy their wares. However, ultimately one would expect that microprocessor computers would take over the mainframe market, and be able to tap the new PC market.

We now turn to explicit dynamics.

Innovation Dynamics

When transistors, and later microprocessors, come into existence, firms have to learn how to design effective computers using these new components. Firms gradually develop competence in using the new technology as a result of the R&D investments they make, and the experience

BOX 17.1 FIRMS' COMPETENCIES AND INNOVATION DYNAMICS

In the model, firms are represented by sets of technological and marketing competencies that are accumulated over time, and by rules of action. The focal competencies in the model are design capabilities: by building incrementally on their past achievements and by accumulating experience, engineers produce successive generations of computers with superior cost/performance attributes. Other actions reflected in the model of the firm concern the pricing of products, R&D and advertising expenditures, the adoption of new technologies and diversification into new markets. There is no explicit representation of production *per se*, or of investments in capacity. It is assumed that the requisite production capabilities can be hired at a price per computer that reflects the 'cheapness' attribute of the design.

Design outcomes are influenced by firm-specific strategies represented by choices of search direction in the capabilities space, but also by latent technological opportunities. Firms are born with different, randomly selected trajectories of technological improvement along the two technological dimensions, costs and performance. In order to capture – in an extreme form – the notion that competencies cannot be changed rapidly and costlessly, in the model it is assumed that this trajectory is firm specific and time invariant.

As firms spend on R&D, they accumulate technical competencies. Technical progress is represented in the model as a change in a computer design along the two technical dimensions, generated by the application of these firm-specific competencies. Technical competencies are represented as a stock that grows over time as a result of R&D expenditures. One can think of competencies as reflecting the shared experience of two types of 'engineers': cost-oriented and performance-oriented engineers. Their mix is defined by the technological trajectory that characterizes each firm. As time goes by, firms hire new engineers, maintaining constant the proportion between the two types and hence the trajectory of advance.

In each period t, R&D expenditures, R_t, are used to pay the stock of engineers of the last period, R_{t-1}. For each of the two design dimensions, if the share of total R&D allocated to one particular type of engineers $R_t^i > R_{t-1}^i$, then the surplus is invested in hiring new engineers, at a given cost c_{eng} per engineer. Conversely, if $R_t^i < R_{t-1}^i$, then 10 percent of the engineers are fired. If $R_t^i < 0.9\, R_{t-1}^i$, the budget B (see Box 17.2) is used to pay for the difference.

Advertising expenditures are considered in a very similar way to R&D expenditures, in that they produce marketing competencies that are accumulated over time. If firms do not invest, their advertising capabilities deteriorate over time – and hence the size of the advertising expenditures effect decreases, for any given amount of expenditure. Moreover, the impact of advertising expenditures is not constant, but follows a logistic curve (see Box 17.3).

they accumulate. Our model of firm learning is meant to capture significant elements of the 'dynamic competence' theory of the firm that has been developed by Winter (1987), Dosi and Marengo (1994), and Teece et. al (1994, 1997). Our model also incorporates the fact that in this industry, and in a number of others, a considerable period may go by after a firm starts trying to operate in a new technology before it is able to sell any product, if it ever achieves that. At the start it must have external financing.

Thus at the beginning of our episode, with the introduction of transistors, we assume that there are a number of firms, endowed by 'venture capitalists' with an initial budget to spend on R&D, who hope to exploit the new technological opportunities. All firms start with the same initial design capabilities, depicted by *Z* in Figure 17.1, and perhaps interpretable as the design characteristics that have been achieved by experimental computers that are in the public domain. Firms start off with randomly assigned initial budgets, which they spend in equal amounts over a prespecified number of periods. Reflecting their bets regarding what is technologically easy and difficult, and what the market will buy, firms assign different fractions of their 'annual' R&D budget to efforts to improve performance, and to reduce the production costs of a computer. Thus, after the initial period, the firms in the industry will be doing different things, and will be achieving computer designs of different characteristics.

From period to period, the quality of the design that a company is able to achieve in each relevant dimension – performance and cheapness – improves according to the following equation:[1]

$$\text{change } X_i = a_0(R_i)^{a1}(T_j)^{a2}(L_i - X_i)^{a3}e \qquad (17.1)$$

The first variable, *R*, is the firm's R&D expenditure aimed at achieving design improvements of a particular sort, where $i = 1$ denotes performance and $i = 2$ denotes cheapness. That expenditure allows the firm to maintain a given stock of engineers dedicated to advancing computer design in each of the two relevant dimensions. That expenditure, in turn, is a constant fraction of its period-by-period R&D expenditures in total. The fraction reflects the firm's 'bet' as to the most useful attribute-mix direction to proceed. As we noted, a firm's total R&D expenditure per period is a constant fraction of the total funds lent to it by its venture capital financiers. After that initial loan is drawn down, a firm either has achieved a commercially viable design, or it is out of business.

The second variable, *T*, is the number of periods that the firm has been working with a particular technology, in this case transistors. For all firms that start with a technology at the same time, this second variable will be the same. However, when later in this exposition we begin to describe the evolution of computers employing microprocessor technology, firms will differ regarding the times when they get into that technology, and thus there will be differences across firms in this experience variable.

The third variable in the equation, L_i–X_i, is the distance of the achieved design from the frontier. As what is achieved comes closer and closer to the limits of what is achievable, a given R&D expenditure will achieve less and less further progress. There is also a random element to what a firm achieves, *e*.

As indicated, if a firm runs through its initial loan before it achieves a marketable product, it simply fails. However, if a firm manages to push its design into the region where customers are buying, it is a new ball game. Now funds from revenues can be invested in R&D.

BOX 17.2 FIRMS' FINANCE, R&D AND PRICING DECISIONS

In this model, firms' finances play a major role. Without a sufficient endowment of R&D funds, firms inevitably fail without ever breaking into either segment of the computer market. Firms that do break into the market may fail nevertheless, because their profits do not sustain the levels of R&D effort required to stay competitive. An investor willing to throw in arbitrarily large amounts of money in support of the R&D of some firm could in principle count on 'winning' in market share terms, but not necessarily in terms of getting his or her money back.

Firms are born with different, randomly selected initial budgets, IB, which are used to finance an R&D project, the length of which is fixed and equal for all firms. During this initial time, in each period firms spend a constant fraction of their budget on R&D. If the funds are exhausted before a marketable design is achieved, firms exit. Otherwise, firms start to spend a constant fraction (15 percent for all firms in this version of the model) of their profits in each period to pay back their debt D_t to investors – that is to say, the initial budget capitalized at the current interest rate, r, until the debt has been fully paid back. What is left is used to invest in R&D and in advertising.

Profits are calculated in each period t as:

$$\pi_t = Mp - Mk,$$

where M is the number of computers sold, p is the computer price and k is production cost of a single computer.

Production costs, k, are determined by the technical progress function. Price is obtained by adding a constant markup, to costs:

$$p = k(1 + \mu).$$

R&D expenditures, R_t, are simply determined as a constant fraction, , of what is left of gross profits, $_t$, after the repayment of the initial budget:

$$R_t = {}_t(1 - \sigma).$$

The parameter ϕ is time invariant and firm specific, although in the simulations of this chapter its value has been set equal for all firms.

Advertising expenditures, A, are calculated in a similar way, but it is assumed that the effect of advertising on sales follows a logistic curve. Specifically, the model first computes advertising expenditures, A^*:

$$A^*_t = \delta\pi_t(1 - \sigma).$$

Then, this value is divided by a number that defines the amount of advertising expenditures beyond which the elasticity of sales to advertising is equal to zero (that is, the asymptote of the logistic curve). This ratio is then inserted into a logistic curve to yield the value of the variable A in the demand equation (equation 17.3).

The excess gross profits after debt repayment, R&D expenditures and advertising is invested in an account, B_t, which yields the interest rate, r, in each period.

Within this model, all firms determine price by setting a constant 'markup' (the same for all firms) over production costs. In turn, the gross margin over production costs is used to cover several things.

This money is used, first of all, to repay its outstanding debt to venture capitalists. Fifteen percent of gross profit is used for repayment, and repayment continues until the debt is eliminated (or the firm fails). At any time the debt owed to venture capitalists is the initial sum, capitalized at a prevailing rate, minus anything it has already paid back. Second, a firm spends a constant fraction of whatever is left from its gross profits, after debt repayment, on R&D, and on advertising. (We shall consider the effects of advertising in the next subsection.) If the firm achieves a marketable product before the end of the time period over which it originally had planned to draw funds from its initial loan, the customary constant amount out of these funds add to the total the firm spends on these activities.

If there is still something left from the gross margin after debt repayment, and expenditure on R&D and advertising, these residual earnings go into a firm's 'account' and are treated in this model as 'reserves'. These reserves will enter the model in an important way for transistor firms that have survived into the era when microprocessors have become available as an alternative component technology. We shall consider what happens next in the fourth and fifth subsections, concerned with transition dynamics.

Market Dynamics

In our earlier discussion, we assumed that the greater the 'merit' M of a machine, the greater the number of machines that will be purchased. We now propose to let M correspond to the number of machines that customers in a submarket (we shall define this concept shortly) will buy, if it is the only machine that meets market threshold requirements. We assume that M is a log-linear function of the extent to which the attributes of that computer exceed threshold requirements in that market:

$$M = b_0(X_1 - X_1\text{min})^{b1}(X_2 - X_2\text{min})^{b2}. \qquad (17.2)$$

If threshold requirements are not met, M = 0.

If there is more than one kind of computer that meets threshold requirements, our analysis of demand involves variables other than M. The appreciative theory put forth by many scholars of the history of the industry to account for the sustained dominance of IBM in the mainframe market includes concepts like bandwagon effects or brand loyalty (or lock-in), and advertising. History-friendly modeling needs to bring these in.

We thus divide each of our broad markets into a large number of submarkets, which the reader may associate with individual customers or homogeneous groups of them. (See Box 17.3) The probability, P_i, that any individual computer buyer or group of them will purchase a particular computer, i, is as follows.

$$P_i = c_0(M_i)^{c1}(m_i + d_1)^{c2}(A_i + d_2)^{c3}. \qquad (17.3)$$

Here, c_0 is specified so that the sum of the probabilities adds to one. As noted, M denotes the 'merit' of a computer; m is the market share, the fraction of total sales revenues accounted for by that computer (note that the market share variable can be interpreted either in terms of a

BOX 17.3 DEMAND

The demand for computers is expressed as a demand for specific product characteristics. Let p be the price charged for a specific computer, then denote 'cheapness' by $X_1 = 1/p = 1/k\,(1 + \mu)$,and 'performance' by X_2. As discussed in the main text of the chapter, computers are demanded by two different user groups, identified as 'big firms' and 'individuals'. The market activity of each type is represented by independent purchasing decisions by a large number of 'submarkets' of that type. Submarket buying behavior reflects the fact that computers are durable goods that deliver services over a period of time, and the demand facing producers is a demand for replacements or increments to the stock of such durables.

The number of submarkets in each main market (mainframes and PCs) is a parameter of the model. Individual submarkets buy computers if they do not have one – either because they have never bought one before or because of breakdowns. Computers have a finite life and surely break down after τ periods. The model keeps track of the average age, G, of the computers held by each submarket. In each period, a fraction G/τ of the submarkets experiences computer breakdowns and becomes ready to buy new computers. Moreover, submarkets buy computers if they 'see' the supply: when there are only a few firms in the market, individual submarkets may not purchase any computers. The probability of buying a computer is equal to one if there are at least S firms selling in the marketplace. When there are only $n < S$ firms, the probability decreases proportionally.

A simple formulation of consumer preferences is the one used in the main text (equation 17.2)).

Consider now some number of customer groups, say two. Let the (integer) number of computers of a particular character that potentially would be purchased by a specific group of customers (if no other competing product were offered in the market) correspond to the level of utility, M. This way, the utility function has a cardinal interpretation and is treated heuristically as a demand curve.

The sum of the exponents in the utility function operates like a sort of generalized demand elasticity reflecting performance as well as price.

Customers select different computer designs as a function of their relative utility, M_i, as it results from the specific mix of price and performance characteristics (see equation (17.3) in the main text). However, various informational constraints, like bandwagon and brand-loyalty effects, affect customers' behavior. These are captured in a compact formulation by the effect of the variables measuring the firms' market shares and advertising.

In the absence of the bandwagon/brand-loyalty effect and of advertising, the demand module would behave similarly to a standard demand curve. Demand would converge to 'best value for the money', although in the limit a positive probability of survival for inferior computers always remains. Convergence is faster the higher is the parameter c_1.

bandwagon effect, or a – probabilistic – lock-in of customers who previously had bought machines of a particular brand); d_1 ensures that computers that have just broken into the market, and have no prior sales, can attract some sales; A is the advertising expenditures of the firm producing the computer; d_2 performs here a similar role to d_1 for firms that have just broken into the market and have not yet invested in advertising.

Given that customers in a particular submarket buy a particular computer, M is the number they buy.

Note the following. First, if there is only one computer that meets threshold requirements, each submarket will buy it with probability 1, and will buy M units of it, as we asserted (assumed) earlier. Second, assume that there is more than one computer that passes the threshold. If c_1 is very high, and c_2 and c_3 are very low, virtually all the customers will buy the computer with the highest merit score. On the other hand, if c_1 is relatively low, or c_2 and c_3 are high, a higher merit computer may be 'out sold' by a rival computer that has the higher existing market share, or which has been advertised more intensively, or both.

Competition Between the Technologies with 'Locked-in' Firms

Within this model, after a number of periods have gone by, and after a number of transistor firms have successfully entered the mainframe market, microprocessors come into existence. A number of new firms start out at point 'Z' in Figure 17.1, with funding provided by venture capitalists, just as earlier new firms had started out at that point using transistor technology. Some of these firms will fail before they get into a market. Others may succeed.

Note that while existing transistor firms provide no 'barrier to entry' for microprocessor firms who have aimed their trajectory toward the PC market, the existence of established transistor firms in the mainframe market creates a significant barrier to entry. First of all, if a microprocessor firm achieves a design that meets threshold requirements in the mainframe market, that computer is in competition with existing transistor-based computers that have already achieved higher than threshold quality levels. Second, the extant transistor mainframe producers have acquired positive market share, and have engaged in significant advertising, and that further disadvantages a newcomer. It is an open question within this model whether a new microprocessor firm can survive in the mainframe market. If not, and if extant transistor firms cannot or do not switch over to making mainframes out of microprocessors, the potential in the mainframe market afforded by microprocessor technology will never be realized.

In fact, we know that microprocessor firms did enter the mainframe market, but did not fare well there, in part because extant mainframe firms themselves adopted microprocessor technologies. Further, some of those old mainframe firms, IBM in particular, then used microprocessor technology to try to enter the PC market. Thus there are two different kinds of transitional dynamics that need to be built into this model, if it is to be 'history friendly'. First, we must enable firms that originally are using one technology to switch over to another. Second, we must enable firms that are in one market to try to diversify into the other.

Transition Dynamics

We noted above our desire to capture in our model a number of aspects of the new understandings about dynamic firm competencies, and competence 'lock-ins'. We have built into

BOX 17.4 ADOPTION OF NEW COMPONENT TECHNOLOGIES AND DIVERSIFICATION INTO NEW MARKETS

Adoption

A key question addressed by the model concerns the conditions at which transistor-based firms can adopt the new integrated circuit technology.

Adoption of the new technology takes place in two steps. First, a firm must 'perceive' microprocessor technology. Perception is a stochastic process that depends on the current technological position of the potential adopter in relation to the technological frontier in transistors and on the progress realized by the new technology:

$$Pr_{perc} = (z_i^{\lambda} + z_{mp}(^{\lambda}/2))$$

where P_{perc} is the probability of perceiving microprocessor technology, z_i is the fraction of the transistors' technological frontier covered by firm i and z_{mp} is the fraction of the microprocessors' frontier covered by the best-practice microprocessors' firm. The parameter measures the general difficulty of perceiving the new technology.

Once firms have perceived the possibility of adoption, they have to invest in order to acquire the new technology. Adoption costs (C_{ad}) entail a fixed cost, F_{ad}, equal for all firms, and the payment of a fraction q of firms' accumulated budget, linked to factors like the training of engineers and the like. Thus,

$$C_{ad} = F_{ad} + q\, B_t.$$

Firms whose budget does not cover the fixed costs or whose profit rate is negative cannot adopt microprocessors. Moreover, the competence-destroying nature of the new technology is captured by the notion that adoption implies that the experience accumulated on the old technology counts now much less. In the model, experience (T) is reduced by a factor which is a parameter of the model.

Once firms have adopted the new technology, they have access to the new technological frontier and can innovate faster. However, they maintain their original trajectory.

Diversification

As the market for PCs becomes large, mainframe companies may contemplate the opportunity to enter a rich and promising market. Diversification can take place only after the adoption of microprocessors. The incentive for diversification is a function of the size of the PC market, defined in terms of the number of computers sold, as compared to the mainframe market. Specifically, diversification becomes possible when the ratio between the size of the PC market and the size of the mainframe market is bigger than a threshold value, which is a parameter of the model.

The procedures governing diversification in the model mimic the actual strategy used by IBM for entering the PC market. In the model, the parent company founds a new division trying to exploit the available competencies specific to PCs, rather than to apply its own competencies to the new market.

The new division inherits from the parent company a fraction of the budget, of technical capabilities and advertising capabilities. The size of these fractions are all parameters of the model. The position of the new division in the design space is determined as the average merit of design prevailing in the PC market at the time diversification occurs. In other words, the parent company exploits 'public knowledge' in the PC market and partly 'imitates' PC firms. The technical progress trajectory (that is, the mix of engineers of the two types) is randomly recalculated. After birth, the new division behaves exactly as a new entrant, with independent products and profits and budget.

the model that firm competencies are 'cumulative': today's design efforts build on what was achieved yesterday. Firms tend to get better and better at the particular things they are doing. On the other hand, it is clear that firms often have a good deal of difficulty when they try to do significantly new things. Thus Tushman and Anderson (1986), and Henderson and Clark (1990), have documented the difficulty that firms often have in coping when the best technologies underlying their products change significantly. Quite often, extant firms cannot switch over rapidly enough to counter the efforts of new firms using the new technology. Christensen and Rosenbloom (1994) have put a spotlight on similar difficulties that extant firms have had in recognizing new markets when they opened up.

In our model, existing transistor-based mainframe firms are able to switch over to microprocessor technology for use in their mainframe designs, but this may be time consuming and costly for them. It is new firms that do the initial work of advancing computer design using microprocessors. The probability that an extant transistor firm will try to switch over is a function of two variables. The first is how far along microprocessor computer designs have been pushed. The second is the closeness of a transistor firm to the technological possibility frontier defined by transistor technology. The former clearly is a signal to extant firms that 'there is a potentially powerful new technology out there, and we may be in trouble if we do not adopt it'. The latter is an indication that 'we cannot get much further if we keep on pushing along the same road' (see Box 17.4).

If an old transistor firm decides to switch over, it faces one significant disadvantage, but also has an advantage. The disadvantage is that the experience that got it to the forefront of transistor technology (recall equation 17.1) counts for little or nothing if it shifts over to microprocessor technology. Thus in its first efforts in microprocessor computer design, it will achieve only about the average for extant microprocessor-based mainframe firms. Further, it must incur a once and for all switchover cost in order to start designing, producing, and marketing microprocessor-based mainframes. However, extant transistor firms have the advantage of large R&D budgets which, with a cost, they can switch over to working with the new technology, and a stock of accumulated earnings on which they can draw to cover any transition costs.

Once an old transistor mainframe firm has switched over to microprocessor technology, it is potentially open to it to diversify by designing and trying to sell computers on the PC market. Its old design trajectory will, in general, not be a good one to pursue if it wants to diversify into PCs. As noted, IBM diversified by setting up an entirely new division, and that is what we assume about diversification of mainframe producers into the PC market in this model.

The new division initially takes a place roughly at the average of the firms already selling in or aiming for the PC market. The new divisional firm also faces the disadvantage that already there are firms selling in the PC market, with designs that already exceed thresholds, positive market shares, established advertising budgets and experience in the PC market. However, the new divisional firm does have the advantage of being able to dip into the 'deep pockets' and resources of its mother firm, which can transfer a sizeable fraction of its extant R&D and advertising budgets to the new division. After the initial infusion of resources the new PC branch firm is on its own.

4 HISTORY-REPLICATING AND HISTORY-DIVERGENT SIMULATIONS

History-replicating Simulations

Start the model going, and it will generate a simulated history of computer technology, and the computer industry. Under a wide range of parameter settings, at least some of the transistor firms that began their operation at the start of the simulated episode will achieve computer designs that will sell on the mainframe market. In general, several will, and they will compete with each other for sales on that market. At least a few of the microprocessor firms, which start out later, will get into the PC market, and some will get into the mainframe market. Faced with their competition, some of the existing transistor-based firms producing mainframes will switch over to microprocessor technology. Some will then go on to enter the PC market.

Some, but not all, of the parameter settings will lead to patterns of industry evolution that, in effect, 'replicate' the industry history being modeled. A dominant transistor-based firm (IBM) will emerge relatively quickly in the mainframe market. That firm will hold on to its large share of the market, even when new microprocessor firms enter that market and challenge it. Part of the reason the dominant firm holds on is that it shifts over to microprocessor technology in a relatively timely manner. That firm then diversifies into the PC market, and gains a non-trivial, but not a dominant share.

Economists who have studied the history of the computer industry have tended to identify the following as key factors behind the pattern that happened. First, the early buyers of IBM equipment tended to feel themselves 'locked in' to IBM for upgrades, extensions, and renewal of their computer capacity, largely because of specialized software. This made entry of new firms difficult. In our model, a firm that has a high market share in mainframes will, because of that, attract a significant share of new purchases. Second, by the time the new technology came along, computer design under the old technology was reasonably advanced, and the leader, IBM, responded rapidly to the availability of new technology. In terms of our model, soon after the first microprocessor firms enter the mainframe market, the dominant transistor firm in that market is induced to switch over to microprocessors. Third, IBM's massive resources enabled it quickly to mount an R&D and advertising effort sufficient for it to diversify and catch up with the earlier entrants into the PC market. However, because the PCs produced by a number of other companies were compatible with the software used by IBM PCs, there was no specific lock-in to IBM. And within the class of IBM compatibles, customers were quite sensitive to the merit of the computers being offered, particularly to price.. In terms of our model, in the PC market the coefficient on quality was high, and the coefficient on specific market share was low.

History-divergent Simulations

Our program of 'history-friendly' modeling obviously involves trying to get some runs that 'replicate', in a stylized manner, the actual industry history. However, once a set of 'history-replicating' parameters is identified, our program involves, as well, changing the parameters that correspond to the key causal factors that analysts have put forth to explain the observed patterns to see if, when these are changed, quite different patterns emerge. The appreciative theory of the historical case, which we have attempted to capture in the model, leads us to try the following experiments, after a 'history-replicating' base case has been achieved.

First, reduce the coefficient on market share in the demand equations for mainframes, to see if this will damp down the tendency of a dominant firm to emerge, and hold on in the face of new stringent competition. Second, have firms using microprocessor technology enter the mainframe market earlier, before a dominant firm has emerged. And make transistor firms more sluggish in shifting over to microprocessors, and make it more costly for them to do so. Third, make demand in the PC market more sensitive to advertising, and less sensitive to computer quality, so that a deep-pockets company diversifying into PCs from mainframes has a chance of quickly capturing a large share of the PC market.

5 THE SIMULATION RUNS

The Basic Case: History Replication

Simulation models are inherently complex. Simulation techniques are used because the model we want to develop is not simple enough to be well posed in a form that admits analytic solution. However, we have tried to keep ours understandable. As a result, we were able to find a set of parameter values that 'replicated' the historical experience. We provide below a set of figures that summarize the behavior of our simulation model with parameters set in a 'history-friendly' way.

First, we provide some pictures of a typical run at various stages in the history of the industry – early in the history when a few 'transistor' firms are just breaking into the mainframe market; somewhat later when one or several transistor firms were well established in that market but several new 'microprocessor' firms were breaking into it, and several microprocessor firms were entering the PC market; and still later when several of the old transistor firms had shifted over to microprocessor technology, and a couple had diversified into the PC market. Figures 17.3–5 depict these stages, respectively. The lines in the figures depict the path of the firms from their start. An x at the end of a line signifies that the firm has failed. Breaks in a line indicate a change in the technology used by firm. We roughly identify a 'period' of the simulation model with a calendar quarter in real time. These figures depict single runs.[2]

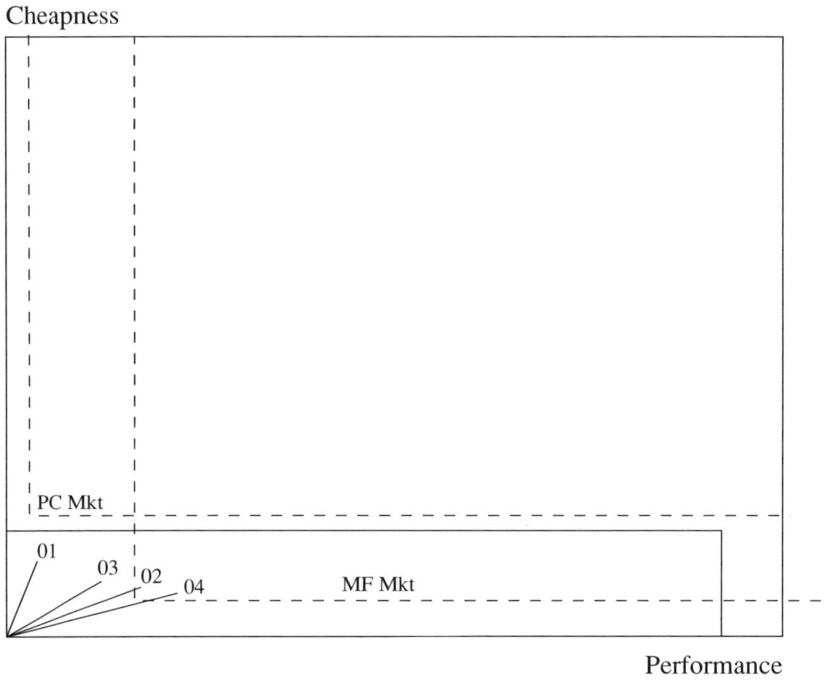

Figure 17.3 Simulation: time = 30

We did 50 runs for each parameter setting. Figures 17.6–9 show our history-replicating results under our 'standard set' of parameter values. Figure 17.6 traces the time path of the Herfindahl index of concentration in the mainframe market averaged over those 50 runs. Given the various random elements in our model, while there was considerable variation from run to run, most runs told a similar story. Transistor firms began to get into the mainframe market around period 30, and a dominant firm quickly emerged. The dip in the concentration ratio beginning around period 60 and its rise again several periods later also was quite common in the runs. This pattern reflects the surge of entry into the mainframe market of new 'microprocessor' firms at the beginning of the dip, and the relatively quick switchover to microprocessors and recovery of market share of the dominant mainframe firm.

Figure 17.6 also depicts the time path of the Herfindahl index in the PC market. As we can see, concentration in that market is much lower than concentration in the mainframe market. Partly that is due to the fact that there are more 'startup' microprocessor firms, many of which enter the PC market, than earlier there were transistor startup firms that entered the mainframe market. But that clearly is only part of the story.

The new microprocessor firms could and did enter the mainframe market as well as the PC market. However, in the mainframe market this did not result in sustained effective competi-

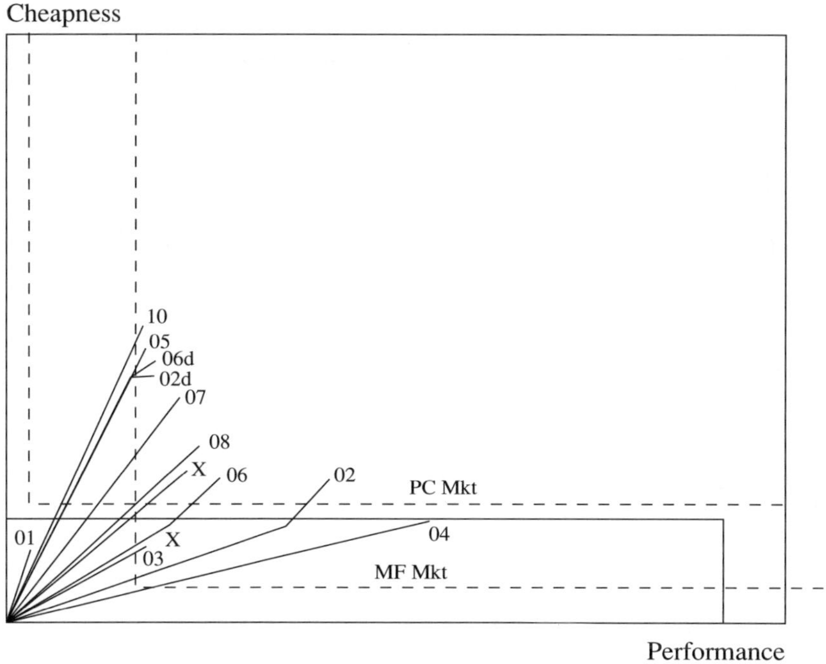

Figure 17.4 Simulation: time = 70

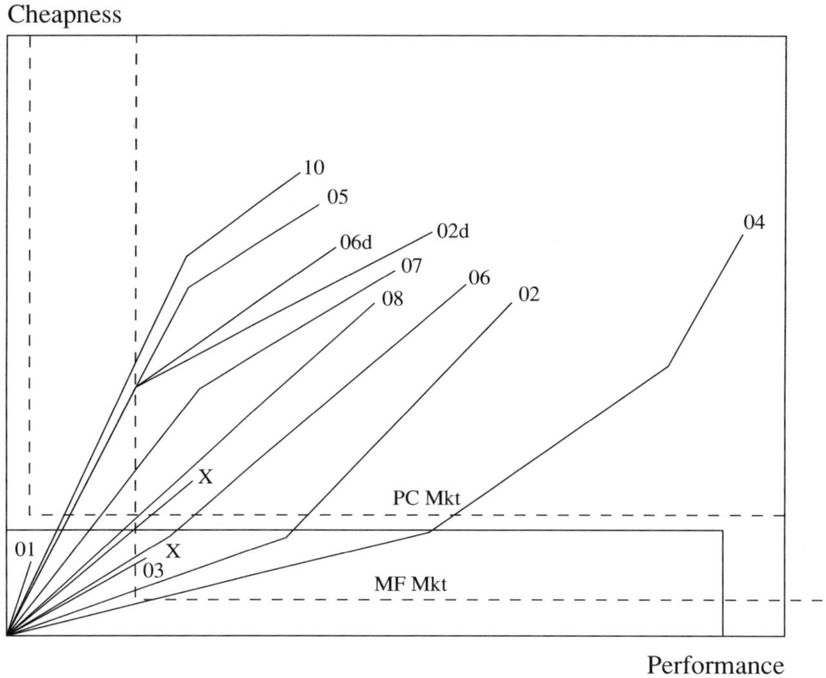

Figure 17.5 Simulation: time = 130

Figure 17.6 Herfindahl index in PC and mainframe markets (standard set)

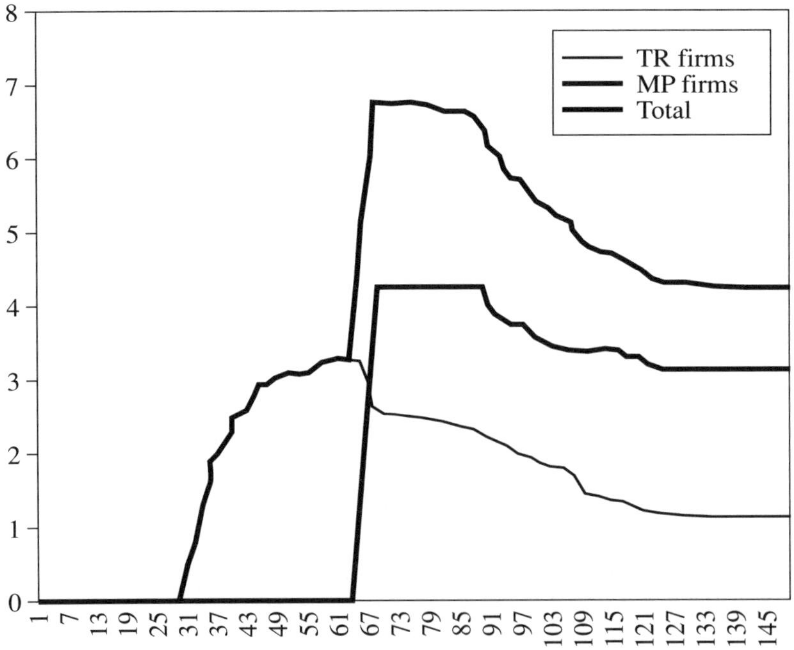

Figure 17.7 Number of firms in mainframe market (standard set)

tion. This fact is depicted in Figure 17.7, which shows the time path of the number of different kinds of firms in the mainframe market. As can be seen, while several new microprocessor firms enter around period 60, on average only three remain in the market for any length of time. As Figure 17.8 (which depicts the number of different kinds of firms in the PC market) shows, significantly more firms that start out with microprocessor technology survive in the PC market, at least until around period 80 when 'IBM' establishes a PC branch.

As shown in Figure 17.8, around period 80 the 'startup' microprocessor firms in the PC market are joined by a branch of the dominant mainframe company, which earlier had switched over to microprocessor technology, and then subsequently entered the PC market. In general, this 'offshoot of IBM' was quite successful in the PC market, but never achieved the dominance there that the firm held in the mainframe market. All this is depicted in Figure 17.9.

The demand equation in runs that generated this 'history-replicating' pattern had a relatively high coefficient on 'market share' in the mainframe market, and a lower one in the PC market. Thus the first firm that achieved a considerable share in the mainframe market was more advantaged than the first firm to achieve considerable market share in the PC market. Microprocessor technology came into existence only after a large firm had emerged in the mainframe market, and it was not too difficult for that firm to switch over to microprocessors once it was challenged. And its ability to marshall R&D resources and advertising to enter the PC market enabled it relatively quickly to overcome its initial technological lag, but the effectiveness of these investments was not so great as to enable it to come to dominate that market.

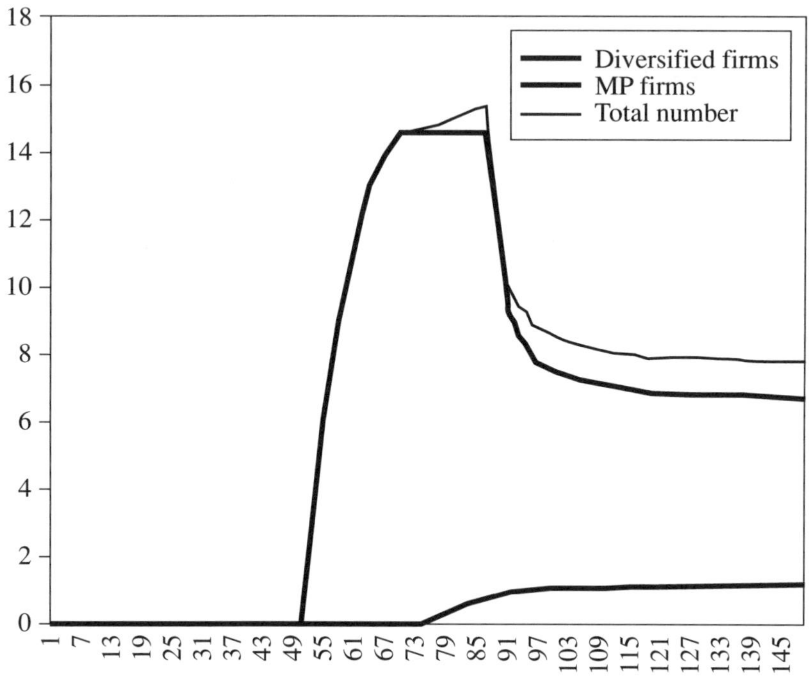

Figure 17.8 Number of firms in PC market (standard set)

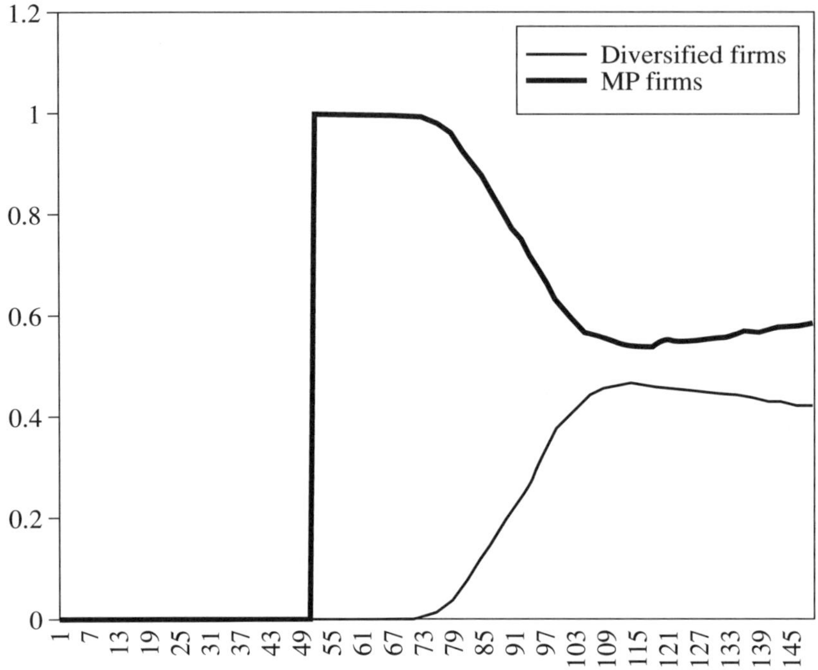

Figure 17.9 Market share in PC market (standard set)

Variations: History-divergent Runs

We stressed above that testing the logic of an appreciative theory called for two things. One was demonstration that a stylized formal model incorporating that theory could generate the observed historical patterns. The other was that incorporation in that model of parameter settings that are counter to those argued as strongly causal in the appreciative theory should yield 'history-divergent' results. Here we describe the workings of the model where we tried first to avoid the rise of a dominant firm in the mainframe market and second to get 'IBM' to come to dominate the PC market.

As we noted earlier, the sustained dominance of IBM in the PC market has been ascribed to two different kinds of factors. One is the importance of 'repeat buying' and lock-in. The other is that IBM achieved dominance in the market before potential 'competence-destroying' new technology emerged, and further, IBM actually was able to adopt that technology relatively quickly. Figure 17.10 shows the time paths of the Herfindahl index in the mainframe market when the exponent on market share in the demand equation is significantly lower (respectively, 0, 0.25 and 0.5) than its setting in our base model case. All other parameter settings are the same as in the base model. Note how the concentration in the market, which largely reflects the share of the leading firm, declines with the reduction in the extent of customer lock-in.

Figure 17.11 depicts the Herfindahl index in the mainframe market for runs in which microprocessor startup firms emerged before IBM was able to come to dominate the mainframe market, and in which transistor firms had great difficulty in switching over to microprocessor

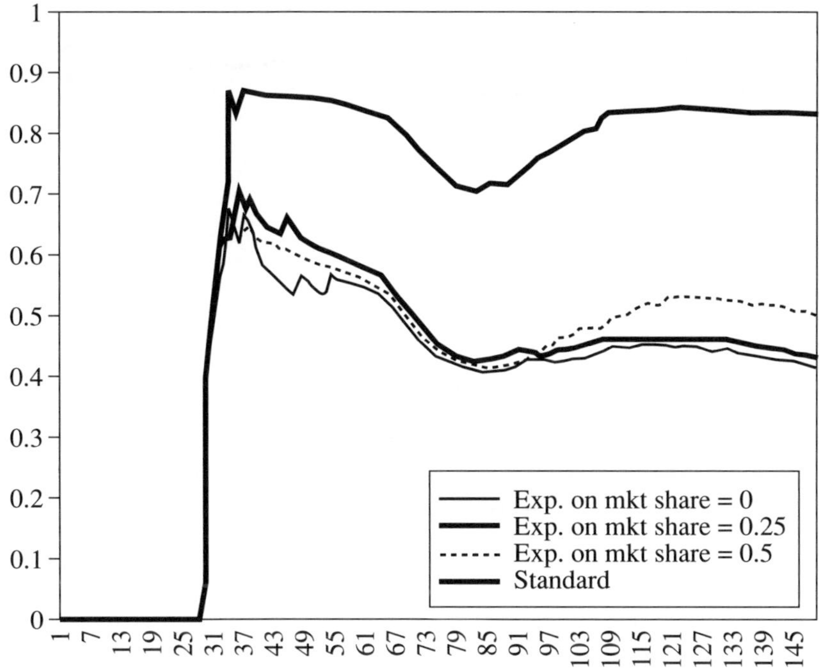

Figure 17.10 Herfindahl index in mainframe market (diminished importance of demand lock-in)

technology, under two different parameter settings regarding the importance of market share in demand – the first as in the base case, the other with zero exponent on the market share in the demand equation. Note that in both cases, the Herfindahl index significantly decreases.

The initial budget plays a major role for the survival of entrants. In the case of a smaller initial budget for microprocessor firms, simulation results (not reported here) show that a smaller number of entrants enter the PC market and no one enters the mainframe market. In addition, the adoption and diversification processes by mainframe firms start later. The effect of entry on adoption and diversification by established firms is even more evident in the case of no microprocessor–PC startup. Simulation results (not reported here) show that without new entrants, established mainframe firms do not adopt microprocessor technology nor do they open up the new PC market (which as a consequence does not take off).

Figure 17.12 depicts the share held by transistor firms and microprocessor firms in the mainframe market under the standard setting and the case in which the exponent on the market share in the demand equation is equal to zero. In this case the share of 'IBM' diminishes and the share of microprocessor firms increases in the mainframe market.

We turn now to attempts at history-divergent modeling of events in the PC market. In particular, we explore what might have happened if IBM's ability to shift large amounts of resources into R&D and advertising in that market had been even more effective than it was in our base case. That is, we try a set of runs in which the coefficient on R in equation (17.1) is higher and the coefficient on T was lower than in the base case, and in which the coeffi-

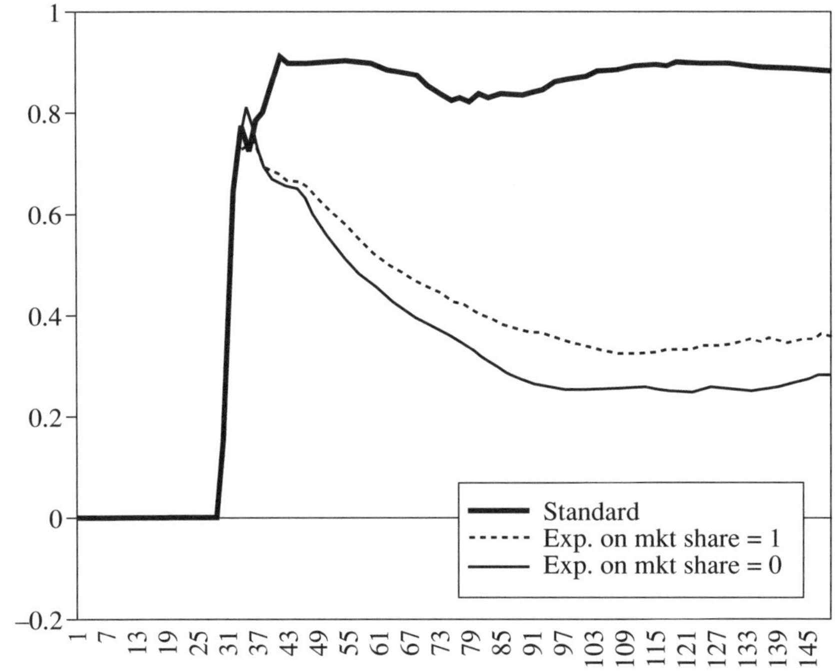

Figure 17.11 Herfindahl index in mainframe market (early entry of MP firms and high difficulty in adoption)

cient on *A* in equation (17.3) is significantly higher than in the base case (set 01). Then we try another set of runs in which (in addition to the changes in parameters stated above) diversification for IBM is easier in terms of cost and of ability to bring a large advertising budget from the mainframe to the PC market (set 02). As Figure 17.13 shows, the first change alone makes little difference for the structure of the PC market. However, when IBM is able to diversify easily or more forcefully, it comes to dominate that market as well as the market for mainframes.

6 THE CONTRIBUTIONS OF HISTORY-FRIENDLY MODELING

In this chapter we have taken a body of appreciative theorizing about a historical episode, developed a formal representation of that theory, and found that the formal version of that theory is consistent and capable of generating the stylized facts the appreciative theory purports to explain. Going through this analytic exercise has significantly sharpened our theoretical understanding of the key factors behind salient aspects of the evolution of the computer industry.

We expect two types of reaction to this chapter. One is that the 'theory' presented here lacks elegance and generality, and scarcely deserves the term 'theory' at all: useful theory in economics needs to be at a much higher level of abstraction. To this complaint we would reply that most of what economists know about the economic world comes in the form of relatively

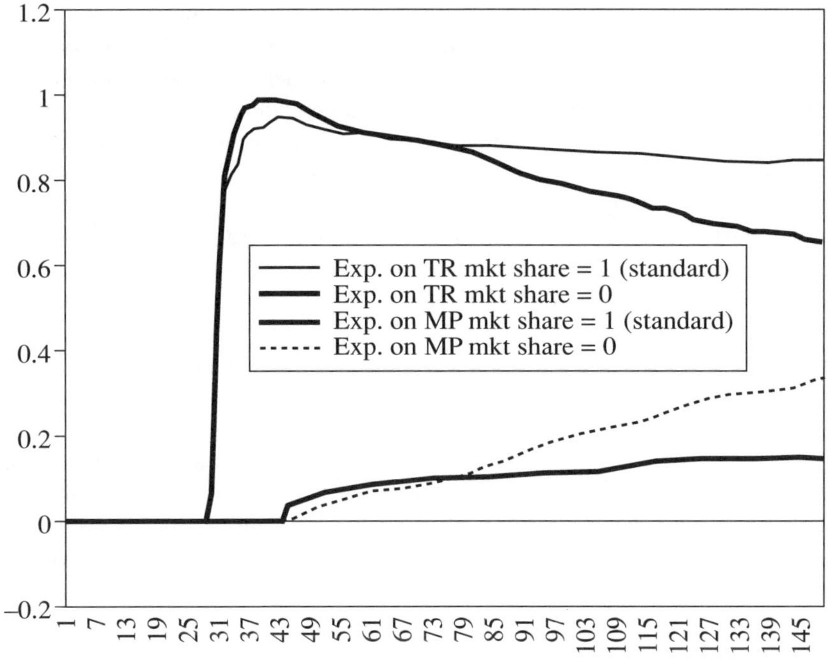

Figure 17.12 Share of TR and MP firms in mainframe market

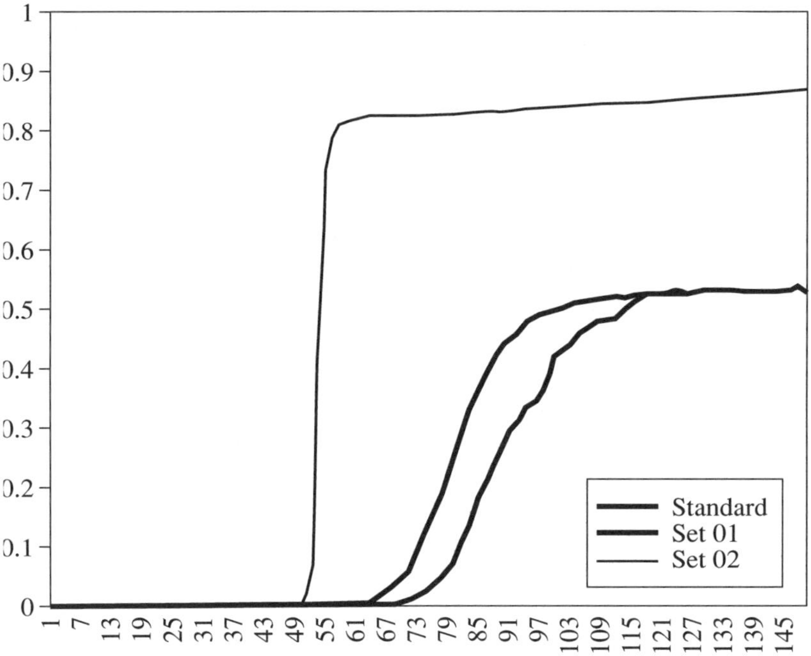

Figure 17.13 Share of diversified firms in PC market

detailed knowledge about particular contexts, like the pattern of evolution of the computer industry, and much of our 'theorizing' is about those particular contexts. General purpose theory provides some broad useful conceptions, and a class of models from which the analyst can pick and choose. But any economist who has tried to understand a particular empirical problem, or come up with a policy prescription that is not laughed out of court by those who know the context, knows that the devil is in the details. And the kind of theorizing that makes sense of the details is derived by paying attention to them.

The details of the industry history we have tried to model are interesting and important to explain, as well as being complex. In particular, in the face of significant changes in the basic underlying technologies, the previously dominant firm was not dislodged from the market where it had been the leader, but was unable to capture the major share of the new market that the new technology opened up. An explanation for this somewhat complicated pattern requires a model of some complexity. It is striking that a model capable of explaining it is as transparent as it is.

We are not arguing here against economic theorizing at a higher level of abstraction. Indeed much of the earlier work in evolutionary theory by some of us has been quite abstract and general. However, we are arguing here for the importance of theory that is close to the empirical details, or rather to the appreciative theory used by knowledgeable empirical scholars to explain those details. We believe that a major advantage of evolutionary economic theory is that it is capable of formulation at this latter level (close to the 'appreciative accounts') as well as in a more abstract mode.

Another reaction to this chapter that we expect is 'big deal'. The verbal model that the formal model aims to capture was well conceived and developed, and it is scarcely surprising, or useful to demonstrate, that a formal representation of it 'works'. And the exercise in formal modeling adds very little, if anything, to the appreciative theory. In response, we would begin by agreeing that carefully developed appreciative verbal theory generally avoids inconsistencies, and can explain what it purports to. That, in fact, is a major reason why it deserves more respect than it typically gets from practitioners of formal theory. But sometimes the logic is incomplete or flawed and, even when it is not, a lot can be learned about what is essential and what is not in the verbal account by trying to build and run a formal representation. More generally, by building and working through a formal model of the verbal account, some results can be brought into view that had not been seen clearly before. We think this definitely was the case here.

In this instance, the formal modeling helps us to see more clearly into at least three important matters: the characteristics of demand, adoption and diversification and entry. The first concerns the major role of demand in affecting market structure and the rate of technological advance. The model clearly separates the role of frictions, inertia and lock-ins in existing demand from emergence of a new demand and a new market. Frictions at the demand level are a powerful reason for the persistence of advantages of incumbent firms. In this respect they play a greater role than the cumulativeness of technical advance at the firm level. By contrast, the emergence of new demand with new features reduces concentration in the overall industry and decreases the advantages of incumbent firms.

The second issue concerns the consequences for incumbent firms of the advent of a new technology and a new market. A new technology and a related new market throw up two different kinds of challenges for incumbent firms: one regarding adoption, the other diversification. The first relates to the use and mastering of the new technology by established firms.

The second concerns the ability of established firms to see and effectively enter new markets that the new technology opens up. The observed body of history and our model tell us that in this case at least the second task was more difficult than the first.

The third issue highlighted by the building and running of the formal model is the important role of entry conditions. New firms not only open up and develop new markets. They also stimulate incumbent firms to adopt and diversify earlier. Because our simulations refer mostly to the American industry, it is reasonable to conclude that the American venture capital market played a major role in generating the history that occurred by enabling new firms to enter, move fast and get established in the new market, thus allowing the new market to take off rapidly. As a consequence of this, international industrial leadership remained with American firms, although the identity of those firms changed. While we did not attempt in this particular model to deal explicitly with what happened outside the United States, the model is consistent with the appreciative view that, lacking strong entrepreneurship and a venture capital market, Europe and Japan were unable to take advantage of the new technologies and opening of new markets that leveled the playing field, and hence unable to have new firms becoming leaders in the new market.

We conclude by noting that these insights, gained from our model, are associated with the explicitly evolutionary nature of that model. Firms try different things, the market selects upon them, and selection takes time. This is a very different theory about firm and industry behavior than the one that presumes that firms always correctly maximize, and the market always is in equilibrium. An essential part of the evolutionary story we have developed here is that firms differed in their level and types of competencies, in their trajectory of advancements and in their ability to see the new market. Another essential part is that entry conditions and financial institutions backing new firms have major consequences on the specific evolution of the industry. Finally, the information that drives firm behavior in the model is the kind of informational feedback that the competitive process actually generates, not the result of 'as if 'equilibrium calculations founded on unrealistically high endowments of *ex ante* information about the structure of the system. In short, technological and industrial change must be understood as an evolutionary process.

7 EVOLUTIONARY ECONOMIC THEORY AND BEHAVIORAL THEORY

As we noted, much of the inspiration for many of the particular structures built into it, as did our work on economic evolutionary theory came from *A Behavioral Theory of the Firm*. Indeed, one of the principal considerations that motivated Nelson and Winter to develop an explicit evolutionary theory was the desire to build a theory capable of explaining questions of the traditional sort that economists had been asking, within a structure that incorporated the theory of firm decision making pioneered by Cyert and March. In our view, *A Behavioral Theory of the Firm* both added to the already powerful collection of evidence challenging the assumption built into standard economic theory – that firm behavior could be accurately deduced from a profit-maximization model – and documented that a behavioral theory of the firm was analytically viable, and could explain what firms actually were doing. We saw, however, three obstacles to using *A Behavioral Theory of the Firm* to rebuild microeconomic theory.

One was the focus of the behavioral theory on the actions of an individual firm. What economists needed was a framework suited for analysis at the level of the industry, or sector. Second, this focus foreclosed the analysis of the viability constraints on a focal firm that arise from the behavior of competitive firms. This both neglected an important source of predictive information and left the vague 'natural selection' rationale for standard theory unanswered. Finally, the analysis in *A Behavioral Theory of the Firm* was, in general, focused on contexts in which the 'routines' built into firms could be considered relatively constant and stable. In contrast, we believed that the most important agenda for deepening understanding lay in the analysis of economic change at the industry level, particularly of industries where technological advance was rapid. Addressing this agenda demanded an explicit treatment of innovation, and of competition based on innovation.

These considerations led to a characterization of firm behavior in *An Evolutionary Theory of Economic Change* that was in most respects simpler and more stylized than the treatment of firm behavior in *A Behavioral Theory of the Firm*. The central focus in evolutionary economic theory was, and is, on change, on innovation, whereas the central orientation of Cyert and March was on how firm behavior is determined by prevailing decision rules (routines) and other characteristic aspects of firms as organizations. And, as noted, the analytical orientation of evolutionary economic theory has been towards patterns of behavior and performance at the level of an industry (as in the model we have just presented) or even at the level of the economy as a whole, rather than on individual firms *per se*. Nonetheless, we intended then, and believe now, that the basic conceptualization of the behavior of individual firms was the same in the two theories.

One central feature of *A Behavioral Theory of the Firm* was its focus on detailed empirical phenomena. While we have preserved that orientation as an objective of evolutionary theory, we confess that it is fair to say that, up until recently, most of the formal evolutionary theory that has been developed has been oriented to explanation of stylized empirical phenomena of a fairly generic kind. In our recent efforts at 'history-friendly modeling', our objectives are much closer to those in *A Behavioral Theory of the Firm* – to develop models that come to grips with the details of observed empirical phenomena at a more detailed level.

NOTES

* Luca Berga and Luca Giorcelli provided an invaluable contribution to the development of the simulation model. This paper benefited from comments of two anonymous referees and from presentations and seminars at the Sixth Conference of the International Joseph A. Schumpeter Society, Bocconi University, BETA, MERIT and SPRU. Support from the Italian National Research Council (CNR), the Bocconi University (Basic Research Program) and the Reginald H. Jones Center of the Wharton School is gratefully acknowledged.

1. We use log-linear equations whenever plausible because most economists have a good feel for their behavior and their quirks. Also, while in most cases the behavior being specified obviously relates to particular firms, to avoid clutter we do not denote that specifically.
2. Firm 02 in Figure 17.4 changes trajectories because with the new microprocessor technology it becomes 'sensitive' to the new MP frontier.

REFERENCES

Bresnahan, T.F. and S. Greenstein (1999), 'Technological competition and the structure of the computer industry', *Journal of Industrial Economics*, **47** (1), pp. 1–40.

Bresnahan, T.F. and F. Malerba (1999), 'Industrial dynamics and the evolution of firms' and nations' competitive capabilities in the world computer industry', in D.C. Mowery and R.R. Nelson (eds), *Sources of Industrial Leadership: Studies of Seven Industries*, New York: Cambridge University Press, pp. 79–132.

Christensen, C.M. and R.S. Rosenbloom (1994), 'Technological discontinuities, organizational capabilities and strategic commitments', *Industrial and Corporate Change* **3**: 655–86.

Cyert, R.M. and J.G. March (1963), *A Behavioral Theory of the Firm*, Englewood Cliffs, NJ: Prentice-Hall.

Dosi, G. and L. Marengo (1994), 'Some elements of an evolutionary theory of organizational competences', in R.W. England (ed.), *Evolutionary Concepts in Contemporary Economics*, Ann Arbor, MI: University of Michigan Press, pp. 157–78.

Flamm, K. (1988), *Creating the Computer*, Washington, DC: Brookings Institution.

Henderson, R. and K. Clark (1990), 'Architectural innovation: the reconfiguration of existing product technologies and the failure of established firms', *Administrative Science Quarterly*, **35**: 9–30.

Langlois, R.N. (1990), 'Creating external capabilities: innovation and vertical disintegration in the microcomputer industry', *Business and Economic History*, **19**: 93–102.

March, J. and H. Simon (1958), *Organizations*, New York: Wiley.

Nelson, R.R. and S.G. Winter (1982), *An Evolutionary Theory of Economic Change*, Cambridge, MA: Harvard University Press.

Teece, D., G. Pisano and A. Shuen (1997), 'Dynamic capabilities and strategic management', *Strategic Management Journal*, **18** (7): 509–33.

Teece, D., R. Rumelt, G. Dosi and S. Winter (1994), 'Understanding corporate coherence: theory and evidence', *Journal of Economic Behavior and Organization*, **23** (January): 1–30.

Tushman, M. and P. Anderson (1986). 'Technological discontinuities and organization environments', *Administrative Science Quarterly*, **31**: 439–65.

Winter, S.G. (1987), 'Knowledge and competence as strategic assets', in D.J. Teece (ed.), *The Competitive Challenge: Strategies for Industrial Innovation and Renewal*, Cambridge, MA: Ballinger, pp. 159–84.

PART IV

Economics of Organization

18. Information, organizational structure and firm strategy

Praveen Kumar*

1 INTRODUCTION

A seminal contribution of the behavioral theory of the firm (Cyert and March 1963, 1992) was to bring a *process-oriented* approach to the study of decision making in firms. Subsequent to the original publication of *A Behavioral Theory of the Firm* (BTF), a large literature has applied this approach to virtually all aspects of decision making in business organizations. But it deserves emphasis that the BTF was substantially ahead of its time in explicitly considering the role of information in business decision making. The main argument of this chapter is that the information search and assimilation process highlighted in the BTF is central to the effective formulation and implementation of firm strategy. However, this link between internal information processing and strategy has become more fully developed only with more recent developments in the economics, organizational behavior and strategic management literatures.

In recent decades, the strategic management literature has advanced considerably. This literature has presented a clear objective for firm strategy: earning economic rents over the long run. It has also identified a core requirement for achieving this objective: the generation and sustenance of competitive advantage (Porter 1981, 1991) or core competencies (Prahalad and Hamel 1991) that give the firm advantage over its competitors. In fact, the outstanding issue in this literature is the determination of firm- or industry-specific factors that facilitate the generation and *sustenance* of competitive advantage. I argue that superior information search and assimilation capabilities are central to both the generation and sustenance of competitive advantage, especially the latter. That is, firms that may achieve a temporary competitive advantage more by good fortune than by design will not be able to sustain it over the longer run unless they have the internal ability to (i) forecast (through information search) shifts in consumer tastes and technology and (ii) translate this information search into market- or production-related strategies in a timely fashion.

This argument bears only a superficial resemblance to the strand of strategic management literature that emphasizes internal resources, rather than external market positioning, as the key to sustainable competitive advantage (Barney 1991; Williamson 1991). The main difference between the argument developed in this chapter and the economizing or 'resource-based competitive advantage' literature is the focus on the information search and assimilation ability. I argue that internal economizing techniques or other strategic assets will only generate uniqueness if they are non-transferable and non-imitable. And, in general, superior information search and assimilation are the only internal assets that are sufficiently intangible and idiosyncratic (due to organizational design reasons) to satisfy these requirements.

Indeed, the important issue is: what can the firm do proactively to develop superior information search and assimilation abilities? I argue that recent developments in the economics of information and organization behavior can speak meaningfully to this issue. The BTF made the important point that information for 'optimal' decisions does not flow frictionlessly in business organizations. It matters who has the information and what are their incentives to reveal this information. These incentive issues can be examined more deeply through agency and contract theory perspectives. This examination has substantive implications for an *organizational strategy* that would develop internal strategic assets relating to superior information search and assimilation abilities. Some of these implications are highlighted below, but clearly much more needs to be done. At the very least, however, the subsequent argument should indicate how the original idea of explicating the information search and assimilation process (in the BTF) has developed – in conjunction with analytic developments in the economics, organizational behavior and strategic management literatures – to address a central issue in strategy.

The structure of the rest of the chapter is the following. Section 2 provides a brief review of the role of information in the BTF. Section 3 then examines the role of information in the various strategy 'paradigms' that are currently dominant in the strategy literature. Section 4 develops the role of internal information processing in the generation and sustenance of competitive advantage. Section 5 examines the incentive issues relating to internal information search and processing, and highlights the implications of these incentive problems for the organizational structure of the firm. Section 6 revisits the issue of economizing versus strategizing in the generation of economic rents, and Section 7 examines the implications of the framework developed here for the role of knowledge in organizations. Section 8 concludes with particular emphasis on future research issues.

2 INFORMATION AND THE BEHAVIORAL THEORY OF THE FIRM

The purpose of this section is to argue that the role of information in firm decision making emphasized in the BTF can be further developed using more recently acquired frameworks in the economics of information and organizational literatures. This development is central to explicitly linking information to organizational structure design and strategy.

The BTF presented a theory of the firm that explicated the actual *process* of decision making in business organizations. Cyert and March identified and examined three major components in this decision process: (i) the formation of organizational objectives, (ii) the evolution of firm strategies to meet these objectives, and (iii) the determination of decisions within those strategies. The implementation of this approach in the BTF, and the large literature that has followed it, have spawned many innovations. One of the most important of these is the distinction between strategy formulation and its implementation when a firm faces uncertainty.

If there is no uncertainty, then *both* the determination of an optimal strategy and its execution follow simply from the existence of a well-defined objective. That is, the choice of strategy is essentially a matter of computation from the objective, and since the environment is always precisely known by assumption, the implementation of the strategy is also straightforward. The presence of uncertainty obviously changes this situation drastically. However, the power of the expected utility theory developed by von Neumann and Morgenstern (1944) and Arrow (1970) was that the determination of the optimal strategy was again made tractable through the maximization of expected welfare. Equally significantly, once the optimal strategy is determined, its implementation, that is, the choice of particular actions or decisions within the strategy, is straightforward since the decision maker is assumed to be sufficiently informed of the environment so as to be precisely able to apply the decision rule.

In BTF, Cyert and March 'broke' this easy equivalence between the choice of strategy and the choice of actions within the strategy. They realistically argued that with a formulated strategy in hand, the firm 'becomes an information-processing and decision rendering system' (Cyert and March 1992, p. 21). To explicate, all members of the firm are typically not simultaneously and equally informed about their business 'situation'. Hence, the determination of a strategy (by whatever fashion) does not imply that the choice of actions or decisions within that strategy is *continually* transparent to the firm. The firm typically has to search and process information before it can determine the best decision or action within the framework of its longer-term strategy.

To be sure, the distinction between determination of decision rules and their implementation is also emphasized in Bayesian decision theory (see, for example, DeGroot 1970), whenever agents are uncertain of the parameters of the decision parameters.[1] In addition, the emphasis on information search in Simon's (1955) work and the BTF finds a formal interpretation in the theory of optimal search in Bayesian decision-making theory (Bernardo and Smith 1995). However, the emphasis in the BTF of fully characterizing firms' decision-making processes identified two central issues that are not generally considered in Bayesian decision theory:

- How is information search conducted within firms? In particular, who searches for information, and what are their incentives?
- How is the new information used or assimilated in the firms? In particular, who gets access to information and what are their incentives for communicating this information?

For truth-in-advertising type reasons, it should be noted that the language of the BTF does not formally use terms like incentives or other items from the agency-theoretic literature, whose development was more than a decade away (from the initial publication of the BTF). However, the development of the incentives literature in economics and the increased emphasis on knowledge-based organizations in the organizational theory literature allow these issues to be addressed with increasing depth and precision. The main thesis of this chapter is that the application of these concepts to issues (i) and (ii) above may lead to new perspectives on the formulation and implementation of firm strategy. Indeed, by focusing on the motivations for the search, communication and assimilation of information, the BTF raised issues that are only beginning to be explored by literatures in economics, organizational theory and strategic management.

Before proceeding, it is worth speculating briefly on why a more formal connection to strategy was not made in the BTF itself. The behavioral theory was intended, not as a theory of market behavior and outcomes, but as a theory of decisions and actions at the level of individual firms.[2] However, Cyert and March appear to be aware of the potential of the BTF to eventually explain and predict market behavior. They argue, for example, that in the longer run, improvements in anti-trust outcomes would be based more on understanding the behavioral basis of decisions and actions *within the firm*, than on the basis of more conventional approaches in industrial organization. A useful perspective on the arguments forwarded by this chapter, then, is that the subsequent developments in the economics and organizational behavior literatures have helped make the connection between the behavioral basis of firm decisions and market outcomes more transparent.[3]

3 INFORMATION AND STRATEGY: SURVEY OF EXISTING PARADIGMS

In this section, I briefly survey the major modern strategy frameworks in strategic management, economics and organization theory with a view to identifying the role of internal information search and assimilation in these frameworks.

Information, Competitive Advantage and Core Competencies

One of the most influential recent ideas in the strategy literature has been the notion of *competitive advantage* (see, for example, Porter 1981, 1991). Competitive advantage allows the firm to achieve superior long-term economic performance; that is, to make long-term economic rents. In the competitive analysis framework developed by Porter and others, the opportunities for, and constraints on, the development of competitive advantage are largely given by the industry structure.[4] The power of this approach is that it gives a relatively precise formulation for the objective of effective strategy; namely, relating the firm to its industry structure and developing competitive advantage through product differentiation or cost advantage or the development of a 'local' monopoly.

The role of information in the industry strategy framework is limited, however. It largely arises in the *signaling* of potential strategies between competitors. In particular, the role of information search and assimilation *within* the firm is not considered in any substantive fashion. The reason for this is that the industry strategy framework is more categorical than operational; that is, it categorizes or classifies industry structures and competitive advantage related strategies into pre-specified groups, but does not provide detailed operational guidance as to the means of achieving and implementing the desirable strategies. Thus, the framework does not really open the opaque 'box' of the firm. It does not ask: how and through what internal incentives does the firm search for product differentiation or cost advantage opportunities? And (presumably) having identified these opportunities, how does the firm provide incentives for the internal communication and assimilation necessary for the exploitation of these opportunities?

The lack of detail on the process of the internal formulation and implementation of strategy is not a minor issue. Indeed, it points to a major weakness in the competitive strategy framework. In a perfectly static world, where industry structure would remain invariant, a structural analysis of the industry may suggest the best strategy (product differentiation versus cost advantage, for example) and then also point to the most effective ways to implement this strategy. But the industry structure is dynamic in practice. It changes as features exogenous to the industry evolve – such as consumer tastes, technology, and the nature of substitutes. More interestingly, the industry structure may also evolve due to the previous strategy choices made by the incumbents. For example, in the instant photographic market, Polaroid for decades maintained its dominance by emphasizing its technological superiority through a strategy of complete focus on research and development. This strategy, while very effective in maintaining Polaroid's technological competitive advantage, also hastened the industry toward a point where further technological leaps were no longer even scientifically possible. By the late 1970s the industry structure 'changed' in the sense that the incumbent could no longer deter entry through the threat of introducing a large technological innovation.

But if the industry structure is evolving, then the internal incentives for information search and assimilation become prominent. A strategy that has proved effective in the past in terms of generating competitive advantage may become ineffectual as the industry structure changes (witness, for example, IBM in the 1980s). Long-term rents can then be guaranteed only if there are internal incentives for the firm's workers to (i) remain alert for market or technology indicators that may predict future weakness in the current strategy, (ii) proactively search for new opportunities for competitive advantage, (iii) effectively communicate potential problems with the current strategy, and (iv) develop viable alternatives and present these to the relevant decision makers in a timely fashion.

The notion of competitive advantage has recently been refined by many authors. A notable refinement has been the idea of *core competencies* (Prahalad and Hamel 1990). Core competencies are the source of growth for the corporation when market boundaries shift due to rapid change in technology. In that sense, the identification and nurturing of core competencies is a recipe for generating competitive advantage within a dynamically evolving industry structure; that is, the notion of core competencies appears to address the weakness with the basic structural analysis framework. Furthermore, Prahalad and Hamel provide illustrations of core competency development that emphasize the role of internal information sharing. However, the core competency framework is still silent on how a firm pro-actively goes about setting the internal organizational incentives and decision-making structure that makes the identification and nurturing of core competencies by its workers a norm rather than an exception. As received, the core competency framework can recognize corporations which have been successful with nurturing core competencies, but cannot present a framework, much less a blueprint, for creating an organization that would have the best chance of developing core competencies.

Another refinement of the competitive advantage idea in the strategic management literature has been the so-called resource-based model of the firm (Barney 1991). This view emphasizes the impact of the idiosyncratic attributes of the firm on its ability to generate sustained competitive advantage. It assumes, first, that firms within a given industry may be heterogeneous with respect to the strategic resources they control and, second, that these resources may not be very mobile across firms. As opposed to the industry structure model, the resource-based model focuses on the internal analysis of the firm.

In principle, the strategic resources of the firm include both assets and capabilities, and hence the information search and processing capabilities of the firm come under the purview of this approach. However, this approach in its current state of development has essentially suggested the variety of tangible and intangible assets that (i) are idiosyncratic to the firm, and (ii) lead to value-creating activities not imitable by current or potential competitors. But, as in the industry structure approach, there is no analytical framework here that allows one to identify organizational structures or worker-related incentives that would allow the firm to pro-actively generate the suitable types of internal strategic assets.[5]

Information in the New Industrial Organization Literature

The 'new' industrial organization literature refers to the large relatively recent output of scholarly work that has analysed oligopolistic competition through the incorporation of non-cooperative game-theoretic techniques (see, for example, Shapiro 1989). The non-cooperative game theory framework is useful because it demands clarity from the modelers regarding the types of decisions being made by firms, the timing conventions regarding these decisions, the information available to the decision makers at every decision point, and so on. Consequently, a number of results, both of theoretical and empirical interest, regarding industry price discipline have been presented by this literature (Shapiro 1989).

However, this entire literature still takes the firm to be an opaque 'box' that takes each and every decision to maximize expected long-term profits. In so doing, this literature has abstracted from the issues of strategy formulation versus strategy implementation. Put differently, the game-theoretic 'lens' has been applied to clarify the nature and consequences of information transmission *between* firms, not *within* firms. Who chooses prices or capacities? What information do these decision makers have? What are their motives and incentives? Issues such as these have still largely been ignored (see, for example, Cyert et al. 1995 and Kumar 1999), but they are often central to understanding oligopolistic competition.

As an illustration, consider the implications of price decentralization. In practice, firms decentralize pricing decisions for a variety of reasons. Indeed, large oligopolistic firms generally present the kinds of technological and organizational complexity that necessitate decentralization of decision making. Price decentralization can have a substantial impact on the implementation of the types of strategies considered in the industrial organization literature. Kumar (1999), for example, shows that there may be a moral hazard on sales personnel who may use price cuts, rather than sales-enhancing efforts, to meet sales goals. Consequently, industry price discipline may not be feasible even if the top management of the firm would seek to tacitly collude due to the fear of price wars. The appropriate pricing strategy under these circumstances may involve price rigidity in order to provide internal incentives.

Information and the Knowledge-based Organization

The strategic management and organizational behavior literature has also recently emphasized information-processing and knowledge-generation activities of firms (Galbraith 1977; Liang and Tan 1994; Rogers et al. 1999). One part of the literature uses formal concepts from the information-management literature and relates them to organizational design and strategy. The other part of the literature seeks to find firm attributes that appear to be most related to knowledge-based strategic advantage (see, for example, DeCarolis and Deeds 1999).

By putting information processing and knowledge generation at the center stage, this literature takes as given that knowledge generation and assimilation is the source of superior economic performance. However, this literature has not yet examined the internal incentive problems in accumulating and applying knowledge for generating long-term competitive advantage. In fact, this literature has attempted either to examine the types of information that are important for strategy implementation (that is, take a management information approach) or to quantify factors that are empirically most related to knowledge generation (for example, geographical proximity to research organizations). Thus, issues such as the self-interested behavior of agents within the organization and the impact of agency conflicts on information generation and knowledge accumulation have not been examined by this literature.

In summary, developments in the strategic management literature subsequent to the (original) publication of the BTF have been enormously insightful. The field now has a well-defined objective for strategy formulation and implementation: the generation of sustainable competitive advantage. While the initial contributions in the competitive advantage framework emphasized industry structure as the source for competitive advantage opportunities, the more recent literature – exemplified in notions like core competencies, resource-based strategies and knowledge-based organizations – has tended to look internally for sources of sustained competitive advantage. This more recent literature has also implicitly or explicitly focused on information processing and knowledge accumulation as an important strategic resource. However, the search and assimilation of information is still largely taken as passive; for example, it apparently happens due to geographical reasons (DeCarolis and Deeds 1999) or due to an organizational structure that *ex post* appears to be just right for information communication within business subunits (Prahalad and Hamel 1990).

I now argue that internal incentive and organizational design issues are central to the effective formulation and implementation of strategies for sustainable competitive advantage. Furthermore, these strategic (in an internal sense) aspects of information search and communication can be usefully examined using the agency and non-cooperative game-theoretic frameworks. Thus, on the one hand, explicit consideration of the decision-making process in firms (as done in the BTF) can fill important gaps in the current strategic management literature.[6] On the other hand, recent developments in the economics of information and strategic management literatures allow a deeper examination of the process of strategy formulation and the determination of decision making within those strategies.

4 INFORMATION, COMPETITIVE ADVANTAGE AND STRATEGY

A firm must continually search for ways to make the firm unique. More precisely, a firm can obtain sustainable competitive advantage only if either the firm's product is unique (or non-imitable) in some dimension crucial to its customers or its cost of product delivery is lower than current and potential competitors due to some uniqueness in its production and organizational structure. Thus, the search for uniqueness must be the underlying objective of a firm's strategy.

But as many observers have noted, if every firm in an industry is searching for uniqueness, then the industry equilibrium will tend toward a perfectly competitive outcome. Successful product designs or production organizations become targets for competitors, and unless there are sustainable entry barriers the equilibrium outcome is one where many producers compete to provide the products most valued by the market. This phenomenon is central to the problem of sustaining, rather than simply generating, a competitive advantage (see, for example, Williams 1992).

The importance of information search and assimilation becomes transparent in this context. If all firms have the same information about consumer preferences or technological and organizational design possibilities, then sustainable competitive advantage will be difficult to achieve without any substantial entry barriers. However, while the literature presents a number of theoretically insurmountable entry barriers such as patents, economies of scale or scope and so on (Scherer 1980; Porter 1981), in practice there are very few examples of 'pure' entry barriers. Given sufficient economic incentive, competitors can work around patents.[7] And there are sufficient theoretical (for example, Milgrom and Roberts 1982) and empirical reasons to question the validity of overcapacity as a credible entry barrier.[8] Thus, if all firms have symmetric access to information regarding consumer preferences and technological and organizational possibilities, then it is difficult to see how a *sustainable* competitive advantage either in product design or cost of delivery can be maintained. A non-information- (or non-knowledge-) based sustainable cost advantage appears possible only due to proprietary access to crucial raw materials, for which there is no technological possibility of substitution.

For most situations of practical or empirical interest, then, sustainable competitive advantage possibilities appear to lie mainly in developing a superior ability to (i) predict the evolution of consumer preferences and technology and (ii) pro-actively exploit this informational advantage in a timely fashion. To explicate, consumer preferences are multidimensional and evolving. This evolution may occur 'exogenously' due to demographic transitions or it may occur 'endogenously' as consumers become aware of new technological possibilities. The complex and dynamic nature of consumer preferences can be vexing for firms with a given product niche. On the other hand, it can also provide opportunities for firms with superior information search and processing abilities as a source of competitive advantage. Meanwhile, the importance of technological forecasting is well-known, and firms routinely invest substantially in this activity.

Of course, information search by itself is not sufficient. There must also be internal incentives in place for the specially informed agents to communicate the results of their information search in a timely fashion to the appropriate decision makers. Unfortunately, and as discussed in greater detail in the next section, the incentives for information search and the timely communication of its results may often be in conflict.

But as the industry technology matures, consumer preferences also begin to stabilize. For example, it is difficult to currently view consumer preferences regarding detergent or toilet soaps as very dynamic. Thus, information search capabilities on product design possibilities will tend to eventually lose steam as an engine of sustainable competitive advantage.[9] Meanwhile, competitive advantage in the cost of delivery (broadly defined) can, and often does, remain a source of sustainable competitive advantage. The reason is that such a competitive advantage typically is based on the availability of non-transferable and non-imitable strategic assets, such as the right incentive and organizational structure for information search and assimilation or proprietary access to specialized raw materials. This implies that over the longer run only firms that have the internal organizational capacity to continually search for and implement opportunities for efficient production and delivery of product value to the market will be able to maintain superior economic performance.

Note that this argument at least superficially supports the resource-based view of strategy: internal information search and processing ability regarding efficient product delivery is viewed to be the central attribute generating long-term competitive advantage. However, the argument here, and its subsequent development below, differs from the resource-based strategy viewpoint in at least two ways.

First, the resource-based school provides a potentially open-ended list of internal strategic assets that can be the source of firm 'heterogeneity' and competitive advantage. In contrast, I have argued that the fundamental 'non-imitable' strategic asset is a superior organizational ability for information search and assimilation. Second, the resource-based approach does not address the issue: what incentive and organizational design allows a firm to develop such superior information-related capabilities? This is an important issue, however. Information search is done by agents with specialized knowledge, placed in situations where they often have a unique view of evolving market and technology conditions. Moreover, these agents have their own objectives and interests, that need not coincide with the firm's overall objectives (see below). A persuasive theory of generating sustainable competitive advantage through superior information search and processing capabilities must, therefore, be explicit regarding the organizational design and incentive strategy of the firm.

Before turning to the organizational design and incentive issues, however, we should clarify further the notion of 'superior' information search and processing ability. If we parameterize the evolving consumer preferences and production technologies, then we can usefully conceptualize the firm's uncertainty about its competitive environment in terms of the parameters governing the evolution of the preferences and technologies. Similarly, the firm may also be uncertain regarding some crucial parameters that determine the objectives, and hence the strategy, of its competitors. Superior information search and processing ability then takes the more precise interpretation of superior parameter estimates.

In a classical inference framework, superior estimation may occur because a firm has the ability to more cost-effectively sample market- or technology-related data than its rivals. A Bayesian framework offers a richer set of possibilities, however. In this framework, a firm may have superior estimation abilities from a given set of observations because its agents have better or more precise prior beliefs and because they may use more accurate likelihood functions; that is, market, technology or strategic models, compared to their rivals. This 'superior estimation' formulation of the information-based competitive advantage is very suggestive in terms of studying pricing, product line, and organizational strategies. The firm's choice of prices, product line or internal organizational design may be motivated by a desire for a better estimation of the unknown preference and technology parameters. The literature in industrial organization, strategic management and organizational behavior has rarely explored this type of learning-motivated strategy formulation, however. This issue deserves much attention in future research.

5 ORGANIZATIONAL STRUCTURE AND STRATEGY

By organizational structure I shall mean the decision and informational hierarchy of the firm. Organizations tend to work with well-defined rules regarding the decision-making authority at various levels of the organization. In addition to this, organizations have formal and informal rules or conventions regarding information communication across various decision-making points. For example, an informational hierarchy or structure is determined by rules – explicit or followed by convention – that determine the types and timing of information communicated by the sales force to their supervisors. In decision-theoretic terms, the organizational structure represents the firm as a decision tree where the decision-making scope and the information availability for every agent (or decision-making level) is specified.

Along with the organizational structure, the firm also has in place a reward and penalty structure for its workers. For example, performance-based bonus schemes and implicit (and sometimes explicit) rules for holding back promotions or outright job terminations. This reward and penalty structure establishes the incentives for workers for superior job performance. Two aspects of worker incentives are particularly important for the issues at hand. These are the incentives for (i) the timely, accurate and complete communication of the information available to the worker, and (ii) adoption of decisions that are consistent with the overall strategy of the firm. Both of these are crucial for effective formulation and implementation of firm strategy, as is explicated below. Furthermore, the two types of incentive problems correspond (respectively) to the situations of 'hidden information' and 'hidden actions', a useful categorization provided by the agency literature (see, for example, Arrow 1984). Indeed, I now argue that the agency framework provides a natural language and analytical framework to study basic issues in the formulation of strategy and its implementation.

Hidden Information and Strategy

As noted above, even protected market positions can be rapidly undermined by changes in consumer preferences, technology and organizational design (for example, contracting) possibilities. The search for information relevant to generate or sustain competitive advantage has two salient characteristics: it is costly and the outcome is uncertain. Learning about preferences and production technologies (broadly defined) incurs direct costs in the form of skilled labor costs, experimentation with prices and product lines, and investment in research and development (R&D). There are also, however, opportunity costs of the organizational time and attention that are devoted to implement such learning and interpreting its results. Uncertainty is inherent because the success of the business policies that are determined by the inflow of the new information can never be guaranteed.

But when a firm searches for information relating to opportunities for competitive advantage, 'pockets' of specialized information are bound to arise within the firm. The reason is that in modern industrial societies economically useful information is complex, and emanates from diverse sources at a fast rate. From a technological or marketing standpoint, it is almost axiomatic that an effective information search for competitive advantage in terms of product differentiation or cost advantage possibilities will require decentralization of the search to agents with special skills and knowledge. If the top or central management can coordinate or control this type of information search, then they do not need to hire specially skilled or informed workers in the first place. That is, information search regarding competitive advantage is necessary only because the firm's current information or skill set, embodied in its management and workers, is perceived to require development or updating.

However, decentralization of information search to specially skilled or informed workers will typically mean that, in due course, these workers become privy to information of potential strategic value. Clearly, effective strategy formulation would require that this private information be communicated to the relevant decision makers in a timely and accurate fashion. But it is by no means clear that the self-interested agents will have the incentives for such information communication.

To fix ideas, consider the 'search' for information regarding the evolution of consumer preferences, specifically the attempt to identify attributes of the industry's basic product that would be given special value by the customers in the future. Typically, the workers with the greatest insight or information on these matters would be those who are *currently* actively interfacing with the customers. But such workers are also the ones who are benefiting most – in terms of compensation, job prestige and so on – from the *existing* marketing or product positioning strategy of the firm. There is a natural conflict of interest, then, if the information search by these workers indicates a need for the firm to radically rethink its product development and marketing strategy. The reason is that any significant changes in the product definition or marketing strategy will likely make the skills of the currently 'valued' employees obsolete. Similar issues also arise when a firm searches for information regarding technological possibilities.

The incentive problems described in the previous paragraphs significantly add to the cost of information search and processing for the firm. The firm will have to suffer costs of providing incentives for timely communication of private information. These types of incentive in practice take many forms. For example, bonuses are sometimes tied to various types of information on customers that are provided by the sales force. Similarly, the communication of technological development ideas to upper management by R&D workers is also sometimes rewarded by bonuses (or more recently the award of stock options) *if* these ideas are perceived to have future commercial value. However, these types of reward schemes will often not address the fundamental incentive problems. The reason is that the scale of the reward must be tied to the *currently* perceived tangible commercial value of the information.

Therefore, there are relatively low-powered incentives available for the communication of information that a particularly knowledgeable worker realizes to be of long-term value, but which does not fit the contemporaneous industry notions of 'value'.[10] One possibility is to provide long-term incentives. The most credible long-term incentives are given through stock options or equity shares in the company. But even such *long-term* incentives do not necessarily 'solve' the information communication incentive problem. Partly, the reason is that, for a variety of accounting and political reasons, equity compensation is generally concentrated in the hands of the senior management, whereas the private information under discussion typically resides with the 'frontline' sales force or R&D workers. And since there is considerable uncertainty regarding the value of the information communicated by these workers, justifying large stock option grants is also politically difficult.

To deal with these complex incentive issues, some firms have adopted the very costly practice of providing 'golden parachutes' (or 'golden handshakes') to workers. Under this arrangement, workers whose jobs may be terminated due to shifts in market or technology focus receive large lump-sum severance payments (see, for example, Cyert and Kumar 1996b). Golden parachutes represent the upper end of the range of the actual costs of information search, when the costs of inducing timely and accurate communication are properly taken into account. They are effective since the firm is essentially transferring to the worker the capitalized value of his or her life-long expected job compensation in the existing (and possibly soon to be outdated) technology and organizational structure. However, it is also clear that these types of incentive cannot be widely given since they would substantially increase the default risk if awarded to a significant proportion of the workforce.

Another useful idea may be to incorporate incentives for information communication in the firm's internal cost allocation or in its performance evaluation of managers of various subunits. For example, the firm could consider imposing a 'capital' charge with an upward drift on its business subunits. This charge would come into effect whenever the actual profit performance of the unit *net of the charge* falls below the profit growth targets (for the unit or the corporation) by a margin that exceeds a threshold value. The threshold value itself should shrink over time; that is, the actual performance would be expected to be closer to the target over time. The capital charge is a lump-sum 'penalty' on the business unit and it represents an opportunity cost of employing the firm's resources elsewhere. It should have an upward drift because over time the estimates of the managers regarding the competitive advantage opportunities in product positioning and efficient production organization must be getting more precise. If front-line managers fail to communicate a likely evolution in the competitive advantage opportunities due to incentive conflicts, then they are more likely to fall short of the given targets since the capital charge is increasing over time. It is noteworthy that while imposing a capital charge or an implicit capital cost in performance evaluation has recently become fashionable due to emphasis on 'value-creating' strategies, the idea of an upward drift in this capital charge due to incentive provision reasons does not appear to have been appreciated in the literature. These types of dynamic incentives for information search and communication deserve much attention, however.

The firm has alternative ways to obtain and process information. In the customer preference realm, top management can follow a strategy of sampling through product line positioning. In this strategy, information on the direction of consumer preference shifts may be obtained by examining consumer response to a variety of product offerings that emphasize different product performance attributes. But this type of sampling is costly. On the other hand, the management has greater control over the informational flows since it is generally easier to monitor, at the top-management level, the financial performance of various product introductions.

Another strategy is to do vertical integration (for obtaining market information) or purchase firms on the 'periphery' of the industry technology to obtain information on the technological evolution. The vertical or horizontal (broadly interpreted) integration generally gives top management a more direct access to technological or marketing related information. Indeed, this strategy appears to be increasingly common in the personal computing and software industries as the pace of technological innovation in those industries has accelerated in recent years.[11]

To summarize, the argument is that in devising a framework for strategy formulation and the determination of decisions within these strategies, the firm must take into account the fact that information search and processing in business organizations is mostly done by self-interested agents who will become privy to strategically relevant information. The firm cannot, therefore, expect to generate and sustain competitive advantage without directly addressing the incentive issues involved in motivating workers to efficiently search for, and then truthfully communicate, consumer- or technology-related information. These incentives generally take the form of contractually specified compensation for particular types of information communicated. However, the firm may be able to avoid some of these incentive costs by:

1. judiciously choosing the organizational structure to minimize the incentive costs of eliciting private information. By paying special attention to the level of decentralization of the information search the firm can minimize potential incentive conflicts;
2. using appropriate internal cost allocation strategies to induce managers of subunits to reveal information to the top management in a timely fashion;
3. using product and pricing strategy that allows information to be channeled directly to the top management; for example, sequential product positioning and pricing decisions whose effects can be relatively easily monitored by the top management; and
4. adapting the 'firm boundary' (for example, through vertical and horizontal integration) to allow more direct access to information sources relating to market or technological conditions.

An important implication of the foregoing argument is that sustainable competitive advantage cannot be generated by focusing on 'external' search alone; that is, by focusing only on the industry structure alone. The internal organization of the firm – organization structure, internal monitoring mechanisms, and choice of firm boundaries – is an integral part of strategy formulation and implementation. This point has only begun to be appreciated by the industrial organization and strategic management literature. The original ideas in the BTF on the process of strategy formulation and the determination of decisions within these strategies, when developed through the application of recent contributions in economics, organizational behavior and strategic management, can provide an analytic framework for integrating internal or organizational strategy with external or competitive strategy.

Hidden Actions and Strategy

Another important type of information asymmetry that relates to strategy formulation and implementation is that of privately observed actions. To fix ideas, consider the following situation that illustrates the issues. Suppose that a firm has crafted a product and pricing strategy based on appropriate cost and differentiation advantage considerations. As is typical, the strategy is implemented by the sales force. Suppose, however, that effective execution of the strategy requires personally costly effort by the sales force.[12] Most plausibly, however, the effort of the sales force cannot be monitored without cost. On the other hand, there is a clear agency problem or objective conflict: the sales force would like to shirk or economize on their effort and use price cuts to obtain sales orders, whereas the firm would like the sales force to maintain price discipline and 'swing' sales orders through personal marketing efforts.[13]

The hidden action (or moral hazard) problem illustrated in the previous paragraph suggests two important problems for strategy formulation and implementation. First, for any given strategy choice the decisions or actions chosen within the strategy will not generally be the right ones because of the presence of agency conflicts. Second, since strategy formulation in a dynamic context requires continual feedback from actual performance, underestimation of the moral hazard problem can lead to substantially erroneous inferences regarding the suitability (or lack thereof) of the formulated strategy. Moreover, these errors of omission or commission may also lead to a situation in which the strategy is realigned in the wrong way from the viewpoint of competitive advantage.

As in the hidden information case, the firm can (i) use contract-based incentives and (ii) devise an appropriate organizational structure to ameliorate this type of agency problem. Contract or organizational structure design will generally not eliminate these agency conflicts, however. With a contractual approach, the firm links workers' short-term and long-term compensation to indicators that are noisily related to their chosen (and unobserved) actions. For example, returning to the example in the beginning of this subsection, the worker's long-term compensation may be adversely affected by falling industry profits when the reduction in profits occurs due to price wars. Here the noisy signal on workers' actions is the onset of the price war which is presumed to be precipitated by 'unjustified' price cutting by the firm's own workers (see, for example, Kumar 1999). But there are a number of costs involved in this approach. Since the rewards or penalties are triggered by noisy indicators, workers may sometimes be unjustly penalized, and this may lead to resignations by valuable workers. Conversely, the workers may be rewarded (with monetary or other costs to the firm) even when they have not contributed to the firm's profits.

Alternative attacks on the said moral hazard problem require appropriate organizational structure design. In particular, the firm can invest in monitoring technologies and integrate these technologies in the organizational hierarchy to obtain information on the workers' actions (see, for example, Holmström and Tirole 1989). The firm can also pay particular attention to the levels at which crucial decisions, such as pricing, are made (Milgrom and Roberts 1992).

6 ECONOMIZING VERSUS STRATEGIZING REVISITED

Williamson (1991) categorizes business strategy under two headings: strategizing and economizing. The former relates to the study of market power, while the latter deals with the firm's effort to reduce or minimize (internal) transaction costs of production and governance. In particular, Williamson emphasizes that effective adaptation is an integral component of economizing by firms. Reinforcing a prior point in this chapter, Williamson notes that strategizing has dominated the strategy literature. He argues, however, that economizing behavior is more fundamental to superior economic performance.

The argument in this chapter furthers the understanding of the type of 'shocks' to which the firm must adapt to, namely new information regarding competitive advantage opportunities. Furthermore, the focus on the role of internal information search and assimilation also clarifies the main problems that come in the way of efficient adaptation, namely the incentive problems that arise due to objective conflicts between informed or pivotal workers and the top management or owners. Indeed, the BTF approach is useful because it indicates that economizing requires both a pro-active search for information (that is, the 'shocks' do not simply arrive randomly at the firm's door) and the establishment of an appropriate organizational structure to deal with the incentive issues. This approach also suggests that the distinction between strategizing and economizing may be somewhat illusory. There can be no effective strategizing by firms unless: (i) they maintain a competitive advantage in understanding their demand and technological environment or evolution in these environments, and (ii) they effectively adapt to these environments or changes in them.

7 KNOWLEDGE, ORGANIZATION AND COMPETITIVE ADVANTAGE

Reinforcing a basic theme of the BTF, Demsetz (1991) argued that future work in the theory of the firm needed to be concerned with the 'economics of acquiring and using knowledge'. He emphasized the importance of economizing on the acquisition and application of knowledge, and derived some implications for the optimal boundary of the firm. However, the foregoing arguments show that there is an interesting, and possibly endemic, tension between the incentives for knowledge acquisition and the incentives for its communication and assimilation within the organization.

Pelikan (1989) and Eliasson (1990) make a useful distinction between *tacit* and *communicable* knowledge. The former relates to the ability of the firm's workers to receive and apply new information or knowledge, is localized to particularly competent groups within the firm, and is not transferable to other firms. The latter, on the other hand, is a skill that can be transferred to other firms by worker mobility. While not parsed in terms of tacit knowledge *per se*, the foregoing argument does recognize the importance of the locally based character of special information. Indeed, an important part of our notion of specialized or private information may be its tacit component. But our perspective also highlights the 'double-edged-sword' nature of tacit knowledge-based sources of competitive advantage. Tacit knowledge may be crucial in the firm's ability to utilize new information, but it may also sometimes impede the efficient adaptation to this information by exacerbating the incentive problems. For example, if the tacit knowledge of a worker is a source of his or her quasi-rents (wages that are higher than those available in alternative job opportunities), then such a worker may resist adaptation to production or organizational innovations if such innovations make some part of that tacit knowledge economically obsolete.

8 CONCLUDING COMMENTS

The research program initiated by the BTF through its emphasis on the internal information search and assimilation in firms has only partially been completed. More recent developments in the economics, organizational behavior and strategic management literatures have clarified the central role of information search and assimilation in the formulation and implementation of firm strategy. However, substantial work remains to be done.

Further work needs to done on the types of informational dispersion that are important, and how these dispersions evolve over time. In other words, what should a firm search for? And, does the focus of the search change systematically with the evolution of the industry? Similarly, should the focus of the search evolve with the organizational efficiency in information processing?

It is also important to develop further the relation of organizational strategy (that is, design of organizational structure) to competitive strategy. The literature has so far only provided an initial glimpse of the incentive problems in information search and assimilation, examining only a few of the settings. Further empirical work (for example, through case analyses) is required to examine these incentive problems in a variety of industrial and organizational contexts. These observations may then provide the material for the theory to arrive at a more general and robust characterization of the link between 'internal' and 'external' strategy.

NOTES

* I thank Mie Augier and Jim March for helpful comments. I would especially like to thank Richard Cyert for many stimulating discussions on the issues discussed in this chapter.

1. A little formal notation may make this issue even clearer. Suppose that the decision rule is written as $\boldsymbol{d}(\tilde{\theta}_t)$, where $\tilde{\theta}_t$ is a vector of parameters at date t, and the range of the function $\boldsymbol{d}(\cdot)$ is some appropriately defined vector subspace. If $\tilde{\theta}_t$ is well known, then the 'implementation' of the decision rule is presumably straightforward. But what if $\tilde{\theta}_t$ is not known with certainty? In this case it may be optimal to conduct costly 'search' for information on $\tilde{\theta}_t$. The point is that the knowledge of $\boldsymbol{d}(\cdot)$ is no longer equivalent to knowing which action to pick from its range.
2. As noted in the BTF: 'Because we see only dimly what lies behind the characteristic behavior of the firm and understand only partly the learning processes within the firm, we can not articulate a serious policy proposal for changing the behavior pattern' (Cyert and March 1963, p. 297).
3. It is also noteworthy that there are contributions in the strategy literature that have behavioral characteristics. See, for example, Selznick (1957).
4. In the competitive strategy framework, five industry attributes (namely, (i) the number of firms competing in the industry, (ii) the existence of substitutes, (iii) the efficacy of entry and exit barriers, (iv) the bargaining power of suppliers, and (v) the bargaining power of buyers), determine the structural opportunities for the development and sustenance of competitive advantage.
5. Some very recent contributions in the resource-based model do emphasize the location of competitive advantage in 'organizational effects' (see, for example, Rouse and Dallenbach 1999).
6. A somewhat different connection between the BTF and strategy is made in Cyert (1998). While taking a different perspective, this paper appears to support the thesis that the BTF was ahead of its time.
7. An interesting example of this is the case of the CT scanner, introduced by EMI in 1973. At the time of product introduction, the company believed that it had a 'lock' on at least five years of patent protection, and its product

development and marketing strategy was based on this assumption. Yet, the first set of competing products were announced within 18 months of the very successful introduction of the CT scanner in the US radiological market. The nature of the competitors' design exemplified the point that there can be no patent protection for basic product development ideas, only for particular methods of implementing those ideas.

8. Typically, excess capacity of the incumbent is not a sufficient deterrent, especially if the entrant can enter with some kind of a technological innovation. If entry is a *fait accompli*, then it is in the self-interest of the incumbent to drawn down the capacity and accommodate with the entrant. As pointed out by Milgrom and Roberts (1982), only a clear and insurmountable cost advantage of the incumbent (in terms of marginal cost) can deter entry.
9. A more formal presentation of this argument is given in Cyert et al. (1993).
10. The value of internet connections is possibly a clichéd example, but nevertheless instructive. Even in the early 1990s, many so-called technologically sophisticated executives and observers viewed the internet as a 'fad' for a miniscule niche of hyper-technological users. Of course, the personal desk-top computer was similarly viewed in the late 1970s and the early 1980s.
11. For example, Microsoft in the mid-1990s acquired controlling stakes in many small firms whose technological competence lies in network computing.
12. The sales force may be required to communicate the comparative advantages of the firm's products or it may be required to pay personal attention to buyers' needs. In most practical situations, due to the presence of informational or market frictions, additional effort by the sales force can have a significant impact on sales. See Scitovsky (1991) for a more formal and elegant exposition of this point.
13. This example, while stylized, is far from unrealistic. See Milgrom and Roberts (1992) and Cyert et al. (1995) for a variety of related examples from actual business situations.

REFERENCES

Arrow, K. (1970), *Essays in the Theory of Risk-bearing*, Amsterdam: North-Holland.

Arrow, K. (1984), 'The economics of agency', Technical Report, Stanford University.

Barney, J. (1991), 'Firm resources and sustained competitive advantage', *Journal of Management*, **17**, 99–120.

Bernardo, J. and A. Smith (1995), *Bayesian Theory*, New York: Wiley.

Cyert, R. (1998), 'Behavioral theory of the firm and strategy', Unpublished manuscript, Carnegie-Mellon University.

Cyert, R. and P. Kumar (1996a), 'Strategies for technological innovation with learning and adaptation costs', *Journal of Economics and Management Strategy*, **5**, 25–67.

Cyert, R. and P. Kumar (1996b), 'Economizing by firms through learning and adaptation', *Journal of Economic Behavior and Organization*, **29**, 211–31.

Cyert, R., P. Kumar and J. Williams (1993), 'Information, market imperfections and strategy', *Strategic Management Journal*, **14**, 47–58.

Cyert, R., P. Kumar and J. Williams (1995), 'Impact of organizational structure on oligopolistic pricing', *Journal of Economic Behavior and Organization*, **26**, 1–15.

Cyert, R. and J. March (1963), *A Behavioral Theory of the Firm*, Englewood Cliffs, NJ: Prentice-Hall.

Cyert, R. and J. March (1992), *A Behavioral theory of the Firm*, Cambridge: Blackwell.

DeCarolis, D. and D. Deeds (1999), 'The impact of stocks and flows of organizational knowledge on firm performance: an empirical investigation of the biotechnology industry', *Strategic Management Journal*, **20**, 953–68.

DeGroot, M. (1970), *Optimal Statistical Decisions*, New York: McGraw-Hill.

Demsetz, H. (1991), The theory of firm revisited', in O. Williamson and S. Winter (eds), *The Nature of the Firm*, Oxford: Oxford University Press, pp. .

Eliasson, G. (1990), 'The firm as a competent team', *Journal of Economic Behavior and Organization*, **13**, 275–98.

Galbraith, J. (1977), *Organization Design*, Reading, MA: Addison-Wesley.

Holmström, B. and J. Tirole (1989), 'The theory of the firm', in R. Schmalensee and R. Willig (eds), *Handbook of Industrial Organization*, Vol. 1, Amsterdam: Elsevier Science, pp. .

Kumar, P. (1999), 'Decentralization, agency, and dynamic oligopoly', mimeo, University of Houston.

Liang, T. and C. Tan (1994), 'Strategic information technology plan: a vital component in the corporate strategies of banks', *Information and Management*, **26**, 265–73.

Milgrom, P. and J. Roberts (1982), 'Limit pricing and entry under incomplete information: an equilibrium analysis', *Econometrica*, **50**, 443–60.
Milgrom, P. and J. Roberts (1992), *Economics, Organization and Management*, Englewood Cliffs, NJ: Prentice-Hall.
Pelikan, P. (1989), 'Evolution, economic competence and the market for corporate control', *Journal of Economic Behavior and Organization*, **12**, 279–303.
Porter, M. (1981), *Competitive Strategy*, New York: Free Press.
Porter, M. (1991), *Competitive Advantage: Creating and Sustaining Superior Performance*, New York: Free Press.
Prahalad, C. and G. Hamel (1990), 'The core competence of organizations', *Harvard Business Review*, May–June, 79–91.
Rogers, P., A. Miller and W. Judge (1999), 'Using information-processing theory to understand planning/performance relationships in the context of strategy', *Strategic Management Journal*, **20**, 567–77.
Rouse, J. and U. Dallenbach (1999), 'Rethinking research methods for the resource-based perspective: isolating sources of sustainable competitive advantage', *Strategic Management Journal*, **20**, 487–94.
Scherer, F. (1980), *Industrial Market Structure and Economic Performance*, Chicago: Rand-McNally.
Scitovsky, T. (1991), 'The benefits of asymmetric markets', *Journal of Economic Perspectives*, 4, 135–48.
Selznick, P. (1957), *Leadership in Administration*, Evanston, IL: Row, Peterson.
Shapiro, C. (1989), 'Theories of oligopoly behavior', in R. Schmalensee and R. Willig (eds), *Handbook of Industrial Organization*, Vol. 1, Amsterdam: Elsevier Science, pp. .
Simon, H. (1955), 'A behavioral model of rational choice', *Quarterly Journal of Economics*, **69**, 99–118.
Von Neumann, J. and O. Morgenstern (1944), *Theory of Games and Economic Behavior*, Princeton, NJ: Princeton University Press.
Williams, J. (1992), 'How sustainable is your competitive advantage', *California Management Review*, **34**, 1–22.
Williamson, O. (1991), 'Strategizing, economizing and economic organization', *Strategic Management Journal*, Winter, 75–94.

19. Organization theory in the age of computers and electronic communication networks

Herbert A. Simon

1 INTRODUCTION

It is a commonplace statement nowadays, and perhaps even a true one, that human business and governmental organizations will be revolutionized by the electronic computer and information systems. In fact, there are already numerous harbingers of the revolution, in the form of the rapidly increasing use of computers and communication networks:

- for keeping and processing the organization's financial and production records and carrying out its market transactions of procuring, selling, delivering and billing; generating in the process the appropriate messages for correspondents, and reading and acting upon the messages received from them;
- for making, or participating in, complex management decisions and carrying out processes of product design, using the tools of artificial intelligence, operations research, and computer-aided design; and
- for transmitting and recording multitudinous communications, with the external environment and among organizational members, in both numerical and natural languages; storing them and information gleaned from them, controlling access to common records and accessible information stores, and facilitating the retrieval of information wanted from them.

In interaction with a fourth category (managing people, which does not directly involve the information technology), these three functions – controlling the flow of transactions, making managerial and design decisions, and processing the information used directly and indirectly in these activities – represent the core of organizational work.

Increasingly, we must think of organizations as large aggregations of people and computers, each contributing to the mutual task of making the organization's decisions and carrying on its activities. Increasingly we must view the computers that participate in the organization not as mindless servants but as intelligent collaborators. We need not argue whether it is philosophically correct to say that computers think; it is enough to observe that they already play an extensive and active role in organizational decision making, and this is only possible because they can play that role intelligently.

At the present time we are beginning to reconsider our theories of how to organize in the light of these new developments in information and computer technology. We are asking how we design effective organizations that have electronic as well as human members with capacities for intelligent behavior and learning.

2 A STARTING BENCHMARK

The mid-decades of the twentieth century saw vigorous research on the nature of organizations, out of which arose new behavioral theories of organizational structure and process, with strong ties to social and cognitive psychology. The research focused particularly on decision-making processes, extending them to include the search for decision alternatives, and thereby seeking to form a realistic picture of human bounded rationality to replace the abstract and unrealistic model of 'economic man'.

The Graduate School of Industrial Administration at Carnegie-Mellon University was an active center of this research in the decades prior to and during the deanship of Dick Cyert, whose memory we honor with this volume. Among the local products of that work were *Administrative Behavior* (Simon, 1947, 1957), *Organizations* (March and Simon, 1958), and *A Behavioral Theory of the Firm* (Cyert and March, 1962), volumes which provide us with a picture of organizations at the very beginning of the computer era, well before computers had any significant impact on organizational design or operation. We shall take these works as a benchmark, from which we can measure the changes that have taken place in organizations and in our theory of them.

3 MOTIVATION AND GOVERNABILITY

Management is concerned with marshalling human and material resources to accomplish collective goals through organized effort. To an important extent, securing collaboration remains the same task no matter how much the goals change and no matter what new technologies arise for attaining them. Knowing how to lead people and to motivate them are central requisites for management whatever one is leading them toward or motivating them to do.

Differences in the levels of skill and knowledge of organization members are, of course, important considerations that may dictate differences in management style, but it is remarkable how much the common sense and folk wisdom of management that has come down from the earliest times of which we have records still applies to leadership and management in today's organizations. Hierarchy and division of work, motivation through material rewards and through recognition of merit, leadership by setting and defining goals, organizational loyalties and identification – these are all clearly present at the beginnings of history some 4000 years ago and retain a central position in our benchmark works of the 1950s. Plutarch's *Lives*, Thucydides' *History* and Xenophon's *Anabasis* still provide us with forceful examples of effective and ineffective leadership and *A Behavioral Theory of the Firm* can still teach us management lessons.

We must be careful not to derive the wrong lessons from this permanence of basic management dimensions. It is true that people have changed little, and that their behavior in organizations retains many resemblances to the behavior of their remote ancestors in the early agricultural kingdoms or the ancient city states. At the same time, our *knowledge* of human behavior has changed a great deal; the folk wisdom has been pruned and augmented by a substantial body of systematic research of varied kinds.

One major focus of the research since the benchmark period has been on organizational behavior (OB), which has given us new insights especially into the relations among participation, morale, motivation and productivity (see, for example, Leavitt and Bahrami, 1988). A second focus has been on the decision-making process and its relation to human problem solving in general (see Kleindorfer et al., 1993). By drawing on this knowledge, managers can enhance their effectiveness significantly.

One way to view the participation of computers in organizations is to say: 'We now have some new members of our organization, and we must include them as participants in all of our organizational practices'. Of course that is too simplistic, for there are important ways in which the computer members are different from human members. The most important differences lie in motivations and controllability.

In anticipating the effects that computers will have upon organizations, or are already having, we must keep firmly in mind that we are dealing with a moving target: the capabilities of computers have changed with great rapidity during the whole period during which they have been entering into our organizations. Today they are performing functions (for example, determining customer creditworthiness) that would have been unthinkable a few years ago. Tomorrow they will be performing functions that most of us would think wholly infeasible today.

In view of this continual flux, it is unrealistic to try to describe the similarities and differences between computers and human employees. Whatever the differences today, they will not be the same tomorrow. The only sure prediction is that the range of functions in organizations that computers can perform has enlarged steadily and rapidly, and will continue to do so for many decades. We should not think that the gestation period of this revolution will be any briefer than were those of the manufacturing revolution or the transportation revolution or the revolution in electrical communication that brought telegraph, wireless and telephone – or that its scope will be any narrower.

Nor should we commit the 'horseless carriage' fallacy of supposing that the computer is simply a way of carrying on old functions by new means. The real products of motor transportation were not better buggy rides but suburbia, continent-crossing family vacations, and interstate trucking that completing altered the railroad industry. The World Wide Web already gives us premonitions of the capacity of computers to create new economic and social activity patterns of wide scope in our society.

Loyalty

Goals can be set for computers without rewarding them, and without worrying about personal goals that might compete with organizational goals. I shall not speculate about a day in which we might concern ourselves with 'computer rights' as we now concern ourselves with 'animal rights'. At present, computers are our slaves, but they raise none of the moral problems that prohibit human slavery. Hence the chapters of the organization manual that deal with morale, rewards and incentives, and goal and group loyalties need not be revised to include computers.

It is quite another matter to ask whether computers can always be expected to do what they were programmed to do. We are already quite aware that they do not always do what we *thought* we programmed them to do! As programs become more complex, and as they penetrate more deeply into an organization's decision processes, we can expect all sorts of behaviors to appear that were not anticipated by the programmers, even without the assistance of viruses introduced by unfriendly antagonists. (The Y2K problem (the problem of the transition into the 21st century), successfully anticipated in its manifold manifestations and mostly solved, was just a specific, quirky instance of (today's) computer fallibilities.)

This divergence of behavior from expectations becomes increasingly apparent as computers are given more and more capability to learn from their experiences. Like people, they may learn more or fewer things than we sought to teach, or quite different things from what we had in mind, and then behave accordingly. They now no longer do what we programmed them to do; they increasingly modify their own programs to incorporate what they have learned to do, through instruction and, to the extent that they are equipped with sensors, from their own experiences.

Consequently, although we do not need to revise the human relations chapters in our manual to accommodate computers, we need to write some new chapters on relations with computers that learn, instructing us how to enforce the adherence of computers to organizational goals and policies, and describing procedures for diagnosing non-compliance and dealing with it. Our Y2K preparations perhaps served as a warm-up for this continuing exercise.

Cognitive Aspects of Identification

If we do not have to *motivate* computers' allegiances to organizational goals, we do have to acculturate them by providing them with the knowledge and foci of attention that are requisite to reaching these goals. Organizational identification is not simply a matter of loyalty; it has a very large, perhaps dominant, cognitive component. Organizations provide people and computers with environments of events and information, and changing contexts within these environments, that strongly influence what they know and learn, and direct their attention to some matters and away from others.

Computers, quite like people, are only boundedly rational – perhaps capable of more rationality than people along some dimensions (for example, numerical computation), less along others (for example, using empathy to predict the behavior of other people). But neither people nor computers ever deal with the real world in its complexity; they deal with highly simplified, abstracted and biased conceptions of it, modified by their knowledge and lack of knowledge, by their computational capacities and limitations, and by their shifting foci of attention. Computers will continue to progress in speed and intelligence, but they will not approach, within many orders of magnitude, an ability to plumb the full complexity of the real world, the world to which action must be adapted. They will not reduce our need to understand and to employ the tools of bounded rationality.

Positions in organizations surround their boundedly rational human and computer occupants with very particular and limited environments of information flow, and screen them from most other information. Positions present particular problems to their occupants, and direct their attention to specific facets of those problems; and the information, problems and facets continue to change even as the problems unfold and are dealt with.

So if loyalty, in the emotional/motivational meaning of that term, becomes less important as computers assume a larger responsibility for decisions, identification, in its cognitive aspects, retains its large influence on decision making, on the agenda and on priorities. What we have learned about the consequences of human identification with subgoals and subgroups and of attention focalized by local physical and social environments will be equally relevant for our understanding of computers and of human-computer systems (Simon, 1997, Chapter X and Commentary to chapter).

Agents

The state of the art of computer participation in organizations is advancing rapidly. We are already writing computer programs that behave as agents: that is, as members of collaborating and competing groups. For the past four years, teams of fully automatic robot players, capable of sensing the physical environment, signaling their teammates and responding to such signals, and kicking and passing miniature soccer balls, have been playing robot soccer against competing robot teams in international competition.

So far, they do not play very skillfully, by human standards; no Pele has made his appearance. But their progress is rapid (as is the progress of chess-playing programs that rely increasingly on intelligence and knowledge instead of brute computing force). Some agents of comparable intelligence have been put to work in business organizations (for example, in determining eligibility for credit), but they are not quite as visible to the outside world as the soccer players. Their numbers will continue to increase steadily.

4 THE AVAILABILITY OF INFORMATION

Those of us who have long been in contact with the world of computers, and more recently, with the World Wide Web, know that the abundance of information they supply is a mixed blessing. Information, once a scarce commodity, now buries us under the masses of paper that are a hallmark of the 'paperless society'. Information is no longer the limiting constraint on our communication; the limit is our inability to absorb, even attend to, more than a trickle of the flood of incoming information. The design of organizations, and the role of computers in organizations must be shaped specifically to cope with the plethora of information relative to the scarcity of human (and computer) attention to deal with it.

Computers will not help us deal with the onslaught of information if they themselves are overwhelmed by it. And they will be overwhelmed unless they can protect both themselves and their human colleagues by screening out irrelevant information and extracting relevant information, and by directing the relevant information to those points in the organization where it can be absorbed and used.

When the matter is put in this way, it becomes obvious that computers must be programmed to understand, or must learn to understand, the information they are screening and extracting. They cannot screen information without distinguishing the relevant from the irrelevant, and understanding what the former is relevant to. They cannot extract information without understanding something of the questions whose answers are being sought and the kinds of information that might answer those questions.

To set some practical initial targets, we might say that we need computer information-processing systems at the levels of skill of good human reference librarians. Research on expert behavior in such tasks as making medical diagnoses or playing chess has shown that the expert must learn to recognize several hundred thousand patterns that appear more or less frequently in the situations that occur in professional practice. The expert then must accumulate knowledge, associated with each pattern, that informs and advises what to do when that pattern appears. Human experts and expert computer programs also require knowledge and problem-solving skills that can deal with genuinely new situations that do not fit the familiar patterns.

If computers are to play a serious role in dealing with the information explosion, we must aim at producing computer experts: that is, programs, and the associated knowledge bases and recognition indexes to these knowledge bases, that are capable of performing at this professional level. Already, we have some demonstrations of such programs – to cite some near-random examples – programs for playing chess, making medical diagnoses, discovering reaction paths in chemical reactions, designing electrical equipment and electronic circuits – and the number, and quality, of such examples will increase rapidly. As they appear, corresponding changes will occur in the division of labor between the human and computer components of organizations.

5 THE ARCHITECTURE OF ORGANIZATIONS

Equally important with making sure that computers pursue the proper goals and procedures is structuring our organizations to accommodate human–computer collaboration. Will these new business and governmental organizations look like those with which we have long been familiar, or will they follow quite different principles of architecture? I would like to argue for a fundamental architectural identity with existing organizations, but also for some very specific differences in detail.

The Continuity of Human Organizations

Human organizations of large size have been with us for four millennia or more, exhibiting a remarkable consistency of form throughout that period. Specifically, they have almost universally been hierarchical pyramids with the successive levels of the pyramid connected by authority relations. But preoccupation with the authority relation in organizations can distract our attention from another very fundamental feature of such hierarchies, to wit: each of the elements of the structure performs a particular subset of the organization's functions, while each of the sub-elements, in turn, performs a smaller, and generally more specialized sub-subset of these functions. Organizational hierarchies are arranged to permit a division of work and specialization (Simon, 1996, Chapter 8).

There has been speculation about whether the introduction of computers into our organizations may lead to a sharp break with this ancient architecture. Cannot our new powers of communication (and transport) allow everyone to communicate with everyone else? Cannot we now achieve a 'flattening', perhaps even a 'democratization', of our organizations that was not possible with the limited technology of previous eras? Let us see what our knowledge of the nature of complex systems can tell us about these possibilities. The earlier discussion of limits on human attention should warn us that there is not an easy answer.

Complex Organizations and Near-decomposability

Not every way of dividing tasks into subtasks is conducive to organizational effectiveness. For effectiveness, sets of employees who need to communicate frequently should generally be assigned to the same subunits, so that only a portion of the organization is concerned with the accomplishment of their particular tasks, and other components of the organization can focus on other tasks.

If we look at any particular level of an organization that is designed in this way, we see that there is a large amount of communication among the members belonging to each of the individual units at that level, and a substantially smaller amount of communication between employees who are members of different units at the same level. Organizations preserve this same appearance at all levels except that the time scale of interaction grows longer as we move from the bottom to the top. Lower levels are predominantly concerned with the here and now; higher levels with implications over longer spans of place and time.

As we find more and more computers as participants in communication networks, we may expect the same principles to apply to these hybrid systems, where computers, like people, have limited capacities (although sometimes large) for processing information. This matter will be considered in more detail in the subsection, below, on computers and organizations.

Markets and organizations

This near-decomposability of the communication net, as this correlation between communication and task specialization is called in the technical literature, is only possible if the tasks are assigned to units in such a way that the knowledge that members of each unit need to have about other units is limited mainly to the inputs and outputs of those other units, and largely excludes their internal processes. Of course, this is an ideal that real-world designs can only approximate.

A much-discussed architecture that aims toward this ideal is the market economy. In a system of competitive markets, in its purest form, a large number of units ('black boxes' called 'firms' or 'consumers') receive inputs from other units and send outputs ('goods' and 'services') to other units, usually in exchange for money. Each unit, in the simplified textbook form of the theory, needs to know only the descriptions and prices of relevant inputs, and needs to provide only the descriptions and prices of its outputs. Such a system is the epitome of flat and 'democratic' organization.

Even a glance at the world's real markets, including those that are competitive, shows how far they are from this ideal. It does not begin to describe the information transactions between building contractors and their clients, or physicians and patients, or automobile manufacturers and their parts suppliers, or ... the list goes on indefinitely. So even in markets, there is usually much more communication than the textbook description suggests, although organizations generally do differ from markets both in their coordinating mechanisms (for example, authority relations versus prices), as well as in the amount of communication between units.

In fact, the continually shifting boundary between organizations and markets in any society is strongly influenced by the relative effectiveness, under different circumstances, of contracts and prices as the coordinating mechanisms, versus authority and the employment relation (a very special form of contract). And this effectiveness depends on how clean a break can be made among functions, or conversely, how much communication is needed in order to coordinate their activities.

There is some evidence that our new electronic communication networks are encouraging the substitution of markets for in-house activities of various kinds – encouraging outsourcing of many kinds. Little is known as yet about the precise trade-offs that make this shift advantageous, or the kinds of activities that are being and will be affected by it.

One might conjecture, as an example, that in cases where interfirm contracts involve exchange of elaborate product designs and specifications, the speed of electronic communication might tip the balance in favor of outsourcing. However, many considerations besides electronics determines what it is advantageous to communicate and what it is not. Today, we are much more aware than ever before that a large part of the world's assets, probably most of them, consist of those intangibles we call 'intellectual property'. The business organization has long served as a relatively thief-proof safe for such property, which even patent and copyright laws cannot always protect.

Computers and organizations

Computer scientists, most of them innocent of organization theory, discovered for themselves, soon after the invention of electronic computers, the same principles of organization that were known to the Pharaoh's generals. They called the organization units 'closed subroutines', and invented the law 'no go-to's between subroutines', which is a way of saying, 'no unauthorized communication between units'. Each routine was supposed to need to know only the inputs and outputs of its subroutines and to remain ignorant of their internal processes. In the end, these principles suffered as many qualifications and exceptions from the textbook theory as do real economic markets and business organizations.

As computers grew larger and faster, so that they had to be shared by many users, time-sharing required the conception of organizations that embraced both the machine and its users – a massive injection of 'parallelism'. Of course, the machine was not really parallel, for in each very brief time interval only a single user had access to it; a control structure assigned separate memory allocations to different users and gave them, in rotation, control for short periods of time over the machine's processes, preserving the independence of information and processes between them. There was no communication between users, but a single control structure (operating system) to manage the memory allocation and switching.

At the same time there were many attempts to create genuine parallelism: computers like factories, in which many processes could be carried on at the same time. Most of the early attempts were failures (or when not complete failures, they presented almost insuperable programming difficulties except for very special kinds of 'decomposable' tasks). To overcome these difficulties (and to understand what caused them and the limits on removing them), researchers in parallel programming again reinvented classical organizations: nearly decomposable systems.

The lesson that was learned, to the extent that it has been learned, is that the problems of parallelism have little to do with people or with electronics; they have much to do with the problems that inevitably arise whenever complex tasks are divided up and assigned to different units, whether those units be humans or machines. What can be done in parallel and what cannot is primarily a function of the structure of the tasks themselves (for example, priorities that constrain what has to be done before other things can be done), and only secondarily of the human or machine architecture that is erected to perform them. When there are genuine connections among tasks, mechanisms must be introduced that are capable of coordinating them, seriality of performance with buffer inventories between them being one such mechanism.

The same lesson was learned, many eons earlier, by Nature. In the course of evolution, virtually all of the complex organisms that have evolved (more accurately, almost all that have survived) are nearly-decomposable systems, whose tissues and organs obey much the same rules of organization as the departments in a factory or the subroutines in a computer program, and almost certainly, for much the same reasons. Each organ, served by one or more circulatory systems, is connected to other organs mainly by the inputs required for its own processes, which it receives from them, and the outputs that it provides to them.

There is one additional very important advantage of near-decomposability. It is much easier for an organism to evolve rapidly if the efficiency of a design for any single component is relatively independent of how the other components are designed – if, for example, the architecture of an efficient heart does not depend very much on the architecture of an efficient liver, except, perhaps, for relative scale (Frenken et al., 1999; Simon 1996, p. 205). In this case, increases in fitness from changes in one organ do not cause decreases in fitness in others, an interaction that would obscure natural selection's detection of the improvements in an organ and make evolution very slow and costly.

For human organizations, and computers, the corresponding principle is that improvement of complex designs is easier if each particular component can be redesigned for greater efficiency without modifying the detail of the internal design of other components. (Recall the earlier discussion of independent subroutines.) As Frenken et al. (1999) show, the principle of near-decomposability can play a crucial role in facilitating technological change in industry.

Coordination

The term 'coordination' has been mentioned several times without any indication of just what it means and how it is brought about. In classical organization theory, various arrangements have been much discussed that are, in fact, devices for achieving one kind or another of coordination of specialized units. Among these devices are staff units (as distinguished from 'line' units), and matrix organization.

Staff units include finance, personnel, and legal departments, and others that are not directly involved in the production and marketing of the organization's products. They owe their existence to recognition that if units are specialized along one dimension (say, by function), activities specialized along other dimensions will be scattered through the organization: for example, as suggested above, financial, personnel and legal functions.

When staff functions are brought together, in whole or part, into their own departments, linkages are needed to the line departments that they serve (and control). These needs are met by various kinds of hybrid authority relations ('dotted-line authority') so that the head of a departmental financial section reports, in some manner, both to the department head ('line authority') and to the chief financial officer ('staff authority'). Such compound relations are hard to define unambiguously, and are a common source of organizational power struggles.

When we observe current medical treatments for heart ailments, we conclude that there is a great deal of sometimes contradictory 'dotted-line' control in biological systems as well as in human organizations. The evolutionary explanation for such violations of near-decomposability is far from clear, but perhaps they represent the same kind of Hobson's choice between competing principles of specialization that we are faced with in subdividing human organization.

To the extent that record-keeping functions of finance and personnel departments are computerized, some of the problems of overlapping jurisdiction can be anticipated in the programs that process the records, so that computerization may somewhat alleviate the difficulties that staff organizations create for unity of command. Of course a price is paid in the level of complexity of the computer programs.

Matrix organization is an extension of the staff/line notion, to allow each subunit to belong to two units. It is most often useful when the organization (for example, a construction company, or a construction division within a large company) has large tasks with a beginning and an end, each of which requires an assignment for some period of time of a team of employees from the whole range of functional departments. In matrix organization, such employees have interactions both with their 'home' functional departments and with the current project, for its duration.

A different kind of complication arises in product design. Here, there will typically be a separate design department, but the design process usually involves essential inputs from and interactions with the marketing departments (to ensure customer satisfaction with designs) and manufacturing departments (to ensure economical manufacturability of the design). Here coordination requires involvement, at appropriate times, of members of all of these departments. If marketing and manufacturing are only brought in after the design department has done its initial work, long delays result in the introduction of new products in the market.

All of the aspects of coordination that have been mentioned arise because, despite the nearly-decomposable structure of organizations, the component parts are not wholly independent but have important relations among them. Coordinate devices are aimed at taking account of these relations without destroying the capacity for the nearly-independent components to operate effectively.

6 ORGANIZATIONS IN TRANSITION

It will be apparent from this discussion why we should not expect the introduction of intelligent computers as components in our organizations, side by side with people, to change drastically the basic principles of organizational architecture and design. The principles of design emerged from the fact that division of work and specialization (combined with means of coordination, because the division can never be wholly clean) depend on the structure of tasks more fundamentally than they do on the anatomies or physiologies of people or computers.

Until the laws of organization are amended or repealed, an event that is not visible on the horizon, the ongoing revolution in our organizations will consist mainly of steady movement of the boundary between tasks performed by humans and those performed by computers, without greatly changing the hierarchical structure of organizations, the assignment of specialized tasks to subunits, and the creation of mechanisms of coordination to manage the interactions among units that remain after specialization.

It will be useful, in conclusion, to comment on several specific predictions that are currently abroad about expected changes in business organizations as the results of the introduction of intelligent computers into our society. What changes may emerge in the shape of organizational hierarchies? To what extent can and will new computer software enable collaboration among employees at different locations? What will be the impact of computers that can learn? Let us examine each of these three issues in the light of our previous discussion.

The Shape and Size of Hierarchies

The claim, repeatedly made in this chapter, that hierarchy and near- decomposability are permanent features of organization architecture does not remove the possibility of changes in the breadth/width ratio of the organizational pyramid. There is already some indication that the span of control (the average number of subunits subordinate to each unit) has increased somewhat, so that business organizations are a bit flatter and broader than before.

Our discussion also does not remove the possibility of shifts in the respective roles of organizations and markets in the economy, or changes in the amounts and kinds of information exchange that are involved in market transactions. The current enthusiasm for, and expansion of, e-markets has suggested to some that the boundary between markets and organizations will move substantially in favor of markets. This is not obvious, for the e-markets have already generated large numbers of both new and expanded organizations to operate in them, and it is not at all clear to what degree these developments favor enhanced competition or enhanced opportunity for large organizations to exploit monopolized advantages.

What we can say with certainty (the certainty associated with past events, but seldom with the future) is that the whole course of the industrial revolution, from Adam Smith to the present, has been characterized by a continual substitution of large organizations for the markets and putting-out system that prevailed in Smith's time in many or most industries. As to the future ... ?

Groupware

There has been much discussion of, and some experiment with, groups of people working together electronically, without the need for physical propinquity in an office; and a number of pieces of computer software undertake to manage the sharing and modification of files by members of a group. Again, we must remind ourselves that this electronic technology does not repeal the laws of task organization. When more than one person is able to alter a file, procedures must be established that specify when that modification is permissible and what information must be provided to group members about successive states of the file and its current status.

The vexing problems must also be dealt with that arise from differences in the software languages that various computers used by group members employ. The thousands of natural languages that have long made a Tower of Babel of our world have now been joined by a comparable number of computer languages that frequently make e-mail and other network communications unreadable.

The same problems of differences in languages and other computer software arise to a considerable degree when we try to maintain documents over the years in the face of continuing rapid change in software. Increasingly, it becomes difficult to read records that are more than two or three years old. Both of these problems of software compatibility must be solved before we can talk of replacing paper by electronic records. Even sulfite-paper books are immensely durable objects (with lives of about 50 years) compared with today's computer records.

Computer Learning and Organizational Change

The concerns with modernization and updating extend far beyond the problems just mentioned, of computer languages and software systems. In addition to the preservation of all kinds of organization memory we must modify memories to incorporate change and innovation. In our organizations of past years, manned by humans, the human life span and the even briefer tenure of personnel in particular organizations and organizational positions within them automatically forced us to preserve important records in hard copy, and to renew organizational memories by training new and old employees. The training process also provided the opportunity to introduce change. So the human learning of both continuing and new employees has been the chief mechanism for updating the organization's knowledge.

When important records and processes are consigned to computer programs, the problem of updating reasserts itself. Economies achieved by replacing human information processing and decision-making procedures by computers are easily wiped out by the costs of updating, and the associated costs of documenting software so that updating is even possible, much less economical.

As early as 1955, Westinghouse engineers wrote Fortran programs for automatically designing motors, generators and transformers that had to be adapted, from standard types, to customer specifications. These programs could handle about 70 percent of the orders requiring such adaptation of standard items, and produced designs as good as or better than those produced by college-trained engineers. Although there was great satisfaction with the programs, within about 15 years they were no longer in use. The cost of updating them, not only to incorporate improvements in design methods but also to maintain their compatibility with constantly changing software, ate up their whole economic advantage.

By now these kinds of experiences have made it clear that the scope of computer applications will be limited by the costs of software obsolescence and updating unless and until computers can be provided with learning programs that will permit programs to be modified more or less continually, and over substantial numbers of years.

Experiments in machine learning are as old as artificial intelligence. An early impressive program that learned to play the game of checkers to a higher and higher skill level was built and tested by Arthur Samuel in the 1950s. In the late 1980s and early 1990s machine learning became a recognized specialization within artificial intelligence, and journals in machine learning have been published ever since. At the present time, machine-learning systems are being developed (and applied) that employ a wide range of learning procedures: connectionist nets, Bayesian and other probabilistic learning systems, adaptive production systems, and genetic algorithms among them.

It is probably not an exaggeration to say that most of the human learning strategies known to psychologists now have their computer counterparts. But this does not mean that we now have systems capable of grasping the structure of complex computer software sufficiently deeply and accurately to improve and update it automatically. This is a major task, which has to be accomplished if we are to remove software inflexibility as a major barrier to the extension of the uses of computers in organizations.

7 ORGANIZATIONS, COMPUTERS AND THE SOCIAL SYSTEM

This chapter has been primarily concerned with the structure and operation of individual organizations, but has also commented upon one important feature of the broader social system: the shifting boundaries between markets and organizations. There is a whole set of additional questions that might be raised about the impact of computers and electronic communications on the structure of society as a whole. These questions cannot be addressed in any detail here, but I should like to indulge in a few reflections.

What Do Organizations Have to Do with the World's 'Big' Problems?

The pattern of my tea leaves does not depict a sharp picture of the future – in fact, it gives me hardly any picture at all – but it does seem to identify some basic features of the social system and its structural problems that are likely to serve as a rather stable backdrop to any scenario that can play itself out. Our task, after all, is not to predict the future but to make it – or less heroically, to seek to move it in desirable directions.

First, there are the global problems that will not magically go away, and which must be addressed, if not tomorrow, then the next day. Two of these head the list: first, how to design a future that reconciles human needs for resources with the limited capacity of the Earth's environment to provide them; second, how to design human societies and a world society that will provide peaceful and equitable allocations of resources and prevent dangerous and possibly irreversible accumulations of power. Neither of these problems has anything obvious – to do with computers or communications, except to the extent that the rapid growth of international communication and interaction forces us to seek solutions that are global in scope and institutional arrangements that permit such solutions to be negotiated and enforced while retaining the substantial freedom of people and their societies to define their own ways of life and futures. We cannot wish away, or cut apart with markets, the real and massive world interdependencies that exist.

The search for problem solutions will depend upon our having effective organizations, and may be accelerated by the assistance that powerful, and preferably intelligent, computing systems can provide to human intelligence. We shall surely need all the intelligence we can get to design acceptable solutions. Those solutions will have to incorporate a sufficient understanding of the natural environment to map a sustainable future, and to contain our population growth within limits that are compatible with maintenance of that environment. Even more difficult, they will have to incorporate social games that all can win, to replace the zero-sum games that characterize so much human interaction, at all scales and levels, in the world today.

The history of this planet gives us no reason to believe that these solutions can be reached solely through market forces. In fact, in the recent past, the most evident change of social structure has been the growth of multinational corporations, no doubt accelerated by the advance of electronic communications, rather than growth in international markets. This change is causing severe problems for the autonomy of governments, problems that call urgently for the restructuring of our weak and inadequate system of international organizations. If my previous analysis is even approximately correct, effective organizations in a modified system will largely have architectures similar to those of the organizations that we know today. The entry of electronics, we have seen, does not alter the basic principles of organizational design.

The System of Organizations-cum-Markets

Let me put the matter in more general, institutional, terms. The twentieth century has seen two Utopian visions of the organization of human society: the Marxist view of central planning (at least until government 'withers away') and the capitalist–libertarian view of societies regulated by free markets with minimal intervention of government to maintain the rule of law. The collapse of the Soviet Union was widely (if briefly) interpreted as a more or less total victory for the second Utopia. Of course, as events quickly revealed and as the history of the past two centuries had already clearly shown, neither extreme alternative is viable.

We live in a world in which organizations are fully as prominent as markets, and where the two are inextricably interwoven. Specialization without organization is impractical whenever sets of activities are not mutually independent but require substantial coordination. And governmental, as well as profit-seeking, organizations are essential as one means for dealing with a host of externalities, both positive and negative, that do not easily yield to simple Coasean treatment by means of prices and changes in the boundaries of legal rights and duties.

The illusion that organizations are collections of building blocks that are easily disassembled and reassembled has been fostered by the frequency of merger and reorganization in today's industrialized world. What has not too often been noticed is that the blocks that are reassembled are quite large blocks, often united only by an investment function of reallocating profits from the units that earned them to other units that promise better future returns. That is basically what 'conglomerate' and 'divisionalized' organization has meant. Peculiarly, reallocation of profits is a function that was traditionally performed by markets (and banks), but in the past half century has been increasingly absorbed by manufacturing organizations. Perhaps the increasing availability of e-markets could reverse this trend, with a consequent reduction in the average size of organizations (but a multiplication of their numbers), but I do not yet see the logic that would predict such a change.

Are Organizations the Drivers of Change?

In most readings of the history of industrialization (including the modernization and industrialization of agriculture), the main driving force has been new technology, and underlying that, new science. I find those readings persuasive. To be sure, modern organizations are also a new (or at least improved) technology, but based upon practical experience more than on science. But their role has been that of adaptive responses, enabling us to make economic and social applications of the new science and technology; they can hardly be regarded as first causes for industrialization.

New knowledge produced by science continues to be a prime mover. The past half-century has introduced two new tools for bringing about fundamental social change – both of them potentially of enormous power, and correspondingly great capacity to do good or harm. One is molecular biology, and especially genetic and developmental biology. The other is artificial intelligence. During the past several decades, we have all become increasingly aware of the potentials of these two bodies of scientific knowledge for good and harm.

Biological knowledge can potentially lead to increases in human intelligence and (probably even more important) improvements in human character and disposition, but only to the yet very uncertain extent to which we can deal with the ethical and psychological problems that are inherent in any attempts to modify our own (and each other's) natures biologically. I have only to mention a word like 'cloning' to conjure up all of the problems. The new technologies will magnify many times the difficulties we already experience whenever we have to decide to what extent our human educational institutions will undertake to change the moral values of their students.

The prospects for artificial intelligence and electronic communications arouse a range of concerns almost identical with those roused by microbiology, extending from protecting privacy and freedom to distributing fairly and productively the world's scarce resources.

On a more optimistic note, we see that the problems listed above are not different from the problems we face today, and would face tomorrow even without technological change. They are the permanent problems associated with the human condition, and we have at least reason to think that we shall have, as we move into the future, more powerful tools than we have today to help us deal with them.

The Outlook

To sum up our discussion of trends in organization and decision making, we can ask: what has changed and what remains the same?

With some confidence, we can assert that 'human nature' remains the same; but our knowledge of human nature has changed considerably in the past half-century, and continues to change as psychological research and computer simulation of the human mind casts new light on the processes of problem solving, decision making and learning. During this same half-century, the appearance on the scene of electronic computers and their rapidly expanding roles in our organizations is the most dramatic change that has taken place and that continues to unfold.

In our fascination with change, we must keep firmly in mind that the structures of effective organizations are at least as much shaped by the tasks they are designed to perform as by the nature of the human and computer resources available for performing them. The permanence of most of these tasks constitutes the most important reason for predicting that the organizations of the future will, in most respects, resemble the organizations of the past and present. They will retain the familiar shape of a hierarchy of semi-independent components and subcomponents. The pyramids of Egypt can symbolize for us both the shape and the venerability of this form of organization, which goes back at least to those same early Egyptian times, and perhaps beyond.

Finally, I have suggested that scientific knowledge, and in particular the scientific knowledge that makes artificial intelligence possible, can play an important, if modest, role in enabling us to tackle the problems that we must address to transform our world into one that can continue to meet our needs, and those of the other living things that cohabit our planet with us. Organizations, with great enhancement of their computer components, will occupy a very prominent position in that world, and we shall have no difficulty in recognizing them, for their requirements for both specialization and coordination will maintain their familiar hierarchical shape.

REFERENCES

Cyert, R.M. and J.G. March (1962), *A Behavioral Theory of the Firm*, Englewood Cliffs, NJ: Prentice-Hall.

Frenken, K., L. Marengo, and M. Valente (1999), 'Interdependencies, near-decomposability and adaptation', Working Paper 1999-03, Department of Economics, University of Trento, Trento, Italy.

Kleindorfer, P.R., H.C. Kunreuther and P.J. Schoemaker (1993), *Decision Sciences*, Cambridge, UK: Cambridge University Press.

Leavitt, H.J. and H. Bahrami (1988), *Managerial Psychology*, Chicago, IL: University of Chicago Press.

March, J.G. and H.A. Simon (1958), *Organizations*, New York: Wiley.

Simon, H.A. (1947, 1957), *Administrative Behavior*, New York: Macmillan (4th edn, 1997, New York: Free Press).

Simon, H.A. (1996), *The Sciences of the Artificial*, 3rd edn. Cambridge, MA: MIT Press.

20. Empirical microeconomics: another perspective

Oliver E. Williamson*

1 INTRODUCTION

What was obvious to many of us at the time has become even more evident since: the Graduate School of Industrial Organization at Carnegie-Mellon (then Carnegie Tech) had assembled an extraordinary group of faculty and students in the 1950s and early 1960s and the PhD program was an inspiring experience. Studies by the Ford Foundation and the Carnegie Foundation record some of the programmatic successes.[1] Nobel Prizes and other awards for research that was done by the Graduate School of Industrial Administration (GSIA) faculty at Carnegie also speak to the intellectual vitality of those years.[2] As a student of Carnegie, I can only marvel at the project.

Of the many distinguished faculty at Carnegie, none cast a larger shadow than Herbert Simon. Everything seemed to be within his purview – as he made contributions to economics, political science, sociology, organization theory, statistics, philosophy, cognitive science and the list goes on. Then and since, he has expressed concerns that economic theories of the firm and of consumer choice worked off of implausible cognitive assumptions. Both were deeply problematic as a consequence. The common response that a theory should be judged not by the reasonableness of its assumptions but by the 'comparison of its predictions with experience' (Friedman 1953, p. 9) does not wash, moreover, if the resulting predictions are few in number and often bear a weak relation to the phenomena of interest, and if the empirical tests are limited and/or ambiguous or contradictory.

Simon continues his criticisms of orthodoxy in the recent book, *An Empirically Based Microeconomics* (1997). The recent criticisms, moreover, go beyond orthodoxy to indict the New Institutional Economics (NIE), of which transaction cost economics is a part.

Without question, transaction cost economics (TCE) is different from the behavioral economics program that flourished at Carnegie in the late 1950s/early 1960s. But while TCE is 'more neoclassical', it nevertheless relates to the Carnegie project in many respects – or at least that is my position (as developed elsewhere and repeated here). Also, contrary to Simon, transaction cost economics is *an empirical success story*. I have no illusions, however, that mine is the last word. TCE always stands to benefit from good critics, of which Simon has been one and Mark Granovetter (1985) is another. The dialogue will continue and the outcome will be decided by others.

The Simon critique of orthodoxy and of TCE is briefly summarized in Section 2. The ways in which the TCE perspective draws on and differs from the work of Simon and Carnegie are reviewed in Section 3. As set out in Section 4, TCE and Simon/Carnegie deal with different phenomena and are often complementary. The empirical research accomplishments of TCE are summarized in Section 5. Concluding remarks follow.

2 THE SIMON CRITIQUE

Simon is a self-described 'scold' of orthodoxy, going back at least to *Models of Man* (1957b). Although some mainline economists immediately took issue (Solow 1958), many have recognized that uncritical use of heroic assumptions (especially hyperrationality) by orthodoxy could lead to implausible constructions. Not only has Simon received recognition and awards from economists – witness his publications in leading economics journals, his presentation of the prestigious 1978 Richard T. Ely Lecture before the American Economics Association and the award of the Nobel Prize in Economics in 1978 – but there is growing appreciation for the need to find ways to model bounded rationality (Rubinstein 1998; Kreps 1999; Maskin and Tirole 1999). Simon nevertheless despairs that the applied and theoretical efforts of economists will truly come to terms with bounded rationality (Simon 1991, 1997; Rubinstein 1998, Ch. 11).

Core Position

If 'Nothing is more fundamental in setting our research agenda and informing our research methods than our view of the nature of the human beings whose behavior we are studying' (Simon 1985, p. 303), then social scientists should be prepared to name the key attributes of human actors. Both the condition of cognition and self-interestedness need to be addressed.

Simon early took the position that the hyperrationality assumption out of which orthodox economics works should be supplanted by the less demanding cognitive condition of bounded rationality – according to which human actors are intendedly rational but only limitedly so. The issue of self-interest has received less attention, but Simon has described it as 'frailty of motive' (1985, p. 303) and has also featured docility, identification, and loyalty in describing human behavior in organization (Simon 1991, 1997).

Theory and Evidence

Simon distinguishes three uses of economic theory: curiosity; a guide to the management and operation of firms; and a guide to the operation of the economy (1997, p. 63). Achieving these three goals (ibid.):

> requires building an adequate, empirically based, theory of bounded rationality. ... The knowledge that economic actors possess and do not possess, the computations that economic actors can make and cannot make must not enter as ad hoc assumptions ... but must be shaped and tested by the sharpest empirical methods that we can devise.

Although both the 'experience-based tests' on which Adam Smith relied and more recent econometric tests are instructive, neither are judged to be adequate to the sharpness needs to which Simon refers. He therefore recommends that these be supplemented by turning to and testing 'the validity of some or all of the specific assumptions that are built into the models as well as the models as wholes' (Simon 1997, p. 23). Laboratory experiments and 'empirical studies that observe the behavior of consumers or of business firms directly' are what he proposes (Simon 1947, p. 23).

He observes in this connection that 'When we look at organization in the real world, we find much more structure and complexity than is hinted at in the theory of the firm, whether in its classical or its "New Institutional" versions' (Simon 1997, p. 38).[3] That orthodoxy is remiss in dealing with 'real-world' organizations is widely conceded. But Simon's view that the TCE and orthodox theories of the firm are two peas in a pod comes not only as a surprise to me but to many others as well – which includes not only NIE economists but Kenneth Arrow, Avinash Dixit, Oliver Hart, Bengt Holmström, David Kreps, Jean Tirole and the list goes on. That is because there are truly fundamental differences between the TCE theory of the firm as governance structure (which is an organizational construction) and the orthodox theory of the firm as production function (which is a technological construction). I return to these issues in Section 3.

Simon's contention that TCE has been remiss in empirical respects – it being his view that, awaiting empirical testing, 'the new institutional economics and related approaches are acts of faith, or perhaps piety' (Simon 1991, p. 27) – is likewise one with which I (and others) take exception. Empirical research in behavioral economics and in transaction cost economics is examined in Sections 4 and 5.

The comparative study of firms and markets requires that the strengths and limitations of each be identified and explicated. Simon describes the strength of firms as follows: 'The need for coordination, along with the possibility of creating organizational loyalties are perhaps the two most important factors that give organizations an advantage over markets in many situations, and that accounts for the large role of organizations in the economic activity of a society like ours' (Simon 1997, p. 49). That is instructive, but a predictive theory of economic organization would advise on when and why the needs for coordination and the support of organizational loyalties *vary* with the circumstances, whereupon an empirical research program focused on the key features could be undertaken. (The possibility that some of these features reside in the microanalytic attributes of transactions is nowhere admitted, whence none are identified or explicated by Simon.)

Also, if all feasible modes of organization are flawed (Coase 1964; Demsetz 1969; Williamson 1996), then symmetrical attention to the *strengths and weaknesses* of each is needed. Simon is silent on the weaknesses of firms. More generally, Simon's propensity to operate at a very high level of generality helps to explain Ariel Rubinstein's remark that 'The book is missing a chapter with a detailed example where Simon demonstrates the implementation of his approach, starting with data about human reasoning, and ending with its valuable conclusions' (1999, p. 1712).

Simon does, however, invite us to 'consider the hypothesis that failures in skills of organizing and in enlisting organizational loyalties play a major role in Russian economic difficulties today, and very likely played such a role before *perestroika* began. Organizations are at least as large a part of the story of Russian disorganization and failure as are markets' (Simon 1997, p. 45). He also discusses the comparative performance of private ownership, non-profits and government agencies, where he interprets the evidence on the efficiency of government providers of public utilities (such as water, electric power and communications services) as compared with private (usually regulated) firms as inconclusive (ibid., p. 49). This lack of a 'consistent relation between forms of ownership and their operational efficiency' is explained by the fact that 'direct participation in profits plays only a small role in motivating the loyalty of employees to business and other organizations' (ibid., p. 50). He therefore expresses skepticism over the need for the privatization of firms in moving from a centralized to a market economy (ibid., p. 51).

Conclusion

Simon concludes that the economics profession needs to be more attentive to the needs of the many students who view 'mathematical tools with distrust and deplore the necessity of devoting their research time to formalisms that they regard as mainly sterile' (1997, p. 90).[4] Inasmuch as young scholars 'desire to explore new paths, including the path of empirical research ... we need to revise the curriculum so that students of economics will be exposed to the range of empirical techniques that I have described' (ibid., p. 91).

Some of the earlier work at Carnegie to which Simon makes favorable reference includes (i) an examination of how the policy recommendations of business executives responding to the same set of facts are strongly influenced by their training and the business functions (marketing, production, legal, and so on) to which they were assigned (Dearborn and Simon 1958), (ii) a study of the size distribution of firms, which takes the form of a Pareto distribution and can be generated by the assumption that the growth of a firm is proportional to its current size (Ijiri and Simon 1977), (iii) a study of the compensation of executives, according to which span of control and fairness considerations are combined to predict that the salaries of executives will vary directly with the logarithm of the number of subordinates (Simon [1947] 1957a), and (iv) a series of studies of the specific business practices of individual business firms, of which the department store pricing study by Richard Cyert and James March (1963) is an example.

Examples from cognitive and experimental psychology include tests of the postulates of rationality by Daniel Kahneman and Amos Tversky (1973), which demonstrate that human actors are poor Bayesians, and the use of verbal protocols and computer simulation of thinking to produce 'an extensive and well-tested theory of human cognitive performance over a wide range of tasks', both laboratory and practical (Simon 1997, p. 80). Other empirical work to which Simon makes favorable reference include the laboratory experiments on markets by Vernon Smith (1991) and his colleagues, experimental game theory, Alfred Chandler's studies of business story (1962), and survey techniques by George Katona (1951) and others. Econometric tests of macroeconomic theory using quantitative data are also mentioned, with special emphasis on the limits of the data and the estimating procedures (Simon 1997, pp. 23, 72–4, 96–7).

3 THE TRANSACTION COST ECONOMICS PERSPECTIVE

Transaction cost economics can be variously described. I describe it as an interdisciplinary joinder of law, economics and organization theory, where the organization theory is predominantly of a Simon/Carnegie kind and economics is the first among equals. Although TCE and Carnegie may divide on how closely to hew to the 'rational spirit' to which Arrow refers (1974, p. 16), there is no question but that TCE draws extensively on organization theory – although some have questioned the value added.[5]

I begin with a sketch of the Carnegie contributions on which TCE rests and then turn to some of the significant respects in which Carnegie and TCE differ.

Carnegie Origins

First and foremost, Carnegie featured interdisciplinary social science. Even if economics is the queen of the social sciences (opinions differ), no single social science is able, by itself, to explain the range of complex organizational phenomena with which Carnegie was concerned.

As I have described it elsewhere, the imperative at Carnegie was to be disciplined, be interdisciplinary and have an active mind (Williamson 1996). Rather than pronounce 'This is the law here', Carnegie encouraged the student of organization to ask 'What's going on here?'. Not only does TCE ask that question but it is furthermore indebted to Carnegie by subscribing to the following: (1) bounded rationality; (2) process matters; (3) near-decomposability; (4) discrete structural analysis; and (5) adaptation. Also, TCE works out of (6) weak-form selection. Consider each.

1. *Bounded rationality* TCE subscribes to the proposition that human behavior is intendedly rational but only limitedly so (Simon [1947] 1961, p. xxiv). Economic actors are thus assumed to be attempting effectively to cope but lack the wits to maximize.

   To concede bounded rationality is one thing. What to make of it is another. TCE holds that the principal ramification of bounded rationality for the study of economic organization is that *all complex contracts are unavoidably incomplete*. 'New questions' are swept in by the move from complete to incomplete contracts. Posing and answering these new questions is where the distinctive TCE contributions reside (Arrow 1987, p. 734).
2. *Process matters* If organization, like the law, has a life of its own, then intertemporal process transformations that predictably recur need to be discovered and the ramifications for organizational design wrung out. Unintended consequences and the imperatives of bureaucracy (March and Simon 1958) are among the more important conditions of which the student of economic organization needs to be apprised. Failing to be alert to the chief intertemporal propensities of organization, students and practitioners will fail to make allowance for unrecognized costs and benefits. As Robert Michels puts it in the context of oligarchy, 'nothing but a serene and frank examination of the oligarchical dangers of democracy will enable us to minimize these dangers' (1962, p. 370). This serenity and candor apply to the study of organization more generally.
3. *Near-decomposability* The now widely recognized importance of modularity was anticipated by Simon's work on nearly-decomposable systems. The main ideas here are these (Simon 1962, p. 474):

   > (a) in a nearly decomposable system, the short-run behavior of each of the component subsystems is approximately independent of the short-run behavior of the other components; (b) in the long-run, the behavior of any one of the components depends in only an aggregative way on the behavior of the other subcomponents.

   Near-decomposability is a widely observed design principle in complex social systems and reflects respect for the cognitive overload (bounded rationality) and ease of disclaiming responsibility (opportunism) in fully connected systems. Given near-decomposability, the microanalytic mechanisms of governance, rather than an overarching theory of organization, become the object of analysis, which is broadly congruent with Jon Elster's dictum that 'explanations in the social sciences should be organized around (partial) *mechanisms* rather than (general) *theories*' (1994, p. 75; emphasis in original).

4. *Discrete structural* Simon's idea of discrete structural, as against marginal, analysis is also one to which TCE subscribes. Because alternative modes of organization differ in kind rather than degree, marginal analysis plays a less significant role in the choice among alternative modes of governance than it does in the analysis of market equilibria (Simon 1978, p. 6).

   Not only does TCE view alternative modes of governance – markets, firms, bureaus, and so on – in discrete structural terms, but it takes three additional steps. It asks (i) what are the principal attributes with respect to which governance structures differ, (ii) how is each generic mode of organization (market, hybrid, firm, bureau, and so on) defined in terms of these attributes and (iii) what resulting strengths and weaknesses accrue to each generic mode (Williamson 1991). The rudiments of a predictive theory of comparative economic organization reside in the answers to these.
5. *Adaptation* TCE also subscribes to the view that 'Interdependence by itself does not cause difficulty if the pattern of interdependence is stable and fixed. For, in that case, each subprogram can be designed to take into account all the subprograms with which it interacts' (March and Simon 1958, p. 159). This argument is akin to one expressed earlier by Frank Knight, to the effect that, but for unanticipated disturbances (uncertainty), organization reduces to repetition ([1921] 1957, pp. 267–8).

   The central problem of organization on which TCE focuses is that of adaptation, of which two kinds are distinguished: autonomous and cooperative. The first of these was featured by Friedrich von Hayek (1945), who emphasized spontaneous adaptation realized through markets. Chester Barnard, by contrast, emphasized cooperative adaptation of a 'conscious, deliberate, purposeful' kind (1938, p. 4), working through administration.[6] TCE makes provision for adaptations of both kinds and holds that alternative modes of governance differ in their capacities to deliver autonomous and cooperative adaptations (Williamson 1991).
6. *Weak-form selection* TCE relies in a general, background way on competition to perform a sort between more and less efficient modes of governance. As against selection of the fittest, it subscribes instead to weak-form selection: 'in a relative sense, the *fitter* survive, but there is no reason to suppose that they are *fittest* in any absolute sense' (Simon 1983, p. 69; emphasis in original).

In all six of these respects, TCE is an exercise in close reasoning (which I take to be the Carnegie tradition) as opposed to the tight reasoning of mathematical economic theory – which routinely sacrifices plausibility in the name of logical consistency and mathematical rigor. Albeit worthy values, 'not everything that is logically consistent is credulous' (Kreps 1999, p. 125). TCE, like Carnegie, gives greater priority to plausibility[7]

Interestingly, Tjalling Koopmans also has a broad (Carnegie-like) conception of the economic enterprise. Thus Koopmans describes the four 'skills within the economics profession' as follows: (i) detailed knowledge of the realities of economic life, thereby to link observations with concepts, (ii) the logical and mathematical skills of reasoning from postulates to conclusions, (iii) subtle procedures of statistical inference to perform empirical testing and

(iv) 'most important of all, the appraisal of postulates with regard to their plausibility, their realism and the relevance or usefulness of the conclusions they lead to' (Koopmans 1957, p. 145). As discussed elsewhere (Williamson 2000), the close reasoning out of which TCE works is acutely attuned to the detailed knowledge to which Koopmans refers, is very conscious about the plausibility of postulates and the relevance of conclusions, invites empirical testing, and encourages logical and mathematical reasoning. Also, in the spirit of Koopmans, this last (full formalism) does not trump all others (Kreps 1999).

Some Differences

The significant reliance of TCE on Carnegie notwithstanding, there are also differences. The most consequential of these are (1) choice and operationalization of the unit of analysis, (2) the main lesson for economic analysis of bounded rationality, (3) the description of self-interest, (4) the condition of foresight and (5) the role of informal organization. By reason of these differences, TCE gives different and more prominent attention to contract. One of the consequences is that TCE and Simon/Carnegie often deal with different microanalytic phenomena and inform different issues of public policy.

1. *Unit of analysis: decision premise or transaction* Both the choice of a unit of analysis and the subsequent dimensionalization thereof are important to a progressive research agenda. Of these two steps, naming a unit is easier than dimensionalization, whence the latter is often scanted. Simon, for example, notes that while the concept of role has been proposed as a sociological unit of analysis, 'the term has never been given sufficiently precise definition' (1957b, p. xxx). He recommends instead that the decision premise be made the unit of analysis and avers that 'Behavior can be predicted ... when the premises of the decision are known (or can be predicted) in sufficient detail' (ibid.). Although subsequent work on human problem solving by Simon (in collaboration with Alan Newell) is in this spirit, in that the human actor is postulated to behave as an information processing system (Newell and Simon 1972), the systematic application of the decision premise as the unit of analysis has yet to produce a widely applicable theory of organization to which predictions about firm and market organization accrue and the data have been applied.

   A more composite variant of the decision premise is to treat the 'routine' – the decision rules and procedures – as the unit of analysis. Not only do the computer simulation models of *A Behavioral Theory of the Firm* (Cyert and March 1963) operate out of routines, but Richard Nelson and Sidney Winter make the bold claim that routines are to the evolutionary theory of the firm what genes are to the biological evolutionary theory (1982, p. 14). That sounds very fundamental, and may prove to be precisely that. To date, however, neither *A Behavioral Theory of the Firm* nor evolutionary economic theory has seriously addressed itself to the daunting challenge of dimensionalizing the routine.

   The unit of analysis out of which transaction cost economics works is the transaction – which John R. Commons features in his overarching statement on the study of economic organization: 'The ultimate unit of activity ... must contain in itself the three principles of conflict, mutuality, and order. This unit is a transaction' (1932, p. 4). Not only does TCE view governance as the means by which to infuse order, thereby to mitigate conflict and realize mutual gains, but it takes the transaction to be the basic unit of analysis and names asset specificity (in its various forms), uncertainty, and frequency as the critical dimensions with respect to which transactions differ.

This effort to dimensionalize transactions in combination with the aforementioned effort to name the principal attributes with respect to which governance structures differ become the basis for the discriminating alignment hypothesis, to wit: transactions, which differ in their attributes, are aligned with governance structures, which differ in their cost and competence, so as to effect a transaction cost economizing result. The large and growing body of empirical research discussed in Section 5 involves the application of this hypothesis to a wide range of phenomena.

2. *Bounded rationality: satisficing or incomplete contracting* Simon holds that 'the replacement of the goal of *maximizing* by the goal of *satisficing*, of finding a course of action that is good enough ... is an essential step in the application of the principle of bounded rationality' (1957b, pp. 204–5; emphasis in original). Such a reformulation appeals to reason and has broad analytical ramifications. Simon's 1955 article, 'A behavioral model of rational choice' – which appeared in the *Quarterly Journal of Economics* and has been described by Simon as his 'chief epistle to the economists' (1985, p. 293) – uses a satisficing setup and potentially heralded a new era. Alas, the apparatus out of which satisficing works is very cumbersome, which helps to explain Robert Aumann's conclusion that the satisficing approach is not presently broadly applicable (Aumann 1985). Awaiting satisficing apparatus that is easier to implement, economists can be thought of as analytical satisficers: they use a short-cut form of analysis (maximizing) that often qualifies as 'good enough.'[8]

   As hitherto indicated, TCE holds that the chief lesson of bounded rationality for the study of economic organization is that all complex contracts are unavoidably incomplete. Faced with contractual incompleteness, the question is how best to cope when unanticipated disturbances arise. Such disturbances push the parties to an incomplete contract off of the contract curve, whence inefficiency arises for which relief is sought. But while inefficiency invites its own demise, that can be costly. Among other things, the appropriate corrective action can be delayed or defeated by a propensity to bargain over the disposition of the potential gains (see the discussion of self-interest, which follows). The upshot is that an issue of efficient governance is posed. If, conditional on the attributes of transactions, some governance structures have superior adaptive properties to others, then the mitigation of contractual hazards through the *ex ante* choice of a better mode of governance will yield efficiency gains. The discriminating alignment hypothesis thus applies. In contrast with satisficing, numerous refutable implications accrue thereto.[9]

3. *Self-interest: frailty of motive or opportunism* My interpretation of Simon's description of self-interest seeking as 'frailty of motive' (Simon 1985, p. 303) is that most people will do what they say (and some will do more) without self-consciously asking whether the effort is justified by expected discounted net gains. If they slip, it is a normal friction and often a matter of bemusement. The proposition that routines describe the behavior of most individuals most of the time contemplates (non-strategic) benign behavior.

   But while accurate descriptions of what is going on 'most of the time' are plainly essential, much of what is interesting about human behavior in general and organizations in particular has reference not to routines but to exceptions. Indeed, once good routines have been developed, the chief role of management is to deal with the exceptions. Such exceptions arise from contractual incompleteness in combination with the disturbances referred to above, the effects of which are to push the parties to an agreement off of the contract curve. *Strategic considerations* – which arise by reason of information asymmetries, bilateral dependencies, weaknesses of property rights, the costliness of court enforcement of contracts, and so on – will now come into play if, rather than frailty of motive, *opportunism* is the operative condition.

To be sure, opportunism is an unflattering behavioral assumption. Serenity and candor nevertheless require us to entertain the possibility that foreseeable contractual hazards will be missed or suppressed by frailty of motive. Opportunism, I submit, takes us into the deep structure of contract and organization in ways that frailty of motive does not. Accordingly, even if frailty of motive describes day-to-day activity most of the time, candid reference to opportunism serves to uncover strategic issues that are ignored only at peril.

Rather, therefore, than pose the issue as frailty of motive (routines) *or* opportunism (strategic behavior), provision needs to be made for *both*. Note, moreover, that the odium associated with opportunism is relieved by the main lesson of opportunism, which is not to celebrate this condition but to mitigate it. Recall that Michels's Iron Law of Oligarchy had its origins in his efforts to understand democracy: 'it is [hierarchical] organization which gives birth to the dominion of the elected over the electors, of the mandatories over the mandators, of the delegates over the delegators. Who says organization, says oligarchy' (Michels 1962, p. 365). One response to unwanted oligarchical outcomes would be to eschew all proposals to introduce democracy in favor of the status quo, but that is extreme. A more constructive and deeper lesson is to make allowance for all such predictable regularities at the outset, whereupon it may be possible to mitigate foreseeable oligarchical propensities at the initial design stage.

That very same lesson applies more generally, whence an important part of the study of economic organization is to look ahead, perceive hazards and fold these back into the organizational design – in all significant contractual contexts whatsoever (intermediate product market, labor market, capital market, and so on). Attenuating the *ex post* hazards of opportunism through the *ex ante* choice of governance is central to the transaction cost economics exercise. Michels had it right: nothing but a serene and frank examination of the hazards of opportunism will enable us to mitigate these hazards.

4. *Foresight: myopic or farsighted* Degrees of foresight can be placed on a continuum. At one extreme is myopia – as postulated by *A Behavioral Theory of the Firm* (Cyert and March 1963): local search, trial-and-error learning, fire-department model of firm behavior. At the other extreme is the comprehensive contracting model, which entails 'a single gigantic once-for-all forward 'higgle-haggle' in which all contingent goods and services (i.e., all goods and services at each possible time-cum-environmental condition) are bought and sold once and for all now for money payments made now' (Meade 1971, p. 166). TCE postulates 'feasible foresight', which is located in between.

The proposition that 'The future influences the present ... [may seem] like a violation of the laws of causality, but what is really meant is that our expectations of the future affect what we do in the present' (Arrow 2000, p. 12; emphasis omitted). George Shultz's reflection on the importance of his training in economics is pertinent: 'my training in economics has had a major influence on the way I think about public policy tasks, even when they have no particular relationship to economics. Our discipline makes one think ahead, ask about indirect consequences, take note of variables that may not be directly under consideration' (Shultz 1995, p. 1). Similar skills have value elsewhere. As the businessman Rudolf Spreckels once put it, 'Whenever I see something badly done or not done at all, I see an opportunity to make a fortune'. Alert practitioners, consultants and public policy analysts who are alert to the lessons of experience and who possess the skills for and practice the art of feasible foresight will frequently be able to implement discriminating alignment by looking ahead, recognizing potential hazards and choosing governance structures appropriately.[10] That is the TCE construction.[11]

Again, a forced choice is not needed. Theories of the firm that deal with short-run operating behavior will feature myopia, while theories that are more concerned with periodic governance alignments will invoke foresight.

5. *Informal organization* Barnard argued that formal and informal organization always and everywhere coexist (1938, p. 20) and that informal organization contributes to the viability of formal organization in three significant respects:

> One of the indispensable functions of informal organization in formal organizations ... [is] that of communication. ... Another function is that of maintaining the cohesiveness in formal organizations through regulating the willingness to serve and the stability of objective authority. A third function is the maintenance of the feeling of personal integrity, of self-respect, and independent choice. (Barnard 1938, p. 122)

The informal effects to which Barnard refers occur spontaneously, as a consequence of or in conjunction with formal organization. Because firm and market organization differ in these respects, informal differences should be taken into account in the decision to use one or the other. According to Simon, organizational loyalties are one of the two most important factors that give firms an advantage over markets (the other being coordination). 'When we speak of organization as having high morale, a principal criterion we have in mind is the loyalty and devotion of the employees to the organizational goals' (Simon 1997, p. 44). He goes on to observe that 'Loyalty has not only a motivational component – internalization of the organization's goals – but also a cognitive component' (ibid.). The latter has its origins in bounded rationality, whereupon the enterprise is factored into manageable parts in which 'an employee ... acquires the goals appropriate to the position' (ibid.). 'Because organizational attachments have this powerful cognitive component, as well as a motivational one, it is customary to speak of organizational *identification* rather than loyalty' (Simon 1997, p. 45).

The benefits of identification notwithstanding, there is also a 'dark side' to the subgoal pursuit that arises from functional specialization and career concerns: the overarching goals of the organization can be and sometimes are subverted. No less of an authority than Philip Selznick – who has a deep and abiding interest in identification – treats 'Michels' theory about democratic organization ... as a *special case* of the general recalcitrance of the human tools of action. The tendency for goals to be subverted through the creation of new centers of interest and motivation *inheres in all organizations*' (Selznick 1950, p. 162; emphasis added). In that event, provision for beneficial identification and subversive subgoal pursuit are both needed.

The TCE response to loyalty/identification comes down to this: (i) yes, these considerations are unarguably important; (ii) awaiting a more complete description of the mechanisms through which they work, they remain vague; and (iii) because loyalty and identification can have both benefits and costs, efforts to ascertain the factors that influence the net effects are needed. In the end, considerations of loyalty and identification should be incorporated within the economizing calculus.[12]

4 PHENOMENA OF INTEREST

Both Carnegie and TCE subscribe to bounded rationality and advance the proposition that organization matters. Both deal with more microanalytic phenomena than orthodoxy. As is apparent from the foregoing, however, Carnegie and TCE also differ from one another in consequential ways. Some of the phenomena of interest to Carnegie are therefore different from those dealt with by TCE.

By way of locating these phenomena on a continuum, Carnegie is interested in very micro phenomena (individual decision making), some issues of price and output, very few issues of firm and market organization (and public policy that pertains thereto), and some macroeconomic issues. TCE, by contrast, had its origins with the vertical integration problem and antitrust lessons that accrue thereto, thereafter studying the governance of contractual relations more generally – including the lessons for regulation/deregulation, corporate governance and corporate finance, labor market organization, vertical market restrictions and public policy more generally (Dixit 1996).

As compared with Carnegie, TCE has focused on *semi*-microanalytic contractual phenomena, many of them of long-standing interest and puzzlement among applied microeconomists.

Microanalytics

Individual decision making

According to Simon, 'The most important data that could lead us to an understanding of economic processes and to empirically sound theories of them reside inside human minds. ... [Accordingly] we must seek to discover what went on in the heads of those who made the relevant decision' (Simon 1997, pp. 70–71). One example is the aforementioned study by Dearborn and Simon (1958) of the reactions of 23 executives enrolled in an executive training program. The basic finding was that executives responded to the case study that was presented to them very much in line with their functional responsibilities – legal, accounting, production, marketing, and so on. This 'is a vivid demonstration of how strongly identifications by particular functions ... focus attention on some phenomena and away from others' (Simon 1997, p. 64).

Experimental tests of the postulate of rationality, along the lines of work by Kahneman and Tversky (1973), and laboratory studies of human problem solving, as in Newell and Simon (1972), also operate at the level of the individual. Simon summarizes as follows: experimental tests show that 'people do not make consistent judgments about uncertain events, violating the axioms of utility maximization and frequently violating the laws of probability' (1997, p. 78); and computer simulations of cognitive process 'provide little evidence ... [for] utility maximization' (ibid., p. 81).

These are noteworthy findings, but evolutionary psychologists have begun to challenge the way in which probability events have been posed in the laboratory. Whereas the usual practice is to model the mind as a general-purpose problem solver, evolutionary psychology works differently (Cosmides and Tooby 1994, p. 328):

> By identifying and modeling the adaptive problems humans faced during their evolution, researchers can make educated guesses about the designs of the complex computational devices the human brain embodies, and about many of the specific design features they required to be able to solve these

> problems. Armed with these models, researchers can then design experiments that can detect and map the features of these complex devices – features that no one would otherwise have thought to test for.

That it makes a difference whether we view the mind as a specialized problem solver, as against a general-purpose system (using methods drawn from logic, mathematics and probability theory), is evident from alternative ways of posing probabilistic problems, some of which are more transparent and arguably relate more to evolutionary success than do others (see especially the exchange between Gerd Gigerenzer (1996) and Kahneman and Tversky (1996)). For example, many individuals perform better when probabilities are expressed in frequentist rather than point estimate terms. Leda Cosmides and John Tooby observe in this connection that (1996, pp. 15–16):

> What was available in the environment in which we evolved was the encountered frequencies of actual events – for example, that we were successful 5 out of the last 20 times that we hunted in the north canyon. Our hominid ancestors were immersed in a rich flow of observable frequencies that could be used to improve decision-making, given procedures that could take advantage of them ...
>
> There are advantages to storing and operating on frequentist representations because they preserve important information that would be lost by conversion to a single-event probability.

That is, five out of 20 contains more information and is easier to update than is 0.25. Cosmides and Tooby thereafter 'suggest that the human mind may contain a series of well-engineered competences capable of being activated under the right conditions, and that a frequentist competence is prominent among these' (1996, p. 17). Given that 'framing' plays such a prominent role in laboratory experiments, the puzzle is that experimental psychologists framed their experiments in non-intuitive (point estimate) ways.

The possibility that many of the limitations of individuals are relieved by specialization also warrants remark. If mind is a scarce resource, then organizing so as to deploy this scarce resource to best advantage has a lot to recommend it. Edwin Hutchins expresses 'surprise that the division of cognitive labor has played such a very minor part in cognitive anthropology' (1995, p. 176) and subsequently observes that 'the cognitive properties of groups are produced by interaction between structures internal to individuals and structures external to individuals ... [and that] the performance of cognitive tasks that exceed individual abilities is always shaped by a social organization of distributed cognition' (1995, p. 262). The division of cognitive labor is also underdeveloped in economics. Mean, variance, variety and group interaction effects are all relevant. The obvious propositions here are these: (i) very complex problems can sometimes be broken down into 'subassemblies', within which specialization can take place and composite solutions worked up (March and Simon 1958, p. 151); (ii) upon recognizing that individuals differ in raw ability and expertise, better than average results can be realized by conferring 'leadership' (through delegation or imitation) on those with greater ability; and (iii) because cognitive ability can take various forms, such variations should be factored in.

Transactions/governance

TCE is predominantly concerned with choice of governance structures by organizations (some of which are very large) rather than by individuals. Economies of specialization thereby arise. As compared with individual consumers, intermediate product market transactions differ in the following respects: (i) firms can be presumed to be more nearly on a parity in information respects and can employ specialists (for example, engineers, lawyers) to represent their interests more effectively; (ii) considerations of differential risk aversion are of second-order importance; (iii) end games aside, reputation effects can be presumed to be more effective; and (iv) experienced as they are with a wide variety of transactions to which differential hazards accrue, firms can be presumed to craft contractual safeguards in differential degree.

The canonical problem of vertical integration out of which TCE works is illustrated by the simple contractual schema shown in Figure 20.1. Thus assume that a good or service can be supplied by either of two alternative technologies. One is a general-purpose technology, the other a special-purpose technology. The special-purpose technology requires greater investment in transaction-specific durable assets and is more efficient for servicing steady-state demands. Contractual complications prospectively arise when there is a need to adapt to disturbances.

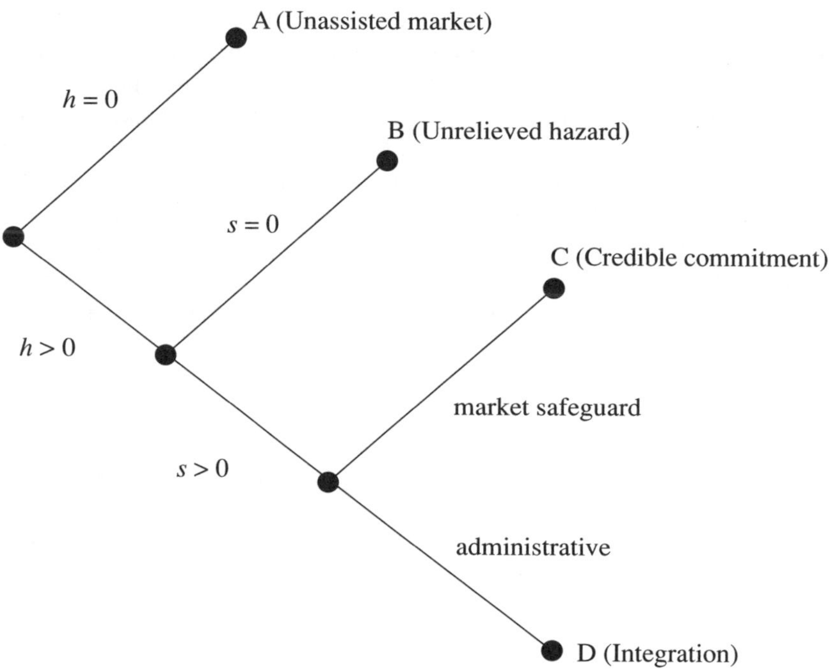

Figure 20.1 Simple contracting schema

Using h as a measure of contractual hazards, transactions that use the general-purpose technology are ones for which $h = 0$. If instead transactions use the special-purpose technology, an $h > 0$ condition exists. Assets here are specialized to the particular needs of the parties. Productive values would therefore be sacrificed if $h > 0$ transactions were to be prematurely terminated. A bilateral dependency condition applies to such transactions. Parties have an incentive to devise safeguards to protect investments for transactions of the latter kind. Let s denote the magnitude of any such safeguards. An $s = 0$ condition is one in which no safeguards are provided; a decision to provide safeguards is reflected by an $s > 0$ result.

Safeguards can take either of two forms. One would be to provide interfirm contracts with added support: penalties to deter breach are introduced, added information disclosure is provided and specialized dispute settlement machinery (for example, arbitration) is devised.

This is the credible interfirm commitment option. A second would be to take transactions out of markets and organize them under unified ownership within which hierarchy (to include fiat) is used to effect coordination.

Node A corresponds to the ideal transaction in law and economics: there being an absence of dependency ($h = 0$), such transactions benefit from the safeguard of competition. Node B poses contractual hazards, in that specialized investments are exposed ($h > 0$) for which no safeguards ($s = 0$) have been provided. Such hazards will be recognized by farsighted players, who will price out the implied risks. Nodes C and D are those for which additional contractual support has been provided ($s > 0$), either in the form of contractual safeguards (node C) or unified ownership (node D).

That an outside supplier will supply on better terms (supply at a lesser price) at node C than node B is not because it has received 'simple assurances' that the buyer will adapt cooperatively should an adverse state realization materialize during the contract implementation interval. Rather, suppliers are viewed as hard-headed businesspeople who will respond to what they perceive to be *credible commitments*, of which the use of hostages to support exchange is an example (Williamson 1983).

In the event that problems of crafting credible interfirm commitments are perceived to be especially great, the transaction may be taken out of the market and organized under unified ownership (vertical integration) instead. In consideration, however, for the added bureaucratic costs that accrue upon taking a transaction out of the market and organizing it internally, internal organization is usefully thought of as the organization form of last resort: try markets, try hybrids and have recourse to the firm only when all else fails. Node D, the firm, thus comes in only as higher degrees of asset specificity and added uncertainty pose greater needs for cooperative adaptation.

The schema, moreover, applies not merely to intermediate product market contracts but much more generally. Friedrich von Hayek's assessment applies: 'whenever the capacity of recognizing an abstract rule which the arrangement of those attributes follows has been acquired in one field, the same master mould will apply when the signs for those attributes are evoked by altogether different elements' (1967, p. 50). Labor markets, capital markets, regulation/deregulation, and, more generally, any issue that arises as or can be restated as a contracting problem are variations on a theme.

Whereas the unifying theme for TCE is that of discriminating alignment, for Simon it is bounded rationality. The latter has broad scope and, possibly for that reason, does not name a canonical problem to which variations on a theme can be referred.

Theory of the Firm

If, as Arrow has observed, 'Any standard theory, not only the neoclassical, starts from the existence of firms' (1999, p. vii), then would-be theories of economic organization should be expected to name the theory of the firm out of which they work.

1. *Carnegie* Simon's theory of the employment relation (1951) relates closely to Coase's (1937) earlier treatment. That has been instructive but, awaiting further work, some of which is in progress (Baron and Kreps 1999), the employment relation is more in the nature of an incipient theory of the firm.

Two other theories that have Carnegie origins or connections are the 'behavioral theory of the firm' and the more recent work on 'competence'. Both differ from orthodoxy.

Harold Demsetz contends that 'It is a mistake to confuse the firm of economic theory with its real-world namesake. The chief mission of neoclassical economics is to understand how the price system coordinates the use of resources, not to understand the inner workings of real firms' (Demsetz 1983, p. 377). Attention is thus focused on supply and demand, prices and output.

Because Carnegie was plainly interested in the inner workings of real firms, it might be expected to de-emphasize price and output. The first research commitment listed by Cyert and March, however, reads as follows (1963, p. 2; emphasis in original): '*Focus on a small number for key economic decisions made by the firm*. In the first instance, these were price and output decisions; subsequently they included internal allocation and market strategy decisions'.

As against the orthodox prescription to set prices on the basis of marginal costs and demand elasticities, Cyert and March maintain that they are set by simple routines. Their department store pricing study correctly predicts prices 'to the exact penny' for 384 out of 404 items, which is astonishing (Cyert and March 1963, Ch. 7). Yet despite their view that their computer model 'lends itself to further elaboration and testing' (ibid., p. 148), few economists or organization theorists have followed that empirical lead.

The reason for this, I believe, is that few economists are interested in exact prices. Rather, economists are more interested in comparative statics: what changes in the parameters will move prices how and why? Awaiting a display of why they should be interested in pricing routines that predict to the exact penny, such results simply do not change the way in which economics gets done.

As I have discussed elsewhere (Williamson 1999), the core competence perspective draws inspiration from Edith Penrose's influential book on *The Theory of the Growth of the Firm* (1959) and Joseph Schumpeter's earlier work on *Capitalism, Socialism, and Democracy* (1942), especially as it relates to technical and organizational innovation. George Richardson's article on 'The organization of industry' (1972) is seminal. The Cyert and March book (1963) makes the case for a 'realism in process' approach to the study of organization, as does Richard Nelson and Sidney Winter's book on *An Evolutionary Theory of Economic Change* (1982). All have had a significant influence on the strategy literature, the overarching theme of which is the importance of process. It is not obvious, however, how to bring the more important processes together in a coherent way. Not only is process analysis hard to do, but there are many important processes. What are the priorities?

Awaiting operationalization, the concept of core competence suffers from a tautological reputation (Porter 1994; Mosakowski and McKelvey 1997). As matters stand presently, the competence perspective relies primarily on success stories to make its case.

2. *TCE* TCE views the firm as a governance structure (which is an organizational construction) rather than as a production function (which is a technological construction). Also, rather than

> consist primarily of giving new answers to the traditional questions of economics – resource allocation and the degree of utilization ... it consists of [asking and] answering *new questions*, why economic institutions have emerged the way they did and not otherwise; it merges into economic

> history, but brings *sharper nanoeconomic ... reasoning to bear than as been customary.* (Arrow 1987, p. 734; emphasis added)

One of the lessons of Carnegie is that firms have structure and that this structure arises for some reason (Arrow 1999, p. vii). Always and everywhere, TCE examines governance structures comparatively, whereby each discrete mode of governance is described as a syndrome of attributes to which distinctive strengths and weaknesses accrue. The decision to take a transaction out of the market and organize it hierarchically follows from the logic of the simple contractual schema set out above. More generally, the discriminating alignment hypothesis invites and has benefitted from empirical testing.[13]

Public Policy Toward Business

General

The governance structure approach to economic organization has numerous ramifications for public policy toward business: vertical integration, vertical market restrictions, non-standard forms of contracting more generally (to include exchange agreements, reciprocity, take-or-pay agreements), corporate governance and corporate finance, labor market organization, the limits of legal centralism, aspects of economic development and reform, the modern corporation (both domestic and multinational) and public policy toward business (antitrust and regulation/deregulation) more generally. Note that these non-standard practices are very different from the resource allocation issues with which the orthodox theory of the firm was concerned (Demsetz 1983). Neither individually nor collectively does orthodox appeal to price-theoretic 'wrinkles' – double-marginalization, price discrimination, differential risk aversion – deal with these matters in a systematic way.

TCE has responded to this lapse by examining non-standard and unfamiliar organization and contractual practices through the lens of transaction cost economizing. Simon (and Carnegie) express little interest in public policy as it relates to such matters.

Public and private

March and Simon's famous book on *Organizations* opens as follows: 'This book is about the theory of formal organizations. ... The United States Steel Corporation is a formal organization; so is the Red Cross, the corner grocery store, the New York State Highway Department' (March and Simon 1958, p. 1). They thereafter observe that 'Transactions that take place within organizations, far more than in markets, are preplanned and precoordinated' and that 'the high specificity of structure and coordination within organizations ... marks off the individual organization as a sociological unit comparable in significance to the individual organism in biology' (ibid., p. 4).

Differences among private for-profit firms, non-profits, regulated firms, public bureaus, and so on get short shrift in this quest for a common theory of formal organizations. Simon's views that public and private firms are indistinguishable in supplying public utility services (1997, p. 49), that the 'managers of charitable organizations are subject to the same discipline as the managers of the profit-making firm' (ibid., p. 50), and that 'in the transfer from centralized planning to a market economy it is not obvious to what extent the production organizations need to be privatized' (ibid., p. 51) are plainly in the common theory tradition.

TCE, by contrast, views markets, firms, regulation, and public bureaus as discrete structural modes of organization that differ in their attributes. Because, moreover, transactions also differ, the choice of mode will be *contingent on the transactions to be organized* (Williamson 1991, 1999).

TCE furthermore holds that public utility transactions are intrinsically difficult to organize (as Milton Friedman has put it, there is 'no good solution' for natural monopoly (1962, p. 128)), whence the lack of sharp differences between public and private operation of public utilities is not altogether surprising (although, upon making provision for variation in the institutional environment – polity, judiciary, bureaucracy – differences appear (Levy and Spiller 1994, 1996)). By contrast, a finding that public and private ownership has no impact on the manufacture of personal computers or the operation of grocery stores would be a big surprise to TCE (if not to Simon). Relatedly, TCE holds that competition in both product and capital markets does have disciplinary consequences, whence charitable organizations will be reserved for a subset of transactions different from profit-making enterprise (Hansmann 1996).

Finally, TCE concurs with Oskar Lange that 'the real danger of socialism is that of a bureaucratization of economic life' (1935, p. 109). Lange, however, relegated bureaucratization to the field of sociology rather than economic theory and bureaucratic differences between capitalism and socialism were neglected by economists for the next 50 years. Given an institutional environment in which property and contract enjoy legal and constitutional supports, the idea that privatization encourages economizing (discourages bureaucratizing) is now broadly conceded.[14]

Macroeconomics

One of the reasons that Simon advances for 'building an adequate, empirically based, theory of bounded rationality' is to better 'understand and guide the operation of the economy' (1997, p. 63). Neoclassical theory, in his judgment, is 'grossly inadequate ... for either understanding the events that occur in the whole economy or providing a basis for macroeconomic policy' (ibid., p. 89). I do not disagree, but a unified theory from micro through macro is very ambitious.

This is not, however, to say that we cannot make piecemeal progress in this direction. Persistent application of the comparative contractual approach to economic organization holds promise for such a purpose. My paper with Michael Wachter on 'Obligational markets and the mechanics of inflation' (Wachter and Williamson 1978) is illustrative of how this can be done. But there has been little effort to date – by Wachter, me, or others – to follow this up with empirical work.

5 EMPIRICAL TCE

Bengt Holmström and Jean Tirole once described the theory of the firm as a field where 'the evidence/theory ratio ... is currently very low' (1989, p. 126). Sam Peltzman (1991) holds a similar view of industrial organization more generally. Simon's statement that, awaiting empirical testing, TCE was an act of faith or perhaps piety (1991, p. 27) is broadly in this spirit.

Those who are closer to empirical TCE (have *done* empirical work) have a different opinion, Thus Scott Masten remarks that

> [Whereas] Ronald Coase could justifiably lament the dearth of research on the organization of industry in 1972 ... the transaction cost literature today [1995] contains scores of empirical studies on the topics

> Coase viewed as central to our understanding of industrial organization – studies of the allocation of activities among firms, of the structure of contractual arrangements between firms, and of the role and extent of participation by government agencies in industry. (1995, p. xi)

It could have been otherwise, but the theory and evidence display a remarkable congruity: 'Progress in the application and testing of transaction cost economics can only be described as phenomenal' (ibid.). Subsequent empirical surveys – by Howard Shelanski and Peter Klein (1995), Bruce Lyons (1996), Keith Crocker and Scott Masten (1996) and Aric Rindfleisch and Jan Heide (1997), where this last focuses on empirical applications of transaction cost economics to marketing – agree.

A still more recent review of the relative contributions of agency theory and TCE to the empirical literature on contracting also bears remark, The theoretical TCE and agency theory literatures both took shape in the 1970s and both have undergone refinements since. But where TCE has advanced numerous refutable implications, agency theory is notable for 'its failure to generate testable hypotheses ... [or even] to account for ... the more basic features of real world contracts' (Masten and Saussier 2000, p. 10). Not only are there few empirical tests of agency theory, but 'evidence from transaction cost economics, where variables of interest in the [two] theories overlap, offers little support for agency theory' (ibid.).[15]

A survey of empirical TCE currently in progress (Boerner and Macher 2000) estimates that the cumulative number of empirical TCE studies has grown from 200 in 1994 to over 600 in the year 2000. Econometric refinements, moreover, are being introduced as this work has progressed. To be sure, transaction cost economics, like everything else, will benefit from more and better empirical work. I have no hesitation, however, in declaring that transaction cost economics is an empirical success story. Judged comparatively, 'this empirical work is in much better shape than much of the empirical work in industrial organization generally' (Joskow 1991, p. 81).

It is furthermore noteworthy that those who have done this empirical TCE work have often collected *original* data specifically attuned to the microanalytic phenomena in question. Progress in science is normally attended by the collection of new and original data (Kuhn 1970), yet that is demanding work – for which TCE empirical researchers deserve enormous credit. But for this empirical research, TCE would merely join the list of plausible but conjectural theories of firm and market organization.[16]

6 CONCLUSIONS

TCE aspires to be both a 'rational spirit' and a 'Carnegie spirit' construction. Economizing on transaction costs is on the rational spirit side of the ledger. Feasible foresight, sometimes buttressed by learning from own-experience and that of others, also supports the idea of efficient alignment (as does weak form selection). Furthermore, TCE addresses itself to many of the long-standing puzzles of orthodoxy. It is one thing to tell economists that their framework is self-limiting. It is another to tell economists something different and consequential about phenomena that are of interest to them. Economists being very pragmatic people, the latter will get their attention.

Carnegie has had a powerful influence on TCE efforts to understand non-standard structures and practices for which orthodoxy was poorly suited (Coase 1972). For one thing, TCE subscribes to bounded rationality, whence focuses on incomplete contracting. Also, and related, TCE eschews hypothetical ideals in favor of feasible alternatives, all of which are flawed and need to be examined comparatively. Such comparative institutional analysis invites the description of alternative modes of governance not in technological but in organizational terms. Given the limits of legal centralism, much of the action resides in the mechanisms of private ordering, to which the lessons of organization theory apply. Also, like Carnegie, TCE moves to a more microanalytic unit of analysis. But the unit of analysis for TCE is the transaction, rather than the decision premise or the routine.

Although TCE does not attempt to implement the program described by Simon, I would nevertheless describe it as an empirically based microeconomics. It deals always and everywhere with feasible modes of organization; it yields numerous refutable implications on a wide range of real-world issues; the data have been generally corroborative. I am confident that those who have been working the transaction cost economics domain will continue their modest, slow, molecular, definitive' efforts – piling block upon block until the value added cannot be denied.

NOTES

* This chapter has benefitted from the helpful remarks of James March and Mie Augier, for which I am grateful, It will not go unnoticed that the chapter deals almost entirely with Simon, vis-à-vis transaction cost economics. The larger Carnegie project, in which *A Behavioral Theory of the Firm* (Cyert and March 1963) played a central role, is dealt with only in part and often only in passing. To address this larger project would require a much longer and more ambitious study. Suffice it to observe here that four of the central ideas of the 'Carnegie tradition' – bounded rationality, intra-firm conflict and strategic action, rule-based action and organizational learning – have been important to modern economic thinking about the firm. All four are featured prominently by Cyert and March (1963). Of these four, transaction cost economics works principally off of the first two (but concedes merit to all, Williamson 1999).

1. The Ford Foundation study was done by Robert Aaron Gordon and James Howell (1959). The Carnegie Foundation study was done by Franklin Pierson (1959).
2. Nobel Prizes in Economic Science were awarded to Herbert Simon (1978), Franco Modigliani (1985), Merton Miller (1990) and Robert Lucas (1995) for work they did while on the faculty at the GSIA.
3. Although economics is an expansive enterprise, 'Any standard economic theory, not just neoclassical, starts from the existence of firms' (Arrow 1999, p. vii).
4. These views differ from those he took much earlier (Simon 1957b, pp. 89–90) and presumably reflect his assessment of the way in which mathematical social science has taken shape over the period from 1957 to 1997.
5. See the exchange between Richard Posner (1993) and myself (1993) on this issue.
6. Recall that cooperation is one of the two chief advantages that Simon ascribes to organizations in relation to markets (1997, p. 49).
7. For a broader discussion of close reasoning, see Williamson (2000).
8. To be sure, short-cut forms of analysis can be and are sometimes used uncritically. See Tjalling Koopmans (1957, pp. 140–41). Overuse of maximizing, like overuse of natural selection, is a chronic hazard. Both work well in some circumstances but break down in others, whence there is a need to *delimit* the use of such methods to the 'appropriate subset'.
9. Neither Aumann's (1985) negative assessment of satisficing nor Arrow's judgment that TCE has made headway where the Simon agenda and older-style institutional economics did not (1987, p. 734) are dispositive, but both Aumann and Arrow are thoughtful students of economic organization.
10. As Richard Dawkins observes, it is the 'capacity to simulate the future in imagination ... [that saves] us from the worst consequences of the blind replicators' (1976, p. 200).
11. Learning through experience and imitation are also relevant. Both benefit from a reflective rather than myopic interpretation of events.
12. As matters stand presently, my efforts to curtail the excesses of calculativeness to which zealous economic reasoning leads have mainly been limited to 'the economics of atmosphere' (Williamson 1975, pp. 37–9, 79; 1996, pp. 270–72).

13. Whereas Simon has given prominent attention to the size distribution of firms (Simon and Bonini 1958; Ijiri and Simon 1977), TCE has been concerned with the boundary of the firm. Both are interesting questions. As between the two, boundary issues are closer to the subject of firm structure.
14. Interestingly, Richard Pipes holds that 'the very principles of Communism violated everything that we have learned from sociobiology, anthropology, and the psychology of human nature, the building blocks of every social order', whereupon he focuses on 'the abolition of private property ... [as] the quintessence of [the] movement' (1996, p. 38).
15. Michael Whinston made similar observations in comparing TCE with the 'property rights theory of the firm' (2000).
16. There being many plausible theories, there is a need to sort the sheep from the goats. That is accomplished by asking each candidate theory to advance refutable implications and ascertain whether the data are corroborative or not. Theories that cannot pass this test are eventually relegated to the history of economic thought.

REFERENCES

Arrow, Kenneth (1974), *The Limits of Organizations*, New York: Norton.

Arrow, Kenneth (1987), 'Reflections on the essays', in George Feiwel (ed.), *Arrow and the Foundations of the Theory of Economic Policy*, New York: New York University Press, pp. 727–34.

Arrow, Kenneth (1999), Foreword, in G. Carroll and D. Teece (eds), *Firms, Markets and Hierarchies*, New York: Oxford University Press, pp. vii–viii.

Arrow, Kenneth (1999), 'Technical information and industrial structure', in G. Carroll and D. Teece (eds), *Firms, Markets, and Hierarchies: The Transaction Cost Economics Perspective*, New York: Oxford University Press, pp. 121–55.

Arrow, Kenneth (2000), 'Economic transition: speed and scope', *Journal of Institutional and Theoretical Economics*, **156** (1), 9–18.

Aumann, R. (1985), 'What is game theory trying to accomplish?', in K. Arrow and S. Honkapohja (eds), *Frontiers of Economics*, Oxford: Basil Blackwell, pp. 28–78.

Barnard, C. (1938), *The Functions of the Executive*, Cambridge, MA: Harvard University Press.

Baron, James N., and David M. Kreps (1999), *Strategic Human Resources: Frameworks for General Managers*, John Wiley & Sons.

Boerner, C. and J. Macher (2000), 'Transaction cost economics: a review and assessment of the empirical literature', Unpublished manuscript.

Chandler, Alfred (1962), *Strategy and Structure*, Cambridge, MA: MIT Press.

Coase, Ronald H. (1937), 'The nature of the firm', *Economica N.S*, **4**, 386–405.

Coase, Ronald H. (1964), 'The regulated industries discussion', *American Economic Review*, **54** (May), 194–7.

Coase, Ronald H. (1972), 'Industrial Organization: A Proposal for Research', in V.R. Fuchs (ed.), *Policy Issues and Research Opportunities in Industrial Organization*, New York: National Bureau of Economic Research, pp. 59–73.

Commons, John R. (1932), 'The problem of correlating law, economics and ethics', *Wisconsin Law Review*, **8**, 3–26.

Cosmides, Leeda and John Tooby (1994), 'Better than rational: evolutionary psychology and the invisible hand', *American Economic Review*, **84** (2), 327–32.

Cosmides, Leeda and John Tooby (1996), 'Are human beings good intuitive statisticians after all?', *Cognition*, **58**, 1–73.

Crocker, Keith and Scott Masten (1996), 'Regulation and administered contracts revisited: lessons from transaction cost economics for public utility regulation', *Journal of Regulatory Economics*, **9** (1), 5–39.

Cyert, Richard M. and James G. March (1963), *A Behavioral Theory of the Firm*, Englewood Cliffs, NJ: Prentice-Hall.

Dawkins, Richard (1976), *The Selfish Gene*, New York: Oxford University Press.

Dearborn, D. and Herbert Simon (1958), 'Selective perception: a note on the departmental identification of executives', *Sociometry*, **21**, 140–44.

Demsetz, Harold (1969), 'Information and efficiency: another viewpoint', *Journal of Law and Economics*, **12** (April), 1–27.

Demsetz, Harold (1983), 'The structure of ownership and the theory of the firm', *Journal of Law and Economics*, **26** (2), 375–90.

Dixit, Avinash (1996), *The Making of Economic Policy: A Transaction Cost Politics Perspective*, Cambridge, MA: MIT Press.

Elster, Jon (1994), 'Arguing and bargaining in two constituent assemblies', Unpublished manuscript. Remarks given at the University of California, Berkeley.

Friedman, Milton (1953), *Essays in Positive Economics*, Chicago, IL: University of Chicago Press.

Friedman, Milton (1962), *Capitalism and Freedom*, Chicago, IL: University of Chicago Press.

Gigerenzer, Gerd (1996), 'On Narrow Norms and Vague Heuristics: A Reply to Kahneman and Tversky', *Psychological Review*, **103** (3), 592–96.

Gigerenzer, G. (1996), 'On Narrow Norms and Vague Heuristics: a rebuttal to Kahneman and Tversky', *Psychological Review*, **103** (3), 582–91.

Gigerenzer, G. and V. Hoffrage (1995), 'How to improve Bayesian reasoning without instruction: frequency formats', *Psychological Review*, **102** (4), 684–704.

Gordon, R. and J. Howell (1959), *Higher Education for Business*, New York: Columbia University Press.

Granovetter, Mark (1985), 'Economic action and social structure: the problem of embeddedness', *American Journal of Sociology*, **91** (November): 481–501.

Hansmann, H. (1996), *The Ownership of Enterprise*, Cambridge, MA: Harvard University Press.

Hayek, Friedrich von (1945), 'The use of knowledge in society', *American Economic Review*, **35** (September), 519–30.

Hayek, Friedrich von (1967), *Studies in Philosophy, Politics and Economics*, London: Routledge & K. Paul.

Holmström, Bengt and Jean Tirole (1989), 'The theory of the firm', in R. Schmalensee and R. Willig (eds), *Handbook of Industrial Organization*, New York: North-Holland, pp. 61–133.

Hutchins, E. (1995), *Cognition in the Wild*, Cambridge, MA: MIT Press.

Ijiri, Y. and Herbert Simon (1977), *Skew Distributions and the Sizes of Business Firms*, New York: North-Holland.

Joskow, Paul (1991), 'The role of transaction cost economics in antitrust and public utility regulatory policies', *Journal of Law, Economics and Organization*, **7** (Special Issue), 53–83.

Kahneman, Daniel and Amos Tversky (1973), 'On the psychology of prediction', *Psychology Review*, **80**, 237–51.

Kahneman, Daniel and Amos Tversky (1996), 'On the reality of cognitive illusions: a reply to Gigerenzer's critique', *Psychological Review*, **103**, 582–91.

Katona, G. (1951), *Psychological Analysis of Economic Behavior*, New York: McGraw-Hill.

Knight, Frank [1921] (1957), *Risk, Uncertainty and Profit*, New York: Harper & Row.

Koopmans, Tjalling (1957), *Three Essays on the State of Economic Science*, New York: McGraw-Hill.

Kreps, David (1999), 'Markets and hierarchies and (mathematical) economic theory', in G. Carroll and D. Teece (eds), *Firms, Markets, and Hierarchies: The Transaction Cost Economics Perspective*, New York: Oxford University Press, pp. 121–55.

Kuhn, Thomas (1970), *The Structure of Scientific Revolutions*, 2nd edn, Chicago: University of Chicago Press.

Lange, Oskar (1938), 'On the Economic Theory of Socialism', in Benjamin Lippincott (ed.), *On the Economic Theory of Socialism*, Minneapolis: University of Minnesota Press, pp. 55–143.

Levy, Brian and Pablo Spiller (1994), 'The institutional foundations of regulatory commitment', *Journal of Law, Economics and Organization*, **9** (Fall), 201–46.

Levy, Brian and Pablo Spiller (1996), 'A framework for resolving the regulatory problem', in Levy and Spiller (eds), *Regulatory Institutions and Commitment: Comparative Studies of Telecommunications*, Political Economy of Institutions and Decision Series, New York: Cambridge University Press, pp. 1–35.

Lyons, Bruce (1996), 'Empirical relevance of efficient contract theory: inter-firm contracts', *Oxford Review of Economic Policy*, **12** (4), 27–52.

March, James G. and Herbert A. Simon (1958), *Organizations*, New York: Wiley.

Maskin, Eric and Jean Tirole (1999), 'Unforeseen contingencies and incomplete contracts', *Review of Economic Studies*, **66** (1), 83–114.
Masten, Scott (1995), 'Introduction', in O.E. Williamson and S.E. Masten (eds), *Transaction Cost Economics, Volume 2: Policy and Applications*, Aldershot, UK and Brookfield, VT: Edward Elgar pp. xi–xxii.
Masten, Scott and S. Saussier (2000), 'Econometrics of contracts: an assessment of developments in the empirical literature on contracting', Unpublished manuscript.
Meade, J.E (1971), *The Controlled Economy*, London: Allen & Unwin.
Michels, R. (1962), *Political Parties*, Glencoe, IL: Free Press.
Mosakowski, Elaine and Bill McKelvey (1997), 'Predicting Rent Generation in Competence Based Competition', in A. Meene and R. Sandes (eds), *Competence-Based Strategic Management*, Chichester: John Wiley, pp. 65–85.
Nelson, R. and S. Winter (1982), *An Evolutionary Theory of Economic Change*, Cambridge, MA, Harvard University Press.
Newell, A. and H. Simon (1972), *Human Problem Solving*, Englewood Cliffs, NJ: Prentice-Hall.
Peltzman, S. (1991), 'The *Handbook of Industrial Organization*: Review Article', *Journal of Political Economy*, **99** (1), 201–17.
Penrose, Edith (1959), *The Theory of the Growth of the Firm*, New York: John Wiley.
Pierson, F. (1959), *The Education of American Businessmen: A Study of University-College Programs in Business Administration*, New York: McGraw-Hill.
Pipes, R. (1996), 'Human nature and the fall of communism', *Bulletin of The American Academy of Arts and Sciences*, **54** (January), 38–53.
Porter, Michael (1994), 'Toward a Dynamic Theory of Strategy', in R. Rumelt, D. Schendel and D. Teece (eds), *Fundamental Issues in Strategy: A Research Agenda*, Boston, Harvard University Press, pp. 423–61.
Posner, R. (1993), 'The New Institutional Economics meet law and economics', *Journal of Institutional and Theoretical Economics*, **149** (March), 73–87.
Richardson, George (1972), 'The Organization of Industry', *Economic Journal*, **82**, pp. 883–96.
Rindfleisch, A. and J. Heide (1997), 'Transaction cost analysis: past, present and future applications', *Journal of Marketing*, **61** (4), 30–54.
Rubinstein, A. (1998), *Modeling Bounded Rationality*, Cambridge, MA: MIT Press.
Rubinstein, A. (1999), 'Review of *An Empirically Based Microeconomics*', *Journal of Economic Literature*, **37** (4), 1711–12.
Schumpeter, Joseph (1942), *Capitalism, Socialism, and Democracy*, New York: Harper & Row.
Shultz, G. (1995), 'Economics in action: ideas, institutions, policies', *American Economic Review*, **85** (May), 1–8.
Selznick, P. (1950), 'The iron law of bureaucracy', *Modern Review*, **3**, 157–65.
Shelanski, H. and P. Klein (1995), 'Empirical research in transaction cost economics: a review and assessment', *Journal of Law Economics and Organization*, **11**, 335–61.
Simon, H.A. (1947), *Administrative Behavior*, New York: Macmillan.
Simon, H.A. (1951), 'A formal theory of the employment relationship', *Econometrica*, **19**, 293–305.
Simon, H.A. (1955), 'A behavioral model of rational choice', *Quarterly Journal of Economics*, **69** (February), 99–118.
Simon, H.A. (1957a), *Administrative Behavior*, 2nd edn, New York: Macmillan.
Simon, H.A. (1957b), *Models of Man*, New York: Wiley.
Simon, H.A. (1961), *Administrative Behavior*, 2nd edn, New York: Macmillan.
Simon, H.A. (1962), 'The architecture of complexity', *Proceedings of the American Philosophical Society*, **106** (December), 467–82.
Simon, H.A. (1978), 'Rationality as process and as product of thought', *American Economic Review*, **68** (May), 1–16.
Simon, H.A. (1983), *Reason in Human Affairs*, Stanford, CA: Stanford University Press.
Simon, H.A. (1985), 'Human nature in politics: a dialogue of psychology with political science', *American Political Science Review*, **79**, 293–304.
Simon, H.A. (1991), 'Organizations and markets', *Journal of Economic Perspectives*, **5** (Spring), 25–44.
Simon, H.A. (1997), *An Empirically Based Microeconomics*, New York, Cambridge University Press.

Simon, H.A. and C. Bonini (1958), 'The size distribution of business firms', *American Economic Review*, **48** (4), 607–17.

Smith, V. (1991), 'Rational choice: the contrast between economics and psychology', *Journal of Political Economy*, **99** (4), 877–97.

Solow, R.M. (1958), 'Review of: *Models of Man – Social and Rational*', *Review of Economics and Statistics*, **40** (1), 81–4.

Wachter, M. and 0. Williamson (1978), 'Obligational markets and the mechanics of inflation', *Bell Journal of Economics*, **9** (Autumn), 549–71.

Whinston, M. (2000), 'On the transaction cost determinants of vertical integration', Unpublished manuscript.

Williamson, O.E. (1975), *Markets and Hierarchies: Analysis and Antitrust Implications*, New York: Free Press.

Williamson, O.E. (1983), 'Credible Commitments: Using Hostages to Support Exchange', *American Economic Review*, **73**: 519–40.

Williamson, O.E. (1991), 'Comparative economic organization: the analysis of discrete structural alternatives', *Administrative Science Quarterly*, **36** (June), 269–96.

Williamson, O.E. (1993), 'Transaction cost economics meets Posnerian law and economics', *Journal of Institutional and Theoretical Economics*, **149** (March), 99–118.

Williamson, O.E. (1996), *The Mechanisms of Governance*, New York: Oxford University Press.

Williamson, O.E. (1999), 'Strategy research: governance and competence perspectives', *Strategic Management Journal*, **20**, 1087–108.

Williamson, O.E. (2000), 'Close reasoning and economic organization', Unpublished manuscript.

Index